Applied Cryptography

This book systematically explores modern cryptography, bridging the gap between theoretical frameworks and engineering practices, and transforming complex mathematical concepts into accessible, real-world algorithms.

Applied Cryptography: Principles, Analysis, and Python Implementation begins with classic cryptographic systems, such as symmetric ciphers (including stream and block ciphers) and public-key cryptography (e.g., RSA and ECC). Then, it advances to specialized post-quantum topics, including lattice-based cryptography and homomorphic encryption. Unlike purely theoretical treatments, this book integrates programming examples and hands-on exercises that transform abstract mathematics into tangible, logical applications. Additionally, it addresses essential security protocols, including hash functions and digital signatures, equipping readers with a structured approach to securing system design.

Designed for students, researchers, and professionals in computer science and cybersecurity, this book connects foundational theory with practical engineering. Its accessible style also makes it a valuable resource for academic libraries, professional training programs, and individuals building secure systems in the digital age.

Zhuo Liu is a Senior Engineer at AVIC General Aircraft Research Institute. His research interests include quantum cryptography, quantum communication, and quantum artificial intelligence.

Yongkun Zhao is a Marie Skłodowska-Curie Actions Postdoctoral Researcher at the University of Oulu, Finland, focusing on neural engineering and human–machine interaction.

Lingcai Huang is a professor-level Senior Engineer and Chief Designer of the AG600 large amphibious aircraft. In addition to his leadership in aviation engineering, he is the Dean of the College of General Aviation and Flight at Nanjing University of Aeronautics and Astronautics (NUAA).

Applied Cryptography

Principles, Analysis, and Python Implementation

Zhuo Liu, Yongkun Zhao, and Lingcai Huang

CRC Press
Taylor & Francis Group
Boca Raton London New York

CRC Press is an imprint of the
Taylor & Francis Group, an informa business

人民邮电出版社
POSTS & TELECOM PRESS

Designed cover image: Shutterstock (ID: 109769693)

First edition published 2027
by CRC Press
2385 NW Executive Center Drive, Suite 320, Boca Raton, FL 33431

and by CRC Press
4 Park Square, Milton Park, Abingdon, Oxon, OX14 4RN

CRC Press is an imprint of Taylor & Francis Group, LLC

English Version by permission of Posts and Telecom Press Co., Ltd.

ISBN: 978-1-041-37939-3 (hbk)
ISBN: 978-1-041-38027-6 (pbk)
ISBN: 978-1-042-01108-7 (ebk)

DOI: 10.1201/9781042011087

Typeset in CMR10 font
by KnowledgeWorks Global Ltd.

Publisher's note: This book has been prepared from camera-ready copy provided by the authors.

*Zhuo Liu: To my dearest wife, Yiyun Liu,
and my lovely daughters, Yubai and Yuzhen.*

Contents

Part II Symmetric Cryptography

Preface

WHY WRITE THIS BOOK

Sun Tzu's *The Art of War* teaches us, "Know yourself and know your enemy, and you will never be defeated in a hundred battles". In the context of contemporary offensive and defensive engagements within the digital realm, this timeless wisdom serves as a paramount guiding principle. From the core assets of multinational corporations to the operational underpinnings of financial systems, extending to the protection of individual digital privacy, proficiency in information encryption and decryption has emerged as the decisive factor determining success or failure. In today's world, leveraging deep insights into underlying algorithms to combat large organizations, or decrypting critical intelligence to shift the landscape of technological competition, is no longer a fictional scenario from science fiction—it is a reality that is happening now.

As we advance into the 21st century, the world confronts unprecedented challenges in digital security. With rapid advancements in computational power and increasing interconnectedness, the scope of information security has expanded beyond traditional network boundaries to cover every line of code and data storage unit. From edge computing that safeguards personal privacy to distributed ledgers facilitating global trade, cryptographic technology forms the strongest supporting wall of digital civilization. In today's world, where "zero trust" has become the norm, cryptography is precisely the cornerstone for building digital trust.

This book is specially written for undergraduates new to cryptography, with the goal of establishing a strong theoretical foundation rather than focusing solely on engineering implementation. Beginning with classical cryptography, it progressively covers topics such as information-theoretic security, symmetric encryption, and public-key cryptosystems, and extends to forward-looking topics such as post-quantum cryptography. As quantum computing is poised to reshape security rules, this section will become your knowledge reserve to face future technological upheavals. A notable feature of this work is its extensive coverage of cryptanalysis. Because we deeply understand that without knowing how shields are pierced, one can never forge an unbreakable defense.

To bridge the gap between theory and practice, the book incorporates a large number of practical Python and SageMath code examples. You will have the opportunity to generate keys, carry out encryption and verification processes, explore the inner mechanics of the RSA algorithm, and even replicate security failures arising from random number generation flaws. These "code experiments" will provide you with a profound understanding that security is not an automatic feature but an art meticulously crafted through deliberate design.

This book has been thoughtfully tailored to serve three primary audiences:

1) **Explorers of Digital Sovereignty**: This book aims to break down the mysterious barriers of cryptography. Whether you are a technology enthusiast or an industry observer, if you wish to deeply understand the security logic behind the digital world, this book will be your ideal guide. While ensuring the accuracy of core concepts, we strive to avoid getting bogged down in obscure mathematics, using intuitive language to reveal how cryptography works, allowing you to grasp the key knowledge to protect digital sovereignty with ease.
2) **Practitioners on the Security Frontier**: Whether you are a frontline engineer responsible for core data protection or a decision-maker designing overall security architecture, this book will be a highly valuable technical reference. From security analysis of hash functions to engineering practices of digital signature technologies, the knowledge system, analytical tools, and practical experience provided in this book will help you build rigorous defensive thinking and empower you with professional confidence to construct high-strength security systems.
3) **STEM Students**: Undergraduate and graduate students in computer science, mathematics, and related disciplines will find this book both a comprehensive supplement to cryptography coursework and a self-study guide for practical application. To bridge the gap between theory and practice, this text includes numerous detailed examples and Python/SageMath code implementations. These "hands-on" sections will help you quickly master algorithmic processes, transforming abstract mathematical formulas into runnable code logic.

Readers who persist in studying this book will ultimately gain not only a profound understanding of encryption algorithms and cryptanalysis but also a comprehensive toolkit for confidently exploring advanced topics such as post-quantum and fully homomorphic encryption.

ERRATA AND SUPPORT

Finally, due to the highly specialized and rapidly evolving nature of this subject, and the authors' limited personal capacity, we apologize in advance for any limitations or outdated content that may be present. If you have any valuable feedback or suggestions, please do not hesitate to reach out to the author at

`ethanliuzhuo@outlook.com`

Your communication would be greatly appreciated and welcomed for further discussion.

ACKNOWLEDGMENTS

The authors would like to extend my heartfelt gratitude to my wife, Professor *Yiyun Liu*, and my beloved daughters. Their support and encouragement have been instrumental in the completion of this book. I am especially thankful to my wife for her invaluable contributions throughout the writing process. She participated in the content development and structural organization of this book as well as meticulously proofreading and revising the manuscript. I sincerely appreciate her dedication and assistance.

Special thanks are also due to Aviation Industry Corporation of China, Ltd., for their invaluable support of this book. The co-authors, *Yongkun Zhao* and *Lingcai Huang*, made tremendous contributions during the writing process, providing important assistance for the smooth completion and quality improvement of this text. *Yongkun Zhao* joined the team during the initial drafting phase and authored Chapters 2, 3, and 14, bringing greater structure and rigor to the content. Chief engineer *Lingcai Huang*, with his extensive experience in the aviation industry, served as the technical advisor, offering us a wealth of insightful guidance and suggestions. He also facilitated connections with numerous industry experts, contributing many practical case studies and technical support. Here, I would like to extend my deepest appreciation and respect to these two collaborators. I would also like to extend my sincere gratitude to *Jie She* and the editorial team at People's Posts & Telecom Press for their efforts in publishing this text. Their professionalism and dedication have left a profound impression on me. It is with their invaluable support that this book was successfully brought to publication. I dedicate this work to my cherished family and to all friends who share a passion for cryptography.

The authors would like to thank the following individuals for the many corrections and helpful suggestions: *Yuejia Cheng* (University of Sussex), *Yuntian Chen*, *Marhaba Mamtimin*, *Jin Peng*, *Linyu Zheng*, *Rui Hu*, *Chun Zhang*, *Songlin Xiang*, *Jianming Li*, *Zhongtian Jing*, *Tianyi Feng*, *Yiying Fang*, *Jie Jiang*, *Zhennan Fei*, and *Yixin Tang*.

The journey ahead is long and unending; yet, with unwavering determination, I'll search with my will unbending!

Notation

Symbol	Meaning
& or $\wedge$	bitwise AND operator
$\vee$	bitwise OR operator
$\neg$	bitwise NOT operator
$\oplus$	exclusive-or (XOR) operator
$\in$	the membership of an element in a set
`0x`	prefix indicating hexadecimal notation
$b\|a$	b divides a or a is divisible by b
$a\|\|b$	concatenation of the strings a and b
$\gcd(a, b)$	the greatest common divisor of a and b
$a \pmod m$	the remainder of a is divided by m
$a^{-1} \pmod m$	the multiplicative inverse of a modulo m
$a \equiv b \pmod m$	the integers a and b are congruent modulo m
$a \not\equiv b \pmod m$	the integers a and b are not congruent modulo m
$R[x]$	the set of polynomials with coefficients in a commutative ring R
$\mathbb{Z}$	the set of integers
$\mathbb{Z}/m\mathbb{Z}$	the ring of integers modulo m
$\mathcal{M}$	plaintext space
$\mathcal{C}$	ciphertext space
$\mathcal{K}$	key space
E_k	the encrypting function under key k
D_k	the decrypting function under key k
IV	initialization vector
$\mathcal{O}$	used in computer science and mathematics to describe the asymptotic behavior of functions; or the point at infinity in ECC
τ	the non-linear transformation in SM4
$\star$	binary operation
GF(p)	the finite field of order p, where p is prime
GF(2^n)	the finite field of order 2^n
$\varphi(n)$	Euler's totient function, the number of positive integers less than n and relatively prime to n
$\left(\frac{a}{b}\right)$	the Legendre symbol

(Continued)

Symbol	Meaning
$J(a, n)$	the Jacobi symbol
$\mu(d)$	the Möbius function
$\Phi_n(x)$	the cyclotomic polynomial
$ord_r(n)$	the multiplicative order of n modulo r
$\mathrm{MAC}_K(M)$	message authentication code of message M using secret key K
$\lvert\cdot\rvert$	absolute value
$\lVert\cdot\rVert$	the Euclidean norm
$\lfloor\cdot\rceil$	rounding to the nearest integer
$\lfloor\cdot\rfloor$	rounding down to the nearest integer
$\lceil\cdot\rceil$	rounding up to the nearest integer
$H(X)$	the entropy of a random variable X
P	probability
$P(n, k)$	permutation
$C(n, k)$	combination
$\det(\mathbf{A}) \pmod m$	the determinant of an $n \times n$ matrix $\mathbf{A}$ modulo m
Δ	the discriminant of the elliptic curve
$\mathrm{NAF}(k)$	non-adjacent form of a positive integer k
$\mathcal{L}$	lattice

I

Fundamental Background Knowledge

Throughout human history, cryptography, as an ancient discipline, embodies humanity's desire for secret communication and the challenge of unraveling mysteries. Its origins trace back to ancient civilizations, where people began using simple substitution and transposition ciphers to conceal information, marking the birth of classical cryptography. Over time, particularly during the Renaissance, more sophisticated polyalphabetic ciphers emerged, transforming cipher creation into a skilled craft. A major revolution in cryptography, however, took place in the 20th century. The rapid advancement of computer technology, coupled with *Claude Shannon*'s ground-breaking information theory, ushered in a new era. *Shannon* introduced information-theoretic concepts, including entropy, into cryptographic analysis, providing mathematical tools to measure system security, but also elevated cryptography from an "art" relying on clever tricks to a "science" based on rigorous mathematical proofs. On this theoretical foundation, modern symmetric cryptography continued to develop, followed by the emergence of public-key cryptography, greatly advancing the field.

The expansion of the Internet has underscored the critical importance of cryptography, making secure communication and privacy paramount in the digital age. Modern cryptography extends beyond algorithm design and cryptanalysis to include protocols, digital signatures, and authentication mechanisms. It safeguards digital communication by ensuring confidentiality, integrity, authentication, and non-repudiation. The evolution of the field, from ancient substitution ciphers to advanced contemporary algorithms, reflects the enduring pursuit of information security.

CHAPTER 1

Introduction to Cryptography

Cryptography, from Ancient Greek "kryptós" (hidden) and "gráphein" (write), is the study of the codes and ciphers used to create secret writing. As defined in the *Oxford English Dictionary*, cryptography is "a secret way of writing, especially one in which a set of letters or symbols is used to represent others". More formally, cryptography involves the use of mathematical algorithms to transform plaintext (readable data) into ciphertext (unreadable data) via a process known as encryption. The original message is recovered through a reversible process called decryption, which typically requires possession of a secret key.

Cryptography is the mathematical study of techniques for securing digital communication in the presence of adversaries. While its roots trace back over three millennia, the discipline has evolved significantly from an art form into a rigorous science. Historically, the development of cryptography can be categorized into three distinct phases: classical cryptography, early modern cryptography, and modern cryptography. Classical cryptography primarily focused on confidentiality, ensuring that information remained secret during transmission, and relied heavily on linguistic patterns and heuristic methods. In contrast, modern cryptography has expanded its scope beyond mere secrecy. It formally addresses a broader set of security goals, including data integrity, authentication, and non-repudiation. Furthermore, modern frameworks rigorously define security against various adversarial models, considering both external attacks and internal threats within complex computing systems.

This chapter introduces a structured overview of cryptographic history, delineating the earliest operational contexts of cryptographic practice and pivotal evolutionary milestones in modern cryptography. It systematically provides the fundamental concepts underpinning contemporary cryptosystems, while also enumerating their essential components, foundational principles, and standardized cryptanalytic methodologies. Designed to equip readers with operational encoding knowledge, this foundational exposition ensures comprehensive preparation for subsequent technical discussions.

DOI: 10.1201/9781042011087-1

1.1 BRIEF HISTORY OF CRYPTOGRAPHY

1.1.1 Development of Ancient Cryptography

China boasts a rich tradition of cryptographic practices dating back centuries. In his seminal work *The Art of War*, Sun Tzu emphasizes the importance of intelligence: "*If you know the enemy and know yourself, you need not fear the result of a hundred battles. If you know yourself but not the enemy, for every victory gained you will also suffer a defeat. If you know neither the enemy nor yourself, you will succumb in every battle*" [2]. This wisdom underscores the critical role of understanding an opponent's strengths, weaknesses, strategies, and tactics. Indeed, the quantity and accuracy of intelligence can often be the deciding factor in warfare. Throughout history, warfare has been the primary driver of cryptographic innovation, with cipher verification serving as a quintessential example. Ancient Chinese armies developed sophisticated, standardized methods for secure communication and identity authentication. One of the most notable was the "Tiger Tally", a credential used for military deployment and a classic form of identity verification in ancient China. During the tumultuous Spring and Autumn and Warring States periods (2000 years ago), Lord *Xinling* of *Wei* (a state name) famously exploited this system by stealing the king's Tiger Tally. In an era of limited communication, this audacious act allowed him to verify his identity, seize military command, and ultimately lead troops to victory against the *Qin* (a state name) army, breaking the siege of the capital in *Zhao* (a state name).

The *Six Secret Teachings: Dragon Secret Teaching: Secret Commander's Seal*, a military treatise from the same era, provides further insight into the clandestine communication methods employed by ancient Chinese rulers and their generals. When King *Wu* sought advice from his adviser on maintaining contact with troops behind enemy lines, the adviser recommended the use of the Secret Commander's Seal. This ingenious method comprised eight distinct types of seals [3]:

- The one which signifies great victory is one foot long.
- The one which signifies defeating the enemy and capturing their general is nine inches long.
- The one which signifies the surrender of the enemy's army and the occupation of their cities is eight inches long.
- The one which signifies repelling the enemy and reporting the situation is seven inches long.
- The one which motivates the soldiers and people to enhance the defenses is six inches long.
- The one which requests supplies and additional support is five inches long.
- The one which reports the defeat and death of the general is four inches long.
- The one which reports defeat and the loss of soldiers is three inches long.

For those who are in charge of delivering commanding seals, any delay or leak of information will mean a death sentence. These eight secret commanding seals are used by the ruler and general to pass information in secret without revealing any details. Even though the enemy is wise, the seals cannot be decoded.

The effectiveness and security of the Secret Commander's Seal led to its continued use and improvement over generations, evolving into more advanced forms such as the "Fu Qi" (Authentication Seal) and "Yin Shu" (Secret Letters). In practice, the "Fu" (Tally) was crafted from bamboo and split into two interlocking parts. When authentication was needed, the two halves were reunited. The perfect fit occurred only between matching parts.

Military strategists in subsequent eras made significant advancements in intelligence transmission. During the Northern Song Dynasty (1000 years ago), *Zeng Gongliang*, *Ding Du*, and *Yang Weide*, who were government officials, refined the Secret Commander's Seal while compiling the *Wujing Zongyao (Complete Essentials for the Military Classics)* [4]. This renowned ancient Chinese military treatise was the first officially commissioned military manual in China. Volume 15 of its first part contains three sections: "Fu Qi" (Authentication Seal), "Xin Pai" (Credentials), and "Zi Yan" (Character Verification), which detail methods of secret communication and identity authentication in the military, as illustrated in Figure 1-1. The "Fu Qi" evolved from the Tiger Tally used for troop mobilization during the Qin and Han dynasties. The imperial court used the "Fu" to deploy local troops, while the "Qi", a fish-shaped credential split into upper and lower halves, was used by military commanders to mobilize their subordinates. The commander-in-chief controlled the "Fu Qi", and its use required documented records by a designated scribe, followed by secure delivery and verification by another specialist.

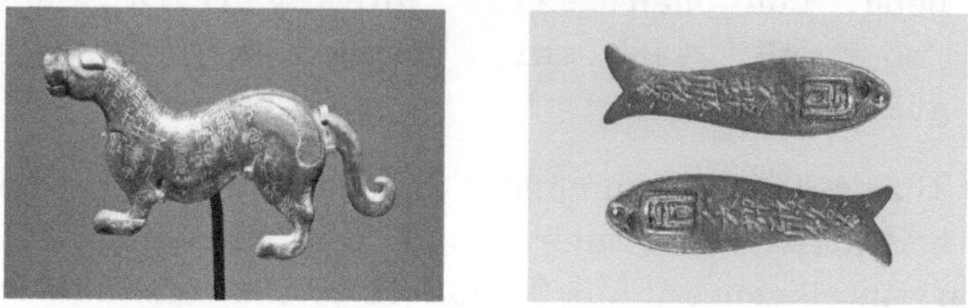

(a) Tiger Tally[1] (b) Xin Pai [2]

Figure 1-1: Secret Communication Methods in *Wujing Zongyao*

"Xin Pai" (Credentials), also called Golden Fish Tally, was primarily employed for transmitting urgent orders during front-line battles. Initially utilizing split copper coins, it later evolved to use inscribable wooden tablets.

"Zi Yan" (Character Verification) was a sophisticated military communication code based on poetry, analogous to modern military codebooks. The *Wujing Zongyao, Regulations 15 · Zi Yan*, outlined its usage: communication items were prearranged as technical terms, which commanders memorized. Prior to each battle, the commander-in-chief and deputy commanders would agree on a five-character regulated verse without repeated characters as their "Zi Yan". To report an event, one would compose an ordinary letter, with the order of the reported item corresponding to a specific

[1]Du Tiger Tally. The artifact is in the collection of the Shannxi History Museum; image by the author.

[2]Xin Pai. The artifact is in the collection of the Liaoning Provincial Museum; image via Huitu.

character's position in the poem. A subtle mark would then be added next to that character in the letter.

For instance, the *Wujing Zongyao · Regulations 15 · Zi Yan* [4] documented a comprehensive list of standardized communication items and their sequence for military operations. These items include: Requests for equipment: (1) bows, (2) arrows, (3) swords, (4) armor, (5) spears and flags, (6) cooking utensils and tents, (7) horses, (8) clothing, (9) provisions, (10) fodder, (11) ox carts, (12) boats, and (13) siege machinery. Tactical commands: (14) call for reinforcements, (15) relocate camp, (16) advance, (17) retreat, and (18) maintain position. Intelligence reports: (19) no enemy sighted, (20) enemy detected, (21) enemy outnumbers us, (22) enemy forces are few, (23) enemy strength matches ours, (24) enemy reinforced, (25) enemy camp relocated, (26) enemy advancing, (27) enemy retreating, and (28) enemy holding position. Battle updates: (29) enemy city under siege, (30) our siege lifted, (31) our forces besieged, (32) escaped enemy siege, (33) battle lost, (34) major victory achieved, (35) decisive triumph, (36) forces surrender, (37) troop mutiny, (38) widespread illness among soldiers, (39) commanding officers incapacitated, and (40) minor victory secured.

To illustrate, suppose the commander-in-chief and deputy commander agreed to use the poem *Shizhi Saishang* (Envoy to the Frontier, one famous Chinese poem) as their "Zi Yan". This poem, containing 40 unique characters without punctuation, perfectly suited the requirements. The full text of *Shizhi Saishang* reads as follows:

dān chē yù wèn biān, shǔ guó guò jū yán.
zhēng péng chū hàn sài, guī yàn rù hú tiān.
dà mò gū yān zhí, cháng hé luò rì yuán.
xiāo guān féng hòu jì, dū hù zài yān rán.

In the event that a deputy commander discovered during the battle that enemy reinforcements had arrived and their troops were surrounded, they would need to report military intelligence items 24 and 31 to the commander-in-chief. To do this, they would incorporate the characters "yān" and "xiāo" into their report, marking them subtly with a black dot or water droplet. If the commander-in-chief, upon receiving this message, wished the deputy to hold their position while he attempted to break the siege, he would include and mark the characters "rù" (item 18) and "yuán" (item 30) in his reply. This process completed the communication between the commanders. Even if intercepted by the enemy, the vast number of ancient poems made it virtually impossible for messengers or foes to decipher the code without knowing which specific poem was being used. Compared to the Secret Commander's Seal, this method could express a wider range of military situations, thus facilitating better decision-making by the commander. Later, *Shu Li*, who was another government official, enhanced the security of military intelligence transmission by adapting the system to use seven-character quatrains, employing less widely known folk verses.

During the Ming Dynasty (450 years ago), the renowned general *Qi Jiguang*, employed the *fanqie code* as an encryption method on the battlefield. "Fanqie", a phonetic notation system, was used by Qi to compile a codebook. This ensured that only authorized intelligence personnel and commanders could understand the true meaning of the messages, while couriers and ordinary soldiers remained unaware of their contents.

The famous late Ming and early Qing (400 years ago) military theorist *Jie Xuan* also detailed secret military communication methods in his work *Bingjing Baiyan* (One Hundred Sayings on the Art of War). In the *Techniques* chapter, he argued that armies operating separately would face defeat if unable to communicate, and would be vulnerable to enemy plots if their communications were not secure. Thus, in addition to using conventional signaling methods such as gongs, drums, banners, cannon fire, horse messengers, signal arrows, fire, and smoke signals, armies meeting in the field also needed to use passwords. For armies separated by great distances, confidential letters were recommended. These took three forms: altering the usual writing or reading method of characters; steganography; and writing messages on special, inconspicuous media rather than regular paper. These methods ensured that even the messengers were unaware of the message contents, while the intended recipients could decipher them. This demonstrates the high importance placed on secure communications in ancient Chinese warfare.

Ciphers were frequently used not only on Chinese battlefields but also in foreign wars. The famous Caesar cipher, for instance, was invented in ancient Rome to ensure effective and reliable secret communication during wartime. According to Suetonius's Lives of *The Twelve Caesars*: "When something confidential was to be written, a cipher was used, that is, the order of the letters was so changed that not a word could be made out. To read and understand these, one had to substitute the fourth letter of the alphabet for the first, that is, D for A, and so on".

For centuries, this encryption system remained unbreakable until the 9th century CE, when Arab scholar Al-Kindi discovered that frequency analysis could be used to break the Caesar cipher. He documented this method in his book, *A Treatise on Decrypting Cryptographic Messages.*

Figure 1-2: Scytale[3]

Around 700 BCE, the Spartans used a wooden rod called "Scytale" (also known as cipher stick) for secure communication, as illustrated in Figure 1-2. The method was simple: Take a long strip of parchment paper and wrap it around a cylindrical wooden rod, then inscribe the intended message. When the writing is completed and the parchment is unwound from the rod, the characters become scrambled in

[3]Image by Eivind Lindbråten via Wikimedia Commons.

sequence. Only by rewinding the parchment onto another wooden rod of identical diameter in the same manner can the original message be properly deciphered.

1.1.2 Development of Early Modern Cryptography

1. Zimmermann Telegram

The early modern cryptography covers the period from World War I (1914–1976).

In the 19th century, the invention of the telegraph sped up communication. Later, in 1893, *Nikola Tesla* invented radio communication for the first time in St. Louis, Missouri. This marked the start of the radio era, allowing people to communicate instantly over long distances. In wartime, this was a game-changer. Commanders could get updates from the front lines and issue orders immediately.

Unlike wired telephone lines that facilitate dedicated point-to-point transmission, radio signals are broadcast by nature. Within a given range, these signals can be received by anyone, including the enemy, making them susceptible to interception. Consequently, the need to encrypt information transmitted over radio became urgent. With the outbreak of World War I, the demand for skilled personnel in coding and decoding rose sharply, initiating a global struggle for secure communication. During the later stages of the war, the British cryptanalytic section known as "*Room 40*" utilized captured German codebooks to decipher the famous "*Zimmermann Telegram*", as illustrated in Figure 1-3. This event significantly altered the course of the war.

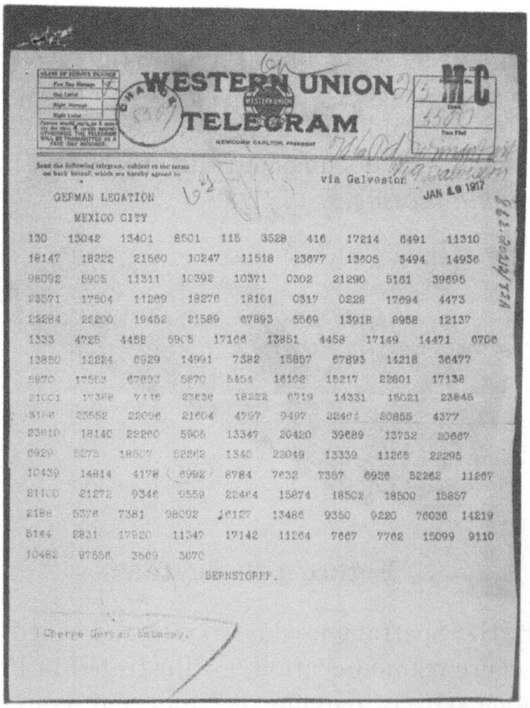

WESTERN UNION TELEGRAM

NEWCOMB CARLTON, PRESIDENT

Send the following telegram, subject to the terms on back hereof, which are hereby agreed to

via Galveston

JAN 19 1917

GERMAN LEGATION

MEXICO CITY

130 13042 13401 8501 115 3528 416 17214 6491 11310
18147 18222 21560 10247 11518 23677 13605 3494 14936
98092 5905 11311 10392 10371 0302 21290 5161 39695
23571 17504 11269 18276 18101 0317 0228 17694 4473
22284 22200 19452 21589 67893 5569 13918 8958 12137
1333 4725 4458 5905 17166 13851 4458 17149 14471 6706
13850 12224 6929 14991 7382 15857 67893 14218 36477
5870 17553 67893 5870 5454 16102 15217 22801 17138
21001 17388 7446 23638 18222 6719 14331 15021 23845
3156 23552 22096 21604 4797 9497 22464 20855 4377
23610 18140 22260 5905 13347 20420 39689 13732 20667
6929 5275 18507 52262 1340 22049 13339 11265 22295
10439 14814 4178 6992 8784 7632 7357 6926 52262 11267
21100 21272 9346 9559 22464 15874 18502 18500 15857
2188 5376 7381 98092 16127 13486 9350 9220 76036 14219
5144 2831 17920 11347 17142 11264 7667 7762 15099 9110
10482 97556 3569 3670

BERNSTORFF.

Charge German Embassy.

Figure 1-3: Zimmermann Telegram[4]

At the onset of the war, the United States maintained a policy of neutrality and abstained from combat in Europe. Great Britain, seeking American intervention, actively monitored traffic on transatlantic cables. This surveillance led to the interception of numerous communications, most notably the Zimmermann Telegram. Sent by German Foreign Minister *Arthur Zimmermann* to the German Ambassador in Mexico, the message proposed a military alliance between Germany and Mexico should the United States enter the conflict. Since the encrypted message was routed through transatlantic cables controlled by the Allies, British intelligence was able to intercept it. Utilizing codebooks captured earlier in the war, British cryptanalysts successfully deciphered the message. Recognizing the strategic value of this intelligence, Britain shared the plaintext with the United States. The revelation provoked widespread public outrage across America, solidifying the perception of Germany as a hostile power. Three months after the telegram was sent, the United States declared war. This episode serves as a quintessential example of how cryptanalysis and information security can influence the geopolitical landscape and determine the fate of nations.

2. Enigma Machine

Drawing from the intelligence failures of World War I, Germany recognized the critical necessity of secure communications. Consequently, they adopted the Enigma machine, as illustrated in Figure 1-4, an electromechanical rotor cipher device invented in 1918. The Enigma was considered one of the most secure systems in history. Its vast key space made it appear computationally infeasible to break using the methods of the time. This cryptographic superiority gave the German military a significant advantage at the onset of World War II, leaving the Allied forces initially blind to German strategic plans. The German Navy utilized Enigma to coordinate their U-boat "wolf packs" in the Atlantic, devastating Allied supply lines and placing Britain in a perilous position.

Figure 1-4: Enigma Machine[5]

However, the intersection of advanced mathematics and nascent computing technology provided new tools for cryptanalysis. At Bletchley Park, the British

[4]Image by the U.S. National Archives via Wikimedia Commons.

[5]Image by Bob Lord via Wikimedia Commons.

Government Code and Cypher School, a team led by the mathematician *Alan Turing* exploited a critical design flaw in the Enigma: the machine's inability to encrypt a letter to itself. By developing the Bombe, Turing and his colleagues successfully broke the Enigma cipher. This breakthrough allowed the British Navy to decrypt German communications, anticipate U-boat movements, and turn the tide of the Battle of the Atlantic.

3. The Pacific War

On the morning of December 7, 1941, the Japanese Navy launched a surprise military strike on the Pearl Harbor naval base in Hawaii, inflicting heavy casualties. The attack severely incapacitated the US Pacific Fleet and precipitated the USA direct entry into World War II, expanding the conflict into a global war against the Axis powers.

Retrospectively, the catastrophe at Pearl Harbor is often cited as a monumental intelligence failure. The inability to detect the impending attack stemmed from a fragmentation of intelligence data and insufficient emphasis on cryptanalysis. The Japanese military employed sophisticated Operational Security (OPSEC) measures, most notably maintaining strict radio silence during the fleet's approach. Instead of standard encrypted traffic, they utilized pre-arranged signals broadcast over public radio to issue final attack orders, thereby evading traditional traffic analysis.

Following this disaster, the United States prioritized the interception and decryption of Japanese communications in the Pacific theater. By successfully breaking the Japanese Naval Code, US cryptanalysts provided critical tactical advantages. This intelligence superiority allowed the US Navy to anticipate enemy movements, leading to decisive victories such as the Battle of Midway, which fundamentally altered the trajectory of the war.

4. Herbert Osborn Yardley

During the War of Resistance Against Japanese Aggression (1931-1945), Japanese bombed Chongqing, temporary capital of China, for several years to make China surrender, which was called the "**Chongqing Bombing**". Chongqing is famous for being a foggy city, so the weather is usually bad for flying planes. However, Chinese intelligence found that Japan always bombed when it was sunny, so they never failed. They suspected there were spies in Chongqing sending messages to the Japanese, but they could not find them. So China invited the American Yardley to help find the spies.

His full name was *Herbert Osborn Yardley* who was an American cryptologist. He was born in Worthington, Indian, USA. He was very good at math when he was a child. At age 13, he learned how to use the telegraph from his father who was a station master, so he became very interested in codes. He accepted a Signal Corps Reserve commission and served as a cryptologic officer with the American Expeditionary Forces in France during WWI. In 1917, *Yardley* started the first "American Black Chamber" called MI-8, which was the beginning of the National Security Agency. Later, the government changed, and the new leader closed the

Figure 1-5: Herbert Osborn Yardley[6]

department. Yardley lost his job and had to write novels to make money for a long time. At the start of World War II, Yardley was not doing well, so he accepted the job to be an advisor in China.

During this period, counter-intelligence operations in China successfully apprehended numerous espionage agents, including the notorious figure known as the "*One-armed Bandit*". These operatives had infiltrated various critical sectors, ranging from the military and intelligence agencies to high-ranking government offices. As these networks were dismantled, *Herbert Yardley*'s cover was eventually compromised. Due to escalating security concerns, he returned to the United States. Yardley later authored a manuscript titled *The Chinese Black Chamber*, detailing his experiences; however, the US government suppressed its publication for decades. Yardley passed away in Washington, D.C., in 1958. His manuscript was finally published posthumously in 1983, allowing the public to learn the details of his assignment.

In conclusion, it is evident that advancements in cryptography and cryptanalysis played a decisive role in determining the outcome of World War II.

1.1.3 Development of Modern Cryptography

The development of modern cryptography is inextricably linked to the rapid advancement of computer science and electronic communication technologies. This era witnessed a theoretical renaissance, where the design of cryptosystems and the development of cryptanalytic techniques engaged in a cycle of mutual reinforcement. Consequently, the field saw a proliferation of encryption algorithms and increasingly sophisticated analysis methods. Furthermore, the application of cryptography expanded beyond exclusive military domains into commercial and civilian sectors, leading to the establishment of ubiquitous encryption standards that underpin the security of modern networks.

Central to this transformation is Dr. *Claude Elwood Shannon*, widely recognized as one of the founding fathers of modern cryptography. An alumnus of the Massachusetts Institute of Technology (MIT), *Shannon* was a distinguished mathematician and

[6]Image by NSA via Wikimedia Commons.

electrical engineer, best known as the progenitor of Information Theory. While he made significant contributions to breaking enemy ciphers during World War II, his most enduring legacy lies in providing the rigorous mathematical framework that transitioned cryptography from an intuitive art into a systematic science.

In 1948, Shannon published a famous paper [5]. Starting from the essence of communication system transmission, this article scientifically defined information and described it qualitatively and quantitatively. It serves as the foundation of modern information theory. In 1949, Shannon published another famous paper [6] This work pushed cryptography, which had a history of thousands of years, onto a scientific track based on information theory. It is one of the theoretical foundations of modern cryptography. However, it was not widely applied at the beginning of its publication. It was not until the birth of block ciphers decades later that its value was fully demonstrated.

In 1976, *Bailey Whitfield Diffie* and *Martin Edward Hellman* published a paper [7]. They proposed the concept of "Public-key Cryptography". This opened up a new field of public key cryptography. From that moment on, the history of cryptography was divided into two parts: symmetric cryptography and asymmetric (public key) cryptography. Before this, all cryptosystems were symmetric. It can be said that without research on public key cryptography, there would be no modern cryptography.

In 1977, three professors from MIT, *Rivest*, *Shamir*, and *Adleman* introduced the RSA cryptographic algorithm [8]. This marked the birth of the first public-key algorithm that was relatively comprehensive and had no obvious weaknesses. The public-key algorithm is a significant milestone in the history of cryptography. Subsequently, public-key cryptosystems such as ElGamal, Elliptic Curve Cryptography (ECC), and Lattice-based cryptography were proposed successively. Modern cryptography entered a new period of rapid development.

Parallel to these developments, the Data Encryption Standard (DES) was adopted as a federal standard in 1977. The standardization of DES facilitated the transition of cryptography from exclusive government use to the civilian and commercial sectors. DES possesses significant pedagogical value for understanding the fundamental theories and design principles of block ciphers, influencing the architecture of many subsequent algorithms. Due to their high computational efficiency and throughput, symmetric cryptosystems remain widely deployed today. They are essential infrastructures in diverse sectors, including government, finance, and telecommunications.

Since then, countries and regions such as China, the United States, and the European Union have all intensified their research in the field of cryptography. In the field of symmetric cryptography, algorithms such as SM4 and AES have been proposed successively. In the field of asymmetric cryptography, algorithms such as SM2 and ECC have also been proposed. Furthermore, attention has turned to quantum-resistant cryptography, such as quantum cryptography and lattice-based cryptography. Cutting-edge cryptographic technologies like post-quantum cryptography are gradually becoming research hotspots.

1.2 BASIC CONCEPTS OF CRYPTOGRAPHY

1.2.1 Security Goals of Cryptography

1) **Confidentiality**. Cryptosystems provide secrecy against an eavesdropping adversary, only an authorized recipient should be able to recover the plaintext from the ciphertext. This is the most fundamental security service provided by cryptography and is typically achieved through encryption algorithms.
2) **Authentication**. Authentication is used to verify the authenticity of the communicating entities or messages. It typically involves two types:
   (a) **Entity Authentication**. Verifies that the received message truly originates from the claimed sender.
   (b) **Data Authentication**. Verifies that the received messages come from the claimed source and have not been altered.
3) **Integrity**. Integrity ensures that information has not been modified in an unauthorized manner (including insertion, deletion, substitution, or reordering) during storage or transmission. This is typically achieved through cryptographic hash functions or message authentication codes (MACs).
4) **Non-repudiation**. Non-repudiation ensures that communicating entities cannot deny their previously transmitted messages. This typically achieved through Digital Signatures.

The four objectives outlined above constitute the fundamental elements of cryptography and serve as the cornerstones of information security, as illustrated in Figure 1-6. These elements provide a rigorous framework for defining security requirements. Consequently, when designing cryptographic systems or evaluating

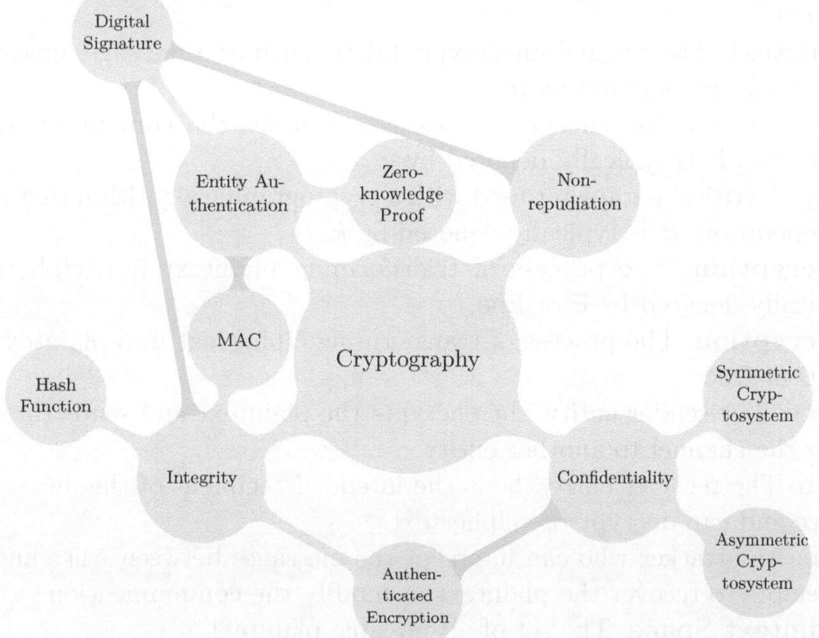

Figure 1-6: Security Goals of Cryptography

their security strength, these fundamental elements are treated as key considerations to comprehensively address the problems encountered.

While the **CIA triad** (Confidentiality, Integrity, and Availability) constitutes the foundational framework of information security, cryptography is primarily concerned with the first two. **Availability** is defined as the assurance of timely and reliable access to data and resources by authorized entities. However, availability is typically achieved through system engineering and network architecture rather than mathematical algorithms. Therefore, as an engineering challenge rather than a cryptographic one, it will not be the focus of this book.

1.2.2 Basic Principles of Cryptography

In the process of classical cryptography evolving toward modern cryptography, a critically important design principle was gradually established, namely **Kerckhoffs' Principle**, which says that a cryptosystem should be secure when the attacker knows all the details of the encryption and decryption algorithms but does not know the secret key. This principle was introduced by the Dutch cryptographer *Auguste Kerckhoffs* in 1883.

This principle serves as the cornerstone of modern cryptography. Modern cryptographic algorithms are typically open and standardized. Public algorithm design allows for extensive analysis and testing by cryptographers worldwide, thereby better ensuring security. With the advancement of computer and communication technologies, universal encryption standards based on this principle have greatly facilitated the widespread adoption of network information technology.

Before formally describing a cryptographic system, we first define the following core concepts:

1) **Plaintext**. The original unencrypted data, such as a message, image, or video. It is typically denoted by m.
2) **Ciphertext**. The encrypted message, it hides the content of the original plaintext. It is typically denoted by c.
3) **Key**: A critical parameter used with a cryptographic algorithm that determines its operation. It is typically denoted by k.
4) **Encryption**. The process of transforming plaintext into ciphertext. It is typically denoted by E or Enc.
5) **Decryption**. The process of transforming ciphertext into plaintext, denoted by D or Dec.
6) **Alice**. The sender entity, she encrypts the plaintext and sends the ciphertext over the channel to another entity.
7) **Bob**. The receiver entity, he is the intended recipient of the message sent by Alice and can decrypt the ciphertext.
8) **Eve**. An attacker who can intercept the messages between Alice and Bob and attempts to recover the plaintext or modify the communication.
9) **Plaintext Space**. The set of all possible plaintext.
10) **Ciphertext Space**. The set of all possible ciphertext.
11) **Key Space**. The set of all possible keys.

Alice and Bob first appeared in the paper published by *Rivest* in 1978 [8]. Prior to this, the field of cryptography typically used "A" to denote the data sender and "B" to denote the data receiver. Compared to the impersonal "A" and "B", Alice and Bob are more personal. They are the world's most famous cryptographic couple and were used to explain how cryptography works. The communication process between Alice and Bob is illustrated in Figure 1-7.

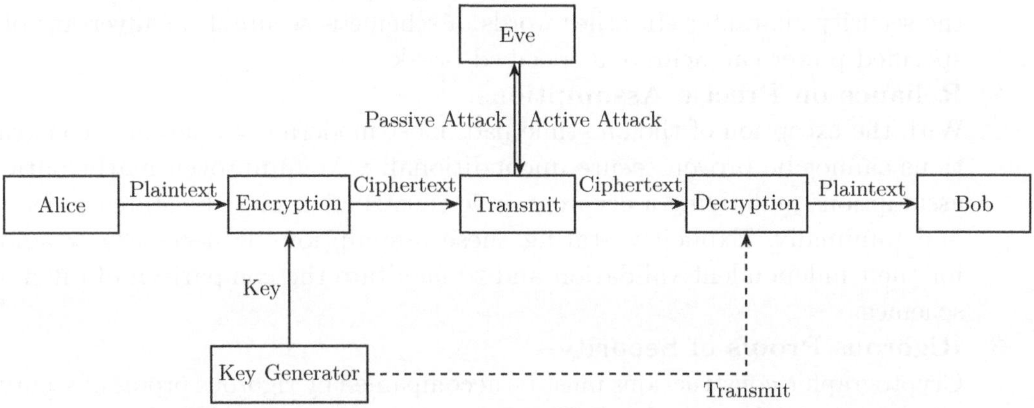

Figure 1-7: Communication Over an Insecure Channel

In the ensuing years, more characters have joined their cryptographic family. Including but not limited to Mallory, Trent, Victor. Mallory is a malicious attacker; Trent is a trusted authority, who acts as a neutral third party; Victor is a verifier. In cryptographic tradition, Eve is only a passive eavesdropper who listens to the channel but does not interfere, while Mallory is an active attacker who can modify, replay, or inject messages. In this book, for simplicity, we will use the name Eve to represent the generic adversary performing any type of attack.

In the encryption and decryption process, Alice encrypts the plaintext using a key, transforming it into ciphertext. This ciphertext is transmitted to Bob via a selected channel. Finally, Bob decrypts the ciphertext using the key to retrieve the original plaintext. A cryptosystem is a five-tuple $(\mathcal{M},\mathcal{C},\mathcal{K},E_k,D_k)$, where $\mathcal{M}$, $\mathcal{C}$, $\mathcal{K}$ are respectively the plaintext space, ciphertext space, and key space. Let $k \in \mathcal{K}$ denote the encryption and decryption key, $m \in \mathcal{M}$ and $c \in \mathcal{C}$. The key is generated by a key-generation algorithm, denoted by KeyGen. This is a probabilistic algorithm according to a specified distribution.

The encryption algorithm is given by the formula

$$\mathsf{E}_k(m) = c \tag{1-1}$$

The decryption algorithm is given by the formula

$$\mathsf{D}_k(c) = m \tag{1-2}$$

Therefore, $\mathrm{D}_k(\mathrm{E}_k(m)) = m$ for each $m \in \mathcal{M}$ in a symmetric cryptosystem.

In general, Alice and Bob communicate via an **Insecure Channel**. To prevent Eve from accessing the content of the information, they employ cryptographic algorithms to encrypt the data. It is worth noting that, in accordance with Kerckhoffs' Principle, the security of modern cryptography relies entirely on the secrecy of the

Key, rather than the secrecy of the encryption algorithm. Once Eve knows the key, she can decrypt the ciphertext, effectively breaching the security of the system.

There are three basic principles of modern cryptography.

1) **Formulation of Exact Definitions.**
   A cryptographic scheme for a given task is considered secure only if it satisfies a formal definition. This definition must clearly specify the threat model and the security guarantee. In other words, a scheme is secure if no adversary of a specified power can achieve a specified break.
2) **Reliance on Precise Assumptions.**
   With the exception of the one-time pad, most modern cryptographic constructions cannot be proven secure unconditionally. Any unproven mathematical assumptions underlying a cryptographic construction must be stated precisely and minimally. Explicitly stating these assumptions is necessary to allow for their independent validation and to facilitate the comparison of different schemes.
3) **Rigorous Proofs of Security.**
   Cryptographic constructions must be accompanied by rigorous proofs of security relative to the formulated definitions and assumptions, rather than relying on ad-hoc intuition. These proofs typically employ a reductionist approach, demonstrating that any adversary capable of breaking the scheme could be effectively used to solve the underlying hard mathematical problem.

1.2.3 Cryptanalysis and Security Definitions

Constructing a reliable cryptosystem requires more than merely guaranteeing the correctness of the encryption algorithm. A rigorously defined secure encryption algorithm must satisfy **semantic security**. This property ensures that an attacker cannot obtain any partial information about the plaintext from the intercepted ciphertext. In other words, for a computationally bounded adversary, the ciphertext should appear indistinguishable from random string, and no statistical characteristics of the plaintext should be derivable from it.

Except for the One-Time Pad scheme, which possesses perfect secrecy, the vast majority of modern practical cryptosystems do not possess unconditional security but rely on computational security. This implies that although the ciphertext theoretically contains information about the plaintext, the computational resources or time required to extract this information are **computationally infeasible**, far exceed the feasible limits of current technology.

The process of attempting to recover the original plaintext or the secret key from the ciphertext, without authorized access to the key, is called **cryptanalysis**. This process typically relies on advanced mathematical tools and computational resources. A specific attempt to execute cryptanalysis on a system is formally referred to as an **attack**.

Cryptanalysis is a core branch of cryptography that serves as the necessary counterpart to cryptographic design. Far from being a purely destructive activity, it acts as the primary mechanism for validating the security of cryptographic algorithms.

The objective of cryptanalysis is to discover potential mathematical flaws or side-channel vulnerabilities within algorithms.

After any new cryptographic algorithm is proposed, it must undergo rigorous public scrutiny and extensive evaluation by the academic/industrial community. Only algorithms that have withstood various types of attacks over a long period without being broken can be accepted by the industry and standardized. This adversarial interplay between design (defense) and analysis (attack) constitutes the fundamental driving force behind the evolution of modern cryptography.

In general, cryptanalysis can be divided into the following three methods:

1) **Classical Cryptanalysis.**

   Classical Cryptanalysis also can be divided into brute-force attacks, which the adversary tries to use all possible keys to find the secret key, and cryptanalytic attacks. The latter can be further classified into the following four attack models:

   (a) **Ciphertext-only Attack**: The adversary knows only a set of ciphertexts. The goal is to determine the plaintexts or the secret key.

   (b) **Known-plaintext Attack**: The adversary knows some pairs of ciphertext and corresponding plaintext. The goal is to determine the secret key or decrypt additional ciphertexts.

   (c) **Chosen-plaintext Attack**: The adversary can choose a set of plaintexts and obtain the ciphertexts. The goal is to determine the secret key or to gain information about a target ciphertext.

   (d) **Chosen-ciphertext Attack**: The adversary can choose a set of ciphertexts and obtain the plaintexts. The goal is to determine information about the underlying plaintext of some other ciphertext or the secret key.

   From the perspective of the adversary, the amount of information required for these four methods of analysis increases sequentially.

2) **Implementation Attacks.**

   Approaches that do not target the cryptographic algorithm itself but instead perform analysis through other channels are also called **Side-Channel Attacks**. For example, an attacker might infer the key by measuring the power consumption of the CPU while it processes the plaintext or by analyzing electromagnetic signal strength. In the vast majority of cases, the implementation of such attacks targets cryptographic systems to which the attacker has physical access. Consequently, this method is generally not considered when employing remote systems for encryption.

3) **Social Engineering Attacks**. Social Engineering Attacks do not target vulnerabilities in the software but rather vulnerabilities in human beings. For example, obtaining the key through espionage behaviors, such as bribery, theft, stalking, phishing, etc. methods. There is a joke: A certain company was blackmailed by a hacker, cutting off the internet every 20 minutes, using technical means could not find it no matter what. Finally discovered it was the hacker bought off the security guard, pulling the network cable every 20 minutes. This is a typical example of social engineering attack.

The security analysis and evaluation of a cryptosystem are generally based on data complexity (Plaintext Space, Ciphertext Space, and Key Space), time complexity, space complexity, and success probability. Generally, the computational complexity commonly discussed in cryptanalysis mainly refers to **Time Complexity** and **Space Complexity**.

The attacker, Eve, seeks the weakest link in the application of cryptography. This includes not only the algorithm itself but also the transmission, management, and other application aspects of cryptography. In other words, users must not only employ sufficiently secure algorithms but also ensure defense against implementation attacks and social engineering attacks. This book will focus on classic cryptanalysis methods while briefly introducing implementation attacks and social engineering.

For any encryption scheme to be considered computationally secure, its key space $\mathcal{K}$ must be large enough to render brute-force attacks computationally infeasible. Furthermore, in the context of practical cryptosystems, it is typically required that $|\mathcal{M}| > |\mathcal{K}|$, meaning the plaintext space is larger than the key space. If the set of possible plaintexts is smaller than the set of possible keys, brute-forcing all possible keys would result in a set of candidate plaintexts larger than the plaintext space itself. A sufficiently large key space is a necessary but not sufficient condition for the security. A secure cryptographic algorithm must possess a sufficiently large key space, but a large key space does not guarantee the security of the algorithm.

It is crucial to distinguish between key space and key length, as they represent distinct concepts with an exponential relationship. The key length refers to the number of bits in the key, typically denoted by n. In contrast, the key space is the total number of possible keys, calculated as 2^n. For instance, consider a key 10101010 with a length of 8 bits; its corresponding key space is $2^8 = 256$. If the key length is 16, which is twice the length of an 8-bit key, its key space is far larger than that of the latter. Specifically, the difference in magnitude is $2^{16}/2^8 = 2^8 = 256$ times. A linear increase in key length results in an exponential expansion of the key space.

1.2.4 Symmetric/Asymmetric Ciphers

This volume systematically examines two fundamental paradigms of cryptography: **Symmetric Cryptography** and **Asymmetric Cryptography**. Symmetric Cryptography is also referred to as Private-key Cryptography or One-key Cryptosystem. Asymmetric Cryptography is also referred to as Public-key Cryptography or Two-key Cryptosystem.

In Symmetric Cryptography, a single key is used for both encryption and decryption, the key must be secret. The encryption and decryption function are very similar, not necessary to be the same. This implies that if an attacker intercepts the key, they can easily decrypt the ciphertext. Symmetric encryption algorithms are generally characterized by the following properties:

1) A single secret key is used for both encryption and decryption.
2) The processing speed is extremely fast, making it suitable for encrypting large volumes of data.
3) Safely exchanging keys over an insecure channel is a significant challenge.

4) In a network with n users, pairwise communication requires managing a total of $n(n-1)/2$ keys. This places extremely high demands on the key management center.

Due to bottlenecks in key distribution and management symmetric encryption systems are difficult to adapt directly to the security requirements of large-scale open networks. The DES and AES algorithms are prominent representatives of this class. We can understand symmetric encryption through an intuitive physical analogy where Alice and Bob possess identical physical keys. Alice places information into a safe and locks it while Bob must use the same key to open the safe upon receipt. The limitations of this model are evident as both parties must exchange the key via a secure channel beforehand. Furthermore once the key is stolen an attacker Eve can impersonate a legitimate user and the system consequently fails to provide non-repudiation.

Symmetric encryption can be understood through an intuitive physical model. Alice and Bob possess identical physical keys for a safe. Alice places her information into the safe and locks it; Bob, upon receiving the safe, must use the same key to open it. The limitations of this model are evident: both parties must pre-exchange the key via a secure channel. Furthermore, once Bob's key is stolen, Eve can impersonate a legitimate user, and the system fails to provide non-repudiation verification of the source.

The utilization of computers enables the practical application of these concepts through complex mathematical operations. Algorithms such as DES and AES serve as prominent representatives of symmetric cryptography.

To address the key exchange problem **asymmetric cryptography** emerged. This system uses two different keys for encryption and decryption: a public key for encryption and a private key for decryption. The public key is made available to the entire network and is used for encryption; the private key is kept strictly secret by the receiver and is used for decryption. The two keys have the property that deriving the private key from the public key is computationally infeasible.

Its working mode is as follows: Alice uses Bob's public key to encrypt message, and the ciphertext can only be decrypted by Bob, who holds the corresponding private key. Even if the public key is transmitted over an insecure channel, an attacker cannot derive the private key from the public key. This mechanism thoroughly eliminates the risk of transmitting decryption keys over insecure networks. In a network with n users, only n personal secrets are needed in asymmetric cryptography that address the key exchange problem.

There are significant differences between symmetric cryptography and asymmetric cryptography regarding the relationship between security and key length. Since the underlying attack principles differ the key lengths required to achieve comparable security strengths diverge significantly. For instance an 80-bit symmetric key provides security roughly equivalent to a 1024-bit RSA public key while a 128-bit symmetric key corresponds to an approximately 3072-bit RSA key.

Regarding brute-force attacks on the key space the computational difficulty increases exponentially with key length. Given modern computational capabilities 64-bit symmetric keys are no longer considered secure. Conversely 128-bit keys remain computationally secure under classical computing models while 256-bit keys are sufficient to render brute-force cracking computationally infeasible.

1.3 ENCODING

1.3.1 ASCII

Given the rigorous demands of modern communication for data throughput and timeliness, the majority of information exchange has shifted from traditional physical delivery to network transmission. Computer networks constitute the infrastructure underpinning this mode of communication. At the hardware level, computers can distinguish between 0 and 1 solely through the logic states of semiconductors.

To facilitate human-computer interaction, the American National Standards Institute (ANSI) developed the American Standard Code for Information Interchange (ASCII). This character encoding standard is primarily based on the Latin alphabet. Since computers can process only binary data, ASCII is extensively applied in the field of information technology. Its core function lies in establishing the mapping relationship between Latin letters, Arabic numerals, and binary codes.

Since modern cryptographic algorithms are implemented on digital computers, they process data represented as sequences of zeros and ones. We define a sequence of these bits as a binary string, such as 10010010. Textual data is typically encoded using the ASCII standard which maps characters to numerical values. Table 1-1

Table 1-1: ASCII Codes

Bin	Dec	Hex	Char	Bin	Dec	Hex	Char	Bin	Dec	Hex	Char
0010 0000	32	20	(Space)	0100 0000	64	40	@	0110 0000	96	60	`
0010 0001	33	21	!	0100 0001	65	41	A	0110 0001	97	61	a
0010 0010	34	22	"	0100 0010	66	42	B	0110 0010	98	62	b
0010 0011	35	23	#	0100 0011	67	43	C	0110 0011	99	63	c
0010 0100	36	24	$	0100 0100	68	44	D	0110 0100	100	64	d
0010 0101	37	25	%	0100 0101	69	45	E	0110 0101	101	65	e
0010 0110	38	26	&	0100 0110	70	46	F	0110 0110	102	66	f
0010 0111	39	27	'	0100 0111	71	47	G	0110 0111	103	67	g
0010 1000	40	28	(	0100 1000	72	48	H	0110 1000	104	68	h
0010 1001	41	29	)	0100 1001	73	49	I	0110 1001	105	69	i
0010 1010	42	2A	*	0100 1010	74	4A	J	0110 1010	106	6A	j
0010 1011	43	2B	+	0100 1011	75	4B	K	0110 1011	107	6B	k
0010 1100	44	2C	,	0100 1100	76	4C	L	0110 1100	108	6C	l
0010 1101	45	2D	-	0100 1101	77	4D	M	0110 1101	109	6D	m
0010 1110	46	2E	.	0100 1110	78	4E	N	0110 1110	110	6E	n
0010 1111	47	2F	/	0100 1111	79	4F	O	0110 1111	111	6F	o
0011 0000	48	30	0	0101 0000	80	50	P	0111 0000	112	70	p
0011 0001	49	31	1	0101 0001	81	51	Q	0111 0001	113	71	q
0011 0010	50	32	2	0101 0010	82	52	R	0111 0010	114	72	r
0011 0011	51	33	3	0101 0011	83	53	S	0111 0011	115	73	s
0011 0100	52	34	4	0101 0100	84	54	T	0111 0100	116	74	t
0011 0101	53	35	5	0101 0101	85	55	U	0111 0101	117	75	u
0011 0110	54	36	6	0101 0110	86	56	V	0111 0110	118	76	v
0011 0111	55	37	7	0101 0111	87	57	W	0111 0111	119	77	w
0011 1000	56	38	8	0101 1000	88	58	X	0111 1000	120	78	x
0011 1001	57	39	9	0101 1001	89	59	Y	0111 1001	121	79	y
0011 1010	58	3A	:	0101 1010	90	5A	Z	0111 1010	122	7A	z
0011 1011	59	3B	;	0101 1011	91	5B	[	0111 1011	123	7B	{
0011 1100	60	3C	<	0101 1100	92	5C	\	0111 1100	124	7C	|
0011 1101	61	3D	=	0101 1101	93	5D	]	0111 1101	125	7D	}
0011 1110	62	3E	>	0101 1110	94	5E	^	0111 1110	126	7E	~
0011 1111	63	3F	?	0101 1111	95	5F	_	0111 1111	127	7F	(Delete)

details the mapping for 96 commonly used characters along with their corresponding binary, decimal, and hexadecimal representations.

It can be observed that each character corresponds to values in the **Binary System** (base 2), **Decimal System** (base 10), and **Hexadecimal System** (base 16). How is the conversion between decimal and binary performed?

To convert decimal to binary numbers, proceed with the steps given below

1) Divide the given decimal number by 2 to obtain an integer quotient and a remainder.
2) Record the remainder, which will be either 0 or 1, as the next bit in the sequence.
3) Repeat until the quotient is zero. By placing all the remainders in order the Least Significant Bit (LSB) at the top and Most Significant Bit (MSB) at the bottom, the required binary number will be obtained.

Example 1.3.1 Convert the decimal number 13 to its binary representation. We employ the method of repeated division by 2. The remainders generated at each step correspond to the bits of the binary number, computed from the Least Significant Bit (LSB) to the Most Significant Bit (MSB).
Solution:

$$\begin{aligned} 13 &= 2 \times 6 + \boxed{1} \\ 6 &= 2 \times 3 + \boxed{0} \\ 3 &= 2 \times 1 + \boxed{1} \\ 1 &= 2 \times 0 + \boxed{1} \end{aligned}$$

By arranging the remainders in reverse order (from the last step to the first), the decimal number 13 is represented in binary as 1101. ■

To convert a binary number to decimal, proceed with the steps given below

1) For n-bit binary number, count the powers of 2 from right to left and starting from 0.
2) Write each binary digit from right to left with the corresponding powers of 2 from, such that first binary digit will be multiplied with the greatest power of 2. The highest power is $n - 1$.
3) Add all the products in the previous step.

Example 1.3.2 Convert the binary number 10010011 to its decimal representation.
Solution: The given binary number has 8 bits, the highest power is 7.

$$\begin{aligned} 10010011 &= 1 \times 2^7 + 0 \times 2^6 + 0 \times 2^5 + 1 \times 2^4 + 0 \times 2^3 + 0 \times 2^2 + 1 \times 2^1 + 1 \times 2^0 \\ &= 128 + 16 + 2 + 1 \\ &= 147 \end{aligned}$$

The binary number 10010011 is represented in decimal as 147. ■

In **hexadecimal** (hex for short) system, a digit is represented as **0** to **9** like for decimal. To represent the numbers **10** to **15**, the letters **A** to **F** are used respectively. Each hex digit effectively represents the same numeric count as four binary digits. When a person is looking at long strings of binary numbers, it is much easier to convert to hex. In technical literature and programming, the suffix `0x` is conventionally used to distinguish hexadecimal values from decimal numbers.

A **hexadecimal** number, written as the sequence of digits $d_n d_{n-1} \dots d_0$, represents the value $\sum_{i=0}^{n} d_i 16^i$ in **base 10**. For instance, $\texttt{2C}_{16} = 2 \times 16^1 + 12 \times 16^0 = 44_{10}$. Conversely, converting decimal to hexadecimal involves repeated division: $90 = 5 \times 16 + 10$ (where 10 is `A`) and $5 = 0 \times 16 + \boxed{5}$. Thus, $90_{10} = \texttt{5A}_{16}$.

While binary, decimal, and hexadecimal are the primary systems discussed, other systems such as **quaternary** (base-4), **octal** (base-8), and **base-32** also exist. Since these alternative bases are rarely encountered in this context, we leave their conversion methods as an exercise for the reader.

With the fundamental concepts of data representation now established, we turn our attention to the standard units used to measure digital information.

- **Bit**. The most basic unit of information in computing. A binary digit with a value of 0 or 1.
- **Byte**. A string of bits, regarded as a unit. A byte typically consists of 8 bits.
- **Word**. A sequence of m bits where $m = 2^n$ and $n \geqslant 4$, depending on the computer.
- **Kilobyte**. 1 Kilobyte = 1 KB = 2^{10} bytes = 1024 bytes.
- **Megabyte**. 1 Megabyte = 1 MB = 2^{20} bytes = 1024 KB.
- **Gigabyte**. 1 Gigabyte = 1 GB = 2^{30} bytes = 1024 MB.
- **Terabyte**. 1 Terabyte = 1 TB = 2^{40} bytes = 1024GB.

There are additional units, but they are of little relevance to cryptography. However, note that computer storage units use a conversion factor of 1024 rather than 1000. This is because $1024 = 2^{10}$ is based on the binary system. Nevertheless, in commercial computer products, a factor of 1000 is used for simplicity. For example, a 1 TB external hard drive actually has a capacity of $\frac{1000^4}{1024^3} \approx 931$ GB. This is 90.9% of the labeled capacity.

1.3.2 Exclusive-OR Operation

The exclusive-or operation, commonly denoted as XOR, is defined on binary digits (bits). When applied to other numerical formats, the operation is performed on the corresponding binary representations. Mathematically, the XOR operation is equivalent to modulo 2 addition. The operation is defined as follows:

$$1 \;\; \texttt{XOR} \;\; 1 = 0$$
$$0 \;\; \texttt{XOR} \;\; 0 = 0$$
$$1 \;\; \texttt{XOR} \;\; 0 = 1$$
$$0 \;\; \texttt{XOR} \;\; 1 = 1$$

For convenience, it is denoted by $\oplus$, such that $1 \oplus 1 = 0$. To illustrate this, consider two magnets. Let the value for repulsion be 0 and the value for attraction be 1. Magnets have South and North poles. The South pole represents 1, and the North pole represents 0. If two South poles are placed together, they repel, so the result is 0. The same applies to the North poles. However, if a South pole and a North pole are placed together, they attract, so the result is 1.

The XOR operation possesses several interesting properties

- Self-Inverse: $a \oplus a = 0$
- Identity Element: $a \oplus 0 = a$
- Commutativity: $a \oplus b = b \oplus a$
- Associativity: $a \oplus b \oplus c = a \oplus (b \oplus c) = (a \oplus b) \oplus c$
- Cancellation: $a \oplus b \oplus a = b$

The proof of the cancellation property is straightforward: $a \oplus b \oplus a = a \oplus a \oplus b = 0 \oplus b = b$. This property is very powerful. In certain cryptographic algorithms, it can be utilized to eliminate the key and recover the plaintext.

CHAPTER 2

Mathematical Foundations

This chapter introduces the relevant mathematical content required for the subsequent chapters on cryptography.

Number theory and algebra are branches of mathematics that serve as the cornerstones of cryptographic algorithms. Number theory and algebra have been utilized since the era of classical cryptography, and modern cryptographic algorithms continue to be based on them. In the design of modern cryptosystems, cryptographers design secure cryptosystems based on computational hardness assumptions or mathematically intractable problems from number theory or algebra (such as in RSA). In modern cryptanalysis, mathematical tools from number theory and algebra are used to analyze cryptographic algorithms.

The concepts of number theory and algebra are highly abstract. Without examples, it becomes challenging to intuitively comprehend and master them. Therefore, this chapter contains numerous examples and figures to help readers comprehend these abstract concepts. Readers already familiar with number theory and algebra may skip this chapter completely or partially.

Topics covered in this chapter:

- Number theory: Sets, Division theorem, Euclidean algorithm and Modular arithmetic.
- Asymmetric cryptography relates to: the Euler totient function, Möbius function, and modular exponentiation.
- Algebra: Groups, Rings, Fields, and Finite Fields.
- Operations on Polynomials over Finite Fields

2.1 SETS

Intuitively, a set is a collection of distinct objects known as elements. These elements may be integers, rational numbers, complex numbers, characters, or any combination thereof. Indeed, a set may be empty. The number of elements in a set can range from zero to infinity, with no predefined limitations.

DOI: 10.1201/9781042011087-2

Definition 2.1.1 Sets

A set is a collection of objects, considered as a mathematical object in its own right. The objects in a set are called the ***elements*** *of the set; the elements are said to belong to the set, and the set is said to contain the elements.*

Given a set E, $x \in E$ if x is an element of the set E.

Sets have three fundamental properties: **Definiteness**, **Unorderedness**, and **Uniqueness** [9]. Definiteness: For any given set and a specific element, the element either belongs to the set or it does not—there is no uncertainty. Unorderedness: The order of elements in a set does not matter. If two sets contain the same elements, they are considered equal, regardless of how the elements are arranged. Uniqueness: Each element in a set is unique. Even if an element appears multiple times, it is only counted once within the set.

Sets are classified as finite or infinite based on their element count. In cryptography, the key space and ciphertext space are finite, therefore they are both finite sets. Examples of the important set are as follows:

- $\mathbb{Z} = \{\ldots, -2, -1, 0, 1, 2, \ldots\}$ denotes the set of all integers, which is an infinite set.
- $\mathbb{Z}^+ = \{1, 2, \ldots\}$ denotes the set of all positive integers, which is an infinite set.
- $\mathbb{Q} = \{p/q \mid p, q \in \mathbb{Z}, q \neq 0\}$ denotes the set of all rational numbers, is an infinite set.
- $\mathbb{R}$ denotes the set of all real numbers, is an infinite set.
- $\mathbb{R}^+$ denotes the set of all positive real numbers, is an infinite set.
- $\mathbb{C}$ denotes the set of all complex numbers, is an infinite set.
- $\{0, 1, \ldots, 100\}$ is a finite set.
- $\emptyset$ denotes the empty set, is a finite set.
- $\{x \in \mathbb{R} \mid x^2 - x - 2 = 0\}$ is a finite set.

To further understand the concept of sets, we can categorize them into subsets and proper subsets.

Definition 2.1.2 Subsets

A set A is a ***subset*** *of a set B if and only if every element of A is also an element of B. We denote it by $A \subseteq B$.*

Definition 2.1.3 Proper Subsets

A set A is a proper subset of B if and only if $A \subseteq B$ and $A \neq B$. We denote it by $A \subset B$.

Examples of the subsets and proper subsets are as follows:

- $\mathbb{Q}$ is a subset of $\mathbb{R}$.
- $\mathbb{Z}^+$ is a subset of $\mathbb{Z}$.
- $\emptyset$ is a proper subset of all non-empty set.

If two sets contain exactly the same elements, they are equal. In other words, if $A \subseteq B$ and $B \subseteq A$, then $A = B$.

It is essential to distinguish between the symbols $\in$ and $\subseteq$. The symbol $\in$ denotes the membership of an element in a set, whereas $\subseteq$ represents the subset relation between two sets. Although these concepts are closely related, they describe fundamentally different relationships. Let a be an element of the set A. We express this relationship as

$$a \in A \Leftrightarrow \{a\} \subseteq A \tag{2-1}$$

There are several important operations that can be used to combine sets to obtain other sets.

Definition 2.1.4 Intersection of Sets

Let A and B be sets. The intersection of A and B, denoted by $A \cap B$, is the set that contains those elements that are in both A and B.

$$A \cap B = \{x \mid x \in A \text{ and } x \in B\} \tag{2-2}$$

Definition 2.1.5 Union of Sets

Let A and B be sets. The union of A and B, denoted by $A \cup B$, is the set that contains those elements that are either in A or in B, or in both.

$$A \cup B = \{x \mid x \in A \text{ or } x \in B\} \tag{2-3}$$

If an element x belongs to both set A and set B, then the intersection of A and B is the set containing only that element. The union of A and B consists of all the elements from both sets, with any duplicates removed so that each element appears only once.

Example 2.1.1 Suppose $A = \{1, 2\}$, $B = \{2, 3\}$, find $A \cap B$ and $A \cup B$.
Solution: $A \cap B = \{2\}$, $A \cup B = \{1, 2, 3\}$ ■

Definition 2.1.6 Difference of Sets

The difference of two sets A and B is the collection of objects in A that are not in B. We denote it by $A - B$.

$$A - B = \{x \mid x \in A \text{ and } x \notin B\} \tag{2-4}$$

It is worth noting that, in general, the set A is different from the set B and the set B is different from the set A, these sets are not equal.

Example 2.1.2 Let $A = \{1, 2, 3, 4\}$, $B = \{2, 3, 4, 5\}$, then $A - B = \{1\}, B - A = \{5\}$.

■

Definition 2.1.7 Complement of Sets

Let U be the universal set and let $A \subseteq U$. The set of all elements in U that are not in A is called the complement of A. We denoted it by A^c, defined by:

$$A^c = U - A = \{x \in U \mid x \notin A\} \quad (2\text{-}5)$$

Note that $(A^c)^c = A$.

Example 2.1.3 Let $A = \{x \in \mathbb{R} \mid x > 2\}$, then $A^c = \{x \in \mathbb{R} \mid x \leqslant 2\}$. ■

Intersection, union, difference, and complement of sets are shown in Figure 2-1.

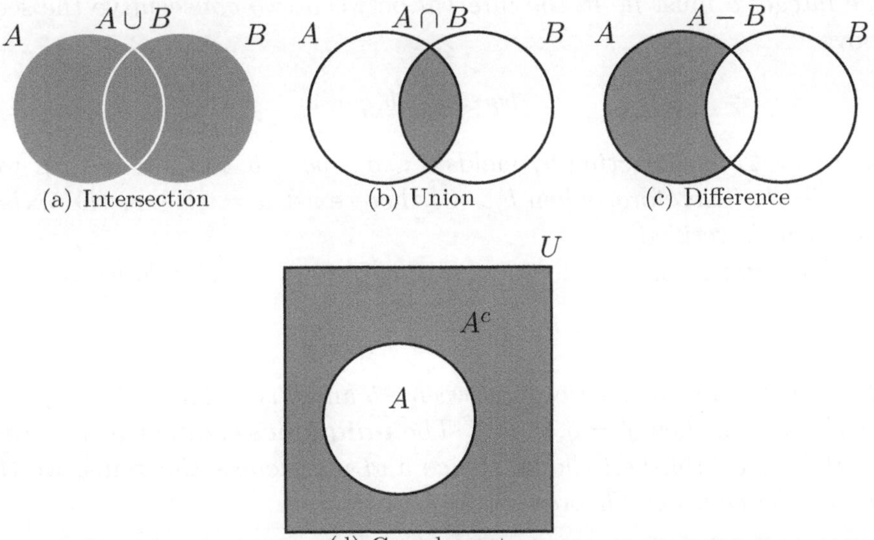

(a) Intersection (b) Union (c) Difference

(d) Complement

Figure 2-1: Operations of Sets

2.2 DIVISION THEOREM

The division theorem is also called division with remainder. Let $a, b \in \mathbb{Z}$, and $b \neq 0$. If $q \in \mathbb{Z}$, there exist $a = qb$, then the integer a is said to be divisible by an integer b, in symbols $b \mid a$. Here, b is called a **divisor** of a, or that a is called a **multiple** of b [9]. We say "b divides a" or "a is divisible by b".

If a is not divisible by b, we can write $b \nmid a$. Since $b \nmid a$, the concept of remainder must be introduced, formally defined by the Division Theorem.

Theorem 2.2.1 Division Theorem

Let $a, b \in \mathbb{Z}$ with $b > 0$. Then there are unique integers q and r such that

$$a = qb + r \tag{2-6}$$

where $0 \leqslant r < b$. The integer q is called the ***quotient*** *and the integer r is called the* ***remainder****.*

The Division Theorem is the fundamental theorem of divisibility, serving as the most essential and frequently utilized tool in number theory proofs. For instance, demonstrating theorems concerning integer representations in various numeral bases necessitates the application of the Division Theorem.

Proof

Let $a, b \in \mathbb{Z}$ with $b > 0$. Suppose there is an integer sequence, such as

$$\cdots - 2b, \; - b, \, 0, \, b, \, 2b \, \cdots \tag{2-7}$$

The integer a must lie in the interval between two consecutive the sequence above

$$bq \leqslant a < b(q+1) \tag{2-8}$$

where $q \in \mathbb{Z}$. Subtracting bq yields $0 \leqslant a - bq < b$. Let $r = a - bq$, we have $0 \leqslant r < b$. Therefore, when $b > 0$, there exist $a = qb + r$, the ***existence*** *statement is verified.*

Now, suppose $q', r' \in \mathbb{Z}$, such as $a = bq' + r'$, $0 \leqslant r' < b$, we get

$$-b < r - r' = b\left(q' - q\right) < b \tag{2-9}$$

The only multiple of b strictly between $-b$ and b is 0. Thus, $b(q' - q) = 0$. We get $r' - r = 0$, then $q' = q$, $r' = r$. The ***uniqueness*** *statement is verified.*

Having established the existence and uniqueness theorems, we thereby proved the Division Theorem.

Example 2.2.1 Find the quotient and remainder when $a = 23542352$ and $b = 234$.
Solution: For these numbers a calculator gives $a/b \approx 100608.34$, thus the quotient $q = 100608$, the remainder is easy to compute $r = a - bq = 80$. ■

Example 2.2.2 Find the quotient and remainder when $a = 12$ and $b = 3$.
Solution: For these numbers a calculator gives $a/b = 4$, thus the quotient $q = 4$, the remainder is easy to compute $r = a - bq = 0$. ■

2.3 EUCLIDEAN ALGORITHM

In China, many people first encounter the Euclidean algorithm [9] during elementary school mathematics. This algorithm originally appeared in *Euclid's Elements*, a foundational work that not only systematically presented plane and solid geometry but also introduced fundamental number theory concepts including divisibility, prime numbers, greatest common divisors, and least common multiples.

Ancient Chinese scholars independently discovered this method as well. For instance, *The Nine Chapters on the Mathematical Art*, one of the earliest surviving mathematical texts from China, describes the "*Yuefen Method*" (reduction method). This technique corresponds algorithmically to the Euclidean algorithm.

"Yuefen Method" is that if the numerator and the denominator of a fraction can be divided by half, just divide them. It they are not divisible by half, a calculation on the numerator and the denominator should be done separately, that is to make the small number subtracted from the large number repeatedly until the difference equals the subtrahend. Then reduce the fraction with the equal number. The equal number also is the greatest common divisor.

It is with regret that *Euclid's Elements* given rigorous proofs of his results, but *The Nine Chapters on the Mathematical Art* was not.

Let a, b be two integers, at least one of them is non-zero. Then the Greatest Common Divisor(GCD) of a and b is denoted by $\gcd(a, b)$, is the positive integer d satisfying the following:

- $d \mid a$ and $d \mid b$
- d is called common divisor and greater than every other common divisor

The Greatest Common Divisor has several lemmas: Suppose $a, b \in \mathbb{Z}$ and $b > 0$, if b divides a then b must be the greatest common divisor of a and b, such as $\gcd(a, b) = b$; Suppose $a, b \in \mathbb{Z}^+$, if $a = bq + r$ where $q, r \in \mathbb{Z}$, then $\gcd(a, b) = \gcd(b, r)$.

The **Euclidean Algorithm** efficiently computes the greatest common divisor. The steps in the following:

1) Let $a, b \in \mathbb{N}$ with $0 < b \leqslant a$. Applying the division algorithm to a and b, we obtain integers q_1 and r_1 such that

$$a = bq_1 + r_1, \quad 0 \leqslant r_1 < b. \tag{2-10}$$

2) If $r_1 = 0$, then b divides a, and $\gcd(a, b) = b$, the algorithm stops. If $r_1 \neq 0$, divide b by r_1 to obtain integers q_2 and r_2 satisfying

$$b = r_1 q_2 + r_2, \quad 0 \leqslant r_2 < r_1. \tag{2-11}$$

3) Proceeding recursively, if $r_k \neq 0$, we divide r_{k-1} by r_k to obtain q_{k+1} and r_{k+1}. The process generates a sequence of remainders

$$r_1 = r_2 q_3 + r_3, \quad 0 \leqslant r_3 < r_2 \tag{2-12}$$

$$\vdots$$

$$r_{n-2} = r_{n-1} q_n + r_n, \quad 0 \leqslant r_n < r_{n-1} \tag{2-13}$$

$$r_{n-1} = r_n q_{n+1} + r_{n+1}, \quad \text{with } r_{n+1} = 0 \tag{2-14}$$

4) The algorithm terminates when the remainder r_{n+1} is zero. The last non-zero remainder, r_n is the greatest common divisor

$$\gcd(a, b) = r_n. \tag{2-15}$$

The algorithm is valid because the sequence of remainders forms a strictly decreasing series $b > r_1 > r_2 > \cdots \geqslant 0$ which can't contain any integer greater than b. For $a = bq + r$, we have $\gcd(a, b) = \gcd(b, r)$. Thus, $\gcd(a, b) = gcd\,(b, r_1) = \cdots = gcd\,(r_{n-1}, r_n) = gcd\,(r_n, 0) = r_n$.

Finally, if $k > 0$, then $\gcd(ka, kb) = k \gcd(a, b)$.

Example 2.3.1 Find the greatest common divisor of 72 and 30.
Solution:

$$72 = 30 \times 2 + 12 \tag{2-16}$$

$$30 = 12 \times 2 + 6 \tag{2-17}$$

$$12 = \boxed{6} \times 2 + 0 \tag{2-18}$$

Thus, $\gcd(72, 30) = 6$. ■

Example 2.3.2 Find the greatest common divisor of 282 and 144.
Solution:

$$282 = 144 \times 1 + 138 \tag{2-19}$$

$$144 = 138 \times 1 + 6 \tag{2-20}$$

$$138 = \boxed{6} \times 23 + 0 \tag{2-21}$$

Thus, $\gcd(282, 144) = 6$. ■

A Python implementation of the Euclidean algorithm is provided below. This function is functionally equivalent to the standard library function **math**.gcd(**a**, **b**).

```python
def gcd(a, b):
    a = abs(a); b = abs(b)

    while b != 0:
        a, b = b, a % b
    return a
```

If $a, b \in \mathbb{Z}$, $a, b \neq 0$, and $\gcd(a, b) = 1$, the integers a and b are called **coprime**.

Now, consider posing a question, given three integers a, b, c and a, b are not both zero, how to find integers m and n for the equation $am + bn = c$? The equation is called "**diophantine equation**". If $c = 0$, the equation is called a homogeneous equation, which is called inhomogeneous if $c \neq 0$.

First, if $c = 0$, then the equation is $am + bn = 0$. So we can begin by dividing through by $\gcd(a, b)$ such as

$$\frac{a}{\gcd(a, b)} m + \frac{b}{\gcd(a, b)} n = Am + Bn = 0 \tag{2-22}$$

where $A = \dfrac{a}{\gcd(a, b)}$, $B = \dfrac{b}{\gcd(a, b)}$, and $\gcd(A, B) = 1$. Since A and B are coprime, B must divide m and A must divide n. This yields infinitely many solutions, we have $m = Bq$, $n = -Aq$, $q \in \mathbb{Z}$, there are infinitely many solutions.

If $c \neq 0$, using the same way above, the equation dividing through by $\gcd(a, b)$ such as

$$\frac{a}{\gcd(a,b)}m + \frac{b}{\gcd(a,b)}n = \frac{c}{\gcd(a,b)} \tag{2-23}$$

Notice that if $\gcd(a, b)$ does not divide c, the equation has no integer solution. If $\gcd(a, b)$ divide c, the equation can rewrite by $Am + Bn = C$, $\gcd(A, B) = 1$. Then, using the Euclidean Algorithm to find the solution (m_1, n_1) of $Am + Bn = 1$. The solutions of $Am + Bn = C$ is (m_p, n_p) equal to (Cm_1, Cn_1). The solutions of $Am + Bn = 0$ is (m_h, n_h) equal to $(Bq, -Aq)$.

Finally, solving the system of equations $am + bn = c$ and $Am + Bn = C$, the solutions such as

$$(m, n) = (m_p + m_h, n_p + n_h) = (m_p + Bq, n_p - Aq) \tag{2-24}$$

Example 2.3.3 Find all the solutions to the equation $4m + 18n = 32$
Solution: Applying the Euclidean Algorithm to find the $\gcd(4, 18)$ is 2, and then 2 divide 32, we can determine there are infinitely many solutions. The equation dividing through by 2 to get

$$2m + 9n = 16 \tag{2-25}$$

Obviously, $(m_1, n_1) = (-1, 2)$ is a particular solution. Thus, the general solution is $(m, n) = (-1 + 9q, 2 - 2q)$, where $q \in \mathbb{Z}$. ■

2.4 MODULAR ARITHMETIC

2.4.1 Definition of Modular Arithmetic

Modular Arithmetic is also called the Theory of Congruences, first introduced by the German mathematician *Carl Friedrich Gauss* in his book *Disquisitiones Arithmeticae* when he was 24 years old. The result of the Modular Arithmetic corresponds to the remainder in the Division Theorem.

According to the Division Algorithm, when a positive integer is divided by 2, there are only two possible remainders: 0 and 1. Specifically, even numbers yield a remainder of 0, while odd numbers yield a remainder of 1. Similarly, when dividing a positive integer by 3, there are three possible remainders: 0, 1, and 2. In modular arithmetic, the quotient obtained from the Division Algorithm is of little concern. As we focus on this context, the quotient may be omitted entirely, it is the remainder that is of primary importance.

There are actually many practical applications of modular arithmetic in daily life. For example, the concept of "weekdays" in timekeeping essentially represents modulo 7 arithmetic. Most people primarily care about what day of the week it is (remainder), while few are interested in which week number of the year it represents (quotient). If we broaden our perspective, any scenario where the focus is solely on the periodic outcome can be viewed as an application of modular arithmetic. Let us now formally define modular arithmetic.

Definition 2.4.1 Congruences

Let $a, b, q \in \mathbb{Z}$, and m be a fixed positive integer. If $a - b = qm$ for some integer q, two integers a and b are said to be **congruent modulo** *m, we write*

$$a \equiv b \pmod{m} \tag{2-26}$$

There are three propositions of modular arithmetic [9]

- Reflexive property: For $a \in \mathbb{Z}$, and $a \equiv a \pmod{m}$.
- Symmetric property: For $a, b \in \mathbb{Z}$, then $a \equiv b \pmod{m} \Rightarrow b \equiv a \pmod{m}$.
- Transitive property: For $a, b, c \in \mathbb{Z}$, if $a \equiv b \pmod{m}$ and $b \equiv c \pmod{m}$, then $a \equiv c \pmod{m}$

For $a, b, c, d \in \mathbb{Z}$, $m \in \mathbb{Z}^+$, if $a \equiv b \pmod{m}$ and $c \equiv d \pmod{m}$, then

- $a \pm c \equiv b \pm d \pmod{m}$
- $ac \equiv bd \pmod{m}$
- $a + c \equiv b + c \pmod{m}$
- $ac \equiv bc \pmod{m}$
- If $k \in \mathbb{Z}^+$, then $a^k \equiv b^k \pmod{m}$

Example 2.4.1 Examples of modular arithmetic.

$$\begin{array}{rlrlrl} 97 \equiv 2 & \pmod{5} & 144 \equiv 4 & \pmod{5} & 99 \equiv 4 & \pmod{5} \\ 100^2 \equiv 0 & \pmod{5} & -144 \equiv 10 & \pmod{11} & 97 \equiv 9 & \pmod{11} \\ -99 \equiv 0 & \pmod{11} & 111^2 \equiv 1 & \pmod{11} & (-123)^2 \equiv 7 & \pmod{11} \end{array}$$

Using "%" modular arithmetic in Python. For example, `99%5`, yielding a result of 4. ■

Example 2.4.2 Find the solution of $\sum_{k=0}^{n=100} k! \pmod{15}$.
Solution: $\sum_{k=0}^{n=100} k! \equiv 0! + 1! + 2! + 3! + 4! + \cdots + 99! + 100! \pmod{15}$. Notice that factorial growth is extremely terrifying. Without the help of modulo operations, this problem would be extremely difficult.

However, $5! \equiv 120 \equiv 0 \pmod{15}$, for $k \geqslant 5$, we have

$$k! \equiv 0 \pmod{15} \tag{2-27}$$

Thus,

$$\sum_{k=0}^{n=100} k! \equiv 0! + 1! + 2! + 3! + 4! + 5! + \cdots + 99! + 100! \pmod{15} \tag{2-28}$$

$$\equiv 0! + 1! + 2! + 3! + 4! + 0 + \cdots + 0 \pmod{15} \tag{2-29}$$

$$\equiv 1 + 1 + 2 + 6 + 24 \pmod{15} \tag{2-30}$$

$$\equiv 4 \pmod{15} \tag{2-31}$$

■

Given $m \in \mathbb{Z}^+$ and $a, b \in \mathbb{Z}$, if $\gcd(a, m) = 1$, there is one and only one solution for congruence $ax \equiv b \pmod{m}$. If $\gcd(a, m) \neq 1$, the congruence $ax \equiv b \pmod{m}$ may or may not have a solution.

How to solve the congruence $ax \equiv b \pmod{m}$? First, check whether $\gcd(a, m)$ can divide b. If not, there is no solution. If yes, solve using the following equations:

We rewrite the congruence to $ax \equiv b \pmod{m} \Rightarrow \frac{a}{\gcd(a,m)}x \equiv \frac{b}{\gcd(a,m)} \bmod \left(\frac{m}{\gcd(a,m)}\right)$, denoted by $Ax \equiv B \pmod{M}$. Using the Euclidean algorithm, we obtain the solution (x_0, y_0) for the congruence $Ax + My = B$. By adjusting this solution, we derive the congruence $Ax_0 \equiv B \pmod{M}$. Therefore, the complete set of solutions is given by $x \equiv x_0 \pmod{M}$.

Example 2.4.3 Solving the congruence $4x \equiv 12 \pmod{14}$ and $290x \equiv 5 \pmod{357}$.

Solution: The first congruence is simple, we get $4x \equiv 12 \pmod{14} \Leftrightarrow 2x \equiv 6 \pmod{7} \Leftrightarrow x \equiv 3 \pmod{7}$. The result is unique solution modulo M, if extended modulo m, another solution is $x \equiv 10 \pmod{14}$.

Solving the second congruence, since $\gcd(290, 357) = 1$, so $\gcd(290, 357)$ can divide 5. The calculation procedure follows the same steps as in Example 2.3.3, yielding the result $(x_0, y_0) = (-80, 65)$, so the solutions are $x \equiv -80 \pmod{357}$ or $x \equiv 277 \pmod{357}$. ■

One can observe that no matter how large the modulus m is, the resulting value is always less than m. Therefore, modular arithmetic can be structured as a ring (see Section 2.9.2 for ring definitions), where remainders remain confined within this ring – their maximum possible value being $m - 1$. We denote the set of integers modulo m as

$$\mathbb{Z}/m\mathbb{Z} = \{0, 1, 2, \ldots, m-1\} \tag{2-32}$$

Moreover, when $\gcd(a, m) = 1$, there exists an inverse element a^{-1} such that $aa^{-1} \equiv 1 \pmod{m}$. It should be noted that in modular arithmetic, a^{-1} is not the arithmetic fraction $1/a$. The following example demonstrates the computation of a^{-1}.

Example 2.4.4 Set the modulus number $m = 13$, $a = 7$, find a^{-1}.

Solution: Obviously, $\gcd(a, m) = 1$ since they are primes. So there must be a^{-1}. We get $7 \times 2 \equiv 1 \pmod{13}$, then $a^{-1} \equiv 2 \pmod{13}$.

Similarly, if $m = 103$, $a = 7$, then $a^{-1} \equiv 59 \pmod{103}$. ■

Therefore, it is established that an integer a has an inverse modulo m if and only if $\gcd(a, m) = 1$. We denote as

$$(\mathbb{Z}/m\mathbb{Z})^* = \{a \in \mathbb{Z}/m\mathbb{Z} : \gcd(a, m) = 1\} \tag{2-33}$$

$(\mathbb{Z}/m\mathbb{Z})^*$ is called the group of units modulo m, this group serves as a fundamental building block in number theory and plays a crucial role in cryptographic systems, particularly in primality testing where it has extensive applications.

Example 2.4.5 Find $(\mathbb{Z}/11\mathbb{Z})^*$ and $(\mathbb{Z}/24\mathbb{Z})^*$.
Solution: Since 11 is a prime number, every positive integer less than 11 is relatively prime to 11. Thus, we have

$$(\mathbb{Z}/11\mathbb{Z})^* = \{1, 2, 3, 4, 5, 6, 7, 8, 9, 10\} \tag{2-34}$$

To determine $(\mathbb{Z}/24\mathbb{Z})^*$, we must identify all integers in $\{1, 2, \ldots, 23\}$ that are coprime to 24. The prime factorization of 24 is $2^3 \times 3$. Therefore, we simply exclude all multiples of 2 (even numbers) and multiples of 3. Following similar reasoning, finally get

$$(\mathbb{Z}/24\mathbb{Z})^* = \{1, 5, 7, 11, 13, 17, 19, 23\} \tag{2-35}$$

■

2.4.2 Examples

When a book is published, it is assigned a number called the **International Standard Book Number (ISBN)**. Until 2007, this number consisted of a 10-digit number, but it now consists of a 13-digit number.

An International Standard Book Number consists of 5 parts (for a 13-digit ISBN):

1) The prefix element, currently this can only be either 978 or 979. The element is 3 digits in length.
2) The registration group element, language-sharing country group, individual country or territory, the element may be between 1 and 5 digits in length.
3) The registrant element, identifies the particular publisher or imprint, up to 7 digits in length.
4) The publication element, identifies a specific edition of a publication by a specific, up to 6 digits in length.
5) Check digit, only 1 digit.

Table 2-1: Example of the Five Parts of an ISBN-13

1	2	3	4	5	6	7	8	9	10	11	12	13
Prefix			Registration group				Registrant			Publication		Check

The ISBN-13 check digit is the final digit of the sequence, ranging from 0 to 9. It is calculated such that the sum of all thirteen digits, weighted by an alternating pattern of 1 and 3, is a multiple of 10. Specifically, it satisfies

$$\begin{aligned}&(x_1 + 3x_2 + x_3 + 3x_4 + x_5 + 3x_6 + x_7 + 3x_8 + x_9 + 3x_{10} + x_{11} + 3x_{12} + x_{13})\\&\quad \equiv 0 \pmod{10}\end{aligned} \tag{2-36}$$

Following the weight table.

Table 2-2: Alternate Weights of 1 and 3

Index	1	2	3	4	5	6	7	8	9	10	11	12	13
Weight	1	3	1	3	1	3	1	3	1	3	1	3	-

Each digit, from left to right, is alternately multiplied by 1 or 3, then those products are summed modulo 10 to give a value ranging from 0 to 9. Subtracted from 10, that leaves a result from 1 to 10. Using zero replaces ten, so, in all cases, a single check digit results.

Example 2.4.6 Calculate the check digit for the ISBN 978-711563571-?
Solution: Determine the sum of the weighted products for the first 12 digits of the ISBN

Table 2-3: ISBN Check Digit Calculation Process

Index	1	2	3	4	5	6	7	8	9	10	11	12	13
ISBN	9	7	8	7	1	1	5	6	3	5	7	1	-
Weight	1	3	1	3	1	3	1	3	1	3	1	3	-
Product	9	21	8	21	1	3	5	18	3	15	7	3	-

The sum of weighted products is **114**. Divide the sum of the weighted products of the first 12 digits of the ISBN calculated by 10, determining the remainder. Thus

$$114 \equiv 4 \pmod{10} \tag{2-37}$$

The resulting difference is the value of the check digit with one exception. If the remainder is 0, the check digit is 0. Thus, the check digit is

$$10 - 4 = 6 \tag{2-38}$$

■

The way of expressing the calculation of the check digit

$$x_{13} \equiv 10 - [(x_1 + 3x_2 + \cdots + x_{11} + 3x_{12}) \pmod{10}] \pmod{10} \tag{2-39}$$

2.5 EULER'S φ FUNCTION

Euler's φ function is one of the most fundamental concepts in number theory. Also known as Euler's totient function, it is named after the renowned mathematician *Leonhard Paul Euler*. The formal definition is given as follows [10].

Definition 2.5.1 Euler's φ Function

For $n \geqslant 1$, let $\varphi(n)$ denote the number of positive integers not exceeding n that are relatively prime to n, defined as

$$\varphi(n) = \#\{m \in \mathbb{Z} : 1 \leqslant m \leqslant n,\ \gcd(m, n) = 1\} \tag{2-40}$$

Notice that in some reference books, $\phi(n)$ is commonly used to represent Euler's phi function, where φ is an alternative typographical form of ϕ. Since ϕ is frequently employed to denote angles, this book adopts φ specifically to represent Euler's phi function throughout its content.

If n is composite, then there exists a factor d of n satisfying $1 < d < n$. This implies that there are at least two integers among $1, 2, 3, \ldots, n$ that are not relatively prime to n. Consequently, Euler's φ function satisfies $\varphi(n) \leqslant n-2$ for composite n. When $n = 1$, $\varphi(n) = 1$. If n is a prime number, then

$$\varphi(n) = n - 1 \tag{2-41}$$

The converse is also true. If $n \in \mathbb{Z}^+$, and $\varphi(n) = n-1$, then n is prime.
If $k \in \mathbb{Z}^+$ and n is prime, then

$$\varphi\left(n^k\right) = n^k - n^{k-1} = n^k\left(1 - \frac{1}{n}\right) \tag{2-42}$$

Theorem 2.5.1 Prime Factorization

Let $n > 1$ be an integer. According to the Fundamental Theorem of Arithmetic, n can be written uniquely in the canonical form

$$n = p_1^{k_1} p_2^{k_2} \cdots p_r^{k_r} = \prod_{i=1}^{r} p_i^{k_i} \tag{2-43}$$

where $r \geqslant 1$, each k_i is a positive integer, and $p_1, p_2, \ldots, p_r$ are distinct prime numbers.

Based on this factorization, the value of $\varphi(n)$ is determined by the formula

$$\varphi(n) = n\left(1 - \frac{1}{p_1}\right)\left(1 - \frac{1}{p_2}\right)\cdots\left(1 - \frac{1}{p_r}\right) \tag{2-44}$$

$$= n\prod_{i=1}^{r}\left(1 - \frac{1}{p_i}\right) \tag{2-45}$$

$$= \prod_{i=1}^{r} p_i^{k_i - 1}\left(p_i - 1\right) \tag{2-46}$$

Example 2.5.1 Calculate the value of $\varphi(360)$.
Solution: First, we determine the prime factorization of 360. We have

$$360 = 2^3 \cdot 3^2 \cdot 5 \tag{2-47}$$

Applying Equation 2-44, we obtain

$$\varphi(360) = 360\left(1 - \frac{1}{2}\right)\left(1 - \frac{1}{3}\right)\left(1 - \frac{1}{5}\right) \tag{2-48}$$

$$= 96 \tag{2-49}$$

■

```
# Euler Totient Function in Python
def gcd(a, b):
    a = abs(a); b = abs(b)

```

```
    while b != 0:
        a, b = b, a % b
    return a

def euler_phi(n):
    """Return Euler's totient function phi(n)."""
    if n <= 0:
        raise ValueError("n must be a positive integer.")
    count = 0
    for k in range(1, n + 1):
        if gcd(k, n) == 1:
            count += 1
    return count
```

Example 2.5.2 The values of the Euler φ function for the first 15 positive integers are illustrated in Table 2-4.

Table 2-4: The Values of the Euler Function for the First 15 Positive Integers

n	1	2	3	4	5	6	7	8	9	10	11	12	13	14	15
$\varphi(n)$	1	1	2	2	4	2	6	4	6	4	10	4	12	6	8

Theorem 2.5.2 Euler's Function is Multiplicative

If $m, n \in \mathbb{N}$, and $\gcd(m, n) = 1$, we have

$$\varphi(mn) = \varphi(m)\varphi(n) \tag{2-50}$$

Proof

Let n, m be positive integers with $\gcd(m, n) = 1$. Let n contain r_1 distinct prime factors and m contain r_2 distinct prime factors, such as

$$\varphi(n) \times \varphi(m) = n \prod_{i=1}^{r_1} \left(1 - \frac{1}{p_i}\right) \times m \prod_{i=1}^{r_2} \left(1 - \frac{1}{p_i}\right) \tag{2-51}$$

$$= nm \times \prod_{i=1}^{r_1+r_2} \left(1 - \frac{1}{p_i}\right) \tag{2-52}$$

$$= \varphi(nm) \quad . \tag{2-53}$$

Let N be a composite number expressed as the product of two primes p and q. Then the following relationship holds:

$$\varphi(N) = (p-1)(q-1) \tag{2-54}$$

Example 2.5.3 Calculate the value of $\varphi(55)$.
Solution: $\varphi(55) = \varphi(5 \times 11) = \varphi(5)\varphi(11) = 4 \times 10 = 40.$ ■

2.6 MÖBIUS FUNCTION

In number theory, one frequently encounters real or complex-valued functions defined on the set of positive integers. Such functions, denoted as $f : \mathbb{N} \to \mathbb{C}$, are collectively known as arithmetic functions; Euler's totient function is a prominent example. An arithmetic function f is said to be **multiplicative** if $f(1) = 1$ and the condition $f(ab) = f(a)f(b)$ holds whenever a and b are coprime. We now introduce another fundamental multiplicative function: the Möbius function [10]. This function is named after the German mathematician *August Ferdinand Möbius.*

Definition 2.6.1 Möbius Function

Given a positive integer d, define μ by the rules

$$\mu(d) = \begin{cases} (-1)^k & \text{if } d = p_1 p_2 \cdots p_k \text{ for distinct primes} \\ 1 & \text{if } d = 1 \\ 0 & p^2 \mid d \text{ for some prime } p \end{cases}$$

The values of $\mu(d)$ for the first 15 positive numbers are shown in Table 2-5.

Table 2-5: The Values of $\mu(d)$ for the First 15 Positive Numbers

d	1	2	3	4	5	6	7	8	9	10	11	12	13	14	15
$\mu(d)$	1	-1	-1	0	-1	1	-1	0	0	1	-1	0	-1	1	1

Example 2.6.1 Explaining the Möbius function through concrete examples.

First, consider $4 = 2 \times 2$. Since this factorization contains repeated prime factors, $\mu(4) = 0$. Next, $12 = 2 \times 2 \times 3$. Here we again have duplicated primes in the factorization, so $\mu(12) = 0$. Third, $15 = 3 \times 5$. This number is factored into distinct prime numbers. The Möbius function then follows the rule: $\mu(15) = (-1)^2 = 1$, where the exponent corresponds to the count of distinct prime factors.

```
def isPrime(n):
    if (n < 2):
        return False
    for i in range(2, n + 1):
        if (i * i <= n and n % i == 0):
            return False
    return True

def mobius(N):
    if (N == 1):
      return 1
    p = 0
    for i in range(1, N + 1):
        if (N % i == 0 and isPrime(i)):
            if (N % (i * i) == 0) : return 0
            else : p = p + 1
    if(p % 2 != 0):
      return -1
    else:
      return 1
```

Theorem 2.6.1 Möbius function is Multiplicative

If either m or n contains a squared prime factor and $gcd(m,n) = 1$, then their product mn also contains a squared prime factor. In this case, $\mu(mn) = 0 = \mu(m)\mu(n)$. Suppose m and n have no common factors. Further assume that m is the product of k different primes and n is the product of r different primes. Then mn will be the product of $k + r$ different primes and

$$\mu(mn) = (-1)^{k+r} = (-1)^k(-1)^r = \mu(m)\mu(n) \tag{2-55}$$

The relationship between $\varphi(n)$ and $\mu(d)$

$$\varphi(n) = \sum_{d|n} \mu(d)\frac{n}{d} \tag{2-56}$$

where $\sum_{d|n} \mu(d)$ is the sum of the Möbius function, and $n \geqslant 1$, the value is the following formula:

$$\sum_{d|n} \mu(d) = \begin{cases} 1 & \text{if } n = 1 \\ 0 & \text{if } n > 1 \end{cases} \tag{2-57}$$

Example 2.6.2 Suppose $n = p_1^{a_1} p_2^{a_2}$, then $p_1^i p_2^j$, $0 \leqslant i \leqslant a_1$, $0 \leqslant j \leqslant a_2$, we have

- $d = p_1^0 p_2^0 = 1 \Rightarrow \mu(1) = (-1)^0 = 1$
- $d = p_1^1 p_2^0 = p_1 \Rightarrow \mu(p_1) = (-1)^1 = -1$
- $d = p_1^0 p_2^1 = p_2 \Rightarrow \mu(p_2) = (-1)^1 = -1$
- $d = p_1^1 p_2^1 = p_1 p_2 \Rightarrow \mu(p_1 p_2) = (-1)^2 = 1$

$$\varphi(n) = \mu(1) \cdot \frac{n}{1} + \mu(p_1) \cdot \frac{n}{p_1} + \mu(p_2) \cdot \frac{n}{p_2} + \mu(p_1 p_2) \cdot \frac{n}{p_1 p_2} \tag{2-58}$$

$$= n - \frac{n}{p_1} - \frac{n}{p_2} + \frac{n}{p_1 p_2} \tag{2-59}$$

$$= n\left(1 - \frac{1}{p_1}\right)\left(1 - \frac{1}{p_2}\right) \tag{2-60}$$

If $n = 10$, by Formula 2-56, obviously, it is easy to calculate that

$$\varphi(10) = \sum_{d|n} \mu(d)\frac{n}{d} = \sum_{d|10} \mu(d)\frac{10}{d} \tag{2-61}$$

$$= 10\left[\mu(1) + \frac{\mu(2)}{2} + \frac{\mu(5)}{5} + \frac{\mu(10)}{10}\right] \tag{2-62}$$

$$= 10\left[1 + \frac{(-1)}{2} + \frac{(-1)}{5} + \frac{(-1)^2}{10}\right] \tag{2-63}$$

$$= 10\left[1 - \frac{1}{2} - \frac{1}{5} + \frac{1}{10}\right] = 4 \tag{2-64}$$

2.7 MODULAR EXPONENTIATION

2.7.1 Euler's Theorem

Building upon the number theory knowledge discussed previously, we now derive a fundamental result in modular arithmetic known as **Euler's theorem**. Although this theorem is closely related to Euler's φ function, they represent distinct concepts. Euler's φ function counts the positive integers less than or equal to n that are relatively prime to n. In contrast, Euler's theorem establishes a profound property of congruence in number theory. Indeed, it is widely regarded as one of the most elegant theorems in mathematics.

Theorem 2.7.1 Euler's Theorem

If $a, n \in \mathbb{Z}^+$ and $\gcd(a,n) = 1$, then

$$a^{\varphi(n)} \equiv 1 \pmod{n} \tag{2-65}$$

where $\varphi(n)$ is Euler's φ function.

Example 2.7.1 Prove that $12659^{88} \equiv 1 \pmod{115}$.
Solution: First, we compute Euler's φ function for the modulus $n = 115$. Since $115 = 5 \cdot 23$, we have

$$115 = 5 \cdot 23 \Rightarrow \varphi(115) = \varphi(5)\varphi(23) = 4 \cdot 22 = 88 \tag{2-66}$$

Next, verify the condition for Euler's theorem, which requires that $\gcd(a,n) = 1$. Applying the Euclidean algorithm to $a = 12659$ and $n = 115$, we find that $\gcd(12659, 115) = 1$. Thus, by Euler's theorem, we conclude

$$\underbrace{12659}_{a}{}^{\overbrace{88}^{\varphi(n)}} \equiv 1 \pmod{\underbrace{115}_{n}} \tag{2-67}$$

■

Theorem 2.7.2 Modular Exponentiation

Let $n \in \mathbb{Z}^+$, and let a, x, y be non-negative integers and $\gcd(a,n) = 1$, then

$$x \equiv y \pmod{\varphi(n)} \Rightarrow a^x \equiv a^y \pmod{n} \tag{2-68}$$

Proof

$$x \equiv y \pmod{\varphi(n)} \tag{2-69}$$

$$= y + k \cdot \varphi(n) \tag{2-70}$$

$$\Rightarrow a^x = a^{y+k\cdot\varphi(n)} \tag{2-71}$$

$$\Rightarrow a^x = a^y \cdot a^{k\cdot\varphi(n)} \tag{2-72}$$

$$\Rightarrow a^x = a^y \cdot (\underbrace{a^{\varphi(n)}}_{\equiv 1 \pmod n})^k \tag{2-73}$$

$$\Rightarrow a^x \equiv a^y \pmod n \tag{2-74}$$

Example 2.7.2 Evaluate $7^{42} \pmod{11}$.
Solution: Since $42 \equiv 2 \pmod{\varphi(11)} \equiv 2 \pmod{10}$, we have $7^{42} \equiv 7^2 \equiv 49 \equiv 5 \pmod{11}$. ■

2.7.2 Fast Modular Exponentiation

A central problem lying at the intersection of cryptography and number theory is the *modular exponentiation problem*. Conceptually, exponentiation is straightforward. For instance, to compute 2^{16}, one might express it as the product $2^{16} = \underbrace{2 \times 2 \times 2 \times \cdots \times 2}_{16 \text{ terms}}$ which requires 15 multiplications. However, for large exponents such as $n = 10^9$, directly calculating high-order powers modulo m becomes computationally infeasible. Such inefficiency would render encryption and decryption processes impractical. To address this challenge, we must optimize the computation to evaluate the target exponent in the minimal number of steps.

The key to optimization lies in the binary representation of the exponent. When expanded in binary, any positive integer decomposes uniquely into a sum of distinct powers of 2, with coefficients restricted to 0 or 1. Recall the computation of 2^{16} (refer to Example 1.3.1 for the decimal-to-binary conversion). In this context, we exploit the method of iterative squaring to achieve efficient computation

$$2^{16} \Rightarrow 2 \xrightarrow{\text{Square}} 2^2 \xrightarrow{\text{Square}} 2^4 \xrightarrow{\text{Square}} 2^8 \xrightarrow{\text{Square}} 2^{16}$$

This approach requires only 4 steps to reach the solution. Compared to performing 15 repeated operations, this technique offers a significant reduction in computational cost.

Consider the case where the exponent is not a power of 2. For example, how do we compute 3^{15}? The solution lies in the method of exponentiation by squaring, which utilizes binary decomposition

$$3^{15} \Rightarrow 3 \xrightarrow{\text{Square}} 3^2 \xrightarrow{\text{Square}} 3^4 \xrightarrow{\text{Square}} 3^8 \xrightarrow{\text{Multiply } 3^4} 3^{12} \xrightarrow{\text{Multiply } 3^2} 3^{14} \xrightarrow{\text{Multiply } 3} 3^{15}$$

This approach requires only 6 steps to reach the solution.

Example 2.7.3 The previous example involves simple computations that can be performed using straightforward arithmetic. However, for modular exponentiation involving large numbers, such as $1915793^{2641} \pmod{5678923}$, direct calculation becomes computationally infeasible due to the sheer magnitude of the intermediate values. This necessitates the use of modular exponentiation algorithms designed to prevent these intermediate results from growing excessively.

Solution: Decompose the exponent $k = 2641$ in the expression $a^k \pmod{n}$ into a sum of powers of 2 by writing it in binary

$$k = 2641 = 2^0 + 2^4 + 2^6 + 2^9 + 2^{11} = 1 + 16 + 64 + 512 + 2048$$

Binary in Python:

```
number = 2641

terms = [
    str(2 ** i)
    for i, bit in enumerate(bin(number)[:1:-1])
        if bit == '1']

print(' + '.join(terms))
```

Step 1: Use the method of **repeated squaring** to calculate the powers of a modulo n, for all powers of 2 less than or equal to k.

Step 2: Given $a = 1915793$, we first calculate $a^2 \equiv 3278564 \pmod{n}$. We avoid direct computation of higher powers by using the previous result. For instance, we compute a^4 by squaring the residue of a^2 such as $a^4 \equiv (a^2)^2 \equiv 3278564^2 \equiv 1631541 \pmod{n}$. This value then serves as the base for computing a^8, yielding $a^8 \equiv (a^4)^2 \equiv 1631541^2 \equiv 4704430 \pmod{n}$. This process is repeated to efficiently compute the residues for all required powers of two, significantly reducing the computational complexity, we have

$$\begin{array}{llllll}
a^2 & \equiv 3278564 \pmod{n} & a^4 & \equiv 1631541 \pmod{n} & a^8 & \equiv 4704430 \pmod{n} \\
a^{16} & \equiv 1424066 \pmod{n} & a^{32} & \equiv 3532287 \pmod{n} & a^{64} & \equiv 3305529 \pmod{n} \\
a^{128} & \equiv 1529537 \pmod{n} & a^{256} & \equiv 5673135 \pmod{n} & a^{512} & \equiv 5106329 \pmod{n} \\
a^{1024} & \equiv 2627277 \pmod{n} & a^{2048} & \equiv 1180227 \pmod{n} & &
\end{array}$$

Step 3: Use the properties of modular multiplication to combine the results obtained in Step 2, selecting only those corresponding to the powers of 2 identified in Step 1

$$a^k \equiv a \cdot a^{16} \cdot a^{64} \cdot a^{512} \cdot a^{2048} \pmod{n} \tag{2-75}$$

$$\equiv 1915793 \cdot 1424066 \cdot 3305529 \cdot 5106329 \cdot 1180227 \pmod{n} \tag{2-76}$$

$$\equiv 1162684 \pmod{n} \tag{2-77}$$

■

This optimized Python implementation demonstrates faster computation than the `a**n%p` operator approach by avoiding redundant calculations. The function below replicates the behavior of Python's built-in `pow(a,n,p)` with the same level efficiency.

```python
def fastExpMod(a, n, p):
    result = 1
    while n != 0:
        if (n&1) == 1:
            # ei = 1, then mul
            result = (result * a) % p
        n >>= 1
        # a, a^2, a^4, a^8, ..., a^(2^n)
        a = (a*a) % p
    return result
```

Let a, k and n be positive integers, the time complexity for computing $a^k \pmod{n}$ is $\mathcal{O}((\log_2 n)^2 \log_2 k)$.

Euler's theorem is not only applied in fast modular exponentiation for large numbers but also provides a method to determine the modular multiplicative inverse. Let $\gcd(a, n) = 1$, according to Euler's theorem, we have $a^{\varphi(n)} \equiv 1 \pmod{n}$. Multiplying both sides by a^{-1}, we obtain $a^{\varphi(n)-1} \equiv a^{-1} \pmod{n}$. Rearranging this congruence yields

$$a^{-1} \equiv a^{\varphi(n)-1} \pmod{n} \tag{2-78}$$

If n is prime, then the equation simplifies to Fermat's Little Theorem

$$a^{-1} \equiv a^{n-2} \pmod{n} \tag{2-79}$$

Example 2.7.4 Find the modular multiplicative inverse for the following expressions of $991^{-1} \pmod{997}$ and $125214^{-1} \pmod{151255}$.

Solution: For the first case, $991^{-1} \pmod{997}$, since $\gcd(991, 997) = 1$, also 997 is prime. By applying Fermat's Little Theorem, we have

$$991^{-1} \equiv 991^{997-2} \equiv 166 \pmod{997} \tag{2-80}$$

For the second case, $125214^{-1} \pmod{151255}$, since $\gcd(125214, 151255) = 1$, we can compute the modular inverse using Euler's theorem. However, the modulus 151255 is not prime, so we must first calculate $\varphi(151255)$.

Since $151255 = 5 \times 13^2 \times 179$. The distinct prime factors are $5, 13$, and 179, it is straightforward to compute

$$\varphi(151255) = 151255\left(1-\frac{1}{5}\right)\left(1-\frac{1}{13}\right)\left(1-\frac{1}{179}\right) = 111072 \tag{2-81}$$

Using Euler's theorem, the inverse is given by

$$\begin{aligned}
125214^{-1} &\equiv 125214^{\varphi(151255)-1} \pmod{151255} \\
&\equiv 125214^{111072-1} \pmod{151255} \\
&\equiv 125214^{1+2+4+8+16+64+128+256+4096+8192+32768+65536} \pmod{151255} \\
&\equiv 125214^{1}125214^{2}\cdots 125214^{65536} \pmod{151255} \\
&\equiv 144709 \pmod{151255}
\end{aligned}$$

■

2.7.3 Solving $x^e \equiv c \pmod{N}$

Consider the following congruence:

$$x^e \equiv c \pmod{N} \tag{2-82}$$

where e, c, N are known integers, and the objective is to solve for x. This congruence plays a crucial role in the RSA encryption system, which will be introduced later. In the general case, solving this congruence is computationally hard. However, if the modulus N is a prime number, the problem becomes significantly more tractable.

Suppose $N = p$ is prime, and let $e > 1$ be an integer such that $\gcd(e, p - 1) = 1$. Then, there exists an integer d such that

$$de \equiv 1 \pmod{p-1} \tag{2-83}$$

We need to consider two cases for solving the congruence. First, suppose $c \equiv 0 \pmod{p}$, then we get $x^e \equiv 0 \pmod{p}$, it follows easily that $x \equiv 0 \pmod{p}$.

Suppose that $c \not\equiv 0 \pmod{p}$. Given the congruence $de \equiv 1 \pmod{p-1}$, we can write $de = 1 + k(p - 1)$ for some integer k. Furthermore, since p is a prime and $\gcd(c, p) = 1$, Fermat's Little Theorem implies that $c^{p-1} \equiv 1 \pmod{p}$. (Note: This theorem is stated and proved in detail in Theorem 7.5.3.) By applying these results, we derive the following:

$$\begin{aligned}
x^e &\equiv c \pmod{p} && (2\text{-}84)\\
&\equiv c \cdot 1^k \pmod{p} && (2\text{-}85)\\
&\equiv c \cdot (c^{p-1})^k \pmod{p} && (2\text{-}86)\\
&\equiv c \cdot c^{k(p-1)} \pmod{p} && (2\text{-}87)\\
&\equiv c^{1+k(p-1)} \pmod{p} && (2\text{-}88)\\
&\equiv c^{de} \pmod{p} && (2\text{-}89)\\
&\equiv \left(c^d\right)^e \pmod{p} && (2\text{-}90)
\end{aligned}$$

Thus, we clearly observe that the congruence $x^e \equiv c \pmod{p}$ has a unique solution

$$x \equiv c^d \pmod{p} \tag{2-91}$$

Example 2.7.5 Solve the following congruence:

$$x^{2345} \equiv 2669 \pmod{8017} \tag{2-92}$$

Solution: Since 8017 is a prime number, the problem can be transformed into another congruence involving the determination of d

$$2345d \equiv 1 \pmod{p-1} \tag{2-93}$$

According to Euler's theorem, we have $d \equiv 2345^{-1} \equiv 1193 \pmod{8016}$. Substituting this value into the formula yields the desired result

$$x \equiv c^d \pmod{p} \equiv 2669^{1193} \equiv 511 \pmod{8017} \tag{2-94}$$

■

2.8 QUADRATIC RESIDUES

Let p be a prime, and let $a, b \in \mathbb{Z}$. If a is not divisible by p and is congruent to a square modulo p, then a is called a quadratic residue modulo p [10]. Conversely, if b is not divisible by p and is not congruent to a square modulo p, then b is called a quadratic non-residue modulo p.

Formally, the set of all quadratic residues modulo p is denoted by $\mathrm{QR}(p)$.

Definition 2.8.1 Quadratic Residues

An integer a is a ***quadratic residue*** *modulo p if the congruence:*

$$x^2 - a \equiv 0 \pmod{p} \tag{2-95}$$

has a solution, where p is an odd prime and $\gcd(a, p) = 1$. Otherwise, a is a ***quadratic non-residue*** *modulo p.*

Example 2.8.1 Find all the quadratic residues modulo $p = 5, 7$ and 11.
Solution: We compute the squares of the integers modulo p for each case. The results are summarized in the following tables, where the distinct quadratic residues are highlighted

(mod 5):

x	1	2	3	4
x^2	1	4	4	1

(mod 7):

x	1	2	3	4	5	6
x^2	1	4	2	2	4	1

(mod 11):

x	1	2	3	4	5	6	7	8	9	10
x^2	1	4	9	5	3	3	5	9	4	1

For modulo 5, we observe that the squares of integers relatively prime to 5 are congruent to either 1 or 4. Thus, the quadratic residues are $\{1, 4\}$, while the quadratic non-residue are $\{2, 3\}$.

Similarly, for modulo 7, the set of quadratic residues is $\{1, 2, 4\}$, and the set of quadratic non-residues is $\{3, 5, 6\}$.

For modulo 11, the quadratic residues are $\{1, 3, 4, 5, 9\}$, and the quadratic non-residues are $\{2, 6, 7, 8, 10\}$. ■

Let p be an odd prime and a is an integer such that $p \nmid a$, then the congruence $x^2 - a \equiv 0 \pmod{p}$ has no solution or has exactly two incongruent solutions modulo p.

Theorem 2.8.1 Number of Quadratic Residues

Let p be an odd prime. Precisely half of the integers in the set $\{1, 2, \ldots, p-1\}$ are quadratic residues modulo p. Thus, the number of quadratic residues *modulo p is equal to $(p-1)/2$. Moreover*

$$1^2, 2^2, \ldots, \left(\frac{p-1}{2}\right)^2 \tag{2-96}$$

are distinct modulo p.

Proof

For any $x \in \{1, 2, \ldots, p-1\}$, the residue $x^2 \bmod p$ is a quadratic residue, we have

$$x^2 - (p-x)^2 \equiv 0 \pmod{p} \tag{2-97}$$

it follows that x^2 and $(p-x)^2$ are equivalent to the same quadratic residue modulo p. Therefore, it suffices to compute $x^2 \pmod{p}$ to find all the distinct quadratic residues.

Next, we verify whether the computed quadratic residues $x^2 \pmod{p}$ are pairwise distinct. Furthermore, let c be an integer such that

$$x^2 \equiv c^2 \pmod{p} \Longrightarrow (x+c)(x-c) \equiv 0 \pmod{p} \tag{2-98}$$

$$\Longrightarrow x \equiv \pm c \pmod{p} \tag{2-99}$$

Since $1 \leqslant x, c \leqslant (p-1)/2$, their sum is bounded by $2 \leqslant x + c \leqslant p-1$. Therefore, p cannot divide $x+c$. It follows that p must divide $x-c$, forcing $x = c$. This confirms the uniqueness of the residues.

The **Legendre symbol**, also known as the quadratic character, was introduced by the French mathematician *Adrien-Marie Legendre*. It serves as a fundamental tool in number theory, extensively used to determine the solvability of quadratic congruences and to analyze the properties of their solutions.

In fields such as algebraic number theory and cryptography, the Legendre symbol plays an indispensable role in studying the properties of integers. For example, in subsequent chapters regarding elliptic curve cryptography, it will be employed to verify the existence of points on a curve.

Definition 2.8.2 Legendre Symbol

The Legendre symbol is defined by

$$\left(\frac{a}{p}\right) = \begin{cases} 1 & \text{if } a \in QR(p) \\ -1 & \text{if } a \notin QR(p) \\ 0 & \text{if } a \equiv 0 \pmod{p} \end{cases} \tag{2-100}$$

where p is an odd prime and a is any integer.

Now if we want to determine whether a number is a quadratic residue modulo p, we can use Euler's criterion. This serves as the most fundamental method for determining quadratic residues.

Theorem 2.8.2 Euler's Criterion

Let p be an odd prime, for all positive integers a, then

$$a^{\frac{p-1}{2}} \pmod{p} \equiv \begin{cases} 1 & \text{if } a \in QR(p) \\ -1 & \text{if } a \notin QR(p) \end{cases} \tag{2-101}$$

According to Euler's criterion mentioned above, we have

$$\left(\frac{a}{p}\right) \equiv a^{(p-1)/2} \pmod{p} \text{ and } \left(\frac{a}{p}\right) = \left(\frac{a \pmod{p}}{p}\right) \tag{2-102}$$

Thus, we obtain the property

$$\left(\frac{ab}{p}\right) = \left(\frac{a}{p}\right)\left(\frac{b}{p}\right) \tag{2-103}$$

The Legendre symbol has the following key properties:

1) If $a \equiv b \pmod{p}$, then $\left(\frac{a}{p}\right) = \left(\frac{b}{p}\right)$.

2) If p does not divide a, then $\left(\frac{a^2}{p}\right) = 1$.

3) $\left(\frac{1}{p}\right) = 1$.

Theorem 2.8.3 Quadratic Reciprocity Law

For any distinct odd primes p and q, we have

$$\left(\frac{p}{q}\right) = (-1)^{\frac{(p-1)(q-1)}{4}} \left(\frac{q}{p}\right) \tag{2-104}$$

Example 2.8.2 Compute the Legendre symbols of $\left(\frac{5}{71}\right)$ and $\left(\frac{3}{79}\right)$

Solution: Applying the Law of Quadratic Reciprocity and the properties of the Legendre symbol, we have

$$\left(\frac{5}{71}\right) = (-1)^{\frac{(5-1)(71-1)}{4}} \cdot \left(\frac{71}{5}\right) = \left(\frac{71}{5}\right) = \left(\frac{71 \pmod{5}}{5}\right) = \left(\frac{1}{5}\right) = 1$$

$$\left(\frac{3}{79}\right) = (-1)^{\frac{(3-1)(79-1)}{4}} \cdot \left(\frac{79}{3}\right) = -\left(\frac{79}{3}\right) = -\left(\frac{79 \pmod{3}}{3}\right) = -\left(\frac{1}{3}\right) = -1$$

■

Suppose p and q are distinct odd primes. If at least one of them is congruent to 1 (mod 4), then the exponent $\frac{(p-1)(q-1)}{4}$ is an even integer. Consequently, the congruence $x^2 \equiv p \pmod q$ has a solution if and only if $x^2 \equiv q \pmod p$ has a solution.

Example 2.8.3 Determine whether 3 and 4 are quadratic residues modulo 5.
Solution: Since $3^{(5-1)/2} = 9 \equiv -1 \pmod 5$, 3 is not a quadratic residue modulo 5.
Since $4^{(5-1)/2} = 16 \equiv 1 \pmod 5$, 4 is a quadratic residue modulo 5.
The Python code for Euler's criterion is as follows:

```
def euler_criterion(n, p):
    n = n % p
    if n == 0:
        return True

    return pow(n, (p - 1) // 2, p) == 1
```

■

The Legendre symbol possesses a significant limitation: its definition is restricted to odd prime moduli. Consequently, when applying the law of quadratic reciprocity to compute the symbol for larger numbers, one is often required to perform prime factorization of the integers involved. This process becomes computationally infeasible as the numbers grow in size. To overcome this obstacle, we employ the Jacobi symbol. Introduced by the German mathematician *Carl Jacobi*, this symbol serves as a generalization of the Legendre symbol. The Jacobi symbol is particularly powerful in computational number theory, as it facilitates the evaluation of Legendre symbols without the need for prime factorization.

Definition 2.8.3 Jacobi Symbol

Let n be an odd positive integer with prime factorization $n = p_1 p_2 \cdots p_k$. For any integer a, the Jacobi symbol, denoted by $J(a, n)$, is defined as

$$J(a,n) = \left(\frac{a}{p_1}\right)\left(\frac{a}{p_2}\right)\cdots\left(\frac{a}{p_k}\right) \tag{2-105}$$

where each factor $\left(\frac{a}{p_i}\right)$ is a Legendre symbol. When n is large and its prime factorization is unknown, direct computation based on this definition is computationally infeasible. But the Jacobi symbol can still be efficiently evaluated using the following recursive properties:

$$J(a,n) = \begin{cases} 0 & \text{if } \gcd(a,n) \neq 1 \\ 1 & \text{if } a = 1 \\ (-1)^{\frac{n^2-1}{8}} J\left(\frac{a}{2}, n\right) & \text{if } a \text{ is even} \\ (-1)^{\frac{(a-1)(n-1)}{4}} J(n \pmod a, a) & \text{if } a \text{ is odd and } a > 1 \end{cases} \tag{2-106}$$

Example 2.8.4 Evaluate $J(24, 601)$
Solution:

$$J(24,601) = (-1)^{(601^2-1)/8} \cdot J(12,601) \tag{2-107}$$
$$= J(12,601) \tag{2-108}$$
$$= (-1)^{(601^2-1)/8} \cdot J(6,601) \tag{2-109}$$
$$= J(6,601) \tag{2-110}$$
$$= J(3,601) \tag{2-111}$$
$$= (-1)^{(3-1)(601-1)/4)} \cdot J(601,3) \tag{2-112}$$
$$= J(601,3) \tag{2-113}$$
$$= J(601 \pmod 3), 3) \tag{2-114}$$
$$= J(1,3) \tag{2-115}$$
$$= 1 \tag{2-116}$$

The Python code for Jacobi Symbol is as follows:

```
#Jacobi Symbol Calculate
def jacobi(a, n):
    assert(n > a > 0 and n%2 == 1)
    t = 1
    while a != 0:
        while a % 2 == 0:
            a /= 2
            r = n % 8
            if r == 3 or r == 5:
                t = -t
        a, n = n, a
        if a % 4 == n % 4 == 3:
            t = -t
        a %= n
    if n == 1:
        return t
    else:
        return 0

j = jacobi(24, 601) #Example
```

■

2.9 ABSTRACT ALGEBRA

2.9.1 Group

In abstract algebra (also known as modern algebra), the primary objects of study are algebraic structures, including but not limited to groups, rings, and fields, which form the fundamental framework of this field [11]. These algebraic structures consist of sets equipped with one or more operations. The operations are subject to certain axioms, which in turn define the properties of the set.

Before formally introducing group theory, we first present the concept of a **binary operation.** Let G be a non-empty set. A binary operation on G is a function $* : G \times G \to G$. In other words, "$*$" is an operation that assigns to each ordered pair of elements $(a, b) \in G \times G$ a unique element $a * b \in G$. The fact that the result $a * b$ lies in G implies that the set G is closed under the operation $*$.

We begin by introducing the concept of a group.

Definition 2.9.1 Group

Let G be a non-empty set, and let $*$ be a binary operation on G. Then G is a group under this operation if the following four properties are satisfied:

1) ***Closure:*** *For any $a, b \in G$, $a * b$ is also in G*
2) ***Associativity:*** *For any $a, b, c \in G$, $(a * b) * c = a * (b * c)$*
3) ***Identity Element:*** *There exists $e \in G$ and for all $a \in G$ such that $a * e = e * a = a$*
4) ***Inverse Element:*** *For any $a \in G$, there exists $a^{-1} \in G$ such that $a * a^{-1} = a^{-1} * a = e$*

For example, the set of integers $\mathbb{Z}$ under the operation of addition forms a group that satisfies the axioms listed above. In this case, the identity element is 0, and the inverse of an element a is $-a$. Elliptic curves provide another critical example in cryptography. As will be detailed in Chapter 9, the points on an elliptic curve, together with a specifically defined geometric operation, form a group. In this context, the group operation satisfies the associative law, and the identity element is the point at infinity, denoted by $\mathcal{O}$.

Groups are classified based on the cardinality of their underlying sets. If the set G contains a finite number of elements, the group is called a **finite group**. The number of elements in G is defined as the **order** of the group, typically denoted by $|G|$ or $\text{ord}(G)$. Conversely, if G contains an infinite number of elements, it is called an **infinite group** (e.g., the integers $\mathbb{Z}$).

Furthermore, if a group satisfies the additional condition that for all $a, b \in G$

$$a * b = b * a \tag{2-117}$$

then the group is called an **Abelian group** (or a commutative group).

Examples of groups:

- The set of integers under ordinary addition($\langle \mathbb{Z}, + \rangle$); the set of rational numbers under ordinary addition($\langle \mathbb{Q}, + \rangle$); the set of real numbers under ordinary addition($\langle \mathbb{R}, + \rangle$), are all groups. In each case, the identity element is 0 and the inverse element is $-a$.
- The set of positive integers $\mathbb{Z}^+$ under ordinary addition, $\langle \mathbb{Z}^+, + \rangle$, is not a group. Since there is no identity element such that $a + e = e + a = a$, $a \in \mathbb{Z}^+$.
- The set of positive integers $\mathbb{Z}^+$ under ordinary multiplication, $\langle \mathbb{Z}^+, \times \rangle$, is not a group. Although the identity element is 1, no element $a > 1$ has a multiplicative inverse in $\mathbb{Z}^+$.

Example 2.9.1 Let $*$ be defined on $\mathbb{Q}^+$ such that $a * b = ab/2$. Show that $\langle \mathbb{Q}^+, * \rangle$ is a group.

Solution: To prove that $\langle \mathbb{Q}^+, * \rangle$ is a group, we must verify that it satisfies the four group properties.

1) **Closure:** For any $a, b \in \mathbb{Q}^+$, the product ab is a positive rational number. Consequently, $a * b = \frac{ab}{2}$ is also in $\mathbb{Q}^+$. Thus, the set is closed under $*$.
2) **Associativity:** For any $a, b, c \in \mathbb{Q}^+$, we have $(a * b) * c = \dfrac{ab}{2} * c = \dfrac{abc}{4} = a * \dfrac{bc}{2} = a * (b * c)$. Since $(a * b) * c = a * (b * c)$, the operation is associative.
3) **Identity Element:** $2 \in \mathbb{Q}^+$, and $2 * a = a = a * 2$, so 2 is an identity element for $*$.
4) **Inverse Element:** For any $a \in \mathbb{Q}^+$, we seek an element a^{-1} such that $a * a^{-1} = e = 2$. Solving $\frac{aa^{-1}}{2} = 2$ gives $a^{-1} = \frac{4}{a}$. Since a is a positive rational number, $\frac{4}{a}$ is also in $\mathbb{Q}^+$. Thus, every element has an inverse.

Since all four group properties are satisfied, $\langle \mathbb{Q}^+, * \rangle$ is a group. ■

Definition 2.9.2 Subgroup

Let G be a group and let H be a non-empty subset of G. If H is a group when equipped with the restriction of $*$, then H is a subgroup of G. We can write

$$H \leqslant G \tag{2-118}$$

Example 2.9.2 Examples of subgroups:

- $\langle \mathbb{Z}, + \rangle$ is a subgroup of $\langle \mathbb{R}, + \rangle$;
- $\langle \mathbb{Q}^+, \times \rangle$ is a subgroup of $\langle \mathbb{R}^+, \times \rangle$;
- Given a group G with identity element denoted e, the set $\{e\}$ is a subgroup of G.

Definition 2.9.3 Cyclic Group

Let G be a group and let $a \in G$. Then

$$H = \langle a \rangle = \left\{ a^k \mid k \in \mathbb{Z} \right\} \tag{2-119}$$

is a subgroup of G and is the smallest subgroup of G which contains a, we say H is the cyclic subgroup $\langle a \rangle$ of G generated by a.

Example 2.9.3 Examples of cyclic groups:

1) $\langle \mathbb{Z}, + \rangle$ is a cyclic group, generated by 1 and -1.
2) $\langle \mathbb{Z}_n, + \rangle$ is a cyclic group that under addition modulo n, generated by 1 and -1, where $-1 = n - 1$.
3) $\langle \mathbb{R}, + \rangle$ is not a cyclic group.

For $n > 2$, the $\mathbb{Z}_n$ be the set $\{0, 1, \ldots, n-1\}$, where addition and multiplication is defined to be addition mod n and multiplication mod n.

2.9.2 Ring

A **ring** is another fundamental type of algebraic structure. While the groups discussed in Section 2.9.1 are defined with respect to a single binary operation—whether addition, multiplication, or another specified operation, rings are more complex. Specifically, a ring is a set equipped with two binary operations, typically referred to as addition and multiplication.

Definition 2.9.4 Ring

A ring R is a set which is **closed** *with two binary operations $+$ (addition) and $\times$ (multiplication), denoted by $\langle R, +, \times\rangle$, satisfying the following properties:*

1) *$\langle R, +\rangle$ is an abelian group under addition.*
2) *$\langle R, \times\rangle$, multiplication is associative, that is, for all $a, b, c \in R$, we have*

$$(a \times b) \times c = a \times (b \times c) \tag{2-120}$$

3) *$\langle R, +, \times\rangle$, the operation satisfies distributive laws: For all $a, b, c \in R$, satisfying the following:*

$$a \times (b + c) = a \times b + a \times c \text{ and } (a + b) \times c = a \times c + b \times c \tag{2-121}$$

Let $\langle R, +, \times\rangle$ be a ring, if the ring in which the multiplication is commutative, that is, $a \times b = b \times a$ for all $a, b \in R$, then the ring is a **commutative ring**.

A ring R with **unity** if there exists a multiplicative identity element, that is, there exists $1 \in R$ such that $a \times 1 = 1 \times a = a$ for all $a \in R$.

Example 2.9.4 Examples of ring:

- $\langle \mathbb{Z}, +, \times\rangle$ is a ring, also is a commutative ring.
- The ring of integers modulo n, $\langle \mathbb{Z}/n\mathbb{Z}, +, \times\rangle$, is a ring.
- All of $\mathbb{R}$, $\mathbb{Q}$ and $\mathbb{C}$ under ordinary addition and multiplication are rings, also are commutative rings.
- $\langle \mathbb{N}, +, \times\rangle$ is not a ring, since there is no element $n \in \mathbb{N}$ such that $1 + n = 0$.

2.9.3 Field

Definition 2.9.5 Field

A Field is a set F which is **closed** *with two binary operations "$+$" (addition) and "$\times$" (multiplication), denoted by $\langle F, +, \times\rangle$, satisfying the following properties:*

1) $\langle F, +\rangle$ is an abelian group under addition.
2) $\langle F \setminus \{0\}, \times\rangle$ is an abelian group under multiplication.
3) The distributive laws hold. That is, for any $a, b, c \in F$, satisfying the following:

$$a \times (b + c) = (a \times b) + (a \times c) \tag{2-122}$$

So a field is a commutative ring with unity in which every nonzero element has a multiplicative inverse.

In a commutative ring, an element $a \neq 0$ is a **zero divisor** if there exists a non-zero element $b \in R$ such that $ab = 0$. If a commutative ring with unity has no zero divisors it is called an **integral domain**.

Example 2.9.5 Examples of field:

- The ring of integers modulo p, $\mathbb{Z}_p$ is a field, where p is a prime.
- The rational numbers $\mathbb{Q}$, the real numbers $\mathbb{R}$, the complex numbers $\mathbb{C}$ are fields.
- The set of integers $\mathbb{Z}$ is not a field, since only 1 and -1 have multiplicative inverse.

Relationship of group, ring and field are shown in Figure 2-2.

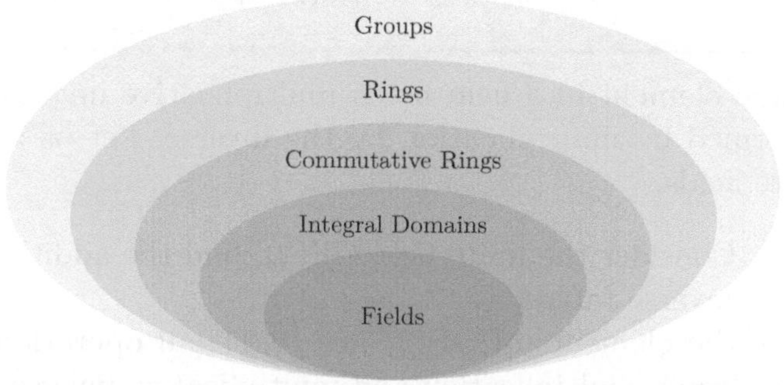

Figure 2-2: Groups, Rings, and Fields

2.10 FINITE FIELDS

A **field** is an algebraic structure in which the operations of addition, subtraction, multiplication, and division (by non-zero elements) are well-defined and satisfy specific properties. Fields are classified by their cardinality. If a field contains a finite number of elements, it is called a **finite field**. Conversely, if it contains infinitely many elements, it is called an **infinite field**.

While elliptic curve operations are often visualized over the real numbers, modern cryptography primarily restricts these operations to finite fields. A finite field is also referred to as a **Galois Field**, typically denoted as $\mathrm{GF}(q)$ or $\mathbb{F}_q$ where $q = p^n$, p is a prime number, and n is a positive integer. It is named in honor of the French mathematician *Évariste Galois*, a founding figure of modern algebra [11].

Finite fields are of fundamental importance in cryptography. A finite field is commonly denoted by GF(p^n) or $\mathbb{F}_{p^n}$, where p is a prime number and n is a positive integer. The **order** of a finite field is defined as the number of elements in the field. Consequently, GF(p^n) is referred to as the Galois field of order p^n. A fundamental property of finite fields is that their order must always be a prime power.

Finite fields are classified based on the value of n:

- When $n = 1$, the field is called a **prime field**, denoted by GF(p).
- When $n > 1$, the field is called an **extension field**, denoted by GF(p^n).

In the context of this book, we primarily focus on fields where $p = 2$. Finite fields of order 2^n are specifically called **binary fields**.

Definition 2.10.1 Prime Fields

Let p be a prime. The set of integers modulo p, denoted by $\{0, 1, \ldots, p-1\}$, equipped with the operations of addition and multiplication modulo p, constitutes a finite field of order p. This field is denoted by GF(p) or $\mathbb{F}_p$.

Theorem 2.10.1 Multiplicative Inverse

For any $w \in \mathbb{F}_p$, if $w \neq 0$, there exists a unique element $z \in \mathbb{F}_p$ satisfying

$$w \cdot z \equiv 1 \pmod{p} \tag{2-123}$$

Every non-zero element in a field has a multiplicative inverse, and division in the field is performed by multiplication by the inverse. Let us now look at a few examples of finite fields.

Example 2.10.1 Consider the finite field GF(2), find the addition, multiplication, and multiplicative inverse tables.

Solution: Since the elements of GF(2) are $\{0, 1\}$, all operations are performed modulo 2. The addition, multiplication and multiplicative inverse tables are shown in Table 2-6, Table 2-7, and Table 2-8:

Table 2-6: GF(2) Addition

+	0	1
0	0	1
1	1	0

Table 2-7: GF(2) Multiplication

×	0	1
0	0	0
1	0	1

Table 2-8: GF(2) Multiplicative Inverse

w	$-w$	w^{-1}
0	0	–
1	1	1

Since the zero element possesses no multiplicative inverse, the value corresponding to w^{-1} is undefined. Furthermore, it is important to observe that in the binary field GF(2), addition corresponds to the bitwise **XOR** (exclusive OR) operation, while multiplication corresponds to the bitwise **AND** operation. ■

Example 2.10.2 Consider the finite field GF(7), find the addition, multiplication, and multiplicative inverse tables.

Solution: Since the elements of GF(7) are $\{0, 1, 2, 3, 4, 5, 6\}$, all operations are performed modulo 7. The addition, multiplication and multiplicative inverse tables are shown in Table 2-9, Table 2-10, and Table 2-11.

Table 2-9: GF(7) Addition

+	0	1	2	3	4	5	6
0	0	1	2	3	4	5	6
1	1	2	3	4	5	6	0
2	2	3	4	5	6	0	1
3	3	4	5	6	0	1	2
4	4	5	6	0	1	2	3
5	5	6	0	1	2	3	4
6	6	0	1	2	3	4	5

Table 2-10: GF(7) Multiplication

×	0	1	2	3	4	5	6
0	0	0	0	0	0	0	0
1	0	1	2	3	4	5	6
2	0	2	4	6	1	3	5
3	0	3	6	2	5	1	4
4	0	4	1	5	2	6	3
5	0	5	3	1	6	4	2
6	0	6	5	4	3	2	1

Table 2-11: GF(7) Multiplicative Inverse

w	$-w$	w^{-1}
0	0	–
1	6	1
2	5	4
3	4	5
4	3	2
5	2	3
6	1	6

■

When the prime p is small, finding multiplicative inverses in a finite field is relatively easy. However, when p is large, how can we efficiently compute multiplicative inverses? One effective method is to use the **Extended Euclidean Algorithm**. This algorithm is an extension of the classical Euclidean Algorithm. Given two integers r and s, the Extended Euclidean Algorithm not only computes their greatest common divisor, but also finds integers a and b such that

Theorem 2.10.2 Extended Euclidean Algorithm

Let r and s be integers not both zero. There exist integers a and b, which can be found by the Extended Euclidean Algorithm such that

$$\gcd(r, s) = ar + bs \tag{2-124}$$

Proof

Let $g = \gcd(r, s)$, so $\gcd(r/g, s/g) = 1$. Consequently, the linear congruence

$$\frac{r}{g}a \equiv 1 \pmod{\frac{s}{g}} \tag{2-125}$$

has a solution and $a \in \mathbb{Z}$. Multiplying congruence 2-125 by g, we have $ar \equiv g \pmod{s}$. There exist $b \in \mathbb{Z}$ such that $ar - g = s(-b)$, then

$$ar + bs = g = \gcd(r, s) \tag{2-126}$$

Let r and s be relatively prime integers. If $\gcd(r, s) = 1$, there exist integers a and b such that $ar + bs = 1$. This equation implies the existence of multiplicative inverses. By reducing the congruence modulo r, we obtain

$$ar + bs \equiv 1 \pmod{r} \tag{2-127}$$
$$0 + bs \equiv 1 \pmod{r} \tag{2-128}$$
$$bs \equiv 1 \pmod{r} \tag{2-129}$$

This congruence shows that b is the multiplicative inverse of s modulo r, denoted as $b \equiv s^{-1} \pmod{r}$. Similarly, reducing modulo s shows that $a \equiv r^{-1} \pmod{s}$.

Therefore, if $\gcd(r, s) = 1$, we can determine these multiplicative inverses by finding the coefficients a and b. This is efficiently achieved using the **Extended Euclidean Algorithm**. We illustrate this algorithm with the following example.

Example 2.10.3 Use the Extended Euclidean algorithm to find integers x and y such that

$$42823x + 6409y = 17 \tag{2-130}$$

Solution: Step 1: We apply the Euclidean algorithm to find the GCD and express the remainders

$$4369 = 42823 - 6409 \times 6 \tag{2-131}$$
$$2040 = 6409 - 4369 \tag{2-132}$$
$$289 = 4369 - 2040 \times 2 \tag{2-133}$$
$$17 = 2040 - 289 \times 7 \tag{2-134}$$

Step 2: Starting from the last equation, we substitute the remainders back up the chain to express 17 as a linear combination of 42823 and 6409

$$17 = 2040 - 289 \times 7 = 2040 - (4369 - 2040 \times 2) \times 7 \tag{2-135}$$
$$= 2040 \times 15 - 4369 \times 7 \tag{2-136}$$
$$= (6409 - 4369) \times 15 - 4369 \times 7 \tag{2-137}$$
$$= 6409 \times 15 - 4369 \times 22 \tag{2-138}$$
$$= 6409 \times 15 - (42823 - 6409 \times 6) \times 22 \tag{2-139}$$
$$= 6409 \times 147 - 42823 \times 22 \tag{2-140}$$

Thus, the solution is $x = -22$, $y = 147$.

The Python code for the Extended Euclidean Algorithm is as follows:

```
def Extended\gcd(a, b):
    if a == 0 :
        return b,0,1

    gcd,x1,y1 = Extended\gcd(b%a, a)
    x = y1 - (b//a) * x1
    y = x1

    return gcd,x,y
```

■

Example 2.10.4 Use the extended Euclidean algorithm to compute the inverse of 8 modulo 11.

Solution: First, use the Euclidean algorithm to compute gcd(8, 11) as follow

$$11 = 8 \times 1 + 3 \Rightarrow 3 = 11 - 8 \tag{2-141}$$

$$8 = 3 \times 2 + 2 \Rightarrow 2 = 8 - 3 \times 2 \tag{2-142}$$

$$3 = 2 \times 1 + 1 \Rightarrow 1 = 3 - 2 \tag{2-143}$$

$$2 = 1 \times 2 + 0 \tag{2-144}$$

Next, we reverse the sequence of equations on the right-hand side in order to perform back-substitution.

$$1 = 3 - 2 \times 1 \tag{2-145}$$

$$= 3 - (8 - 3 \times 2) \times 1 \tag{2-146}$$

$$= 3 - 8 + (3 \times 2) \tag{2-147}$$

$$= 3 \times 3 - 8 \tag{2-148}$$

$$= (11 - 8 \times 1) \times 3 - 8 \tag{2-149}$$

$$= 11 \times 3 - 8 \times 4 \tag{2-150}$$

$$= 11 \times 3 + 8 \times (-4) \tag{2-151}$$

Therefore, $1 \equiv 8 \times -4 \pmod{11}$. We rewrite

$$1 \equiv 8 \times \boxed{7} \pmod{11} \tag{2-152}$$

The inverse of 8 modulo 11 is 7. ■

A finite field is defined as a set containing a finite number of elements, equipped with the operations of addition, subtraction, multiplication, and multiplicative inversion (for non-zero elements). A fundamental theorem states that the number of elements in a finite field is not arbitrary; it must be a prime power. Specifically, the order is of the form $q = p^n$, where p is a prime number and n is a positive integer. For example, $2^7 = 128$ is a valid size for a finite field. When $n = 1$, the field is called a prime field. The smallest possible finite field is GF(2).

For an elliptic curve E defined over a finite field $\mathbb{F}_q$, the curve possesses a well-defined order. The points on the curve, together with the point at infinity, form an Abelian group under the geometric addition operation. Unlike the multiplicative group of a finite field, whose order is trivially $q - 1$, determining the order of an elliptic curve group is a non-trivial problem. The order of E over $\mathbb{F}_q$, denoted by $\#E(\mathbb{F}_q)$, is bounded by Hasse's Theorem, which states that the order lies within the following specific range:

$$q + 1 - g\lfloor 2\sqrt{q} \rfloor \leqslant \#E(\mathbb{F}_q) \leqslant q + 1 + g\lfloor 2\sqrt{q} \rfloor \tag{2-153}$$

where q is a power of a prime p and g denotes the **genus** of the curve. It is crucial to note that for all elliptic curves, the genus is exactly $g = 1$. Informally, the genus measures the topological complexity of the surface; it counts the maximum number of non-intersecting simple closed curves that can be drawn on the surface without disconnecting it. This generalized result is known as the **Hasse-Weil bound**, with a further refinement provided by *Serre* [12]. Consequently, the order of the curve is approximately q.

The Schoof algorithm [13] provides an efficient method for computing the order of elliptic curve over a finite field. Interested readers are encouraged to consult further references for details. In SageMath, a convenient built-in function is available for performing this computation.

Sage ("System for Algebra and Geometry Experimentation") is an open-source computer algebra system for desktop computers and represents a powerful alternative to Mathematica, MATLAB and Magma. Its library contains over 100 additional open-source packages, which are all interfaced via the Python programming language. Therewith, Sage is capable of symbolic as well as numerical computations in analysis, algebra, linear algebra, geometry, cryptography and more. Although Sage is based on Python, it provides a slightly different syntax closer to actual mathematics, which turns it into a perfect tool for mathematicians.

```
p=next_prime(10^3) #Prime
E=EllipticCurve(GF(p),[3,4]) #p A B
E.cardinality_bsgs()   #Order
```

Example 2.10.5 Calculate the orders of the following elliptic curves:
1) The orders of the Elliptic Curve $E : y^2 = x^3 - 3x + 8$ over $\mathbb{F}_{131}$ is 110;
2) The orders of the Elliptic Curve $E : y^2 = x^3 + 4x + 2$ over $\mathbb{F}_{23}$ is 21;

2.11 POLYNOMIAL OPERATIONS

A **polynomial** is a combination of terms containing coefficients and variables raised to positive (or zero) whole number powers. A polynomial $f(x)$ of degree n over a finite field $\mathbb{F}_q$ can be written as

$$f(x) = \sum_{i=0}^{n} f_i x^i = f_n x^n + f_{n-1} x^{n-1} + \ldots + f_1 x + f_0 \tag{2-154}$$

where $f_i \in \mathbb{F}_q$, $i = 0, 1, \ldots, n$, q is a power of a prime p.

The **degree** of polynomial $f(x)$ is the largest $n \in \mathbb{N}$ such that $f_n \neq 0$, denoted by $\deg(f)$. A polynomial of degree n is called **monic** if the leading coefficient $f_n = 1$. A polynomial is called **linear** if its degree $n = 1$. A polynomial is called **constant** if its degree is zero.

Operationally, adding and subtracting polynomials is analogous to combining like terms. When adding polynomials, one simply groups coefficients of the same power. When subtracting, one subtracts the coefficients of the corresponding terms.

Let $f(x) = \sum_{i=0}^{n} f_i x^i$ and $g(x) = \sum_{i=0}^{m} g_i x^i$ be two polynomials where $n \geqslant m$. The addition and subtraction of these polynomials are defined as

$$f(x) \pm g(x) = \sum_{i=0}^{m} (f_i \pm g_i)\, x^i + \sum_{i=m+1}^{n} f_i x^i \tag{2-155}$$

To **multiply** two polynomials, one must distribute each term of the first polynomial to every term of the second. Formally, let $f(x)$ be a polynomial of degree n and $g(x)$ be a polynomial of degree m. The product $f(x) \cdot g(x)$ is a polynomial of degree $n + m$, given by

$$f(x) \cdot g(x) = \sum_{i=0}^{n+m} c_i x^i \tag{2-156}$$

where $c_i = f_0 g_i + f_1 g_{i-1} + \cdots + f_{i-1} g_1 + f_i g_0$.

For **polynomial division**, particularly when the divisor is a non-constant polynomial, we employ polynomial **long division**. This algorithm is analogous to the long division of integers and allows us to express $f(x)$ in terms of a divisor $g(x)$, a quotient $q(x)$, and a remainder $r(x)$.

The polynomials $f(x)$ and $g(x)$ are the **same** if and only if either both are 0 or degree of $f(x)$ and $g(x)$ are the same, and $f_i = g_i$ for all nonnegative integers i.

Example 2.11.1 Let $f(x) = x^3 + 2x^2 + 3x + 1$ and $g(x) = x^2 + x$. Compute $f(x) + g(x)$, $f(x) - g(x)$, $f(x) \cdot g(x)$ and $f(x)/g(x)$.

Solution:

$$f(x) + g(x) = x^3 + 3x^2 + 4x + 1 \tag{2-157}$$

$$f(x) - g(x) = x^3 + x^2 + 2x + 1 \tag{2-158}$$

$$f(x) \cdot g(x) = x^5 + 2x^4 + 3x^3 + x^2 + x^4 + 2x^3 + 3x^2 + x \tag{2-159}$$

$$= x^5 + 3x^4 + 5x^3 + 4x^2 + x \tag{2-160}$$

$$f(x)/g(x) = \begin{array}{r} x + 1 \\ x^2 + x \overline{)\, x^3 + 2x^2 + 3x + 1} \\ -\, x^3 \; - x^2 \qquad\quad \\ \hline x^2 + 3x \quad\;\; \\ -\, x^2 \; - x \quad\;\; \\ \hline 2x + 1 \end{array}$$

■

We now extend the discussion to polynomials defined over a ring, referred to as a **polynomial ring**. The set of polynomials with coefficients in a commutative ring R forms a commutative ring with identity, denoted by $R[x]$. In the context of cryptography, we frequently work with polynomials where the coefficients are elements of $\mathbb{Z}_n$.

Let R be a ring. $R[x]$ is a ring with respect to the standard operations of polynomial addition and multiplication, the ring of all polynomials with coefficients in $\mathbb{Z}_n$. Let $f(x) = \sum_{i=0}^{\infty} f_i x^i$ and $g(x) = \sum_{i=0}^{\infty} g_i x^i$ be two polynomials in $R[x]$, with the strict mathematical condition that only finitely many coefficients are nonzero. The operations are defined as follows:

$$f(x) \pm g(x) = \sum_{i=0}^{\infty} (f_i \pm g_i) x^i \tag{2-161}$$

$$f(x) \cdot g(x) = \sum_{i=0}^{\infty} c_i x^i, \text{where } c_i = \sum_{k=0}^{i} f_k g_{i-k} \tag{2-162}$$

Take GF(2) as an example: addition and subtraction are equivalent to performing modulo 2 on each coefficient. Multiplication of coefficients corresponds to the logical AND operation.

Let F be a field, and let $f(x), g(x) \in F[x]$. If $g(x) \neq 0$, there are unique polynomials $q(x), r(x) \in F[x]$ such that

$$f(x) = q(x) \cdot g(x) + r(x), \text{and either } \deg\ r(x) < \deg\ g(x) \text{ or } r(x) = 0 \tag{2-163}$$

If $r(x) = 0$, then we can say $g(x)$ divides $f(x)$. Here, $g(x)$ is a divisor of $f(x)$. We use the long division to factorize.

Example 2.11.2 Let $f(x) = x^7 + x^5 + x^4 + x^3 + x + 1$ and $g(x) = x^3 + x + 1$ in $\mathbb{Z}_2$. Compute $f(x) + g(x)$, $f(x) - g(x)$, $f(x) \cdot g(x)$ and $f(x)/g(x)$.

Solution:

$$f(x) + g(x) \equiv \underbrace{x^7 + x^5 + x^4 + 2x^3 + 2x + 2}_{\text{coefficient modulo 2}} \equiv x^7 + x^5 + x^4$$

$$f(x) - g(x) \equiv x^7 + x^5 + x^4$$

$$f(x) \cdot g(x) \equiv \underbrace{x^{10} + 2x^8 + 2x^7 + 2x^6 + 2x^5 + 3x^4 + 2x^3 + x^2 + 2x + 1}_{\text{coefficient modulo 2}}$$

$$\equiv x^{10} + x^4 + x^2 + 1$$

$$f(x)/g(x) \equiv \begin{array}{r|l} & \quad x^4 \qquad\qquad\quad + 1 \\ \hline x^3 + x + 1) & x^7 + x^5 + x^4 + x^3 + x + 1 \\ & -x^7 - x^5 - x^4 \\ \hline & \qquad\qquad\quad x^3 + x + 1 \\ & \qquad\qquad -x^3 - x - 1 \\ \hline & \qquad\qquad\qquad\qquad 0 \end{array}$$

Code in Sage

```
R = PolynomialRing(GF(2),'x')
x = R.gen()
f = x^7+x^5+x^4+x^3+x+1
g = x^3+x+1
print(f+g)
print(f-g)
print(f*g)
print(f/g)
```

■

Example 2.11.3 Let $f(x) = 5x^3+3x^2+3x$ and $g(x) = 4x^2+4x+1$ in $\mathbb{Z}_7$. Compute $f(x)+g(x)$, $f(x)-g(x)$, $f(x)\cdot g(x)$ and $f(x)/g(x)$.
Solution:

$$f(x)+g(x) \equiv \underbrace{5x^3+7x^2+7x+1}_{\text{coefficient modulo 7}} \equiv 5x^3+1$$

$$f(x)-g(x) \equiv \underbrace{5x^3-x^2-x-1}_{\text{coefficient modulo 7}} \equiv 5x^3+6x^2+6x+6$$

$$f(x)\cdot g(x) \equiv \underbrace{20x^5+32x^4+17x^3+15x^2+3x}_{\text{coefficient modulo 7}} \equiv 6x^{10}+4x^4+3x^3+x^2+3x$$

$$f(x)/g(x) \Rightarrow f(x) \equiv q(x)\cdot g(x)+r(x) \equiv 3x \times g(x)+5x^2$$

```
R = PolynomialRing(GF(7),'x')
x = R.gen()
f = 5*x^3+3*x^2+3*x
g = 4*x^2+4*x+1
print(f+g,f-g,f*g,f/g)
```

■

Finally, we introduce **irreducible polynomial**. A polynomial of degree $n \geqslant 1$ with coefficients in a field F is said to be irreducible over F if it cannot be written as a product of two non-constant polynomials over F of degree less than n. In other words, a non-constant polynomial is irreducible over F if $f(x)$ cannot be expressed as a product $g(x)\cdot h(x)$ of two polynomials $g(x)$ and $h(x)$ in $F[x]$ both of lower degree than the degree of $f(x)$.

It is crucial to understand that the reducibility of a polynomial depends heavily on the specific field over which it is considered. Note that factoring out a non-zero constant (a unit in the field) does not constitute a reduction. For instance, while $2x^2+1 = 2(x^2+\frac{1}{2})$, this does not make the polynomial reducible, as the factor 2 has degree 0.

The polynomial $x^2 + 1$ is irreducible in $\mathbb{R}[x]$ since it has no real roots. However, it is reducible in $\mathbb{C}[x]$ where it factors as $x^2 + 1 = (x + i)(x - i)$.

2.12 GF(2^N)

The order of a finite field must be a prime power, denoted as p^n, where p is a prime number and n is a positive integer. When $n = 1$, the field is a prime field, commonly denoted as GF(p) or $\mathbb{F}_p$. Why must the modulus p be a prime? The primality of p is essential for the existence of multiplicative inverses. In the structure of integers modulo m (denoted $\mathbb{Z}_m$), a non-zero element a has a multiplicative inverse if and only if $\gcd(a, m) = 1$. If the modulus is composite, the structure contains zero divisors and fails to form a field.

For example, consider $\mathbb{Z}_8$. Since 8 is composite, only 1, 3, 5, and 7, which are coprime to 8, possess multiplicative inverses. Elements such as 2 and 4 do not have inverses. In contrast, in a prime field like GF(7), every non-zero element has a multiplicative inverse.

While mathematically sound, the constraint that p must be prime introduces inefficiency in digital systems, which operate on binary logic. Memory and registers typically store data in blocks of size 2^k (e.g., 8, 16, 32, or 512 bits). If we choose a modulus of 512 (2^9), we cannot simply use arithmetic modulo 512 because 512 is composite. Instead, we would have to choose the largest prime less than 512, which is 509. This results in a "waste" of state space. The values 509, 510, and 511 can be represented by 9 bits but are invalid in GF(509). In massive computations, handling these gaps requires additional checks and reduces data density.

To address this inefficiency, we utilize **Binary Fields**, denoted as GF(2^n). Unlike $\mathbb{Z}_{2^n}$, which is not a field, GF(2^n) is constructed using polynomial arithmetic rather than integer modular arithmetic. This allows us to have a field with exactly 2^n elements, perfectly matching digital representation.

In GF(2^9), for instance

- Representation: Each element corresponds to a 9-bit binary string, representing a polynomial of degree at most 8 with coefficients in $\{0, 1\}$.
- Addition: Polynomial addition corresponds to the bitwise **XOR** operation (since $1 + 1 = 0$ in GF(2)).
- Multiplication: This involves polynomial multiplication followed by reduction modulo an irreducible polynomial of degree n.

This structure ensures that every bit pattern represents a valid element, and every non-zero element has an inverse, making GF(2^n) highly efficient for computer-based arithmetic.

Example 2.12.1 An example of arithmetic over $\mathbb{Z}_4$ and GF(2^2).
Solution: The finite field GF(2^2) uses a set of 2^2 elements, the set is $\{00, 01, 10, 11\}$.

Table 2-12: Addition Over $\mathbb{Z}_4$

+	0	1	2	3
0	0	1	2	3
1	1	2	3	0
2	2	3	0	1
3	3	0	1	2

Table 2-13: Multiplication Over $\mathbb{Z}_4$

×	0	1	2	3
0	0	0	0	0
1	0	1	2	3
2	0	2	0	2
3	0	3	2	1

Table 2-14: Addition Over GF(2^2)

+	00	01	10	11
00	00	01	10	11
01	01	00	11	10
10	10	11	00	01
11	11	10	01	00

Table 2-15: Multiplication Over GF(2^2)

×	00	01	10	11
00	00	00	00	00
01	00	01	10	11
10	00	10	11	01
11	00	11	01	10

■

Arithmetic in GF(2^n) is particularly advantageous for implementation because addition corresponds to the bitwise XOR operation, which is inherently carry-free. This offers significant benefits for encoding and decoding efficiency. At the hardware level, these binary operations map directly onto standard logic gates, minimizing computational resources and reducing hardware costs. Furthermore, intermediate results require no additional storage beyond the binary representation itself, optimizing both memory usage and performance. Consequently, finite fields in cryptographic applications are typically selected to prioritize computational efficiency, hardware friendliness, and algorithmic suitability.

In contrast, extension fields based on small odd primes (e.g., $p = 3$ or 5) are generally avoided in standard implementations. Such fields would require ternary or quinary representations, introducing significant complexity in data storage and arithmetic logic units (ALUs). These non-binary bases are incompatible with standard binary hardware architectures. To simplify algorithm design and minimize hardware complexity, while maintaining compatibility with existing systems, $p = 2$ is the standard choice for the base prime in most extension fields GF(p^n).

We now formally define the structure of these fields. A finite field GF(p^n) is classified based on the exponent n

- If $n = 1$, the field GF(p) is called the **base field** (or prime field).
- If $n > 1$, the field GF(p^n) is called an **extension field** of GF(p).

It is important to distinguish between the finite field GF(p^n) and the ring of integers modulo p^n (denoted $\mathbb{Z}_{p^n}$). Arithmetic in an extension field GF(p^n) cannot be performed using integer arithmetic modulo p^n. The ring $\mathbb{Z}_{p^n}$ contains zero divisors and is not a field. Instead, the field structure of GF(p^n) requires elements to be represented as polynomials. Arithmetic operations are defined modulo an irreducible polynomial of degree n.

Elements in the extension field $GF(2^n)$ are not represented as integers, but rather as polynomials with coefficients in the base field GF(2). The degree of these polynomials is at most $n-1$. For example, any element $A(x)$ of the field $GF(2^8)$ can be expressed as a polynomial of degree at most 7

$$A(x) = a_7x^7 + a_6x^6 + \cdots + a_1x + a_0, \text{where } a_i \in \mathrm{GF}(2) = \{0,1\} \tag{2-164}$$

This polynomial representation allows for a compact digital format. Each element of $GF(2^8)$ corresponds uniquely to an ordered sequence of its coefficients. For $n = 8$, this is an 8-bit vector $A = (a_7, a_6, a_5, a_4, a_3, a_2, a_1, a_0)$.

Generally, an element in $GF(2^n)$ corresponds to a binary vector of length n. Since there are 2^n possible binary vectors of length n, there are exactly 2^n unique elements in the field. Consider the field $GF(2^4)$, the binary vector 1101 corresponds to the polynomial $x^3 + x^2 + 1$.

How are basic arithmetic operations defined for elements in $GF(2^n)$? Let $A(x)$ and $B(x)$ be two polynomials representing elements in $GF(2^n)$. Their addition is defined as follows:

$$C(x) \equiv A(x) + B(x) \equiv \sum_{i=0}^{n-1} c_i x^i, \text{where } c_i \equiv (a_i + b_i) \pmod 2 \tag{2-165}$$

The operations are performed coefficient-wise, following the arithmetic rules of the base field $\mathbb{Z}_2$. Thus, all coefficients are restricted to the values 0 or 1.

In a computer system, this arithmetic is highly efficient. Since polynomial addition in $GF(2^n)$ involves adding corresponding coefficients modulo 2, and since $1 + 1 \equiv 0 \pmod 2$, this operation is identical to the bitwise XOR operation (see Section 1.3.2). Furthermore, in the field GF(2), subtraction is equivalent to addition (since $-1 \equiv 1 \pmod 2$). Therefore, polynomial subtraction is also performed using bitwise XOR. A significant advantage of this arithmetic is that it is carry-free. Addition involves no carry, and subtraction involves no borrow, allowing for high-speed parallel execution in hardware.

Example 2.12.2 Consider the two polynomials $A(x) = x^5 + x^4 + x^3 + x^2 + x + 1$ and $B(x) = x^7 + x^5 + x^3 + x$, where $A(x)$, $B(x) \in GF(2^8)$. Compute $A(x) + B(x)$.
Solution: Add the polynomials and reduce the coefficients modulo 2

$$A(x) + B(x) = x^5 + x^4 + x^3 + x^2 + x + 1 + x^7 + x^5 + x^3 + x \tag{2-166}$$

$$= x^7 + 2x^5 + x^4 + 2x^3 + x^2 + 2x + 1 \tag{2-167}$$

$$= x^7 + x^4 + x^2 + 1 \tag{2-168}$$

Represent each polynomial as an 8-bit vector and perform a bitwise XOR operation

$$00111111 \oplus 10101010 \tag{2-169}$$

$$= 10010101 \tag{2-170}$$

■

Subtraction is similar to addition

$$C(x) \equiv A(x) - B(x) \equiv \sum_{i=0}^{n-1} c_i x^i, \text{ where } c_i \equiv (a_i - b_i) \pmod 2 \qquad (2\text{-}171)$$

Multiplication in GF(2^n) is more intricate than addition. The result is the sum of the multiplication of each term of the first polynomial with each term of the second polynomial. Should this multiplication yield a polynomial of degree exceeding $n-1$, it must be reduced modulo an irreducible polynomial $P(x)$ of degree n. In the context of polynomials over GF(2^n), multiplication is defined as

$$C(x) \equiv A(x) \cdot B(x) \pmod{P(x)} \qquad (2\text{-}172)$$

The irreducible polynomial $P(x)$ is expressed as $P(x) = \sum_{i=0}^{n} p_i x^i$, where each coefficient $p_i \in \{0, 1\}$, and the coefficient multiplication is done over GF(2). If the resulting polynomial $C(x)$ has a degree greater than $n-1$, the operation $C(x) \pmod{P(x)}$ is applied, yielding the remainder $r(x)$ derived from the division of $C(x)$ by $P(x)$.

Example 2.12.3 Consider the two polynomials $A(x) = x^3+x^2+1$ and $B(x) = x^2+x$ in GF(2^4) with irreducible polynomial $P(x) = x^4 + x + 1$. Find the result of $A(x) \cdot B(x) \bmod P(x)$.
Solution: Since the coefficient multiplication is done in GF(2), we have

$$C(x) \equiv A(x) \cdot B(x) \equiv (x^3 + x^2 + 1)(x^2 + x) \pmod{P(x)} \qquad (2\text{-}173)$$

$$\equiv x^5 + \underbrace{x^4 + x^4}_{\text{coefficients mod 2}} + x^3 + x^2 + x \pmod{P(x)} \qquad (2\text{-}174)$$

$$\equiv x^5 + x^3 + x^2 + x \pmod{x^4 + x + 1} \qquad (2\text{-}175)$$

Since the polynomial has a degree greater than 3, we need to find the remainder, the process of division shown below

$$\begin{array}{r|l} & \quad\quad\quad\quad\quad x \\ \hline x^4 + x + 1) & x^5 + x^3 + x^2 + x \\ & -x^5 \quad\quad - x^2 - x \\ \hline & \quad\quad x^3 \end{array}$$

Obviously, the remainder is x^3. Therefore, the result of $A(x) \cdot B(x) \bmod P(x)$ is x^3

$$A(x) \cdot B(x) \equiv x^5 + x^3 + x^2 + x \pmod{x^4 + x + 1} \qquad (2\text{-}176)$$

$$\equiv x^3 \pmod{x^4 + x + 1} \qquad (2\text{-}177)$$

■

Example 2.12.4 Consider the two polynomials $A(x) = x^5 + x^2 + x$ and $B(x) = x^7+x^4+x^3+x^2+x$ in GF(2^8) with irreducible polynomial $P(x) = x^8+x^4+x^3+x+1$. Find the result of $A(x) \cdot B(x) \bmod P(x)$.

Solution: Similarly, the coefficient multiplication is done in GF(2), we have

$$A(x) \cdot B(x) \equiv (x^5 + x^2 + x)(x^7 + x^4 + x^3 + x^2 + x) \pmod{P(x)} \tag{2-178}$$

$$\equiv x^{12} + \underbrace{x^9 + x^9}_{\text{coefficients mod 2}} + \underbrace{x^8 + x^8}_{\text{coefficients mod 2}} + x^7$$
$$+ \underbrace{x^6 + x^6 + x^5 + x^5 + x^4 + x^4 + x^3 + x^3}_{\text{coefficients mod 2}} + x^2 \pmod{P(x)} \tag{2-179}$$

$$\equiv x^{12} + x^7 + x^2 \pmod{x^8 + x^4 + x^3 + x + 1} \tag{2-180}$$

Since the polynomial has a degree greater than 7, we need to find the remainder, the process of division shown below

$$\begin{array}{r|l}
 & x^4 \qquad\qquad\qquad\qquad - 1 \\ \hline
x^8 + x^4 + x^3 + x + 1) & x^{12} \quad + x^7 \qquad\qquad + x^2 \\
 & - x^{12} - x^8 - x^7 - x^5 - x^4 \\ \hline
 & \quad - x^8 \quad - x^5 - x^4 \quad + x^2 \\
 & \quad x^8 \quad + x^4 + x^3 \quad + x + 1 \\ \hline
 & \qquad - x^5 \quad + x^3 + x^2 + x + 1
\end{array}$$

Obviously, the remainder is $-x^5 + x^3 + x^2 + x + 1$. Therefore, we know the result of $A(x) \cdot B(x) \bmod P(x)$

$$A(x) \cdot B(x) \equiv x^{12} + x^7 + x^2 \pmod{P(x)} \tag{2-181}$$
$$\equiv -x^5 + x^3 + x^2 + x + 1 \pmod{P(x)} \tag{2-182}$$
$$\equiv x^5 + x^3 + x^2 + x + 1 \pmod{P(x)} \tag{2-183}$$

From the division above, the remainder is $-x^5 + x^3 + x^2 + x + 1$. Recall that in GF(2), subtraction is equivalent to addition. Therefore, $-x^5 = x^5$.

SageMath code implementation

```
x = PolynomialRing(GF(2^8), 'x').gen()
f = x^5+x^2+x
g = x^7+x^4+x^3+x^2+x
p = x^8+x^4+x^3+x+1

print(f*g%p)
```

■

To compute the multiplicative inverse of a polynomial in GF(2^8), we first formally define the concept. Let $P(x)$ be the irreducible polynomial of degree n defining the field GF(2^n). For any non-zero polynomial $A(x) \in$ GF(2^n), the multiplicative inverse is the unique polynomial $B(x) \in$ GF(2^n) such that

$$A(x) \cdot B(x) \equiv 1 \pmod{P(x)} \tag{2-184}$$

This inverse is commonly denoted as $A^{-1}(x)$.

An efficient method to compute this inverse is the Extended Euclidean Algorithm. The procedure is computationally analogous to the integer case described in Example 2.10.3, with the distinction that arithmetic operations are performed on polynomials over GF(2).

Definition 2.12.1 Generator

For a finite field F of order q, if g is the generator of this finite field, then the finite field can be expressed by the set

$$0, g^0, g^1, \ldots, g^{q-2} \tag{2-185}$$

If g is a generator element, then every element of $\mathrm{GF}(2^n)$, except for the 0 element, can be expressed as some power of g.

2.13 EXERCISES

1) Prove that an integer n is divisible by 7 if and only if n^2 is divisible by 7.
2) Prove the reflexivity, symmetry, and transitivity in modular arithmetic.
3) Solve the following congruences:
   (a) $234 + x \equiv 24 \pmod{51}$
   (b) $x + 23 \equiv 999 \pmod{10003}$
   (c) $2423 + 324 + x + 3452 \equiv 345 \pmod{560}$
4) Prove that for an integer n, n is an even number if and only if n^2 is even.
5) Prove that if a is an integer such that a and m are coprime, then

$$ab_1 \equiv ab_2 \pmod{m} \Leftrightarrow b_1 \equiv b_2 \pmod{m}$$

6) Use the Euclidean algorithm to find the greatest common divisor of
   (a) 165 and 252
   (b) 4282 and 3480
   (c) 11033442 and 1102246
7) Calculate $\varphi(77)$ and $\varphi(\varphi(77))$.
8) Find the smallest positive integer such that $10^{5^{101}} \equiv 10^{5^x} \pmod{77}$.
9) Use the Extended Euclidean algorithm to compute the following multiplicative inverses:
   (a) $101^{-1} \pmod{1009}$
   (b) $307^{-1} \pmod{1511}$
   (c) $907^{-1} \pmod{2897}$
10) Solve the following linear congruence:

$$6x \equiv 15 \pmod{21}$$

11) Let p be a prime, e be a positive integer such that $\gcd(e, p-1) = 1$, and d be the multiplicative inverse of e modulo $p-1$ show the congruence

$$x^e \equiv c \pmod{p}$$

has the unique solution $x \equiv c^d \pmod{p}$ where $c > 0$.

12) Solve the following congruences:
    (a) $x^{11} \equiv 10 \pmod{23}$
    (b) $x^5 \equiv 2 \pmod{43}$
    (c) $x^7 \equiv 18 \pmod{55}$
    (d) $x^{751} \equiv 1145 \pmod{5003}$
    (e) $x^{3727} \equiv 3024 \pmod{8235}$
13) How many integers, greater than 0 but smaller than $n = 2^2 \cdot 3 \cdot 5^3 \cdot 113$, are relatively prime to n?
14) Suppose that $a^x \equiv 1 \pmod{p}$ and $a^y \equiv 1 \pmod{p}$, show that

$$a^{gcd(x,y)} \equiv 1 \pmod{p}$$

15) (a) Give the complete list of quadratic residues modulo 37.
    (b) Find all solutions of the quadratic congruence $x^2+12x+40 \equiv 0 \pmod{37}$.
16) Use repeated squaring to compute $2^{436} \pmod{437}$. Then based on this result, decide whether 437 is a prime number.
17) Calculate the Legendre symbol $\left(\frac{11}{31}\right)$. Use the result to decide whether the congruence $x^2 \equiv 11 \pmod{31}$ has a solution modulo 31.
18) Let p be an odd prime. Assuming p does not divide n, show that

$$\left(\frac{n^2}{p}\right) = 1$$

19) Find the value of the Jacobi symbols of $J(5, 21)$ and $J(17, 866731)$.
20) Compute $101^{4800000023} \pmod{35}$ without calculator.
21) Show that the set of integers $\mathbb{Z}_p = \{0, 1, \ldots, p-1\}$ forms a group under the operation of addition modulo p, with an identity element of 0.
22) Show that if G is a finite group with identity e and with an even number of elements, then there is $a \neq e$ in G such that $a * a = e$.
23) Show that if a group G with identity e satisfies $x * x = e$ for all $x \in G$, then G is abelian.
24) Show that a group containing at least two elements and having no proper nontrivial subgroups is a finite group of prime order.
25) Let $\mathbb{Z}_{18}^{\times}$ be the group of all positive integers less than 18 and relative prime to 18, with the group operation given by the multiplication modulo 18.
    (a) List all the elements of $\mathbb{Z}_{18}^{\times}$.
    (b) Show that $\mathbb{Z}_{18}^{\times}$ is cyclic.
26) Find the number of elements in the given subgroup of $\mathbb{Z}_{40}$.
    (a) $\langle 15 \rangle$
    (b) $\langle 24, 32 \rangle$
27) Show that $\langle \mathbb{Z}, +, \times \rangle$ is a ring.
28) Let a set $\langle M_2\mathbb{Z}, +, \times \rangle$ be a ring, where $M_2\mathbb{Z}$ is the set of all 2×2 matrix with integer entries. Find the identity matrix.
29) Show that for every prime p, $\mathbb{Z}_p$, the ring of integers modulo p is a field.

30) Let $A(x) = x^6 + x^5 + x^4 + x^3 + x^2 + x + 1$ and $B(x) = x^4 + x^2 + x + 1$. Find the greatest common divisor of $A(x)$ and $B(x)$ over GF(2).
31) Let $A(x) = x^7+x^6+x^4+1$ and $B(x) = x^4+x^2+1$. Compute $C(x) = A(x)+B(x)$ over GF (2).
32) Let $A(x) = x^3 + x^2 + x + 1$ and $B(x) = x^3 + x$ with the irreducible polynomial $P(x) = x^4 + x + 1$ over $\mathbb{Z}_2$. Compute $A(x) \cdot B(x)$ over GF (2^4).

CHAPTER 3

Information Theory in Cryptography

This chapter introduces information theory within the context of cryptography. It primarily covers the relationship between the theoretical security and practical security of cryptosystems, the concept of perfect secrecy, and examples of cryptosystems that possess perfect secrecy. The concept of perfect secrecy was first proposed by *Claude Shannon*, the father of information theory, in his 1949 paper "*Communication Theory of Secrecy Systems*". It is primarily applied to cryptosystems that provide confidentiality and is analyzed using information theory concepts such as entropy.

A fundamental principle of perfect secrecy is that no information regarding the plaintext or the key can be obtained from the ciphertext. To accurately define perfect secrecy, we must introduce concepts from information theory, allowing it to be described both qualitatively and quantitatively. We will then compare and discuss this concept with other concepts of secrecy, aiming to explore the issue of information secrecy in depth and to provide readers with comprehensive cryptographic knowledge and practical skills.

Topics covered in this chapter:

- The concept of information theory
- The definition of entropy and entropy in natural language
- How to use Huffman coding for lossless data compression
- An unbreakable cryptographic algorithm
- Perfect secrecy

3.1 ENTROPY

3.1.1 Definition of Entropy

Recall the concept of the "bit" mentioned in Chapter 1. The bit is the smallest unit for measuring information and is a contraction of "Binary Digit". The term was coined by the mathematician *John Tukey* in 1946; he is also credited with the

DOI: 10.1201/9781042011087-3

development of the Fast Fourier Transform (FFT). The concept was first cited and popularized in the famous paper [5] by *Claude Shannon.*

A bit means an entity which can take the value 0 or 1, which can correspond to states such as "off" or "on" in an electric circuit, "true" or "false", and other binary conditions. In information theory, a bit is a measure of information, which depends on the probabilities of occurrence of 0 and 1.

How much information does one bit actually carry? Let's explore this through a few examples.

Example 3.1.1 Consider two alphabets with letter probability in Table 3-1.

Table 3-1: Alphabet Frequency

Letters	A	B	C	D
Alphabet 1 frequency	1/4	1/4	1/4	1/4
Alphabet 2 frequency	1/2	1/4	1/8	1/8

How many yes/no questions do we need to determine a letter in each alphabet?

Solution: The determination method for the Alphabet 1 is illustrated in Figure 3-1. Since in Alphabet 1, each letter has an equal probability of occurring, we can start by asking whether the letter is A or B. This question yields a binary response: yes or no.

- If the answer is "yes", we now know the letter is either A or B.
- If the answer is "no", it must be either C or D.

Next, a second question is asked to distinguish between the two remaining possibilities: If it was A or B, we ask: is it A?

- A "yes" means the letter is A.
- A "no" means the letter is B.

The process for determining C and D follows an identical logic structure.

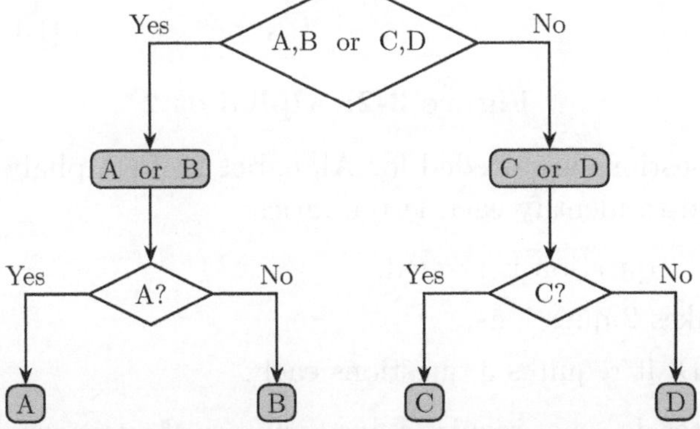

Figure 3-1: Alphabet 1

This binary decision tree leads to the correct result in exactly two steps, leveraging the uniform probability distribution.

For Alphabet 2, a different approach is needed, as illustrated in Figure 3-2.

The first question is: is it A?

- If "yes", the answer is clearly A.
- If "no", we continue to the next letter.

The second question is: Is it B?

- If "yes", the answer is B.
- If "no", we proceed further.

The third question: is it C?

- If "yes", the answer is C.
- If "no", the only remaining possibility is D.

This approach reflects non-uniform probability handling in information theory and often results in fewer average questions when more probable outcomes are placed earlier in the sequence.

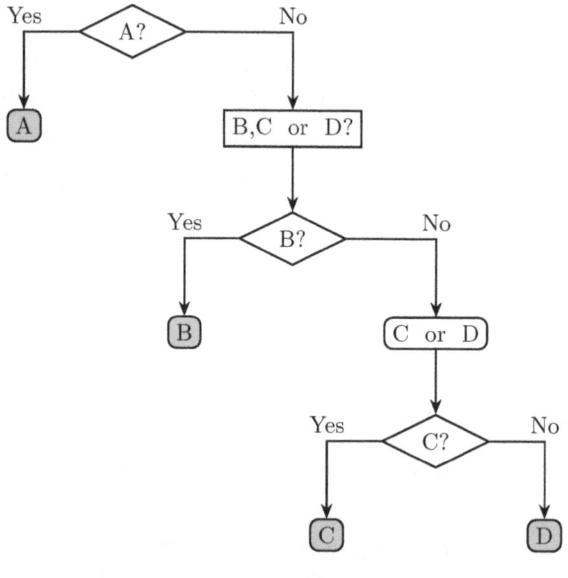

Figure 3-2: Alphabet 2

How many questions are needed for Alphabet 2? In Alphabet 2, the number of questions required to identify each letter varies

- For A, only 1 question is needed.
- For B, it takes 2 questions.
- For C and D, it requires 3 questions each.

Since each letter does not require a fixed number of questions, we calculate the expected number of questions, that is, on average, it takes $\underbrace{1 \cdot \frac{1}{2}}_{A} + \underbrace{2 \cdot \frac{1}{4}}_{B} + \underbrace{3 \cdot \frac{1}{8}}_{C} + \underbrace{3 \cdot \frac{1}{8}}_{D} =$ **1.75** questions to determine a letter from Alphabet 2. ■

By mapping "Yes" to 1 and "No" to 0, the outcome of a binary decision can be expressed as a single binary digit. Generalizing this, if an experiment has N equally likely outcomes, then $\log_2(N)$ bits of information are required to represent the result.

In information theory, the **information content**, also known as self-information, quantifies information gained from the occurrence of an event. Let $X = \{x_0, x_1, \ldots, x_n\}$ be a set of possible outcomes, where each event x_i occurs with probability $P(x_i)$. The information content of x_i, denoted by $I(x_i)$, is defined as

$$I\left(x_i\right) = \log_a \frac{1}{P\left(x_i\right)} \tag{3-1}$$

where $\log_a$ is the logarithm in base a. If $a = 2$, information is measured in **bits**, denoted by $I\left(x_i\right) = \log_2 \frac{1}{P(x_i)}$. If $a = e$, information is measured in **nats**, denoted by $I\left(x_i\right) = \ln \frac{1}{P(x_i)}$. If $a = 10$, information is measured in **hartleys**, denoted by $I\left(x_i\right) = \log_{10} \frac{1}{P(x_i)}$.

According to the change-of-base formula for logarithms, we can deduce that: 1 nat $\approx$ 1.443 bits and 1 hart $\approx$ 3.322 bits.

The less probable an event is, the more information it carries when it happens. The more probable it is, the less new information it brings. For a binary event, when the probability is 0.5, the uncertainty is maximum.

How many bits are required to represent an outcome? Let's look at a few examples

1) A six-sided fair die has $\log_2(6) \approx 2.585$ bits, round up to the nearest integer, 3 bits are required.
2) Roman alphabet has $\log_2(26) \approx 4.7$ bits, round up to the nearest integer, 5 bits are required.
3) The standard ASCII table contains 128 characters. Since $\log_2(128) = 7$, each character requires exactly 7 bits. However, most computer systems use 8 bits (1 byte) to represent a character, with the most significant bit often set to 0.

If the outcomes of an experiment are not equally likely, the number of bits required to represent a specific outcome x_i is given by its self-information that requires $\log_2(1/p_i)$.

Therefore, the expected number of bits required per outcome is

$$\sum_i p_i \cdot \log_2 \frac{1}{p_i} \tag{3-2}$$

Definition 3.1.1 Entropy

The entropy of an event is a measure of the uncertainty we feel about the occurrence of the event. The entropy $H(X)$ of a random variable X is given by

$$H(X) = \sum_a P(X = a) \cdot \log_2 \left(\frac{1}{P(X = a)} \right) \tag{3-3}$$

where X is a discrete random variable, $P(X = a)$ is a probability mass function for X.

In other words, entropy can be used to measure the uncertainty of information, that is, the amount of information contained in a system. When the entropy of a system is high, it means the system contains more information and is therefore more uncertain. Entropy is defined as the expected value of the information content.

Since the probability satisfies $0 \leqslant P(X = a) \leqslant 1$, we have $\log_2\left(\frac{1}{P(X=a)}\right) \geqslant 0$. Thus, the entropy $H(X)$ is always greater than or equal to zero.

Example 3.1.2 Let binary random variable $X = \{0, 1\}$ with distribution $\{p, 1-p\}$, where $0 \leqslant p \leqslant 1$. What is the entropy of X?
Solution: The entropy of X is

$$H(X) = P(0) \cdot \log_2\left(\frac{1}{P(0)}\right) + P(1) \cdot \log_2\left(\frac{1}{P(1)}\right) \tag{3-4}$$

$$= p \cdot \log_2 \frac{1}{p} + (1-p) \cdot \log_2 \frac{1}{1-p} \tag{3-5}$$

$$= H(p) \tag{3-6}$$

The entropy of X depends on p. The graph of $H(p)$ is shown in Figure 3-3. The entropy of X achieves the maximum value when $p = 0.5$, and achieves the minimum value when $p = 0$ or 1. In other words, if $p = 0$ or $p = 1$, the variable X is no longer random but deterministic.

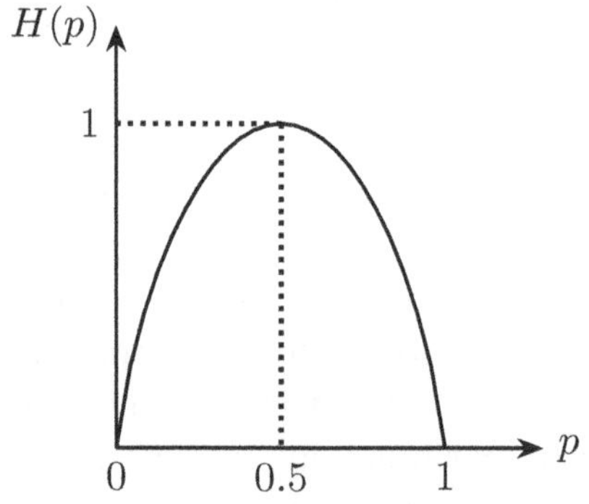

Figure 3-3: Binary Entropy Function $H(p)$

■

As illustrated in Example 3.1.2, the entropy of a random variable X is independent of the values assumed by X. It is determined solely by the probability distribution. Consequently, entropy satisfies the following properties:

1) **Symmetry**. Entropy depends solely on the set of probabilities and is independent of the order of the outcomes.

$$H(p_1, p_2, \ldots, p_q) = H(p_2, p_3, \ldots, p_q, p_1) = \cdots = H(p_q, p_1, \ldots, p_{q-1}) \tag{3-7}$$

2) **Non-negativity**. Entropy is always greater than or equal to zero, that is $H(p) \geqslant 0$. $H(X) = 0$ if and only if X is deterministic.
3) **Certainty**.

$$H(1,0) = H(1,0,0) = \cdots = H(1,0,0,\ldots,0) = 0 \tag{3-8}$$

4) **Continuity**. Events with negligible probability have a vanishing effect on the entropy.

$$\lim_{\varepsilon \to 0} H_{q+1}(p_1, p_2, \ldots, p_q - \varepsilon, \varepsilon) = H_q(p_1, p_2, \ldots, p_q) \tag{3-9}$$

5) **Additivity**. If two random variables X and Y are independent, the joint entropy satisfies

$$H(X, Y) = H(X) + H(Y) \tag{3-10}$$

6) **Maximality**. Entropy is maximized when all the probabilities are equal.

We have considered entropy from the perspective of a single random variable. We now generalize the concept to a pair of random variables X and Y. In this case, entropy can be classified into two types: joint entropy and conditional entropy.

Definition 3.1.2 Joint Entropy

Consider a pair of discrete random variables (X, Y) with joint distribution $P(X = a, Y = b)$, the joint entropy $H(X, Y)$ is given by

$$H(X, Y) = \sum_{a,b} P(X = a, Y = b) \cdot \log_2 \left(\frac{1}{P(X = a, Y = b)} \right) \tag{3-11}$$

The joint entropy measures how much uncertainty there is in the two random variables X and Y taken together.

Definition 3.1.3 Conditional Entropy

Consider a pair of discrete random variables (X, Y), the conditional entropy of X given Y is

$$H(X \mid Y) = \sum_{b} P(Y = b) \cdot H(X \mid Y = b) \tag{3-12}$$

$H(X \mid Y) = H(X)$ if and only if they are independent.

The conditional entropy $H(X \mid Y)$ quantifies the uncertainty remaining about the transmitted message X given the received message Y. This quantity is referred to as the **channel equivocation**.

The conditional entropy $H(Y \mid X)$ measures the uncertainty in the received message Y given that the transmitted message X is known. This is termed the **noise entropy**.

It is important to note that, in general, $H(X \mid Y) \neq H(Y \mid X)$.

Example 3.1.3 Suppose that random variables X, Y, Z are obtained by spinning the wheel below, with X given by the innermost circle, Y given by the intermediate circle, and Z given by the outermost circle, as shown in Figure 3-4. Answer the following questions.

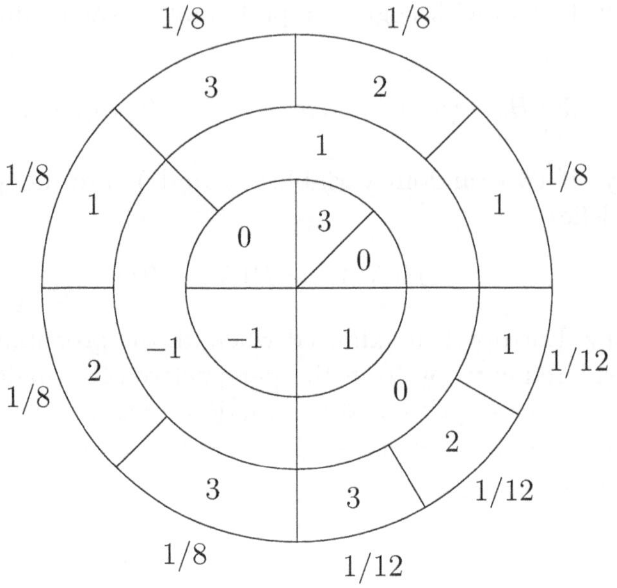

Figure 3-4: Probability of Spinning a Wheel

1) Compute $H(X)$
   Solution: The probability distribution of the innermost circle is shown in Table 3-2.

Table 3-2: Probability of Innermost Circle

a	-1	0	1	3
$P(X=a)$	1/4	3/8	1/4	1/8

$$H(X) = \frac{1}{4} \cdot \log_2(\frac{1}{1/4}) + \frac{3}{8} \cdot \log_2(\frac{1}{3/8}) + \frac{1}{4} \cdot \log_2(\frac{1}{1/4}) + \frac{1}{8} \cdot \log_2(\frac{1}{1/8}) \quad (3\text{-}13)$$
$$\approx 1.906 \quad (3\text{-}14)$$

■

2) How many bits are required to store the results of 100,000 spins of Z?
   Solution:

Table 3-3: Probability of Outermost Circle

a	1	2	3
$P(Z=a)$	1/3	1/3	1/3

$$H(Z) = \frac{1}{3} \cdot \log_2(\frac{1}{1/3}) + \frac{1}{3} \cdot \log_2(\frac{1}{1/3}) + \frac{1}{3} \cdot \log_2(\frac{1}{1/3}) \quad (3\text{-}15)$$
$$= \log_2(3) \approx 1.585 \quad (3\text{-}16)$$
$$100000 \cdot H(Z) = 158,500 \text{ bits} \quad (3\text{-}17)$$

■

3) Calculate the uncertainty of Z given that $X = 0$.
Solution:

$$H(Z \mid X = 0) = \sum_a P(Z = a \mid X = 0) \cdot \log_2 \left(\frac{1}{P(Z = a \mid X = 0)} \right) \tag{3-18}$$

$$= \frac{2}{3} \cdot \log_2 \left(\frac{1}{2/3} \right) + \frac{1}{3} \cdot \log_2 \left(\frac{1}{1/3} \right) \approx 0.9183 \tag{3-19}$$

■

4) Calculate $H(Z \mid Y)$
Solution:

$$H(Z \mid Y) = \sum_y P(Y = y) \cdot H(Z \mid Y = y) \tag{3-20}$$

$$= \frac{3}{8} \cdot H(Z \mid Y = -1) + \frac{3}{8} \cdot H(Z \mid Y = 1) + \frac{1}{4} \cdot H(Z \mid Y = 0) \tag{3-21}$$

The calculation method for $H(Z \mid Y = y)$ is the same as above. ■

5) Calculate $H(X \mid Y, Z)$
Solution: If $X = aY^n + bZ^m$ where $n, m \in \mathbb{Z}$, then $H(X \mid Y, Z) = 0$. This problem satisfies the stated condition. ■

Theorem 3.1.1 Chain Rule

The joint entropy of X and Y is given by the sum of the marginal entropy of X and the conditional entropy of Y given X

$$H(X, Y) = H(X) + H(Y \mid X) \tag{3-22}$$

Proof

Let two random variables X and Y with $P(x, y)$, then:

$$H(X,Y) = \sum_a \sum_b P(X = a, Y = b) \log_2 \left(\frac{1}{P(X = a, Y = b)} \right) \tag{3-23}$$

$$= \sum_a \sum_b P(X = a, Y = b) \log_2 \left(\frac{1}{P(X = a)P(Y = b \mid X = a)} \right) \tag{3-24}$$

$$= \sum_a \sum_b P(X = a, Y = b) \log_2 \left(\frac{1}{P(X = a)} \right)$$

$$+ \sum_a \sum_b P(X = a, Y = b) \log_2 \left(\frac{1}{P(Y = b \mid X = a)} \right) \tag{3-25}$$

$$= \sum_a \sum_b \log_2 \left(\frac{1}{P(X = a)} \right) P(X = a)P(Y = b \mid X = a)$$

$$+ \sum_a \sum_b P(X = a)P(Y = b \mid X = a) \log_2 \left(\frac{1}{P(Y = b \mid X = a)} \right) \tag{3-26}$$

$$= H(X) + H(Y \mid X) \tag{3-27}$$

We can now proceed to derive the general chain rule of entropy

$$H(X_1, X_2, \ldots, X_n) = H(X_1) + H(X_2 \mid X_1) + \cdots + H(X_n \mid X_1, X_2, \ldots, X_{n-1}) \tag{3-28}$$

$$= \sum_{i=1}^{n} H\left(X_i \mid X_1, \ldots, X_{i-1}\right) \tag{3-29}$$

The **mutual information** of two random variables X and Y measures the mutual dependence between them. Specifically, it quantifies the amount of information obtained about one random variable through the observation of the other. For instance, if *Bob* receives a message, he can estimate the probability that it was sent by *Alice*. This is especially useful in authentication mechanisms within cryptography.

Definition 3.1.4 Mutual Information

For random variables X and Y, the mutual information between X and Y is defined by

$$I(X;Y) = \sum_{x,y} P(x,y) \log_2 \frac{P(x,y)}{P(x)P(y)} \tag{3-30}$$

$$= H(Y) - H(Y \mid X) \tag{3-31}$$

$$= H(X) + H(Y) - H(X,Y) \tag{3-32}$$

The relationship between entropy and mutual information is shown in Figure 3-5.

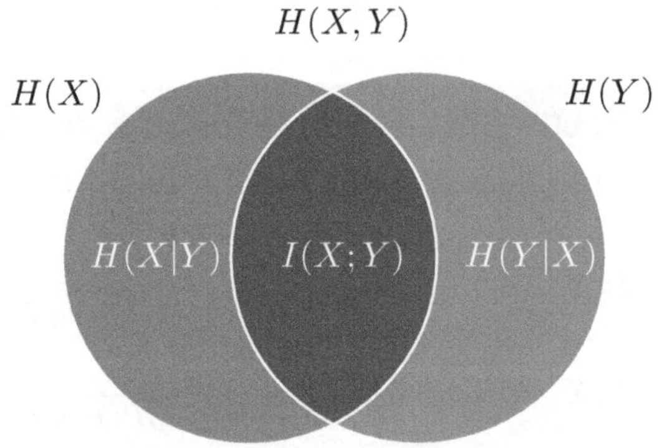

Figure 3-5: Graphical Representation of Entropy and Mutual Information

3.1.2 Important Inequalities

Theorem 3.1.2 Important Inequalities 1

For a random variable X which takes only k values, we have

$$H(X) \leqslant \log_2(k) \tag{3-33}$$

with equality if and only if X takes all its values with equal probability.

Proof

$$H(X) = \sum P(X=a) \cdot \log_2 \left(\frac{1}{P(X=a)} \right) \tag{3-34}$$

$$\leqslant \log_2 \left(\sum P(X=a) \cdot \frac{1}{P(X=a)} \right) \tag{3-35}$$

$$= \log_2(k) \tag{3-36}$$

Theorem 3.1.3 Important Inequalities 2

For any two random variables X and Y, we have

$$H(X,Y) \leqslant H(X) + H(Y) \tag{3-37}$$

and equality holds if and only if X and Y are independent.

Proof

$$H(X,Y) = H(X) + H(Y|X) \leqslant H(X) + H(Y) \tag{3-38}$$

Theorem 3.1.4 Important Inequalities 3

For any two random variables X and Y, we have

$$H(X|Y) \leqslant H(X) \tag{3-39}$$

and equality holds if and only if X and Y are independent.

Proof

$$H(X \mid Y) = \sum_b P(Y=b) H(X \mid Y=b) \tag{3-40}$$

$$= \sum_b \sum_a P(X=a, Y=b) \log_2 \left(\frac{1}{P(X=a \mid Y=b)} \right) \tag{3-41}$$

$$= \sum_a P(X=a) \sum_b P(Y=b \mid X=a) \log_2 \left(\frac{1}{P(X=a \mid Y=b)} \right) \tag{3-42}$$

Since $\log_2(x)$ is concave, Jensen's inequality gives

$$H(X \mid Y) \leqslant \sum_a P(X=a) \log_2 \left(\sum_b P(Y=b \mid X=a) \frac{1}{P(X=a \mid Y=b)} \right) \tag{3-43}$$

$$= \sum_a P(X=a) \log_2 \left(\frac{1}{P(X=a)} \right) \tag{3-44}$$

$$= H(X) \tag{3-45}$$

Thus, $H(X \mid Y) \leqslant H(X)$. Equality holds if and only if $P(X=a \mid Y=b) = P(X=a)$ for all a, b with positive probability, which is equivalent to the independence of X and Y.

3.1.3 Entropy of English

Entropy, as a fundamental measure of information capacity, can quantify any entity containing informational content. Natural language is a prime example. Since language exhibits inherent statistical structure, it is amenable to measurement and quantification using information-theoretic tools. Significant research has been devoted to estimating the entropy of English, establishing methods for its precise quantification.

In paper [14], *Shannon* introduced two methods for estimating the entropy of the English language. One approach relies on N-gram statistics. Natural languages possess inherent redundancy because characters are neither equiprobable nor independent. For instance, the letter "U" frequently follows "Q", and "H" often appears after "T". Consequently, given a sequence of known letters, the subsequent letter can be predicted with varying degrees of certainty. Formally, when the preceding $N-1$ letters are known, we can compute the conditional entropy of the next letter. Let F_N denote the entropy of the N-th letter given the preceding $N-1$ letters. Shannon's calculated values for the entropy of English are presented in Table 3-4.

Table 3-4: Entropy of English

	F_0	F_1	F_2	F_3	F_{word}
26 Letters	4.70	4.14	3.56	3.3	2.62
27 Letters	4.76	4.03	3.32	3.1	2.14

Although the inclusion of the space character expands the alphabet to 27 symbols, we consider the standard 26-letter alphabet for this calculation. Consequently, F_0 represents the maximum possible entropy per character, calculated as $\log_2 26 \approx 4.7$ bits. The term F_N denotes the conditional entropy of the subsequent character given a sequence of $N-1$ preceding characters. As the analysis demonstrates, the entropy values exhibit a monotonic decrease with increasing N, theoretically converging to the true entropy rate of English. However, this theoretical framework faces practical limitations. The computational complexity (Definition 3.5.1) grows exponentially as

$\mathcal{O}(26^N)$, rendering precise calculations computationally intractable for large values of N.

The entropy of English is given by

$$H(X) = \sum_{\alpha=A}^{Z} P(X = \alpha) \cdot \log_2 \left(\frac{1}{P(X = \alpha)} \right) \tag{3-46}$$

where α represents a letter in the alphabet.

Example 3.1.4 Determine the entropy of a 1000-letter English sample based on the frequencies provided in Table 3-5.

Table 3-5: Frequency for the Letters

Letter	A	B	C	D	E	F	G	H	I	J	K	L	M
Frequency	73	9	30	44	130	28	16	35	74	2	3	35	25
Letter	N	O	P	Q	R	S	T	U	V	W	X	Y	Z
Frequency	78	74	27	3	77	63	93	27	13	16	5	19	1

Solution: The entropy of English can be calculated using Equation 3-46.

$$H(X) = \sum_{\alpha=A}^{Z} P(X = \alpha) \cdot \log_2 \left(\frac{1}{P(X = \alpha)} \right) \tag{3-47}$$

$$= P(A) \log_2 \left(\frac{1}{P(A)} \right) + \cdots + P(Z) \log_2 \left(\frac{1}{P(Z)} \right) \tag{3-48}$$

$$= 0.073 \cdot \log_2 \left(\frac{1}{0.073} \right) + \cdots + 0.001 \cdot \log_2 \left(\frac{1}{0.001} \right) \tag{3-49}$$

$$\approx 4.1621 \tag{3-50}$$

The average entropy required to encode a single letter in this example is approximately 4.1621 bits. This value, falling below the theoretical upper bound of 4.7 bits, signifies the inherent redundancy embedded within linguistic structures. ■

The preceding discussion outlined a method for calculating the entropy of English using sequences of fixed length. While the theoretical formulation of linguistic entropy is relatively straightforward, the primary challenge lies in the accurate estimation of the probability of occurrence for each character within a given text. This task becomes considerably more complex when punctuation marks and special characters are taken into account.

We now introduce the fundamental concept of an **information source**. An information source is defined as the origin of messages or sequences of messages. Physically, this source may correspond to a person, an organism, a machine, or any natural system. Mathematically, it is often modeled as a process generating a sequence of states. The output generated by a source is termed a message. Two critical metrics characterizing an information source are the **relative entropy rate** and **redundancy**.

Definition 3.1.5 Relative Entropy Rate

The Relative Entropy Rate is given by

$$\eta = H_\infty / H_0 \tag{3-51}$$

where H_∞ *is the entropy of the set of states, and* $H_0 = \log_2(q)$ *is the maximum entropy for the same number of states,* q *is number of equiprobable outcomes.*

Definition 3.1.6 Redundancy

The formula for redundancy is

$$R = 1 - \eta = 1 - H_\infty / H_0 \tag{3-52}$$

Redundancy provides an effective measure of the strength of statistical dependence among symbols in the sequence emitted by a discrete source. A higher redundancy R implies a lower actual entropy H_∞, indicating stronger inter-symbol dependencies within the source.

Shannon introduced an alternative method for estimating the entropy of the English language based on the frequency distribution of words. By analyzing over 8,000 words, he estimated the entropy per word to be 11.82 bits. Given that the average English word consists of approximately 4.5 letters, this corresponds to an entropy of roughly 2.62 bits per letter. This value is denoted as F_{word} in Table 3-4. Based on this figure, the redundancy of English can be estimated as $1 - \frac{F_{word}}{F_0} \approx 44\%$. Consequently, approximately 44% of English text is statistically redundant. It is crucial to note, however, that this does not imply that arbitrary characters can be removed without loss of intelligibility. Rather, it indicates that efficient lossless compression is feasible.

It is worth noting that the entropy of English varies depending on the historical period and usage context, and accurate estimation requires the selection of appropriate statistical samples. Shannon estimated that the asymptotic entropy of English, measured over sequences of up to 100 characters, lies between 0.6 and 1.3 bits per character [14]. Subsequent studies have refined these estimates: Cover and King reported values between 1.25 and 1.35 [15], Teahan and Cleary calculated 1.46 [16], Kontoyiannis derived 1.77 [17], and Guerrero reported 1.58 [18]. These results collectively suggest that the redundancy of English exceeds 60%. Discrepancies among these values arise primarily from differences in sample selection and analytical methodology.

Similar information-theoretic analyses can be applied to other natural languages composed of alphabetic sequences, such as German and French, to estimate their respective entropy and redundancy.

3.1.4 Entropy of Chinese

Chinese is widely recognized for its semantic conciseness. It is capable of expressing complex meanings using relatively few characters, consequently exhibiting one of the highest entropy rates per symbol among major languages. This implies that, for texts of equivalent content, Chinese carries a higher density of information compared to other languages. Recall the definition of entropy $H(X) = -\sum p_i \log_2 p_i$; a larger alphabet size n increases the maximum potential entropy of the system.

Unlike phonographic alphabetic systems, Chinese utilizes a logographic writing system, where each character (*Hanzi*) typically represents a morpheme or a syllable rather than a single phoneme. This stands in stark contrast to alphabetic scripts. The inventory of Chinese characters is substantially larger than that of any alphabet. While everyday communication may involve only a few hundred characters, the comprehensive set extends to tens of thousands. This expansive symbol space inherently contributes to a significantly higher potential entropy at the character level.

To estimate the entropy of Chinese, we consider the data from the 12th edition of the *Xinhua Dictionary*(a Chinese-language dictionary), which includes approximately 13,000 characters. If we model each character as a unique symbol and assume a uniform distribution (i.e., equal probability) over these 13,000 characters, the maximum entropy (or zero-order entropy) is calculated as follows:

$$H_0 = \log_2(13{,}000) \approx 13.67 \text{ bits} \tag{3-53}$$

Based on statistical analysis of large corpora of modern Chinese text, the entropy of Chinese characters is estimated to be approximately 9.65 bits per character. This value is significantly higher than the character entropy of English. This difference is not merely a quantitative distinction; it reflects a fundamental structural characteristic of the writing system that profoundly influences its information-theoretic properties. The use of a large, morpheme-representing character set establishes a higher baseline of character-level uncertainty compared to alphabetic languages. Consequently, information is encoded more densely at the character level in Chinese, requiring more bits per character to represent the same degree of uncertainty.

A single Chinese character often conveys a morpheme or a complete concept, thereby packing more semantic information into a single unit than a Latin letter. This higher "information density" per orthographic unit inherently necessitates more bits to represent its state, leading to higher entropy at this granular level. In terms of information load, Chinese characters function more like "mini-words" than simple alphabetic letters.

A defining feature of written Chinese is the absence of explicit delimiters, such as spaces, between words. This results in a continuous stream of characters. This contrasts sharply with most Indo-European languages. Consequently, word segmentation becomes an indispensable pre-processing step for any word-level analysis, including entropy calculation. The definition of a "word" in Chinese remains a complex linguistic and computational problem, lacking a universally accepted standard.

To calculate the entropy of Chinese, we need to determine the probability distribution of individual characters. As a simplified example, suppose the 13,000 characters listed in the *Xinhua Dictionary* are divided into five categories. The top 100 most frequently used characters account for 40% of total usage; an additional 500 characters (excluding the previous 100) also contribute 40%; another 2,000 characters account for 19%. A further 8,000 characters make up 0.99%; the remaining characters contribute only 0.01%.

Table 3-6: Probability of Chinese Characters

Categories	Amount	Probability	Probability of Each Character
1	100	0.4	0.004
2	500	0.4	0.0008
3	2000	0.19	9.5×10^{-5}
4	8000	0.0099	1.2375×10^{-6}
5	2400	0.0001	4.167×10^{-8}

Based on the probability distribution provided in Table 3-6, the entropy of Chinese is calculated as follows:

$$H(X) = \sum_{i=1}^{13000} P_i \log_2 \frac{1}{P_i} \tag{3-54}$$

$$= \sum_{a=1}^{100} P_a \log_2 \frac{1}{P_a} + \sum_{b=1}^{500} P_b \log_2 \frac{1}{P_b} + \sum_{c=1}^{2000} P_c \log_2 \frac{1}{P_c} + \sum_{i=d}^{8000} P_d \log_2 \frac{1}{P_d} + \sum_{e=1}^{2400} P_e \log_2 \frac{1}{P_e} \tag{3-55}$$

$$= 0.4 \log_2 (1/0.004) + 0.4 \log_2 (1/0.0008) + 0.19 \log_2 (1/(9.5 \times 10^{-5})) + 0.0099 \log_2 (1/(1.2375 \times 10^{-6})) + 0.0001 \log_2 (1/(4.167 \times 10^{-8})) \tag{3-56}$$

$$\approx 10.036 \tag{3-57}$$

The entropy is calculated to be 10.036 bits per character. Consequently, the redundancy is determined as $R = 1 - \frac{H(X)}{H_0} \approx 0.2656$.

These quantitative results corroborate the structural characteristics discussed earlier. While the high information density of Chinese logograms requires more bits to encode the uncertainty of a single character, it simultaneously yields a significantly lower overall redundancy (approx. 26.56%) compared to the English language (approx. 44%).

A study indicates that the information entropy of Chinese is approximately 9.56, whereas that of English letters is around 3.9 [19].

3.1.5 International Morse Code

Morse code is a character encoding scheme that represents text characters as standardized sequences of two different signal durations, known as dots (•) and dashes (▬). Originally developed for telegraphy in the 1830s and 1840s by *Samuel Morse* and *Alfred Vail*, the system remains in use today in radio communication, aviation, and amateur radio. While *Samuel Morse* conceptualized the idea, *Alfred Vail* is credited with refining the encoding system.

The International Morse Code was standardized in 1865 by the International Telegraph Union (ITU) for global application. In this system, each letter, numeral, and symbol is mapped to a unique sequence; for instance, "A" is represented as • ▬ and "B" as ▬ • • •. The complete International Morse Code is illustrated in Figure 3-6.

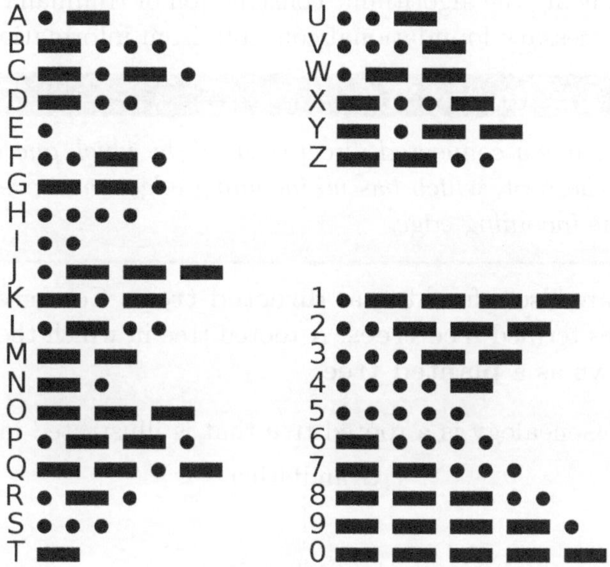

Figure 3-6: Chart of the International Morse Code[1]

The timing of the signals is governed by the following fundamental rules:

1) The duration of a dot (•) is one unit.
2) The duration of a dash (▬) is three units.
3) The space between components within the same character is one unit.
4) The space between characters is three units.
5) The space between words is seven units.

The most universally recognized distress signal is SOS. In Morse code, this is represented as the sequence "• • • ▬ ▬ ▬ • • •". In emergency scenarios, Morse code can be generated via improvised methods, such as modulating a light source, tapping on a solid object, or sounding a horn or whistle. This adaptability renders it one of the most simple and versatile methods of telecommunication. From an information-theoretic perspective, the entropy of Morse code is calculated to be approximately 7.039 bits.

3.2 HUFFMAN CODE

Huffman coding [20], a foundational algorithm in data compression, was developed by *David A. Huffman* in 1952 during his graduate studies at the Massachusetts Institute

[1] Image by Rhey T. Snodgrass and Victor F. Camp via Wikimedia Commons.

of Technology (MIT). Motivated by a course assignment to find the most efficient binary code, *Huffman* devised a method that proved superior to existing approaches, such as Shannon-Fano coding. Since its publication in 1952, the algorithm has become a cornerstone of information theory, establishing Huffman as a pioneer in the field of data compression. The algorithm finds widespread application in diverse domains, including image and audio compression (e.g., JPEG and MP3), communication protocols, and general lossless data compression formats.

Prior to introducing the algorithmic construction of Huffman codes, it is essential to establish the necessary foundational concepts from information theory.

Definition 3.2.1 Rooted Tree

A rooted tree is a connected directed graph in which one vertex has been designated as the root, which has no incoming edges, and every other vertex has exactly one incoming edge.

Rooted trees are also referred to as **directed trees**. Conversely, trees without a root are sometimes termed **free trees**. A rooted tree in which the degree of the root vertex is 1 is known as a **planted tree**.

Example 3.2.1 Genealogy is a rooted tree that is illustrated in Figure 3-7.

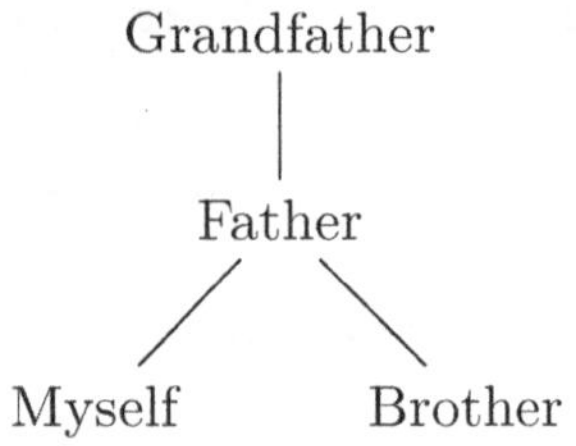

Figure 3-7: Genealogy-Family Tree

Example 3.2.2 A typical rooted tree is illustrated in Figure 3-8.

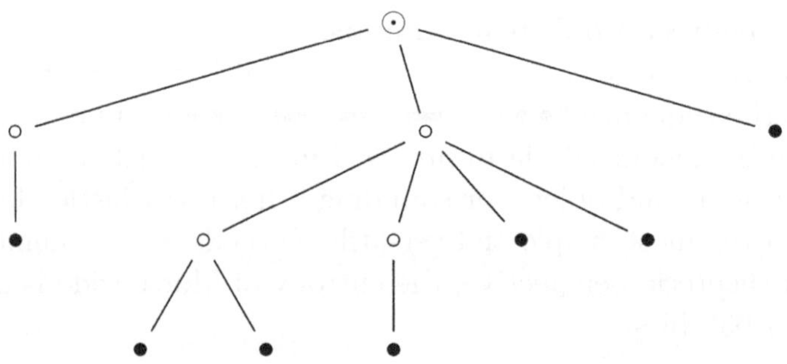

Figure 3-8: A Rooted Tree

where "•" is *Leaves*, ∘ is *Internal Vertex*, ⊙ is *Root*.

Definition 3.2.2 Binary Tree

*A **binary tree** is a rooted tree in which every internal vertex has at most two children. Furthermore, each child is uniquely designated as either a left child or a right child.*

*A **complete binary tree** is a binary tree in which every level, except possibly the last, is completely filled, and all nodes in the last level are as far left as possible.*

*A **full binary tree** is a rooted tree in which every internal vertex has exactly two children. Equivalently, it is a binary tree in which the out-degree of every node is either 0 or 2.*

Example 3.2.3 A Full Binary Tree and a Complete Binary Tree are illustrated in Figure 3-9:

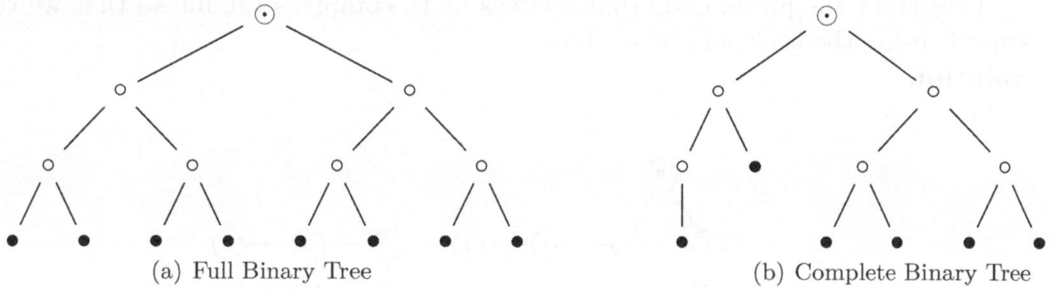

Figure 3-9: Full Binary Tree vs. Complete Binary Tree

Example 3.2.4 Let $A = 000, B = 001, C = 01, D = 10, E = 1100, F = 1101, G = 111$, the tree is illustrated in Figure 3-10.

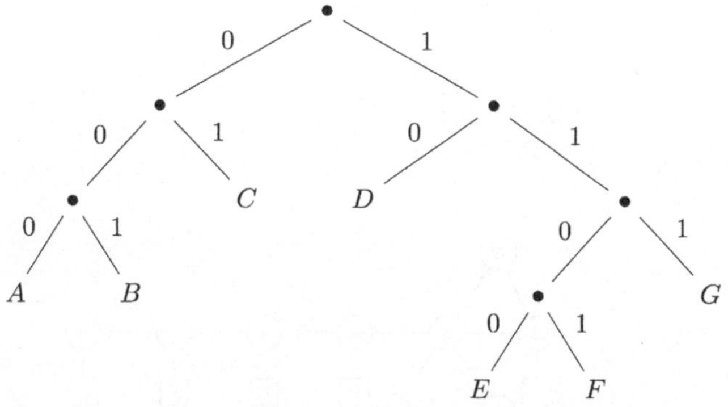

Figure 3-10: A Tree Example

Given the frequency distribution of characters in a file, the objective is to construct a binary tree that minimizes the total number of bits required for encoding. The following algorithm generates such an **optimal tree**:

1) Replace each letter by a node/vertex and label these nodes based on the frequency of each letter. Then sort the nodes by their values in increasing order when reading from left to right.

2) Starting from left to right, group the two smallest numbers together and replace them by their sum.
3) Sort the resulting nodes by their values again. Then repeat these steps until all the nodes are connected.
4) Once we obtain the binary tree, replace the vertex numbers with corresponding letters. Then we label the branches with 0 to the left and 1 to the right.
5) Lastly, we trace along the paths to obtain the code for each letter.

Example 3.2.5 Suppose a certain file contains only the letter with the following frequencies that is shown in Table 3-7.

Table 3-7: Letter Frequency

A	B	C	D	E	F	G
1	2	2	4	4	5	6

Construct the prefix code that enables us to compress the file so that we can store it using the least number of bits.

Solution:

1)

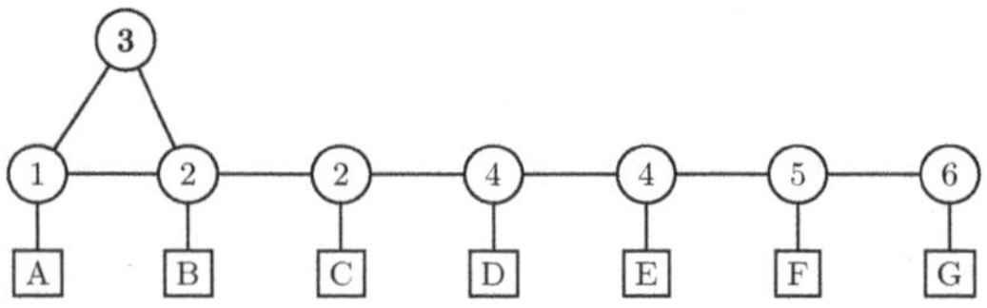

2)

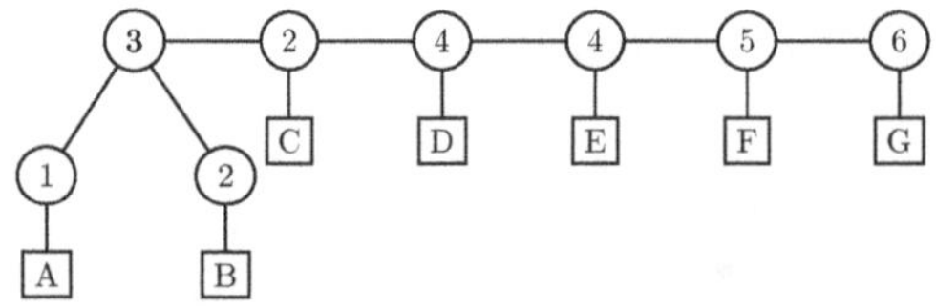

3)

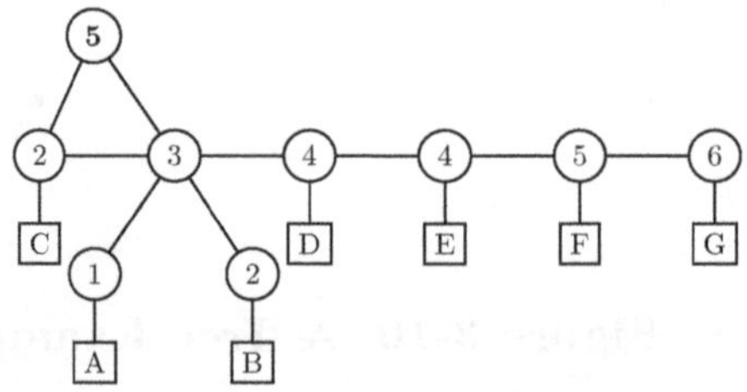

4)

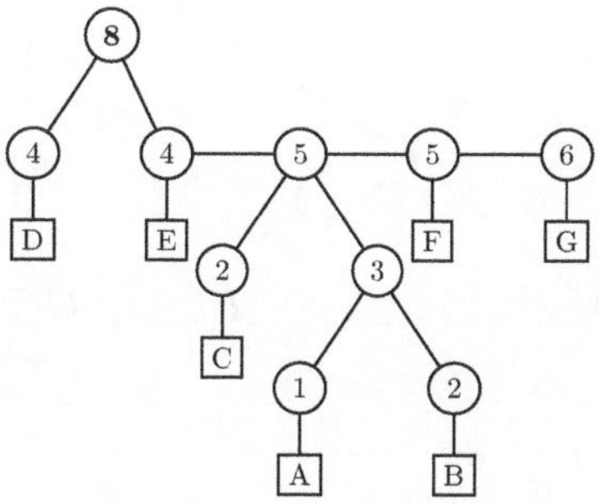
8
4
4
5
5
6
D
E
F
G
2
3
C
1
2
A
B

5)

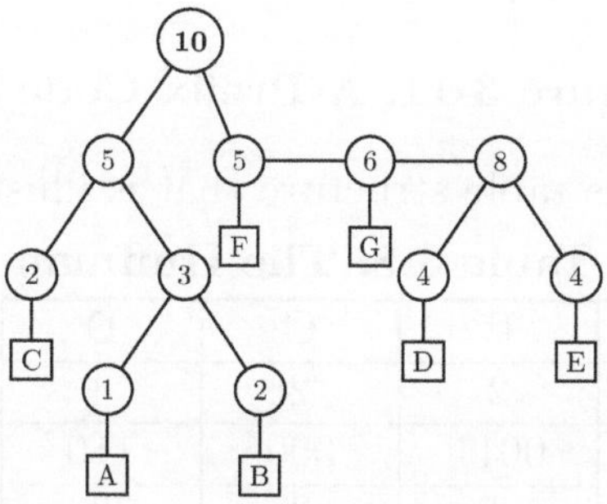
10
5
5
6
8
F
G
2
3
4
4
C
D
E
1
2
A
B

6)

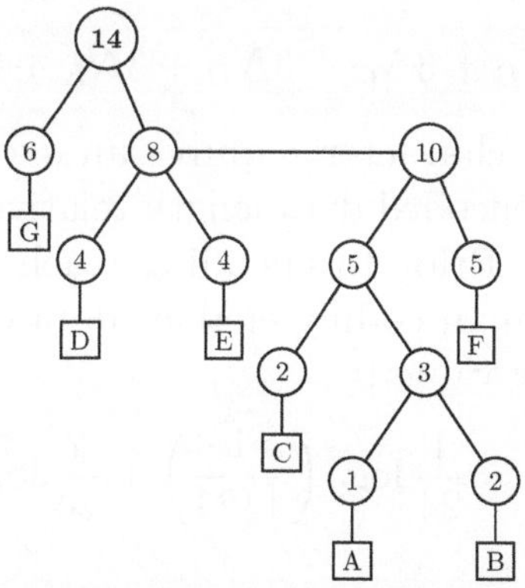
14
6
8
10
G
4
4
5
5
D
E
F
2
3
C
1
2
A
B

7)

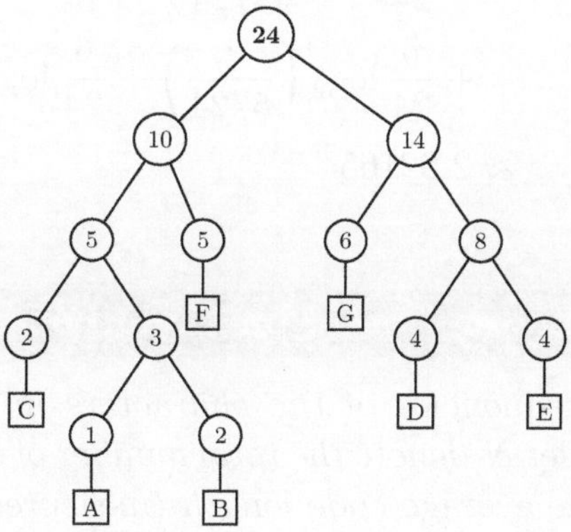
24
10
14
5
5
6
8
F
G
2
3
4
4
C
D
E
1
2
A
B

Representable as tree structure is illustrated in Figure 3-11

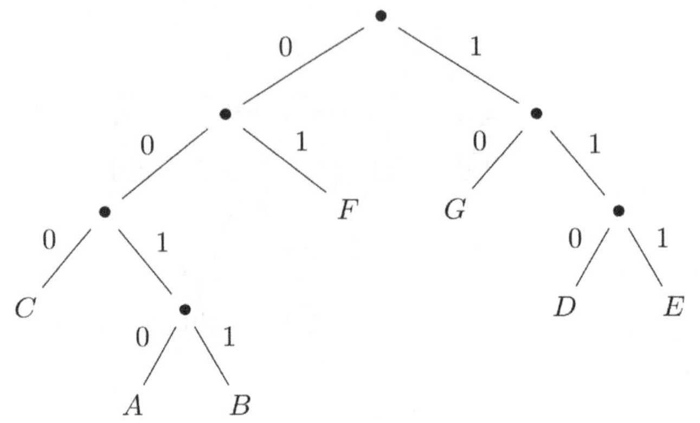

Figure 3-11: A Prefix Code Example

And representable as table structure that is illustrated in Table 3-8.

Table 3-8: The Huffman Code

Letter	A	B	C	D	E	F	G
Frequency	1	2	2	4	4	5	6
Code	0010	0011	000	110	111	01	10
Bits	4	4	3	3	3	2	2

The encoded length is

$$4N_A + 4N_B + 3N_C + 3N_D + 3N_E + 2N_F + 2N_G = 64 \tag{3-58}$$

After encoding, each character requires an average of $64/24 \approx 2.67$ bits. The compression ratio of the encoded data length relative to the original plaintext length is $64/(24 \times 8) \approx 33.3\%$. Prior to encoding, each character required 8 bits (e.g., ASCII) for storage. Huffman coding enables data compression without any loss of information. The entropy value is

$$\sum_{\alpha} P(\alpha)\log_2\left(\frac{1}{P(\alpha)}\right) = \frac{1}{24}\log_2\left(\frac{1}{1/24}\right) + \frac{2}{24}\log_2\left(\frac{1}{2/24}\right) + \frac{2}{24}\log_2\left(\frac{1}{2/24}\right) \tag{3-59}$$

$$+\frac{4}{24}\log_2\left(\frac{1}{4/24}\right) + \frac{4}{24}\log_2\left(\frac{1}{4/24}\right) \tag{3-60}$$

$$+\frac{5}{24}\log_2\left(\frac{1}{5/24}\right) + \frac{6}{24}\log_2\left(\frac{1}{6/24}\right) \tag{3-61}$$

$$\approx 2.62165 \tag{3-62}$$

■

Theorem 3.2.1 Lower Bound on Code Length

Suppose the frequencies of the characters in a plaintext are given by $n_1, n_2, \ldots, n_k$, and let N denote the total number of characters. The theoretical lower bound for the average code length (measured in bits per character) is *given by the entropy*

$$H = \sum_{i=1}^{k} p_i \log_2 \left(\frac{1}{p_i}\right), \tag{3-63}$$

where $p_i = n_i/N$ *represents the probability of the i-th character for all* $1 \leqslant i \leqslant k$.

Theorem 3.2.2 Expected Code Length

The Huffman tree constructed from the probabilities $p_1, p_2, \ldots, p_k$ *yields an expected code length that is within one bit of the entropy.*

Once the redundancy R of a language is quantified, Huffman coding can be utilized to compress the original text to approximately a factor of $1 - R$ of its original length. The algorithmic construction described thus far pertains specifically to **binary Huffman coding**. It is important to note that the method can be generalized to **r-ary Huffman codes**, which utilize an alphabet of size r. Beyond Huffman coding, numerous other **lossless compression** algorithms exist, including **Shannon-Fano coding**, **Run-Length Encoding (RLE)**, **Modified Huffman (MH) coding**, **Arithmetic coding**, and **Dictionary-based coding** (such as LZW). The interested reader is referred to standard literature on information theory for a comprehensive treatment of these techniques.

3.3 ONE-TIME PAD/VERNAM CIPHER

Perfect secrecy represents the ultimate goal in the field of cryptography, a standard that ensures absolute confidentiality. In practice, most cryptographic systems aim for **computational security**, meaning the ciphertext cannot be broken within a reasonable timeframe given current computing power. However, a more rigorous standard exists: if a cipher algorithm remains unbreakable even to an attacker possessing unlimited time and computational resources, such a system is said to possess **unconditional security**.

Does such a cipher exist? Indeed, it does. In classical cryptography, the quintessential example is the **Vernam cipher**, widely known as the **One-Time Pad (OTP)**. This polyalphabetic substitution cipher was invented in 1917 by *Gilbert Vernam*, an engineer at *Bell Labs* in the United States. While implementation errors can compromise its security, the Vernam cipher remains mathematically unbreakable when the key is truly random, as long as the message, and used only once. Consequently, it stands as the only known encryption method that provably achieves perfect secrecy.

To attain this information-theoretic security, the system imposes three stringent requirements on the key relative to the plaintext. First, the key must be generated via a process of true randomness. Second, it must be at least as long as the plaintext. Finally, it must be kept completely secret and used exactly once. Under these rigorous conditions, the ciphertext generated by a one-time pad is information-theoretically unbreakable. This property was mathematically proven by Claude Shannon approximately 30 years after the cipher's invention, in his seminal paper *Communication Theory of Secrecy Systems* [6].

3.3.1 Vernam Cipher

The Vernam cipher consumes one bit of pre-shared key material for every bit of message encrypted and transmitted over a public channel. The operational procedure is defined as follows:

1) (Setup): Convert the plaintext message into a binary sequence (e.g., using 8-bit ASCII encoding).
2) (KeyGen): Generate a random key sequence that is at least as long as the plaintext. This key must be used exactly once.
3) (Key Formatting): Convert the generated key into a corresponding binary sequence.
4) (Encrypt): Compute the ciphertext by performing the logical XOR operation between each bit of the plaintext and the corresponding bit of the secret key.

Example 3.3.1 Suppose the plaintext is "**Dynamics**" and the random key is "**F3aP;]M.**". Try to encrypt using Vernam cipher?

Solution: The encryption process is detailed in Table 3-9.

Table 3-9: Example of Vernam Cipher

M	D	y	n	a	m	i	c	s
Binary	01000100	01111001	01101110	01100001	01101101	01101001	01100011	01110011
K	F	3	a	P	;	]	M	.
Binary	01000110	00110011	01100001	01010000	00111011	01011101	01001101	00101110
C	00000010	01001010	00001111	00110001	01010110	00110100	00101110	01011101

■

Because each bit of the plaintext is encrypted using a new, independently and uniformly generated key bit, and because the key itself is truly random, the resulting ciphertext reveals absolutely no information about the original message. This holds true regardless of any inherent redundancy in the plaintext. Consequently, without the key, the One-Time Pad is information-theoretically unbreakable.

The proof that the one-time pad offers unconditional security is relatively straightforward.

Proof

For one-time pad, each ciphertext works with the congruence

$$c_i \equiv m_i + k_i \pmod 2 \tag{3-64}$$

Since the ciphertext results from the bitwise XOR of the plaintext and a secret key, recovering the plaintext without the key is impossible. Even if an attacker intercepts the ciphertext bit c_i, lacking the corresponding key *bit means they cannot determine whether the original plaintext bit is 0 or 1. Their optimal strategy is guessing, yielding a 50% success rate per bit.*

For a plaintext of length l, the probability of correctly guessing the entire message is only 0.5^l. Assuming each character is encoded using 8-bit ASCII, the chance of correctly guessing a single character is roughly 0.39%.

Is there any way to deduce the key? In short, no. The key must be generated by a true random number generator and cannot be derived algorithmically. This is precisely why the probability of recovering the correct plaintext without the key remains at 50%—a fundamental condition underpinning the security of the one-time pad.

While the preceding reasoning provides an intuitive understanding, it does not constitute a formal mathematical proof. Claude Shannon established a rigorous justification using information theory, demonstrating that the **mutual information** shared between the plaintext and the ciphertext is identically zero. The information gained by an attacker upon observing the ciphertext, denoted by $I(M;C)$, vanishes. For a detailed derivation, see Shannon's foundational work [6].

3.3.2 Consequences of Key Reuse

What happens if the generated key is accidentally reused? Suppose Eve intercepts two distinct ciphertexts, which were encrypted with the same key k: $c_1 = m_1 \oplus k$, $c_2 = m_2 \oplus k$.

Due to the cancellation property of the XOR operation

$$a \oplus b \oplus b = a \tag{3-65}$$

Eve can now determine some partial information about the pair of plaintexts m_1 and m_2, Eve computes

$$c_1 \oplus c_2 = (m_1 \oplus k) \oplus (m_2 \oplus k) \tag{3-66}$$

$$= m_1 \oplus (m_2 \oplus k \oplus k) \tag{3-67}$$

$$= m_1 \oplus m_2 \tag{3-68}$$

Has reader noticed that even without knowing the key, it is possible to learn some information about the plaintext just by knowing the ciphertexts. And this does not require any information about the key. This introduces information redundancy. By computing combinations and permutations of different ciphertexts, more information about the plaintexts can be revealed, and the probability of guessing the plaintext becomes greater than 50%! Consequently, the probability of correctly recovering the plaintext rises significantly above that of a random guess.

Furthermore, key reuse renders the system entirely vulnerable to known-plaintext attacks (KPA) and chosen-plaintext attacks (CPA). The attacker can impersonate a user and send a plaintext m_k, then receive the corresponding ciphertext c_k. Since the attacker knows the plaintext, using the cancellation property, they can deduce the key k, and the encryption is broken.

3.4 PERFECT SECRECY

3.4.1 Theoretic Security

What insights does information theory bring to cryptography?

It establishes the boundary between the ideal and the practical. While **unconditional security** remains the theoretical gold standard, practical constraints necessitate a shift toward **computational security**. A cryptographic system is considered computationally secure if the best known method for breaking it requires computational resources or time that exceeds the value or useful lifespan of the protected information.

Consider the classical **random substitution cipher** as an illustrative example. It boasts a key space of 26!. In terms of raw magnitude, this key space is astronomically large and would theoretically thwart a brute-force attack. However, a large key space is a necessary, but not sufficient, condition for security. Because the cipher preserves the statistical structure of the plaintext (i.e., letter frequencies), it remains vulnerable to **frequency analysis**. Unless the redundancy of the language is masked, a cipher can be broken with relatively little ciphertext, regardless of the key space size.

Another critical framework for evaluating cryptographic strength is **provable security**. Demonstrating that breaking the cryptographic scheme is computationally equivalent to solving a specific mathematical problem believed to be intractable. For instance, the security of the RSA cryptosystem is intrinsically linked to the difficulty of the **Integer Factorization Problem**. Under the assumption that factoring large integers is computationally infeasible, the encryption scheme is considered provably secure.

In conclusion, while modern cryptographic algorithms typically aim for computational or provable security, the One-Time Pad stands out as a unique anomaly. It remains the only cipher that achieves perfect secrecy, offering the highest theoretical level of security.

Theorem 3.4.1 Perfect Secrecy

Let $(\mathcal{M}, \mathcal{C}, \mathcal{K}, E_k, D_k)$ be a cryptosystem where $\mathcal{M}$ is the plaintext space, $\mathcal{C}$ is the ciphertext space, $\mathcal{K}$ is the key space, E_k is the encrypting function and D_k is the decrypting function.

*If the cryptosystem with $|\mathcal{M}| = |\mathcal{C}| = |\mathcal{K}|$, and every key is used with equal probability $1/|\mathcal{K}|$, then the cryptosystem is **perfect secrecy** and unbreakable.*

In other words, a cryptosystem has perfect secrecy if $P(m|c) = P(m)$ for all $m \in \mathcal{M}, c \in \mathcal{C}$.

Proof

For any $m \in \mathcal{M}$, $c \in \mathcal{C}$, there exists a key $k \in K$ such that $E_k(m) = c$. Since $|\mathcal{M}| = |\mathcal{C}| = |\mathcal{K}|$, then the key k must be unique.

Let $l = |\mathcal{M}| = |\mathcal{C}| = |\mathcal{K}|$, given a ciphertext $c \in \mathcal{C}$ and plaintext set $\{m_1, m_2, \ldots, m_l\}$, there exist a unique key $k_i \in \mathcal{K}$ that maps m_i to c where $1 \leqslant i \leqslant l$, and these keys must all be different such that $E_{k_i}(m_i) = c$. Now, we have

$$P_{\mathcal{M}}(m_i|c) = \frac{P_{\mathcal{C}}(c|m_i)P_{\mathcal{M}}(m_i)}{P_{\mathcal{C}}(c)} \tag{3-69}$$

$$= \frac{P_{\mathcal{K}}(k_i)P_{\mathcal{M}}(m_i)}{P_{\mathcal{C}}(c)} \tag{3-70}$$

and we also have that $P_{\mathcal{M}}(m_i|c) = P_{\mathcal{M}}(m_i)$ for $1 \leqslant i \leqslant l$ as the cryptosystem has perfect secrecy.

Hence $P_{\mathcal{K}}(k_i) = P_{\mathcal{C}}(c_i)$ for all i, so the keys are used with equal probability $P_{\mathcal{C}}(c_i)$. Since $|K| = l$, we have $P_{\mathcal{K}}(k_i) = 1/l$ for $1 \leqslant i \leqslant l$.

Note: $P_{\mathcal{M}}$ is the probability distribution on the plaintext space $\mathcal{M}$, and $P_{\mathcal{K}}$ is the probability distribution on the key space $\mathcal{K}$. The plaintext and the key are chosen independently; $P_{\mathcal{C}}$ is the probability distribution on the ciphertext space $\mathcal{C}$.

A cryptosystem achieves perfect secrecy, if Eve possesses full knowledge of the **a priori** probability distribution of the plaintext space, observing a specific ciphertext provides no additional information. In other words, the **a posteriori** probability distribution of the plaintext, conditioned on the ciphertext, must be identical to its **a priori** distribution.

Suppose the length of plaintext is l, the length of key is r and the length of ciphertext is n. The entropy of plaintext is $H\left(m^l\right) = H\left(m_1 m_2 \cdots m_l\right)$; The entropy of key is $H\left(k^r\right) = H\left(k_1 k_2 \cdots k_r\right)$; The entropy of ciphertext is $H\left(c^n\right) = H\left(c_1 c_2 \cdots c_n\right)$.

Recalling Section 1.2.3, in classical cryptanalysis, the ciphertext-only attack is the most commonly used. The attacker hopes to extract information about the plaintext or the key from the intercepted ciphertext. Then, the amount of information about the plaintext that can be extracted from the ciphertext is:

$$I\left(m^l; c^n\right) = H\left(m^l\right) - H\left(m^l \mid c^n\right) \tag{3-71}$$

Therefore, if we want the cryptosystem to achieve perfect secrecy, it is necessary that $I\left(m^l; c^n\right) = 0 \Rightarrow H\left(m^l\right) = H\left(m^l \mid c^n\right)$.

A cryptographic encryption scheme has perfect indistinguishability if, for any two plaintexts of the same length, an adversary who intercepts a ciphertext cannot determine which plaintext was encoded, even with unbounded processing capabilities.

An encryption scheme is said to possess perfect indistinguishability if for every pair of distinct plaintexts m_0 and m_1 of the same length, the probability distribution of the ciphertext generated by encrypting m_0 is identical to that of m_1.

Definition 3.4.1 Perfect Indistinguishability

An encryption scheme E is perfectly indistinguishable if for all plaintext $m_0, m_1 \in M$ of equal length, and for all ciphertext c, we have

$$P[E_k(m_0) = c] = P[E_k(m_1) = c] \tag{3-72}$$

A fundamental lemma for Perfect Indistinguishability: An encryption scheme has Perfect Indistinguishability if and only if it has Perfect Secrecy.

How can we construct an encryption scheme that achieves perfect secrecy? The simplest system with perfect secrecy requires three criteria:

- $|\mathcal{K}| \geqslant |\mathcal{C}| \geqslant |\mathcal{P}|$;
- All the keys must be chosen with equal probability;
- The key can be only used once;

Encryption matrix is a **Latin square** or encryption graph is a **Complete Bipartite graph**.

A latin square is an n ×n array where the integers 1 through n appear exactly once in each row and column.

A complete bipartite graph is a graph whose set of vertices are partitioned into two disjoint subsets such that no two vertices in the same subset are connected, and there is an edge between every pair of two vertices from different subset.

Example 3.4.1 There are 3 plaintexts: m_1, m_2, m_3, 3 keys: k_1, k_2, k_3, and 3 ciphertexts: c_1, c_2, c_3. Latin square and complete bipartite graph are shown in Table 3-10 and Figure 3-12.

Table 3-10: A Latin Square

	m_1	m_2	m_3
k_1	c_1	c_2	c_3
k_2	c_2	c_3	c_1
k_3	c_3	c_1	c_2

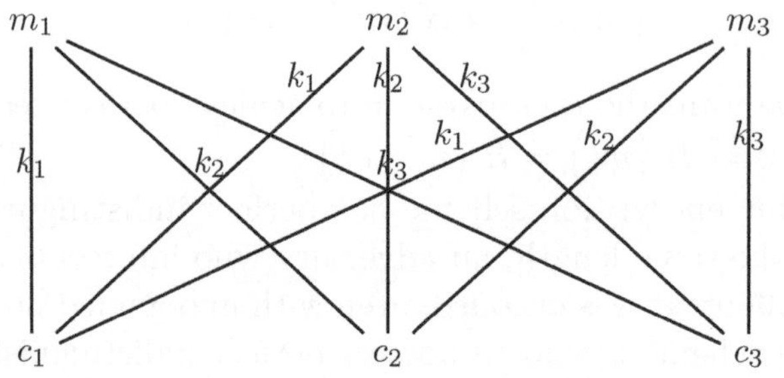

Figure 3-12: A Complete Bipartite Graph $K_{3,3}$

As shown in Figure 3-12, any given ciphertext could have originated from any of the possible plaintexts. This scenario is referred to as *indistinguishability* from an adversary's perspective, meaning the attacker can not tell which plaintext the ciphertext corresponds to.

It is also an equivalent formulation of **perfect secrecy**. Even if the attacker knows the full set of possible plaintexts, the probability of correctly guessing the original message at random remains only 1/3. In other words, indistinguishability implies that the attacker cannot raise this probability above 1/3 through any analysis or strategy.

3.4.2 Unicity Distance

Let the plaintext length be l, the key as k, the key length as r, the ciphertext as c and the ciphertext length as n. Then the information content about key is

$$I(k^r; c^n) = H(k^r) - H(k^r \mid c^n) \tag{3-73}$$

In a ciphertext-only attack, the conditional entropy of the key k, given the ciphertext sequence c^n, is $H(k^r \mid c^n) = H(k^r \mid c_1 c_2 \cdots c_n)$. According to Definition 3-39, it holds that $H(k^r \mid c^n) \leqslant H(k^r)$.

As Eve intercepts more ciphertext (i.e., as n increases), the conditional entropy of the key decreases. This means that the more ciphertext is intercepted, the more information is revealed about the key, making it easier to break the cipher.

When the amount of intercepted ciphertext becomes sufficient for $H(k^r \mid c^n)$ to approach zero, Eve can uniquely determine the encryption key and thus recover the plaintext. This minimum value of n is referred to as the unicity distance.

Definition 3.4.2 The Unicity Distance

The unicity distance is the least amount of ciphertext the opponent needs to know in order to uniquely recover the plaintext, denoted by n_0, is defined as

$$n_0 = \min\{n \in \mathbb{N} : H(k^r \mid c^n) \approx 0\} \tag{3-74}$$

The Equation 3-74 defines n_0 as the smallest integer where the conditional entropy of the key approximates zero.

The unicity distance refers to the minimum amount of intercepted ciphertext required for a cryptanalyst to uniquely determine the encryption key. Once the intercepted ciphertext exceeds n_0, the key used in the cryptographic system can, in principle, be uniquely identified, making decryption possible. Therefore, the unicity distance n_0 serves as a fundamental metric for evaluating the theoretical security of a cryptographic system against ciphertext-only attacks.

In practical scenarios, however, determining the exact point of unicity is complex. Theoretically, under the assumption of a random cipher model, the conditional entropy of the key, $H(K \mid C^n)$, is expected to decrease linearly as the amount of intercepted ciphertext n increases. Yet, as illustrated in Figure 3-13, the behavior often deviates from linearity as the entropy approaches zero. The curve tends to flatten asymptotically, implying that while the majority of incorrect keys are eliminated

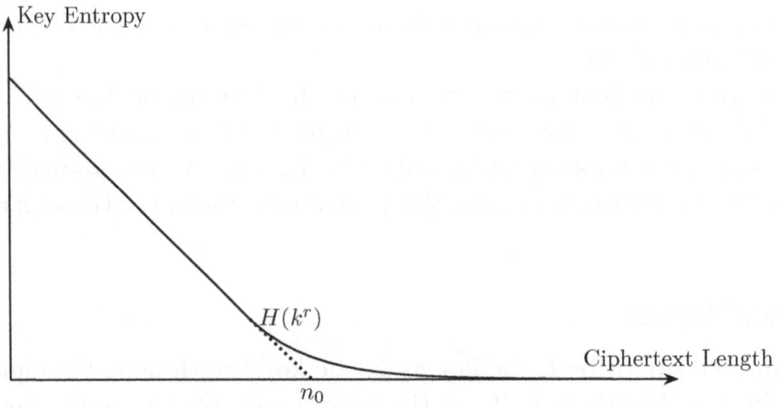

Figure 3-13: Key Entropy vs. Ciphertext Length Curve

quickly, distinguishing among the final few candidates requires a disproportionately larger amount of ciphertext.

The unicity distance n_0 is approximated by the ratio of the key entropy $H(k^r)$ to the absolute redundancy $D = R \cdot H(k^r)$, given by the relation

$$n_0 \approx H(k^r)/D \tag{3-75}$$

Conversely, as the absolute redundancy D of the plaintext approaches zero, the unicity distance n_0 tends toward infinity. In this scenario, the cipher remains theoretically unbreakable, even with access to unlimited ciphertext.

Example 3.4.2 Determine the unicity distance for the shift cipher and random substitution cipher.

Solution: For a shift cipher, the key space size is 26, which yields a key entropy of $H(k^r) = \log_2 26 \approx 4.7$. Assuming the entropy of English text is approximately 1.4 bits per character and observing that the absolute entropy of the 26-letter alphabet is $\log_2 26 \approx 4.7$, the redundancy of English is calculated as $R = 1 - \frac{H_\infty}{H_0} = 1 - \frac{1.4}{4.7} \approx 0.702$.

Hence, $D = R \cdot H(k^r) = 0.702 \cdot 4.7 \approx 3.3$. The unicity distance is estimated by the ratio $n_0 = H(k^r)/D \approx 4.7/3.3 \approx 1.42$. Rounding up to the nearest integer, this implies that intercepting just two ciphertext characters is theoretically sufficient to uniquely determine the key of a shift cipher.

For a random substitution cipher, the key space expands to 26!, resulting in a significantly higher key entropy of $H(k^r) = \log_2(26!) \approx 88.38$ bits. Maintaining the same linguistic redundancy of $D = 3.3$, the unicity distance becomes $n_0 = 88.38/3.3 \approx 26.8$. Consequently, a minimum of 27 ciphertext characters is required to break the cipher.

This comparison highlights that a large key space is a necessary, but not sufficient, condition for strong security. Although the substitution cipher provides a larger unicity distance than the shift cipher, both remain vulnerable to frequency analysis once the ciphertext length exceeds n_0, particularly given the high redundancy of the plaintext. ■

Theoretically, when the intercepted ciphertext exceeds the unicity distance n_0, the encryption key can be uniquely determined, thereby allowing the system to be decrypted. In practice, however, the volume of ciphertext required to successfully break the system is often much greater than n_0. This discrepancy stems primarily from two factors. First, the plaintext used in real-world applications rarely exhibits the full statistical structure of the language, resulting in an actual redundancy R that is lower than theoretical estimates. Second, to enhance security, designers often employ key spaces with high entropy to mitigate brute-force attacks.

Consequently, the unicity distance n_0 is inversely proportional to the redundancy R of the plaintext. A larger unicity distance implies that a longer ciphertext is required for unique decryption, indicating higher theoretical security. Conversely, a small n_0 suggests the system is more vulnerable. Nevertheless, the unicity distance is a theoretical metric and does not fully capture practical resilience. Even if n_0 is large, flaws in algorithm design or insecure key management may still leave the system susceptible to compromise.

3.4.3 Practical Secrecy

Most cryptosystems do not offer **perfect secrecy** in the strict information-theoretic sense; instead, they rely on **computational security**. In practice, deploying a one-time pad is often infeasible due to the sheer volume of data transmission. Modern wireless networks typically communicate billions of bits per second, making it prohibitive for the sender and receiver to pre-share and store an equivalent amount of key material.

Consequently, in real-world applications, the key is significantly shorter than the plaintext. However, this necessitates key reuse or cyclic repetition, which introduces statistical redundancy. Adversaries can exploit this redundancy to detect patterns and potentially recover both the key and the plaintext. Given the impracticality of maintaining a key length equal to the message length, cryptographic design focuses on maximizing algorithmic complexity. If the computational effort required to break the cipher exceeds feasible limits within a reasonable timeframe, the system is considered computationally secure.

In other words, if Eve possessed unlimited time, computing power, and resources, she could theoretically recover the plaintext from any ciphertext exceeding the unicity distance n_0. However, in reality, Eve is constrained by limitations in time, computational resources, and personnel. If the computational effort required to break a cipher exceeds these constraints, the system is said to possess **computational security**. For instance, if recovering the key requires 100 years of computation, the cipher is considered secure for safeguarding information with a useful lifespan significantly shorter than a century.

Public-key cryptography serves as a prime example of computational security. It relies on the computational hardness of mathematical problems, such as integer factorization, to withstand cryptanalytic attacks within any feasible timeframe.

Example 3.4.3 Suppose 3 messages are m_1, m_2, m_3; 4 keys are k_1, k_2, k_3, k_4; 4 ciphertexts are c_1, c_2, c_3, c_4. The complete bipartite graph are shown in Figure 3-14.

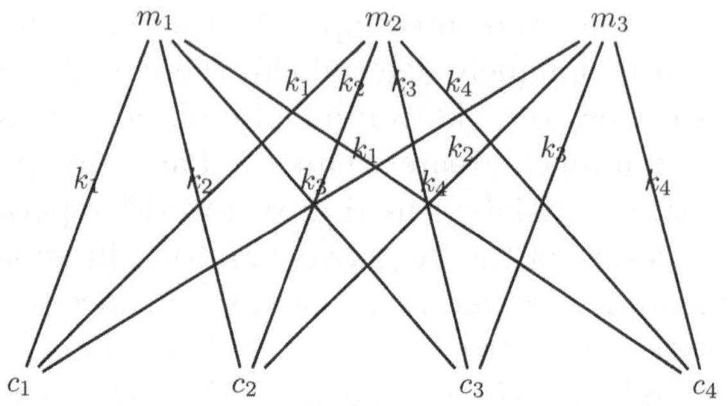

Figure 3-14: Complete Bipartite Graph $K_{3,4}$

A single ciphertext may correspond to three possible plaintexts. Since the ciphertext space is larger than the plaintext space, the difficulty of breaking is increased. ■

3.5 POLYNOMIAL TIME

The security of **perfect secrecy** fundamentally relies on the fact that, even with unlimited computational resources, an attacker lacks the necessary information to perform a successful analysis. To achieve practical implementation, modern cryptography adopts an alternative approach. The goal is to ensure that attackers cannot break the encryption within a reasonable time frame, or effectively guarantee that by the time they succeed, the information has become obsolete.

This approach is known as **computational security**.

Definition 3.5.1 Time Complexity

Let M be a deterministic Turing machine that halts on all inputs. The time complexity of M is the function $f : \mathbb{N} \to \mathbb{N}$, where $f(n)$ is the maximum number of steps that M uses on any input of length n. If $f(n)$ is the running time of M, we say that M runs in time $f(n)$ and that M is an $f(n)$ time Turing machine.

Let f and g be functions. We define $f(n) = \mathcal{O}(g(n))$ if there exist constants c and n_0 such that for all $n > n_0$, we have $f(n) \leqslant cg(n)$. This is illustrated in the Figure 3-15.

$\mathcal{O}(1)$ denotes constant time complexity; $\mathcal{O}(log(n))$ denotes logarithmic time complexity; $\mathcal{O}(n)$ denotes linear time complexity; $\mathcal{O}(n\log(n))$ denotes log-linear time complexity; $\mathcal{O}(n^c)$ denotes polynomial time complexity where c is a constant; $\mathcal{O}(a^n)$ denotes exponential time complexity where a is a constant raised to a power based on input size; $\mathcal{O}(n!)$ denotes factorial time complexity.

Properties of Big-O($\mathcal{O}$) notation:

$$f = \mathcal{O}(f) \tag{3-76}$$

$$\mathcal{O}(cf(n)) = \mathcal{O}(f(n)) \tag{3-77}$$

$$\mathcal{O}(f) + \mathcal{O}(g) = \mathcal{O}(\max(f, g)) \tag{3-78}$$

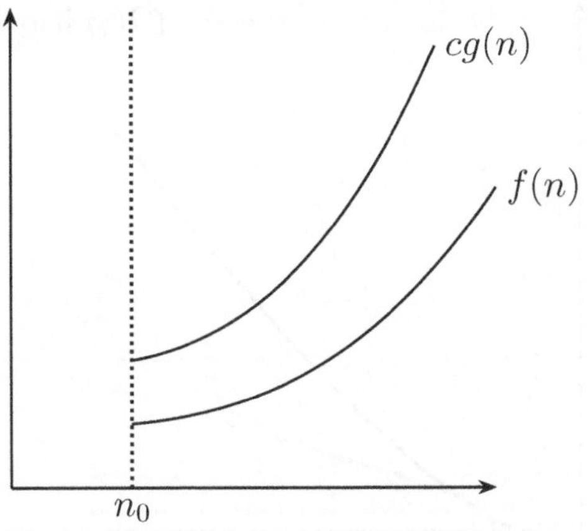

Figure 3-15: $f(n) = \mathcal{O}(g(n))$

$$\mathcal{O}(\mathcal{O}(f)) = \mathcal{O}(f) \tag{3-79}$$

$$\mathcal{O}(f) \cdot \mathcal{O}(g) = \mathcal{O}(f \cdot g) \tag{3-80}$$

To determine the Big-$\mathcal{O}$ complexity, we consider the number of executions the code performs in the worst-case scenario. In practice, we identify the dominant (highest-order or fastest-growing) term of the function $f(n)$ and discard its coefficient to obtain $g(n)$. For example, if $f_1(n) = 3n^2$ and $f_2(n) = 10n^2$, both functions belong to the class $\mathcal{O}(n^2)$. Generally, if $f(n)$ is a polynomial of the form $f(n) = a_k n^k + a_{k-1} n^{k-1} + \cdots + a_0$, we can write $f(n) = \mathcal{O}(n^k)$, where $k \in \mathbb{N}$. We say $g(n)$ is an upper bound on $f(n)$.

If a problem can be solved with a complexity of no more than $\mathcal{O}(n^k)$, it is considered solvable in polynomial time. To estimate the actual wall-clock time required to solve such a problem, one must account for the computer's processing speed. The following formula provides an estimation:

$$\text{Estimated Runtime} \approx \frac{\text{Total Operations}}{\text{Processing Speed}}$$

For instance, "El Capitan", the supercomputer developed by Lawrence Livermore National Laboratory in 2024, is capable of performing up to 2.746×10^{18} FLOPS(exaFLOPS). If a brute-force approach has a time complexity of $\mathcal{O}(n!)$, then for $n = 100$, the runtime on El Capitan would still be astronomically high

$$\frac{100!}{2.746 \times 10^{18}} \approx \frac{10^{157}}{2.746 \times 10^{18}} = 3.64 \times 10^{138} \text{ Seconds} \approx 10^{131} \text{ Years}$$

It is important to note that time complexity characterizes the asymptotic growth rate of an algorithm and does not necessarily reflect practical runtimes.

In computational theory, problems solvable in polynomial time are classified as *easy problems*, whereas those requiring exponential time are classified as **hard problems**. As shown in Figure 3-16, exponential functions grow with extreme rapidity, rendering such problems computationally infeasible beyond a certain input size. Furthermore, beyond these categories, there exist **undecidable problems**. These are problems that cannot be solved by any algorithm or computer, regardless of the available processing time or resources.

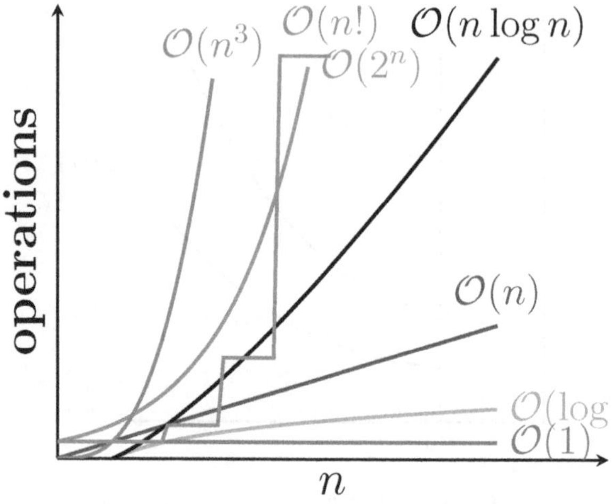

Figure 3-16: Time Complexity

Definition 3.5.2 Deterministic Algorithm

An algorithm is deterministic if, given its current state, the execution of the current instruction uniquely determines the next state.

Definition 3.5.3 Class P

An algorithm solves a decision problem in polynomial time if there exists a non-negative integer k such that for every input of size n, the algorithm completes its execution in time $\mathcal{O}(n^k)$. Note that a decision problem is defined as a problem that yields a strictly "yes" or "no" answer.

The set of all decision problems that can be solved by a deterministic algorithm in polynomial time is the complexity class P.

Definition 3.5.4 Non-deterministic Algorithm

A non-deterministic algorithm solves a decision problem by employing two distinct phases: a guessing stage and a checking stage. The algorithm is considered correct if the following conditions are met:

1) *For every input where the correct answer is "yes", there exists at least one guess in the guessing stage that leads to a "yes" after the checking stage verifies it.*
2) *For every input where the correct answer is "no", no matter what guess is made in the guessing stage, the checking stage will always reject it.*

Definition 3.5.5 Class NP

A non-deterministic algorithm whose input size is n solves a decision problem in polynomial time if there exists a polynomial p such that, for every *input to decision problem for which the answer should be "yes", there is a guess that leads in the checking stage to a yes answer within polynomial time.*

The set of all problems that can be solved by a non-deterministic algorithm in polynomial time is the complexity class NP.

Definition 3.5.6 NP-Hard

A problem is NP-hard if it is at least as hard as any problem in NP.

Definition 3.5.7 NP-complete Problems

A problem is NP-complete if it is NP-hard and also in NP.

Every problem in class P is also in class NP. In mathematical symbol, $P \subseteq NP$, but it is not clear whether $P = NP$.

In combinatorics, there is a famous NP-hard problem: Traveling Salesman Problem(TSP). A traveling salesman wants to visit n distinct cities, starting in his home town and returning to the starting city, and visiting every other city exactly once. With $(n-1)!$ possible routes to traverse all cities, to find a shortest route that visits every city exactly once and returns to the starting city.

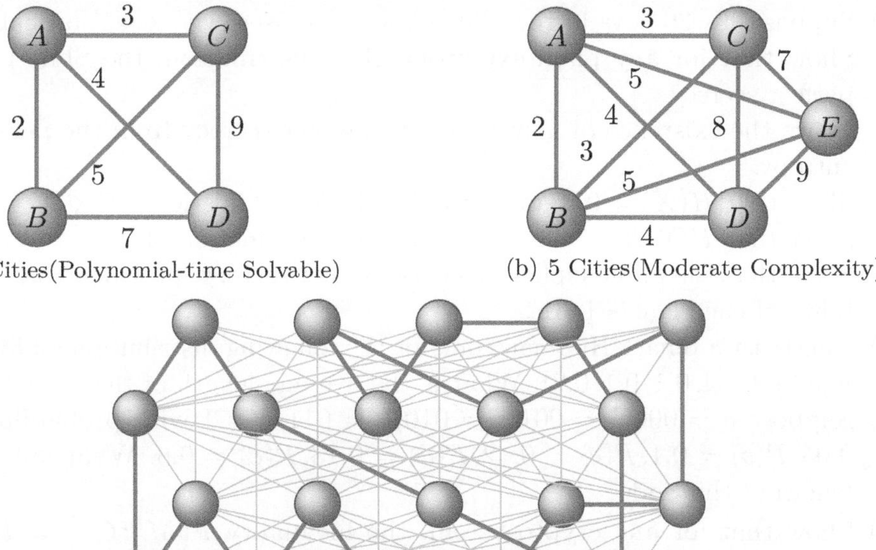

(a) 4 Cities(Polynomial-time Solvable) (b) 5 Cities(Moderate Complexity)

(c) 20 Cities(NP-Complete)

Figure 3-17: Traveling Salesman Problem

When the number of cities is small, the brute-force method is available. For example in Figure 3.17(a) and Figure 3.17(b), starting from City A and know their tour distance: calculate the total distance for routes such as A-B-C-D-A (20 units),

A-C-D-B-A (21 units); or starting from City C: C-A-B-D-C (21 units), similarly 21 more tours, then select the route with the minimum total distance.

There are 6 possible permutations with 4 cities, and 24 possible permutations with 5 cities. If the number of cities increase, computation becomes drastically more challenging. For example in Figure 3.17(c), 20 cities yield $19! \approx 1.216 \times 10^{17}$ permutations, while 30 cities yield $29! \approx 8.84 \times 10^{30}$ permutations. Because TSP is inherently NP-hard, we do not expect a polynomial-time algorithm to exist.

Subset Sum Problem, Boolean Satisfiability Problem, Hamiltonian Cycle Problem, Graph Coloring Problem, Vertex Cover Problem, Longest Path Problem, Maximum Clique Problem, etc., are NP-complete when expressed as decision problems.

In general, if a decision problem is classified as NP-complete, then its corresponding optimization problem is considered NP-hard. NP-hard are those that are at least as difficult as the hardest problems in NP. These problems are widely regarded as some of the most challenging in computational theory. Even with modern computing power, no polynomial-time algorithm is currently known to solve them efficiently. Therefore, most NP-hard are tackled using heuristic or approximation algorithms, or solved exactly only for instances of limited size.

3.6 EXERCISES

1) A one-time pad is provably secure. What makes it hard to use in practice?
2) Suppose the 26 keys in the Shift Cipher are used with equal probability 1/26. Show that for any plaintext probability distribution, the Shift Cipher has perfect secrecy.
3) Prove the existence of a system with perfect secrecy from the perspective of entropy.
4) Show that $H(X) = 0$ if and only if X is deterministic.
5) Show that $H(Y|X) = 0$ if and only if Y is a function of X.
6) Show that the affine cipher achieves perfect secrecy, provided that the probability of each key is 1/312.
7) Construct a binary Huffman code for the following distribution on five symbols $p = (0.2, 0.4, 0.1, 0.1, 0.2)$. What is the average length of this code?
8) Suppose $a = 000, b = 001, c = 010, d = 011, e = 1$ with probability $P(a) = 0.05, P(b) = 0.1, P(c) = 0.12, P(d) = 0.13, P(e) = 0.6$. What is the average length of this code?
9) Show that for any cryptosystem, the inequality $I\left(M^L; C^n\right) \geqslant H\left(M^L\right) - H\left(K^r\right)$ holds, where $H(M^L)$ denotes the plaintext entropy, $H(C^n)$ denotes the ciphertext entropy, and $H(K^r)$ denotes the key entropy.
10) Show that for any $(\mathcal{M}, \mathcal{C}, \mathcal{K}, E_k, D_k)$ cryptosystem, we have
$$H(K \mid C) = H(K) + H(M) - H(C) \tag{3-81}$$
11) Show that the following statement is false. For every encryption scheme that is perfectly secret it holds that for every distribution over the message space $\mathcal{M}$, for any $m, m' \in \mathcal{M}$ and $c \in \mathcal{C}$ such that
$$P(M = m \mid C = c) = P\left(M = m' \mid C = c\right) \tag{3-82}$$

12) Show that if only a single character is encrypted, then the shift cipher is Perfect Secret.
13) Show how to use the Vigenère cipher to encrypt any word of arbitrary length so that perfect secrecy is obtained.
14) In the One-time pad encryption scheme, it can sometimes happen that the key is the all-zero string. That is $m \oplus 0^l = m$, therefore the ciphertext is identical to the message. Do you think the one-time pad scheme should be modified so that the all-zero key is not used?

II

Symmetric Cryptography

Symmetric cryptography is an important branch of the field of cryptography. It encompasses classical cryptography, stream ciphers, and block ciphers. It provides secure and efficient encryption solutions.

Classical cryptography is the origin of symmetric cryptography. Its history traces back to the Caesar cipher. This cipher uses the shifting of letters to perform encryption and decryption. Other ciphers also use simple substitution and transposition to hide messages. However, classical cryptography is vulnerable to statistical analysis and frequency analysis. Therefore, it was gradually replaced by stronger cryptographic methods.

Symmetric cryptography is primarily categorized into two branches: stream ciphers and block ciphers. A stream cipher operates by generating a pseudorandom keystream using a pseudorandom number generator (PRNG). Encryption is achieved by combining this keystream with the plaintext, typically through a bit-wise XOR operation. Characterized by their efficiency and real-time processing capabilities, stream ciphers are particularly advantageous for securing streaming data and high-speed communications.

Block ciphers represent the other primary category of symmetric cryptography. Unlike stream ciphers, these algorithms partition plaintext into fixed-size segments, known as blocks, and encrypt each block utilizing a secret key. Prominent examples include the Data Encryption Standard (DES) and the Advanced Encryption Standard (AES). Block ciphers are renowned for their robust security and versatility. By employing various modes of operation and adjustable key lengths, they can be tailored to meet diverse security requirements.

The fundamental principle of symmetric cryptography relies on a single shared secret key for both encryption and decryption. While this symmetry facilitates high computational efficiency, it necessitates the secure distribution and management of keys between communicating parties. Consequently, the field faces significant challenges regarding key lifecycle management, particularly the secure exchange, storage, and updating of keys. Despite these complexities, symmetric algorithms remain ubiquitous for safeguarding data privacy and integrity. Nevertheless, the discipline must continually evolve to counter emerging threats, including the advent of quantum computing and sophisticated side-channel attacks.

CHAPTER 4

Classical Ciphers

This chapter introduces several classical cryptosystems, ranging from the primitive Caesar cipher to the groundbreaking Merkle Hellman knapsack cryptosystem, providing a detailed overview of their encryption procedures and analysis methods. With the exception of the Merkle Hellman knapsack cryptosystem, all classical algorithms discussed herein are symmetric encryption algorithms, meaning that the keys used for encryption and decryption are identical. This chapter explains the process of encrypting and decrypting information using a single key and explores the various symmetric encryption algorithms developed by cryptographers.

Topics covered in this chapter:

- Encryption and decryption of the Caesar cipher (Shift Cipher).
- Encryption and decryption of the Fanqie cipher.
- Encryption and decryption of the Vigenère cipher.
- Encryption and decryption of the Affine cipher.
- Encryption and decryption of the Hill cipher.
- Encryption and decryption of the Playfair cipher.
- Encryption and decryption of the ADFGVX cipher.

4.1 CAESAR CIPHER/SHIFT CIPHER

The Caesar Cipher, also known as the Shift Cipher, with a history of 2,000 years, is one of the oldest and most widely recognized classical ciphers. It is frequently the first algorithm introduced in the study of cryptography.

Classified as a mono-alphabetic substitution cipher, specifically a shift cipher, it encrypts messages by replacing each letter in the plaintext with a letter a fixed number of positions down the alphabet.

Historically, *Julius Caesar* employed this technique during the *Gallic Wars*. In a notable instance, upon learning that his general *Cicero* was besieged, Caesar dispatched a cryptic message. The courier was instructed to deliver the letter directly or, if necessary, to hurl it attached to a spear into the camp.

Cicero received the urgent message on the third day. He deciphered it by following a prearranged rule where each letter was shifted such that "D" represented "A", "E"

DOI: 10.1201/9781042011087-4

represented "B", and so forth. In this scheme, plaintext characters were replaced by letters positioned three places further down the alphabet. The decrypted message revealed that reinforcements were imminent, which brought great rejoicing to the troops and inspired them to hold out until help arrived.

Caesar later standardized this method with a fixed shift value. The cipher was subsequently named in his honor, securing its significance in the history of cryptography.

4.1.1 Encryption

In the Caesar cipher, the plaintext alphabet typically consists of the 26 letters of the English alphabet. In certain contexts, this domain may be extended to include the 10 Arabic numerals (0–9).

The key in a shift cipher is defined by a specific shift value. For the classical Caesar cipher, the shift value is $K = 3$. Consequently, "A" is replaced by "D", "B" by "E", and so forth. This transformation is cyclic: at the end of the alphabet, "Z" is replaced by "C". This property implies that the alphabet wraps around, mapping characters from the end of the sequence back to the beginning.

Mathematically, the Caesar cipher defines a bijective function over a finite alphabet.

Example 4.1.1 Other shifts could be used. Here is the key for a Caesar cipher with shift 16. "A" is replaced by "Q", "B" is replaced by "R", and so on. The example is illustrated in Figure 4-1.

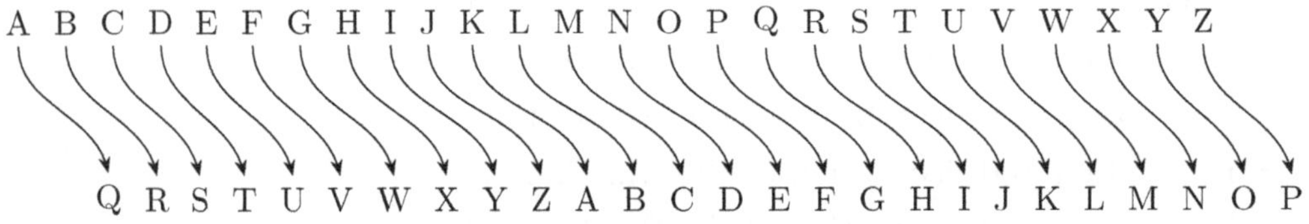

Figure 4-1: Caesar Cipher with Shift 16

Suppose the plaintext is "**MISSILE**", with a shift 16 becomes "**CYIIYBU**". ■

Example 4.1.2 We now encrypt the plaintext "**intelligence**" using Python.

```
plaintext = "intelligence"
key = 16
ciphertext = ""

key %= 26

for letter in plaintext:
    if letter.islower():
        shifted = (ord(letter) - ord('a') + key) % 26
        ciphertext += chr(shifted + ord('a'))
    else:
        ciphertext += letter
```

Output: **ydjubbywudsu.** ■

4.1.2 Cryptanalysis

Given that the English alphabet contains only 26 letters, the Caesar cipher typically utilizes the integers modulo 26 as its key space. This results in a very small key space, denoted as $|\mathcal{K}| = 26$. Furthermore, one of these keys corresponds to a shift of 0 (or equivalently 26), which maps every letter to itself, essentially leaving the plaintext unencrypted. Consequently, there are only 25 effective keys available to secure a message.

Due to this limited key space, Eve can easily recover the plaintext by systematically testing every possible shift. This method is formally known as a **brute-force attack**. With the exception of systems possessing perfect secrecy (see Section 3.4), a brute-force attack can theoretically compromise any encryption scheme. However, for modern cryptosystems with sufficiently large key spaces, this approach becomes computationally infeasible.

Example 4.1.3 Breaking the given ciphertext: **exxegoexsrgi**.
Solution: Breaking the given ciphertext using Python.

```
ciphertext = ''exxegoexsrgi''

for key in range(26):

    plaintext = ''

    for letter in ciphertext:
        shifted = (ord(letter) - ord('a') - key) % 26
        plaintext += chr(shifted + ord('a'))
    print(''Key {:2d}: {}''.format(key, plaintext))
```

The output is shown in the Table 4-1:

Table 4-1: Breaking Table

Caesar Shift	Output
A	exxegoexsrgi
B	dwwdfndwrqfh
C	cvvcemcvqpeg
D	buubdlbupodf
E	**attackatonce**
...	...
Z	fyyfhpfytshj

When the Caesar cipher with shift of E, we can find the plaintext as: **attack at once.** ■

4.1.3 Caesar Cipher Improvements

Because the Caesar cipher is overly simplistic and highly vulnerable to brute-force attacks due to its limited key space, enhancing its cryptographic strength requires expanding the key space. There are three methods to achieve this:

(1) **Randomize the Order of Substitution**

To enhance security, we can move beyond the fixed shift structure of the Caesar cipher. Instead of a simple shift, we employ an arbitrary permutation of the alphabet, where each letter is mapped to another distinct letter in a random fashion. This scheme is illustrated in Figure 4-2.

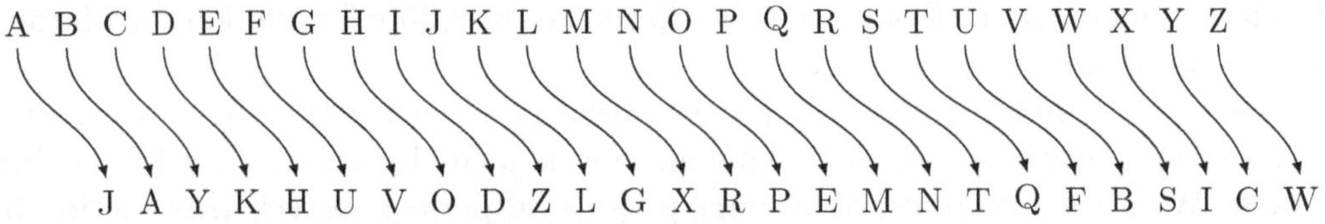

Figure 4-2: Randomize the Order of Substitution

From a combinatorial perspective, the letter "A" can be mapped to any of the 26 letters. Once "A" is assigned, the letter "B" has 25 remaining choices, and so on. Consequently, the simple substitution key space consists of the $26! \approx 2^{88}$ possible permutations of the alphabet which represents a massive increase compared to the 26 keys of the Caesar cipher. Due to this immense search space, a brute-force attack is computationally infeasible.

Generally, a sufficiently large key space is a necessary condition for a secure cryptosystem. However, it is not a sufficient condition.

Despite the large key space, this simple substitution cipher remains vulnerable to **frequency analysis**. Since the mapping is bijective and fixed, the encryption preserves the underlying statistical structure of the language. The ciphertext preserves the statistical structure of the plaintext, although the symbols themselves are permuted.

The standard letter frequencies for English are presented in Figure 4-3, which serves as a baseline for such statistical attacks.

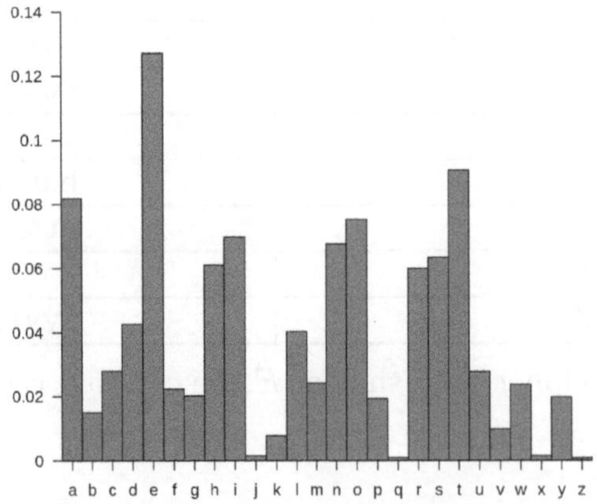

Figure 4-3: English Letter Frequencies[1]

Given a sufficient quantity of ciphertext, an attacker can utilize letter frequencies to identify statistical anomalies. For instance, the letter "Q" is typically infrequent in standard English. However, if "Q" appears with high frequency in the ciphertext,

[1]Image by Nandhp via Wikimedia Commons.

perhaps even exceeding common letters like "E", it implies that the plaintext "E" has been substituted by "Q". By systematically applying this logic, the attacker can achieve a plausible reconstruction of the original plaintext.

(2) **Homophonic Substitution**

In contrast to the Caesar cipher, which utilizes a one-to-one mapping, homophonic substitution maps each plaintext letter to a set of multiple ciphertext symbols. Consequently, there is more than one possible substitution for a given plaintext letter. However, the decryption is unique, each ciphertext symbol can represent only one plaintext letter. By balancing these frequencies, the ciphertext symbols appear with roughly equal probability and consequently makes attacks based on frequency analysis more difficult.

An example of a homophonic substitution cipher is given in Table 4-2.

Table 4-2: Homophonic Substitution Key

Plaintext	A	B	C	D	E	F	G	H	I	J	K	L	M	N	O	P	Q	R	S	T	U	V	W	X	Y	Z
Ciphertext	G	H	M	F	X	S	R	V	A	D	B	K	Y	J	P	T	E	C	N	I	L	O	W	Q	Z	U
	β	δ	ζ	α	η	θ	ι		κ		ν	ξ	π	ρ		σ	τ		υ	ϕ		χ	ψ	ω		λ
	$\pm$	$\triangleright$			$\amalg$	$\unrhd$			$*$			$\sqcap$		$\wedge$		$\bullet$	$\ominus$		$\rhd$	$\bigtriangledown$		$\bigoplus$	$\biguplus$	$\bigotimes$		
	$					&								%					#					@		

As previously established, high-frequency letters are assigned a larger set of homophones to flatten the frequency distribution. We illustrate these encoding principles and their implications for cryptanalysis with the following examples:

1) The ciphertext string $\Diamond\Box\Box\Delta$ exhibits the structural pattern $ABBC$. To break, this structure limits the candidate plaintext words to those with an identical pattern of repetition, such as "**FOOD**" or "**AMMO**".
2) The plaintext **ok** may be encoded as either "**83**" or "**∗3**". This demonstrates that the encryption process is non-deterministic.
3) Specialized encoding rules may be defined. For instance, **ee** $\leftrightarrow \Diamond\Delta$, **oo** $\leftrightarrow \sqcap\Delta$, where Δ denotes a repeated character.

The brute-force attack and frequency analysis are out of the method. An available attack way relies on examining the structural information that leaks from the plaintext into the ciphertext, as demonstrated in the first example.

(3) **Poly-alphabetic Substitution**

In 1467, *Leon Battista Alberti* invented the cipher disk which allowed the sender to use different alphabets for different portions of the plaintext. He used more than one alphabet, switching between them systematically. This type of cipher is called a Poly-alphabetic substitution cipher ("Poly" is the Greek root for "many").

Leon is celebrated as the "Father of Western Cryptography" for his groundbreaking 1467 invention of the this cipher, revealed in his treatise *De Cifris*, which introduced revolutionary concepts like cipher disks and frequency analysis countermeasures that defined encryption for centuries.

Example 4.1.4 Let the keyword be "**REV**". Encrypt the plaintext "**Avenged Sevenfold**". The method involves applying three separate Caesar ciphers using the key "**REV**", arranged vertically beneath the plaintext starting from the letter A. Specifically, the first cipher maps $A \to R$ (shift 17), the second maps $A \to E$ (shift 4), and the third maps $A \to V$ (shift 21), as illustrated in Table 4-3.

Table 4-3: Poly-Alphabetic Substitution

A	B	C	D	E	F	G	H	I	J	K	L	M	N	O	P	Q	R	S	T	U	V	W	X	Y	Z
R	S	T	U	V	W	X	Y	Z	A	B	C	D	E	F	G	H	I	J	K	L	M	N	O	P	Q
E	F	G	H	I	J	K	L	M	N	O	P	Q	R	S	T	U	V	W	X	Y	Z	A	B	C	D
V	W	X	Y	Z	A	B	C	D	E	F	G	H	I	J	K	L	M	N	O	P	Q	R	S	T	U

Solution: The plaintext is processed in blocks of length three, corresponding to the length of the keyword. Spaces between words are typically omitted. In each group, the first letter is encrypted using the first letter of the key as the Caesar cipher shift; the second letter uses the second letter of the key, and the third letter uses the third. The encryption process for the plaintext "**Avenged Sevenfold**" is illustrated in Table 4-4.

Table 4-4: Poly-Alphabetic Substitution Encryption Process

Plaintext	A	V	E	N	G	E	D	S	E	V	E	N	F	O	L	D
Shift 1 (R)	**R**			**E**			**U**			**M**			**W**			**U**
Shift 2 (E)		**Z**			**K**			**W**			**I**			**S**		
Shift 3 (V)			**Z**			**Z**			**Z**			**I**			**G**	
Ciphertext	R	Z	Z	E	K	Z	U	W	Z	M	I	I	W	S	G	U

Thus, the ciphertext is "**RZZEKZUWZMIIWSGU**". ■

The key space of a poly-alphabetic substitution cipher is 26^N, where N is the length of the key. For example, with a key such as "**WATER**", then the key space equals 26^5.

The standard frequency analysis no longer works to break the cipher. The cipher was eventually compromised in the 19th century. Although *Charles Babbage* is believed to have solved it privately around 1854, his work was never published. It was not until 1863 that *Friedrich Kasiski* independently published a general solution. By identifying repeated patterns in the ciphertext to deduce the key length, he established the method now known as the Kasiski test (discussed in Section 4.3.4).

4.2 FANQIE CODE

The Fanqie code uses the "Fanqie" pronunciation method of Chinese characters for encoding. What is "Fanqie"? It is a method created by ancient Chinese to indicate the pronunciation of Chinese characters following methods like "Zhiyin" (using a homophone) and "Duruo" (using a similar-sounding character).

The basic principle of Fanqie is to use two Chinese characters from the same language or dialect to form the pronunciation of another character: the first character provides the initial consonant, and the second contributes the final and tone.

The basic principle of Fanqie is to use two Chinese characters from the same language or dialect to form the pronunciation of another character: the first character provides the initial consonant, and the second contributes the final and tone. For example, the character "Hong" ("Red" in Chinese) is represented by the combination "He Gong" in Fanqie. "He" provides the initial "H", and "Gong" contributes the final "ong", forming the pronunciation "Hong", which reads as "red", as shown in Figure 4-4.

In Volume 14 of *Yunlu Manchao* (a classic scholarly note) by *Zhao Yanwei* from the Song Dynasty (in the 13th century, a dynastic states name of China), it is noted that "Sun Yan was the creator of the **Fanqie** method". It originated in the Han Dynasty (in the 1st century) and became a popular, common pronunciation method during the Tang Dynasty (in the 7th century). But how can this well-known pronunciation method be used to encrypt information? That's where dialects come into play. Due to inconvenient transportation and underdeveloped communication in ancient times, pronunciations varied even within short distances. Many remote areas and ethnic groups used unique phonetic systems that outsiders found hard to understand.

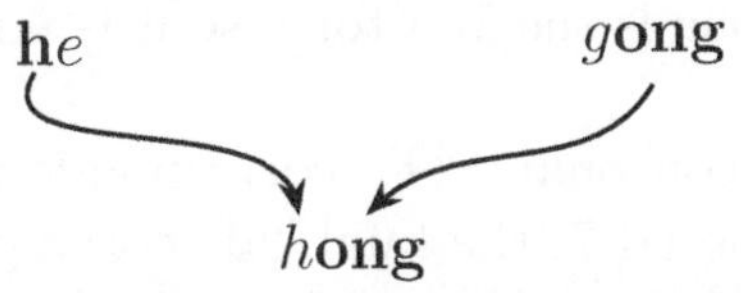

Figure 4-4: "He Gong" in Fanqie Code

For example, the dialect of Taizhou (a coastal city in East China) is highly distinctive. Therefore, *Qi Jiguang*, who was a Chinese military general during the Ming Dynasty (in the 16th century, a dynastic states name of China). For fighting against Japanese pirates, used Fanqie codes based on Taizhou dialect to transmit messages to various military units. He composed two poems as keys. The first one is (the Romanization of Chinese):

Liŭ biān qiú qì dī, Bō tā zhēng rì shí.
Yīng méng yŭ chū xī, Dă zhăng yŭ jūn zhī.

The second one is:

Chūn huā xiāng, Qiū shān kāi,
Jiā bīn huān gē xū jīn bēi, Gū dēng guāng huī shāo yín gāng.
Zhī dōng jiāo, Guò xī qiáo,
Jī shēng cuī chū tiān, Qí méi wāi zhē gōu.

These two poems, which lack real literary value, served as a codebook for intelligence personnel to master.

The Chinese phonrtics consists of initials, finals and tones. The Fanqie Code works like this: the 20 characters in the first poem provide initial consonants and are numbered 1 to 20; the 36 characters in the second poem supply finals and are numbered 1 to 36. Then, the four tones of character(for example: ā, á, ǎ, à) pronunciation are also numbered sequentially from 1 to 4.

By converting plaintext into Fanqie Code, messengers can transmit messages. Since the pronunciation of these two poems is not based on standard Mandarin, but rather on the dialect from northern Fujian and southeastern Zhejiang(two coastal provinces in East China) during the Ming Dynasty, the pronunciation differs from that of modern Mandarin. To facilitate readers' understanding, the following examples use standard Mandarin pronunciation and modern Chinese Pinyin for reference.

Example 4.2.1 Suppose Taizhou authorities discover Japanese pirates near Taizhou and want to send the message "Dí Tāi Zhōu" (meaning enemy at Taizhou) back to the headquarters. How should this be done?

Solution: Break down "Dí Tāi Zhōu" character by character. The first character is pronounced "Dí". The initial consonant "D" corresponds to the character "dī" in the first poem, which is numbered 5 (similarly, 16th can also be chosen); the final "i" corresponds to the character "xī" in the second poem, which is numbered 25 (27th can also be chosen); the tone is the 2nd tone, so it is numbered 2. These combine to form the code 5-25-2.

For "Tāi", the initial consonant "T" corresponds to the character "tā" in the first poem, which is numbered 7; the final "ai" corresponds to the character "wāi" in the second poem, which is numbered 34 (similarly, 6th can also be chosen); the tone is the 1st tone, so it is numbered 1. These combine to form the code 7-34-1.

For "Zhōu", the initial "Zh" consonant corresponds to the character "zhēng" in the first poem, which is numbered 8 (similarly, 17th can also be chosen); the final "ōu" corresponds to the character "gōu" in the second poem, which is numbered 36; the tone is the 1st tone, so it is numbered 1. These combine to form the code 8-36-1. Hence, the messenger only needs to transmit "5-25-2, 7-34-1, 8-36-1" to the headquarters. The intelligence personnel there will decrypt it using the same poems. ■

By modern standards, the Fanqie Code is not secure, as its keyspace is limited to only $20 \times 36 \times 4 = 2880$ combinations. Although combining pronunciations with dialects can enhance the security of the code to some extent, making it difficult for attackers using foreign languages to understand, the entire encryption system will become insecure once the two poems are obtained by attackers. Due to the limitations of the keyspace, methods like frequency analysis can be employed to decipher the plaintext. Consequently, under the conditions of that time, to ensure the security of the code, these two poems must be strictly shared by intelligence personnel and not leaked to outsiders.

4.3 VIGENÈRE CIPHER

The Vigenère Cipher is a classical example of a poly-alphabetic substitution cipher. It generalizes the principle of the Caesar cipher by employing a sequence of shifts determined by a repeating keyword. This structure significantly increases resistance to standard frequency analysis, representing a major advancement over mono-alphabetic schemes.

Historically, the mechanism was first described by the Italian cryptographer *Giovan Battista Bellaso* in 1553. *Bellaso* introduced the innovative concept of using a periodic key to control the letter substitution. However, his contribution was overshadowed for centuries due to a misattribution to the French diplomat *Blaise de Vigenère*. Consequently, the cipher became universally known as the "Vigenère Cipher", a name that persists to this day.

4.3.1 Encryption/Decryption

1) **(Setup)**: Translate the given plaintext into numbers. Starting from zero, encoding each letter, as shown in Table 4-5.

Table 4-5: Alphabet

0	1	2	3	4	5	6	7	8	9	10	11	12	13	14	15	16	17	18	19	20	21	22	23	24	25
A	B	C	D	E	F	G	H	I	J	K	L	M	N	O	P	Q	R	S	T	U	V	W	X	Y	Z

2) **(KeyGen)**: Randomize two short keys U and V and compute the long key K, as follows:

$$K_i \equiv (U_i + V_i) \pmod{26} \tag{4-1}$$

for each $1 \leqslant i \leqslant n$ where n is the length of the plaintext.

3) **(Encrypt)**: Compute the ciphertext C, as follows:

$$C_i \equiv (M_i + K_i) \pmod{26} \tag{4-2}$$

for each i, and use substitute each M_i by the corresponding letter in the alphabet.

4) **(Decrypt)**: Compute the plaintext M, as follows:

$$M_i \equiv (C_i - K_i) \pmod{26} \tag{4-3}$$

Example 4.3.1 Encrypt the plaintext "**NO MORE AMMO**" using the composite keys $\{U, V\} = \{(3, 1, 2), (7, 3, 8, 4, 5)\}$.

Solution: First, we determine the combined key stream K. The period of K is the least common multiple (LCM) of the lengths of the components U and V. We align U and V cyclically and compute the key using the congruence $K \equiv U + V \pmod{26}$, as illustrated in Table 4-6.

Table 4-6: The Encryption Process of the Vigenère Cipher (1)

U	**3**	**1**	**2**	3	1	2	3	1	2	3	1	2	3	1	2
V	**7**	**3**	**8**	**4**	**5**	7	3	8	4	5	7	3	8	4	5
$K \equiv U + V \pmod{26}$	10	4	10	7	6	9	6	9	6	8	8	5	11	5	7

Next, we convert the plaintext letters into their corresponding numerical values M. The key stream K is aligned with the plaintext. Since the plaintext length is shorter than the key period, we simply use the first 10 values of K. The ciphertext values C are computed using $C \equiv M + K \pmod{26}$ and then converted back to letters. This process is detailed in Table 4-7.

The resulting ciphertext is "**XSWVXNGVSW**". ■

Example 4.3.2 Implement a Python script to encrypt the plaintext "**MYNAMEISBOB**" using the composite keys {U, V} = {(3, 1, 2),(7, 3, 8, 4, 5)},

Table 4-7: The Encryption Process of the Vigenère Cipher (2)

Plaintext	N	O	M	O	R	E	A	M	M	O
M	13	14	12	14	17	4	0	12	12	14
K	10	4	10	7	6	9	6	9	6	8
$C \equiv M + K \pmod{26}$	23	18	22	21	23	13	6	21	18	22
Ciphertext	X	S	W	V	X	N	G	V	S	W

```
plaintext = "MYNAMEISBOB"

U = [3 ,1 ,2 ,5 ,5 ,7 ,7 ,5 ,7]
V = [5 ,4 ,2 ,3 ,5 ,6 ,4 ,23 ,99 ,12]

ciphertext = ""
index = 0

for letter in plaintext:
    if letter.isalpha():
        m = ord(letter) - ord('A')
        u = U[index % len(U)]
        v = V[index % len(V)]

        k = (u + v) % 26
        c = (m + k) % 26

        ciphertext += chr(c + ord('A'))
        index += 1
    else:
        ciphertext += letter

print("Plaintext: ", plaintext)
print("Ciphertext:", ciphertext)
```

The resulting ciphertext is "**UDRIWRTUDDH**". ■

Example 4.3.3 Implement a Python script to decrypt the ciphertext "**UDRIWRTUDDH**".

```
ciphertext = ''UDRIWRTUDDH''

U = [3, 1, 2, 5, 5, 7, 7, 5, 7]
V = [5, 4, 2, 3, 5, 6, 4, 23, 99, 12]

plaintext = ''''
index = 0

for letter in ciphertext:
    if letter.isalpha():
        c = ord(letter) - ord('A')
        u = U[index % len(U)]
        v = V[index % len(V)]

        k = (u + v) % 26
        m = (c - k) % 26

```

```
            plaintext += chr(m + ord('A'))
            index += 1
        else:
            plaintext += letter
print(''Plaintext:'', plaintext)
```

The resulting plaintext is "**MYNAMEISBOB**". ■

4.3.2 Cryptanalysis

The Vigenère cipher remains a subject of enduring interest in the field of cryptography. Following its formulation by *Giovan Battista Bellaso* in 1553, generations of cryptanalysts attempted to compromise the system. While isolated successes were recorded, a general systematic solution remained elusive until 1854. In that year, the British mathematician *Charles Babbage* successfully devised a structured method to break the cipher. However, Babbage did not publish his findings. It was *Friedrich Kasiski* who first published a similar independent solution in 1863.

Although the Vigenère cipher is theoretically breakable, its resistance to cryptanalysis increases significantly with the length of the key. Since the polyalphabetic nature of the cipher masks the underlying letter statistics, simple frequency analysis is rendered ineffective. Consequently, a systematic attack typically proceeds in two stages. The first step involves determining the key length. The second step focuses on recovering the specific key components. A primary statistical tool employed in this recovery phase is the chi-squared test.

The following section introduces the mathematical tools required for this analysis.

Definition 4.3.1 Permutation

If an ordered list or permutation of k objects is to be formed by selecting from a collection of n objects, where $k \leqslant n$, then there are

$$P(n,k) = n \cdot (n-1) \cdot (n-2) \cdots (n-k+2) \cdot (n-k+1) = \frac{n!}{(n-k)!} \quad (4\text{-}4)$$

ways to form this list.

Definition 4.3.2 Combination

The number of unordered selections of combinations of n objects selected k at a time is given by

$$C(n,k) = \frac{P(n,k)}{k!} = \binom{n}{k} = \frac{n!}{k!(n-k)!} \quad (4\text{-}5)$$

Definition 4.3.3 Probability

For an experiment where there are n different equally likely possible outcomes, then the probability of a result that can occur in k possible ways is

> *given by*
>
> $$P = \frac{k}{n} \tag{4-6}$$

Example 4.3.4 Suppose there are 45 cards in a deck. Of those cards, 20 are labeled with "X", 15 are labeled with "Y", and 10 "Z". Suppose we pick a card at random, put it back, then shuffle the deck and pick another card at random. Find the probability that

1) The first letter is X and the second is Z.
Solution: Since they are independently, the probability is

$$P(X_1 \cap Z_2) = P(X_1) \cdot P(Z_2) = \frac{20}{45} \cdot \frac{10}{45} = \frac{8}{81} \tag{4-7}$$

■

2) The two letters are X and Z.
Solution: $P(\{X, Z\}) = P(X_1 \cap Z_2) + P(Z_1 \cap X_2) = \frac{8}{81} + \left(\frac{10}{45} \cdot \frac{20}{45}\right) = \frac{8}{81} + \frac{8}{81} = \frac{16}{81}$ ■

3) The two letters are Y.
Solution: $P(Y \cap Y) = P(Y) \cdot P(Y) = \frac{15}{45} \cdot \frac{15}{45} = \frac{1}{9}$ ■

Example 4.3.5 Birthday problem is very interesting, it is based on the well known "**birthday paradox**" which says that if there are n people in a classroom, what is the probability that at least two have the same birthday(ignore leap year)?
Solution: The best way to do this is to compute the probability that no two of these n people have the same birthday. By subtracting this result from one, we obtain the probability that at least two people have the same birthday.

The first person's birthday can occur on 365 possible days, so his probability is $\frac{365}{365}$. The second person's birthday must be born on one of the remaining 364 days, the probability that 2 people have different birthdays is $\frac{364 \times 365}{365^2}$. The third person's birthday can occur on 363 possible days, the probability that 3 people have different birthdays is $\frac{363 \times 364 \times 365}{365^3}$, and so on.

Assume there are n people in this classroom, the probability that n people have different birthdays is $P = \frac{365}{365} \times \frac{364}{365} \times \frac{363}{365} \times \cdots \times \frac{365-n+1}{365}$.

By the rule of complements, the probability that at least two have the same birthday is given by

$$P(\text{same}) = 1 - \frac{P(365, n)}{365^n} \tag{4-8}$$

$$= 1 - \frac{365 \times 364 \times \cdots \times (365 - n + 1)}{365^n} \tag{4-9}$$

Table 4-8 presents the probability that at least two people have the same birthday for various group sizes. In the table, n denotes the number of people, and p is the probability that at least two have the same birthday.

Table 4-8: Probability of Having Shared Birthdays

n	1	2	3	5	10	20	30	40	50
p	0	0.0027	0.0082	0.027	0.117	0.411	0.706	0.891	0.97

Assume there are 50 people in a classroom, the data indicates a probability of approximately 0.97, meaning it is nearly guaranteed that at least two people have the same birthdays. It is important to note that if $n > 365$, the probability becomes exactly 1. This certainty is a direct application of the Pigeonhole Principle. In cryptographic terms, this event is referred to as a collision. This concept is fundamental to the security of hash functions, which will be discussed in detail in later chapters.

How many people are required for the probability that at least two share the same birthdays to over 50%?

$$1 - C(365, n) = 1 - \frac{P(365, n)}{365^n} \tag{4-10}$$

$$= 1 - \frac{365 \times 364 \times \cdots \times (365 - n + 1)}{365^n} \tag{4-11}$$

$$= 0.5 \tag{4-12}$$

By solving this inequality, we find that $n = 23$ is sufficient. For 23 people, the probability is approximately $0.507 \geqslant 0.5$. ■

Example 4.3.6 Table 4-9 gives the relative frequency of the English alphabet letters in a 7834-letter sample of English writing.

Table 4-9: Relative Frequency of the English Alphabet (%)

Letter	Relative frequency	Letter	Relative frequency
A	8.399	N	6.778
B	1.442	O	7.493
C	2.527	P	1.991
D	4.800	Q	0.077
E	12.150	R	6.063
F	2.132	S	6.319
G	2.323	T	8.999
H	6.025	U	2.783
I	6.485	V	0.996
J	0.102	W	2.464
K	0.689	X	0.204
L	4.008	Y	2.157
M	2.566	Z	0.025

Use the table to find the probability that two randomly selected letters in English are identical.

Solution: The calculation proceeds as follows:

$$P(2Letter) = P(A)^2 + P(B)^2 + \cdots + P(Z)^2 \tag{4-13}$$
$$= 0.08399^2 + 0.01442^2 + \cdots + 0.00025^2 = 6.5\% \tag{4-14}$$

Thus, the probability is approximately 6.5%. ■

Example 4.3.7 Suppose we use the Caesar cipher where $A \rightarrow D$. Answer the following questions.

1) What is the probability of randomly selecting the letter "A" from the ciphertext?
   Solution: $P(\text{A in ciphertext}) = P(\text{X in plaintext}) = P(X) = 0.204\%$ ■
2) What is the probability of randomly selecting the letter "B" from the ciphertext?
   Solution: $P(\text{B in ciphertext}) = P(\text{Y in plaintext}) = P(Y) = 2.157\%$ ■

Example 4.3.8 Suppose we use the Vigenère cipher with key "**DN**". Answer the following questions.

1) What is the probability of selecting an "A" in the ciphertext?
   Solution:

$$\begin{aligned} P(\text{A in ciphertext}) &= P(X \text{ in the plaintext at odd}) \\ &+ P(N \text{ in the plaintext at even}) \\ &= \frac{P(X)}{2} + \frac{P(N)}{2} = 3.491\% \end{aligned}$$

■

2) What is the probability of selecting an "B" in the ciphertext?
   Solution:

$$\begin{aligned} P(\text{B in ciphertext}) &= P(Y \text{ in the plaintext at odd}) \\ &+ P(O \text{ in the plaintext at even}) \\ &= \frac{P(Y)}{2} + \frac{P(O)}{2} = 4.825\% \end{aligned}$$

■

In the Vigenère cipher with sufficiently long key, the probabilities of seeing any letter in the ciphertext will converge to a uniform distribution, where $Pr(C) = 1/26 \approx 3.8\%$ for any given letter.

4.3.3 Friedman Test

The index of coincidence (for a ciphertext), denoted by I, is the probability that two randomly selected letters in the ciphertext are identical. If $I \approx 0.0385$ then the cipher is more likely to be a poly-alphabetic substitution. If $I \approx 0.065$ then the cipher is more likely to be a mono-alphabetic substitution. The value of I typically falls within the range $0.0385 \leqslant I \leqslant 0.065$.

Let $n_0, n_1, n_2, \ldots, n_{24}, n_{25}$ be the respective counts of the letters $A, B, C, \ldots, Y, Z$. Let $n = \sum n_i$ be the total number of letters in the text then

$$I = \frac{1}{n(n-1)} \sum_{i=0}^{25} n_i(n_i - 1), \text{ where } 0 \leqslant i \leqslant 25 \tag{4-15}$$

Now if an English plaintext is encrypted using a Vigenère cipher with key of length k, estimate it, we can use Friedman Test:

$$\text{Index of coincidence} = I \approx \frac{0.0385 \times n(k-1) + 0.065(n-k)}{k(n-1)} \tag{4-16}$$

$$\text{key Length} = k \approx \frac{0.0265n}{(0.065 - I) + n(I - 0.0385)} \tag{4-17}$$

Unfortunately, the Friedman test can only estimate key of length k and cannot directly recover the key. Moreover, it requires a sufficiently long ciphertext to be effective.

Example 4.3.9 Suppose a ciphertext is encrypted with a Vigenère cipher with key of length k. The total number of letters in the ciphertext is $n = 337$ and the frequency count of the ciphertext is given by the table below. Estimate the key length k.

Table 4-10: Frequency Counts of the English Text

Letter	Count	Letter	Count	Letter	Count	Letter	Count
A	13	H	9	O	17	V	8
B	18	I	16	P	21	W	14
C	12	J	8	Q	9	X	8
D	15	K	9	R	16	Y	20
E	26	L	18	S	7	Z	6
F	4	M	22	T	8		
G	15	N	11	U	7		

Solution: We compute the Index of Coincidence I using equations 4-16 and 4-17 yields

$$I = \frac{1}{n(n-1)} \sum_{i=0}^{25} n_i(n_i - 1) = \frac{1}{337 \times 336}(13 \times 12 + 18 \times 17 + \cdots + 6 \times 5) = 0.0428 \tag{4-18}$$

$$k = \frac{0.0265 \times 337}{(0.065 - 0.0428) + 337 \times (0.0428 - 0.0385)} \approx 6.07 \approx 6 \tag{4-19}$$

We estimate the length of the key is 6. ■

4.3.4 Kasiski Test

The Kasiski test is another way of estimating the length of the key for Vigenère cipher. It obtains possible key lengths from the GCD of the spacing between repeated letter groups in the ciphertext.

Example 4.3.10 Consider the ciphertext **IVEVYGARMLMYIVEKFDIVE-FRL**. Estimate the key length for the ciphertext.

Solution:

$$\underbrace{\text{IVE}VYGARMLMY}_{12}\underbrace{\text{IVE}KFD}_{6}\underbrace{\text{IVE}FRL}_{6}$$

$$k \approx \gcd(12, 6) = 6$$

Therefore, the key length is 6. ■

Both Friedman and Kasiski tests only give the key length, but not the keyword itself. Furthermore, they are not very accurate when the ciphertext is small (usually less than 400 characters).

Suppose we have estimated the key length of Vigenère cipher, denoted by m, using either the Friedman test or the Kasiski test. This implies that the ciphertext is composed of m distinct, interleaved Caesar ciphers. We must now determine the exact key K, a task that is non-trivial. However, the analysis can proceed systematically as follows.

Let the ciphertext C have a total length of n. We divide the ciphertext into m subciphertexts, denoted as $C_1, C_2, \ldots, C_m$. Each substring c_i consists of every m-th character, starting from the i-th position, for $1 \leqslant i \leqslant m$.

$$\begin{aligned}
\text{Ciphertext} : C &= c_1 c_2 \cdots c_n \\
\text{Subciphertext } 1 : C_1 &= c_1 c_{m+1} \cdots c_{n-m+1} \\
\text{Subciphertext } 2 : C_2 &= c_2 c_{m+2} \cdots c_{n-m+2} \\
&\vdots \\
\text{Subciphertext } m : C_m &= c_m c_{2m} \cdots c_n
\end{aligned}$$

Let each subciphertext have a length of approximately $l = n/m$ and $f_0, f_1, \ldots, f_{25}$ denote the frequency counts of the letters A–Z in a specific subciphertext c_i. The empirical frequency distribution is given by the vector

$$\mathbf{q} = \left(\frac{f_0}{l}, \frac{f_1}{l}, \ldots, \frac{f_{25}}{l}\right) \tag{4-20}$$

Since the subciphertext is generated by shifting the plaintext letters by a fixed amount k, this distribution $\mathbf{q}$ is simply a cyclically shifted version of the original plaintext distribution.

If the substring is sufficiently long, its frequency distribution (when shifted back by the correct key) should approximate the standard English distribution shown in Table 4-9. To find the correct shift, we compute the mutual index of coincidence, denoted as M_g, for each candidate shift g ($0 \leqslant g \leqslant 25$). Let p_i represent the expected probability of the i-th letter in standard English. The measure M_g is defined as

$$M_g = \sum_{i=0}^{25} p_i \cdot \frac{f_{(i+g) \bmod 26}}{l} \tag{4-21}$$

This calculation effectively represents the dot product between the standard English frequency vector and the ciphertext frequency vector shifted by g. In natural English text, M_g is approximately 0.065, whereas for random text, it is approximately 0.0385. Therefore, if $M_g \approx 0.065$, it implies that g is likely the correct key shift k for this subciphertext. The recovery process involves computing M_g for all possible shifts $g \in \{0, \ldots, 25\}$ and selecting the value g that maximizes M_g. By repeating this procedure for all m subciphertexts, we can recover each component of the keyword. Once the full keyword K is reconstructed, the ciphertext can be decrypted.

Example 4.3.11 Consider the following ciphertext obtained from a Vigenère cipher and decrypt the given message.

```
CQKATIYRCZXEGVXPCTEWDCBJVCIDTWFRJMUYUQVAQUIMPMGRUWYUKVZQHCLCNIZCUBTG
NCGGVATLFKHLVZHJUCKDCKXQVPXPGIKCXIKGCBBMPABLRIKRKKNJCZTGTKKYHBYMTMQY
OXECCLXJVIPGPOTGTKKYHBPMWTWLQBGCEMLQCZBJAXHQUMLQCPHPKHHLVIERCQEYNBAM
WOARJQLGUXKCUMGRKVTACVTPFKHLHQZSTIMGQVLSEPTQVPTRQNMFGMNPQNBEJBXPGIVF
EWFNQVXLVPTQQVXMTUHPGAICEQYGENNLEBBMPATLFUNQVJXBGABEPMWRQMGQWZXRJIMG
VKTLEIKPAWNRVPXQGNNLEBBMPALYHMEWKVMFKAVFCXMCTEXBGAVPKJXRJMOYTQHSUTHY
FAMMYPBAJIBPEZTDVKHKRWGCPBLYTMLSDRXAVMWRJMBPHCGAVQHLCVWDCJKGEIMGQVTL
FBACFMLGIVHDEWGLGKMGQVLQRIVCEZTDVIIYTBYPQUMFGAIYEMLFWBMJGEAGEPAYFIFM
TMHPNMLQEWGTGVMGQVTJNIRMWBVMPABQVOXLGZTJNGHDCTHLIVTPTWPRWJXAQVMYKVBL
IBACVPKSUBLRTCVRWZXDWMERCVDQCVWNCGEMCLPCUPTJNMQYOQGCUCVFUBKSEBNPGABL
UWFCFMMYKTTJVPHSIPTAQUIPGPXLUQOCUBNBAWYQRIVCEZTDVLXQKOGGUWNRUQWCVPXQ
EWICQNMFKAUMQSYMTANAJAMSFQXQTMYCTMGAGAAMWTWZGUTBGBHYPGHDVPXQGDXPCTMC
ZBLYXIBJCJECVGIGEIEMHEAGEPBQVPTRDGPGLSXP
```

Solution: In the first step, we determine the key length, use Friedman Test. The given message has 856 letters, by Equation 4-16 and Equation 4-17, we have

$$I = \frac{1}{n(n-1)} \sum_{i=0}^{25} n_i(n_i - 1) = \frac{1}{856 \times 855}(37 \times 36 + \cdots + 15 \times 14) = 0.04405 \tag{4-22}$$

$$k = \frac{0.0265 \times 856}{(0.065 - 0.04405) + 856 \times (0.04405 - 0.0385)} \approx 4.75 \tag{4-23}$$

We estimate the key length. Based on the result of Equation 4-23, the estimated key length is likely 4 or 5. (Note that this estimation does not always rely on simple rounding; either rounding up or down may be appropriate.) Next, we proceed to calculate the mutual index of coincidence M_g.

Assuming the key length is determined to be 4, the ciphertext is partitioned into four subciphertexts of approximately equal length. The first subciphertext consists of every fourth character, commencing from the first position of the ciphertext. The first subciphertext is

```
CTCGCDVTJUQPUKHNUNVFVUCVGXCPRKCTHTOCVPTHWQECAUCKVCNWJUUKCF
HTQEVQGQJGEQVQTGEEEPFVGPQWJVEAVGEPHKKCTGKJTUFYJEVRPTDVJHVC
CEQFFIEGQREVTQGEWGEFTNEGQNWPVGNCITWQKIVUTWWCCCCUNOUUEGUFKV
IQGUUAREVKUUVEQKQTJFTTGWGGPVGCZXCVEHEVDL
```

We then compute the frequency of each letter in this subciphertext. For example, in this case, the letter A appears 3 times, B appears 0 times, and so on. The length of this subciphertext is 214, hence

$$\mathbf{q} = (\frac{3}{214}, \frac{0}{214}, \frac{21}{214}, \ldots, \frac{1}{214}) \tag{4-24}$$

Next, we calculate the mutual index M_g by circularly shifting this empirical ciphertext frequency vector $\mathbf{q}$ by g positions and taking the dot product with the expected standard English frequency vector $\mathbf{p}$. This computation is repeated for $g = 0$ to 25, yielding 26 different M_g values, which listed follow.

$$g = 0,\ M_0 = 0.082 \times \frac{3}{214} + 0.015 \times \frac{0}{214} + \cdots + 0.001 \times \frac{1}{214} \approx 0.040 \tag{4-25}$$

$$g = 1,\ M_1 = 0.082 \times \frac{0}{214} + 0.015 \times \frac{21}{214} + \cdots + 0.001 \times \frac{3}{214} \approx 0.040 \tag{4-26}$$

$$\vdots$$

$$g = 25,\ M_{25} = 0.082 \times \frac{1}{214} + 0.015 \times \frac{3}{214} + \cdots + 0.001 \times \frac{1}{214} \approx 0.034 \tag{4-27}$$

M_g	0.040	0.040	0.062	0.040	0.036	0.030	0.040	0.032	0.036
	0.038	0.031	0.037	0.040	0.045	0.039	0.044	0.044	0.048
	0.037	0.034	0.032	0.035	0.034	0.033	0.041	0.034	

Among these, the value at $g = 2$ (i.e., $M_2 = \mathbf{0.062}$) is the closest to 0.065. This suggests with high confidence that the first key letter is likely **C**.

By applying the same method to the second, third, and fourth subciphertexts, we can determine the remaining letters of the key. The full recovered key is **CITY**. The corresponding plaintext is

Aircraft are generally built up from the basic components of wings, fuselages, tail units, and control surfaces. There are variations in particular aircraft: for example, a delta wing aircraft would not necessarily possess a horizontal tail, although this is present in a canard configuration, such as that of the Eurofighter. Each component has one or more specific functions and must be designed to ensure that it can carry out these functions safely. In this chapter, we describe the various loads to which aircraft components are subjected, their function and fabrication, and the design of connections. Spacecraft, apart from the Space Shuttle, which had a more or less conventional layout, consist generally of a long narrow tube containing the thrust structure, fuel tanks, and payload. We shall examine such structures in some detail, although a comprehensive study of spacecraft design is outside the scope of this book. For such studies reference should be made to any of the several texts available, typical of which is that by Wijker. [21] ■

4.4 AFFINE CIPHER

The affine cipher is a type of mono-alphabetic substitution cipher and represents a specific form of substitution encryption, it is essentially a mathematical generalization of the Caesar cipher while the Caesar cipher relies solely on modular addition, the affine cipher incorporates both modular multiplication and addition.

While it offers lower security than the Vigenère cipher and is particularly susceptible to frequency analysis making it relatively easy to break, it serves as an excellent introduction for beginners to understand the basic principles of cryptography. For this reason, it remains a popular teaching tool in the study of classical ciphers.

4.4.1 Encryption/Decryption

When encrypting with the affine cipher, several conditions must be satisfied

1) A key is given by a pair of integers (a, b);
2) Integer a relatively prime to 26 such that $\gcd(a, 26) = 1$, so must be one of the following numbers: $\{1, 3, 5, 7, 9, 11, 15, 17, 19, 21, 23, 25\}$.
3) Integer b exists $0 \leqslant b \leqslant 25$;

For each plaintext number m and ciphertext number c, the encryption function is given by

$$c \equiv E(m) \equiv am + b \pmod{26} \tag{4-28}$$

The decryption function given by

$$m \equiv D(c) \equiv a^{-1}(c - b) \pmod{26} \tag{4-29}$$

Example 4.4.1 Encrypt the word "**SWORD**" using the affine cipher mod 26 for $a = 9$ and $b = 15$.

Solution: Since a and b are integers, and they are coprime. We have

0	1	2	3	4	5	6	7	8	9	10	11	12	13	14	15	16	17	18	19	20	21	22	23	24	25
A	B	C	D	E	F	G	H	I	J	K	L	M	N	O	P	Q	R	S	T	U	V	W	X	Y	Z

Table 4-11: Affine Cipher Encryption

Plaintext	S	W	O	R	D
m	18	22	14	17	3
$c \equiv am + b \pmod{26}$	**21**	**5**	**11**	**12**	**16**
Ciphertext	**V**	**F**	**L**	**M**	**Q**

The ciphertext is "**VFLMQ**". ■

Example 4.4.2 Decrypt the word "**SYLNH**" using the affine cipher mod 26 for $a = 19$ and $b = 13$.

Solution: Since the encryption function is $c \equiv 19m + 13 \pmod{26}$. Try to solve the congruence, we are added 13 to both sides of the congruence to get $c + 13 \equiv 19m + 26 \equiv 19m \pmod{26}$. By modular inversion, we have $19^{-1} \equiv 11 \pmod{26}$, this is equivalent to

$$19^{-1}(c + 13) \equiv 19^{-1} \cdot 19m \pmod{26} \tag{4-30}$$

$$11(c + 13) \equiv m \pmod{26} \tag{4-31}$$

$$\Rightarrow m \equiv 11c + 13 \pmod{26} \tag{4-32}$$

Table 4-12: **Affine Cipher Decryption**

Ciphertext	S	Y	L	N	H
c	18	24	11	13	7
$m \equiv 11c + 13 \pmod{26}$	**3**	**17**	**4**	**0**	**12**
Plaintext	D	R	E	A	M

The plaintext is "**DREAM**". ■

Example 4.4.3 Implement a Python script to encrypt the plaintext "**I CAN PLAY**".

```
Plaintext = 'ICANPLAY'#Capital Letter
a = 7;b = 25

Ciphertext = ''
for i in Plaintext:
    x = ord(i) -65
    y = (a*x + b)%26
    Ciphertext += chr(y+ 65)
```

Output: **DNZMAYZL**

4.4.2 Cryptanalysis

The affine cipher offers a marginal improvement in security over the Caesar cipher. However, since only 12 values of a are coprime with 26, its total key space is limited.

For a general modulus r with the prime factorization $r = \prod_{i=1}^{n} p_i^{e_i}$, where p_i are distinct primes and e_i are positive integers, then the count of integers coprime to r is given by Euler's φ function

$$\varphi(r) = \prod_{i=1}^{n} \left(p_i^{e_i} - p_i^{e_i - 1}\right) \tag{4-33}$$

Consequently, the size of the key space is $r \cdot \phi(r) = 26 \times 12 = 312$ possible keys (or 311 if we exclude the trivial identity case where $a = 1$ and $b = 0$). This key space is significantly smaller than that of the Vigenère cipher, making the affine cipher vulnerable. With the help of modern computation, it's easy to break it via brute-force. Even worse, like other substitution ciphers, it is highly susceptible to frequency analysis when the ciphertext is sufficiently long.

Example 4.4.4 Decrypt the ciphertext "**EKTWQMRVRVWQMTF**" knowing that the plaintext starts with "**GO**" and it was encrypted with an affine cipher modulo 26.

Solution: We know

$$G(6) \to E(4)$$
$$O(14) \to K(10)$$

Then we find (a, b) that were used to encrypt this plaintext, use the encryption function, solve the system in mod 26

$$\begin{cases} 6a + b \equiv 4 \\ 14a + b \equiv 10 \end{cases} \pmod{26} \tag{4-34}$$

$$\begin{cases} 6a + b \equiv 4 \\ 14a + b \equiv 10 \end{cases} \pmod{26} \Rightarrow \begin{cases} a \equiv 4 \\ b \equiv 6 \end{cases} \pmod{26} \text{ or } \begin{cases} a \equiv 17 \\ b \equiv 6 \end{cases} \pmod{26}$$

We must verify the valid key condition $\gcd(a, 26) = 1$. If $a = 4$, the condition fails because $\gcd(4, 26) = 2 \neq 1$, making it an invalid multiplier. If $a = 17$, $\gcd(17, 26) = 1$, so $a = 17$, $b = 6$.

By decryption function, the plaintext is "**GONE WITH THE WIND**". ■

Example 4.4.5 Decrypt the given ciphertext and it was encrypted with an affine cipher.

```
QSFHZFAJRNANERDXDLAAFGOPLAOMDJXWMFSXDALODLFNDRYFJNZDFX
OXDALONDZYDOXOZOXLAJXWMFSXAXOOMFDNPFWENXAOFGOEFOOFSJNA
YFFAJSRWOFUOLNARLAFLQDFKFSNEUXQQFSFAOJXWMFSOFGOEFOOFSD
UFWFAUXABLAXODWLDXOXLAXAOMFPFDDNBF
```

Solution: If we attempt a brute-force attack, we may need to try up to 312 combinations in the worst case (but quickly with computer help).

Instead, let's try frequency analysis. The ciphertext is fairly long, containing 196 characters. Assuming it was derived from English plaintext, we can analyze it using known letter frequency statistics. With Python's `str.count()` method, we can tally letter frequencies in the ciphertext: "A" appears 20 times, "B" appears 2 times, "C" appears 0 times, "G" appears 17 times, and so on. As shown in Figure 4-3, letters "E" and "T" are the most common in typical English text. Comparing these patterns, we can reasonably hypothesize that ciphertext "F" represents plaintext "E", and ciphertext "O" represents plaintext "T".

A	B	C	D	E	F	G	H	I	J	K	L	M	N	O	P	Q	R	S	T	U	V	W	X	Y	Z
20	2	0	17	5	30	3	1	0	7	1	12	6	11	24	3	4	5	9	0	4	0	7	18	3	4

This leads us to the following system of congruences:

$$\begin{cases} 4a + b \equiv 5 \\ 19a + b \equiv 14 \end{cases} \pmod{26} \tag{4-35}$$

Solving the system, we have $a = 11, b = 13$. We must verify that the key is valid by checking $\gcd(11, 26) = 1$, which holds true. The plaintext is: *Frequency analysis on next month's cipher is not so easy because it is not a substitution cipher in it the same plain text letter can be encrypted to any one of several different cipher text letters depending on its position in the message.* ■

4.5 HILL CIPHER

The Hill cipher is a block cipher where pairs of plaintext letters are encrypted by matrix. *Lester S. Hill* invented it in his 1929 paper [22], thus becoming known as the Hill cipher.

4.5.1 Matrix Arithmetic

The Hill cipher is a polygraphic substitution cipher fundamentally based on linear algebra. Before describing the Hill cipher, let us first establish fundamental concepts of linear algebra.

Definition 4.5.1 Matrix Addition

Let $\mathbf{A} = (a_{ij})$ *and* $\mathbf{B} = (b_{ij})$ *be two* $r \times n$ *matrices. Then the matrix addition* $\mathbf{A} + \mathbf{B}$ *is the* $m \times n$ *matrix whose* (i, j) *entry is* $a_{ij} + b_{ij}$ *for each pair* (i, j).

Definition 4.5.2 Scalar Multiplication

Let $\mathbf{A} = (a_{ij})$ *be an* $r \times n$ *matrix and* α *be a scalar. Then the scalar multiplication* $\alpha\mathbf{A}$ *is the* $r \times n$ *matrix whose* (i, j) *entry is* αa_{ij}.

Definition 4.5.3 Matrix Multiplication

Let $\mathbf{A} = (a_{ij})$ *be an* $r \times s$ *matrix and* $\mathbf{B} = (b_{ij})$ *be an* $s \times n$ *matrix. Then the product* $\mathbf{AB} = \mathbf{C} = (c_{ij})$ *is the* $r \times n$ *matrix whose* (i, j) *entries are defined by*

$$c_{ij} = \sum_{k=1}^{s} a_{ik} b_{kj} \tag{4-36}$$

Example 4.5.1 Let $\mathbf{A} = \begin{bmatrix} 4 & 5 \\ 7 & -2 \end{bmatrix}$ and $\mathbf{B} = \begin{bmatrix} -1 & 3 \\ 5 & 6 \end{bmatrix}$. Given the scalar $\alpha = 2$, find $\mathbf{A} + \mathbf{B}$, $\alpha\mathbf{A}$ and $\mathbf{AB}$.
Solution:

$$\mathbf{A} + \mathbf{B} = \begin{bmatrix} 4 & 5 \\ 7 & -2 \end{bmatrix} + \begin{bmatrix} -1 & 3 \\ 5 & 6 \end{bmatrix} = \begin{bmatrix} 3 & 8 \\ 12 & 4 \end{bmatrix} \tag{4-37}$$

$$\alpha\mathbf{A} = 2\begin{bmatrix} 4 & 5 \\ 7 & -2 \end{bmatrix} = \begin{bmatrix} 8 & 10 \\ 14 & -4 \end{bmatrix} \tag{4-38}$$

$$\mathbf{AB} = \begin{bmatrix} 4 & 5 \\ 7 & -2 \end{bmatrix}\begin{bmatrix} -1 & 3 \\ 5 & 6 \end{bmatrix} = \begin{bmatrix} 21 & 42 \\ -17 & 9 \end{bmatrix} \tag{4-39}$$

■

If **A** and **B** are both $n \times n$ matrices, then **AB** and **BA** will also be $n \times n$ matrices. In general, matrix multiplication is not commutative.

Definition 4.5.4 Modulo Arithmetic on Matrices

Let $\mathbf{A} = (a_{ij})$ *and* $\mathbf{B} = (b_{ij})$ *be two* $r \times n$ *matrices, and all the entries of the matrices are integers. If*

$$a_{i,j} \equiv b_{i,j} \pmod{m} \tag{4-40}$$

for all entries $a_{i,j}$, $b_{i,j}$, *the matrices* $\mathbf{A}$ *and* $\mathbf{B}$ *are congruent modulo* m, *we denoted by* $\mathbf{A} \equiv \mathbf{B} \pmod{m}$.

If there exist two $n \times n$ *integer matrices* $\mathbf{A}$ *and* $\mathbf{B}$ *such that*

$$\mathbf{AB} \equiv \mathbf{I} \pmod{m} \text{ and } \mathbf{BA} \equiv \mathbf{I} \pmod{m} \tag{4-41}$$

where $\mathbf{I}$ *is the identity matrix. Then we say* $\mathbf{B}$ *is the inverse of* $\mathbf{A}$ *modulo* m, *denoted by* $\mathbf{A}^{-1} \equiv \mathbf{B} \pmod{m}$.

Example 4.5.2 Let $m = 5$, $\mathbf{A} = \begin{bmatrix} 2 & 3 \\ 2 & 1 \end{bmatrix}$ and $\mathbf{B} = \begin{bmatrix} 1 & 2 \\ 3 & 2 \end{bmatrix}$, find $\mathbf{A}+2\mathbf{B} \pmod{5}$ and $\mathbf{BA} \pmod{5}$.

Solution:

$$\mathbf{A} + 2\mathbf{B} \pmod{5} \equiv \begin{bmatrix} 2 & 3 \\ 2 & 1 \end{bmatrix} + \begin{bmatrix} 2 & 4 \\ 6 & 4 \end{bmatrix} \pmod{5} \tag{4-42}$$

$$\equiv \begin{bmatrix} 4 & 2 \\ 3 & 0 \end{bmatrix} \pmod{5} \tag{4-43}$$

$$\mathbf{BA} \pmod{5} \equiv \begin{bmatrix} 1 & 2 \\ 3 & 2 \end{bmatrix}\begin{bmatrix} 2 & 3 \\ 2 & 1 \end{bmatrix} \pmod{5} \tag{4-44}$$

$$\equiv \begin{bmatrix} 1 & 0 \\ 0 & 1 \end{bmatrix} \pmod{5} \tag{4-45}$$

■

Definition 4.5.5 Determinant

The determinant of an $n \times n$ *matrix* $\mathbf{A}$ *computed modulo* m *is denoted by*

$$\det(\mathbf{A}) \pmod{m} \tag{4-46}$$

If $\mathbf{A} = \begin{bmatrix} a & b \\ c & d \end{bmatrix}$ is an integer entries then the determinant of $\mathbf{A}$ under modulo m is given by

$$\det(\mathbf{A}) \equiv ad - bc \pmod{m} \tag{4-47}$$

Example 4.5.3 Evaluate the following determinants:

$$\mathbf{A} \equiv \begin{bmatrix} 3 & 4 \\ -9 & 8 \end{bmatrix} \pmod{10} \tag{4-48}$$

Solution: $\det(\mathbf{A}) \equiv ad - bc \equiv (3)(8) - (-9)(4) \equiv 60 \equiv 0 \pmod{10}$. ■

Definition 4.5.6 Multiplicative Inverse

Let $\mathbf{A}$ *be an* $n \times n$ *matrix, if* $\mathbf{A}$ *is said to be nonsingular, then there exists a matrix* $\mathbf{B}$ *such that* $\mathbf{AB} = \mathbf{BA} = \mathbf{I}$*. The matrix* $\mathbf{B}$ *is said to be a multiplicative inverse of* $\mathbf{A}$*, where* $\mathbf{I}$ *is an* $n \times n$ *identity matrix.*

If $\mathbf{A} = \begin{bmatrix} a & b \\ c & d \end{bmatrix}$ is a 2×2 matrix with integer entries, then $\mathbf{A}$ is invertible modulo m if and only if $\det(\mathbf{A})$ is relatively prime to m. The inverse is given by

$$\mathbf{A}^{-1} \equiv \frac{1}{ad - bc} \begin{bmatrix} d & -b \\ -c & a \end{bmatrix} \pmod{m} \tag{4-49}$$

For an $n \times n$ matrix with $n > 2$ is to use elementary row operations(Gauss-Jordan elimination). One constructs an augmented matrix $[\mathbf{A} \quad \mathbf{I}_n]$ by placing the identity matrix $\mathbf{I}_n$ alongside $\mathbf{A}$, and then performs row operations to transform it into the form $[\mathbf{I}_n \quad \mathbf{B}]$, where $\mathbf{B}$ is the inverse of $\mathbf{A}$. However, this method has a time complexity of $\mathcal{O}(n^3)$.

Example 4.5.4 Let $\mathbf{A}_1 = \begin{bmatrix} 5 & 6 \\ 7 & 8 \end{bmatrix}$, $\mathbf{A}_2 = \begin{bmatrix} 1 & 0 & -2 \\ -3 & 1 & 4 \\ 2 & -3 & 4 \end{bmatrix}$, find the inverse of each of the above matrices over the real numbers.
Solution:

$$\mathbf{A}_1^{-1} = \frac{1}{5 \cdot 8 - 6 \cdot 7} \begin{bmatrix} 8 & -6 \\ -7 & 5 \end{bmatrix} = \begin{bmatrix} -4 & 3 \\ 7/2 & -5/2 \end{bmatrix} \tag{4-50}$$

$$\mathbf{A}_2^{-1} = \begin{bmatrix} \mathbf{A} & \mathbf{I}_3 \end{bmatrix} \tag{4-51}$$

$$= \left[\begin{array}{ccc|ccc} 1 & 0 & -2 & 1 & 0 & 0 \\ -3 & 1 & 4 & 0 & 1 & 0 \\ 2 & -3 & 4 & 0 & 0 & 1 \end{array}\right] \sim \left[\begin{array}{ccc|ccc} 1 & 0 & -2 & 1 & 0 & 0 \\ 0 & 1 & -2 & 3 & 1 & 0 \\ 0 & -3 & 8 & -2 & 0 & 1 \end{array}\right] \tag{4-52}$$

$$\sim \left[\begin{array}{ccc|ccc} 1 & 0 & -2 & 1 & 0 & 0 \\ 0 & 1 & -2 & 3 & 1 & 0 \\ 0 & 0 & 2 & 7 & 3 & 1 \end{array}\right] \sim \left[\begin{array}{ccc|ccc} 1 & 0 & 0 & 8 & 3 & 1 \\ 0 & 1 & 0 & 10 & 4 & 1 \\ 0 & 0 & 2 & 7 & 3 & 1 \end{array}\right] \tag{4-53}$$

$$\sim \left[\begin{array}{ccc|ccc} 1 & 0 & 0 & 8 & 3 & 1 \\ 0 & 1 & 0 & 10 & 4 & 1 \\ 0 & 0 & 1 & 7/2 & 3/2 & 1/2 \end{array}\right] = \begin{bmatrix} \mathbf{I}_3 & \mathbf{B} \end{bmatrix} \tag{4-54}$$

■

4.5.2 Encryption/Decryption

The Hill cipher takes a message then converts it to numbers assigned to each letter in that message. This message is then transformed into a matrix, which is then multiplied by a key matrix that is invertible. Then, the matrix does modulo operation of the size of alphabet

$$\mathbf{C} \equiv \mathbf{KM} \pmod{26} \tag{4-55}$$

where $\mathbf{K}$ is an 2×2 invertible key matrix modulo 26. Then we need to obtain 2 messages with 2 entries each and their corresponding encryptions, the plaintext denoted by $\mathbf{M} = [m_1\ m_2]^T$, and the ciphertext denoted by $\mathbf{C} = [c_1\ c_2]^T$.

The key matrix of Hill cipher is not always 2×2 matrix, it can be $n \times n$ matrix. The block length is n. Furthermore, the modulus in the Hill cipher is not necessarily 26, 26 is the default for English, if we use other languages, the modulus can be different. For example, 27 is the default for Spanish and 33 is the default for Russian. Thus, the modulus is the size of the character set used for the plaintext message.

The Hill cipher operates on blocks of a fixed dimension n. Consequently, if the total length of the plaintext is not a multiple of n, **padding** is required to complete the final block, it is customary to replace it with the integer representing a plaintext letter. While the specific padding scheme is subject to agreement between the communicating parties. In this section, the letter "**K**" is chosen to fill remaining positions.

Example 4.5.5 Let the key matrix $\mathbf{K} = \begin{bmatrix} 22 & 13 \\ 11 & 5 \end{bmatrix}$, encrypt the message **MISSING** using a Hill cipher with this key.

Solution: Using the conversion table

0	1	2	3	4	5	6	7	8	9	10	11	12	13	14	15	16	17	18	19	20	21	22	23	24	25
A	B	C	D	E	F	G	H	I	J	K	L	M	N	O	P	Q	R	S	T	U	V	W	X	Y	Z

The plaintext is divided into 2×1 column vectors. Consider the pair "**MI**", we have

$$\mathbf{C}_1 \equiv \mathbf{KM} \pmod{26} \tag{4-56}$$

$$\equiv \begin{bmatrix} 22 & 13 \\ 11 & 5 \end{bmatrix} \begin{bmatrix} 12 \\ 8 \end{bmatrix} \equiv \begin{bmatrix} 368 \\ 172 \end{bmatrix} \equiv \begin{bmatrix} 4 \\ 16 \end{bmatrix} \pmod{26} \implies \text{"EQ"} \tag{4-57}$$

Similarly, encrypt the remaining column vectors

$$\text{"}\mathbf{SS}\text{"}: \quad \mathbf{C}_2 \equiv \begin{bmatrix} 22 & 13 \\ 11 & 5 \end{bmatrix} \begin{bmatrix} 18 \\ 18 \end{bmatrix} \equiv \begin{bmatrix} 630 \\ 288 \end{bmatrix} \equiv \begin{bmatrix} 6 \\ 2 \end{bmatrix} \pmod{26} \implies \text{"GC"} \tag{4-58}$$

$$\text{"}\mathbf{IN}\text{"}: \quad \mathbf{C}_3 \equiv \begin{bmatrix} 22 & 13 \\ 11 & 5 \end{bmatrix} \begin{bmatrix} 8 \\ 13 \end{bmatrix} \equiv \begin{bmatrix} 345 \\ 153 \end{bmatrix} \equiv \begin{bmatrix} 7 \\ 23 \end{bmatrix} \pmod{26} \implies \text{"HX"} \tag{4-59}$$

$$\text{"}\mathbf{GK}\text{"}: \quad \mathbf{C}_4 \equiv \begin{bmatrix} 22 & 13 \\ 11 & 5 \end{bmatrix} \begin{bmatrix} 6 \\ 10 \end{bmatrix} \equiv \begin{bmatrix} 262 \\ 116 \end{bmatrix} \equiv \begin{bmatrix} 2 \\ 12 \end{bmatrix} \pmod{26} \implies \text{"CM"} \tag{4-60}$$

The ciphertext is "**EQGCHXCM**". ■

The decryption function of the Hill cipher given by

$$\mathbf{M} \equiv \mathbf{K}^{-1}\mathbf{C} \pmod{26} \tag{4-61}$$

Example 4.5.6 Decrypt the message "**ZGWQ**", knowing it was encrypted using Hill cipher modulo 26 with the key matrix $\mathbf{K} = \begin{bmatrix} 3 & 7 \\ 9 & 10 \end{bmatrix}$.

Solution:

$$\mathbf{K}^{-1} \equiv \det(\mathbf{K})^{-1} \begin{bmatrix} d & -b \\ -c & a \end{bmatrix} \pmod{26} \tag{4-62}$$

$$\equiv (3 \cdot 10 - 7 \cdot 9)^{-1} \begin{bmatrix} 10 & -7 \\ -9 & 3 \end{bmatrix} \pmod{26} \tag{4-63}$$

$$\equiv (-33)^{-1} \begin{bmatrix} 10 & 19 \\ 17 & 3 \end{bmatrix} \equiv 19^{-1} \begin{bmatrix} 10 & 19 \\ 17 & 3 \end{bmatrix} \pmod{26} \tag{4-64}$$

$$\equiv 11 \begin{bmatrix} 10 & 19 \\ 17 & 3 \end{bmatrix} \equiv \begin{bmatrix} 110 & 209 \\ 187 & 33 \end{bmatrix} \pmod{26} \tag{4-65}$$

$$\equiv \begin{bmatrix} 6 & 1 \\ 5 & 7 \end{bmatrix} \pmod{26} \tag{4-66}$$

$$\begin{aligned} \text{“ZG”:} \quad & \begin{bmatrix} 25 \\ 6 \end{bmatrix} \equiv \begin{bmatrix} 6 & 1 \\ 5 & 7 \end{bmatrix} \begin{bmatrix} 25 \\ 6 \end{bmatrix} \pmod{26} \equiv \begin{bmatrix} 0 \\ 11 \end{bmatrix} \implies \text{“AL”} \\ \text{“WQ”:} \quad & \begin{bmatrix} 22 \\ 16 \end{bmatrix} \equiv \begin{bmatrix} 6 & 1 \\ 5 & 7 \end{bmatrix} \begin{bmatrix} 22 \\ 16 \end{bmatrix} \pmod{26} \equiv \begin{bmatrix} 18 \\ 14 \end{bmatrix} \implies \text{“SO”} \end{aligned} \tag{4-67}$$

The plaintext is "**ALSO**". ■

Example 4.5.7 Decrypt the message "**COKE**", knowing it was encrypted using Hill cipher modulo 26 with the key matrix $\mathbf{K} = \begin{bmatrix} 22 & 13 \\ 11 & 5 \end{bmatrix}$.

```
import numpy as np
ciphertext = ''COKE''
K_inv = np.array([[22, 13], [11,  5]])

plaintext = ''''

for i in range(0, len(ciphertext), 2):
    C = np.array([
        ord(ciphertext[i]) - ord('A'),
        ord(ciphertext[i + 1]) - ord('A')])

    M = K_inv @ C % 26
    plaintext += ''.join(chr(x + ord('A')) for x in M)

print(''Plaintext:'', plaintext)
```

The ciphertext is **SOMA**.

4.5.3 Cryptanalysis

To analyze the Hill cipher, it is essential to understand the size of its key space. For a key matrix **K** of size $n \times n$, there are 26^{n^2} possible combinations. This yields a theoretical key length of approximately $\log_2(26^{n^2})$ bits. However, not every matrix is invertible, so this number overestimates the actual number of usable keys. Even with this reduction, the key space remains sufficiently large to render standard brute-force attacks computationally expensive for large n. Furthermore, its polygraphic nature masks single-letter distributions, making standard frequency analysis ineffective compared to mono-alphabetic ciphers.

However, the Hill cipher's reliance on linear algebra introduces a critical vulnerability. It is highly susceptible to a known-plaintext attack. If an attacker possesses a segment of plaintext and its corresponding ciphertext, the system can be broken algebraically. First, since the dimension n is unknown, the attacker may iterate through all possible values. Assume a block size of n. The attacker identifies n linearly independent plaintext block vectors to form an $n \times n$ plaintext matrix **M**, and the corresponding ciphertext matrix **C**. Provided that the plaintext matrix **M** is invertible, the key matrix **K** can be recovered by multiplying the ciphertext matrix by the inverse of **M**.

Example 4.5.8 Eve has intercepted the ciphertext "**DLHIVDLZHIPNEU**", which she knows to be produced by a Hill cipher modulo 26 using a 2×2 matrix. Moreover, she strongly suspects that the first four letters of the message are the word "**DEAR**". Decrypt the message.

Solution: First, arrange the ciphertext according to the table below, and then align it with "**DEAR**", as shown in Table 4-13.

Table 4-13: Hill Cipher Analysis

D	L	H	I	V	D	L	Z	H	I	P	N	E	U
3	11	7	8	21	3	11	25	7	8	15	13	4	20
D	E	A	R										
3	4	0	17										

The plaintext DEAR is divided into two 2×1 column vectors: $\mathbf{P}_1 = \begin{bmatrix} 3 \\ 4 \end{bmatrix}$ (representing "DE") and $\mathbf{P}_2 = \begin{bmatrix} 0 \\ 17 \end{bmatrix}$ (representing "AR"). These encrypt to the corresponding ciphertext vectors $\mathbf{C}_1 = \begin{bmatrix} 3 \\ 11 \end{bmatrix}$ ("DL") and $\mathbf{C}_2 = \begin{bmatrix} 7 \\ 8 \end{bmatrix}$ ("HI"), respectively.

Next, find the key matrix **K**

$$\begin{aligned} \mathbf{K}^{-1} \begin{bmatrix} D \\ L \end{bmatrix} &\equiv \mathbf{K}^{-1} \begin{bmatrix} 3 \\ 11 \end{bmatrix} \equiv \begin{bmatrix} 3 \\ 4 \end{bmatrix} \pmod{26} \\ \mathbf{K}^{-1} \begin{bmatrix} H \\ I \end{bmatrix} &\equiv \mathbf{K}^{-1} \begin{bmatrix} 7 \\ 8 \end{bmatrix} \equiv \begin{bmatrix} 0 \\ 17 \end{bmatrix} \pmod{26} \end{aligned} \tag{4-68}$$

Since

$$\mathbf{K}^{-1}\begin{bmatrix} 3 & 7 \\ 11 & 8 \end{bmatrix} = \begin{bmatrix} 3 & 0 \\ 4 & 17 \end{bmatrix} \tag{4-69}$$

Then the inverse matrix $\mathbf{K}^{-1}$ is

$$\mathbf{K}^{-1} \equiv \begin{bmatrix} 3 & 0 \\ 4 & 17 \end{bmatrix} \cdot \begin{bmatrix} 3 & 7 \\ 11 & 8 \end{bmatrix}^{-1} \tag{4-70}$$

$$\equiv \begin{bmatrix} 3 & 0 \\ 4 & 17 \end{bmatrix} \cdot \begin{bmatrix} 18 & 7 \\ 11 & 23 \end{bmatrix} \equiv \begin{bmatrix} 2 & 21 \\ 25 & 3 \end{bmatrix} \pmod{26} \tag{4-71}$$

The plaintext is "**Dear Bob Marry Me**". ■

4.6 MERKLE-HELLMAN KNAPSACK CRYPTOSYSTEM

Unlike the previous encryption schemes, which rely on keeping the encryption key secret to prevent unauthorized access, the Merkle–Hellman Knapsack Cryptosystem[2] adopts a different approach by making the key public while still ensuring the confidentiality of the transmitted data.

Proposed by *Ralph C. Merkle* and *Martin Edward Hellman* in their 1978 IEEE paper [23], the Merkle–Hellman knapsack cryptosystem was one of the earliest public-key cryptosystems.

However, in 1982, *Adi Shamir* published a breakthrough paper [24], *Shamir* successfully breaking the system.

4.6.1 Encryption/Decryption

The Knapsack Problem is a classic combinatorial optimization problem. It can be illustrated with a simple analogy: imagine a thief who breaks into a diamond store which is showcasing various diamonds. Each diamond has a weight and a different value. If the thief wants to fill his knapsack, which diamonds should he steal in order to maximize the cumulative value?

When the value of each diamond is equal to its size and then finding a subset of the diamonds that sum to a given capacity. This is commonly known as the **Subset Sum Problem** in cryptography. While the problem statement is simple, the general subset sum problem is computationally hard because it is NP-complete. This implies that for a large number of items, determining whether a solution exists or finding one that is computationally infeasible in the worst case, as the time required grows exponentially.

The Merkle–Hellman knapsack cryptosystem is founded on this mathematical difficulty. It utilizes the Subset Sum Problem as a trapdoor function, relying on the disparity between the difficulty of the general problem and a specific, easily solvable instance.

[2]Unlike the other classical ciphers discussed in this chapter, this cryptosystem is not a symmetric cipher. This section is provided as optional reading and may be skipped.

Definition 4.6.1 Subset-Sum Problem (SSP)

Given an increasing sequence $a_1 < a_2 < \cdots < a_n$ and a "target" number M. Determine if there is a subsequence of the $a_i's$ whose sum is M.

Formally, we want to find the values $x_1, x_2, \ldots, x_n$, where each $x_i \in \{0,1\}$ such that

$$x_1a_1 + x_2a_2 + \cdots + x_na_n = M \tag{4-72}$$

A ***super-increasing sequence*** *is a sequence where each number in the sequence is greater than the sum of all preceding terms.*

Formally, $a_1, a_2, \ldots, a_n$ is a super-increasing sequence if for all $1 \leqslant k \leqslant n$, such that

$$a_k > \sum_{i=1}^{k-1} a_i \tag{4-73}$$

Note that sometimes there can be multiple sets of solutions or no solution.

Example 4.6.1 Solve the SSP for $[3, 5, 11, 23, 51]$ and $M = 67$.
Solution: Since $67 = 51 + 11 + 5 = a_2 + a_3 + a_5$, then $\mathbf{x} = [0, 1, 1, 0, 1]$, which means that 51,11 and 5 are in the knapsack. ■

Example 4.6.2 Solve the SSP for $[13, 18, 35, 72, 155, 301, 595]$ and $M = 1003$.
Solution: Since $1003 = 595 + 301 + 72 + 35 = a_3 + a_4 + a_6 + a_7$, then $\mathbf{x} = [0, 0, 1, 1, 0, 1, 1]$, which means that 595, 301, 72 and 35 are in the knapsack. ■

Encryption with the Merkle-Hellman knapsack cryptosystem given by

1) **(KeyGen)**: Bob chooses
   - A super-increasing sequence $\mathbf{a} = (a_1, a_2, ..., a_n)$;
   - A prime modulus $p > \sum_{i=1}^{n} a_i$;
   - An encrypting factor A with $2 \leqslant A \leqslant p - 1$;
   - For each $1 \leqslant i \leqslant n$, Bob then computes the vector $\mathbf{b}$ by $b_i \equiv A \cdot a_i \pmod{p}$.

   The public key is the vector $\mathbf{b}$; The private key is $\mathbf{a}$, p and A.
2) **(Encrypt)**: Now suppose Alice wants to send a binary message $m_1m_2 \cdots m_n$ of n-bits. She then uses Bob published vector $\mathbf{b}$ and compute

   $$C = m_1b_1 + m_2b_2 + \cdots + m_nb_n \tag{4-74}$$

   then she transmits the ciphertext C to Bob.
3) **(Decrypt)**: To decrypt Alice's message, Bob computes

   $$M \equiv A^{-1}C \pmod{p} \tag{4-75}$$

   then solves the subset-sum problem

   $$m_1a_1 + m_2a_2 + \cdots + m_na_n = M \tag{4-76}$$

   to recover the binary string $m_1m_2 \cdots m_n$.

Example 4.6.3 Bob picks the super-increasing sequence

$$(a_1, a_2, \ldots, a_8) = (2, 5, 9, 22, 47, 99, 203, 409) \tag{4-77}$$

and chooses the prime $p = 997$ and the encryption factor $A = 60$.

1) The public key is $\mathbf{b}$

$$\mathbf{b} \equiv 60 \times (2, 5, 9, 22, 47, 99, 203, 409) \tag{4-78}$$

$$\equiv (120, 300, 540, 323, 826, 955, 216, 612) \pmod{997} \tag{4-79}$$

2) Alice wants to send the lower letter "**d**", the ASCII code of the letter "d" is 01100100 that is the plaintext. The ciphertext C is

$$C = 0 \cdot b_1 + 1 \cdot b_2 + \ldots + 0 \cdot b_8 = 1795 \tag{4-80}$$

3) Bob receives C from Alice, try to decrypt using Python function pow$(A, -1, p)$

$$A^{-1} \equiv 781 \pmod{p} \tag{4-81}$$

4) Compute $M \equiv A^{-1} \cdot C \pmod{p}$

$$M \equiv 781 \cdot 1795 \equiv 113 \pmod{997}$$

5) Solve the subset-sum problem

$$113 = 5 + 9 + 99 = a_2 + a_3 + a_6 \tag{4-82}$$

$$X = (0, 1, 1, 0, 0, 1, 0, 0) \tag{4-83}$$

6) Recover the binary string as "**d**".

■

Encrypt the given plaintext using a Python program: **AGREE**

```
plaintext = ''AGREE''
private_key = [2, 5, 9, 22, 47, 99, 203, 409]
p, A = 997, 60

public_key = [(A * x) % p for x in private_key]

# Encryption
ciphertext = [
    sum(int(bit) * b for bit, b in zip(format(ord(ch), ''08b''),
   public_key))
    for ch in plaintext
]

# Decryption
A_inv = pow(A, -1, p)
decrypted = ''''

for c in ciphertext:
    s = (c * A_inv) % p
    bits = [0] * 8
```

```

    for i in range(7, -1, -1):
        if private_key[i] <= s:
            bits[i] = 1
            s -= private_key[i]

    decrypted += chr(int("".join(map(str, bits)), 2))

print(‘‘Ciphertext:’’, ciphertext)
print(‘‘Decrypted plaintext:’’, decrypted)
```

4.6.2 Cryptanalysis

After publishing the cipher, *Merkle* remained confident in its security. He publicly offered a \$100 reward to anyone who could successfully break the first-generation knapsack cryptosystem. In 1982, *Adi Shamir* developed a polynomial-time algorithm capable of breaking this system. *Merkle* subsequently honored his promise and awarded *Shamir* the prize. However, *Shamir*'s method was limited in scope; it was ineffective against keys generated through multiple iterations. In response, *Merkle* introduced a modified version, known as the iterated knapsack cryptosystem, to counter such attacks. Confident in the strength of this hardened variant, *Merkle* increased the challenge reward to \$1,000. Despite these improvements, the system was broken in 1985 by *Ernest F. Brickell.* His method successfully broke a 40-iteration version of the cryptosystem in approximately one hour [25]. Following this breakthrough, other cryptanalysts proposed various approaches that further demonstrated the insecurity of the system.

The LLL algorithm was first introduced in 1982 by Lenstra, Lenstra, and Lovász [26]. Its original intent was not to break cryptosystems, but to factor polynomials with rational coefficients. Additionally, it improved upon existing lattice reduction algorithms to solve integer linear programming problems, this topic we will examine in detail in the following chapters. However, due to its polynomial-time complexity, the algorithm found immediate application in the field of cryptanalysis. By 1984, cryptanalysts had successfully employed it to break the iterated version of the Merkle–Hellman knapsack cryptosystem.

For the moment, we will defer the technical intricacies of the LLL algorithm, as they require a foundational understanding of lattice-based cryptography, which will be introduced in Chapter 10.

To illustrate the attack, let n denote the key length. Let $\mathbf{b}$ be an $1 \times n$ column vector representing the public key, and let $\mathbf{C}$ be the ciphertext block. The encryption relationship is defined by $\mathbf{bX} = \mathbf{C}$, where $\mathbf{X}$ is an $n \times 1$ binary vector consisting of elements 0 and 1. If such a vector $\mathbf{X}$ exists, we can construct a larger block matrix such that

$$\mathbf{MV} = \begin{bmatrix} \mathbf{I}_{n\times n} & \mathbf{0}_{n\times 1} \\ \mathbf{b}_{1\times n} & -\mathbf{C}_{1\times 1} \end{bmatrix} \begin{bmatrix} \mathbf{X}_{n\times 1} \\ \mathbf{I}_{1\times 1} \end{bmatrix} = \begin{bmatrix} \mathbf{X}_{n\times 1} \\ \mathbf{0}_{1\times 1} \end{bmatrix} = \mathbf{W} \tag{4-84}$$

where $\mathbf{I}_{n\times n}$ is an $n \times n$ identity matrix. We want to determine $\mathbf{X}_{n\times 1}$. Apply the LLL Algorithm to the matrix $\mathbf{M}$ and get the new matrix $\mathbf{M}'$. Check the vector of the matrix $\mathbf{M}'$, if it has the special form required, which is a column vector where the first n elements are all 0 or 1 and last element is 0. The LLL algorithm does not always produce the target vector, so the attack is not always successful. Nevertheless, the LLL algorithm has proven highly effective in practice for breaking the Merkle–Hellman knapsack cryptosystem.

Example 4.6.4 Assume Bob picks the super-increasing sequence

$$a_i = (1, 7, 14, 30, 57, 120, 251, 509), \text{ where } 1 \leqslant i \leqslant 8 \tag{4-85}$$

with $p = 1009$ and the encrypting factor $A = 310$.

He computes the public key $\mathbf{b}$

$$\mathbf{b} \equiv A \times a_i \equiv (310, 152, 304, 219, 517, 876, 117, 386) \pmod{p} \tag{4-86}$$

Suppose Alice wants to encrypt the letter "**L**", the ASCII code of "**L**" is **01001100**. Therefore, the ciphertext is $\mathbf{C} = 1545$ and sends to Bob. However, Eve intercepts this ciphertext and she wants to recover the plaintext.

Solution: Since she knows the public key $\mathbf{b}$, she constructs the matrix such that

$$\mathbf{M} = \begin{bmatrix} \mathbf{I}_{n\times n} & \mathbf{0}_{n\times 1} \\ \mathbf{b}_{1\times n} & -\mathbf{C}_{1\times 1} \end{bmatrix} = \left[\begin{array}{cccccccc|c} 1 & 0 & 0 & 0 & 0 & 0 & 0 & 0 & 0 \\ 0 & 1 & 0 & 0 & 0 & 0 & 0 & 0 & 0 \\ 0 & 0 & 1 & 0 & 0 & 0 & 0 & 0 & 0 \\ 0 & 0 & 0 & 1 & 0 & 0 & 0 & 0 & 0 \\ 0 & 0 & 0 & 0 & 1 & 0 & 0 & 0 & 0 \\ 0 & 0 & 0 & 0 & 0 & 1 & 0 & 0 & 0 \\ 0 & 0 & 0 & 0 & 0 & 0 & 1 & 0 & 0 \\ 0 & 0 & 0 & 0 & 0 & 0 & 0 & 1 & 0 \\ \hline 310 & 152 & 304 & 219 & 517 & 876 & 117 & 386 & -1545 \end{array}\right] \tag{4-87}$$

Using the LLL Algorithm(Sage Command: `Mt.LLL()` where `Mt` is the transpose of $\mathbf{M}$, Eve obtains the reduced basis matrix $\mathbf{M}'$

$$\mathbf{M}' = \begin{bmatrix} 0 & 1 & 0 & 0 & 1 & 1 & 0 & 0 & 0 \\ 0 & -1 & 1 & 0 & 1 & 1 & 0 & 0 & 0 \\ 0 & -1 & 0 & 0 & 0 & 0 & -2 & 1 & 0 \\ 1 & 1 & 0 & -1 & 1 & -1 & 1 & 0 & 1 \\ 1 & 0 & 0 & 0 & -1 & 2 & 0 & 0 & 0 \\ 1 & 0 & -2 & -1 & 1 & 0 & 0 & 0 & 0 \\ 0 & 0 & 0 & 1 & 0 & -1 & -1 & -2 & -1 \\ 0 & 0 & -1 & -1 & -1 & 0 & -1 & -1 & 2 \\ -2 & -1 & 0 & -3 & 0 & 0 & -1 & 0 & -1 \end{bmatrix}$$

The entries in the first row of $\mathbf{M}'$ only 0 or 1 that is correct form to be a solution. The code is 01001100 the same as the ASCII code of the letter "**L**", Eve successfully intercepted the plaintext. ■

As previously discussed, the Merkle–Hellman cryptosystem, along with most knapsack-based variants has been successfully broken. Nevertheless, unlike integer factorization and the discrete logarithm problem, the general knapsack problem is mathematically proven to be NP-complete. While it is conceivable that future breakthroughs might yield polynomial-time algorithms for factorization or discrete logarithms, the knapsack problem is expected to remain NP-complete.

However, it is important to note that NP-completeness applies only to the worst-case scenario. From the perspective of average-case complexity, or for specific instances constructed with trapdoors, the knapsack problem may be significantly easier to solve. Consequently, current knapsack-based cryptosystems have failed to reach their full security potential because the trapdoor structures often leak information.

If a new system could effectively leverage the inherent hardness of the knapsack problem through robust algorithms and undetectable trapdoors, it could theoretically surpass existing systems based on factorization or discrete logarithms. Neither of the latter is currently known to be NP-complete. Over the years, numerous improvements have been proposed to achieve this goal, including the Morii–Kasahara multiplicative knapsack [27], schemes based on Diophantine equations [28], and multi-iteration dense knapsack systems.

Moreover, the Merkle–Hellman scheme offered remarkable computational efficiency. For key lengths where $n \gg 100$, it can outperform legacy RSA implementations (such as those with a 500-bit modulus) by a factor of over 100. This efficiency stems from the fact that encryption requires only simple addition rather than modular exponentiation, making it comparable in speed to symmetric cryptosystems in both hardware and software [29].

Despite these advantages, the IEEE reviewed three mainstream cryptographic foundations in 2000: discrete logarithms modulo primes, elliptic curve discrete logarithms, and integer factorization. The consensus was clear. Due to their susceptibility to lattice reduction attacks, knapsack-based cryptosystems were deemed largely obsolete. Barring significant mathematical advances, the cryptographic community has shown little interest in further pursuing them, and the future of classical knapsack cryptosystems currently appears limited.

4.7 OTHER CLASSICAL CIPHERS

4.7.1 Playfair Cipher

The Playfair cipher, a foundational symmetric encryption scheme, was invented in 1854 by the British physicist *Charles Wheatstone*, who is also renowned for the Wheatstone bridge. However, the cipher takes its name from his friend *Lyon Playfair*, who was instrumental in its popularization [30]. *Playfair* demonstrated the cipher at a formal dinner attended by prominent figures, including *Prince Albert*, the husband of Queen Victoria, and *Lord Palmerston*, the Home Secretary. Their enthusiastic endorsement helped bring the system to public attention. Subsequently, the cipher saw widespread operational use by British forces during the Second Boer War

(1899–1902) and World War I (1914–1918). It was also later adopted by Australian forces for field operations against Japan during World War II (1939–1945).

In 1917, Britain's newspaper *The Times* published a public challenge to crack Playfair. Cryptographer *William Friedman* succeeded without the key. Today, Playfair remains a staple in cryptography education and historical puzzle games.

As the first practical cipher to encrypt pairs of letters, known as digraphs, the Playfair cipher represents a significant advancement over simple mono-alphabetic substitution ciphers.

To begin encryption, a secret key must first be defined. In general, a key or preset string of letters, which must remain confidential. The following example illustrates how to construct the 5 × 5 Playfair key grid.

Example 4.7.1 Construct the Playfair key square using the keyword **DIVERGENT**. The letters are placed into a 5 × 5 grid, omitting duplicates. For this keyword, skip the 7-th letter **E**. The letters **I** and **J** combined in the same cell of the square. Beginning with the first row, enter the keyword from left to right skipping letters previously used and continuing on to the second row, and so on. As shown in Table 4-14.

Table 4-14: Playfair Key

D	I / J	V	E	R
G	N	T	A	B
C	F	H	K	L
M	O	P	Q	S
U	W	X	Y	Z

The key space is 25!.

Then, break the plaintext into 2-grams

- Use a letter "**X**" to break up repeated letters;
- Put a letter "**Q**" at the end if there is an odd number of letter (some references put "**X**" or "**Z**" at the end);

Example 4.7.2 Applying the formatting rules described above, we obtain the following digraph sequences:

- For the input **PLAN**, break into **PL** || **AN**
- For the input **CHEEG**, break into **CH** || **EX** || **EG**
- For the input **ACT**, break into **AC** || **TQ**

Encrypt the plaintext using the Playfair key square

1) If two letters of the 2-gram are in the same row, shift right(letter is the rightmost cycling back to the first letter in same row).
2) If two letters of the 2-gram are in the same column, shift down(letter is the downmost cycling back to the first letter in same row).

3) If two letters of the 2-gram are in the opposite corner of a rectangle, each letter is replaced by the letter at the intersection of its row and the other letter's column.

The decryption process reverses the process of encryption. However, the decoder needs to determine the plaintext letter is "**I**" or "**J**".

Example 4.7.3 According to the Table 4-14 in Example 4.7.1.

- By rule 1, the letters are in the same row, **GT** is encrypted as **NA**; **TG** is encrypted as **AN**; **NB** is encrypted as **TG**;
- By rule 2, the letters are in the same column, **MG** is encrypted as **UC**; **DC** is encrypted as **GM**; **GU** is encrypted as **CD**;
- By rule 3, the letters are in a diagonal, **AO** is encrypted as **NQ**; **OA** is encrypted as **QN**; **NZ** is encrypted as **BW**;

D	I/J	V	E	R
G	**N**	**T**	**A**	B
C	F	H	K	L
M	O	P	Q	S
U	W	X	Y	Z

D	I/J	V	E	R
G	N	T	A	B
C	F	H	K	L
M	O	P	Q	S
U	W	X	Y	Z

D	I/J	V	E	R
G	**N**	T	**A**	B
C	F	H	K	L
M	**O**	P	**Q**	S
U	W	X	Y	Z

Example 4.7.4 Encrypt the following message "**Their most potent weapon was the Nuclear Bomb**" using the key "**aerospace**".
Solution: The Playfair key square is

A	**E**	**R**	**O**	**S**
P	**C**	**B**	**D**	**F**
G	**H**	**I/J**	**K**	**L**
M	**N**	**Q**	**T**	**U**
V	**W**	**X**	**Y**	**Z**

Ignore punctuation and spaces, divided into 2-grams

TH	EI	RM	OS	TP	OT	EN	TW	EA	PO	NW
AS	TH	EN	UC	LE	AR	BO	MB			

The plaintext would be encrypted as

NK	RH	AQ	SA	MD	DY	CW	NY	RE	DA	WE
EA	NK	CW	NF	HS	EO	DR	QP			

The ciphertext is "**NKRHAQSAMDDYCWNYREDAWEEANKCWN-FHSEODRQP**". ■

Encrypt using a Python program:

```
def encrypt_RowRule(matr, e1r, e1c, e2r, e2c):
    "In the same row"
    char1 = '';char2 = ''
    if e1c == 4: char1 = matr[e1r][0]
    else: char1 = matr[e1r][e1c+1]
```

```
    if e2c == 4: char2 = matr[e2r][0]
    else: char2 = matr[e2r][e2c+1]

    return char1, char2


def encrypt_ColumnRule(matr, e1r, e1c, e2r, e2c):
    "In the same column"
    char1 = '' ;char2 = ''
    if e1r == 4: char1 = matr[0][e1c]
    else: char1 = matr[e1r+1][e1c]

    if e2r == 4: char2 = matr[0][e2c]
    else: char2 = matr[e2r+1][e2c]

    return char1, char2


def encrypt_RectangleRule(matr, e1r, e1c, e2r, e2c):
    "In the Diagonal"
    char1 = '';char2 = ''
    char1 = matr[e1r][e2c]
    char2 = matr[e2r][e1c]

    return char1, char2
```

We discuss the security of the Playfair cipher. From a combinatorial standpoint, the key space consists of all possible permutations of the 25 letters in the matrix, totaling 25!, or approximately 1.55×10^{25} possible keys. Unlike mono-alphabetic substitution ciphers, which operate on single characters, the Playfair cipher encodes pairs of letters. This property significantly alters the statistical profile of the ciphertext. Since the frequency distribution is spread across $25 \times 24 = 600$ possible digraphs rather than just 26 individual letters, the distribution is much flatter. This makes the cipher resistant to basic frequency analysis techniques that rely on single-letter statistics. Due to its relative strength, combined with its ease of use and lack of specialized equipment requirements, the Playfair cipher saw extensive use by Allied forces for tactical communications during World War II.

While it is significantly more secure than the Caesar cipher, the Playfair cipher is not unbreakable. During World War II, Australian forces employed the cipher, but Japanese cryptanalysts successfully deciphered many intercepted messages. Fortunately, the compromised intelligence was generally of low strategic value, minimizing the operational impact. Encrypted Playfair messages possess distinctive characteristics that make them identifiable to cryptanalysts, that is

- They use only 25 different letters (excluding **J**).
- The length of the ciphertext is always even.
- No single ciphertext digraph contains repeated letters.

These patterns make the cipher susceptible to digraph frequency analysis, especially when the ciphertext is long enough. By comparing the frequency of letter pairs to standard English digraph distributions and using contextual clues, experienced cryptanalysts can often recover the plaintext.

In 1914, U.S. Army Lieutenant *Joseph O. Mauborgne* published a 19-page book [31], detailing a method for breaking the Playfair cipher. It was the first cryptography publication officially issued by the U.S. government. Mauborgne later became a Major General and played a key role in American military intelligence during World War II.

4.7.2 ADFGVX Cipher

The ADFGVX system was introduced by the German Colonel *Fritz Nebel* in 1918, the ADFGVX cipher is a modified version of the ADFGX cipher [32], sharing similarities with the Playfair cipher in that both utilize matrix-based spatial arrangements, but ADFGVX goes significantly further by incorporating fractionating and transposition techniques. When the system was first introduced in March 1918, only five letters: **A, D, F, G,** and **X** were used. The letter **V** was added later to strengthen the cipher's security.

The letters "ADFGVX" were specifically chosen for this cryptosystem because their International Morse code equivalents are highly distinct. This deliberate selection minimized the risk of operator confusion during transmission. Since the output ciphertext consists exclusively of these six characters, the scheme acts as a fractionating cipher. Conceptually, it can be viewed as a hybrid system that combines a substitution step with a columnar transposition. Like the Playfair cipher, ADFGVX cipher was applied on the battlefield for secure military communications.

The ADFGVX encryption process

1) Construct a 6×6 ADFGVX matrix with entries taken from 26 alphabet letters and 10 number digits;
2) Convert each letter in the plaintext into its coordinates in the ADFGVX table. Coordinates are ordered as (row index, column index);
3) Transpose the converted text, row-by-row from left to right, into a table with n columns and permute the columns using a chosen permutation of length n; To do the transposition, a keyword or a permutation is needed.
4) Write the permuted table column-by-column from top to bottom to obtain the ciphertext that results from considering the letters of the keyword in alphabetical order or numerical order;

The key space is $36! \approx 3.7 \times 10^{41}$, greater than Playfair. An example key grid is as follow.

Example 4.7.5 Suppose a word is "**SUMMER**", ignore repeated letter, the ADFGVX square as shown in Table 4-15.

Table 4-15: ADFGVX Square 1

	A	D	F	G	V	X
A	S	U	M	E	R	*A*
D	B	C	D	F	G	H
F	I	J	K	L	N	O
G	P	Q	T	V	W	X
V	Y	Z	0	1	2	3
X	4	5	6	7	8	9

■

Example 4.7.6 Encrypt the following plaintext "**from one day to another in battle**" using the permutation **8 4 3 2 7 6 1 5** and the key square as shown in Table 4-16.

Table 4-16: ADFGVX Square 2

	A	D	F	G	V	X
A	I	W	O	U	L	D
D	E	F	R	Y	0	A
F	9	B	C	1	G	H
G	J	K	2	M	N	7
V	P	3	Q	S	6	T
X	4	V	X	5	Z	8

Solution: Convert each letter into its coordinates, the plaintext becomes the intermediate ciphertext as shown in Table 4-17.

Table 4-17: Convert Each Letter

f	r	o	m	o	n	e	d	a
DD	DF	AF	GG	AF	GV	DA	AX	DX
y	t	o	a	n	o	t	h	e
DG	VX	AF	DX	GV	AF	VX	FX	DA
r	i	n	b	a	t	t	l	e
DF	AA	GV	FD	DX	VX	VX	AV	DA

After encryption, the length of the message is doubled. The next step is **transposition**. The intermediate ciphertext is rewritten into the 8 columns grid, row by row. There are two empty cells remaining in the grid. Using message "**X**" as a filler, convert to "**XF**" have been added to the end of the message to complete the square.

8	4	3	2	7	6	1	5
D	D	D	F	A	F	G	G
A	F	G	V	D	A	A	X
D	X	D	E	V	X	A	F
D	X	G	V	A	F	V	X
F	X	D	A	D	F	A	A
G	V	F	D	D	X	V	X
B	X	A	V	D	A	**X**	**F**

The ciphertext is created by going down columns by numerical order: **GAAVAVX FVGVADV DGDGDFA DFXXXVX GXFXAXF FAXFFXA ADVADDD DADDFGB** ■

Decryption process:

1) Fill the letters of the ciphertext into a table of n columns, where n is the length of the permutation. Fill the entries column-by-column, top-to-bottom, and left-to-right.
2) Label each column from left to right with $1, 2, \ldots, n$. Then rearrange the columns so that the given permutation appears.
3) Read the text from step 2 row-by-row, left-to-right, and top-to-bottom. Then break the resultant text into pairs.
4) Translate each pair into the plaintext using its coordinates in the ADFGVX square. Coordinates are ordered as (row index, column index);

The ADFGVX cipher is not hard to ascertain in practical use because the cipher only six letters appear in the ciphertext and every ciphertext message is even.

Theoretically, the ADFGVX cipher is a very difficult cipher to break. First, the cipher with huge key space, making brute-force attacks practically impossible. Second, the transposition is hard to analyze. Every plaintext letter is substituted by a digraph. When placed into the rectangular array for transposition, the first letter of the digraph will be placed in a column and the second letter of the digraph will put in another column. After transposition, these letters will be separated. Therefore, it is hard to find the relationship between ciphertext letters and plaintext letters.

However, the cipher was successfully broken not long after its deployment. In early 1918, as both Germany and France were entrenched in the brutal stalemate of World War I, the *German High Command* devised a bold spring offensive aimed at ending the war. Secrecy was paramount to its success, and to securely transmit battle orders, Germany adopted the ADFGX cipher.

French intelligence intercepted these encrypted messages and forwarded them to *Georges Painvin*, a skilled cryptanalyst. At first, the cipher appeared impenetrable, standard methods failed, and the limited volume of intercepted data ruled out frequency-based analysis. Worse still, the encryption keys appeared to change daily, adding another layer of complexity.

On March 21, 1918, the German offensive began with 6,000 artillery guns pounding French positions along the Somme River. The front line quickly collapsed.

As panic spread, Painvin's burden grew. Reinforcements were assigned to assist him. One day, he realized that cracking the cipher required multiple ciphertexts captured on the same day because he guessed that the two plaintexts agree for several words.

On April 1st, a breakthrough came: French forces intercepted several messages, some of which contained overlapping content. He found that the top few entries of the columns for one are the same as for the other. Search through the ciphertexts and find places where they same. Using these redundancies, *Painvin* successfully broke the ADFGX cipher by April 26. By May 31, he was able to decrypt messages from the previous day.

Then came an unexpected hurdle. On June 1, the newly intercepted ciphertexts could no longer be broken. Analysis revealed that the cipher had been strengthened. Germany had expanded it into the ADFGVX cipher by adding the letter "**V**", significantly increasing the system's complexity. Uncertain whether the new matrix incorporated homophones, duplicate letters, or digits, *Painvin* found himself starting from scratch.

But he refused to give up. After days of relentless work, he cracked the upgraded cipher as well. Armed with Painvin's decrypted intelligence, French forces fortified the exact sector of the expected German attack—and successfully repelled it. That battle marked the end of Germany's ability to launch major offensives.

The decryption effort took a heavy toll: *Painvin* lost over 30 pounds due to stress and exhaustion. After the war, he enjoyed a successful business career, serving as CEO of the French chemical company Ugine and later as President of the Paris Chamber of Commerce.

Today, the ADFGVX cipher can be broken using modern techniques such as hill-climbing algorithms, reflecting both the ingenuity of early cryptanalysts and the evolution of cipher-breaking tools.

4.7.3 Rectangular Transposition Ciphers

The Rectangular Transposition Cipher, also known as a permutation cipher, works by rearranging the order of the characters in the plaintext rather than altering the characters themselves. Its core principle lies in reordering the plaintext in a structured way to obscure the original message.

Unlike substitution ciphers, transposition ciphers do not modify the identity of the characters. Consequently, the statistical frequency distribution of individual letters in the ciphertext remains identical to that of the plaintext. This property allows cryptanalysts to easily distinguish transposition ciphers from substitution schemes. However, breaking them requires reconstructing the original order, often by analyzing the disruption of common letter pairs (digraphs) rather than single-letter statistics. The security of the scheme relies entirely on the secrecy of the rearrangement pattern, which is determined by the cipher key.

Example 4.7.7 Encrypt the plaintext **"The airliner took off on time"**. using a Rectangular Transposition Cipher with the keyword "**lunch**".

Solution: The key has a length of 5. We begin by organizing the plaintext into a rectangular grid with 5 columns. The text is inscribed from left to right, top to bottom. Before proceeding, we must ensure the total length of the message is a multiple of the key length. If the number of plaintext characters is not divisible by 5, padding characters are appended to complete the final row. These padding characters should be distinct to facilitate accurate decryption. In this example, we use the character "**X**" as padding.

Next, we reorder the columns by the alphabetical order of the letters in the keyword. For instance, suppose the key is "lunch", whose alphabetical order corresponds to the permutation **3 5 4 1 2**. This means the 1st character in each row moves to position 3, the 2nd character moves to position 5, the 3rd to position 4, and so on.

```
lunch        lunch        chlnu
35412        35412        12345
-----        -----        -----
theai        theai        aiteh
rline   ⇒    rline   ⇒    neril
rtook        rtook        okrot
offon        offon        onoff
time         timex        extmi
```

Once the plaintext has been reordered according to the key, multiple ciphertext extraction methods are possible.

1) Left to right, then top to bottom: `aiteh neril okrot onoff extmi`
2) Top to bottom, then left to right: `anooe ieknx trrot eiofm hltfi`
3) Right to left, then top to bottom: `hetia liren torko ffono imtxe`
4) Top to bottom, then right to left: `hltfi eiofm trrot ieknx anooe`
5) Vertical alternating, left to right: `anooe xnkei trrot mfoie hltfi`
6) Horizontal alternating, top to bottom: `aiteh liren okrot ffono extmi`

Note: The ciphertexts are transmitted without spaces; spaces here are for readability only. Typically, the first two methods are adopted.

Assuming method 1 (left-to-right, then top-to-bottom) is selected for extraction. To decrypt: Set the rectangle width using the key length. Rearrange the ciphertext into a rectangle with five letters per line, top to bottom. For the key Lunch (alphabetical order: 3, 5, 4, 1, 2), per row doing: Move the 3rd letter to position 1; Move the 5th letter to position 2; Move the 4th letter to position 3, and so on. For other methods, rearrange according to their specific patterns. ■

The key space of the rectangular transposition cipher depends on the length of the key. If the key has an effective length of 20, then there are a total of $20! \approx 2.43 \times 10^{18}$ possible permutations. Such a huge number makes brute-force attacks computationally infeasible. However, this represents only the theoretical upper bound of the key space. In practical applications, the effective key space is often significantly smaller.

A significant reduction in security occurs when the keyword is not a random permutation but a common English word containing repeated letters. For instance, consider the word "apple". While the key length is 5, the two repeated "P"s make the corresponding columns indistinguishable in the permutation process. This reduces the total number of unique permutations from 120 to 60. Similarly, for the keyword "tooth" (length 5, with two "O"s and two "T"s), the key space is reduced to $5!/(2!2!) = 30$. If a longer phrase is used as the key, such as "What do you think of the movie?" The key space could be $24!/((2!)^2(3!)^2(4!)) \approx 1.8 \times 10^{20}$.

To enhance the cipher's security, the use of padding to complete the final row of the grid is generally discouraged. This variant is known as regular columnar transposition. If padding is used, the length of the ciphertext becomes a multiple of the key length, providing cryptanalysts with a structural hint. For example, if a ciphertext contains exactly 22 characters, an attacker might infer a grid size of 2×11 or 11×2, narrowing the potential key lengths to 2 or 11. By not padding, such structural hints are eliminated, making cryptanalysis more difficult.

Another technique to enhance the cipher's strength is to use double transposition, where the same key is used twice to perform two rounds of transposition encryption. This approach significantly increases the confusion and diffusion, making the ciphertext more resistant to pattern detection. During World War I, the Germans developed the Übchi transposition cipher, which applied such double transpositions. However, in November 1914, French cryptanalysts successfully broke this system, prompting the Germans to abandon it.

Example 4.7.8 Consider a double transposition. Encrypt the following message: "**Thanks to Queqiao, the communication problem between Earth and ChangE has been well solved**". Using the key "**spacecraft**".

```
spacecraft      The First Encrypt      spacecraft      The Second Encrypt
thankstoqu      aiuredbl oetmrge       aiuredbloe      urvobsee lneeqea
eqiaotheco ⇒    nanoecev stcleand ⇒    tmrgenanoe ⇒    rgsitomh dncnlhtl
mmunicatio      koibnhee qcibtel       cevstclean      eetbetnh ooaemas
nproblembe      hqmpwnso thaeanw       dkoibnheeq      imekinto balhhaa
tweenearth      temntaas uooehhl       cibtelhqmp      atcdcwwo eenqpnu
andchangeh                             wnsothaean
asbeenwell                             wtemntaasu
solved                                 ooehhl
```

To further strengthen the cipher, there are five more basic transposition patterns. These patterns vary the way in which text is filled into and extracted from the transposition grid, such as

Orthogonal	Diagonal	Spiral
ABCDE	ABDGL	ABCDE
FGHIK	CEHMQ	QRSTF
LMNOP	FINRU	PYZUG
QRSTU	KOSVX	OXWVH
VWXYZ	PTWYZ	NMLKI

Boustrophedon	Diagonal Boustrophedon	Central Spiral
ABCDE	ABFGP	ZYXWV
KIHGF	CEHOQ	KIHGU
LMNOP	DINRW	LBAFT
UTSRQ	KMSVX	MCDES
VWXYZ	LTUYZ	NOPQR

4.7.4 Cryptanalysis

Definition 4.7.1 Conditional Probability

The conditional probability of an event A is the probability that this event will occur, given the knowledge that another event B has already occurred. We have

$$P(A \mid B) = \frac{P(A \cap B)}{P(B)} \tag{4-88}$$

where $P(B) > 0$.

Example 4.7.9 Consider a rare disease known as the Z-virus, which affects approximately 5% of the population. A biotechnology company claims to have developed a test that detects this virus with 95% accuracy. Suppose that someone is tested positive for having the virus, what is the probability that the person actually carries the disease?
Solution: This problem illustrates the classic statistical concept of "False Positives". To visualize the probabilities, let us assume a hypothetical population of 10,000 people. Given the prevalence rate, 500 individuals are infected with the pathogen, while the remaining 9,500 are healthy.

- Infected individuals: Among the 500 infected individuals, the number who test positive is $500 \times 0.95 = 475$; the number who test negative is $500 \times 0.05 = 25$.
- Healthy individuals: Among the 9,500 healthy individuals, the number who receive a false positive is $9500 \times (1 - 0.95) = 475$; the number who test negative is $9500 \times 0.95 = 9025$.

The conditional probability that a person who tested positive is truly infected is:

$$P(\text{Infected} \mid \text{Positive}) = \frac{P(\text{True Positive})}{P(\text{Tested Positive})} = \frac{475}{475 + 475} = \frac{1}{2}$$

This result implies that if an individual tests positive, there is only a 50% chance that they actually carry the disease. Despite the test's high accuracy of 95%, the positive predictive value is low because the disease is rare. In this scenario, the number of false alarms (healthy people wrongly identified as sick) equals the number of actual detections.

A common error is to focus solely on the 95% accuracy while overlooking the fact that infected individuals constitute only a small fraction of the total population. This cognitive bias is known as the base rate fallacy, which serves as a reminder of how easily probabilities can be misinterpreted when the underlying population distribution (the base rate) is ignored. ■

Example 4.7.10 Given a ciphertext "$\star\star\star\star\star\star\mu\lambda\star\star\star\star\star\star$" and known the plaintext is English. What is the probability that a randomly chosen letter λ is "A''?
Solution: By the Table 4-9, we know $P(\lambda = A) = P(A) = 0.08399$. ■

Example 4.7.11 Now suppose that μ and λ are far apart. What is the probability that μ is "L" and λ is "A"?
Solution: If the letter are far apart, they are independent. Thus, $P(\lambda = A \mid \mu = L) = P(L)P(A)$. ■

Definition 4.7.2 Mean Value

If X is a discrete random variable with a probability mass function $P(x)$, then the mean value of X is denoted by $\mathbb{E}(X)$, is defined by

$$\mathbb{E}(X) = x_1P(X = x_1) + \cdots + x_kP(X = x_k), \text{ where } P(X = x_i) \geqslant 0 \quad (4\text{-}89)$$

Example 4.7.12 Suppose we roll two fair 6-sided dice. Find the mean value of the sum of the two faces.
Solution: The all possible of two faces are shown in the Table 4-18.

Table 4-18: All Possible Sums of Two Dice

(1,1)=2	(1,2)=3	(1,3)=4	(1,4)=5	(1,5)=6	(1,6)=7
(2,1)=3	(2,2)=4	(2,3)=5	(2,4)=6	(2,5)=7	(2,6)=8
(3,1)=4	(3,2)=5	(3,3)=6	(3,4)=7	(3,5)=8	(3,6)=9
(4,1)=5	(4,2)=6	(4,3)=7	(4,4)=8	(4,5)=9	(4,6)=10
(5,1)=6	(5,2)=7	(5,3)=8	(5,4)=9	(5,5)=10	(5,6)=11
(6,1)=7	(6,2)=8	(6,3)=9	(6,4)=10	(6,5)=11	(6,6)=12

Using the Table 4-19 to find the mean value. There are 11 possibles, the mean

Table 4-19: Probability Distribution of the Sum

Sum	2	3	4	···	12
Probability	1/36	2/36	3/36	···	1/36

the expected value is computed as

$$\mathbb{E}(X) = \sum_{i=1}^{11} x_iP_i = 2 \times \frac{1}{36} + \cdots + 12 \times \frac{1}{36} = 7$$

■

Theorem 4.7.1 Bayes' Theorem

The conditional probability of event A given event B is defined by $P(A \mid B)$, using the formula was provided for finding $P(A \mid B)$ is given by

$$P(A \mid B) = \frac{P(A)P(B \mid A)}{P(B)} \quad (4\text{-}90)$$

where $P(B) > 0$ exists.

Proof

According to Definition 4.7.1, we know the conditional probability of event A given event B is defined by $P(A \mid B)$

$$P(A \mid B) = \frac{P(A \cap B)}{P(B)} \tag{4-91}$$

By chain rule

$$P(A \cap B) = P(A \mid B)P(B) \tag{4-92}$$

Note that since

$$P(A \cap B) = P(B \mid A)P(A) \tag{4-93}$$

We get that

$$P(A \mid B)P(B) = P(B \mid A)P(A) \tag{4-94}$$

We will get the most common version

$$P(A \mid B) = \frac{P(A)P(B \mid A)}{P(B)} \tag{4-95}$$

Example 4.7.13 Over the past year, a spillway in a given region was activated on 3 separate days due to flooding, with at most one activation per day. Persistent rainfall has led to the implementation of a flood warning system; however, its sensor is faulty, triggering an alarm one day per week on average. The probability that the sensor correctly signals an actual flood is 0.9. If the sensor triggers an alarm, what is the probability that a real flood is approaching?

Solution: Let $P(B)$ be the probability that the sensor issues a warning on any given week, which is $1/7$. Let $P(A)$ be the probability of a flood occurring $3/365$. The probability that the sensor responds given a flood, $P(B \mid A)$ is 0.9. Therefore, the probability that a flood occurs given that the sensor has triggered an alarm, $P(A \mid B)$ is

$$P(A \mid B) = \frac{P(A)P(B \mid A)}{P(B)} \approx 5.2\% \tag{4-96}$$

The probability of a true positive prediction is less than 10%, indicating that the sensor must be promptly repaired or replaced. ■

Definition 4.7.3 Convex Function

A function $y = f(x)$ is convex on an interval $[a, b]$ provided that $f''(x) \geqslant 0$ for all $a \leqslant x \leqslant b$. In particular, the first derivative $f'(x)$ is increasing on the interval $[a, b]$.

In other words, $f : \mathbb{R}^n \to \mathbb{R}$ is a function, if the domain of f is convex set for all x, y in its domain, and all $\lambda \in [0, 1]$, we say f is convex. We have

$$f(\lambda x + (1 - \lambda)y) \leqslant \lambda f(x) + (1 - \lambda)f(y) \tag{4-97}$$

As shown in Figure 4-5.

A function f is **strictly convex** if whenever for all x, y in its domain, $x \neq y$, and $\lambda \in (0, 1)$, strict inequality holds, we have

$$f(\lambda x + (1 - \lambda)y) < \lambda f(x) + (1 - \lambda)f(y) \tag{4-98}$$

Similarly, it is said to be **concave** if $f''(x) \leqslant 0$. Thus, if $f(x)$ is convex, then $-f(x)$ is concave.

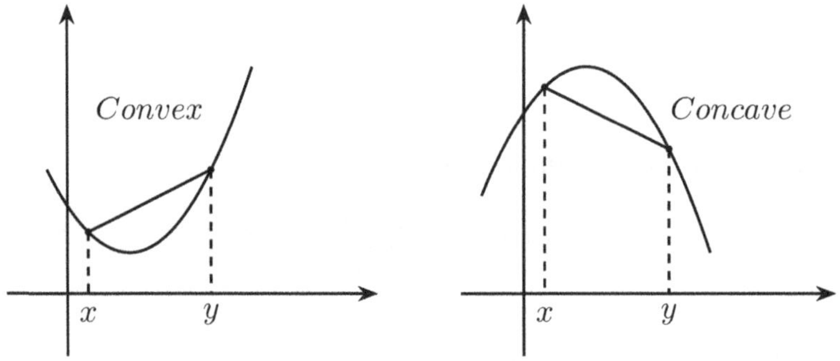

Figure 4-5: An Illustration of a Convex Function and a Concave Function

Some examples of convex or concave functions

1) $f(x) = ax + b$ is convex function, for all $a, b \in \mathbb{R}$ and defined on $\mathbb{R}$;
2) $f(x) = e^{ax}$ is convex function, for all $a \in \mathbb{R}$ and defined on $\mathbb{R}$;
3) $f(x) = |x|^a$ is convex function, for all $a \geqslant 1$ and defined on $\mathbb{R}$;
4) $f(x) = x^\alpha$ is concave function, for all $0 \leqslant \alpha \leqslant 1$ and defined on $\mathbb{R}^+$;
5) $f(x) = \sqrt[n]{\prod_{i=1}^{n} x_i}$ is concave function, for all $n \geqslant 1$ and defined on $x_i \geqslant 0$.

Theorem 4.7.2 Jensen's Inequality

Let $x_1, x_2, \ldots, x_n \in [a, b]$, and $\lambda_1, \lambda_2, \ldots, \lambda_n \geqslant 0$, satisfy $\lambda_1 + \lambda_2 + \cdots + \lambda_n = 1$. If $f(x)$ is a convex function, then

$$f(\lambda_1 x_1 + \lambda_2 x_2 + \cdots + \lambda_n x_n) \leqslant \lambda_1 f(x_1) + \lambda_2 f(x_2) + \cdots + \lambda_n f(x_n) \tag{4-99}$$

Furthermore, if $f(x)$ is a strictly convex function and $\lambda_i > 0$ for all i, equality holds if and only if $x_1 = x_2 = \cdots = x_n$.

Proof

We prove Jensen's Inequality by induction.

Base case. Let $n = 1$, since $\lambda_1 = 1$, thus $f(\lambda_1 x_1) = f(x_1) \leqslant \lambda_1 f(x_1)$, the inequality holds.

Let $n = 2$, the inequality holds from the definition of convexity. Assume that it is true for $n-1$ points. We prove it is true for n points. Inductive step. Let $\lambda_1, \lambda_2, \ldots, \lambda_n \geqslant 0$, $\sum_{k=1}^{n} \lambda_k = 1$, and

$$y = \sum_{k=1}^{n-1} \frac{\lambda_k}{1-\lambda_n} x_k \in [a, b] \tag{4-100}$$

We have

$$\begin{aligned} f\left(\lambda_1 x_1 + \cdots + \lambda_n x_n\right) &= f\left(\sum_{i=1}^{n-1} \lambda_i x_i + \lambda_n x_n\right) && (4\text{-}101) \\ &= f\left(\left(1-\lambda_n\right) y + \lambda_n x_n\right) && (4\text{-}102) \\ &\leqslant \left(1-\lambda_n\right) f(y) + \lambda_n f\left(x_n\right) && (4\text{-}103) \\ &= \left(1-\lambda_n\right) f\left(\sum_{k=1}^{n-1} \frac{\lambda_k}{1-\lambda_n} x_k\right) + \lambda_n f\left(x_n\right) && (4\text{-}104) \\ &\leqslant \left(1-\lambda_n\right) \sum_{k=1}^{n-1} \frac{\lambda_k}{1-\lambda_n} f\left(x_k\right) + \lambda_n f\left(x_n\right) && (4\text{-}105) \\ &= \sum_{k=1}^{n} \lambda_k f\left(x_k\right) && (4\text{-}106) \end{aligned}$$

Let $f(x) = \log(1/x)$, since this function is strictly convex for $x > 0$, Jensen's inequality takes the form

$$\log\left(\frac{1}{\lambda_1 x_1 + \lambda_2 x_2 + \cdots + \lambda_n x_n}\right) \leqslant \lambda_1 \log\left(\frac{1}{x_1}\right) + \cdots + \lambda_n \log\left(\frac{1}{x_n}\right) \tag{4-107}$$

Theorem 4.7.3 Extension of Jensen's Inequality

For two positive probability distributions $\lambda_1, \lambda_2, \ldots, \lambda_n$ and $q_1, q_2, \ldots, q_n$, they satisfy $\lambda_1 + \lambda_2 + \cdots + \lambda_n = 1$ and $q_1 + q_2 + \cdots + q_n = 1$, then

$$\sum_{i=1}^{n} \lambda_i \log(q_i) \leqslant \sum_{i=1}^{n} \lambda_i \log(\lambda_i) \tag{4-108}$$

The steps for breaking rectangular transposition:

1) Guess a length for the decrypting permutation, denoted by K.
2) Arrange the ciphertext into K columns and let N be the height of the resulting rectangle.
3) For each pair $1 \leqslant i \neq j \leqslant K$, extract the columns i and j and count the number of occurrence of the pair of letters α, β and call it as $n_{\alpha,\beta}^{ij}$.
4) For each pair α, β, let $P_{\alpha,\beta}$ be the probability of the pair α, β in English (or other languages). Compute

$$C_{i,j} = \sum_{\alpha,\beta} P_{\alpha,\beta} \log(n_{\alpha,\beta}^{ij}) \tag{4-109}$$

Example 4.7.14 We know a message that was encrypted using rectangular transposition, the length of ciphertext is 230. First, we guess the key length is 10. Thus, $K = 10, N = 23$. As an example, let $i = 3, j = 7$. As shown in Table 4-20.

Table 4-20: The Resulting Rectangle

E	C	T	I	H	N	O	H	G	I		T	O
O	K	R	O	B	C	A	O	H	F		R	A
E	I	N	S	G	N	N	S	A	A		N	N
E	T	C	N	I	I	E	C	N	H		C	E
O	A	S	R	E	E	H	C	T	L		S	H
H	S	A	A	T	E	I	B	N	E		A	I
S	F	N	E	U	C	N	O	E	R		N	N
R	E	T	I	U	S	S	S	A	A		T	S
R	E	O	C	U	W	S	O	I	F		O	S
M	N	D	A	O	D	I	D	V	A		D	I
T	E	C	H	E	X	O	T	T	E		C	O
H	O	F	E	T	C	E	R	L	A		F	E
I	I	A	T	S	O	E	S	M	S	⇒	A	E
M	S	T	E	I	O	N	K	W	N		T	N
N	I	C	S	O	S	F	S	O	T		C	F
X	Y	S	T	I	U	H	F	R	O		S	H
A	R	E	G	X	S	A	A	E	M		E	A
S	M	C	Y	H	L	Z	B	I	O		C	Z
B	A	E	Y	D	R	I	P	T	A		E	I
L	R	C	A	U	R	N	A	A	R		C	N
M	N	G	E	E	F	I	T	S	O		G	I
T	A	X	R	S	H	A	I	T	G		X	A
B	O	N	R	D	N	I	K	L	E		N	I

We verify the adjacency of columns by analyzing the frequency of digraphs formed between them. Let $n_{\alpha\beta}^{(i,j)}$ denote the number of occurrences of the letter pair (α, β), where α appears in the i-th column and β appears in the j-th column of the same row within the ciphertext blocks.

Suppose the sequence of digraphs formed by these rows is given by: **TO**, **RA**, **NN**, **CE**, ..., **NI**. Counting these pairs, we observe $n_{\mathrm{TO}}^{(3,7)} = 1, n_{\mathrm{RA}}^{(3,7)} = 1, n_{\mathrm{NN}}^{(3,7)} = 2, \ldots, n_{\mathrm{NI}}^{(3,7)} = 1$. The correlation score $C_{i,j}$ is defined as the weighted sum of logarithmic counts

$$C_{i,j} = \sum_{\alpha,\beta} P_{\alpha\beta} \log\left(n_{\alpha\beta}^{(i,j)}\right) \tag{4-110}$$

Applying this to the rows $i = 3$ and $j = 7$, we obtain

$$
\begin{aligned}
C_{3,7} &= P_{TO} \cdot \log(n^{3,7}_{TO}) + P_{RA} \cdot \log(n^{3,7}_{RA}) + \cdots + P_{NI} \cdot \log(n^{3,7}_{NI}) && \text{(4-111)}\\
&= P_{TO} \cdot \log(1) + P_{RA} \cdot \log(1) + P_{NN} \cdot \log(2) + \cdots + P_{NI} \cdot \log(1) && \text{(4-112)}\\
&= P_{TO} \cdot 0 + P_{RA} \cdot 0 + P_{NN} \cdot \log(2) + \cdots + P_{NI} \cdot 0 && \text{(4-113)}
\end{aligned}
$$

Using the method described above, compute all values of $C_{i,j}$ for $0 \leqslant i, j \leqslant K$ with $i \neq j$.

Define a function $f^{(i,j)}_{\alpha,\beta} = n^{(i,j)}_{\alpha,\beta}/N$, by the Theorem 4.7.4, we have

$$
\begin{aligned}
C_{i,j} &= \sum_{\alpha,\beta} P_{\alpha\beta} \cdot \log\left(N \cdot f^{(i,j)}_{\alpha\beta}\right) && \text{(4-114)}\\
&= \log(N) + \sum_{\alpha,\beta} P_{\alpha\beta} \cdot \log\left(f^{(i,j)}_{\alpha\beta}\right) && \text{(4-115)}\\
&\leqslant \sum_{\alpha,\beta} P_{\alpha\beta} \cdot \log\left(P_{\alpha\beta}\right) && \text{(4-116)}
\end{aligned}
$$

If two columns i and j were not consecutive in the plaintext, then the value of $C_{i,j}$ will be much smaller than comparing to when two columns i and j were consecutive in the plaintext. Otherwise, for $C_{i,j}$, where $1 \leqslant i \neq j \leqslant K$, its value has a substantially bigger number in each row, except one This leads to the following conclusion:

- If $C_{i,j}$ is the substantially big number on row i then j follows i in the decryption permutation.
- If row K is the only row with no substantially big entry, then K is the first entry in the decryption permutation.

If the key K is correctly identified, the resulting correlation matrix will exhibit a distinct contrast between values. This distribution pattern is illustrated in Table 4-21.

Table 4-21: Breaking Rectangular Transposition Matrix

	1	2	3	4	5	6
1		s	B	s	s	s
2	s		s	s	B	s
3	s	B		s	s	s
4	s	s	s		s	B
5	s	s	s	s		s
6	B	s	s	s	s	

Here, B denotes a large value and s denotes a small value. The procedure to determine the decryption permutation is as follows:

1) We look for the row that contains no big values, as this implies the column has no successor. Since row 5 contains only small values, column 5 is the final column. Hence, we set $a_6 = 5$.

2) To find a_5: Given that $a_6 = 5$, look for the big value in column 5, which is in row 2. Hence, $a_5 = 2$.
3) To find a_4: Given that $a_5 = 2$, look for the big value in column 2, which is in row 3. Hence, $a_4 = 3$.
4) To find a_3: Given that $a_4 = 3$, look for the big value in column 3, which is in row 1. Hence, $a_3 = 1$.
5) To find a_2: Given that $a_3 = 1$, look for the big value in column 1, which is in row 6. Hence, $a_2 = 6$.
6) To find a_1: Given that $a_2 = 6$, look for the big value in column 6, which is in row 4. Hence, $a_1 = 4$.
7) Observing column 4 in the table, we see it contains no big values, confirming it is the first column. The reconstructed permutation is $4 \to 6 \to 1 \to 3 \to 2 \to 5$.

Example 4.7.15 The following message was encrypted using rectangular transposition. Decrypt it.

```
ENFOT HIILN GOWLI EONCT SPTHY HESLI MECAS IHSMA NCEOA
TFHSA LREOW FUISS SCDDD REANE ERNTE SPETF OIVAA MSFUL
RTRIM ESOGT HEINA ATNST RAAET ERRFH IEHNT SVPEL ERYYC
REITO AIREM EGERN TESPE DNATH ETTIO ENTOI CUSFN NETHD
OSHMO DETEL EOYMP SODRD INEPR ROTOE AENDC TTTOH EOLCA
UCERF SNOAI FASFC TORAR SASIM IREL
```

Solution: Start by estimating the key length, beginning with 2, and calculate $C_{i,j}$ in the matrix. Check for any big values. Unfortunately, for key lengths of 2, 3, or 4, none of the values show a clear distinction from the others.

0	27
20	0

0	21	16
14	0	22
14	17	0

0	13	12	14
9	0	16	11
13	13	0	15
12	11	11	0

Until $K = 7$, certain values in the matrix stand out from the rest. The final decryption sequence is illustrated in Figure 4-6, with the decryption order being $7 \to 2 \to 5 \to 6 \to 1 \to 3 \to 4$.

Consequently, we can determine the original encryption permutation. Since the 1st block of plaintext was routed to column 7, the 2nd block to column 2, and so on, the corresponding encryption key permutation π is exactly equivalent to this reading sequence: $(7, 2, 5, 6, 1, 3, 4)$. Conversely, the inverse permutation $\pi^{-1} = (5, 2, 6, 7, 3, 4, 1)$ reveals the original plaintext column index residing in each ciphertext column from left to right.

0	18	33	19	20	20	26
22	0	20	19	35	19	28
21	18	0	35	21	21	18
20	22	20	0	22	20	24
19	23	18	22	0	34	16
37	22	18	22	20	0	20
19	33	19	23	16	19	0

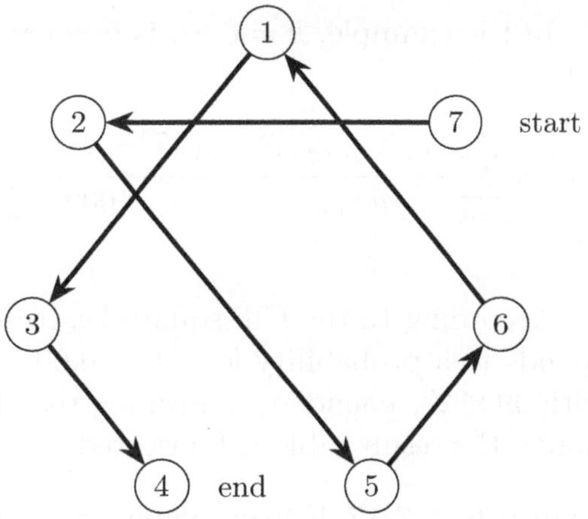

Figure 4-6: Breaking Rectangular Transposition

■

4.7.5 Breaking Mono-Alphabetic Substitution

Example 4.7.16 A supposedly fair die rolled 1000 times produced the following outcome (Table 4-22).

Table 4-22: Outcome of Rolling a Die

Result	1	2	3	4	5	6
Frequency	171	186	174	170	192	107

Should we believe this outcome?

Solution: The Chi-square statistic shows the discrepancies observed frequencies are from their theoretical values.

Definition 4.7.4 Chi-Squared Test

The chi-square test is a hypothesis test where the test statistic approximately follows a chi-square distribution when the null hypothesis holds. In the absence of other conditions or explanations, the term "chi-square test" usually refers to Pearson's chi-square test. It is denoted by

$$\chi^2 = \sum_{i=1}^{k} \frac{(n_i - n \cdot p_i)^2}{n \cdot p_i} \tag{4-117}$$

where k is the total number of entries; n_i is the observed frequency of the i-th entry; n is the total number of observations; p_i is the theoretical probability of the i-th entry.

In the example, $k = 6$, n_i is frequency, $n = 1000$ and $p_i = 1/6$. The chi-square value is

$$\chi^2 = \sum_{i=1}^{6} \frac{(n_i - n \cdot p_i)^2}{n \cdot p_i} = \frac{\left(171 - 1000 \times \frac{1}{6}\right)^2}{1000 \times \frac{1}{6}} + \frac{\left(186 - 1000 \times \frac{1}{6}\right)^2}{1000 \times \frac{1}{6}} + \cdots = 27.95 \tag{4-118}$$

According to the Chi-square Distribution Table, we see that $\chi^2 \geqslant 27.95$ corresponds to a probability less than 0.001%. Thus, we can reject the null hypothesis with 99.999% confidence, meaning that this result is virtually impossible. In other words, the result table is fabricated. ■

Example 4.7.17 Known plaintext attack of mono-alphabetic substitution. Given the letter frequencies of a certain ciphertext as follows:

Table 4-23: Ciphertext Letter Frequencies

Ciphertext	L	H	A	W	D	Q	O	N	F	S	Z	K	P
Frequency	80	61	55	46	44	40	39	35	33	26	22	26	22
Ciphertext	I	T	V	Y	R	X	U	M	C	G	J	B	E
Frequency	18	17	12	11	9	9	8	7	5	3	1	0	0

Known that the word "**WHERE**" was in the plaintext. We found in the ciphertext the two strings "**HDFKF**" and "**PDLHL**" that match the pattern of "**WHERE**". Using the chi-square test, decide which of these two strings is the image of "**WHERE**".

Solution: First, find the probability of each letter that is calculated using the frequencies from Table 4-9.

$$P(W) = P(W|W \text{ or } H \text{ or } E \text{ or } R) \tag{4-119}$$

$$= \frac{0.02464}{0.02464 + 0.06025 + 0.1215 + 0.06063} = 0.0923 \tag{4-120}$$

Applying the same method, we obtain $P(H) = 0.226, P(E) = 0.455, P(R) = 0.227$.

The second step is to compute the chi-square statistic for "**HDFKF**", as shown in Table 4-24.

Table 4-24: HDFKF Chi-Square Test

	W=H	H=D	E=F	R=K
P_i	0.0923	0.226	0.455	0.227
n_i	61	44	33	26

Here, $n = 164$, $k = 4$, n_i represents the observed frequency, and p_i is the probability of each letter's occurrence. Substituting these values into Equation 4-117, we have

$$\chi^2_{HDFKF} = \frac{(61 - 164 \times 0.0923)^2}{164 \times 0.0923} + \cdots + \frac{(26 - 164 \times 0.227)^2}{164 \times 0.227} \tag{4-121}$$

$$\approx \mathbf{166.79} \tag{4-122}$$

Similarly, we perform the same calculation for "**PDLHL**".

$$\chi^2_{PDLHL} \approx \mathbf{6.91} \tag{4-123}$$

By comparing the results with the chi-square table, we choose the string with the smaller χ^2 value as the correct match. A slightly larger p-value implies that we do not reject the null hypothesis. Therefore, "**PDLHL**" is correct. ■

4.8 EXERCISES

1) Implement the Caesar cipher using Python to obtain all 26 possible Caesar shifts for the plaintext
   (a) Latex;
   (b) Air-to-air missile;
   (c) aircraft;
2) Consider the Vigenère cipher, answer following questions:
   (a) Suppose the cipher with the short keys $U = (10, 5)$ and $V = (17, 23, 6)$. Encrypt the plaintext **the base is under attack**.
   (b) It is also known that the ciphertext **XJNRJ QPISY BZGZM AJHCL LZ** and the short keys U and V were of length 3 and 4, respectively. Also known the original plaintext starts with **KEEPCA**. Decrypt the message
3) Consider the following ciphertext obtained from a Vigenère cipher, answer following questions:

   YVJFJ KJFJH MFJSG SJGFH YVJSS RTTYV JTJBHS

   (a) Suppose the keyword has two letters. Perform the frequency analysis and decide which Caesar shifts have been used in the encryption process.
   (b) Decrypt the given message.
4) Suppose Eve intercepted Bob's message and learned that he is using a Vigenère cipher with a keyword of length less than 12. Eve applied the chosen plaintext attack and learned that the plaintext **AAAAAAAA** is encrypted as **BCDEBCDE**. What are all the possible values for the length?
5) Consider the following ciphertext obtained from a rectangular transposition:

   ET HX FO DA NE TH AG RS PE

   (a) What are all the possible dimensions for the rectangle used?
   (b) Decide the correct rectangle dimension and decrypt the given message.
6) Suppose Alice and Bob want to use the Playfair cipher to communicate.
   (a) Construct the Playfair square with the keyword **IRENEADLER**.
   (b) Decrypt the following message **EUFN ICRF RAFK KRGN RU**.
7) Suppose Alice and Bob want to use the ADFGVX cipher to communicate. Construct the ADFGVX substitution matrix using the keyword **OPHELIA**.
8) Determine the key space size for the following cryptographic algorithms:
   (a) The Vigenère cipher using keyword of length 8.
   (b) The ADFGVX cipher.

(c) The Playfair cipher.
(d) The Affine cipher in modulo 13.
(e) The 2×2 Hill cipher in modulo 2.

9) Using the Euclidean algorithm, compute $B^{-1} \pmod{A}$.
   (a) $A = 11393, B = 229$.
   (b) $A = 25207, B = 163$.
   (c) $A = 2639, B = 391$.
10) Suppose Alice and Bob want to use the Merkle-Hellman Knapsack Cryptosystem to communicate. Bob chooses the prime $p = 43$ and the encryption factor $A = 2$. Bob picks a sequence $(3, 5, 11, 23)$. Answer the following questions:
   (a) Show that the sequence $(3, 5, 11, 23)$ is indeed a super-increase sequence.
   (b) What is the public key that Bob sends to Alice.
   (c) Suppose Eve intercepts and overrides the sequence of integers that Bob sends to Alice. Eve then sends to Alice a new sequence (4, 8, 15, 33). Without knowing the authenticity of this data, Alice uses Eve's sequence to encrypt her message $(1, 1, 0, 1)$. What is the ciphertext that Alice sends out?
   (d) Eve then tricks Bob by sending out to Bob the ciphertext $c' = 10$. What message will Bob decrypt from c'?
11) Find the inverse of the following matrices in modulo 26:

$$\text{(a)} \begin{bmatrix} 1 & 4 \\ 8 & 11 \end{bmatrix} \qquad \text{(b)} \begin{bmatrix} 2 & 5 \\ 9 & 5 \end{bmatrix} \qquad \text{(c)} \begin{bmatrix} 1 & 11 & 12 \\ 4 & 23 & 2 \\ 17 & 15 & 9 \end{bmatrix}$$

12) Suppose Alice and Bob want to use Affine cipher to communicate. The plaintext is encrypted by the formula

$$c \equiv 11m + 4 \pmod{26}$$

   Answer the following questions:
   (a) Encrypt the plaintext **tanker is ready**.
   (b) Give the decryption formula.
   (c) Decrypt the ciphertext **GRWI**.
   (d) Suppose the ciphertext **QJKESREOGHGXXREOXEO**, has been encrypted using an affine cipher. However, we do not know the key (a, b) that was used. Fortunately, we know that the plaintext letter "T" becomes ciphertext "H" and the plaintext letter "O" becomes "E". Break the message.
13) Consider the Hill cipher. The key matrix is $\begin{bmatrix} 11 & 13 \\ 2 & 3 \end{bmatrix}$, and the resulting ciphertext was **YGFI**. What is the plaintext?
14) Consider the Hill cipher with a 2×2 key matrix, the cipher encrypted the plaintext **SOLVED** to give the ciphertext **GEZXDS**. Determine the key matrix.
15) Solve each of the following subset-sum problems or explain if no solution:
   (a) Let $[3, 7, 19, 43, 89, 195]$ and $M = 260$.
   (b) Let $[5, 23, 54, 101, 304]$ and $M = 124$.

(c) Let [3, 6, 13, 29, 61, 132, 258] and $M = 303$.
(d) Let [6, 14, 17, 38, 77, 164] and $M = 240$

16) Consider the Merkle-Hellman Knapsack Cryptosystem. Bob sets up the cryptosystem with the following private parameters: the super-increasing sequence $\mathbf{a} = (14, 16, 32, 66, 131, 260)$, the prime modulus $p = 521$, and the encrypting factor $A = 53$. Answer following questions:
    (a) Compute the public key vector $\mathbf{b} = (b_1, \ldots, b_6)$ where $b_i \equiv A \cdot a_i \pmod{p}$.
    (b) Alice wishes to send the message $m = 49$ to Bob. Convert m into a 6-bit binary string $m_1 \ldots m_6$ and compute the ciphertext.
    (c) Bob receives the ciphertext C. Given the modular inverse $A^{-1} \equiv 59 \pmod{521}$, compute the intermediate value $M \equiv A^{-1}C \pmod{p}$. Then, solve the subset-sum problem $\sum_{i=1}^{6} x_i a_i = M$ to recover the original binary message.
17) The plaintext **NOODLE** is encrypted into **OVUAKK** under an unknown cipher. We know that this unknown cipher must be one of the following five possibilities: Caesar, Vigenère, ADFGVX, Playfair, or mono-alphabetic substitution. Determine which cipher was used and briefly justify why the other four ciphers cannot be the encrypting method in this case.
18) For the matrix $A = \begin{bmatrix} a & b \\ c & d \end{bmatrix} \pmod{2}$, determine the total number of possible matrices. Furthermore, how many of these matrices are invertible?
19) Prove that $a \pmod{m} \equiv b \pmod{m}$ if and only if $a \equiv b \pmod{m}$.
20) Suppose we color 7 boxes using a pallet of 61 colors. What is the probability that at least two boxes have the same color?
21) An box initially contains 5 white and 7 black balls. Each time a ball is selected, its color is noted and it is replaced in the box along with 2 other balls of the same color. Compute the probability that
    (a) The first 2 balls selected are black and the next 2 are white.
    (b) of the first 4 balls selected, exactly 2 are black.
22) Suppose that an ordinary deck of 52 cards is shuffled and the cards are then turned over one at a time until the first ace appears. Given that the first ace is the 20th card to appear, what is the conditional probability that the card following it is the
    (a) ace of clubs?
    (b) two of spades?
23) Suppose the probability of a missile launch failure is 0.01%. Determine the number of launches required for the probability of at least one failure to exceed 95%.
24) Let p be a prime number. Prove that the number of 2×2 invertible matrices over $\mathbb{Z}_p$ is $(p^2 - 1)(p^2 - p)$.
25) Assume that $p_1, p_2, \ldots, p_n$ and $q_1, q_2, \ldots, q_n$ are probability distributions, with $p_1 \geqslant p_2 \geqslant \cdots \geqslant p_n$. Let $q'_1, q'_2, \ldots, q'_n$ be a permutation of the distribution $q_1, q_2, \ldots, q_n$. Prove that to maximize the sum $\sum_{i=1}^{n} p_i q'_i$, the condition $q'_1 \geqslant q'_2 \geqslant \cdots \geqslant q'_n$ must be satisfied.

CHAPTER 5

Stream Ciphers

This chapter introduces stream ciphers, a fundamental class of symmetric-key algorithms that uses the same key for both encryption and decryption. In the context of modern symmetric cryptography, cryptosystems are primarily classified into two categories: block ciphers and stream ciphers.

A block cipher operates on fixed-length groups of bits, referred to as blocks. Specifically, a plaintext block m of length n is represented as a vector of bits $(m_1, m_2, \ldots, m_n)$, where each $m_i \in \{0, 1\}$. The encryption algorithm transforms this input into a corresponding ciphertext block $c = (c_1, c_2, \ldots, c_n)$ of the same length n. Because these algorithms rely on a shared secret key, they are formally known as symmetric block ciphers.

A stream cipher can be conceptually viewed as a specialized case of a block cipher where the block length is reduced to a single bit ($n = 1$). Also known as a sequence cipher, a stream cipher processes the plaintext bit by bit to generate the ciphertext. As discussed in Section 3.3, while the Vernam cipher offers perfect secrecy, it requires a key length equal to that of the plaintext. This requirement imposes significant challenges regarding key generation, distribution, and storage. Consequently, the development of practical stream ciphers was driven by the urgent need to address these logistical limitations while maintaining a high level of security.

Topics covered in this chapter:

- The definition and basic operation mode of stream ciphers.
- The encryption and decryption steps of the RC4 cipher.
- The encryption and decryption steps of the ZUC cipher.

5.1 RC4

The operational mode of a stream cipher is illustrated in Figure 5-1. Let the plaintext be denoted by $M = (m_1, m_2, \ldots, m_l)$, where l is a positive integer, and let K represent the secret key. In a stream cipher, the key K typically has a fixed length that is significantly shorter than the plaintext. To perform encryption, a keystream generator is employed to expand the key into a long keystream $(k_1, k_2, k_3, \ldots, k_l)$ of the same length as the plaintext.

DOI: 10.1201/9781042011087-5

The ciphertext is obtained by computing the bitwise exclusive-OR (XOR) of the plaintext and the keystream, denoted as $c_i = m_i \oplus k_i$. The decryption process mirrors the encryption phase. It requires the receiver to possess both the same secret key and the identical keystream generator to reproduce the keystream. Example 5.1.1 demonstrates the special case where the key length equals the plaintext length.

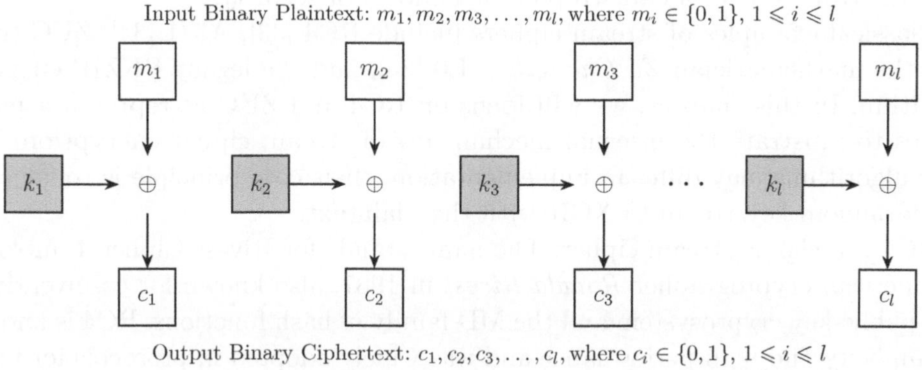

Figure 5-1: Stream Cipher

The fundamental distinction between a practical stream cipher and the Vernam cipher lies in the nature of the keystream. While the Vernam cipher requires a truly random keystream, modern stream ciphers rely on a pseudorandom keystream generated from the seed key. For a formal definition of pseudorandomness, please refer to Section 13.5.

Example 5.1.1 Encrypt the decimal plaintext **704** using a basic stream cipher with the key stream **100101011001**.
Solution: First, convert the decimal plaintext 704 into its binary representation, that is $704_{10} = 001011000000_2$. Then, perform a bitwise exclusive-OR (XOR) operation between the binary plaintext and the key. The detailed calculation process is illustrated in Table 5-1.

Table 5-1: Simple Stream Cipher Encryption

Plaintext	0	0	1	0	1	1	0	0	0	0	0	0
Key	1	0	0	1	0	1	0	1	1	0	0	1
Operation	$\oplus$	$\oplus$	$\oplus$	$\oplus$	$\oplus$	$\oplus$	$\oplus$	$\oplus$	$\oplus$	$\oplus$	$\oplus$	$\oplus$
Ciphertext	1	0	1	1	1	0	0	1	1	0	0	1

The resulting ciphertext in binary form is **101110011001**, which corresponds to the decimal value **2969**. ■

We begin by examining the security implications of stream ciphers. Consider a scenario where an adversary, Eve, successfully obtains a segment of the plaintext. In the context of stream ciphers, possession of both a plaintext segment and its corresponding ciphertext allows for the immediate recovery of the keystream segment used for encryption. This vulnerability implies that the security of a stream cipher relies fundamentally on the properties of its keystream, rather than the complexity of the mixing operation. To ensure security, the keystream must exhibit cryptographically strong pseudorandomness, necessitating the use of a cryptographically secure random number generator.

This characteristic highlights the critical importance of keystream management. If a keystream is ever reused, attackers can exploit the linear relationship between two ciphertexts to eliminate the keystream and potentially recover the plaintext. Such an error leads to a catastrophic breakdown of security.

Classical examples of stream ciphers include RC4 [33], A5/1 [34], ZUC (named after the mathematician *Zu Chongzhi*), E0 [35], and the legacy PKZIP encryption algorithm. In this chapter, we will focus on RC4 and ZUC as representative case studies to illustrate the internal mechanisms of stream cipher encryption. While other algorithms may differ in implementation, their core principle is to generate a pseudorandom keystream to XOR with the plaintext.

RC4 is a classic stream cipher. The name stands for Rivest Cipher 4, introduced by American cryptographer *Ronald Rivest* in 1987, also known for co-inventing the RSA public-key cryptosystem and the MD family of hash functions. RC4 is known for its simplicity and high-performance and was widely adopted in protocols for internet security (such as SSL/TLS) and wireless local area networks (WEP). Initially, the algorithm was maintained as a trade secret with its internal specifications undisclosed. However, in 1994, the code was reverse-engineered and anonymously posted to the Cypherpunks mailing list, effectively placing it in the public domain.

5.1.1 Encryption/Decryption

The RC4 consists of two parts

1) Key Scheduling Algorithm (KSA).
2) Pseudo-Random Generation Algorithm (PRGA).

The initialization phase of RC4 employs a variable-length secret key, often referred to as the seed, to configure the internal state vector, or permutation S. Typically, this permutation S contains 256 elements, initially populated with the identity permutation $\{0, 1, 2, \ldots, 255\}$. During the Key-Scheduling Algorithm (KSA), the user-provided key, typically ranging from 1 to 256 bytes in length, is utilized to permute the values within the S-box.

The specific algorithmic steps are detailed below.

1) **Initialization of Permutation S**: Let $n = 8$ be the word size. The state vector S is initialized with integers ranging from 0 to 255. Let i and j be two 8-bit indices used to reference elements within the vector. Note that each location in S stores exactly one byte. This initial structure is depicted in Figure 5-2.

Permutation S	0	1	2	3	$\cdots$	254	255

Figure 5-2: Initialization of State Vector S

2) **Key Expansion**: The input key (seed) can be of arbitrary length. Conceptually, if the key is shorter than 256 bytes, it is cyclically repeated until it fills a temporary vector of length 256. In implementation, this is handled efficiently using modulo arithmetic. This process is illustrated in Figure 5-3.

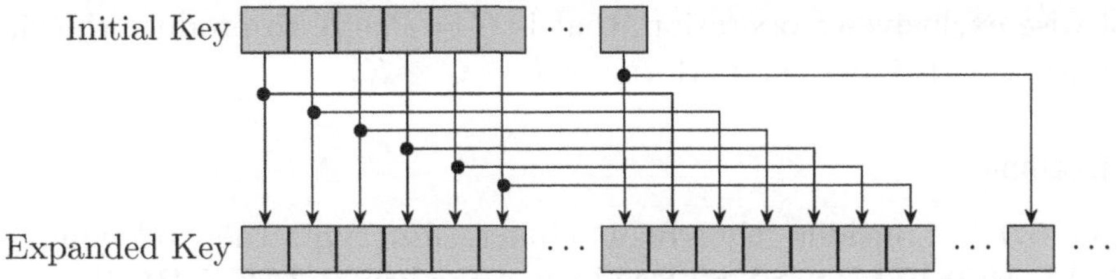

Figure 5-3: Key Expansion Concept

3) **Key-Scheduling Algorithm (KSA)**: The KSA transforms the initial state and the secret key into a scrambled random permutation S. The logic is shown in Figure 5-4 and the Python implementation below.

```
def KSA(key):
    """Initialization of State Vector S"""
    key_length = len(key)
    S = [i for i in range(256)]
    j = 0
    """Scrambling S based on the Key"""
    for i in range(256):
        j = (j + S[i] + key[i % key_length]) % 256
        S[i], S[j] = S[j], S[i]  # Swap values
    return S
```

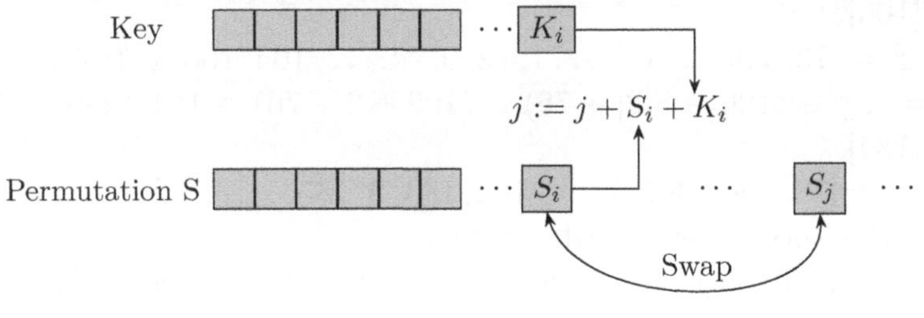

Figure 5-4: RC4 Key-Scheduling Algorithm Diagram

4) **Pseudo-Random Generation Algorithm (PRGA)**: This phase generates the keystream byte-by-byte. Before generation begins, the algorithm must strictly reset both indices i and j to zero. It then executes a continuous loop: updating indices, swapping elements in S, and outputting a keystream byte K. The Python code is provided below.

```
def PRGA(S):
    i = 0
    j = 0
    while True:
        i = (i + 1) % 256
        j = (j + S[i]) % 256
        S[i], S[j] = S[j], S[i]  # Swap values
        K = S[(S[i] + S[j]) % 256]
        yield K  # Output keystream byte
```

5) **Encryption/Decryption**: The algorithm outputs an n-bit byte K as the keystream. This byte is then combined with the plaintext byte P using the

bitwise exclusive-or operation, that is $C = P \oplus K$ to produce the ciphertext. Decryption is identical, performing $P = C \oplus K$.

5.1.2 Example

Example 5.1.2 Consider the RC4 cipher. Encrypt the following message "**GLOBAL POSITION SYSTEM**" using the key "**I LIKE RC4**".

Solution: First, we process the key. Since the key length is 10 bytes, it must be repeated to fill the 256-byte state vector during the KSA phase. The conversion of the key characters into their corresponding ASCII byte values is shown in Table 5-2.

Table 5-2: RC4 Keystream

Index	0	1	2	3	4	5	6	7	8	9	10	11	12	13	14	···
Character	I		L	I	K	E		R	C	4	I		L	I	K	···
Value (Dec)	73	32	76	73	75	69	32	82	67	52	73	32	76	73	75	···

Based on the key generated above, the Permutation S is initialized. Starting with the identity permutation, we update the state. We detail the first few iterations of the loop ($i = 0, 1, 2$).

1) For $i = 0$, $j \equiv (0 + S[0] + 73) \equiv 73 \pmod{256}$. Swap $S[0]$ and $S[73]$.
   State: $S = [73, 1, 2, 3, \ldots, 71, 72, \mathbf{0}, 74, 75, \ldots, 254, 255]$.
2) For $i = 1$, $j \equiv (73 + S[1] + 32) \equiv (73 + 1 + 32) \equiv 106 \pmod{256}$. Swap $S[1]$ and $S[106]$.
   State: $S = [73, \mathbf{106}, 2, 3, \ldots, 71, 72, 0, 74, \ldots, 104, 105, \mathbf{1}, 107, \ldots, 254, 255]$.
3) For $i = 2$, $j \equiv (106 + S[2] + 76) \equiv (106 + 2 + 76) \equiv 184 \pmod{256}$. Swap $S[2]$ and $S[184]$.
   State: $S = [73, 106, \mathbf{184}, 3, \ldots, 182, 183, \mathbf{2}, 185, \ldots, 255]$.
4) Repeat the above steps until $i = 255$.

The final state of the Permutation S after the KSA phase is shown in Table 5-3.

Table 5-3: RC4 Permutation S Values

Index	0	1	2	3	4	5	6	7	8	9	10	11	12	13	14	15
0	73	75	244	50	87	156	41	27	193	163	26	165	146	81	40	15
1	172	124	100	143	25	32	74	80	98	192	250	83	178	208	112	36
2	70	164	153	62	130	251	21	189	102	93	211	71	89	115	117	23
3	111	212	10	76	214	213	135	3	245	254	51	108	241	132	149	4
4	168	126	31	35	16	86	6	203	147	220	119	173	176	121	248	29
5	5	207	92	95	106	158	91	82	22	190	145	67	148	194	206	68
6	42	161	239	97	155	8	232	199	19	202	99	197	167	252	104	103
7	85	159	96	72	219	230	237	113	107	127	60	114	141	209	116	123
8	249	210	142	1	154	188	191	105	222	185	20	218	184	94	46	247
9	238	18	77	166	136	59	52	217	39	118	66	225	49	169	229	150
10	53	134	34	79	129	120	139	37	38	43	28	122	187	177	160	17
11	109	64	242	13	61	7	234	182	246	216	174	196	223	9	57	138
12	227	56	180	200	240	151	54	226	243	0	162	133	175	131	125	2
13	63	204	233	181	101	170	224	11	201	33	45	110	215	235	236	47
14	253	179	48	221	231	205	65	183	255	198	152	14	12	88	24	84
15	58	78	186	137	140	30	228	171	55	44	90	69	195	157	128	144

Next, we generate the keystream. We reset indices i and j to zero and begin the generation loop.

1) **For Loop 1**: $i \equiv (0+1) \equiv 1 \pmod{256}$; $j \equiv (0+S[1]) \equiv (0+75) \equiv 75 \pmod{256}$.
   Swap $S[1]$ and $S[75]$. Now $S[1]=173, S[75]=75$.
   $t \equiv (S[1]+S[75]) \equiv (173+75) \equiv 248 \pmod{256}$.
   Keystream $K = S[248] = \mathbf{55}$.
2) **For Loop 2** : $i \equiv (1+1) \equiv 2 \pmod{256}$; $j \equiv (75+S[2]) \equiv (75+244) \equiv 63 \pmod{256}$.
   Swap $S[2]$ and $S[63]$. Now $S[2]=4, S[63]=244$.
   $t \equiv (S[2]+S[63]) \equiv (4+244) \equiv 248 \pmod{256}$.
   Keystream $K = S[248] = \mathbf{55}$.
3) **For Loop 3**: $i \equiv (2+1) \equiv 3 \pmod{256}$; $j \equiv (63+S[3]) \equiv (63+50) \equiv 113 \pmod{256}$.
   Swap $S[3]$ and $S[113]$. Now $S[3]=159, S[113]=50$.
   $t \equiv (S[3]+S[113]) \equiv (159+50) \equiv 209 \pmod{256}$.
   Keystream $K = S[209] = \mathbf{204}$.
4) This process repeats until we have generated enough keystream bytes to match the plaintext length.

The final step is the bitwise XOR of the plaintext and the generated keystream. The result is illustrated in Table 5-4.

Table 5-4: Example Process of RC4

Index	0	1	2	3	4	5	6	7	8	9	⋯	19	20	21
Plaintext	71	76	79	66	65	76	32	80	79	83	⋯	84	69	77
Key	55	55	204	119	3	105	126	218	213	23	⋯	12	217	233
Ciphertext	112	123	131	53	66	37	94	138	154	68	⋯	88	156	164
Hexadecimal	70	7B	83	35	42	25	5E	8A	9A	44	⋯	58	9C	A4

The ciphertext in hexadecimal is `0x707B833542255E8A9A449AD12760C75D5FE3C3589CA4`.

Decryption is computationally identical to encryption. The receiver generates the same keystream using the secret key and performs a bitwise XOR with the ciphertext to recover the plaintext. ■

5.1.3 Cryptanalysis

RC4 design avoids the use of Linear Feedback Shift Registers (LFSRs), the idea of RC4 is to manipulate the elements by swapping them to achieve superior randomness. Unlike the One-Time Pad, RC4 is a computational cipher whose security relies on the generator's ability to produce a keystream that is indistinguishable from a truly random sequence. Theoretically, if an adversary can distinguish the RC4 keystream from a truly random sequence with probability significantly better than random guessing, the cipher is considered broken. Unfortunately, extensive research has demonstrated that RC4 fails to meet this standard of indistinguishability.

In 1997, *Golic* [36] described a linear statistical weakness of RC4, showing that by analyzing multiple output values, one could distinguish RC4's keystream from a truly random sequence.

Finney [37] discovered a class of internal states is called "Finney states", that the RC4 algorithm can never enter. This discovery proved that the state transition graph of RC4 is not uniform and provided early evidence of the algorithm's non-random structural properties.

Knudsen [38] proposed efficient state-guessing attacks. These methods involve guessing a portion of the unknown internal state and verifying the guess against the observed keystream. If successful, this allows the attacker to reconstruct the entire internal state and predict all future keystream bytes.

In 2001, *Fluhrer, Mantin, and Shamir* published the seminal paper [39]. They introduced the **FMS attack**, which exploits correlations between the visible IVs and the values in the internal Permutation S. This vulnerability allows an attacker to reconstruct the secret key by passively collecting a sufficient number of encrypted packets.

In 2015, the IETF officially prohibited the use of RC4 in TLS implementations. [40].

5.2 ZUC STREAM CIPHER

The ZUC stream cipher, is named after the renowned ancient Chinese astronomer, inventor and mathematician *Zu Chongzhi*(429 – 500). The ZUC stream cipher was jointly specified and designed by the *Beijing Institute of Information Science and Technology*, the *Institute of Software at the Chinese Academy of Sciences*, and the *Research and Education Center for Data and Communication Protection at the Chinese Academy of Sciences*. The design team was led by Professor *Feng Dengguo*, a prominent academician at CAS.

ZUC is primarily used in wireless communication. In September 2011, it was standardized by the 3rd Generation Partnership Project (3GPP) as the encryption algorithm for 4G mobile communication (Long Term Evolution, LTE), under the standard designation TS 35.221, making it the first cryptographic algorithm from China to be internationally recognized. Later, ZUC was issued as the Cryptography StandardizationTechnical Committee of China (GM/T 0001-2012) [41] in March 2012, and was formally published as a national standard (GB/T 33133-2016) [42] in October 2016, demonstrating the algorithm's robustness and global acceptance.

5.2.1 Encryption/Decryption

The overall structure of the ZUC algorithm is shown in Figure 5-5. The ZUC algorithm consists of three parts: the top part is a Linear Feedback Shift Register (LFSR) of 16 stages; the middle part is Bit Reorganization(BR); the bottom part is the non-linear function F.

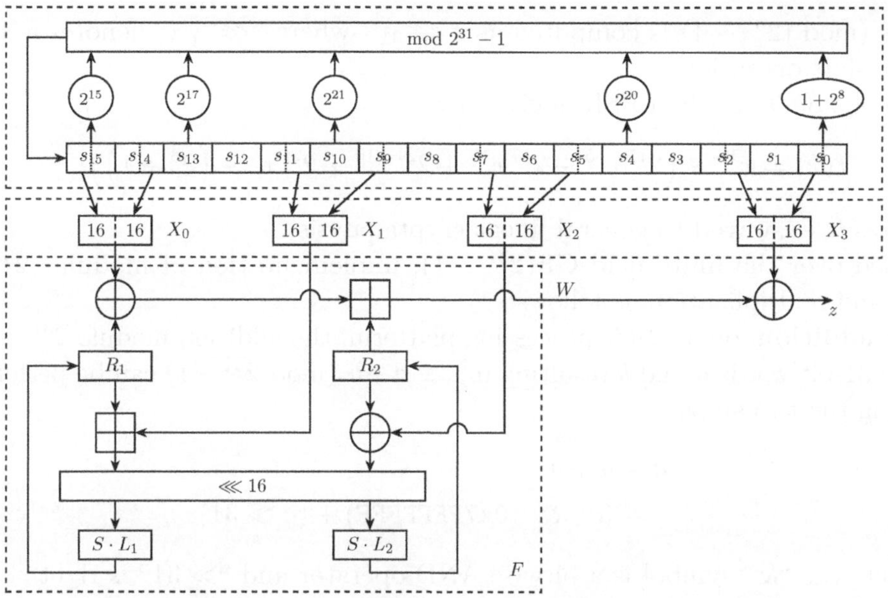

Figure 5-5: General Structure of ZUC [1][1]

We introduce **LFSR** first. The LFSR consists sixteen of 31-bit cells s_i, where $0 \leqslant i \leqslant 15$, giving 496 bits in total. The LFSR operations have two modes: initialization mode and working mode.

In the **initialization mode**, the LFSR receives a 31-bit input word u and updates the register cells s_i where $0 \leqslant i \leqslant 15$ and giving 496 bits in total. The computation process is as follows:

$$v \equiv 2^{15}s_{15} + 2^{17}s_{13} + 2^{21}s_{10} + 2^{20}s_4 + \left(1 + 2^8\right)s_0 \pmod{2^{31}-1} \quad (5\text{-}1)$$

$$s_{16} \equiv (v + u) \pmod{2^{31}-1} \quad (5\text{-}2)$$

If $s_{16} = 0$, then set $s_{16} = 2^{31} - 1$

$$(s_1, s_2, \ldots, s_{15}, s_{16}) \rightarrow (s_0, s_1, \ldots, s_{14}, s_{15})$$

where "→" is element-wisely assign left vector to right vector.

In the **working mode**, the LFSR does not receive any input, updates the register cells s_i where $0 \leqslant i \leqslant 15$ only, as follows:

$$s_{16} \equiv 2^{15}s_{15} + 2^{17}s_{13} + 2^{21}s_{10} + 2^{20}s_4 + \left(1 + 2^8\right)s_0 \pmod{2^{31}-1} \quad (5\text{-}3)$$

If $s_{16} = 0$, then set $s_{16} = 2^{31} - 1$

$$(s_1, s_2, \ldots, s_{15}, s_{16}) \rightarrow (s_0, s_1, \ldots, s_{14}, s_{15})$$

Every value in the LFSR cells is an element defined over the finite field GF($2^{31}-1$), it can be written in a binary representation as

$$x = x_0 2^0 + x_1 2^1 + \cdots + x_{30} 2^{30}, \text{ where } x_i \in \{0,1\} \text{ and } 0 \leqslant i \leqslant 30 \quad (5\text{-}4)$$

[1]Liu, Fukang, et al. "New cryptanalysis of ZUC-256 initialization using modular differences". IACR Transactions on Symmetric Cryptology (2022): 152-190.

Then $2^i x \pmod{(2^{31}-1)}$ is computed as $x \lll_{31} i$ where "$\lll_{31} i$" denotes a 31-bit left cyclic shift operation.

The polynomial of the LFSR is given by

$$f(x) = x^{16} - \left(2^{15}x^{15} + 2^{17}x^{13} + 2^{21}x^{10} + 2^{20}x^4 + \left(2^8+1\right)\right) \tag{5-5}$$

This makes it unswayed to general linear cryptanalysis.

Defined over the finite field GF($2^{31}-1$), implementation of modular $2^{31}-1$ addition and multiplication as follows:

1) For **addition**, on a 32-bit processing platform, the addition modulo $2^{31}-1$ for two 31-bit words a and b resulting in $c \equiv a+b \pmod{2^{31}-1}$ can be performed using the two steps

$$c = a + b \tag{5-6}$$

$$c = (c \quad \& \quad \texttt{0x7FFFFFFF}) + (c \gg 31) \tag{5-7}$$

where the "&" symbol is a bitwise AND operator and "$\gg 31$" is right shift of a 32-bit word by 31 bits.

2) For **multiplication**, $ab \pmod{2^{31}-1}$ can be computed as

$$ab \pmod{2^{31}-1} \equiv (a \lll_{31} i) + (a \lll_{31} j) + (a \lll_{31} k) \pmod{2^{31}-1} \tag{5-8}$$

where $b = 2^i + 2^j + 2^k$, "$\lll_{31} i$" is the 31-bit left circular shift of a 32-bit word by i bits.

Next, we introduce **Bit Reorganization**(BR). The input consists 128 bits from the LFSR register cells $s_0, s_2, s_5, s_7, s_9, s_{11}, s_{14}, s_{15}$ and output four 32-bit words X_0, X_1, X_2, X_3. The first three outputs used by the Non-linear function F and the last one XOR-ed with the output of F. The BR process is performed as follows:

$$X_0 = s_{15H} \| s_{14L} \quad X_1 = s_{11L} \| s_{9H} \quad X_2 = s_{7L} \| s_{5H} \quad X_3 = s_{2L} \| s_{0H} \tag{5-9}$$

where s_{iH}(or s_{iL}) mean that extract the most(or least) significant 16 bits of a word, $0 \leqslant i \leqslant 15$, and "$\|$" is string concatenation operator.

The final part is **Non-linear function** F. The function F contains two 32-bit memory unit variables R_1 and R_2. Taking X_0, X_1, X_2 as the input and the output is one 32-bit word W. The computation process is as follows:

$$W = (X_0 \oplus R_1) \boxplus R_2 \tag{5-10}$$

$$W_1 = R_1 \boxplus X_1 \tag{5-11}$$

$$W_2 = R_2 \oplus X_2 \tag{5-12}$$

$$R_1 = S\left[L_1\left(W_{1L} \| W_{2H}\right)\right] \tag{5-13}$$

$$R_2 = S\left[L_2\left(W_{2L} \| W_{1H}\right)\right] \tag{5-14}$$

Here, "$\boxplus$" is the modular 2^{32} addition and $S = (S_0, S_1, S_0, S_1)$ is a 32×32 S-box. S-box composed of four smaller S-boxes, where S_0 and S_1 are two different 8 to 8 bits S-boxes, they are shown in Table 5-5 and Table 5-6 of hexadecimal. Let the

32-bit input to the S-Box be X and the 32-bit output be Y. They can be represented as

$$X = x_0 \| x_1 \| x_2 \| x_3 \tag{5-15}$$
$$Y = y_0 \| y_1 \| y_2 \| y_3 \tag{5-16}$$

L_1, L_2 are two 32×32 linear transformations which are defined as follows:

$$L_1(X) = X \oplus (X \lll 2) \oplus (X \lll 10) \oplus (X \lll 18) \oplus (X \lll 24) \tag{5-17}$$
$$L_2(X) = X \oplus (X \lll 8) \oplus (X \lll 14) \oplus (X \lll 22) \oplus (X \lll 30) \tag{5-18}$$

where "$\lll i$" is circular left shift of a 32-bit word by i bits.

Table 5-5: ZUC S-Box S_0

	0	1	2	3	4	5	6	7	8	9	A	B	C	D	E	F
0	3E	72	5B	47	CA	E0	00	33	04	D1	54	98	09	B9	6D	CB
1	7B	1B	F9	32	AF	9D	6A	A5	B8	2D	FC	1D	08	53	03	90
2	4D	4E	84	99	E4	CE	D9	91	DD	B6	85	48	8B	29	6E	AC
3	CD	C1	F8	1E	73	43	69	C6	B5	BD	FD	39	63	20	D4	38
4	76	7D	B2	A7	CF	ED	57	C5	F3	2C	BB	14	21	06	55	9B
5	E3	EF	5E	31	4F	7F	5A	A4	0D	82	51	49	5F	BA	58	1C
6	4A	16	D5	17	A8	92	24	1F	8C	FF	D8	AE	2E	01	D3	AD
7	3B	4B	DA	46	EB	C9	DE	9A	8F	87	D7	3A	80	6F	2F	C8
8	B1	B4	37	F7	0A	22	13	28	7C	CC	3C	89	C7	C3	96	56
9	07	BF	7E	F0	0B	2B	97	52	35	41	79	61	A6	4C	10	FE
A	BC	26	95	88	8A	B0	A3	FB	C0	18	94	F2	E1	E5	E9	5D
B	D0	DC	11	66	64	5C	EC	59	42	75	12	F5	74	9C	AA	23
C	0E	86	AB	BE	2A	02	E7	67	E6	44	A2	6C	C2	93	9F	F1
D	F6	FA	36	D2	50	68	9E	62	71	15	3D	D6	40	C4	E2	0F
E	8E	83	77	6B	25	05	3F	0C	30	EA	70	B7	A1	E8	A9	65
F	8D	27	1A	DB	81	B3	A0	F4	45	7A	19	DF	EE	78	34	60

Table 5-6: ZUC S-Box S_1

	0	1	2	3	4	5	6	7	8	9	A	B	C	D	E	F
0	55	C2	63	71	3B	C8	47	86	9F	3C	DA	5B	29	AA	FD	77
1	8C	C5	94	0C	A6	1A	13	00	E3	A8	16	72	40	F9	F8	42
2	44	26	68	96	81	D9	45	3E	10	76	C6	A7	8B	39	43	E1
3	3A	B5	56	2A	C0	6D	B3	05	22	66	BF	DC	0B	FA	62	48
4	DD	20	11	06	36	C9	C1	CF	F6	27	52	BB	69	F5	D4	87
5	7F	84	4C	D2	9C	57	A4	BC	4F	9A	DF	FE	D6	8D	7A	EB
6	2B	53	D8	5C	A1	14	17	FB	23	D5	7D	30	67	73	08	09
7	EE	B7	70	3F	61	B2	19	8E	4E	E5	4B	93	8F	5D	DB	A9
8	AD	F1	AE	2E	CB	0D	FC	F4	2D	46	6E	1D	97	E8	D1	E9

(Continued)

Table 5-6 ZUC S-Box S_1(Continued)

	0	1	2	3	4	5	6	7	8	9	A	B	C	D	E	F
9	4D	37	A5	75	5E	83	9E	AB	82	9D	B9	1C	E0	CD	49	89
A	01	B6	BD	58	24	A2	5F	38	78	99	15	90	50	B8	95	E4
B	D0	91	C7	CE	ED	0F	B4	6F	A0	CC	F0	02	4A	79	C3	DE
C	A3	EF	EA	51	E6	6B	18	EC	1B	2C	80	F7	74	E7	FF	21
D	5A	6A	54	1E	41	31	92	35	C4	33	07	0A	BA	7E	0E	34
E	88	B1	98	7C	F3	3D	60	6C	7B	CA	D3	1F	32	65	04	28
F	64	BE	85	9B	2F	59	8A	D7	B0	25	AC	AF	12	03	E2	F2

The Python implementation of the F function is shown below.

```
def l1(x):
    return (x ^ rotl_uint32(x, 2) ^ rotl_uint32(x, 10) ^ rotl_uint32(x, 18) ^ rotl_uint32(x, 24))

def l2(x):
    return (x ^ rotl_uint32(x, 8) ^ rotl_uint32(x, 14) ^ rotl_uint32(x, 22) ^ rotl_uint32(x, 30))

def make_uint32(a, b, c, d):
    return ((a << 24) & 0xffffffff) | ((b << 16) & 0xffffffff) | ((c << 8) & 0xffffffff) | d

def f(self):
        W = ((x[0] ^ r[0]) + r[1]) & 0xffffffff
        W1 = (r[0] + x[1]) & 0xffffffff
        W2 = r[1] ^ x[2]
        u = l1(((W1 & 0x0000ffff) << 16) | (W2 \gg  16))
        v = l2(((W2 & 0x0000ffff) << 16) | (W1 \gg  16))
        r = [make_uint32(S0[u \gg  24], S1[(u \gg  16) & 0xFF],S0[(u \gg  8) & 0xFF], S1[u & 0xFF]),
            make_uint32(S0[v \gg  24], S1[(v \gg  16) & 0xFF],S0[(v \gg  8) & 0xFF], S1[v & 0xFF])]
        return W
```

Just like other stream ciphers, ZUC has **key loading** K. It uses an initialization phase before generating a keystream sequence, to fully mix the secret key and the **Initialization Vector** (**IV**). During the initialization phase, K and **IV** are loaded into the LFSR registers. Let K and **IV** be

$$K = K_0 \| K_1 \| \cdots \| K_{15} \tag{5-19}$$

and

$$\mathbf{IV} = \mathbf{IV}_0 \| \mathbf{IV}_1 \| \cdots \| \mathbf{IV}_{15}, \tag{5-20}$$

where K_i and $\mathbf{IV}_i$ are all bytes, $0 \leqslant i \leqslant 15$. Let s_i be

$$s_i = K_i \| d_i \| \mathbf{IV}_i \tag{5-21}$$

where d_i is a 15-bit constant string, as shown in Table 5-7.

Table 5-7: ZUC d_i Constants(in Binary)

d_0 = 100010011010111	d_8 = 100110101111000
d_1 = 010011010111100	d_9 = 010111100010011
d_2 = 110001001101011	d_{10} = 110101111000100
d_3 = 001001101011110	d_{11} = 001101011110001
d_4 = 101011110001001	d_{12} = 101111000100110
d_5 = 011010111100010	d_{13} = 011110001001101
d_6 = 111000100110101	d_{14} = 111100010011010
d_7 = 000100110101111	d_{15} = 100011110101100

Running algorithm, the cipher runs 32 iterations with the output from the F function being feedback to the LFSR instead of producing keystream symbols, perform the following **initialization steps**:

1) Load the initial key K and Initialization Vector **IV** into the LFSR register unit variables $(s_0, s_1, \ldots, s_{14}, s_{15})$, to form the initial state of the LFSR.
2) Set the 32-bit memory unit variables R_1 and R_2 to zero.
3) Repeat the following process 32 times, do following:
   (a) Bit Reorganization;
   (b) $W = F(X_0, X_1, X_2)$;
   (c) Output the 32-bit word W;
   (d) LFSR with Initialization Mode($W \gg 1$) where "$\gg 1$" denotes a logical right shift.

After the initialization, the cipher enters the keystream mode, with the first output word from F being discarded and the following outputs forming the keystream symbols by XOR-ing with X_3. Perform the following **working steps**:

1) Execute the following process:
   (a) Bit Reorganization;
   (b) $F(X_0, X_1, X_2)$;
   (c) LFSR with Work Mode;
2) Repeat the following process L times. Here L is the length of the plaintext, do following:
   (a) Bit Reorganization;
   (b) $Z = F(X_0, X_1, X_2) \oplus X_3$;
   (c) Output the 32-bit key word Z;
   (d) LFSR with Work Mode;

5.2.2 Example

Example 5.2.1 Consider the ZUC cipher. Encrypt the message "**WE ARE UNDER ATTACK**" using the key "**YOU CAN TRY ZUC**", with the **IV** being the same as the key.

Consider the ZUC stream cipher. Encrypt the plaintext message "**WE ARE UNDER ATTACK**" using the secret key "**YOU CAN TRY ZUC**". Assume the Initialization Vector (**IV**) is same as the key.

Solution: The standard ZUC algorithm mandates that both the secret key and the Initialization Vector (**IV**) be exactly 16 bytes (128 bits) in length. The provided key string consists of only 15 bytes. Therefore, padding is required to meet the 16-byte specification. For this example, we append a single byte with the value `0x30` (corresponding to the ASCII character "0") to the end of the string. The resulting 16-byte Key and **IV** are detailed in Table 5-8.

Table 5-8: ZUC Key and IV

Index	0	1	2	3	4	5	6	7	8	9	10	11	12	13	14	15
Character	Y	O	U		C	A	N		T	R	Y		Z	U	C	0
Hexadecimal	59	4F	55	20	43	41	4E	20	54	52	59	20	5A	55	43	30

The first step is **initialization**. The secret key K and the initialization vector **IV** are loaded into the LFSR state cells. Compute s_i for $0 \leqslant i \leqslant 15$. As an example, let us compute s_0. Given the inputs $K_0 = \texttt{0x59}$ and $\mathbf{IV}_0 = \texttt{0x59}$, and $d_0 = \underbrace{100010011010111}_{\text{binary}} = \underbrace{\texttt{0x44D7}}_{\text{hex}}$, the state variable is constructed by concatenating these components. The calculation can be implemented in Python as follows:

```python
def make_uint31(a, b, c):
    return ((a << 23) & 0x7fffffff) | ((b << 8) & 0x7fffffff) | c
```

Thus, $s_0 = K_0 \| d_0 \| \mathbf{IV}_0 = \texttt{0x2CC4D759}$. The resulting initial values for all state variables s_i are listed in Table 5-9.

Table 5-9: Initial State of LFSR

$s_0 = \texttt{2CC4D759}$	$s_4 = \texttt{21D78943}$	$s_8 = \texttt{2A4D7854}$	$s_{12} = \texttt{2D5E265A}$
$s_1 = \texttt{27A6BC4F}$	$s_5 = \texttt{20B5E241}$	$s_9 = \texttt{292F1352}$	$s_{13} = \texttt{2ABC4D55}$
$s_2 = \texttt{2AE26B55}$	$s_6 = \texttt{2771354E}$	$s_{10} = \texttt{2CEBC459}$	$s_{14} = \texttt{21F89A43}$
$s_3 = \texttt{10135E20}$	$s_7 = \texttt{1009AF20}$	$s_{11} = \texttt{101AF120}$	$s_{15} = \texttt{1847AC30}$

Then, initialize the 32-bit state variables R_1 and R_2 to 0. Run 32 rounds of bit reorganization and evaluation of the F function, producing a 32-bit output $W = F(X_0, X_1, X_2)$, followed by the initialization of the LFSR.

As an example, consider the computation of the first two W values. Let $X_0 = s_{15H}|s_{14L} = \texttt{0x308F9A43}$ and set $R_0 = R_1 = 0$. Then, the non-linear function F output is

$$W = (X_0 \oplus R_1) \boxplus R_2 = \texttt{0x308F9A43} \tag{5-22}$$

$$W_1 = R_1 \boxplus X_1 = \texttt{0xF120525E} \tag{5-23}$$

$$W_2 = R_2 \oplus X_2 = \texttt{0xAF20416B} \tag{5-24}$$

$$R_1 = S[L_1(W_{1L}|W_{2H})] = \texttt{0x78BB22FA} \tag{5-25}$$

$$R_2 = S[L_2(W_{2L}|W_{1H})] = \texttt{0x96821FE9} \tag{5-26}$$

Table 5-10, Table 5-11 summarizes the values of key variables during the initialization process.

Table 5-10: ZUC Initialization Steps 1

	S_0	S_1	S_2	S_3	S_4	S_{10}	S_{13}	S_{15}
0	2CC4D759	27A6BC4F	2AE26B55	10135E20	21D78943	2CEBC459	2ABC4D55	1847AC30
1	27A6BC4F	2AE26B55	10135E20	21D78943	20B5E241	101AF120	21F89A43	1A0636EF
2	2AE26B55	10135E20	21D78943	20B5E241	2771354E	2D5E265A	1847AC30	58162259
⋮	⋮	⋮	⋮	⋮	⋮	⋮	⋮	⋮
29	331DD688	4375395C	6B088417	736A5F04	07C3B8FA	1985E837	3F31FDA7	18B1372A
30	4375395C	6B088417	736A5F04	07C3B8FA	0FAD413C	6BDDCA4B	2B147C3A	18F2F7D9
31	6B088417	736A5F04	07C3B8FA	0FAD413C	73ED15D2	2977AEEE	18B1372A	626097AC

Table 5-11: ZUC Initialization Steps 2

	X_0	X_1	X_2	X_3	R_1	R_2	W	S_{15}
0	308F9A43	F120525E	AF20416B	6B555989	78BB22FA	96821FE9	308F9A43	1A0636EF
1	340CAC30	265A59D7	78544EE2	5E204F4D	B09F6E31	8BCF3A81	E339AEB3	58162259
2	B02C36EF	4D552035	13522013	894355C4	3617D25A	21D0AF2D	8C82935F	5D4C893F
⋮	⋮	⋮	⋮	⋮	⋮	⋮	⋮	⋮
29	31627C3A	CA4B63AC	B6301F5A	8417663B	C471E9DB	BA92BFE2	35265300	18F2F7D9
30	31E5372A	AEEE330B	91CFE7DA	5F0486EA	33021FCA	111DA585	B0279ED3	626097AC
31	C4C1F7D9	FDA7D7BB	0D3DA097	B8FAD611	018364B2	8DAA7BD4	08E18D98	6D21036D

The next step is to enter the **working steps**. The number of working steps is equal to the length of the plaintext, which is 19 in this example. Perform the bit reorganization operation, followed by the calculation of the F function. However, the result of the F function is discarded. Then, enter the LFSR working mode. The LFSR values in working mode are shown in Table 5-12.

Table 5-12: ZUC Working Steps

	S_0	S_1	S_2	S_3	S_4	S_{10}	S_{13}	S_{15}
0	736A5F04	07C3B8FA	0FAD413C	73ED15D2	504BB630	3F31FDA7	18F2F7D9	6D21036D
1	07C3B8FA	0FAD413C	73ED15D2	504BB630	6BD691CF	2B147C3A	626097AC	672C8ACE
2	0FAD413C	73ED15D2	504BB630	6BD691CF	31D60D3D	18B1372A	6D21036D	6485E3A9
⋮	⋮	⋮	⋮	⋮	⋮	⋮	⋮	⋮
16	672C8ACE	6485E3A9	6EBB7D74	33F461A3	2E7D40BC	647453FE	5D503F4D	3B2148C7
17	6485E3A9	6EBB7D74	33F461A3	2E7D40BC	3A50C249	2C268D4D	7D2B4943	425576BC
18	6EBB7D74	33F461A3	2E7D40BC	3A50C249	60A08625	15A55B88	3B2148C7	06921831

Finally, the keystream is generated. Internal State of the Finite State is $R_1 =$ 0x018364B2 and $R_2 =$ 0x8DAA7BD4. The result is shown in Table 5-13.

Table 5-13: ZUC Keystream

	X_0	X_1	X_2	X_3	R_1	R_2	Z	S_{15}
0	DA4297AC	7C3A52EF	E837D7AD	413CE6D4	0C3F1931	96F87048	28508826	672C8ACE
1	CE59036D	372A7E63	CA4B63AC	15D20F87	82048543	87A32827	4C8C8523	6485E3A9
2	C90B8ACE	F7D95628	AEEE330B	B6301F5A	1AD19CA5	B8E4C6A1	648228EE	6EBB7D74
⋮	⋮	⋮	⋮	⋮	⋮	⋮	⋮	⋮
17	76424943	8D4DA029	3E0874A1	7D74CE59	665F28FE	3CA31E4F	7E3BB783	425576BC
18	84AA48C7	5B88C8E8	E145C141	61A3C90B	632B7B12	65AE9556	93017E72	06921831
19	0D2476BC	3F4D584D	C9B839B0	40BCDD76	57A87F54	A41B4A0A	C70FD687	1B41E2D1

The keystream is

```
4C8C8523  648228EE  1143A277  76B9EE30  078EA868  6D8BFFD6  3D1BFC17
26219F69  5FDC48BF  CA592D7C  9FB58AC6  835C5FE4  FF1C192B  87062BF0
68F8DE31  53A754AF  7E3BB783  93017E72  C70FD687
```

The ciphertext is

```
4C8C8574 648228AB 1143A257 76B9EE71 078EA83A 6D8BFF93 3D1BFC37
26219F3C 5FDC48F1 CA592D38 9FB58A83 835C5FB6 FF1C190B 87062BB1
68F8DE65 53A754FB 7E3BB7C2 93017E31 C70FD6CC
```

■

5.2.3 Cryptanalysis

There is no obvious weakness that the ZUC cipher, with a 256-bit key, has a key space of 2^{256}. A cryptologist introduces several analysis methods targeting ZUC [44], including

1) Weak key analysis
2) Linear distinguishing analysis
3) Algebraic analysis
4) Guess-and-determine analysis
5) Time-memory-data tradeoff analysis

However, none of these approaches are sufficient to significantly reduce the difficulty of breaking the cipher. Since ZUC operates over the finite field GF$(2^{31} - 1)$, it possesses a high level of cryptographic security. The best known attacks can only reduce the exhaustive search complexity to approximately $\mathcal{O}(2^{126})$ [45]. As a result, ZUC remains resistant to all currently known public cryptanalytic techniques targeting stream ciphers.

5.3 EXERCISES

1) If a sufficiently long keystream is generated, the keystream must eventually repeat. Why?
2) Why does a repeating keystream pose a security risk?
3) Let $\mathcal{P} = \mathcal{C} = \mathcal{K} = \{0,1\}^n$ be the plaintext, ciphertext, and key spaces, respectively. Consider a stream cipher where the ciphertext is generated by $c = p \oplus k$, where $\oplus$ denotes the bitwise XOR operation.
   (a) Show that perfect secrecy implies that for a fixed ciphertext c, every plaintext p is equally likely if the key k is chosen uniformly at random from $\{0,1\}^n$.
   (b) Suppose the same keystream k is used to encrypt two different plaintexts p_1 and p_2, resulting in ciphertexts c_1 and c_2. Show that if Eve intercepts c_1 and c_2 can compute the XOR sum of the two plaintexts. Explain why this is a security vulnerability.
4) Consider a simplified version of RC4, denoted as "Mini-RC4", where the state vector S has a length of $N = 4$ (instead of 256). The elements of S are integers in $\mathbb{Z}_4 = \{0, 1, 2, 3\}$. The Key Scheduling Algorithm (KSA) for Mini-RC4 initializes S as the identity permutation and then updates it using a secret key K.

Input: Key K of length L

Initialization:

For $i = 0$ to $N - 1$:

$S[i] = i$

$j = 0$

Scrambling:

For $i = 0$ to $N - 1$:

$j = (j + S[i] + K[i \pmod{L}]) \pmod{N}$

$\text{Swap}(S[i], S[j])$

Given a key $K = (1, 3)$ with length $L = 2$:

(a) Perform the KSA step-by-step. List the state of the array S and the value of j after each iteration of the loop (for $i = 0$ to 3).

(b) Write down the final permuted state vector S after the KSA is complete.

5) Consider the RC4 stream cipher and answer the following questions:

(a) Reduce the length of the Permutation S to $n = 8$. Given the initial key $K = [1, 2, 3, 6]$, determine the generated keystream.

(b) Suppose the plaintext is $M = [1, 2, 2, 2]$. What is the resulting ciphertext after encryption?

6) Write the code for the RC4 encryption algorithm using the Python or SageMath.

7) Implement the RC4 algorithm. Suppose the key consists of the following 7 bytes: (`0x1A`, `0x2B`, `0x3C`, `0x4D`, `0x5E`, `0x6F`, `0x77`). For each of the following, give S in the form of a 16×16 array where each entry is in hex. Answer the following questions:

(a) List the permutation S and indices i and j after the initialization phase has completed.

(b) List the permutation S and indices i and j after the first 100 bytes of keystream have been generated.

(c) List the permutation S and indices i and j after the first 1000 bytes of keystream have been generated.

8) Consider the RC4 stream cipher and determine the upper bound of its state space.

9) A stream cipher employs a single LFSR with a length of 256 as its keystream generator. Determine the number of plaintext/ciphertext pairs required to mount a successful attack.

10) The ZUC algorithm relies on a LFSR defined over a prime field (specifically modulo $2^{31} - 1$). Consider a simplified LFSR over the field $\mathbb{Z}_{13}$ (integers modulo 13) with length $L = 3$. Let the state of the LFSR at time t be denoted by $S_t = (s_t, s_{t+1}, s_{t+2})$, where each $s_i \in \mathbb{Z}_{13}$. The feedback loop is governed by the recurrence relation

$$s_{t+3} = (3s_t + 5s_{t+1}) \pmod{13}$$

Note that s_{t+2} does not participate in the feedback in this simplified model.

(a) Given the initial state $S_0 = (2, 1, 6)$, calculate the next feedback value s_3.

(b) Determine the subsequent state vector S_1 (which consists of s_1, s_2, s_3).

(c) Calculate the value s_4 and write down the state vector S_2.

11) Consider the ZUC cipher. Given a 32-bit input of `0x1A2B3C4D` to the S-Box-0, determine the output of the S-Box-0.

12) Consider the ZUC cipher. Generate a keystream using the initial key (key seed)

$$K = \texttt{0xffffffffffffffffffffffffffffffff}$$

and the initialization vector

$$\mathbf{IV} = \texttt{0xffffffffffffffffffffffffffffffff}$$

13) Consider the ZUC cipher. Generate a keystream using the initial key (key seed)

$$K = \texttt{0x3d4c4be96a82fdaeb58f641db17b455b}$$

and the initialization vector

$$\mathbf{IV} = \texttt{0x84319aa8de6915ca1f6bda6bfbd8c766}$$

CHAPTER 6

Block Ciphers

This chapter introduces block ciphers, a fundamental primitive of symmetric encryption and a cornerstone of modern cryptography. Unlike stream ciphers that process data bit-by-bit or byte-by-byte, a block cipher operates on a fixed-size block of plaintext as a single unit to produce a ciphertext block of equal size. Typical block lengths are integer multiples of eight bits. For example, the Data Encryption Standard (DES) employs a 64-bit block size.

Block ciphers exhibit various architectural designs. Conceptually, they can be viewed as an "electronic substitution table" or an "electronic codebook". Specifically, an l-bit plaintext block is mapped to a ciphertext block of the same length, and the decryption process applies the inverse transformation. Compared to traditional paper-based codebooks, electronic implementations are easier to update and offer significantly higher security provided the key remains secret.

The theoretical foundations of block cipher design trace back to *Claude E. Shannon*'s seminal 1949 paper, Communication Theory of Secrecy Systems. Shannon introduced two principles that remain central to modern cryptography. **Confusion** seeks to obscure the relationship between the secret key and the ciphertext, typically achieved through substitution. **Diffusion** seeks to obscure the relationship between the plaintext and the ciphertext, typically achieved through permutation.

Representative examples of block ciphers include DES, AES, and SM4. The DES developed by IBM in 1973 and adopted by the *US National Bureau of Standards* (NBS, now called NIST) in 1976, was once the dominant algorithm [46]. However, due to advances in computing power and cryptanalysis, DES is now considered insecure. Its variant, Triple DES extended its lifespan but has largely been superseded by the Advanced Encryption Standard (AES). Designed in 1998 by Belgian cryptographers *Joan Daemen* and *Vincent Rijmen* [47], AES is widely adopted for its robust security and efficiency. SM4 is the Chinese national standard for commercial encryption, commonly used in wireless networks as well as government and financial data protection systems.

From a mathematical perspective, a block cipher constitutes a bijection. Encryption defines a one-to-one mapping from the plaintext space to the ciphertext space, while decryption performs the inverse mapping to ensure distinct recoverability of the plaintext.

DOI: 10.1201/9781042011087-6

Topics covered in this chapter:

- Block cipher modes of operation and their applications
- The fundamental structure of block ciphers: the Feistel cipher
- The encryption and decryption processes of DES
- The encryption and decryption processes of AES
- The encryption and decryption processes of SM4

6.1 BLOCK CIPHER MODES OF OPERATION

6.1.1 ECB

Block ciphers employ various modes of operation to provide confidentiality for messages of arbitrary length. Common modes include **ECB**, **CBC**, **CFB**, **OFB**, **CTR**, and **PCBC** [46]. Among these, the **Electronic Codebook** (ECB) mode represents the most straightforward approach. Unlike modes that chain blocks together or generate a keystream, ECB processes each plaintext block independently. Specifically, the encryption function is applied directly to each block using the same secret key, and decryption is performed by applying the inverse transformation. The operational structure of ECB mode is illustrated in Figure 6-1.

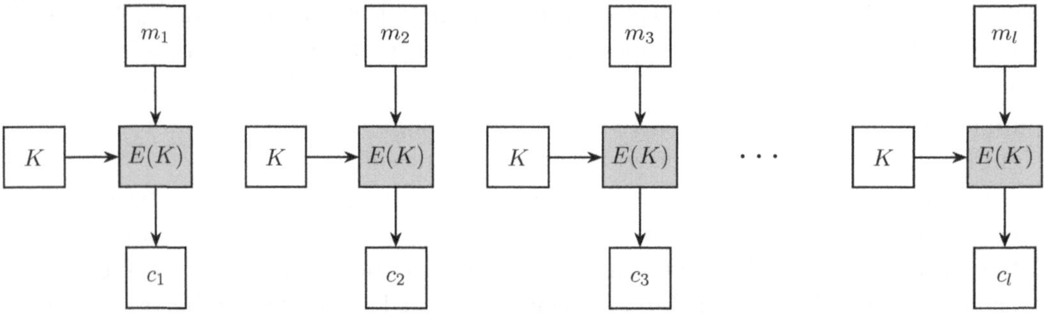

Figure 6-1: ECB Mode

Given a sequence of plaintext blocks $m_1, m_2, \ldots, m_l$ and a fixed secret key K, ECB establishes a deterministic mapping from plaintext to ciphertext blocks. This implies that identical plaintext blocks are transformed into identical ciphertext blocks. If the total length of the message is not an exact multiple of the block size, the final block must be padded according to a specified padding scheme. Formally, let E denote a block cipher with block size n, where m_i and c_i represent bit strings of length n.

The encryption process is given by

$$c_i = E_K(m_i), \quad \text{where } 1 \leqslant i \leqslant l \tag{6-1}$$

The decryption process is given by

$$m_i = E_K^{-1}(c_i), \quad \text{where } 1 \leqslant i \leqslant l \tag{6-2}$$

or equivalently

$$m_i = D_K(c_i) = D_K(E_K(m_i)) \tag{6-3}$$

Advantages of ECB mode include its computational simplicity, suitability for parallel processing, immunity to error propagation between blocks, and its one-to-one correspondence between plaintext and ciphertext.

However, ECB mode has some weaknesses. The same input block always output the same output block. That is, if $m_i = m_j$ then we have $c_i = c_j$. Moreover, because ciphertext blocks are independent, suffers from possible deletion and insertion attacks. A one-bit error in ciphertext gives one whole block error in the decrypted plaintext. Except for special purposes, we never use ECB mode.

6.1.2 CBC

To overcome the deficiencies of ECB, where identical plaintext blocks produce identical ciphertext blocks, the **Cipher Block Chaining** (CBC) mode is used. CBC is an **IV**-based encryption scheme that introduces randomization into the encryption process. As the name implies, this mode chains blocks together: each plaintext block is combined with the preceding ciphertext block via an XOR operation before being encrypted. Consequently, the value of each ciphertext block depends not only on the current plaintext block but also on the entire history of preceding blocks. This chaining mechanism ensures that identical plaintext sequences are encrypted into distinct ciphertext sequences.

To initiate the chaining process for the first block, a non-secret Initialization Vector (**IV**) serves as a pseudo-ciphertext block, denoted as c_0. While the **IV** need not be kept secret from third parties, it must be unpredictable to ensure semantic security. The **IV** must be generated randomly and must not bear any relationship to the plaintext; otherwise, the scheme may be vulnerable to chosen-plaintext attacks [48].

The chaining structure of CBC makes it superior to ECB for encrypting long messages. However, this dependency also implies specific error propagation characteristics. During encryption, a single bit error in a plaintext block will cascade through all subsequent ciphertext blocks. Conversely, during decryption, an error in a received ciphertext block c_i will corrupt the corresponding plaintext block m_i and flip the exact corresponding bits in the subsequent plaintext block m_{i+1}. As with ECB, the last block padded if needed.

Formally, let E be a block cipher with block size n, where m_i and c_i denote bit strings of length n. Let the **IV** be a bit string of length n, defined as $c_0 = \mathbf{IV}$. The operation of CBC mode is illustrated in Figure 6-2.

The encryption process is given by

$$c_1 = E_K\left(m_1 \oplus \mathbf{IV}\right) \tag{6-4}$$

$$c_i = E_K\left(m_i \oplus c_{i-1}\right), \text{ where } 2 \leqslant i \leqslant l \tag{6-5}$$

The decryption process is given by

$$m_1 = D_K\left(c_1\right) \oplus \mathbf{IV} \tag{6-6}$$

$$m_i = D_K\left(c_i\right) \oplus c_{i-1}, \text{ where } 2 \leqslant i \leqslant l \tag{6-7}$$

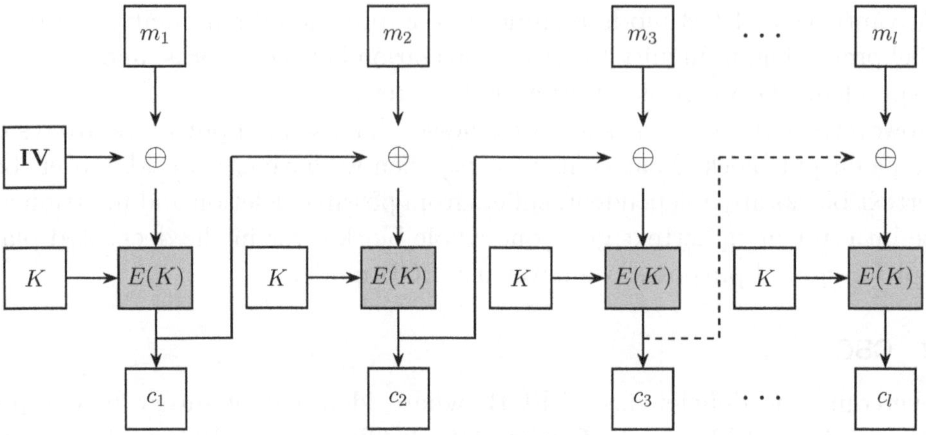

Figure 6-2: CBC Mode

If a ciphertext block encrypted in CBC mode is damaged, due to hard disk failure, network transmission errors, etc., and the block length remains unchanged, then during decryption, at most two plaintext blocks will be corrupted. However, if any data within the ciphertext block is lost, even a single bit, the block length changes, causing all subsequent blocks to be misaligned. As a result, none of the following blocks can be decrypted. Therefore, the ciphertext length in CBC mode must be carefully preserved, and in communication, the plaintext length information should be sent along with the ciphertext to help receiver determine whether the ciphertext has been corrupted.

The CBC mode works not only for encryption but also for ensuring data integrity and authenticity. In this configuration, known as a Message Authentication Code based on CBC (CBC-MAC), Alice processes the plaintext blocks $m_1, m_2, \ldots, m_l$ using a shared secret key K. Unlike CBC encryption, the initialization vector (**IV**) in a standard CBC-MAC is fixed rather than random.

Alice performs the encryption steps but discards all intermediate ciphertext blocks, retaining only the final block C_l. This final block serves as MAC. She transmits the plaintext message and the tag C_l to Bob. Upon receipt, Bob recomputes the CBC-MAC using the same key K and fixed **IV** on the received message. He then compares his computed tag C_l' with the received tag C_l. If $C_l' = C_l$, the message is verified as authentic and unmodified since any alteration to the plaintext bits would result in an unpredictable change to the MAC value.

6.1.3 CFB

The **Cipher Feedback** (CFB) mode operates as a self-synchronizing stream cipher. It utilizes an n-bit shift register, initialized with an Initialization Vector (**IV**), to generate a keystream. This mode also turns a block cipher into a stream cipher. A single bit error in the ciphertext affects both this block and the next, just as in CBC mode. In each step, the register content is encrypted, and the first s bits of the output ($1 \leqslant s \leqslant n$) are XORed with the plaintext segment to produce the ciphertext. This s-bit ciphertext is then shifted into the register to update the state. CFB relies solely on the encryption function for both encryption and decryption and inherently recovers synchronization after transmission errors. The flexibility of s enables low-latency processing suitable for real-time applications.

CFB mode can be divided into several submodes depending on the value of s.

1) CFB-n (known as **full-block feedback** mode, $s = n$), processes an entire block at a time; offers stronger security but introduces higher latency.
2) CFB-1 (known as **bit feedback** mode, $s = 1$), encrypts data one bit at a time, suitable for very low-bandwidth channels.
3) CFB-8 (known as **byte feedback** mode, $s = 8$), encrypts data one byte at a time, widely used in byte-oriented protocols.
4) CFB-s (known as **partial feedback** mode, $1 \leqslant s \leqslant n$), allows tuning s to balance security, performance, and latency.

The underlying mechanism of these submodes is the same. They differ only in how many output bits are taken in each encryption cycle, allowing adaptation to different application scenarios.

Formally, let E be a block cipher with block size n, where m_i and c_i denote bit strings of length n. Let the **IV** be a bit string of length n, defined as $c_0 = \mathbf{IV}$. The operation of full-block CFB mode is illustrated in Figure 6-3.

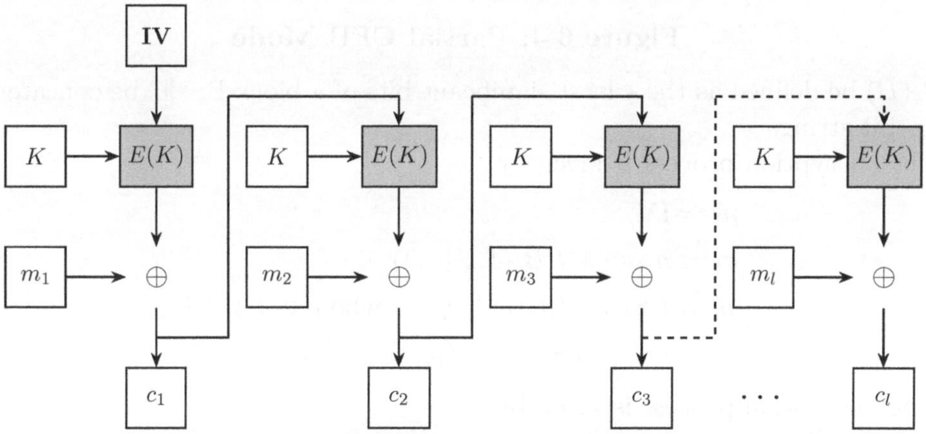

Figure 6-3: CFB Mode

The encryption process is given by

$$c_1 = E_K(\mathbf{IV}) \oplus m_1 \tag{6-8}$$

$$c_i = E_K(c_{i-1}) \oplus m_i, \quad \text{where } 2 \leqslant i \leqslant l \tag{6-9}$$

The decryption process is given by

$$m_1 = E_K(\mathbf{IV}) \oplus c_1 \tag{6-10}$$

$$m_i = E_K(c_{i-1}) \oplus c_i, \quad \text{where } 2 \leqslant i \leqslant l \tag{6-11}$$

Let E be a block cipher of block size n, and the plaintext is divided into segments of s. The partial CFB mode is illustrated in Figure 6-4.

In partial CFB mode, the previous block input is shifted by s positions to the left, and the s least significant positions of the input register are filled with the ciphertext. Let $MSB_s(B)$ be defined as the s most significant bits of a block B;

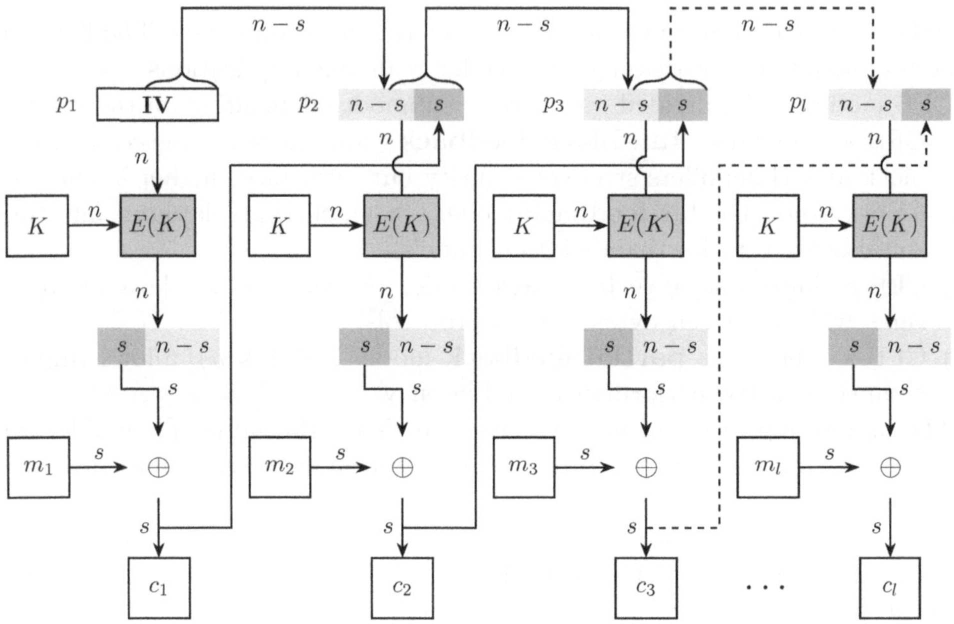

Figure 6-4: Partial CFB Mode

$LSB_s(B)$ be defined as the s least significant bits of a block B; "$\|$" be concatenation of two bit strings.

The encryption process is given by

$$p_1 = \mathbf{IV} \tag{6-12}$$

$$c_1 = m_1 \oplus MSB_s(E_K(p_1)) \tag{6-13}$$

$$p_i = LSB_{n-s}(p_{i-1}) \parallel c_{i-1}, \quad \text{where } 2 \leqslant i \leqslant l \tag{6-14}$$

$$c_i = m_i \oplus MSB_s(E_K(p_i)), \quad \text{where } 2 \leqslant i \leqslant l \tag{6-15}$$

The decryption process is given by

$$p_1 = \mathbf{IV} \tag{6-16}$$

$$m_1 = c_1 \oplus MSB_s(E_K(\mathbf{IV})) \tag{6-17}$$

$$p_i = LSB_{n-s}(p_{i-1}) \parallel c_{i-1}, \quad \text{where } 2 \leqslant i \leqslant l \tag{6-18}$$

$$m_i = c_i \oplus MSB_s(E_K(p_i)), \quad \text{where } 2 \leqslant i \leqslant l \tag{6-19}$$

In CFB-1 mode, the output resembles a random sequence in a one-time pad. However, because the cipher output is generated by computation using pseudorandom numbers, CFB mode cannot achieve the theoretically unbreakable security of a one-time pad.

6.1.4 Other Modes

In addition to the ECB, CBC, and CFB modes described above, several other block cipher modes of operation are widely used, including **Output Feedback** (OFB) mode, **Counter** (CTR) mode [49], and **Propagating Cipher-Block Chaining** (PCBC) mode.

The **Output Feedback** (OFB) mode is similar in structure to that of CFB. In OFB, the output of the encryption function is fed directly back as the input for the next round, whereas CFB uses the previous ciphertext block. This internal feedback mechanism isolates the keystream generation from the plaintext data. Consequently, OFB possesses excellent error containment properties. If a bit error occurs in ciphertext only gives a bit error in the decrypted plaintext.

Because the keystream is generated by a deterministic process driven solely by the secret key and the Initialization Vector (**IV**), it is completely independent of the plaintext. A significant advantage of this design is that the keystream can be precomputed before the message is available. This allows the final encryption or decryption step to be a simple and fast XOR operation. However, this independence also implies that the system is malleable and vulnerable to bit-flipping attacks, where an adversary can manipulate specific bits in the ciphertext to cause predictable changes in the plaintext. To maintain security, the **IV** must be a nonce; reusing an **IV** with the same key would result in keystream reuse, catastrophically compromising confidentiality.

Formally, let E be a block cipher with block size n, where m_i and c_i denote bit strings of length n. Let the **IV** be a bit string of length n, defined as $c_0 = \mathbf{IV}$. The operation of OFB mode is illustrated in Figure 6-5.

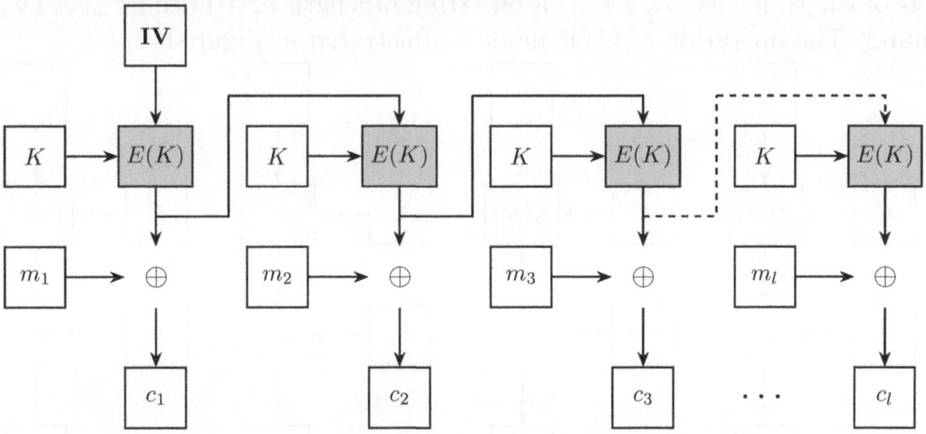

Figure 6-5: OFB Mode

The encryption process of OFB mode is given by

$$p_1 = E_K(\mathbf{IV}) \tag{6-20}$$

$$c_1 = p_1 \oplus m_1 \tag{6-21}$$

$$p_i = E_K(p_{i-1}), \text{ where } 2 \leqslant i \leqslant l \tag{6-22}$$

$$c_i = p_i \oplus m_i, \text{ where } 2 \leqslant i \leqslant l-1 \tag{6-23}$$

$$c_l = MSB_s(p_l) \oplus m_l \tag{6-24}$$

If the last block of plaintext contains s bits and $s < n$, the most significant s bits of the last output block p_l are used for the XOR operation. The remaining $n - s$ bits of p_l are discarded.

The decryption process of OFB mode is given by

$$s_1 = E_K(\mathbf{IV}) \tag{6-25}$$
$$m_1 = s_1 \oplus c_1 \tag{6-26}$$
$$s_i = E_K(s_{i-1}), \ \text{where } 2 \leqslant i \leqslant l \tag{6-27}$$
$$m_i = s_i \oplus c_i, \ \text{where } 2 \leqslant i \leqslant l-1 \tag{6-28}$$
$$m_l = MSB_s(p_l) \oplus c_l \tag{6-29}$$

The **Counter** (CTR) mode is the simplest of the confidentiality-only schemes. The CTR mode is similar in concept to CBC, it is another form of stream cipher. In CTR mode, the input to the encryption function is a counter whose length matches the block size of the cipher. The counter can be thought of as a sequence of unique and nonce, each encryption round uses a completely different counter value. For each block, the counter is encrypted with the key, and the resulting output is XORed with the plaintext block to produce the ciphertext block. This design allows for precomputation of the keystream and enables parallel encryption and decryption, making CTR mode highly efficient for high-throughput applications.

Formally, let E be a block cipher with block size n, where m_i and c_i denote bit strings of length n. Let the **IV** be a bit string of length n, defined as $c_0 = \mathbf{IV}$, T_i be a counter. The operation of CTR mode is illustrated in Figure 6-6.

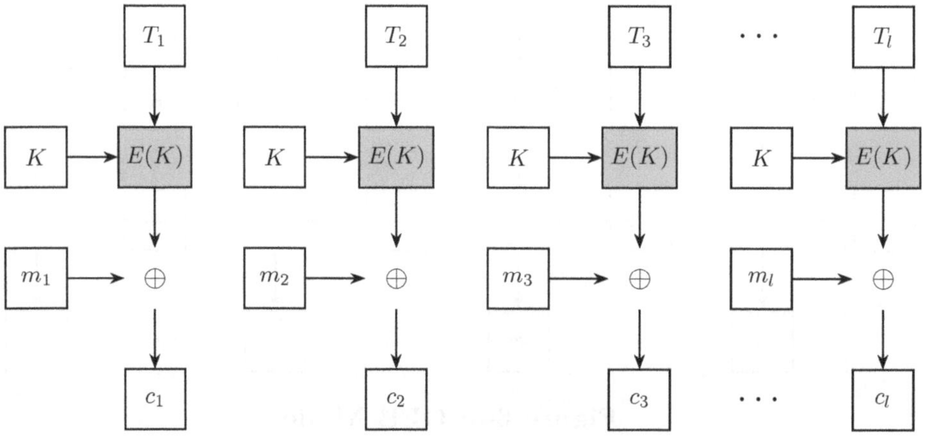

Figure 6-6: CTR Mode

The encryption process of CTR mode is given by

$$c_i = E_K(T_i) \oplus m_i, \ \text{where } 1 \leqslant i \leqslant l-1 \tag{6-30}$$
$$c_l = MSB_s(E_K(T_l)) \oplus m_l \tag{6-31}$$

Similar to OFB mode, if the last block of plaintext contains s bits and $s < n$, the most significant s bits of the last output block p_l are used for the XOR operation.

The decryption process of CTR mode is given by

$$m_i = E_K(T_i) \oplus c_i, \ \text{where } 1 \leqslant i \leqslant l-1 \tag{6-32}$$
$$m_l = MSB_s(E_K(T_l)) \oplus c_l \tag{6-33}$$

The **Propagating Cipher-Block Chaining** (PCBC) mode is a variant of CBC designed to extend error propagation properties. While standard CBC XORs the current plaintext only with the previous ciphertext, PCBC introduces a dual-feedback mechanism. Specifically, before encryption, the current plaintext block is XORed with both the previous plaintext block and the previous ciphertext block.

The defining characteristic of PCBC is its unbounded error propagation. In standard CBC, a bit error in a ciphertext block affects only the corresponding plaintext block and the immediate next block. In contrast, PCBC ensures that a single bit change in a ciphertext block corrupts the decryption of that block and propagates the error to all subsequent blocks in the message. However, this mode has largely fallen out of favor due to its vulnerability to specific swap attacks and the lack of standard semantic security proofs compared to modern authenticated encryption schemes.

Formally, let E be a block cipher with block size n, where m_i and c_i denote bit strings of length n. Let the **IV** be a bit string of length n, defined as $c_0 = \mathbf{IV}$. The operation of PCBC mode is illustrated in Figure 6-7.

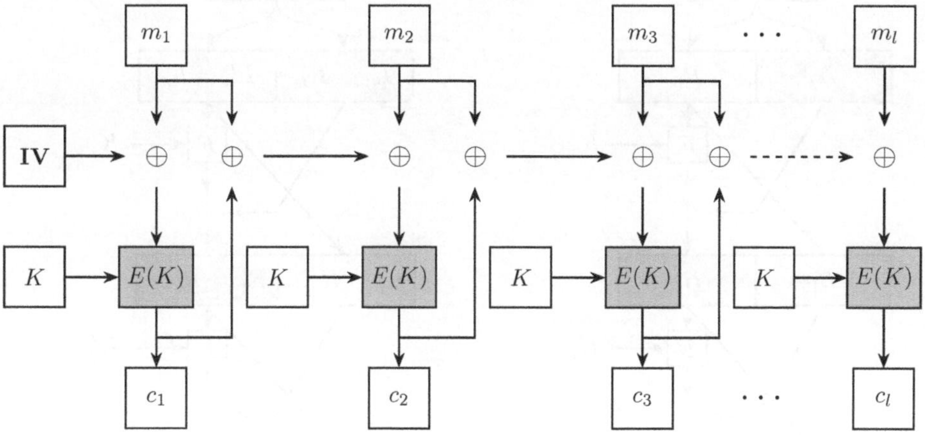

Figure 6-7: PCBC Mode

The encryption process of PCBC mode is given by

$$c_1 = E_K(m_1 \oplus \mathbf{IV}) \tag{6-34}$$

$$c_i = E_K(m_i \oplus m_{i-1} \oplus c_{i-1}), \text{ where } 2 \leqslant i \leqslant l \tag{6-35}$$

The decryption process of PCBC mode is given by

$$m_1 = E_K^{-1}(c_1) \oplus \mathbf{IV} \tag{6-36}$$

$$m_i = E_K^{-1}(c_i) \oplus m_{i-1} \oplus c_{i-1}, \text{ where } 2 \leqslant i \leqslant l \tag{6-37}$$

6.2 FEISTEL CIPHER STRUCTURE

The Feistel structure is a symmetric architectural pattern used in the construction of block ciphers. It was invented in 1973 by IBM cryptographer *Horst Feistel* [50] and inspired by Shannon's principles of **confusion** and **diffusion**, it remains a fundamental design paradigm in modern cryptography. A Feistel structure consists of multiple rounds of an identical round function, applied to one half of the data block, followed by a swap of the two halves. A crucial property of this structure is that the round function itself need not be invertible for the overall cipher to be reversible.

The initial secret key is expanded into a schedule of round subkeys, ensuring that each round utilizes a distinct key derived from the master key. This architecture was famously implemented in the Data Encryption Standard (DES) and its successor, Triple DES (3DES), which were adopted by the *U.S. National Bureau of Standards* (NBS, now known as NIST) as federal standards for government and commercial data protection.

The structure is illustrated in Figure 6-8. Initialization step, split the plaintext block m into a left half L_0 and a right half R_0

$$m = (L_0 \| R_0) \tag{6-38}$$

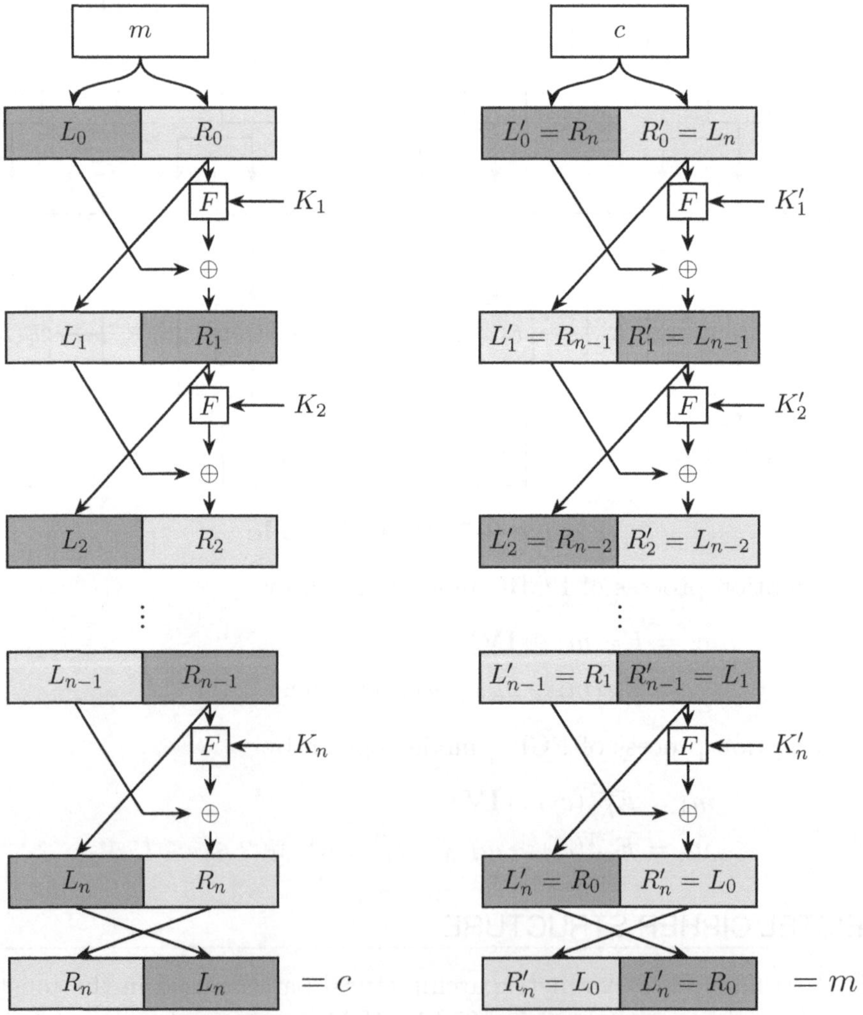

Figure 6-8: Illustration of the Feistel Structure

The **round computation** steps, let F denote the **round function**. For $i = 1, 2, \ldots, n$, the processing steps are defined as follows:

$$L_i = R_{i-1} \tag{6-39}$$
$$R_i = L_{i-1} \oplus F\left(R_{i-1}, K_i\right) \tag{6-40}$$

where K_i is the subkey for round i and "$\oplus$" denotes bitwise XOR operation.

The **finalization** step. After n rounds, the Feistel cipher produces the output pair $(L_n \parallel R_n)$. There are two standard conventions for the finalization step

1) Direct output: Output $(L_n \parallel R_n)$ without any additional processing.
2) Final swap: Perform one additional swap of the two halves and outputs $(R_n \parallel L_n)$, thereby restoring the left and right halves to their original input order relative to the decryption process.

Both conventions are mathematically equivalent regarding security. However, strictly adhering to the specification is essential for interoperability. This textbook adopts the "final swap" convention. Consequently, the final ciphertext c is defined as

$$c = (R_n \parallel L_n) \tag{6-41}$$

The **decryption** process is structurally same as encryption, with the sole exception that the subkeys are applied in reverse order. Starting with the ciphertext $c = (R_n \parallel L_n)$, we initialize the decryption variables as $(L'_0, R'_0) = (R_n, L_n)$. The same round function and swapping logic are then used to reconstruct the plaintext. For $i = 1, 2, \ldots, n$

$$L'_i = R'_{i-1} \tag{6-42}$$
$$R'_i = L'_{i-1} \oplus F(R'_{i-1}, K_i) \tag{6-43}$$

Finally, obtain the plaintext $m = (L_0 \parallel R_0) = (R'_n \parallel L'_n)$.

The **round function** F is not constrained to a fixed formulation; instead, its structure is flexible and varies across distinct cipher designs. Generally, greater complexity in F correlates with improved resistance to cryptanalytic attacks. A poorly designed function, for example, the linear mapping $F(R_{i-1}, K_i) = R_{i-1}$ would yield a system with negligible security.

A fundamental property of the Feistel network is its structural invertibility. We must know that the entire cipher remains reversible even if the round function F itself is non-invertible. This property guarantees that the ciphertext can always be uniquely decrypted back into the plaintext. This requires proving that the Feistel cipher is **reversible**. From the encryption process, we can see that the left and right parts of the ciphertext equal $L'_0 = R_n$ and $R'_0 = L_n$. Assuming $1 \leqslant i \leqslant n$, we have

$$L'_{i-1} = R_{n-i+1} \tag{6-44}$$
$$R'_{i-1} = L_{n-i+1} \tag{6-45}$$

From Equation 6-42, we can derive

$$L'_i = R'_{i-1} \tag{6-46}$$
$$= L_{n-i+1} \tag{6-47}$$
$$= R_{n-i+1-1} \tag{6-48}$$
$$= R_{n-i} \tag{6-49}$$

At the same time, we have

$$R'_i = L'_{i-1} \oplus F\left(R'_{i-1}, K_{n-i+1}\right) \tag{6-50}$$
$$= R_{n-i-1} \oplus F\left(L_{n-i+1}, K_{n-i+1}\right) \tag{6-51}$$
$$= \left[L_{n-i} \oplus F\left(R_{n-i}, K_{n-i+1}\right)\right] \oplus F\left(R_{n-i}, K_{n-i+1}\right) \tag{6-52}$$

By the self-inverse property of the XOR operation ($A \oplus B \oplus B = A$), the two F terms cancel out

$$R'_i = L_{n-i} \tag{6-53}$$

Thus, $(L'_i, R'_i) = (R_{n-i}, L_{n-i})$. This demonstrates that each decryption step systematically recovers the state of the data from the previous encryption round. After n rounds, the original plaintext (L_0, R_0) is fully restored.

The Feistel cipher typically uses a 64-bit plaintext block and a 64-bit key length. A key that is too long reduces encryption and decryption speed, while a key that is too short leads to insufficient key space and reduced security. However, with the continuous improvement of computing speed, 128-bit key lengths are now in use. The number of iterations is not fixed at 16 rounds. In theory, more rounds provide greater security.

Applications of the Feistel cipher can be seen in DES, which will be introduced in the next section.

6.3 DATA ENCRYPTION STANDARD

The Data Encryption Standard (DES) stands as one of the most influential block ciphers of the 20th century. Originally developed by IBM in the early 1970s, it was published as a draft *Federal Information Processing Standard* (FIPS) in the *Federal Register* in March 1975. It was officially adopted by the *U.S. National Bureau of Standards* (now NIST) as FIPS PUB 46 in 1977. Following its federal adoption, DES was recognized by the *American National Standards Institute* (ANSI) as ANSI X3.92 in 1981 and was subsequently incorporated into international standards by the ISO. DES saw widespread deployment across government sectors, banking systems, and industry, marking a significant milestone in the standardization and engineering of modern cryptography.

DES is a classic implementation of the Feistel cipher [51]. It operates on a 64-bit plaintext block and uses a 56-bit effective key (extended with 8 parity bits to form a 64-bit key). The encryption process transforms a 64-bit plaintext block into a 64-bit ciphertext block through 16 identical Feistel rounds, each employing a distinct 48-bit subkey derived from the main key.

Within each round, the data block is divided into a 32-bit left half and a 32-bit right half. The 32-bit right half is processed by the round function F. The output of the round function is then XORed with the left half (L_{i-1}), and the halves are swapped for the next round. After the completion of all 16 rounds, the left and right halves are rejoined (incorporating a final swap to ensure structural invertibility), and a Final Permutation (FP) which is the inverse of the Initial Permutation is applied to produce the ciphertext block.

The detailed structure of DES is illustrated in Figure 6-9.

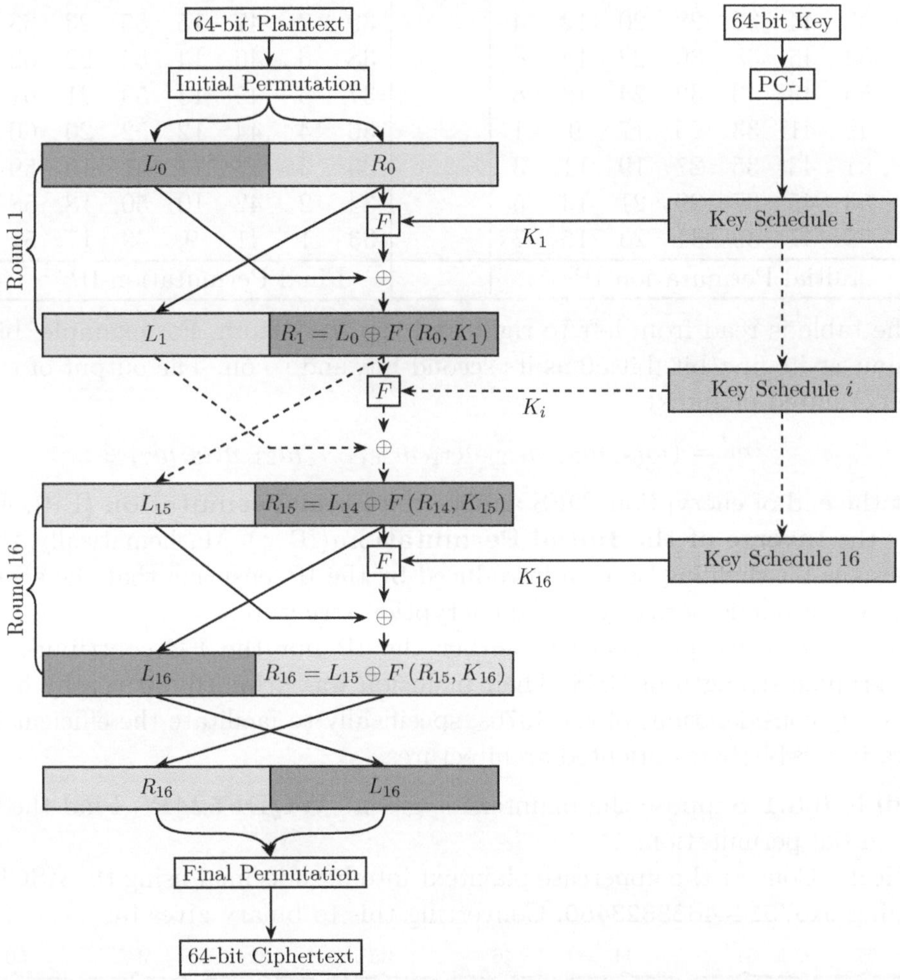

Figure 6-9: The Overall Structure of DES

Although DES is no longer considered secure against modern brute-force attacks and cryptanalysis, its historical impact is profound. As the first widely adopted public standard, DES transformed cryptography from a secretive military domain into an open scientific discipline. Its structure spurred the development of critical cryptanalytic techniques, most notably differential cryptanalysis and linear cryptanalysis, which remain foundational tools in evaluating the security of modern block ciphers.

6.3.1 DES Encryption

6.3.2 Initial and Final Permutation

The **Initial Permutation** (IP) requires permuting each 64-bit plaintext block bit by bit. The permutation operation rearranges the original 64-bit binary plaintext according to a predefined permutation table. The initial permutation table is shown in Table 6-1, consisting of 64 numbers, and is used only before the first round. Other initial permutation tables are also allowed.

Table 6-1: Initial and Final Permutation Tables

58	50	42	34	26	18	10	2		40	8	48	16	56	24	64	32
60	52	44	36	28	20	12	4		39	7	47	15	55	23	63	31
62	54	46	38	30	22	14	6		38	6	46	14	54	22	62	30
64	56	48	40	32	24	16	8		37	5	45	13	53	21	61	29
57	49	41	33	25	17	9	1		36	4	44	12	52	20	60	28
59	51	43	35	27	19	11	3		35	3	43	11	51	19	59	27
61	53	45	37	29	21	13	5		34	2	42	10	50	18	58	26
63	55	47	39	31	23	15	7		33	1	41	9	49	17	57	25
Initial Permutation IP									Final Permutation IP^{-1}							

The table is read from left to right and top to bottom. For example, bit 58 of the input as its first bit, bit 50 as its second bit, and so on. The output of this step is the permuted plaintext

$$m' = (m_{58}, m_{50}, m_{42}, m_{34}, m_{26}, \ldots, m_{23}, m_{15}, m_7) \tag{6-54}$$

At the end of encryption, DES applies the **Final Permutation** (FP), which is simply the **Inverse of the Initial Permutation** (IP^{-1}). Mathematically, this step reverses the bit-shuffling pattern introduced by the IP, ensuring that the decryption process corresponds perfectly to the encryption structure.

From a security perspective, neither the IP nor the FP contributes to the cryptographic strength of DES. Their inclusion was primarily driven by hardware engineering considerations of the 1970s, specifically to facilitate the efficient loading of data into 8-bit(byte) oriented architectures.

Example 6.3.1 Suppose the plaintext is given "**WQDF524P**". Find the output of the initial permutation.

Solution: Convert the uppercase plaintext into hexadecimal using the ASCII table, obtaining `0x5751444635323450`. Converting this to binary gives by

$$\overbrace{01010111}^{57}\overbrace{01010001}^{51}\overbrace{01000100}^{44}\overbrace{01000110}^{46}\overbrace{00110101}^{35}\overbrace{00110010}^{32}\overbrace{00110100}^{34}\overbrace{01010000}^{50}$$

Then, using Table 6-1 to reorder via the initial permutation, the result in hexadecimal is `0x8FF35D1300700029`. ■

6.3.3 Round Function

The DES encryption process through 16 rounds of iteration, as illustrated in Figure 6-10. In each round, the left and right halves from the previous round,

(L_{i-1}, R_{i-1}), are used to compute the next pair (L_i, R_i). For the first round, the plaintext block (after the initial permutation) is divided into (L_0, R_0). After the 16th round, (R_{16}, L_{16}) are concatenated, and the result undergoes the final permutation (IP^{-1}) to produce the final ciphertext $c = \mathrm{IP}^{-1}(R_{16} \parallel L_{16})$. The final permutation table defined by the Table 6-1.

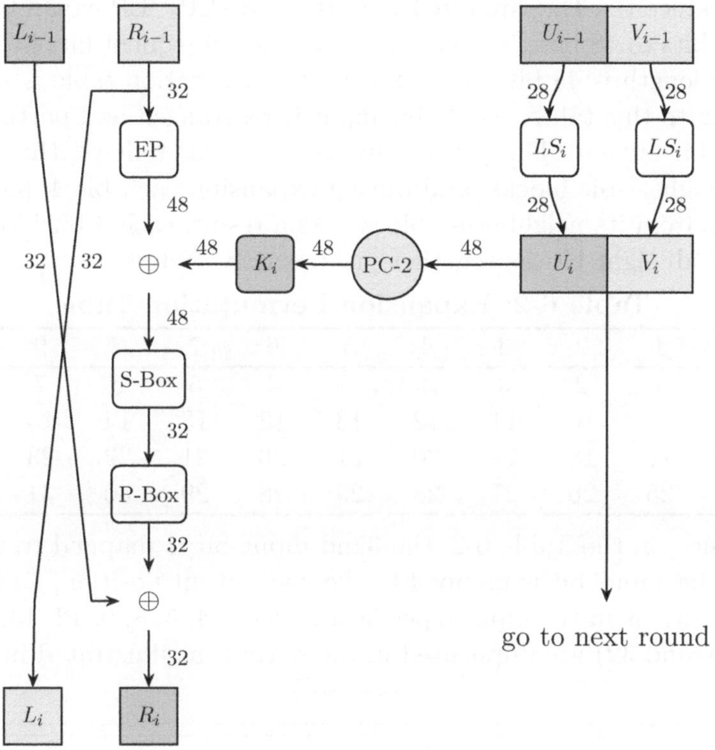

Figure 6-10: Structure of a Single DES Round

While the structural layout of a single round appears straightforward, the cryptographic strength of DES relies predominantly on its S-boxes that is non-linear components of the cipher, S-boxes prevent the algorithm from collapsing into a linear system that would be trivial to break. The round function applies the following transformations:

1) **Expansion Permutation**: Expand the 32-bit right half input R_{i-1} to 48 bits using a fixed table.
2) **XOR with round subkey**: The expanded 48-bit block is XORed with the round subkey K_i.
3) **S-box substitution**: The 48-bit result is divided into 8 groups of 6 bits each, which are input into 8 distinct S-boxes for substitution. The combined result is 32 bits.
4) **P-box permutation**: Rearrange the 32-bit output of the S-boxes according to a fixed permutation table, redistributing bits across different positions to maximize diffusion.

The round function expresses in formula

$$F(R_{i-1}, K_i) = P(S(\mathrm{EP}(R_{i-1}) \oplus K_i)) \text{ where } i = 1, 2, \ldots, 16 \qquad (6\text{-}55)$$

where "**EP**" denotes the Expansion Permutation, "**S**" denotes the S-box, "**P**" denotes the P-box.

Expansion Permutation

Now, we introduce the **Expansion Permutation** (EP). EP expands the right half R_{i-1} from 32 bits to 48 bits, in preparation for the subsequent bitwise XOR with the subkey K_i its length is 48 bits. The expansion permutation table is shown in Table 6-2. According to this table, the 32-bit input is rearranged and partially duplicated to form a 48-bit output. The predetermined rule is as follows: the 32-bit input is divided into eight 4-bit blocks, and during expansion each block incorporates the boundary bits from its neighboring blocks. As a result, each 4-bit block is extended to 6 bits, and all eight blocks together yield exactly 48 bits.

Table 6-2: Expansion Permutation Table

	0	1	2	3	4	5	6	7	8	9	10	11
0	32	1	2	3	4	5	4	5	6	7	8	9
1	8	9	10	11	12	13	12	13	14	15	16	17
2	16	17	18	19	20	21	20	21	22	23	24	25
3	24	25	26	27	28	29	28	29	30	31	32	1

For instance, in the Table 6-2, the 32nd input bit is mapped to the 1st output position, the 1st input bit is mapped to the 2nd output position, and so on. Consequently, 16 positions in the input (specifically bits 1, 4, 5, 8, 9, 12, 13, 16, 17, 20, 21, 24, 25, 28, 29, and 32) are duplicated in the output, as illustrated in Figure 6-11.

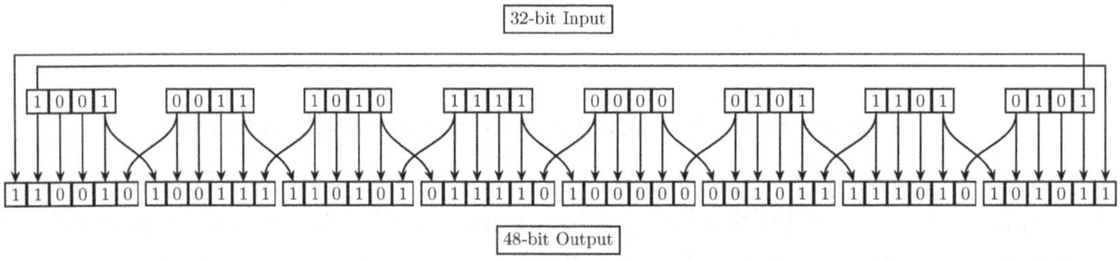

Figure 6-11: DES Expansion Permutation

The expansion permutation serves two primary objectives.

1) Length Matching: Since R_{i-1} is a 32-bit input and subkey K_i is a 48-bit key. Expansion ensures that R_{i-1} is extended to 48 bits so it can be XORed with the subkey.
2) Diffusion and Avalanche Effect: By duplicating boundary bits, the expansion forms an overlapping structure. Each bit of the 32-bit input maps to two positions in the 48-bit output. Thus, one input bit can influence two distinct S-box outputs in the subsequent substitution phase. This mechanism boosts diffusion, induces the avalanche effect, ensuring that even a one-bit change in the plaintext propagates rapidly to produce drastic changes in the ciphertext.

Example 6.3.2 Assume the input to the Expansion Permutation (EP) step is the hexadecimal block `0x93AF05D5`. What is the expanded output?

Solution: Converting `0x93AF05D5` to binary yields 1001 0011 1010 1111 0000 0101 1101 0101. According to the EP table, the positions 1, 4, 5, 8, 9, 12, 13, 16, 17, 20, 21, 24, 25, 28, 29, 32 are duplicated via boundary overlap, see Figure 6-11, the 32-bit input is expanded into eight 6-bit groups as: 110010 100111 110101 011110 100000 001011 111010 101011.

Converting this 48-bit value in hexadecimal is `0xCA7D5E80BEAB`. ■

S-box

Next, the result of the XOR operation is passed into the S-boxes for substitution and compression, reducing the 48-bit input to 32 bits. DES has eight S-boxes in total, whose definitions are listed in Table 6-3. The 48-bit input is divided into eight 6-bit blocks, each processed by its corresponding S-box. Each S-box is organized as a 4-row by 16-column table. For a given 6-bit input, written as $a_0a_1a_2a_3a_4a_5$, the outer bits (a_0a_5) represent in base 2 a row number in the range **0-3**, while the inner four bits ($a_1a_2a_3a_4$) represent in base 2 a column number in the range **0-15**. The S-box output is the 4-bit value located at the intersection of row and column. Figure 6-12 illustrates this addressing mechanism.

Table 6-3: DES S-Box

a_0a_5	$a_1a_2a_3a_4$															
S-Box 1	**0**	**1**	**2**	**3**	**4**	**5**	**6**	**7**	**8**	**9**	**10**	**11**	**12**	**13**	**14**	**15**
0	14	4	13	1	2	15	11	8	3	10	6	12	5	9	0	7
1	0	15	7	4	14	2	13	1	10	6	12	11	9	5	3	8
2	4	1	14	8	13	6	2	11	15	12	9	7	3	10	5	0
3	15	12	8	2	4	9	1	7	5	11	3	14	10	0	6	13
S-Box 2	**0**	**1**	**2**	**3**	**4**	**5**	**6**	**7**	**8**	**9**	**10**	**11**	**12**	**13**	**14**	**15**
0	15	1	8	14	6	11	3	4	9	7	2	13	12	0	5	10
1	3	13	4	7	15	2	8	14	12	0	1	10	6	9	11	5
2	0	14	7	11	10	4	13	1	5	8	12	6	9	3	2	15
3	13	8	10	1	3	15	4	2	11	6	7	12	0	5	14	9
S-Box 3	**0**	**1**	**2**	**3**	**4**	**5**	**6**	**7**	**8**	**9**	**10**	**11**	**12**	**13**	**14**	**15**
0	10	0	9	14	6	3	15	5	1	13	12	7	11	4	2	8
1	13	7	0	9	3	4	6	10	2	8	5	14	12	11	15	1
2	13	6	4	9	8	15	3	0	11	1	2	12	5	10	14	7
3	1	10	13	0	6	9	8	7	4	15	14	3	11	5	2	12
S-Box 4	**0**	**1**	**2**	**3**	**4**	**5**	**6**	**7**	**8**	**9**	**10**	**11**	**12**	**13**	**14**	**15**
0	7	13	14	3	0	6	9	10	1	2	8	5	11	12	4	15
1	13	8	11	5	6	15	0	3	4	7	2	12	1	10	14	9
2	10	6	9	0	12	11	7	13	15	1	3	14	5	2	8	4
3	3	15	0	6	10	1	13	8	9	4	5	11	12	7	2	14
S-Box 5	**0**	**1**	**2**	**3**	**4**	**5**	**6**	**7**	**8**	**9**	**10**	**11**	**12**	**13**	**14**	**15**
0	2	12	4	1	7	10	11	6	8	5	3	15	13	0	14	9
1	14	11	2	12	4	7	13	1	5	0	15	10	3	9	8	6

(Continued)

Table 6-3: DES S-Box (Continued)

a_0a_5	$a_1a_2a_3a_4$															
	0	**1**	**2**	**3**	**4**	**5**	**6**	**7**	**8**	**9**	**10**	**11**	**12**	**13**	**14**	**15**
2	4	2	1	11	10	13	7	8	15	9	12	5	6	3	0	14
3	11	8	12	7	1	14	2	13	6	15	0	9	10	4	5	3
S-Box 6	**0**	**1**	**2**	**3**	**4**	**5**	**6**	**7**	**8**	**9**	**10**	**11**	**12**	**13**	**14**	**15**
0	12	1	10	15	9	2	6	6	0	13	3	4	14	7	5	11
1	10	15	4	2	7	12	9	5	6	1	13	14	0	11	3	8
2	9	14	15	5	12	8	12	3	7	0	0	10	12	13	11	6
3	4	3	12	12	9	5	15	10	11	14	1	7	6	0	8	13
S-Box 7	**0**	**1**	**2**	**3**	**4**	**5**	**6**	**7**	**8**	**9**	**10**	**11**	**12**	**13**	**14**	**15**
0	4	11	2	14	15	0	8	13	3	12	9	7	5	10	6	1
1	13	0	11	7	4	9	1	10	14	3	5	12	2	15	8	6
2	1	4	11	13	12	3	7	14	10	15	6	8	0	5	9	2
3	6	11	13	8	1	4	10	7	9	5	0	15	14	2	3	12
S-Box 8	**0**	**1**	**2**	**3**	**4**	**5**	**6**	**7**	**8**	**9**	**10**	**11**	**12**	**13**	**14**	**15**
0	13	2	8	4	6	15	11	1	10	9	3	14	5	0	12	7
1	1	15	13	8	10	3	7	4	12	5	6	11	0	14	9	2
2	7	11	4	1	9	12	14	2	0	6	10	13	15	3	5	8
3	2	1	14	7	4	10	8	13	15	12	9	0	3	5	6	11

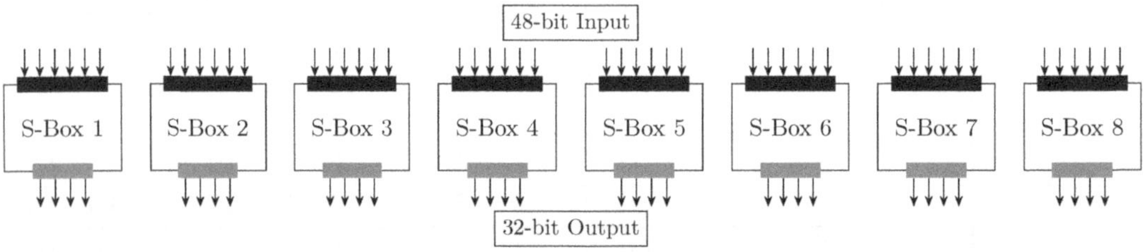

Figure 6-12: DES S-Boxes

When DES was first developed, the contents of the S-boxes were kept secret. Later, through the work of independent cryptographers, the S-box design was reverse-engineered and eventually made public. The S-boxes form the very heart of DES's security. This is because they are the only non-linear operation in this cipher. that is, $\text{Sbox}(x) \oplus \text{Sbox}(y) \neq \text{Sbox}(x \oplus y)$.

All other steps in DES, permutations, expansions, and XOR operations are all linear and comparatively easy to analyze. The careful construction of the S-boxes, therefore, provides the main method of strength against cryptanalysis, making them the most critical component of DES.

Example 6.3.3 Assume a random 48-bit input is provided to the S-box layer and is compressed to 32 bits. How is this computed?

Solution: For illustration, consider only the first S-box, see Table 6-3. Suppose the first 6-bit group of the 48-bit input is 101010. The row index is determined by the outer bits a_0a_5. Here $a_0a_5 = 10$ in binary, which is 2 in decimal. The column index is determined by the inner four bits $a_1a_2a_3a_4$, 0101 in binary, which is 5 in decimal.

Using zero-based indexing, we select the entry at row 2 and column 5 whose S-box value is 6 in decimal, 0110 in binary.

The other seven S-boxes operate in the same way on their respective 6-bit groups. ■

P-box Permutation

The last step of the round function is P-box permutation, also known as the **straight permutation**. Its purpose is to rearrange the 32-bit output produced by the S-boxes according to a fixed mapping table, thereby redistributing the bit positions and improving diffusion for the next round. The process is similar to the initial permutation: each input bit is remapped to a specific output position. The P-box is shown in Table 6-4 and follows the same general rule as previous.

Table 6-4: DES P-Box

	0	1	2	3	4	5	6	7	8	9	10	11	12	13	14	15
0	16	7	20	21	29	12	28	17	1	15	23	26	5	18	31	10
1	2	8	24	14	32	27	3	9	19	13	30	6	22	11	4	25

Unlike the S-boxes, the P-box introduces no new information and no nonlinearity. Every output bit is simply a reordering of the input, with no duplication or omission. It ensures that the outputs of a single S-box are scattered across different regions in subsequent rounds, where they are mixed with outputs from other S-boxes. This interleaving prevents strong local correlations and greatly strengthens the cipher's diffusion property. Without the P-box, DES would suffer from much weaker diffusion, making it more vulnerable to differential and linear cryptanalysis.

The Python code for DES encryption is as follows:

```
def permute(k, arr, n): #Permutation
    permutation = ""
    for i in range(0, n):
        permutation = permutation + k[arr[i] - 1]
    return permutation

def shift_left(k, nth_shifts): #Shift Left
    s = ""
    for i in range(nth_shifts):
        for j in range(1, len(k)):
            s = s + k[j]
        s = s + k[0]
        k = s
        s = ""
    return k

# Initial Permutation Table
initial_perm = [58, 50, 42, 34, 26, 18, 10, 2,...]

# Expansion Permutation Table
exp_d = [32, 1, 2, 3, 4, 5, 4, 5,...]

# Straight Permutation Table
per = [16, 7, 20, 21,29, 12, 28, 17,..]
```

```
# S-Boxes
sbox = [[[14, 4, 13, 1, 2, 15, 11, 8, 3, 10, 6, 12, 5, 9, 0, 7],
         [0, 15, 7, 4, 14, 2, 13, 1, 10, 6, 12, 11, 9, 5, 3, 8],
         [4, 1, 14, 8, 13, 6, 2, 11, 15, 12, 9, 7, 3, 10, 5, 0],
         [15, 12, 8, 2, 4, 9, 1, 7, 5, 11, 3, 14, 10, 0, 6, 13]],
         ...]

# Final Permutation
final_perm = [40, 8, 48, 16, 56, 24, 64, 32,...]


def encrypt(pt, rkb, rk):
    pt = hex2bin(pt)

  # Initial Permutation Step
    pt = permute(pt, initial_perm, 64)

  # divided two block
    left = pt[0:32]
    right = pt[32:64]
    for i in range(0, 16):
        right_expanded = permute(right, exp_d, 48)
        xor_x = xor(right_expanded, rkb[i])# XOR

    # S-Box
        sbox_str = ""
        for j in range(0, 8):
            row = bin2dec(int(xor_x[j * 6] + xor_x[j * 6 + 5]))
            col = bin2dec(
                    int(xor_x[j * 6 + 1] + xor_x[j * 6 + 2] + xor_x[j
    * 6 + 3] + xor_x[j * 6 + 4]))
            val = sbox[j][row][col]
            sbox_str = sbox_str + dec2bin(val)

        sbox_str = permute(sbox_str, per, 32) #Straight Permutation

    # XOR
        result = xor(left, sbox_str)
        left = result
    # Swap
        if(i != 15):
            left, right = right, left
    combine = left + right
    cipher_text = permute(combine, final_perm, 64) #Final Permutation
    return cipher_text
```

In the code, functions such as **hex2bin**, **bin2hex**, **bin2dec**, **dec2bin**, and **xor** responsible for conversions between different numeral systems are omitted.

6.3.4 Key Schedule

The standard DES key length is 64 bits. However, the algorithm relies on a Key Schedule, or is called round-key generator to create sixteen subkeys. The input key consists of 56 effective bits and 8 parity bits. Specifically, every eighth bit (bits 8, 16, 24, ..., 64) is a parity bit generated from the preceding seven bits. These bits are reserved solely for error detection during key transmission and loading. The arrangement of the key bits is illustrated in Figure 6-13.

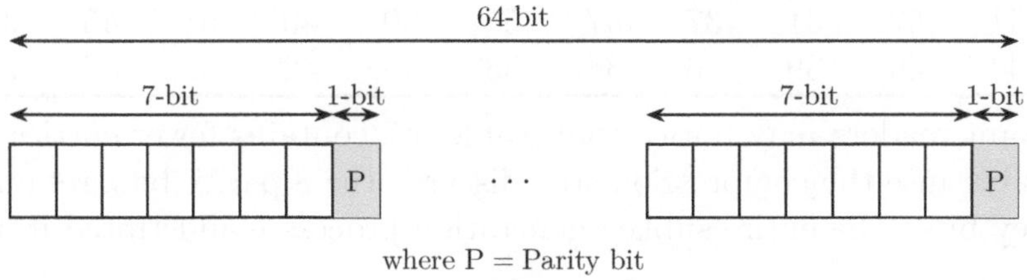

Figure 6-13: DES Key Arrangement

The subkey generation process begins by discarding these parity bits. The remaining 56 bits are then subjected to the **Permuted Choice** 1 (PC-1), as specified in Table 6-5. This permutation is defined by a fixed lookup table that performs two functions simultaneously: it strips away the parity bits and reorders the remaining 56 effective bits to form the initial state for the key schedule.

Table 6-5: DES PC-1 Table

	0	1	2	3	4	5	6	7	8	9	10	11	12	13
0	57	49	41	33	25	17	9	1	58	50	42	34	26	18
1	10	2	59	51	43	35	27	19	11	3	60	52	44	36
2	63	55	47	39	31	23	15	7	62	54	46	38	30	22
3	14	6	61	53	45	37	29	21	13	5	28	20	12	4

After PC-1, the 56-bit key is divided into two equal halves, denoted U_0 and V_0. U_0 is the leftmost 28 bits after permutation and V_0 is the rightmost 28 bits after permutation. In other words, according to Table 6-5, the first two rows define the left half U_0, corresponding to key bits at positions $57, 49, 41, \ldots, 36$ from the original 64-bit key. The last two rows define the right half V_0, corresponding to key bits at positions $63, 55, 47, \ldots, 4$ from the original key.

For $1 \leqslant i \leqslant 16$, each half U_{i-1} and V_{i-1} is shifted left one or two bits, producing U_i and V_i. The left shift is an operation in which the bit string is rotated leftward, and the bits shifted out from the leftmost positions are wrapped around to the rightmost end. The number of rotations depends on the round index, as given in Table 6-6.

Table 6-6: Left Shift for DES

Round	1	2	3	4	5	6	7	8	9	10	11	12	13	14	15	16
Shift	1	1	2	2	2	2	2	2	1	2	2	2	2	2	2	1

In rounds $1, 2, 9$, and 16, shifting is one bit. In the other rounds, shifting is two bits. Across all 16 rounds, the total number of shifting is $4 \times 1 + 12 \times 2 = 28$.

The rotated halves U_i and V_i are then merged, compressed and permuted into a 48-bit subkey, denoted K_i, which is injected into the round function. We call the permutation operation as **Permuted Choice**(PC-2), this operation selects a permuted subset of 48 bits of 56 bits. The permutation is defined by Table 6-7.

Table 6-7: DES PC-2 Table

	0	1	2	3	4	5	6	7	8	9	10	11
0	14	17	11	24	1	5	3	28	15	6	21	10
1	23	19	12	4	26	8	16	7	27	20	13	2
2	41	52	31	37	47	55	30	40	51	45	33	48
3	44	49	39	56	34	53	46	42	50	36	29	32

Observant readers may notice that Table 6-7 contains fewer entries than Table 6-5; this is because the compression step discards the 8 parity bits, retaining only 48 effective key bits. The entire subkey generation process is illustrated in Figure 6-10.

Example 6.3.4 Given a random key `0x9CBFC60F6B8FAC11`, what is the first-round subkey K_1 produced by the DES key schedule?
Solution: To illustrate the derivation of the first-round subkey K_1, consider the following 64-bit input key K:

10011100 10111111 11000110 00001111 01101011 10001111 10101100 00010001

In DES each of the 64 bits contains a parity bit at the end of each byte. Consequently, these 8 bits are discarded during the initial processing stage.

Step 1: The 64-bit key (including 8 parity bits) is reduced to 56 effective bits using the PC-1 table. The result is divided into two 28-bit halves

$$U_0 = \texttt{0110011100010100010100101000} \tag{6-56}$$

$$V_0 = \texttt{0011111001101111011110110011} \tag{6-57}$$

Step 2: For round 1, both halves are shifted left by one bit

$$U_1 = \texttt{1100111000101000101001010000} \tag{6-58}$$

$$V_1 = \texttt{0111110011011110111101100110} \tag{6-59}$$

Step 3: The concatenation $U_1 \parallel V_1$ is permuted and processed by the by PC-2, this compression permutation selects 48 bits to form the first-round subkey K_1.

$$K_1 = \texttt{1010 0001 1001 0010 0010 0010 1000 1000 1000 0011 0011 0101} \tag{6-60}$$

$$= \texttt{0xA19222888335} \tag{6-61}$$

■

The Python implementation of the DES key schedule is provided below.

```
#Given Key
key = " "
key = key.upper()
key = hex2bin(key)

# PC-1
keyp = [57, 49, 41, 33, 25, 17, 9,...]
key = permute(key, keyp, 56)

```

```
# Left Shift
shift_table = [1, 1, 2, 2,2, 2, 2, 2,1, 2, 2, 2,2, 2, 2, 1]

# Key- Compression Table : Compression of key from 56 bits to 48 bits
key_comp = [14, 17, 11, 24, 1, 5,...]

# Splitting
left = key[0:28];right = key[28:56]

rkb ,rk = [],[]
for i in range(0, 16):
  # Round Key
    left = shift_left(left, shift_table[i])
    right = shift_left(right, shift_table[i])
    combine_str = left + right
    round_key = permute(combine_str, key_comp, 48)
    rkb.append(round_key)
    rk.append(bin2hex(round_key))
```

6.3.5 Examples

Working through a round of DES by hand is highly instructive, as it helps readers grasp the overall encryption workflow. For clarity, we will use hexadecimal throughout the calculations.

Example 6.3.5 Consider the encryption of the plaintext message "**VELOCITY**" using the DES algorithm with the key "**SIDESLIP**". Determine the resulting ciphertext.

Solution: First, convert the plaintext to hexadecimal using the ASCII table, as shown in Table 6-8.

The first step is to convert the plaintext string into its hexadecimal representation using the ASCII standard, as detailed in Table 6-8.

Table 6-8: Plaintext to Hexadecimal

Plaintext	V	E	L	O	C	I	T	Y
Hexadecimal	56	45	4C	4F	43	49	54	59

Thus, the plaintext block is 0x56454C4F43495459. Converting this value into binary yields

010101100 10001010 10011000 10011110 10000110 10010010 10101000 1011001.

The **Initial Permutation** (IP) is applied to this binary block according to the standard specification refer to Table 6-1. The resulting permuted block is 0xFFC14FBA0000AC19.

This 64-bit permuted block is then divided into two 32-bit halves, the left half L_0 and the right half R_0

$$L_0 = \texttt{0xFFC14FBA}, \quad R_0 = \texttt{0x0000AC19}$$

Encryption proceeds through 16 rounds, with the intermediate states and generated subkeys summarized in Table 6-9. In each round i, the fundamental Feistel relation $L_i = R_{i-1}$ is maintained.

Table 6-9: DES Encryption Example

Round	L_i	R_i	K_i
0	FFC14FBA	0000AC19	-
1	0000AC19	3B291DE4	B0924AA54028
2	3B291DE4	A45F1AA2	A01AD2134E80
3	A45F1AA2	F9A321B6	347250580111
4	F9A321B6	2051E8B1	06555083600C
5	2051E8B1	A275DAEA	4E4155603380
6	A275DAEA	259B9236	0FC109B0002F
7	259B9236	A1668FF4	0B01AB461A82
8	A1668FF4	4978E4E6	B90889142179
9	4978E4E6	3829FFE3	19188AE44405
10	3829FFE3	D7E2E925	3028CC4A02CA
11	D7E2E925	EE2EAE27	106C0494D109
12	EE2EAE27	AEAFE1C6	402D34021660
13	AEAFE1C6	A7D608AF	C4A425D8A920
14	A7D608AF	B6624599	C38622204E18
15	B6624599	D46D0BA1	E892A2593012
16	4FEA1F39	D46D0BA1	A19222888335

Upon completion of the 16th round, the ciphertext is constructed by applying the IP^{-1}. Crucially, consistent with the Feistel structure defined earlier, the left and right halves are swapped one final time before this permutation.

The results of the last rounds L_{16} and R_{16} are combined that produces the 64-bit block `0x4FEA1F39D46D0BA1`. The result goes through IP^{-1}, as defined in Table 6-1, gives the final ciphertext is `0x6F5CE47D8533F092`. ■

Since DES is Feistel cipher structure, is a symmetric cipher, meaning that the same round function is used for both encryption and decryption. The only difference lies in the order of subkey application: during decryption, the subkeys are applied in reverse sequence $K_{16}, K_{15}, K_{14}, \ldots, K_1$. In addition, the rotations in the key schedule are performed to the right rather than to the left, while the number of shifts remains unchanged, exactly as specified in Table 6-6.

Example 6.3.6 We now proceed to decrypt the ciphertext generated in Example 6.3.5. To conserve space, a condensed summary of the process is presented in Table 6-10.

Solution: Inspection of Table 6-10 reveals two critical features. First, the round subkeys are applied in reverse order: the subkey utilized in decryption round 1 is identical to the subkey from encryption round 16 (as shown in Table 6-9). Second, the initial decryption inputs L_0 and R_0 correspond to the swapped encryption outputs R_{16} and L_{16}, respectively. This reversal highlights the inherent symmetry of the Feistel structure, demonstrating why the same hardware or software implementation can perform both encryption and decryption.

Table 6-10: DES Decryption Process

Round	L_i	R_i	K_i
0	4FEA1F39	D46D0BA1	
1	D46D0BA1	B6624599	A19222888335
2	B6624599	A7D608AF	E892A2593012
3	A7D608AF	AEAFE1C6	C38622204E18
4-13	...	...	...
14	A45F1AA2	3B291DE4	347250580111
15	3B291DE4	0000AC19	A01AD2134E80
16	FFC14FBA	0000AC19	B0924AA54028

The result of the last round is `0xFFC14FBA0000AC19`, then goes through IP^{-1}, then the final text is `0x56454C4F43495459`. ■

6.3.6 Cryptanalysis

The security of DES rests primarily on its 16-round iterative structure, its 56-bit key length, and the design of its S-boxes. The most immediate weakness lies in the limited key length: the effective key space is only $2^{56} \approx 7.2 \times 10^{16}$. While this was sufficient to resist brute-force attacks in the 1970s, it has long been inadequate under modern computing conditions. In 1998, the *Electronic Frontier Foundation* (EFF) built a special-purpose machine that succeeded in brute-forcing DES in just 56 hours. This demonstrated that DES can be broken by straightforward exhaustive search, without the need for advanced cryptanalytic techniques. For this reason, contemporary cryptographic research no longer focuses on developing new attacks against DES since its key space itself is simply too small.

Historically, DES was proposed in 1973. At the time, computing technology was still in its infancy, and information security was mainly a concern of the U.S. military and government. Neither academia nor industry had yet devoted significant resources to the field. Against this backdrop, IBM's DES design, valued for its simplicity and efficiency, was quickly adopted by the National Bureau of Standards (NBS) as the first true national encryption standard.

During the standardization process, the NBS lacked the expertise to evaluate the algorithm's security and therefore enlisted the *National Security Agency* (NSA) to perform the assessment. The NSA's involvement sparked two major controversies: the reduction of the key length from 128 bits to 56 bits, and modifications to the S-box design. Some researchers speculated that the NSA had inserted backdoors into the S-boxes for its own benefit. The NSA and IBM later jointly denied this allegation, claiming that the changes were intended to strengthen security. In retrospect, the publication of differential cryptanalysis in the 1990s revealed that the DES S-boxes were indeed resistant to this powerful attack method. The striking fact, however, is that differential cryptanalysis had not been known in academia in the 1970s, suggesting that IBM and the NSA may already have been aware of it that perhaps a decade or more ahead of public research.

However, the shortening of the key length unquestionably reduced security. A 128-bit key would have rendered brute-force attacks infeasible in that era, whereas a 56-bit key quickly became inadequate as computing power advanced. Many have concluded that the NSA pushed for this reduction in order to retain the ability to attack DES when necessary. The suspicion that DES was deliberately weakened has remained a topic of debate ever since.

Finally, the S-boxes are the cornerstone of DES security. They are the sole source of nonlinearity in the round function, preventing the cipher from being reduced to a system of linear equations. Their careful construction ensures strong avalanche properties and resistance to both differential and linear cryptanalysis across multiple rounds. Whatever the controversies surrounding their origin, the S-boxes endowed DES with an impressive level of security for its time.

The relevant criteria for the S-boxes are as follows [52]:

1) Every S-box has 6 bits of input and 4 bits of output.
2) Every output bit of an S-box should NOT be too close to a linear function of the input bits.
3) The leftmost and rightmost input bits of the S-box and modify the 4 middle bits, each possible 4-bit output is attained exactly once as the middle four input bits range over their 16 possibilities.
4) If two inputs to an S-box differ in exactly one bit, the outputs must differ in at least two bits.
5) If two inputs to an S-box differ in the two middle bits exactly, the outputs must differ in at least two bits.
6) If two inputs to an S-box differ in their first two bits and are identical in their last two bits, the two outputs must not be the same.
7) For any non-zero 6-bit difference between inputs, no more than eight of the 32 pairs of inputs exhibiting may result in the same output difference.
8) The conflict (zero output difference) in the 32-bit output corresponding to the 8 S-boxes is only possible in the case of three adjacent S-boxes.

Later revisions to the S-box design provided some improvements in security [53]. Beginning in 1977, the NSA conducted periodic evaluations of DES. By 1997, a brute-force attack could be carried out within several months [54], and by 1999 the same task could be accomplished in only 22 hours [55]. As a result, DES had become effectively obsolete by the year 2000, supplanted by Triple DES (3DES) and the Advanced Encryption Standard (AES).

To enhance security, increasing the key length was the natural approach. One early idea was Double DES (2DES) [56], which expanded the key space to 2^{112}, making brute-force attacks seemingly infeasible. In theory, searching all possible keys would require $2^{56} \times 2^{56} = 2^{112}$ operations. However, it was soon discovered that a meet-in-the-middle attack (see Figure 6-14) could reduce the effective time complexity

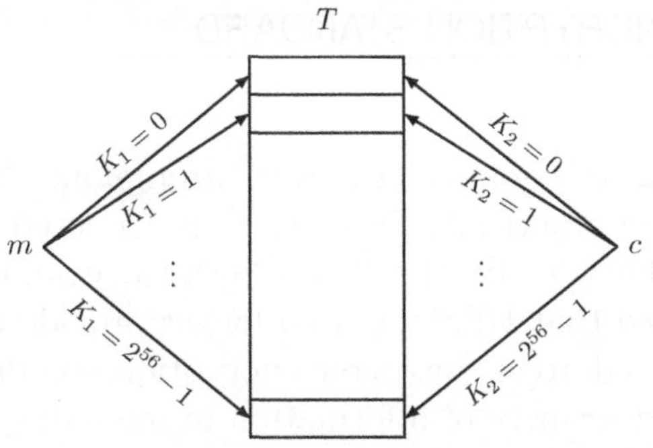

Figure 6-14: Meet-in-the-Middle Attack

to about $\mathcal{O}(2^{57})$, only slightly higher than that of single DES. Although 2DES offered somewhat better security, its theoretical vulnerability led to its abandonment.

To counter the vulnerabilities of single DES, specifically brute-force attacks, cryptographers introduced Triple DES (3DES or TDES) [34]. However, 3DES does not simply perform three encryption operations in sequence. Instead, it typically employs an Encrypt–Decrypt–Encrypt (EDE) structure. This design was chosen for backward compatibility: if the keys are identical, the operation collapses to a single DES implementation.

The most common variant is commonly known as 2-key Triple DES, that uses two independent keys K_1 and K_2. Formally, the ciphertext c is derived as

$$c = E_{K_1}\left(D_{K_2}\left(E_{K_1}(m)\right)\right), \quad \text{where } K_1 \neq K_2 \tag{6-62}$$

This scheme extends the effective key length to 112 bits, resulting in a theoretical key space of 2^{112}.

The use of three unique keys is defined for the Triple DES is commonly known as 3-key Triple DES. NIST suggested that 2-key Triple DES shall not be used to apply cryptographic protection.

The rationale for 3DES is best understood by analyzing the meet-in-the-middle attack on Double DES. Consider a 2DES scheme where $c = E_{K_2}(E_{K_1}(m))$, and $K_1 \neq K_2$. Suppose an attacker **Eve** obtains two plaintext–ciphertext pairs (m_1, c_1) and (m_2, c_2). She computes $D_{K_2}(c_i) = X_i = E_{K_1}(m_i)$, and checks for matches across both pairs. Practically, **Eve** constructs two tables of size 2^{56}. One holding encryptions of candidate K_1 values, the other holding decryptions under candidate K_2. A match on X_i implies a candidate (K_1, K_2). The attack thus requires about $2^{56} + 2^{56} = 2^{57}$ operations, which is only slightly harder than brute-forcing single DES.

For a single plaintext–ciphertext pair, the expected number of spurious key pairs is $\frac{2^{112}}{2^{64}} = 2^{48}$. With two pairs, this drops to $\frac{2^{48}}{2^{64}} = 2^{-16}$, so the probability of recovering the correct key pair is essentially $1 - 2^{-16} \approx 100\%$.

However, as computing power has continued to increase, its effective 2^{112}-bit key space has gradually become unsafe, and 3DES has been progressively phased out in favor of stronger algorithms such as AES. All versions of DES were officially retired before 2024.

6.4 ADVANCED ENCRYPTION STANDARD

6.4.1 Introduction

With the advancement of computing power throughout the 20th century, **brute-force attacks** became practically feasible. This rendered the 56-bit key space of DES increasingly insufficient. By the 1990s, both the computing and cryptographic communities recognized that DES could no longer provide long-term security. Consequently, a critical need arose for a new encryption standard capable of ensuring the confidentiality and security of information in modern computing environments.

In 1997, NIST initiated a rigorous process to select a successor to DES, designating the project as the **Advanced Encryption Standard** (AES). NIST mandated that candidate algorithms support a block size of 128 bits and support key lengths of 128, 192, and 256 bits to accommodate varying security requirements. The baseline configuration, AES-128, utilizes a 128-bit block and a 128-bit key. Furthermore, the submission requirements stipulated that all algorithms be publicly specified and open to global scrutiny. This principle of openness fostered extensive participation and analysis from the international cryptographic community.

With technical assistance from the NSA, NIST narrowed the initial 21 submissions down to 15 first-round candidates. Following multiple rounds of international review and benchmarking against candidates such as CAST-256, E2, FROG, and RC6, the **Rijndael algorithm** was selected as the winner. Designed by Belgian cryptographers *Joan Daemen* and *Vincent Rijmen*, Rijndael distinguished itself through its balance of security, performance, hardware and software efficiency, and implementation flexibility. In 2000, NIST announced Rijndael as the proposed AES algorithm. On November 26, 2001, AES was formally adopted as the new U.S. Federal Information Processing Standard, replacing DES as the international benchmark for symmetric encryption.

Due to the transparency of the AES selection process, cryptographers worldwide were able to freely scrutinize the candidate algorithms. Any potential weaknesses would likely have been identified in the early stages of analysis. As a result, the NSA restricted its role to evaluation and testing without direct involvement in the design phase. This approach stands in contrast to the historical development of DES and has reinforced the consensus within the academic community that AES does not contain a cryptographic "backdoor".

Structurally, AES represents a departure from the 23 classical **Feistel structure**. In a Feistel cipher, the data block is split into two halves where one half is modified by a round function while the other passes through unchanged. This design allows for symmetry between encryption and decryption. In contrast, AES employs a **Substitution-Permutation Network** (SPN). The decryption process in an SPN mirrors the structure of encryption but is not identical, as it requires the sequential application of inverse transformations. Although this introduces additional implementation complexity, modern techniques such as lookup tables and optimized instruction sets largely mitigate the computational overhead [57]. The structure of AES is illustrated in Figure 6-15.

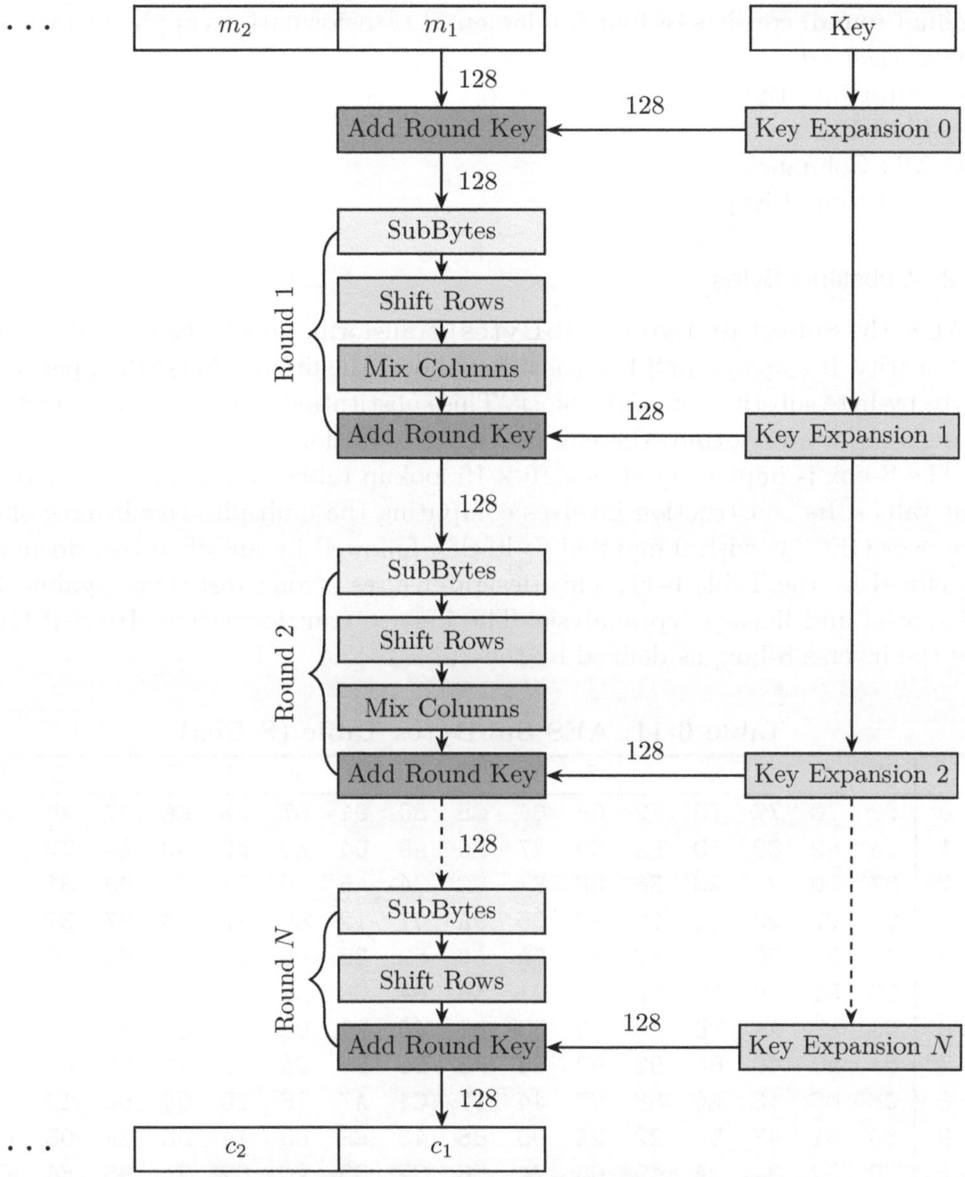

Figure 6-15: The Overall Structure of AES

AES differs from the original **Rijndael** specification primarily in its parameter definitions. While Rijndael supports block and key sizes in 32-bit increments ranging from 128 to 256 bits, the AES standard fixes the block size strictly at 128 bits. The key lengths can be 128, 192, or 256 bits, which is referred to as AES-128, AES-192, and AES-256. The length of the key directly determines the number of rounds required: 10 rounds for a 128-bit key, 12 rounds for a 192-bit key, and 14 rounds for a 256-bit key.

In encryption, plaintext is divided into 128-bit blocks, each expressed as a 4×4 state matrix of bytes. If the final block is shorter than 128 bits, standard padding methods (e.g., PKCS#7; in simple illustrations, arbitrary filler characters such as "Z" may be used) must be applied. Each encryption round, with the exception of the final round, consists of four fundamental transformations applied to the state matrix, they are

1) Substitute Bytes
2) Shift Rows
3) Mix Columns
4) Add Round Key

6.4.2 Substitute Bytes

In AES, the Substitute Bytes (**SubBytes**) transformation is the critical source of nonlinearity. It employs an S-box constructed over the finite field GF(2^8), performing a byte-by-byte substitution of the block. This substitution disrupts linear correlations between input and output, thereby providing confusion.

The S-box is implemented as a 16×16 lookup table containing all possible 256 8-bit values. Its construction involves computing the multiplicative inverse of each byte over GF(2^8) (with 0 mapped to itself), followed by an affine transformation, as defined by the Table 6-11. This design ensures strong resistance against both differential and linear cryptanalysis. The inverse transformation, **InvSubBytes**, uses the inverse S-box, as defined by the Table 6-12.

Table 6-11: AES SubBytes Table (S-Box)

	0	1	2	3	4	5	6	7	8	9	A	B	C	D	E	F
0	63	7C	77	7B	F2	6B	6F	C5	30	01	67	2B	FE	D7	AB	76
1	CA	82	C9	7D	FA	59	47	F0	AD	D4	A2	AF	9C	A4	72	C0
2	B7	FD	93	26	36	3F	F7	CC	34	A5	E5	F1	71	D8	31	15
3	04	C7	23	C3	18	96	05	9A	07	12	80	E2	EB	27	B2	75
4	09	83	2C	1A	1B	6E	5A	A0	52	3B	D6	B3	29	E3	2F	84
5	53	D1	00	ED	20	FC	B1	5B	6A	CB	BE	39	4A	4C	58	CF
6	D0	EF	AA	FB	43	4D	33	85	45	F9	02	7F	50	3C	9F	A8
7	51	A3	40	8F	92	9D	38	F5	BC	B6	DA	21	10	FF	F3	D2
8	CD	0C	13	EC	5F	97	44	17	C4	A7	7E	3D	64	5D	19	73
9	60	81	4F	DC	22	2A	90	88	46	EE	B8	14	DE	5E	0B	DB
A	E0	32	3A	0A	49	06	24	5C	C2	D3	AC	62	91	95	E4	79
B	E7	C8	37	6D	8D	D5	4E	A9	6C	56	F4	EA	65	7A	AE	08
C	BA	78	25	2E	1C	A6	B4	C6	E8	DD	74	1F	4B	BD	8B	8A
D	70	3E	B5	66	48	03	F6	0E	61	35	57	B9	86	C1	1D	9E
E	E1	F8	98	11	69	D9	8E	94	9B	1E	87	E9	CE	55	28	DF
F	8C	A1	89	0D	BF	E6	42	68	41	99	2D	0F	B0	54	BB	16

For a 128-bit plaintext block, the data is divided into 16 bytes and arranged into a 4×4 **state matrix** that is an intermediate result of the AES block cipher. The matrix is populated in **column-major order**, meaning the bytes fill the first

Table 6-12: AES InvSubBytes Table

	0	1	2	3	4	5	6	7	8	9	A	B	C	D	E	F
0	52	09	6A	D5	30	36	A5	38	BF	40	A3	9E	81	F3	D7	FB
1	7C	E3	39	82	9B	2F	FF	87	34	8E	43	44	C4	DE	E9	CB
2	54	7B	94	32	A6	C2	23	3D	EE	4C	95	0B	42	FA	C3	4E
3	08	2E	A1	66	28	D9	24	B2	76	5B	A2	49	6D	8B	D1	25
4	72	F8	F6	64	86	68	98	16	D4	A4	5C	CC	5D	65	B6	92
5	6C	70	48	50	FD	ED	B9	DA	5E	15	46	57	A7	8D	9D	84
6	90	D8	AB	00	8C	BC	D3	0A	F7	E4	58	05	B8	B3	45	06
7	D0	2C	1E	8F	CA	3F	0F	02	C1	AF	BD	03	01	13	8A	6B
8	3A	91	11	41	4F	67	DC	EA	97	F2	CF	CE	F0	B4	E6	73
9	96	AC	74	22	E7	AD	35	85	E2	F9	37	E8	1C	75	DF	6E
A	47	F1	1A	71	1D	29	C5	89	6F	B7	62	0E	AA	18	BE	1B
B	FC	56	3E	4B	C6	D2	79	20	9A	DB	C0	FE	78	CD	5A	F4
C	1F	DD	A8	33	88	07	C7	31	B1	12	10	59	27	80	EC	5F
D	60	51	7F	A9	19	B5	4A	0D	2D	E5	7A	9F	93	C9	9C	EF
E	A0	E0	3B	4D	AE	2A	F5	B0	C8	EB	BB	3C	83	53	99	61
F	17	2B	04	7E	BA	77	D6	26	E1	69	14	63	55	21	0C	7D

column, then the second, and so on.

$$\begin{bmatrix} a_{00} & a_{01} & a_{02} & a_{03} \\ a_{10} & a_{11} & a_{12} & a_{13} \\ a_{20} & a_{21} & a_{22} & a_{23} \\ a_{30} & a_{31} & a_{32} & a_{33} \end{bmatrix} \xrightarrow{\text{SubBytes}} \begin{bmatrix} b_{00} & b_{01} & b_{02} & b_{03} \\ b_{10} & b_{11} & b_{12} & b_{13} \\ b_{20} & b_{21} & b_{22} & b_{23} \\ b_{30} & b_{31} & b_{32} & b_{33} \end{bmatrix}$$

To determine the substitution value, each byte is interpreted as two hexadecimal digits. The left digit (the leftmost 4 bits) specifies the row index, while the right digit (the rightmost 4 bits) specifies the column index of the S-box.

Example 6.4.1 Consider that each byte is the hexadecimal value, let a_{00} = 0x42, a_{01} = 0xE6, a_{02} = 0x4F, what are the substituted values?
Solution: Since a_{00} = 0x42, so it references the row 4 and the column 2 of the S-box. According to Table 6-11, b_{00} = 0x2C.

Similarly, b_{01} = 0x8E, b_{02} = 0x84. ■

Example 6.4.2 Consider that each byte is the hexadecimal value, let b_{00} = 0x6E, b_{01} = 0x46, b_{02} = 0xA3, what are the original values?
Solution: Since b_{00} = 0x6E, so it references the row 6 and the column E of the inverse S-box. According to Table 6-12, a_{00} = 0x45.

Similarly, a_{01} = 0x98, a_{02} = 0x71. ■

In AES, a single fixed S-box is used consistently across all rounds, which is a distinctive feature of the algorithm. This S-box defines a one-to-one mapping for all 256 possible byte values, ensuring that every input byte corresponds uniquely to an output byte. As a bijective transformation, it is also fully reversible.

Example 6.4.3 Given a state matrix, show an example of the SubBytes transformation using the S-box.

$$\begin{bmatrix} \mathtt{7E} & \mathtt{DE} & \mathtt{C2} & \mathtt{09} \\ \mathtt{06} & \mathtt{F4} & \mathtt{67} & \mathtt{FA} \\ \mathtt{4A} & \mathtt{FE} & \mathtt{B3} & \mathtt{DD} \\ \mathtt{91} & \mathtt{86} & \mathtt{DB} & \mathtt{C0} \end{bmatrix} \xrightarrow{\text{SubBytes}} \begin{bmatrix} \mathtt{F3} & \mathtt{1D} & \mathtt{25} & \mathtt{01} \\ \mathtt{6F} & \mathtt{BF} & \mathtt{85} & \mathtt{2D} \\ \mathtt{D6} & \mathtt{BB} & \mathtt{6D} & \mathtt{C1} \\ \mathtt{81} & \mathtt{44} & \mathtt{B9} & \mathtt{BA} \end{bmatrix}$$

The specific values within the AES S-box are not chosen arbitrarily; rather, they are rigorously derived using algebraic properties defined over the finite field GF(2^8). The construction of the S-box involves two distinct stages

1) Compute the multiplicative inverse of the input byte in GF(2^8);
2) Apply a fixed affine transformation;

AES defines the GF(2^8) field with the irreducible polynomial $P(x) = x^8 + x^4 + x^3 + x + 1$. Every 8-bit binary value corresponds uniquely to a polynomial with coefficients in GF(2). This mapping ensures that every non-zero byte possesses a unique multiplicative inverse, a property that renders the S-box a bijective function. Since the byte zero has no inverse in GF(2^8), it is mapped to itself.

Following the inversion, an affine transformation is applied to the result. This step is designed to obscure the algebraic relationship between the inputs and outputs. Conceptually, this transformation consists of a fixed linear matrix multiplication over GF(2) followed by the addition (via XOR) of a constant vector. The combination of multiplicative inversion and the affine transformation provides the necessary nonlinearity and ensures robust resistance against both differential and linear cryptanalysis.

Let us now illustrate this with an example.

Example 6.4.4 Define two polynomials, $A(x) = x^6 + x^4 + x^2 + x + 1$ and $B(x) = x^7 + x + 1$ in GF(2^8), the coefficients of the polynomials that represent the elements are added modulo 2, we have

$$A(x) + B(x) \equiv \left(x^6 + x^4 + x^2 + x + 1\right) + \left(x^7 + x + 1\right) \pmod{P(x)} \tag{6-63}$$

$$\equiv x^7 + x^6 + x^4 + x^2 \pmod{P(x)} \tag{6-64}$$

$$A(x) \cdot B(x) \equiv \left(x^6 + x^4 + x^2 + x + 1\right)\left(x^7 + x + 1\right) \pmod{P(x)} \tag{6-65}$$

$$\equiv x^{13} + x^{11} + x^9 + x^8 + x^6 + x^5 + x^4 + x^3 + 1 \pmod{P(x)} \tag{6-66}$$

$$\equiv C(x) \pmod{P(x)} \tag{6-67}$$

Since the degree of $C(x)$ exceeds 8, we perform polynomial long division of $C(x)$ by $P(x)$ to obtain the remainder

$$\begin{array}{r|l}
 & x^5 + x^3 \\ \hline
x^8 + x^4 + x^3 + x + 1 & x^{13} + x^{11} + x^9 + x^8 + x^6 + x^5 + x^4 + x^3 + 1 \\
 & -x^{13} - x^9 - x^8 - x^6 - x^5 \\ \hline
 & x^{11} + x^4 + x^3 \\
 & -x^{11} - x^7 - x^6 - x^4 - x^3 \\ \hline
 & -x^7 - x^6 + 1
\end{array}$$

The remainder is $-x^7 - x^6 + 1$. Coefficients of the polynomials are reduced modulo 2, the coefficients -1 is equivalent to the coefficients 1. Substituting this result back into $C(x)$, we obtain

$$A(x) \cdot B(x) \equiv x^{13} + x^{11} + x^9 + x^8 + x^6 + x^5 + x^4 + x^3 + 1 \pmod{P(x)} \quad (6\text{-}68)$$

$$\equiv -x^7 - x^6 + 1 \pmod{x^8 + x^4 + x^3 + x + 1} \quad (6\text{-}69)$$

$$\equiv x^7 + x^6 + 1 \pmod{x^8 + x^4 + x^3 + x + 1} \quad (6\text{-}70)$$

This step endows the SubBytes transformation with its non-linear property. Table 6-13 presents the multiplicative inverses in GF(2^8), listing all elements and their inverses modulo the irreducible polynomial $P(x)$.

Table 6-13: Multiplicative Inverses in GF(2^8)

	0	1	2	3	4	5	6	7	8	9	A	B	C	D	E	F
0	00	01	8D	F6	CB	52	7B	D1	E8	4F	29	C0	B0	E1	E5	C7
1	74	B4	AA	4B	99	2B	60	5F	58	3F	FD	CC	FF	40	EE	B2
2	3A	6E	5A	F1	55	4D	A8	C9	C1	0A	98	15	30	44	A2	C2
3	2C	45	92	6C	F3	39	66	42	F2	35	20	6F	77	BB	59	19
4	1D	FE	37	67	2D	31	F5	69	A7	64	AB	13	54	25	E9	09
5	ED	5C	05	CA	4C	24	87	BF	18	3E	22	F0	51	EC	61	17
6	16	5E	AF	D3	49	A6	36	43	F4	47	91	DF	33	93	21	3B
7	79	B7	97	85	10	B5	BA	3C	B6	70	D0	06	A1	FA	81	82
8	83	7E	7F	80	96	73	BE	56	9B	9E	95	D9	F7	02	B9	A4
9	DE	6A	32	6D	D8	8A	84	72	2A	14	9F	88	F9	DC	89	9A
A	FB	7C	2E	C3	8F	B8	65	48	26	C8	12	4A	CE	E7	D2	62
B	0C	E0	1F	EF	11	75	78	71	A5	8E	76	3D	BD	BC	86	57
C	0B	28	2F	A3	DA	D4	E4	0F	A9	27	53	04	1B	FC	AC	E6
D	7A	07	AE	63	C5	DB	E2	EA	94	8B	C4	D5	9D	F8	90	6B
E	B1	0D	D6	EB	C6	0E	CF	AD	08	4E	D7	E3	5D	50	1E	B3
F	5B	23	38	34	68	46	03	8C	DD	9C	7D	A0	CD	1A	41	1C

How can Table 6-13 be applied in practice? Consider the following example.

Example 6.4.5 In GF(2^8), with respect to the irreducible polynomial $P(x) = x^8 + x^4 + x^3 + x + 1$, compute the inverse of the polynomial $f(x) = x^5 + x^3 + x$.
Solution: The coefficients of $f(x) = x^5 + x^3 + x$ are 00101010, which corresponds to the hexadecimal value `0x2A`. According to Table 6-13, we find that the inverse of `0x2A` is `0x98`, the binary string 10011000. In polynomial form, this corresponds to $f^{-1}(x) = x^7 + x^4 + x^3$.

To verify correctness, we can compute the product

$$f^{-1}(x) \cdot f(x) \equiv (x^7 + x^4 + x^3)(x^5 + x^3 + x) \pmod{P(x)} \quad (6\text{-}71)$$

$$\equiv x^{12} + x^{10} + x^9 + 2x^8 + x^7 + x^6 + x^5 + x^4 \pmod{P(x)} \quad (6\text{-}72)$$

Since the degree of $f^{-1}(x) \cdot f(x)$ exceeds 8, we perform polynomial long division of $C(x)$ by $P(x)$ to obtain the remainder

$$
\begin{array}{r|l}
 & x^4 + x^2 + x - 1 \\
\hline
x^8+x^4+x^3+x+1 & x^{12}+x^{10}+x^9+x^7+x^6+x^5+x^4 \\
 & -x^{12} - x^8 - x^7 - x^5 - x^4 \\
\cline{2-2}
 & x^{10}+x^9-x^8+x^6 \\
 & -x^{10} - x^6 - x^5 - x^3 - x^2 \\
\cline{2-2}
 & x^9 - x^8 - x^5 - x^3 - x^2 \\
 & -x^9 - x^5 - x^4 - x^2 - x \\
\cline{2-2}
 & -x^8 - 2x^5 - x^4 - x^3 - 2x^2 - x \\
 & x^8 + x^4 + x^3 + x + 1 \\
\cline{2-2}
 & -2x^5 - 2x^2 + 1
\end{array}
$$

Since all coefficients are taken from the finite field GF(2), hence

$$f^{-1}(x) \cdot f(x) \equiv 1 \pmod{P(x)} \tag{6-73}$$

■

The construction of the AES S-box is not yet complete. Its 8-bit input can be denoted as $(b_7, b_6, b_5, b_4, b_3, b_2, b_1, b_0)$. These bits are then processed through an affine transformation represented by a fixed matrix operation

$$
\begin{bmatrix} b'_0 \\ b'_1 \\ b'_2 \\ b'_3 \\ b'_4 \\ b'_5 \\ b'_6 \\ b'_7 \end{bmatrix}
=
\begin{bmatrix}
1 & 0 & 0 & 0 & 1 & 1 & 1 & 1 \\
1 & 1 & 0 & 0 & 0 & 1 & 1 & 1 \\
1 & 1 & 1 & 0 & 0 & 0 & 1 & 1 \\
1 & 1 & 1 & 1 & 0 & 0 & 0 & 1 \\
1 & 1 & 1 & 1 & 1 & 0 & 0 & 0 \\
0 & 1 & 1 & 1 & 1 & 1 & 0 & 0 \\
0 & 0 & 1 & 1 & 1 & 1 & 1 & 0 \\
0 & 0 & 0 & 1 & 1 & 1 & 1 & 1
\end{bmatrix}
\begin{bmatrix} b_0 \\ b_1 \\ b_2 \\ b_3 \\ b_4 \\ b_5 \\ b_6 \\ b_7 \end{bmatrix}
\oplus
\begin{bmatrix} 1 \\ 1 \\ 0 \\ 0 \\ 0 \\ 1 \\ 1 \\ 0 \end{bmatrix}
\tag{6-74}
$$

It is important to emphasize that this matrix multiplication is not conventional arithmetic but is defined over GF(2^n). Thus, each entry of the resulting vector is obtained by performing XOR operations between the corresponding row and column elements. In summary, the affine transformation to each bit of each byte in the S-box

$$b'_i = b_i \oplus b_{(i+4) \pmod 8} \oplus b_{(i+5) \pmod 8} \oplus b_{(i+6) \pmod 8} \oplus b_{(i+7) \pmod 8} \oplus c_i \tag{6-75}$$

where $0 \leqslant i < 8$, and c_i is the i-th bit of constant byte $\texttt{c} = 01100011 = \texttt{0x63}$. This constant plays a crucial role. Without it, the all-zero input byte would remain unchanged under the affine transformation. By introducing c, the input `0x00` is mapped instead to `0x63`. At the same time, the transformation still preserves a one-to-one correspondence for all other byte values.

Example 6.4.6 Without Table 6-11, suppose the input byte is `0x10`. What is its S-box substitution?

Solution: From Table 6-13, the multiplicative inverse in GF(2^8) of `0x10` is `0x74`, 01110100 in binary. Substitute it into matrix above

$$\begin{bmatrix} b'_0 \\ b'_1 \\ b'_2 \\ b'_3 \\ b'_4 \\ b'_5 \\ b'_6 \\ b'_7 \end{bmatrix} = \begin{bmatrix} 1 & 0 & 0 & 0 & 1 & 1 & 1 & 1 \\ 1 & 1 & 0 & 0 & 0 & 1 & 1 & 1 \\ 1 & 1 & 1 & 0 & 0 & 0 & 1 & 1 \\ 1 & 1 & 1 & 1 & 0 & 0 & 0 & 1 \\ 1 & 1 & 1 & 1 & 1 & 0 & 0 & 0 \\ 0 & 1 & 1 & 1 & 1 & 1 & 0 & 0 \\ 0 & 0 & 1 & 1 & 1 & 1 & 1 & 0 \\ 0 & 0 & 0 & 1 & 1 & 1 & 1 & 1 \end{bmatrix} \begin{bmatrix} 0 \\ 0 \\ 1 \\ 0 \\ 1 \\ 1 \\ 1 \\ 0 \end{bmatrix} \oplus \begin{bmatrix} 1 \\ 1 \\ 0 \\ 0 \\ 0 \\ 1 \\ 1 \\ 0 \end{bmatrix} = \begin{bmatrix} 0 \\ 1 \\ 0 \\ 1 \\ 0 \\ 0 \\ 1 \\ 1 \end{bmatrix}$$

This yields the binary result 11001010, which is `0xCA` in hexadecimal. This calculated result matches Table 6-11. ■

6.4.3 Shift Rows

The Shift Rows (**ShiftRows**) transformation is applied to the 4×4 state matrix. Specifically, the i-th row is cyclically shifted to the left by $(i - 1)$ bytes, $1 \leqslant i \leqslant 4$. The ShiftRows of AES is illustrated in Figure 6-16.

Its inverse, **InvShiftRows**, performs the opposite: the i-th row is cyclically shifted to the right by $(i - 1)$ bytes.

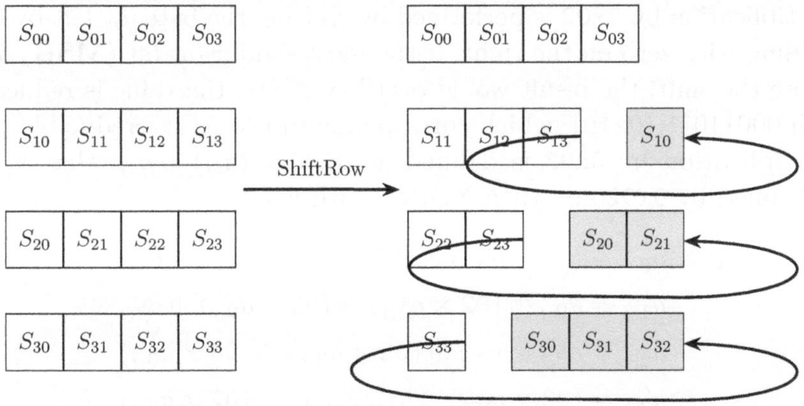

Figure 6-16: The ShiftRows of AES

In other words, the number of shifts depends on the row index. For the first row of state matrix, is not shifted; the second row does one byte circular shift to left; the third row does two byte circular shift to left; the fourth row does three byte circular shift to left. The purpose of this step is to enhance diffusion within AES, ensuring that small changes in the input propagate rapidly across the entire state.

Example 6.4.7 Example of ShiftRows is as follow.

$$\begin{bmatrix} \texttt{F2} & \texttt{4C} & \texttt{63} & \texttt{72} \\ \texttt{CA} & \texttt{FA} & \texttt{B7} & \texttt{27} \\ \texttt{09} & \texttt{2C} & \texttt{5A} & \texttt{D0} \\ \texttt{8C} & \texttt{A1} & \texttt{98} & \texttt{9E} \end{bmatrix} \xrightarrow{\text{ShiftRows}} \begin{bmatrix} \texttt{F2} & \texttt{4C} & \texttt{63} & \texttt{72} \\ \texttt{FA} & \texttt{B7} & \texttt{27} & \texttt{CA} \\ \texttt{5A} & \texttt{D0} & \texttt{09} & \texttt{2C} \\ \texttt{9E} & \texttt{8C} & \texttt{A1} & \texttt{98} \end{bmatrix}$$

6.4.4 Mix Columns

The Mix Columns(**MixColumns**) transformation represents a critical linear transformation applied to the state matrix. It is implemented as a matrix multiplication over GF(2^8), which involves polynomial multiplication and bitwise XOR addition.

In this process, AES operates on the state matrix column by column, mapping each column of four bytes to a new column of four bytes. The transformation is designed to maximize diffusion. Every byte in the output column depends on all four bytes of the input column. Consequently, changing a single bit in the input results in changes to all four output bytes. This mixing effect is achieved by interpreting the column as a vector and multiplying it by fixed constants in GF(2^8).

This operation corresponds to left-multiplying the state matrix by a fixed constant matrix.

$$\begin{bmatrix} \texttt{02} & \texttt{03} & \texttt{01} & \texttt{01} \\ \texttt{01} & \texttt{02} & \texttt{03} & \texttt{01} \\ \texttt{01} & \texttt{01} & \texttt{02} & \texttt{03} \\ \texttt{03} & \texttt{01} & \texttt{01} & \texttt{02} \end{bmatrix} \times \begin{bmatrix} a_{00} & a_{01} & a_{02} & a_{03} \\ a_{10} & a_{11} & a_{12} & a_{13} \\ a_{20} & a_{21} & a_{22} & a_{23} \\ a_{30} & a_{31} & a_{32} & a_{33} \end{bmatrix} = \begin{bmatrix} a'_{00} & a'_{01} & a'_{02} & a'_{03} \\ a'_{10} & a'_{11} & a'_{12} & a'_{13} \\ a'_{20} & a'_{21} & a'_{22} & a'_{23} \\ a'_{30} & a'_{31} & a'_{32} & a'_{33} \end{bmatrix} \tag{6-76}$$

At this stage, finite field multiplication is applied as described in Section 2.10. Since all operations are carried out in GF(2), addition corresponds to bitwise XOR.

1) Multiplication by `0x01` leaves the byte unchanged, that is $\texttt{0x01} \times a_{ij} = a_{ij}$;
2) Multiplication by `0x02` is performed by shifting the byte a_{ij} left by one bit and padding with zero on the right. If the most significant bit (**MSB**) of a_{ij} is one before the shift, the result would overflow 8 bits, the value is reduced by XOR with 00011011 (`0x1B`), which corresponds to the AES irreducible polynomial;
3) Multiplication by `0x03` is defined as $\texttt{0x02} \times (a_{ij}) \oplus a_{ij}$, that is a_{ij} is first multiplied by `0x02` and then XORed with itself.

$$a'_{0,j} = (\texttt{02} \times a_{0,j}) \oplus (\texttt{03} \times a_{1,j}) \oplus a_{2,j} \oplus a_{3,j} \tag{6-77}$$

$$a'_{1,j} = a_{0,j} \oplus (\texttt{02} \times a_{1,j}) \oplus (\texttt{03} \times a_{2,j}) \oplus a_{3,j} \tag{6-78}$$

$$a'_{2,j} = a_{0,j} \oplus a_{1,j} \oplus (\texttt{02} \times a_{2,j}) \oplus (\texttt{03} \times a_{3,j}) \tag{6-79}$$

$$a'_{3,j} = (\texttt{03} \times a_{0,j}) \oplus a_{1,j} \oplus a_{2,j} \oplus (\texttt{02} \times a_{3,j}) \tag{6-80}$$

Example 6.4.8 Compute the result of the following matrix multiplication representing the MixColumns transformation:

$$\begin{bmatrix} \texttt{02} & \texttt{03} & \texttt{01} & \texttt{01} \\ \texttt{01} & \texttt{02} & \texttt{03} & \texttt{01} \\ \texttt{01} & \texttt{01} & \texttt{02} & \texttt{03} \\ \texttt{03} & \texttt{01} & \texttt{01} & \texttt{02} \end{bmatrix} \times \begin{bmatrix} \texttt{87} & \texttt{F2} & \texttt{4D} & \texttt{97} \\ \texttt{6E} & \texttt{4C} & \texttt{90} & \texttt{EC} \\ \texttt{46} & \texttt{E7} & \texttt{4A} & \texttt{C3} \\ \texttt{A6} & \texttt{8C} & \texttt{D8} & \texttt{95} \end{bmatrix}$$

Solution: First, $a'_{00} = (\texttt{02} \times \texttt{87}) \oplus (\texttt{03} \times \texttt{6E}) \oplus (\texttt{01} \times \texttt{46}) \oplus (\texttt{01} \times \texttt{A6})$.

As an example, let us compute the first term. The constant `0x02` is represented in binary as 0000 0010, while the byte $a_{00} = \texttt{0x87}$ corresponds to the binary string 1000 0111. Since the MSB is 1, shifting left results in an overflow. We must discard the

MSB, shift left, and then perform an XOR operation with the reduction polynomial constant 0x1B, as illustrated in Figure 6-17.

$$(\texttt{0x87} \ll 1) \oplus \texttt{0x1B} = 0000\,1110 \oplus 0001\,1011 = 0001\,0101\ (\texttt{0x15}) \tag{6-81}$$

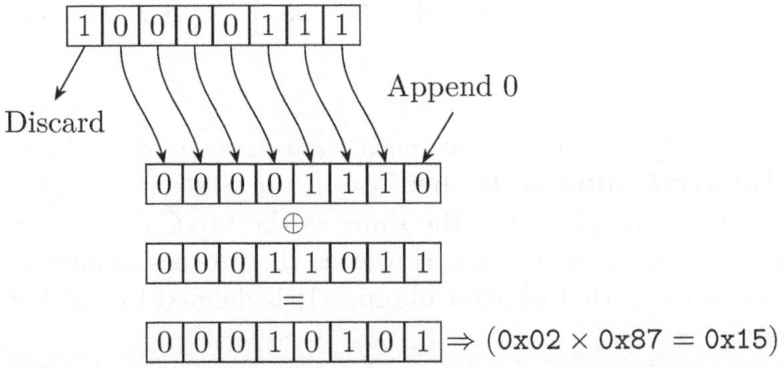

Figure 6-17: Example of MixColumns

Consider the second case (0x03 × 0x6E). The constant 0x03 is represented in binary as 0000 0011, and the byte 0x6E corresponds to 0110 1110. By definition, multiplication by 0x03 is given by (0x03 × 0x6E) = (0x02 × 0x6E) ⊕ 0x6E.

First, compute 0x02 × 0x6E. Since MSB of 0x6E is 0, no reduction with 0x1B is required. We simply shift left to get 0x02 × 0x6E = 1101 1100 (0xDC). Then, (0x02 × 0x6E) ⊕ 0x6E = 1101 1100 ⊕ 0110 1110 = 1011 0010 (0xB2). Hence, 0x03 × 0x6E = 0xB2.

The third and fourth case are easy to solve, this is the identity operation. 01 × 46 = 0100 0110(0x46), 01 × A6 = 1010 0110(0xA6).

Finally, we sum the four intermediate results using bitwise XOR

$$\begin{array}{rl} \texttt{02} \times \texttt{87} = & 0001\,0101 \\ \texttt{03} \times \texttt{6E} = & 1011\,0010 \\ \texttt{01} \times \texttt{46} = & 0100\,0110 \\ \texttt{01} \times \texttt{A6} = & 1010\,0110 \\ \hline \text{Sum}(\oplus) = & 0100\,0111 \end{array}$$

Thus, $a'_{00} = \underbrace{\underline{01000111}}_{\text{Binary}} = \underbrace{\underline{71}}_{\text{Dec}} = \underbrace{\underline{\texttt{0x47}}}_{\text{Hex}}$.

The remaining entries a'_{ij} are computed analogously. The calculations for the first row and first column are shown below

$$a'_{10} = (\texttt{01} \times \texttt{87}) \oplus (\texttt{02} \times \texttt{6E}) \oplus (\texttt{03} \times \texttt{46}) \oplus (\texttt{01} \times \texttt{A6}) = \texttt{0x37} \tag{6-82}$$

$$a'_{20} = (\texttt{01} \times \texttt{87}) \oplus (\texttt{01} \times \texttt{6E}) \oplus (\texttt{02} \times \texttt{46}) \oplus (\texttt{03} \times \texttt{A6}) = \texttt{0x94} \tag{6-83}$$

$$a'_{30} = (\texttt{03} \times \texttt{87}) \oplus (\texttt{01} \times \texttt{6E}) \oplus (\texttt{01} \times \texttt{46}) \oplus (\texttt{02} \times \texttt{A6}) = \texttt{0xED} \tag{6-84}$$

$$a'_{01} = (\texttt{01} \times \texttt{F2}) \oplus (\texttt{02} \times \texttt{4C}) \oplus (\texttt{03} \times \texttt{E7}) \oplus (\texttt{01} \times \texttt{8C}) = \texttt{0x40} \tag{6-85}$$

$$a'_{02} = (\texttt{01} \times \texttt{4D}) \oplus (\texttt{02} \times \texttt{90}) \oplus (\texttt{03} \times \texttt{4A}) \oplus (\texttt{01} \times \texttt{D8}) = \texttt{0xA3} \tag{6-86}$$

$$a'_{03} = (\texttt{01} \times \texttt{97}) \oplus (\texttt{02} \times \texttt{EC}) \oplus (\texttt{03} \times \texttt{C3}) \oplus (\texttt{01} \times \texttt{95}) = \texttt{0x4C} \tag{6-87}$$

The resulting state matrix after the MixColumns transformation is given by

$$\begin{bmatrix} \texttt{02} & \texttt{03} & \texttt{01} & \texttt{01} \\ \texttt{01} & \texttt{02} & \texttt{03} & \texttt{01} \\ \texttt{01} & \texttt{01} & \texttt{02} & \texttt{03} \\ \texttt{03} & \texttt{01} & \texttt{01} & \texttt{02} \end{bmatrix} \times \begin{bmatrix} \texttt{87} & \texttt{F2} & \texttt{4D} & \texttt{97} \\ \texttt{6E} & \texttt{4C} & \texttt{90} & \texttt{EC} \\ \texttt{46} & \texttt{E7} & \texttt{4A} & \texttt{C3} \\ \texttt{A6} & \texttt{8C} & \texttt{D8} & \texttt{95} \end{bmatrix} = \begin{bmatrix} \texttt{47} & \texttt{40} & \texttt{A3} & \texttt{4C} \\ \texttt{37} & \texttt{D4} & \texttt{70} & \texttt{9F} \\ \texttt{94} & \texttt{E4} & \texttt{3A} & \texttt{42} \\ \texttt{ED} & \texttt{A5} & \texttt{A6} & \texttt{BC} \end{bmatrix}$$

■

During the decryption process, we need to do Inverse MixColumns transformation, called **InvMixColumns**. It operates on the State column-by-column. The inverse MixColumns matrix is not the same as the MixColumns matrix, they are multiplicative inverses of each other. However, the process of inverse MixColumns is basically the same as that of MixColumns. It is defined by the following matrix multiplication:

$$\begin{bmatrix} \texttt{0E} & \texttt{0B} & \texttt{0D} & \texttt{09} \\ \texttt{09} & \texttt{0E} & \texttt{0B} & \texttt{0D} \\ \texttt{0D} & \texttt{09} & \texttt{0E} & \texttt{0B} \\ \texttt{0B} & \texttt{0D} & \texttt{09} & \texttt{0E} \end{bmatrix} \times \begin{bmatrix} a'_{00} & a'_{01} & a'_{02} & a'_{03} \\ a'_{10} & a'_{11} & a'_{12} & a'_{13} \\ a'_{20} & a'_{21} & a'_{22} & a'_{23} \\ a'_{30} & a'_{31} & a'_{32} & a'_{33} \end{bmatrix} = \begin{bmatrix} a_{00} & a_{01} & a_{02} & a_{03} \\ a_{10} & a_{11} & a_{12} & a_{13} \\ a_{20} & a_{21} & a_{22} & a_{23} \\ a_{30} & a_{31} & a_{32} & a_{33} \end{bmatrix}$$

6.4.5 Add Round Key

The Add Round Key (**AddRoundKey**) transformation can be contrasted with MixColumns, whereas MixColumns involves matrix multiplication, AddRoundKey corresponds to matrix addition, where addition is defined as bitwise XOR in GF(2). This step is simple, the 128 bits of state matrix are bitwise XORed with the 128 bits of the round key.

It is important to note the initial round, the plaintext is combined directly with the original, unmodified cipher key before any of the subsequent AES transformations are applied, that is

$$K \oplus A = \begin{bmatrix} k_{00} \oplus a_{00} & k_{01} \oplus a_{01} & k_{03} \oplus a_{03} & k_{04} \oplus a_{04} \\ k_{10} \oplus a_{10} & k_{11} \oplus a_{11} & k_{12} \oplus a_{12} & k_{13} \oplus a_{13} \\ k_{20} \oplus a_{20} & k_{21} \oplus a_{21} & k_{22} \oplus a_{22} & k_{23} \oplus a_{23} \\ k_{30} \oplus a_{30} & k_{31} \oplus a_{31} & k_{32} \oplus a_{32} & k_{33} \oplus a_{33} \end{bmatrix} \tag{6-88}$$

where K is round key and A is state matrix.

If AES employs a 192-bit or 256-bit key, the key matrix consists of 6 and 8 columns, respectively. Consequently, the initial cipher key comprises 6 and 8 words. For example, a 256-bit key can be written as

$$K = \begin{bmatrix} k_{00} & k_{01} & k_{02} & k_{03} & k_{04} & k_{05} & k_{06} & k_{07} \\ k_{10} & k_{11} & k_{12} & k_{13} & k_{14} & k_{15} & k_{16} & k_{17} \\ k_{20} & k_{21} & k_{22} & k_{23} & k_{24} & k_{25} & k_{26} & k_{27} \\ k_{30} & k_{31} & k_{32} & k_{33} & k_{34} & k_{35} & k_{36} & k_{37} \end{bmatrix} \tag{6-89}$$

Example 6.4.9 Suppose

$$K = \begin{bmatrix} \texttt{8F} & \texttt{E2} & \texttt{3B} & \texttt{29} \\ \texttt{7C} & \texttt{BC} & \texttt{11} & \texttt{84} \\ \texttt{4B} & \texttt{A3} & \texttt{9C} & \texttt{09} \\ \texttt{E0} & \texttt{4E} & \texttt{D6} & \texttt{CA} \end{bmatrix} \quad A = \begin{bmatrix} \texttt{35} & \texttt{56} & \texttt{81} & \texttt{DA} \\ \texttt{EB} & \texttt{36} & \texttt{C1} & \texttt{71} \\ \texttt{87} & \texttt{71} & \texttt{61} & \texttt{3C} \\ \texttt{F9} & \texttt{2A} & \texttt{3D} & \texttt{23} \end{bmatrix} \tag{6-90}$$

What is the result after the AddRoundKey transformation?

Solution:

$$K \oplus A = \begin{bmatrix} \texttt{59} & \texttt{D2} & \texttt{BA} & \texttt{F3} \\ \texttt{97} & \texttt{8A} & \texttt{D0} & \texttt{F5} \\ \texttt{CC} & \texttt{D2} & \texttt{FD} & \texttt{35} \\ \texttt{19} & \texttt{64} & \texttt{EB} & \texttt{E9} \end{bmatrix} \tag{6-91}$$

■

Then how is its inverse operation carried out? In XOR operations, since $P \oplus K \oplus K = P$, it means that performing the AddRoundKey operation once again will suffice.

6.4.6 Key Expansion

The key expansion in AES is more complex than in DES. AES utilizes a specialized algorithm to generate a distinct round key for each round of the encryption process. In the initial phase, the original cipher key is applied directly using the AddRoundKey transformation. In all subsequent rounds, the specific round keys derived from the expansion process are introduced during the final step of the round function. For AES-128, the key expansion algorithm accepts a 4-word key as input and expands it word by word to produce a total of 44 words.

To begin the process, the provided 128-bit binary key is typically represented in hexadecimal notation. It is then arranged into a 4×4 key matrix of bytes, populated in column-major order, as illustrated in Figure 6-18.

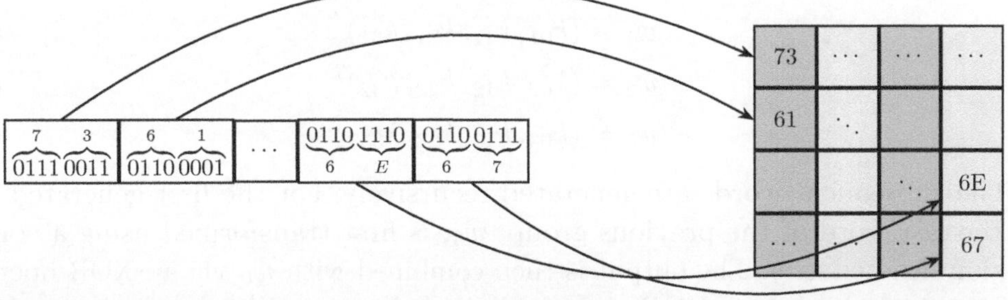

Figure 6-18: Conversion of a 128-bit Key into a 4×4 Matrix

Subkey generation in AES is performed on a column-by-column basis. Each column consists of 32 bits (4 bytes), and four consecutive columns collectively form a 128-bit (16-byte) round key. In the context of key expansion, these columns are referred to as words. We denote the element k_{ij} as the byte in row i and column j.

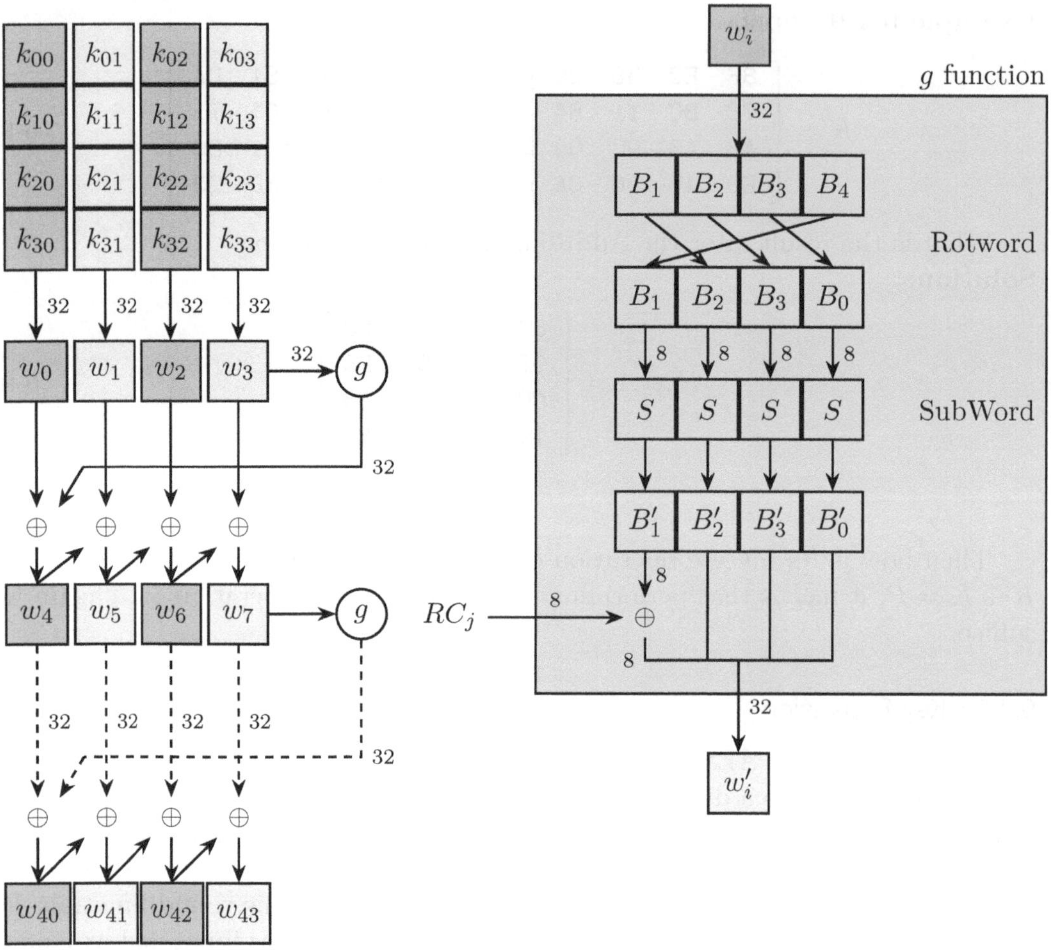

Figure 6-19: AES Key Schedule for 128-bit Key Size

As illustrated in Figure 6-19, each word w_i is composed of the four bytes $(k_{0i}, k_{1i}, k_{2i}, k_{3i})$. That is

$$w_0 = (k_{00}, k_{10}, k_{20}, k_{30})^T \tag{6-92}$$

$$w_1 = (k_{01}, k_{11}, k_{21}, k_{31})^T \tag{6-93}$$

$$w_2 = (k_{02}, k_{12}, k_{22}, k_{32})^T \tag{6-94}$$

$$w_3 = (k_{03}, k_{13}, k_{23}, k_{33})^T \tag{6-95}$$

The subsequent words are generated recursively. For the first generated word, w_4, the last word of the previous group, w_3, is first transformed using a complex function denoted as g. The output is then combined with w_0 via an XOR operation. Once w_4 is derived, it is XORed with the previous word w_1 to produce w_5. This chain of dependency continues for the rest of the block. Formally, the expansion for the first new round key can be expressed as

$$w_4 = w_0 \oplus g(w_3) \tag{6-96}$$

$$w_5 = w_1 \oplus w_4 \tag{6-97}$$

$$w_6 = w_2 \oplus w_5 \tag{6-98}$$

$$w_7 = w_3 \oplus w_6 \tag{6-99}$$

The expansion continues by updating each word w_i for $4 \leqslant i \leqslant 43$. The recurrence is defined as follows:

$$w_i = \begin{cases} w_{i-1} \oplus w_{i-4}, & \text{if } i \bmod 4 \not\equiv 0, \\ w_{i-4} \oplus g(w_{i-1}), & \text{if } i \bmod 4 \equiv 0. \end{cases} \tag{6-100}$$

Here, the g function is a composite function, consisting of three subfunctions. It can be expressed by the following formula:

$$g = \text{WordSub}\left(\text{RotWord}\left(w_{i-1}\right)\right) \oplus \text{RC}_j \tag{6-101}$$

1) The first subfunction of the g function is **RotWord**, a simple byte-wise cyclic shift: $[B_0, B_1, B_2, B_3] \longrightarrow [B_1, B_2, B_3, B_0]$. It is similar to the ShiftRows transformation, but applies to only one row rather than the entire state.
2) The second subfunction is **SubWord**, which substitutes each byte of the rotated word using the AES S-box (Table 6-11). For each byte, the higher 4 bits are taken as the row index and the lower 4 bits as the column index, yielding a substituted word $[B'_0, B'_1, B'_2, B'_3]$. This is similar to the SubBytes transformation, but applies to only four bytes rather than the entire state.
3) The third subfunction is doing XOR operation, introduces the **round constants** [57] RC_j, the RC_j is a word whose three rightmost bytes are all zero. Specifically, the first byte of the substituted word B'_1, is XORed with RC_j, where j denotes the round number. The RC_j listed in Table 6-14 that are predefined hexadecimal values. After this step, the transformed word w'_i is obtained.

Table 6-14: The Round Constant RC_j in Hexadecimal

Round	1	2	3	4	5	6	7	8	9	10
Constant	01	02	04	08	10	20	40	80	1B	36

A brief discussion of how the RC_j are determined. They are computed in GF(2^8), using the same irreducible polynomial $P(x) = x^8 + x^4 + x^3 + x + 1$. The procedure is as follows:

Round 1: $x^{1-1} \equiv x^0 \pmod{P(x)} \equiv 1 \Rightarrow 00000001 \Rightarrow$ 0x01

Round 2: $x^{2-1} \equiv x^1 \pmod{P(x)} \equiv x \Rightarrow 00000010 \Rightarrow$ 0x02

Round 3: $x^{3-1} \equiv x^2 \pmod{P(x)} \equiv x^2 \Rightarrow 00000100 \Rightarrow$ 0x04

Round 4: $x^{4-1} \equiv x^3 \pmod{P(x)} \equiv x^3 \Rightarrow 00001000 \Rightarrow$ 0x08

Round 5: $x^{5-1} \equiv x^4 \pmod{P(x)} \equiv x^4 \Rightarrow 00010000 \Rightarrow$ 0x10

Round 6: $x^{6-1} \equiv x^5 \pmod{P(x)} \equiv x^5 \Rightarrow 00100000 \Rightarrow$ 0x20

Round 7: $x^{7-1} \equiv x^6 \pmod{P(x)} \equiv x^6 \Rightarrow 01000000 \Rightarrow$ 0x40

Round 8: $x^{8-1} \equiv x^7 \pmod{P(x)} \equiv x^7 \Rightarrow 10000000 \Rightarrow$ 0x80

$$\text{Round 9:} \quad x^{9-1} \equiv x^8 \pmod{P(x)} \equiv x^4 + x^3 + x + 1 \Rightarrow 00011011 \Rightarrow \texttt{0x1B}$$
$$\text{Round 10:} \quad x^{10-1} \equiv x^9 \pmod{P(x)} \equiv x^5 + x^4 + x^2 + x \Rightarrow 00110110 \Rightarrow \texttt{0x36}$$

Example 6.4.10 Given a key $\begin{bmatrix} \texttt{73} & \texttt{73} & \texttt{69} & \texttt{72} \\ \texttt{61} & \texttt{68} & \texttt{73} & \texttt{69} \\ \texttt{74} & \texttt{63} & \texttt{62} & \texttt{6E} \\ \texttt{69} & \texttt{6A} & \texttt{6F} & \texttt{67} \end{bmatrix}$, what are the generated round subkeys?

Solution: Step 1, the first 32 bits of the key constitute the word w_0, the next 32 bits form w_1, and so so. Extracting the columns from the matrix yields

$$w_0 = \begin{bmatrix} \texttt{73} \\ \texttt{61} \\ \texttt{74} \\ \texttt{69} \end{bmatrix}, w_1 = \begin{bmatrix} \texttt{73} \\ \texttt{68} \\ \texttt{63} \\ \texttt{6A} \end{bmatrix}, w_2 = \begin{bmatrix} \texttt{69} \\ \texttt{73} \\ \texttt{62} \\ \texttt{6F} \end{bmatrix}, w_3 = \begin{bmatrix} \texttt{72} \\ \texttt{69} \\ \texttt{6E} \\ \texttt{67} \end{bmatrix}$$

Step 2, to generate w_4, we need to compute $g(w_3)$. This involves three substeps

1) **RotWord**: Applying a cyclic left shift to w_3 results in the vector $[\texttt{69}, \texttt{6E}, \texttt{67}, \texttt{72}]^T$.
2) **SubWord**: Substituting each byte using the S-box (Table 6-11) yields $[\texttt{F9}, \texttt{9F}, \texttt{85}, \texttt{40}]^T$.
3) **AddRoundConstant**: We XOR the first byte of the result with the round constant for the first round (`0x01`). That is$\texttt{F9} \oplus \texttt{01} = 1111\,1001_2 \oplus 0000\,0001_2 = 1111\,1000_2$ (`F8`).

Thus, the transformed word is $g(w_3) = w_3' = [\texttt{F8}, \texttt{9F}, \texttt{85}, \texttt{40}]^T$.

Step 3, compute $w_0 \oplus w_3'$. Proceed similarly to obtain the subsequent words. In Python, this XOR can be performed with code such as

```
hex(int('73',16)^int('f8',16))
```

It is straightforward to compute $\texttt{73} \oplus \texttt{F8} = \texttt{8B}$, hence $w_4 = [\texttt{8B}, \texttt{FE}, \texttt{F1}, \texttt{29}]^T$. Next, XOR w_4 with w_1 to obtain $w_4 \oplus w_1 = w_5 = [\texttt{F8}, \texttt{96}, \texttt{92}, \texttt{43}]^T$, similarly, $w_6 = [\texttt{91}, \texttt{E5}, \texttt{F0}, \texttt{2C}]^T$, $w_7 = [\texttt{E3}, \texttt{8C}, \texttt{9E}, \texttt{4B}]^T$.

Step 4, the first round of the key expansion now completes, and the words (w_4, w_5, w_6, w_7) serve as the input to the next round. Continue with $w_8 = w_4 \oplus g(w_7)$, and proceed analogously until all 10 rounds are generated, up to w_{43} for AES-128.

A key expansion for AES Example as shown in Table 6-15.

Table 6-15: Key Expansion for AES

Round	g Function	$w_i(i \equiv 0 \bmod 4)$	$w_i(i \equiv 1 \bmod 4)$	$w_i(i \equiv 2 \bmod 4)$	$w_i(i \equiv 3 \bmod 4)$
k_1	F89F8540	8BFEF129	F8969243	91E5F02C	E38C9E4B
k_2	660BB311	EDF54238	1563D07B	84862057	670ABE1C
k_3	63AE9C85	8E5BDEBD	9B380EC6	1FBE2E91	78B4908D
k_4	85605DBC	0B3B8301	90038DC7	8FBDA356	F70933DB

Continued on Next Page

Table 6-15: Key Expansion for AES (Continued)

Round	g Function	$w_i(i \equiv 0 \bmod 4)$	$w_i(i \equiv 1 \bmod 4)$	$w_i(i \equiv 2 \bmod 4)$	$w_i(i \equiv 3 \bmod 4)$
k_5	11C3B968	1AF83A69	8AFBB7AE	054614F8	F24F2723
k_6	A4CC2689	BE341CE0	34CFAB4E	3189BFB6	C3C69895
k_7	F4462A2E	4A7236CE	7EBD9D80	4F342236	8CF2BAA3
k_8	09F40A64	43863CAA	3D3BA12A	720F831C	FEFD39BF
k_9	4F1208BB	0C943411	31AF953B	43A01627	BD5D2F98
k_{10}	7A15467A	7681726B	472EE750	048EF177	B9D3DEEF

■

6.4.7 Example

Manually performing a complete round of AES encryption is a valuable exercise that facilitates a deeper understanding of the overall algorithmic workflow. To ensure clarity and compactness, we will utilize hexadecimal notation throughout the following calculations.

Example 6.4.11 We will encrypt the message "**Airgroundmissile**" with AES-128 using the key "**defence missile**" and determine the resulting ciphertext.
Solution: First, we convert the key into its hexadecimal representation using the standard ASCII table. Note that to meet the fixed length requirement of 128 bits. The conversion is detailed in Table 6-16.

Table 6-16: Key to Hexadecimal

Key	d	e	f	e	n	c	e		m	i	s	s	i	l	e	
Hexadecimal	64	65	66	65	6E	63	65	20	6D	69	73	73	69	6C	65	20

Thus, the key matirx is $\begin{bmatrix} 64 & 6E & 6D & 69 \\ 65 & 63 & 69 & 6C \\ 66 & 65 & 73 & 65 \\ 65 & 20 & 73 & 20 \end{bmatrix}$. Then $w_0 = [64, 65, 66, 65]^T$, $w_1 = [6E, 63, 65, 20]^T$, $w_2 = [6D, 69, 73, 73]^T$, $w_3 = [69, 6C, 65, 20]^T$.

Then compute $g(w_3)$ following the procedure described in Example 6.4.10, $w_3' = [51, 4D, B7, F9]^T$.

Compute $w_0 \oplus w_3'$. Therefore, $w_4 = [35, 28, D1, 9C]^T$, then $w_4 \oplus w_1 = w_5 = [5B, 4B, B4, BC]^T$. Similarly, $w_6 = [36, 22, C7, CF]^T$, $w_7 = [5F, 4E, A2, EF]^T$.

Step 4, the first round of the key expansion now completes, and the words (w_4, w_5, w_6, w_7) serve as the input to the next round. Continue with $w_8 = w_4 \oplus g(w_7)$ and so on, until all 44 words required for the 10 rounds of AES-128 (up to w_{43}) are generated. The overall key expansion procedure is illustrated in Figure 6-19, while the single-round computation follows the same steps as described in Example 6.4.10. The complete set of generated subkeys is summarized in Table 6-17.

Table 6-17: Round Keys

Round	$w_i(i \equiv 0 \bmod 4)$	$w_i(i \equiv 1 \bmod 4)$	$w_i(i \equiv 2 \bmod 4)$	$w_i(i \equiv 3 \bmod 4)$
k_0	64656665	6E636520	6D697373	696C6520
k_1	3528D19C	5B4BB4BC	3622C7CF	5F4EA2EF
k_2	18120E53	4359BAEF	757B7D20	2A35DFCF
k_3	8A8C84B6	C9D53E59	BCAE4379	969B9CB6
k_4	9652CA26	5F87F47F	E329B706	75B22BB0
k_5	B1A32DBB	EE24D9C4	0D0D6EC2	78BF4572
k_6	99CD6D07	77E9B4C3	7AE4DA01	025B9F73
k_7	E016E270	97FF56B3	ED1B8CB2	EF4013C1
k_8	696B9AAF	FE94CC1C	138F40AE	FCCF536F
k_9	F886321F	0612FE03	159DBEAD	E952EDC2
k_{10}	CED31701	C8C1E902	DD5C57AF	340EBA6D

The plaintext is then converted into its hexadecimal. It is important to note that, in the ASCII encoding scheme, the codes for uppercase letters differ from those of their lowercase counterparts, as shown in Table 6-18.

Table 6-18: Plaintext to Hexadecimal

Plaintext	A	i	r	g	r	o	u	n	d	m	i	s	s	i	l	e
Hexadecimal	41	69	72	67	72	6F	75	6E	64	6D	69	73	73	69	6C	65

The initial round, the plaintext is combined with the cipher key through the AddRoundKey operation.

$$\begin{bmatrix} 41 & 72 & 64 & 73 \\ 69 & 6F & 6D & 69 \\ 72 & 75 & 69 & 6C \\ 67 & 6E & 73 & 65 \end{bmatrix} \oplus \begin{bmatrix} 64 & 6E & 6D & 69 \\ 65 & 63 & 69 & 6C \\ 66 & 65 & 73 & 65 \\ 65 & 20 & 73 & 20 \end{bmatrix} \xrightarrow{\text{AddRoundKey}} \begin{bmatrix} 25 & 1C & 09 & 1A \\ 0C & 0C & 04 & 05 \\ 14 & 10 & 1A & 09 \\ 02 & 4E & 00 & 45 \end{bmatrix} \tag{6-102}$$

The first round, the SubBytes transformation is applied by substituting each byte through the AES S-box, as specified in Table 6-11. The resulting state matrix is then processed by ShiftRows and MixColumns, with the latter computed following the procedure in Example 6.4.8. Finally, the state is combined with the round key k_1 through the AddRoundKey operation.

$$\begin{bmatrix} 25 & 1C & 09 & 1A \\ 0C & 0C & 04 & 05 \\ 14 & 10 & 1A & 09 \\ 02 & 4E & 00 & 45 \end{bmatrix} \xrightarrow{\text{SubBytes}} \begin{bmatrix} 3F & 9C & 01 & A2 \\ FE & FE & F2 & 6B \\ FA & CA & A2 & 01 \\ 77 & 2F & 63 & 6E \end{bmatrix} \tag{6-103}$$

$$\begin{bmatrix} 3F & 9C & 01 & A2 \\ FE & FE & F2 & 6B \\ FA & CA & A2 & 01 \\ 77 & 2F & 63 & 6E \end{bmatrix} \xrightarrow{\text{ShiftRow}} \begin{bmatrix} 3F & 9C & 01 & A2 \\ FE & F2 & 6B & FE \\ A2 & 01 & FA & CA \\ 6E & 77 & 2F & 63 \end{bmatrix} \tag{6-104}$$

$$\begin{bmatrix} 02 & 03 & 01 & 01 \\ 01 & 02 & 03 & 01 \\ 01 & 01 & 02 & 03 \\ 03 & 01 & 01 & 02 \end{bmatrix} \times \begin{bmatrix} 3F & 9C & 01 & A2 \\ FE & F2 & 6B & FE \\ A2 & 01 & FA & CA \\ 6E & 77 & 2F & 63 \end{bmatrix} \xrightarrow{\text{MixColumns}} \begin{bmatrix} AB & 58 & 6A & EF \\ 4B & 17 & ED & 63 \\ 2C & F5 & F4 & 76 \\ C1 & A2 & CC & 0F \end{bmatrix} \tag{6-105}$$

$$\begin{bmatrix} AB & 58 & 6A & EF \\ 4B & 17 & ED & 63 \\ 2C & F5 & F4 & 76 \\ C1 & A2 & CC & 0F \end{bmatrix} \oplus \begin{bmatrix} 35 & 5B & 36 & 5F \\ 28 & 4B & 22 & 4E \\ D1 & B4 & C7 & A2 \\ 9C & BCC & CF & EF \end{bmatrix} \xrightarrow{\text{AddRoundKey}} \begin{bmatrix} 9E & 03 & 5C & B0 \\ 63 & 5C & CF & 2D \\ FD & 41 & 33 & D4 \\ 5D & 1E & 03 & E0 \end{bmatrix} \tag{6-106}$$

In the equation above, the first matrix is state matrix, and the second matrix is the round key. After repeated iterations, the process concludes with Round 10. In this final round, the MixColumns transformation is omitted. The overall procedure can be summarized as follows:

The **SubBytes** operation is detailed in Table 6-19.

Table 6-19: SubBytes Process

Round	1	2	3	4	5	6	7	8	9	10	11	12	13	14	15	16
Sub_1	3F	FE	FA	77	9C	FE	CA	2F	01	F2	A2	63	A2	6B	01	6E
Sub_2	0B	FB	54	4C	7B	4A	83	72	4A	8A	C3	7B	E7	D8	48	E1
Sub_3	89	23	87	72	18	56	76	07	8D	FA	3E	90	82	57	ED	8F
Sub_4	E8	43	95	39	8F	10	3D	13	1C	AD	97	F1	67	FC	DA	6E
Sub_5	22	B1	D5	58	FC	6B	23	8C	2C	EF	ED	3C	37	D9	FF	0B
Sub_6	E4	51	6C	E3	CD	CF	C6	21	10	D0	06	56	78	C2	78	78
Sub_7	F3	1D	25	01	6F	BF	85	2D	D6	BB	6D	C1	81	44	B9	BA
Sub_8	CA	5D	32	2E	CC	71	9B	77	0B	C5	26	9B	2A	E4	B4	6A
Sub_9	12	1A	66	F9	6D	B7	1C	F3	F5	38	00	3D	84	40	08	2D
Sub_{10}	C3	4B	E1	1C	4D	28	62	3C	C8	C8	DD	40	E6	0F	FE	A5

The **ShiftRows** operation is detailed in Table 6-20.

Table 6-20: ShiftRows Process

Round	1	2	3	4	5	6	7	8	9	10	11	12	13	14	15	16
$Shift_1$	3F	FE	A2	6E	9C	F2	01	77	01	6B	FA	2F	A2	FE	CA	63
$Shift_2$	0B	4A	C3	E1	7B	8A	48	4C	4A	D8	54	72	E7	FB	83	7B
$Shift_3$	89	56	3E	8F	18	FA	ED	72	8D	57	87	07	82	23	76	90
$Shift_4$	E8	10	97	6E	8F	AD	DA	39	1C	FC	95	13	67	43	3D	F1
$Shift_5$	22	6B	ED	0B	FC	EF	FF	58	2C	D9	D5	8C	37	B1	23	3C
$Shift_6$	E4	CF	06	78	CD	D0	78	E3	10	C2	6C	21	78	51	C6	56
$Shift_7$	F3	BF	6D	BA	6F	BB	B9	01	D6	44	25	2D	81	1D	85	C1
$Shift_8$	CA	71	26	6A	CC	C5	B4	2E	0B	E4	32	77	2A	5D	9B	9B
$Shift_9$	12	B7	00	2D	6D	38	08	F9	F5	40	66	F3	84	1A	1C	3D
$Shift_{10}$	C3	28	DD	A5	4D	C8	FE	1C	C8	0F	E1	3C	E6	4B	62	40

The **MixColumns** operation is detailed in Table 6-21. Note that the last round there is not MixColumns.

Table 6-21: MixColumns Process

Round	1	2	3	4	5	6	7	8	9	10	11	12	13	14	15	16
Mix_1	AB	4B	2C	C1	58	17	F5	A2	6A	ED	F4	CC	EF	63	76	0F
Mix_2	EA	20	E4	4D	77	E0	B5	D7	C1	6F	AC	B6	3B	EF	8C	BC
Mix_3	42	E8	29	ED	BA	A9	B5	DB	78	B6	C6	52	9C	CE	E6	F3
Mix_4	02	04	7F	78	0A	82	C6	8F	A1	48	E4	6B	C7	57	56	2E
Mix_5	1F	D3	95	F6	6E	7B	1E	BF	71	6D	CB	7B	B9	17	84	B3
Mix_6	E7	13	AF	0E	71	1D	D3	39	30	1A	69	DC	93	DD	44	B3
Mix_7	F0	9B	43	B3	B0	D3	BE	B1	73	1C	AF	5A	7A	EE	D5	99
Mix_8	50	28	49	C6	4D	B4	08	62	64	F9	12	25	B3	BD	EC	95
Mix_9	CB	4A	D2	DB	63	FC	55	6E	A4	2C	77	DF	1C	A9	E1	EB

The **AddRoundKey** operation is detailed in Table 6-22, where R_0 denotes the initial plaintext input and R_{11} represents the final ciphertext output.

Table 6-22: AddRoundKey Process

Round	1	2	3	4	5	6	7	8	9	10	11	12	13	14	15	16
R_0	41	69	72	67	72	6F	75	6E	64	6D	69	73	73	69	6C	65
R_1	25	0C	14	02	1C	0C	10	4E	09	04	1A	00	1A	05	09	45
R_2	9E	63	FD	5D	03	5C	41	1E	5C	CF	33	03	B0	2D	D4	E0
R_3	F2	32	EA	1E	34	B9	0F	38	B4	14	D1	96	11	DA	53	73
R_4	C8	64	AD	5B	73	7C	8B	82	C4	18	85	2B	0A	55	7A	45
R_5	94	56	B5	5E	55	05	32	F0	42	61	53	6D	B2	E5	7D	9E
R_6	AE	70	B8	4D	80	5F	C7	7B	7C	60	A5	B9	C1	A8	C1	C1
R_7	7E	DE	C2	09	06	F4	67	FA	4A	FE	B3	DD	91	86	DB	C0
R_8	10	8D	A1	C3	27	2C	E8	02	9E	07	23	E8	95	AE	C6	58
R_9	39	43	D3	69	B3	20	C4	7E	77	76	52	8B	4F	72	BF	FA
R_{10}	33	CC	E0	C4	65	EE	AB	6D	B1	B1	C9	72	F5	FB	0C	29
R_{11}	0D	FB	CA	A4	85	09	17	1E	15	53	B6	93	D2	45	D8	2D

The ciphertext in Hexadecimal is `0x0DFBCAA48509171E1553B693D245D82D`.

The Python code for AES encryption is as follows:

```
import numpy as np

MIX_C   = [[0x2, 0x3, 0x1, 0x1], ...]
I_MIX_C = [[0xe, 0xb, 0xd, 0x9], ...]
RCon    = [0x01000000, 0x02000000, ...]
SBOX = [[0x63, 0x7C,...]]
I_SBOX = [[0x52, 0x09, ...]]

def SubBytes(State): #SubBytes
    return [SBOX[i][j] for i, j in [(_ >> 4, _ & 0xF) for _ in State
    ]]
```

```
def ShiftRows(S): #ShiftRows
    return [S[ 0], S[ 5], S[10], S[15], S[ 4], S[ 9], S[14], S[ 3],
            S[ 8], S[13], S[ 2], S[ 7], S[12], S[ 1], S[ 6], S[11]]

def MixColumns(State):  # MixColumns
    return Matrix_Mul(MIX_C, State)

def RotWord(block): # RotWord
    return ((block & 0xffffff) << 8) + (block >> 24)

def SubWord(block): # SubWord
    result = 0
    for position in range(4):
        i = block >> position * 8 + 4 & 0xf
        j = block >> position * 8 & 0xf
        result ^= SBOX[i][j] << position * 8
    return result

def mod(poly, mod = 0b100011011):
    while poly.bit_length() > 8:
        poly ^= mod << poly.bit_length() - 9
    return poly

def mul(poly1, poly2):# Polynomial multiplication
    result = 0
    for index in range(poly2.bit_length()):
        if poly2 & 1 << index:
            result ^= poly1 << index
    return result

def Matrix_Mul(MIX_C, State):  # matirx multiplication
    M = [0] * 16
    for row in range(4):
        for col in range(4):
            for Round in range(4):
                M[row + col*4] ^= mul(MIX_C[row][Round], State[Round+
      col*4])
            M[row + col*4] = mod(M[row + col*4])
    return M

def round_key_generator(key):# Key Expansion
    w = [key >> 96, key >> 64 & 0xFFFFFFFF, key >> 32 & 0xFFFFFFFF,
         key & 0xFFFFFFFF] + [0]*40
    for i in range(4, 44):
        temp = w[i-1]
        if not i % 4:
            temp = SubWord(RotWord(temp)) ^ RCon[i//4-1]
        w[i] = w[i-4] ^ temp
    return [num_2_bytes(
                sum([w[4 * i] << 96, w[4*i+1] << 64,
                     w[4*i+2] << 32, w[4*i+3]])) for i in range(11)]

def xor( State, RoundKeys):
    return [State[i] ^ RoundKeys[i] for i in range(16)]
```

```python

def AddRoundKey( State, RoundKeys, index):# AddRoundKey
    return xor(State, RoundKeys[index])

def bytes2num( _16bytes):#bytes to int
    return int.from_bytes(_16bytes, byteorder = 'big')

def num_2_bytes( num):# int to bytes
    return num.to_bytes(16, byteorder = 'big')

def aes_encrypt(plaintext, RoundKeys):
    State = plaintext #initial
    State = AddRoundKey(State, RoundKeys, 0)
    for Round in range(1, 10): #Round
        State = AddRoundKey(MixColumns(ShiftRows(SubBytes(State))), RoundKeys, Round)
    State = AddRoundKey(ShiftRows(SubBytes(State)), RoundKeys, 10) # last round
    return State

if __name__ == '__main__':
    RoundKeys = round_key_generator(0x646566656E6365206D697373696C6520) #key
    plaintext = num_2_bytes(0x41697267726F756E646D697373696C65) # plaintext
    ciphertext = aes_encrypt(plaintext, RoundKeys) #encryption
    print('ciphertext = ' + hex(bytes2num(ciphertext))[2:].upper())
```

■

6.4.8 AES Application

A Virtual Private Network (VPN) establishes a private network over the public Internet by utilizing public network infrastructure. To ensure the confidentiality of transmitted data, VPNs require robust encryption techniques, along with reliable authentication mechanisms to verify remote users. The security of a VPN depends fundamentally on the strength of its encryption algorithms and the length of the encryption keys.

IPSec, developed by the IETF, is a suite of Internet security standards designed to deliver interoperable, cryptography-based protection for both IPv4 and IPv6 traffic. Within IPSec VPNs, the Encapsulating Security Payload (ESP) is responsible for ensuring data confidentiality. To guarantee interoperability, communicating parties must adhere to the same Domain of Interpretation (DOI). The DOI is a namespace defined by IANA that specifies permissible encryption algorithms, security protocols, and key exchange identifiers. ESP mandates a set of default encryption and authentication algorithms. By extending the IPSec DOI to include AES, both endpoints can support AES as a common encryption algorithm, provided the negotiation fields are updated accordingly.

In 2006, the Wi-Fi Alliance officially adopted WPA2 as the global standard for wireless LAN security, marking the third generation of Wi-Fi protection. WPA2 replaced the legacy RC4 cipher with AES as the foundation for its encryption. This implementation, often referred to as WPA2-AES, divides message payloads into blocks and applies the AES algorithm's multiple rounds of transformation. Despite its robustness, the algorithm executes efficiently on limited hardware resources and allows for rapid key setup. Its algebraic structure significantly complicates brute-force and reverse-engineering attempts. Furthermore, WPA2-AES incorporates enhanced integrity verification through the CCMP protocol (based on AES in CCM mode), which provides a stronger Message Integrity Code (MIC) compared to its predecessors. WPA2 remains a dominant Wi-Fi encryption protocol, ensuring key separation across sessions and users to provide strong isolation of encrypted communications.

Beyond networking, AES is widely applied in mobile applications, such as instant messaging platforms, to secure multimedia and text messages. Compression and archiving utilities, such as WinZip and RAR, integrate AES to prevent unauthorized data access. Additionally, within the U.S. government, AES is employed in specific operating system components to reinforce overall system security.

6.4.9 Cryptanalysis

To strengthen security, AES was specifically designed to exhibit the **avalanche effect**. This property ensures that a small change in plaintext or key produces a large change in the ciphertext. In practice, flipping one bit of the plaintext typically alters approximately half of the ciphertext bits. Similarly, changing one bit of the key affects roughly half of the output bits. This behavior is optimal; indeed, if every bit of the ciphertext were flipped, it would be equivalent to no change at all, as an attacker could simply invert the transformation to recover the original state.

In Example 6.4.11, if the plaintext input changes from `0x41697267726F756E646D697373696C65` to `0x40697267726F756E646D697373696C65`, the resulting ciphertext becomes `0x21D67A10A2EE126258480F843C393852`. Compared to the original ciphertext, 69 bits differ that is close to half of the total, exactly as the avalanche principle predicts.

To date, no practical or credible cryptanalytic attacks have broken AES. A brute-force attack against 128-bit AES would require trillions of years, rendering it computationally infeasible. However, side-channel techniques (e.g., cache-based timing attacks [58]) pose a real threat by exploiting implementation details rather than algorithmic weaknesses. If an attacker can execute unprivileged code on a target system, even AES-128 could be compromised [59]. Since AES was designed with lessons learned from DES, resistance to differential cryptanalysis and linear cryptanalysis was built in, and no effective methods of this type have yet been discovered.

Today, the most significant risks to AES lie not in the encryption algorithm itself, but in key management. Securely generating, distributing, and storing keys remains the foremost challenge in protecting cryptographic systems.

6.5 SM4

ShangMi4 (SM4) is a symmetric block cipher. It was developed under the leadership of *Lu Shuwang* at the *Data Assurance and Communication Security Center* (DCS Center) of the Chinese Academy of Sciences, with drafting conducted by the *Commercial Cryptography Testing Center of the State Cryptography Administration.* First released to the public in 2006, SM4 was standardized in March 2012 as industry specification GM/T 0002-2012. It was subsequently upgraded to the national standard GB/T 32907-2016 [60] in August 2016 and formally adopted by ISO as an international standard (ISO/IEC 18033-3 AMD2) in 2017.

The SM4 cipher was designed as a Chinese alternative to internationally adopted algorithms such as DES and AES, intended primarily for deployment in wireless LAN products. Like AES, it operates with a 128-bit key and a 128-bit block size (16 bytes, or 4 words). The cipher adopts unbalanced Feistel structure, where both the encryption and key expansion algorithms rely on 32 rounds of non-linear iteration followed by a final reverse transformation. Decryption follows the same process as encryption, with the exception that the round keys are applied in reverse order [61].

The structure of SM4 is illustrated in Figure 6-20.

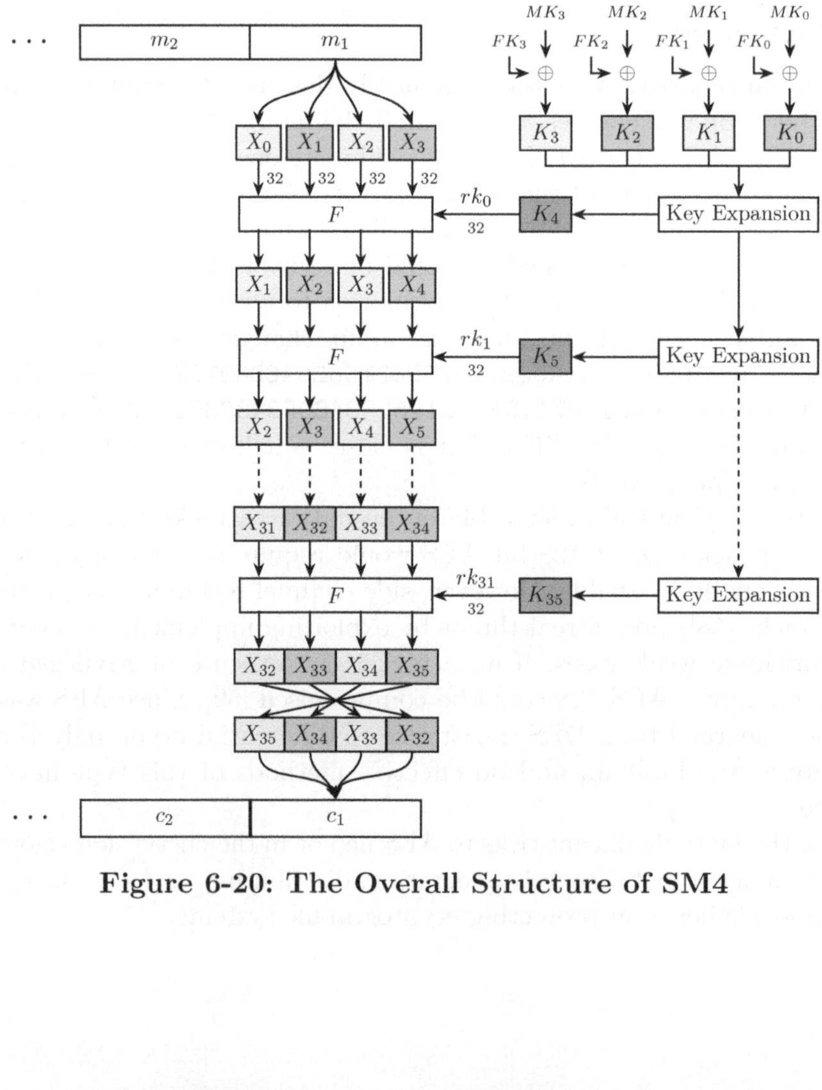

Figure 6-20: The Overall Structure of SM4

6.5.1 Encryption

The encryption algorithm contains two steps.

In the first step, the encryption procedure begins with an iterative computation consisting of 32 rounds. Since SM4 is a block cipher with a 128-bit block size and a 128-bit key size, the input is divided into four 32-bit words (X_0, X_1, X_2, X_3). Let the round keys be denoted by rk_i for $i = 0, 1, \ldots, 31$, where each rk_i is a 32-bit word. The **round function** F is defined as

$$X_{i+4} = F\left(X_i, X_{i+1}, X_{i+2}, X_{i+3}, rk_i\right) \tag{6-107}$$
$$= X_i \oplus T\left(X_{i+1} \oplus X_{i+2} \oplus X_{i+3} \oplus rk_i\right) \text{ where } i = 0, 1, \ldots, 31 \tag{6-108}$$

where "T" represents the mixed substitution function that contains reversible permutation and "$\oplus$" represents bitwise XOR. T permutation is composed of a **non-linear transformation function** τ and a **linear function** L, that is $T(\bullet) = L(\tau(\bullet))$. The function maps 32-bit inputs to 32-bit output.

The non-linear transformation function τ indicates four parallel S-boxes. Let the 32-bit input of τ be $A = (a_0, a_1, a_2, a_3)$, each a_i is a 8-bit block. The output of τ is $B = (b_0, b_1, b_2, b_3)$, each b_i is a 8-bit block. Then

$$(b_0, b_1, b_2, b_3) = \tau(A) = \left(Sbox\left(a_0\right), Sbox\left(a_1\right), Sbox\left(a_2\right), Sbox\left(a_3\right)\right) \tag{6-109}$$

The entries of the SM4 S-box are listed in Table 6-23. The substitution procedure is identical to the SubBytes transformation in AES. For each byte, the leftmost 4 bits specifies the row index, while the rightmost 4 bits specifies the column index of the S-box. The corresponding table entry is then retrieved, producing the substituted output byte.

Table 6-23: SM4 S-Box

	0	1	2	3	4	5	6	7	8	9	A	B	C	D	E	F
0	D6	90	E9	FE	CC	E1	3D	B7	16	B6	14	C2	28	FB	2C	05
1	2B	67	9A	76	2A	BE	04	C3	AA	44	13	26	49	86	06	99
2	9C	42	50	F4	91	EF	98	7A	33	54	0B	43	ED	CF	AC	62
3	E4	B3	1C	A9	C9	08	E8	95	80	DF	94	FA	75	8F	3F	A6
4	47	07	A7	FC	F3	73	17	BA	83	59	3C	19	E6	85	4F	A8
5	68	6B	81	B2	71	64	DA	8B	F8	EB	0F	4B	70	56	9D	35
6	1E	24	0E	5E	63	58	D1	A2	25	22	7C	3B	01	21	78	87
7	D4	00	46	57	9F	D3	27	52	4C	36	02	E7	A0	C4	C8	9E
8	EA	BF	8A	D2	40	C7	38	B5	A3	F7	F2	CE	F9	61	15	A1
9	E0	AE	5D	A4	9B	34	1A	55	AD	93	32	30	F5	8C	B1	E3
A	1D	F6	E2	2E	82	66	CA	60	C0	29	23	AB	0D	53	4E	6F
B	D5	DB	37	45	DE	FD	8E	2F	03	FF	6A	72	6D	6C	5B	51
C	8D	1B	AF	92	BB	DD	BC	7F	11	D9	5C	41	1F	10	5A	D8
D	0A	C1	31	88	A5	CD	7B	BD	2D	74	D0	12	B8	E5	B4	B0
E	89	69	97	4A	0C	96	77	7E	65	B9	F1	09	C5	6E	C6	84
F	18	F0	7D	EC	3A	DC	4D	20	79	EE	5F	3E	D7	CB	39	48

L is a **linear transformation function**, the 32-bit output of τ will be the input of L. Suppose the input is a 32-bit word B, and the corresponding output is a 32-bit word C, the function L is defined as follows:

$$C = L(B) = B \oplus (B \lll 2) \oplus (B \lll 10) \oplus (B \lll 18) \oplus (B \lll 24) \qquad (6\text{-}110)$$

where "$\lll i$" is circular shift of a 32-bit word, with i bits shifted left. After applying the non-linear transformation τ and the linear transformation L, one full round of iteration is completed. The output of this round then serves as the input to the next round.

One single round of F function is illustrated in Figure 6-21.

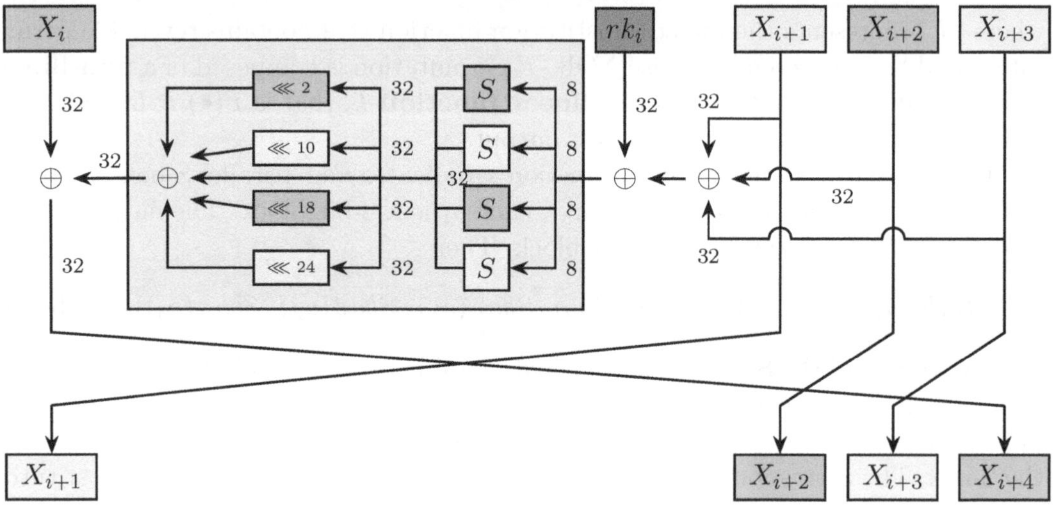

Figure 6-21: The Round Function of SM4

The second step, the **reverse transformation**. A reverse-order transformation is applied to the output of the final round to produce the ciphertext, and this operation is performed only once. Specifically, the four 32-bit words (X_{32}, X_{33},X_{34}, X_{35}) are reversed to yield the final ciphertext output

$$(C_0, C_1, C_2, C_3) = Reverse(X_{32}, X_{33}, X_{34}, X_{35}) = (X_{35}, X_{34}, X_{33}, X_{32}) \qquad (6\text{-}111)$$

6.5.2 Key Expansion

The key expansion of SM4 is structured similarly to the encryption process. As the encryption involves 32 iterations, each round requires a unique 32-bit round key. The objective is to derive these 32 round keys from the initial 128-bit key. This is accomplished via the key expansion algorithm, as illustrated in Figure 6-22.

Let the 128-bit initial key be represented as $MK = (MK_0, MK_1, MK_2, MK_3)$, each $MK_i(i = 0, 1, 2, 3)$ is 32 bits long. The round keys are represented by $(rk_0, rk_1, \ldots, rk_{31})$, where each $rk_i(i = 0, 1, \ldots, 31)$ is 32 bits long.

SM4 defines two sets of constants: the system parameter FK and the fixed parameter CK.

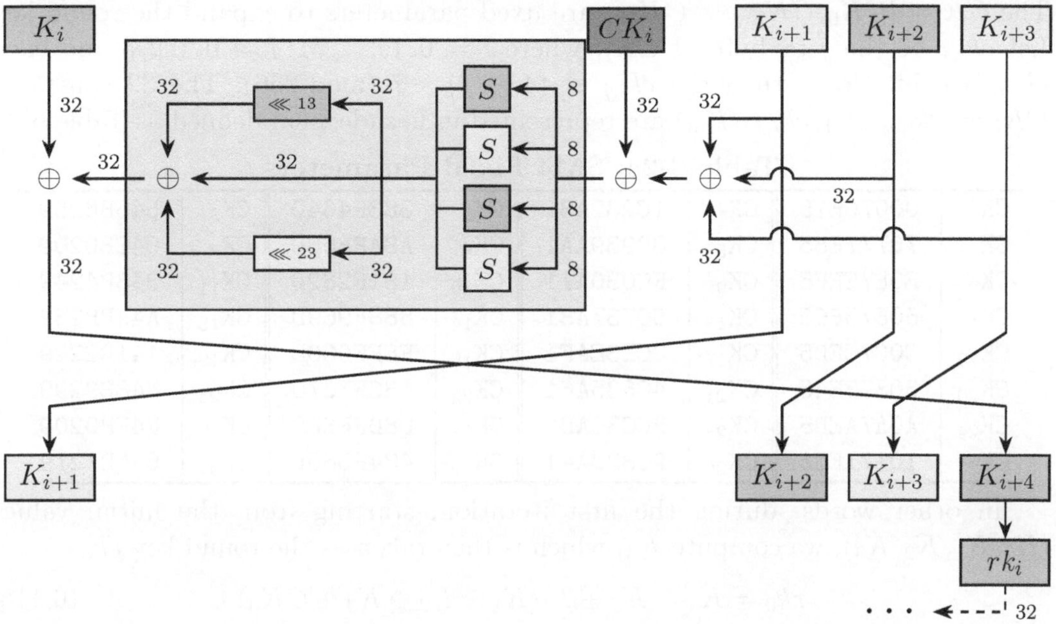

Figure 6-22: Key Expansion of SM4

The system parameter four 32-bit words $FK = (FK_0, FK_1, FK_2, FK_3)$ is used to initialize the seed key, which are represented in hexadecimal as follows:

$$FK_0 = \texttt{0xA3B1BAC6}$$
$$FK_1 = \texttt{0x56AA3350}$$
$$FK_2 = \texttt{0x677D9197}$$
$$FK_3 = \texttt{0xB27022DC}$$

1) The 128-bit initial key is represented as $MK = (MK_0, MK_1, MK_2, MK_3)$, each MK_i is XORed with the system parameter FK_i, that is

$$(K_0, K_1, K_2, K_3) = (MK_0 \oplus FK_0, MK_1 \oplus FK_1, MK_2 \oplus FK_2, MK_3 \oplus FK_3) \tag{6-112}$$

2) Starting from these four 32-bit words, 32 rounds of iteration are carried out to derive the 32 round keys. The round key rk_i is defined as

$$rk_i = K_{i+4} = K_i \oplus T'\left(K_{i+1} \oplus K_{i+2} \oplus K_{i+3} \oplus CK_i\right), \text{ where } i = 0, 1, \ldots, 31 \tag{6-113}$$

where "T'" is similar to the transformation T used in the encryption process. T' is composed of a non-linear transformation τ and a linear transformation L'. The non-linear transformation τ is the same as in T. However, the linear transformation L' differs from the L transformation used in encryption. Given a 32-bit input word B, the computation of L' is defined as

$$L'(B) = B \oplus (B \lll 13) \oplus (B \lll 23) \tag{6-114}$$

The $CK = (CK_0, CK_1, \ldots, CK_{31})$ are fixed parameters to expand the round key. Let $ck_{i,j}$ be the j-th byte of CK_i, where $i = 0, 1, \ldots, 31; j = 0, 1, 2, 3$ and each $ck_{i,j}$ is 8 bits long, then the $ck_{i,j} \equiv (4i + j) \times 7 \pmod{256}$. The 32 constants $CK_i = (ck_{i,0}, ck_{i,1}, ck_{i,2}, ck_{i,3})$ are represented in hexadecimal defined as Table 6-24.

Table 6-24: SM4 Fixed Parameters

CK_0	00070E15	CK_1	1C232A31	CK_2	383F464D	CK_3	545B6269
CK_4	70777E85	CK_5	8C939AA1	CK_6	A8AFB6BD	CK_7	C4CBD2D9
CK_8	E0E7EEF5	CK_9	FC030A11	CK_{10}	181F262D	CK_{11}	343B4249
CK_{12}	50575E65	CK_{13}	6C737A81	CK_{14}	888F969D	CK_{15}	A4ABB2B9
CK_{16}	C0C7CED5	CK_{17}	DCE3EAF1	CK_{18}	F8FF060D	CK_{19}	141B2229
CK_{20}	30373E45	CK_{21}	4C535A61	CK_{22}	686F767D	CK_{23}	848B9299
CK_{24}	A0A7AEB5	CK_{25}	BCC3CAD1	CK_{26}	D8DFE6ED	CK_{27}	F4FB0209
CK_{28}	10171E25	CK_{29}	2C333A41	CK_{30}	484F565D	CK_{31}	646B7279

In other words, during the first iteration, starting from the initial values (K_0, K_1, K_2, K_3), we compute K_4, which is then taken as the round key rk_0

$$rk_0 = K_4 = K_0 \oplus T'(K_1 \oplus K_2 \oplus K_3 \oplus CK_0) \tag{6-115}$$

In the second iteration, K_5 is computed, and K_5 is used as the round key rk_1

$$rk_1 = K_5 = K_1 \oplus T'(K_2 \oplus K_3 \oplus K_4 \oplus CK_1) \tag{6-116}$$

and so on, we can derive all 32 round keys required for the SM4 algorithm.

Example 6.5.1 Let the initial key be given by 0x0123456789ABCDEF0123456789A BCDEF, what is round key for the first round?

Solution: The 128-bit initial key is divided into four 32-bit words. Each word is expressed in binary form and then XORed with the corresponding system parameter FK_i. That is

$$MK_0 = \mathtt{01234567} \tag{6-117}$$

$$MK_1 = \mathtt{89ABCDEF} \tag{6-118}$$

$$MK_2 = \mathtt{01234567} \tag{6-119}$$

$$MK_3 = \mathtt{89ABCDEF} \tag{6-120}$$

The first round key is generated as follow

$$K_0 = MK_0 \oplus FK_0 = \mathtt{01234567} \oplus \mathtt{A3B1BAC6} = \mathtt{A292FFA1} \tag{6-121}$$

$$K_1 = MK_1 \oplus FK_1 = \mathtt{89ABCDEF} \oplus \mathtt{56AA3350} = \mathtt{DF01FEBF} \tag{6-122}$$

$$K_2 = MK_2 \oplus FK_2 = \mathtt{01234567} \oplus \mathtt{677D9197} = \mathtt{665ED4F0} \tag{6-123}$$

$$K_3 = MK_3 \oplus FK_3 = \mathtt{89ABCDEF} \oplus \mathtt{B27022DC} = \mathtt{3BDBEF33} \tag{6-124}$$

Next, we compute $K_4 = K_0 \oplus T'(K_1 \oplus K_2 \oplus K_3 \oplus CK_0)$, which yields the first round key. Given the intermediate value $K_1 \oplus K_2 \oplus K_3 \oplus CK_0 =$ 8283CB69, this 32-bit word is divided into four bytes and substituted using the S-box. Consequently, the output of the non-linear transformation τ is obtained

$$Sbox(\mathtt{82}) = \mathtt{8A} \quad Sbox(\mathtt{83}) = \mathtt{D2} \quad Sbox(\mathtt{CB}) = \mathtt{41} \quad Sbox(\mathtt{69}) = \mathtt{22} \tag{6-125}$$

For the linear transformation L', we first concatenate the binary representations of the S-box outputs. Since `0x8A` = 1000 1010, `0xD2`= 1101 0010, `0x41` = 0100 0001, `0x22` = 0010 0010, then

$$B = 10001010\,11010010\,01000001\,00100010 \quad (6\text{-}126)$$

$$B \lll 13 = 01001000\,00100100\,01010001\,01011010 \quad (6\text{-}127)$$

$$B \lll 23 = 10010001\,01000101\,01101001\,00100000 \quad (6\text{-}128)$$

$$B \oplus (B \lll 13) \oplus (B \lll 23) = 01010011\,10110011\,01111001\,01011000 \quad (6\text{-}129)$$

Thus, $T'(K_1 \oplus K_2 \oplus K_3 \oplus CK_0)$ = `0x53B37958`, we get the rk_0

$$rk_0 = K_4 = K_0 \oplus T'(K_1 \oplus K_2 \oplus K_3 \oplus CK_0) \quad (6\text{-}130)$$

$$= \texttt{A292FFA1} \oplus \texttt{53B37958} \quad (6\text{-}131)$$

$$= \texttt{F12186F9} \quad (6\text{-}132)$$

■

Example 6.5.2 Consider the plaintext is `0x0123456789ABCDEF0123456789ABCDEF` with the round key from Example 6.5.1, determine the first round output.
Solution: The plaintext is divided into four 32-bit words, that is

$$X_0 = \texttt{01234567} \quad X_1 = \texttt{89ABCDEF} \quad X_2 = \texttt{01234567} \quad X_3 = \texttt{89ABCDEF} \quad (6\text{-}133)$$

Since the round key rk_0 = `0xF12186F9`, $X_1 \oplus X_2 \oplus X_3 \oplus rk_0$ = `0xF002C39E`.

Next, apply the S-box to compute the non-linear transformation τ and then the linear transformation L, following the same procedure as in Example 6.5.1, hence the details are omitted here. The non-linear transformation τ yields the hexadecimal tuple (`18`, `E9`, `92`, `B1`). The linear transformation L produces the 32-bit value `0x26D99622`.

Substituting this result into the round function F, we obtain

$$X_4 = F(X_0, X_1, X_2, X_3, rk_0) = X_0 \oplus T(X_1 \oplus X_2 \oplus X_3 \oplus rk_0) \quad (6\text{-}134)$$

$$= \texttt{01234567} \oplus \texttt{26D99622} \quad (6\text{-}135)$$

$$= \texttt{27FAD345} \quad (6\text{-}136)$$

The output is `0x27FAD345`. ■

6.5.3 Example

Working through a round of SM4 by hand is highly instructive, as it helps readers grasp the overall encryption workflow. For clarity, we will use hexadecimal throughout the calculations.

Example 6.5.3 Encrypt the message "**Airgroundmissile**" with SM4 using the key "**defence missile**" and determine the resulting ciphertext.
Solution: First, convert the plaintext and key to hexadecimal using the ASCII table, as shown in Table 6-25.

Table 6-25: Plaintext and Key to Hexadecimal

Plaintext	41	69	72	67	72	6F	75	6E	64	6D	69	73	73	69	6C	65
Key	64	65	66	65	6E	63	65	20	6D	69	73	73	69	6C	65	20

As illustrated in Examples 6.5.1 and 6.5.2, the computational procedure for a single round key and its corresponding output can be explicitly derived.

Consequently, the subkeys and outputs for all 32 rounds are summarized in Table 6-26.

Table 6-26: SM4 Encryption Process

rk_0	054C5E35	X_4	FB417BC9	rk_{16}	56CAC57E	X_{20}	E711E8C6
rk_1	D5CA646D	X_5	2C062A6F	rk_{17}	BB1EC2AA	X_{21}	C1935C3B
rk_2	20F19E0C	X_6	85872F26	rk_{18}	10FE3761	X_{22}	D4C9DC6C
rk_3	A9A17DF0	X_7	094BE574	rk_{19}	BD60D9F9	X_{23}	30C96C8C
rk_4	20915AC5	X_8	4583BDB9	rk_{20}	14E31BE4	X_{24}	EF3ECB45
rk_5	5229EDCA	X_9	1062CB90	rk_{21}	292C208E	X_{25}	D410EF15
rk_6	F0C0130A	X_{10}	6F830AAD	rk_{22}	2539A6DB	X_{26}	B4C6D8A2
rk_7	C618FA33	X_{11}	45C9DC88	rk_{23}	51F84070	X_{27}	C567663C
rk_8	60120180	X_{12}	094D5AB7	rk_{24}	AB06B971	X_{28}	0469D80E
rk_9	A31992BA	X_{13}	6141B4DA	rk_{25}	9057398F	X_{29}	DA59D208
rk_{10}	2B399F0A	X_{14}	326A27C0	rk_{26}	CE0E6BAD	X_{30}	68C4398E
rk_{11}	2C143934	X_{15}	169E31CA	rk_{27}	11934A33	X_{31}	043D60BB
rk_{12}	A15C759C	X_{16}	C07103A0	rk_{28}	DDC0509A	X_{32}	82FDF168
rk_{13}	20E04447	X_{17}	95D47DE9	rk_{29}	86D7697F	X_{33}	74F9FAB5
rk_{14}	311C4EFB	X_{18}	8ACCA4DE	rk_{30}	FDC2F9BC	X_{34}	273179AE
rk_{15}	0D512DF7	X_{19}	7FD7AF4A	rk_{31}	166C45DF	X_{35}	73668047

The ciphertext in Hexadecimal is 0x73668047273179AE74F9FAB582FDF168.

The Python code for SM4 encryption is as follows:

```
class SM4Cipher:
    def __init__(self, key):
        if not len(key) == 16:
            raise ValueError("Length of SM4 Key must be 16")
        self._round_key = self._generate_key(key)
        self.block_size = 16

    def encrypt(self, plaintext):
        return self.process(plaintext, self._round_key)

    def process(self, text, round_key: list):
        text_ = [0 for _ in range(4)]
        for i in range(4):
            text_[i] = int.from_bytes(text[4 * i:4 * i + 4], 'big')
        for i in range(32):
            sbox_input = text_[1] ^ text_[2] ^ text_[3] ^ round_key[i]
            sbox_out = self._s_box(sbox_input)
            temp = text_[0] ^ sbox_out ^ self.shift_left(sbox_out, 2) ^ self.shift_left(sbox_out, 10)
```

```
            temp = temp ^ self.shift_left(sbox_out, 18) ^ self.shift_left(sbox_out, 24)
            text_ = text_[1:] + [temp]
            print(i,hex(text_[3])[2:].upper().zfill(8))
        text_ = text_[::-1]
        result = bytearray()
        for i in range(4):
            result.extend(text_[i].to_bytes(4, 'big'))
        return bytes(result)

    def _generate_key(self, key):
        """Key Expansion"""
        round_key, key_temp = [0 for i in range(32)], [0 for i in range(4)]
        FK = [0xa3b1bac6, 0x56aa3350, 0x677d9197, 0xb27022dc]
        CK = [0x00070e15, 0x1c232a31, 0x383f464d, 0x545b6269,...]
        for i in range(4):
            temp = int.from_bytes(key[4 * i:4 * i + 4], 'big')
            key_temp[i] = temp ^ FK[i]
        for i in range(32):
            sbox_input = key_temp[1] ^ key_temp[2] ^ key_temp[3] ^ CK[i]
            sbox_out = self._s_box(sbox_input)
            round_key[i] = key_temp[0] ^ sbox_out ^ self.shift_left(sbox_out, 13) ^ self.shift_left(sbox_out, 23)
            key_temp = key_temp[1:] + [round_key[i]]
            print('//', i,hex(key_temp[3])[2:].upper().zfill(8))
        return round_key

    @staticmethod
    def _s_box(n: int):
        SBOX = [0xD6, 0x90, 0xE9, 0xFE, 0xCC, 0xE1, 0x3D, 0xB7,...]
        result = bytearray()
        for item in list(n.to_bytes(4, 'big')):
            result.append(SBOX[item])
        return int.from_bytes(result, 'big')

    @staticmethod
    def shift_left(n, m):
        """shift left"""
        return ((n << m) | (n >> (32 - m))) & 0xFFFFFFFF
key = bytes.fromhex("646566656E6365206D697373696C6520")#128bit key
plaintext = bytes.fromhex("41697267726F756E646D697373696C65")#128bit plaintext
sm4 = SM4Cipher(key)
print(sm4.encrypt(plaintext).hex())
```

■

6.5.4 Decryption

To decrypt the ciphertext of SM4, we define two transformations: S transformation and R transformation, for $i = 0, 1, \ldots, 31$, we have

$$S_{rk_i}(a, b, c, d) = (b, c, d, a \oplus T\,(b \oplus c \oplus d \oplus rk_i)) \tag{6-137}$$

$$R(a, b, c, d) = (d, c, b, a) \tag{6-138}$$

It is easy to prove that $R \circ S_{rk_i} \circ R \circ S_{rk_i}(a,b,c,d)$ is an **identity transformation**

$$R \circ S_{rk_i}(a,b,c,d) = (a \oplus T(b \oplus c \oplus d \oplus rk_i), d, c, b) \tag{6-139}$$

$$\begin{aligned} S_{rk_i} \circ R \circ S_{rk_i}(a,b,c,d) &= (d, c, b, a \oplus T(b \oplus c \oplus d \oplus rk_i) \oplus T(d \oplus c \oplus b \oplus rk_i)) \\ &= (d, c, b, a) \end{aligned} \tag{6-140}$$

$$R \circ S_{rk_i} \circ R \circ S_{rk_i}(a,b,c,d) = (a,b,c,d) \tag{6-141}$$

Thus, the inverse of the transformation S can be readily obtained as $S_{rk_i}^{-1} = R \circ S_{rk_i} \circ R(a,b,c,d)$. Likewise, it is easy to verify that $R \circ R = (a,b,c,d)$.

According to the encryption procedure of the SM4 algorithm, and assuming the round keys are ordered as $(rk_0, rk_1, \ldots, rk_{31})$, the overall encryption process can be expressed as

$$c = \mathrm{E}_{rk}(m) = R \circ S_{rk_{31}} \circ S_{rk_{30}} \circ \cdots \circ S_{rk_0}(a,b,c,d) \tag{6-142}$$

Therefore, the overall decryption process can be expressed as:

$$\mathrm{D}_{rk}(c) = \mathrm{E}_{rk}^{-1}(c) = (R \circ S_{rk_{31}} \circ S_{rk_{30}} \circ \cdots \circ S_{rk_0}(a,b,c,d))^{-1} \tag{6-143}$$

$$= S_{rk_0}^{-1} \circ S_{rk_1}^{-1} \circ \cdots \circ S_{rk_{31}}^{-1}(a,b,c,d) \circ R^{-1} \tag{6-144}$$

$$= R \circ S_{rk_0} \circ R \circ R \circ S_{rk_1} \circ R \circ R \cdots R \circ R \circ S_{rk_{31}} \circ R \circ R^{-1} \tag{6-145}$$

$$= R \circ S_{rk_0} \circ S_{rk_1} \circ \cdots \circ S_{rk_{31}} \tag{6-146}$$

The decryption process of SM4 is the same as the encryption process, except that the round keys are used in the reverse order of $(rk_{31}, rk_{30}, \ldots, rk_0)$.

6.5.5 Cryptanalysis

The SM4 encryption algorithm provides a key strength comparable to that of AES, with a key space of 2^{128} defining its theoretical security level. This places SM4 distinctively above 3DES in terms of overall cryptographic strength.

To date, several types of cryptanalytic attacks have been explored against SM4, including linear cryptanalysis and differential cryptanalysis [62] [63] [64]. Research indicates that linear cryptanalysis can reduce the effective breaking complexity to approximately $2^{106.8}$ [65], while differential cryptanalysis can reduce it to $2^{112.3}$ [66]. Other methods, such as integral cryptanalysis and algebraic (matrix-based) techniques, have also been investigated. Nevertheless, public evaluations indicate that SM4 remains resistant to all currently known practical attacks and retains sufficient security margins.

However, SM4 is not entirely immune to implementation vulnerabilities. When implemented in hardware, it may be exposed to side-channel attacks [67], particularly power analysis, where an attacker exploits correlations between round keys and masking values to recover secret information. To mitigate these threats, hardware-oriented countermeasures have been proposed [68]. In principle, when SM4 is implemented in hardware, parameters and keys should be generated with randomness to avoid fixed correlations. With proper hardware enhancements, SM4 can effectively resist such implementation-level attacks.

6.6 EXERCISES

1) Consider the ECB mode. Based on the characteristic that each plaintext block is encrypted independently, devise an attack strategy.
2) Consider the CBC mode. Prove that if the n-th ciphertext block is corrupted, the $(n+2)$-th ciphertext block can still be decrypted to recover the plaintext.
3) Consider the CFB mode. How many blocks are affected by a single-bit error in transmission?
4) Consider the CFB mode. Explain why encryption cannot commence from the middle of the plaintext.
5) Consider the OFB mode. Suppose a transmission error occurs in the ciphertext block c_i, flipping exactly one bit. Show that this error affects only the corresponding bit in the decrypted plaintext m_i and does not propagate to subsequent blocks m_{i+j} for $j > 0$.
6) Consider the CTR mode. Show that the decryption function D_K is never invoked during the recovery of m_i.
7) Consider the PCBC mode. The mode was designed to ensure that any change in the ciphertext or plaintext would propagate indefinitely. Suppose a single-bit error occurs in c_i. Show that every subsequent decrypted block m_{i+j} will be corrupted for $j \geqslant 1$.
8) Prove that decryption in a Feistel cipher is performed by applying the encryption algorithm to the ciphertext with reversed key schedule.
9) Consider a block cipher using 8-bit blocks that is based on the Feistel structure with two rounds and no initial and final permutation. The round function is $f_i(x, k) = (2i \cdot k)^x \pmod{15}$ for $i = 1, 2$, where $k \in \mathbb{Z}_{15}$. If $k = 7$ and the ciphertext is 00111111, what is the plaintext?
10) Given the Feistel structure $L_i = R_{i-1}$ and $R_i = L_{i-1} \oplus f(R_{i-1}, K_i)$, if a single bit is flipped in L_0, in which round i will this error first affect the output of the f-function?
11) Suppose a sequence of plaintext blocks is encrypted using DES, producing a corresponding sequence of ciphertext blocks. Let one ciphertext block be transmitted incorrectly. Show that the number of plaintext blocks that will be decrypted incorrectly is equal to one if ECB or OFB modes were used for encryption; and equal to two if CBC or CFB modes were used.
12) Consider the DES cipher, answer the following questions:
    (a) For the first S-box, given the input 100011, determine the output.
    (b) For the third S-box, given the input 001100, determine the output.
    (c) For the fifth S-box, given the input 111111, determine the output.
    (d) For the seventh S-box, given the input 110101, determine the output.
13) Consider the DES cipher, if S-box is linear, it must satisfy $S(\mathbf{a} \oplus \mathbf{b}) = S(\mathbf{a}) \oplus S(\mathbf{b})$. Using two test vectors from the same row of S-box 1, prove by counterexample that S-box 1 is a non-linear mapping.
14) Consider the DES cipher. Suppose the plaintext and key are

$$\text{plaintext} : \texttt{0x123456ABCD132536}$$

$$\text{key} : \texttt{0xAABB09182736CCDD}$$

Answer the following questions:

(a) What is the key after the initial permutation?

(b) What are the respective outputs U and V of the Permuted Choice 1 (PC-1)?

(c) After 16 rounds of encryption, determine the ciphertext.

15) Consider the DES cipher. Suppose the plaintext and key are

plaintext : `0x0000000000000000`

key : `0x22234512987ABB23`

resulting in the ciphertext `0x4789FD476E82A5F1`. If the plaintext is changed to `0x0000000000000001`, determine the number of differing bits between the new ciphertext and the original ciphertext.

16) Consider the DES cipher. Show the result of `0xAAAABBBBCCCCDDDD` after passing it through the final permutation box.

17) Show that DES decryption is the inverse of DES encryption.

18) Compare the substitution in DES and AES. Why does AES use only one S-box, while DES uses eight?

19) Consider the AES cipher. Is the AES S-box static or dynamic? Explain.

20) Consider a simplified AES cipher over the field GF(2^4) defined by the irreducible polynomial $P(x) = x^4 + x + 1$. Let the input element be represented by the polynomial $A(x) = x^3 + x$. Using the Extended Euclidean Algorithm, find its multiplicative inverse $A^{-1}(x) \pmod{P(x)}$.

21) Consider a simplified AES cipher with a 2×2 state matrix S where each entry is an element of GF(2^4). The MixColumns step is defined as the matrix multiplication $S' = M \times S$, where

$$M = \begin{bmatrix} x & x+1 \\ x+1 & x \end{bmatrix}$$

All operations are performed in GF(2^4) modulo $x^4 + x + 1$. Given the first column of the state vector $s = \begin{bmatrix} 1 \\ x^2 \end{bmatrix}$, compute the resulting column s' after the MixColumns transformation.

22) What are the advantages and disadvantages of AES over DES?

23) Consider the AES cipher. Show that

$$\text{SubBytes } (a \oplus b) \neq \text{ SubBytes } (a) \oplus \text{ SubBytes } (b)$$

where a and b are bytes.

24) Arithmetic in GF(2^4) with the irreducible polynomial $P(x) = x^4 + x + 1$. Compute $A(x) + B(x) \pmod{P(x)}$ and $A(x) \cdot B(x) \pmod{P(x)}$, where

(a) $A(x) = x^2 + x, \quad B(x) = x^3 + x^2 + 1$

(b) $A(x) = x^2 + x, \quad B(x) = x + 1$

25) Consider the AES cipher. Given the SubBytes transformation inputs `0xA4`, `0x7B`, and `0x69`, determine their respective SubBytes transformation outputs.

26) Consider the AES cipher. Given the ASCII-encoded plaintext **AESUSESAMATRIXZZ** and the key **ABCDEFGHABCDEFGH**, answer the following questions:

(a) Show the original contents of state matrix.
(b) Show the value of state matrix after initial AddRoundKey.
(c) Show the value of state matrix after SubBytes.
(d) Show the value of state matrix after ShiftRows.
(e) Show the value of state matrix after MixColumns

27) Consider the AES-128 cipher. Suppose the plaintext and key are

plaintext : `0x24252627282930313233343536373839`

key : `0x21222324252627282930313233343536`

Show the ciphertext.

28) Consider the SM4 cipher. Given the initial state $X_0 = X_1 = X_2 = X_3 =$ `0x00000000` and the first round key $rk_0 =$ `0x12345678`, calculate the value of X_4 by executing one complete round of the F function.

29) Consider the SM4 cipher. The fixed constants CK_i are defined by $ck_{i,j} = (4i + j) \times 7 \pmod{256}$. Calculate the 32-bit hexadecimal value of the first constant CK_0.

30) Consider the SM4 cipher. Let the intermediate key state be (K_0, K_1, K_2, K_3). Calculate the first round key rk_0 using the formula $rk_0 = K_0 \oplus T'(K_1 \oplus K_2 \oplus K_3 \oplus CK_0)$, assuming all K_i are zero words.

III

Asymmetric Cryptography

Asymmetric cryptography, also known as public-key cryptography, constitutes a pivotal branch of the field, offering robust security guarantees through unique encryption and decryption mechanisms. The fundamental concept relies on a mathematically related key pair: a public key and a private key. The public key is disseminated openly for encrypting messages, whereas the private key is kept confidential for decryption. This architecture eliminates the requirement for a pre-shared secret between communicating parties, thereby significantly simplifying key management. The discipline encompasses several prominent algorithms, including RSA, ElGamal, Elliptic Curve Cryptography (ECC), and lattice-based cryptography, each characterized by distinct mathematical foundations and application domains.

The RSA algorithm is one of the most well-known and widely used schemes in asymmetric cryptography. Its security relies on the difficulty of the integer factorization problem. Even with powerful computational resources, an attacker would require an impractical amount of time to break it. RSA is widely used in digital signatures and data encryption to ensure secure communication.

Similar to RSA, the ElGamal encryption algorithm bases its security on the difficulty of the discrete logarithm problem modulo a large prime.

Beyond RSA and ElGamal, ECC is another prominent area in asymmetric cryptography. It utilizes the discrete logarithm problem on elliptic curves for encryption and decryption. Compared to traditional RSA, ECC uses shorter keys for the same security level. This results in higher efficiency and lower storage costs. Consequently, ECC is an ideal solution for resource-constrained environments, such as mobile devices and Internet of Things (IoT) applications.

Lattice-based cryptography constitutes a vital and rapidly evolving branch of modern cryptography. Grounded in lattice theory and the geometry of high-dimensional spaces, these schemes rely on the computational hardness of specific lattice problems for their security. A distinguishing feature of lattice-based systems is their inherent resistance to quantum computing attacks, rendering them a cornerstone of post-quantum cryptography (PQC) and essential for future-proofing security infrastructure. Beyond standard encryption, this field has garnered significant attention for enabling advanced primitives; notably, fully homomorphic encryption is predominantly realized through lattice-based constructions.

Beyond standard encryption, asymmetric cryptography encompasses critical protocols such as the Diffie-Hellman key exchange. Collectively, these primitives act as foundational elements for digital signatures, identity authentication, and secure key establishment, thereby ensuring data integrity and security. The evolution of asymmetric cryptography has fundamentally driven progress in information security, providing essential fortification for the digital ecosystem. However, the field faces escalating challenges stemming from increasing computational power and novel attack vectors. Consequently, continuous algorithmic innovation remains imperative to withstand these emerging security threats.

CHAPTER 7

RSA Cryptosystem

This chapter introduces the RSA cryptosystem, a seminal public-key algorithm founded on the difficulty of integer factorization. Prior to the advent of RSA, the field of cryptography was dominated by symmetric-key algorithms. The introduction of RSA provided an elegant solution to the fundamental problem of key distribution. Unlike symmetric systems, RSA utilizes a pair of distinct keys for encryption and decryption. The specific mathematical relationship between these keys eliminates the requirement for a secure channel to transmit the decryption key.

Topics covered in this chapter:

- Introduction to RSA
- RSA Encryption and Decryption Process
- RSA Cryptanalysis
- Prime Numbers: Definition and Properties
- Primality Testing

7.1 INTRODUCTION

In 1977, *Ronald Rivest*, *Adi Shamir*, and *Leonard Adleman* of the Massachusetts Institute of Technology introduced the first fully practical public-key cryptosystem, RSA, in their seminal paper [8]. The acronym "RSA" named for its inventors. The security of RSA rests on the computational difficulty of factoring large integers.

Ronald Rivest, who obtained his Ph.D. at Stanford University and is a professor at MIT, is a renowned cryptographer. In addition to co-inventing RSA, he designed the well-known RC (Rivest Cipher) family of symmetric encryption algorithms and the MD (Message Digest) family of hash functions. He is also a leading advocate for computer science education, most notably as a co-author of the authoritative textbook *Introduction to Algorithms*.

Adi Shamir, born in Israel, obtained his Ph.D. at the Weizmann Institute of Science, where he serves as a professor. Shortly after completing his doctorate in 1977, he joined MIT as a researcher, where he collaborated with *Rivest* and *Adleman* on the RSA algorithm. Beyond RSA, *Shamir* has made foundational contributions to cryptanalysis, particularly in the development of differential cryptanalysis.

DOI: 10.1201/9781042011087-7

Leonard Adleman, who obtained his Ph.D. from the University of California, Berkeley, is a professor at the University of Southern California. He is not only a computer scientist but also an active researcher in molecular biology. For their joint work on RSA, *Rivest, Shamir*, and *Adleman* were awarded the 2002 *Turing Award*, the most prestigious honor in computer science.

The RSA algorithm is a prototypical asymmetric cryptosystem and remains one of the most extensively studied public-key schemes to date. Since its introduction in 1978, RSA has withstood decades of cryptanalytic scrutiny and has been widely adopted across both academia and industry. It continues to serve as a cornerstone of modern security, underpinning protocols such as HTTPS.

The theoretical foundation for RSA was laid in 1976, when *Whitfield Diffie* and *Martin Hellman* published their landmark paper, "*New Directions in Cryptography*" [7]. This seminal work introduced the concept of public-key cryptography, which was rapidly accepted by the research community.

At its mathematical core, RSA relies on the concept of a trapdoor one-way function. Informally, a one-way function is a mapping that is efficient to compute in the forward direction but computationally infeasible to invert without specific auxiliary information. This "trapdoor" property facilitates the separation of encryption and decryption processes, thereby enabling secure public-key exchange.

Definition 7.1.1 One-way Function

A function $f\colon \{0,1\}^n \to \{0,1\}^n$ *is a one-way function if*
1) $y = f(x)$ *is easy to evaluate;*
2) $x = f^{-1}(y)$ *is hard to evaluate;*

To formalize the notions of "easy" and "hard" in a cryptographic context, we rely on the concept of Probabilistic Polynomial Time (PPT). A function is considered "easy" to evaluate if there exists a PPT algorithm that computes it for every input. Conversely, a task is regarded as "hard" if no PPT algorithm can solve it with non-negligible probability.

RSA utilizes these concepts through the framework of a trapdoor one-way function. While the generation of the RSA modulus involves multiplying two large primes, an operation that is computationally efficient, reversing this process (integer factorization) is computationally infeasible on classical computers. Consequently, without the private key, inverting the encryption function is considered hard.

However, a standard one-way function alone is insufficient for a cryptosystem. If we were to "encrypt" using a strictly one-way function, even the legitimate receiver would be unable to recover the plaintext. The solution lies in the trapdoor function that is easy to compute in one direction and hard to invert, unless a specific piece of secret information is provided.

Definition 7.1.2 Trapdoor One-way Function

A function $f\colon \{0,1\}^* \to \{0,1\}^*$ is strictly designated as a trapdoor one-way function if it is a standard one-way function strictly possessing the following auxiliary structural property: while computing the inverse mapping $f^{-1}(y)$ is globally intractable for any arbitrary Probabilistic Polynomial Time (PPT) adversary, there exists a specific piece of secret auxiliary information t (the trapdoor) such that knowledge of t renders the exact recovery of $x = f^{-1}(y)$ computationally efficient.

To ensure confidentiality, a cipher must rely on computations that are computationally infeasible for an adversary to reverse. However, this requirement presents a dilemma: if decryption were inherently difficult, the intended recipient would also be unable to recover the plaintext efficiently. The resolution to this problem involves equipping the algorithm with a trapdoor, denoted as t.

A trapdoor function is a specific type of one-way function widely used in public-key cryptography. It is constructed such that the forward evaluation is efficient for any party, whereas inversion is computationally hard without specific auxiliary information. However, possession of the trapdoor t renders the inversion process efficient. This property ensures that decryption is feasible only for the designated receiver, as illustrated in Figure 7-1.

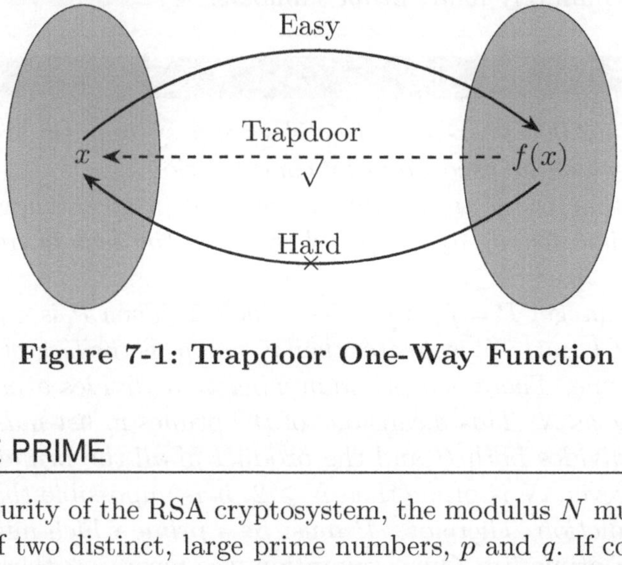

Figure 7-1: Trapdoor One-Way Function

7.2 WHY USE PRIME

To ensure the security of the RSA cryptosystem, the modulus N must be constructed as the product of two distinct, large prime numbers, p and q. If composite numbers were used instead, the fundamental mathematical structure of key generation would be invalid. Specifically, the standard formula for Euler's totient function holds only when p and q are prime. Using composite factors would render this formula incorrect, resulting in a malfunction of the encryption-decryption cycle.

More importantly, the use of composite factors would weaken the security of the system. The security of RSA relies on the integer factorization problem. If p and q were composite, the modulus N would inherently contain smaller prime factors. Cryptanalytic algorithms can isolate small factors with significantly lower computational complexity than is required to factor the product of two large primes. Therefore, RSA explicitly requires p and q to be large primes to ensure that the modulus resists factorization attacks by maximizing the size of its prime factors.

Definition 7.2.1 Prime Numbers

*A positive integer n is said to be **prime** when $n > 1$ and the only positive divisors of n are 1 and n.*

If an integer $n > 1$ is not prime, it is called **composite**. If n is composite, then there exists a prime p such that $p|n$ and $1 < p < n$.

Example 7.2.1 List of prime numbers up to 100. They are: 2, 3, 5, 7, 11, 13, 17, 19, 23, 29, 31, 37, 41, 43, 47, 53, 59, 61, 67, 71, 73, 79, 83, 89, 97.

Apart from the numbers listed above, all the other numbers within 100 are composite.

By definition of the prime number, which states that a number should have exactly two factors for it. But, number 1 has one and only one factor which is 1 itself. Thus, 1 is not a prime number, and is not a composite number.

Theorem 7.2.1 The Infinitude of Primes

There are infinitely many prime numbers.

Proof

More than 2,000 years ago, Euclid gave a systematic argument in the Elements, in which he used proof by contradiction.

Suppose that there are a finite number of primes. Then we can write them in a prime list $p_1, p_2, \ldots, p_r$ where p_r is the last prime number and $p_1 < p_2 < \cdots < p_r$.

Define an integer $P = p_1 \times p_2 \times \cdots \times p_r + 1$. Then P is a positive integer greater than 2. Clearly, P is greater than p_r and p_r is the largest prime number, P is not a prime. There is a prime number that divides evenly into P. We call this prime as N. This means one of the primes in list must divide P,

Since N divides both P and the product of all the primes, it must also divide 1. However, N is prime then $N \geqslant 2$, it is impossible that N divides 1, it is a contradiction. Therefore, P must be a prime which must then not be an element of prime list. Our assumption was incorrect, there are infinitely many prime numbers.

7.2.1 Integer Factorization

Given two prime factors p and q, multiplication and factoring, we have

$$p = 16347336458092538484431338838650908598417836700330923121811108523893331001045081512121181675115 79$$

$$
\begin{aligned}
q = {} & 190087128166482211312685157393541397547189678996851549366663 8\\
& 5390880271038021044989571912614655 71\\
N = p \cdot q = {} & 310741824049004372135075003588856793003734602284272754572016 1\\
& 948823206440518081504556346829671723286782437916272838033415 4\\
& 710731085019195485290073377248227835257423864540146917366024 7\\
& 7652346609
\end{aligned}
$$

It is straightforward to compute $N = p \cdot q$. However, attempting to factor N into its components p and q is difficult. With no clear strategy to follow. Several classical methods for integer factorization are introduced below.

Trial Division

The most elementary approach to primality testing is trial division. Given an integer n, the method involves attempting to divide n by every integer d less than n. If no such integer divides n, then n is declared prime.

However, if n is a composite number, it must possess a prime divisor less than or equal to $\sqrt{n}$. Consequently, to determine whether n is prime, only needs to test all integers up to $\sqrt{n}$. The time complexity of this algorithm is $\mathcal{O}(\sqrt{n})$. This efficiency can be further improved if a pre-computed table of primes is available; in that case, one needs only to test prime divisors up to $\sqrt{n}$.

```
def is_prime(a):
    if a == 1:
        return False
    for i in range(2, int(a**0.5)+1):
        if a % i == 0:
            return False
    return True
a = '67280421310721 '
b = is_prime(int(a))
print(b)
```

General Number Field Sieve

The General Number Field Sieve (GNFS) stands as the most efficient algorithm known today for factoring large integers. It was developed as a generalization of the Special Number Field Sieve (SNFS). The conceptual foundations were originally established by *John M. Pollard* [69] and later refined by *Hendrik Lenstra* [26]. Building upon these works, GNFS emerged as a powerful tool that dramatically reduced the computational difficulty of factoring arbitrary large integers.

Prior to the advent of modern sieve methods, factoring large numbers was computationally prohibitive. The SNFS demonstrated the potential of these techniques by successfully factoring the ninth Fermat number. Its generalization, GNFS, subsequently became the standard method for practical large-scale factorization efforts.

The complexity of GNFS can be expressed as

$$L_n\left[\frac{1}{3}, \sqrt[3]{\frac{64}{9}}\right] = \exp\left(\left(\sqrt[3]{\frac{64}{9}} + o(1)\right)(\ln n)^{\frac{1}{3}}(\ln \ln n)^{\frac{2}{3}}\right) \tag{7-1}$$

where $L_n[\alpha, c] = e^{(c+\mathcal{O}(1))(\ln n)^{\alpha}(\ln \ln n)^{1-\alpha}}$, $\alpha \in [0,1]$, $c \in \mathbb{R}^{+}$. The running time of GNFS is a sub-exponential bound that, among all currently known methods, comes closest to linear growth.

Shor's Algorithm

In the realm of quantum computing, Shor's Algorithm presents a paradigm shift in integer factorization. Originally introduced by Peter Shor in 1994 [70] and subsequently published in the SIAM Journal on Computing in 1997, this algorithm demonstrated that integer factorization can be executed in polynomial time on a quantum computer. This efficiency represents an exponential advantage over the best known classical algorithm, the General Number Field Sieve (GNFS).

The implications for cryptography are profound. Since Shor's algorithm solves the factorization problem efficiently, simply increasing the RSA key length fails to provide adequate security. Once sufficiently powerful quantum computers exist, they will be capable of breaking RSA keys of any practical size.

However, a significant gap remains between theory and practice. The implementation of Shor's Algorithm requires large-scale, fault-tolerant quantum hardware. To date, experimental realizations have been limited to proof-of-concept demonstrations on small-scale quantum processors, capable of factoring only very small integers. Despite these practical limitations, the theoretical existence of Shor's Algorithm underscores a fundamental vulnerability: the security of RSA is not absolute but relies entirely on the limitations of classical computing architectures.

7.2.2 Difficulty of Integer Factorization

In cryptography, the **MIPS-Year** [71] (Million Instructions Per Second-Year) is a classical unit used to quantify computational workload. It is defined as the amount of computation performed by a processor sustaining one million instructions per second over the course of a year. Analogous to the "light-year" in physics, the MIPS-Year does not measure time duration but rather serves as a standard metric for computational magnitude.

One standard MIPS-Year corresponds to approximately 2^{45} elementary instructions. In early cryptographic literature, this metric was extensively used to estimate the feasibility of factorization attacks. For instance, factoring a 512-bit RSA modulus using the GNFS requires approximately 8,000 MIPS-Years. In contrast, factoring a 1024-bit RSA modulus is estimated to demand roughly 98 billion MIPS-Years, illustrating the exponential growth in difficulty relative to key length.

In contemporary high-performance computing, performance is more commonly quantified in FLOPS. For example, the El Capitan supercomputer achieves a peak performance of approximately 2.746 exaFLOPS (2.746×10^{18} calculations per second).

It is important to note, however, that integer factorization relies primarily on integer arithmetic rather than floating-point operations. Yet, even assuming such immense computational power could be fully utilized, attacking a modern 2048-bit RSA modulus by brute force would still require billions of years, rendering the task computationally infeasible.

One might consider an alternative cryptanalytic strategy: precomputing a massive table of primes to facilitate quick lookup. However, due to the sheer density of prime numbers, this approach provides no reduction in computational difficulty. According to the **Prime Number Theorem** (PNT), the **prime-counting function**, denoted as $\pi(x)$ [72], describes the distribution of primes less than or equal to a real number x. It provides the specific approximation

$$\pi(x) = Li(x) + \mathcal{O}\left(xe^{-\frac{1}{15}\sqrt{\log(x)}}\right) \approx \frac{x}{\log(x)} \tag{7-2}$$

where $Li(x) = \int_2^x \frac{dt}{\log t}$ is the logarithmic integral function, and $\mathcal{O}\left(xe^{-\frac{1}{15}\sqrt{\log(x)}}\right)$ is error estimation. The approximation $\pi(x) \approx x/\log(x)$ was first demonstrated in the 19th century by the Russian mathematician *Chebyshev*.

Theorem 7.2.2 Prime Number Theorem

Let $\pi(x)$ be the number of primes, then $\pi(x)$ is asymptotically equivalent to $\frac{x}{\log x}$ as $x \to \infty$, formally

$$\lim_{x\to+\infty} \frac{\pi(x)\log(x)}{x} = 1 \tag{7-3}$$

The proof of the Prime Number Theorem was first given independently by *Hadamard* [73] and *de la Vallée Poussin* [74] in 1896, using methods from complex analysis. About fifty years later, *Erdős* [75] and *Selberg* [76] provided an alternative elementary proof.

The theorem asserts that as x large, the ratio $\pi(x)/(x/\log x)$ approaches 1. In other words, the number of primes less than x is approximately $x/\log x$. For instance, if RSA-1024 is used, the modulus has a size of about 10^{309}, within which roughly 10^{306} primes exist. This number far exceeds the estimated number of atoms in the observable universe, rendering brute-force factorization virtually impossible.

Today, RSA-2048 has become the standard key size for most practical deployments. The largest integer successfully factored to date is the RSA-250 number, which consists of 250 decimal digits (approximately 829 bits). Historically, RSA challenge numbers were categorized by their decimal length, such as RSA-100 through RSA-500. As hardware capabilities evolved, the naming convention shifted to specify bit length, starting with numbers like RSA-576.

The security of RSA rests on the hardness of large integer factorization and the computational intractability of the RSA problem itself. To strengthen resistance against factorization attacks, its prime factors are typically chosen as strong primes or safe primes. Moreover, if the two primes p and q are chosen too close together, the modulus $N = pq$ becomes more vulnerable to specialized factoring techniques. Since the entire encryption scheme collapses once the factors of N are revealed, ensuring adequate security requires the adoption of larger key sizes, such as RSA-4096.

RSA is designed with the requirement that its factors be large prime numbers. When both p and q are prime, the modulus N has exactly two prime factors. By contrast, if composites were chosen instead, N would contain at least four prime factors, giving attackers additional avenues to accelerate factorization and thereby undermining security. For this reason, practical implementations of RSA rely on the use of strong primes or safe primes, which are selected specifically to maximize the difficulty of factorization.

Definition 7.2.2 Strong Primes

A prime p is called a strong prime if there exist integers r, s, and t satisfying the following conditions:

- *$p - 1$ has a large prime factor r.*
- *$p + 1$ has a large prime factor s.*
- *Both $r \pm 1$ and $s \pm 1$ have a large prime factor t.*

Definition 7.2.3 Safe and Sophie Germain Primes

A prime p is called a safe prime if it can be written as $p = 2p' + 1$, where p' is also prime.

Example 7.2.2 The prime $p = 107$ is a safe prime, since $107 = 2 \times 53 + 1$ and 53 is prime.

By contrast, $p = 103$ is not a safe prime, because $103 = 2 \times 51 + 1$ and 51 is not prime, so the condition is not satisfied.

Safe primes are particularly important because in many factorization algorithms, the runtime depends on the relative size of the prime factors. Using safe primes makes the factorization significantly harder than if the factors were chosen randomly. Moreover, safe primes must be sufficiently long in bit length to ensure robust cryptographic security.

7.3 RSA

7.3.1 Encryption/Decryption

1) (KeyGen):
   (a) Bob selects two distinct large prime numbers, p and q, and computes the modulus $N = p \cdot q$.
   (b) Bob computes Euler's totient function

$$\varphi(N) = (p - 1)(q - 1) \tag{7-4}$$

(c) Bob selects an integer e such that $1 < e < \varphi(N)$ and

$$\gcd(e, \varphi(N)) = 1 \tag{7-5}$$

This integer e serves as the **encryption exponent**.

(d) (PrivateKeyGen): Bob computes the **decryption exponent** d, the relationship between e and d can be expressed as

$$d \equiv e^{-1} \pmod{\varphi(N)} \tag{7-6}$$

Bob keeps the values p, q, and d secret.

(e) (PublicKeyGen): Bob publishes the pair (N, e) as his public key.

2) (Encrypt): To send a message to Bob, Alice represents her plaintext as an integer m, where $0 \leqslant m < N$. She uses Bob's public key (N, e) to compute the ciphertext c

$$c \equiv m^e \pmod{N} \tag{7-7}$$

Alice transmits the ciphertext c to Bob.

3) (Decrypt): Upon receiving the ciphertext c, Bob recovers the original plaintext m using his private key exponent d

$$m \equiv c^d \pmod{N} \tag{7-8}$$

The condition $\gcd(e, \varphi(N)) = 1$ is critical for the correctness of the algorithm. This coprimality constraint ensures the existence of the modular multiplicative inverse $d \equiv e^{-1} \pmod{\varphi(N)}$ [77]. Without this inverse, the decryption process defined in congruence (7-8) would be mathematically impossible. If the condition is not met, a different value of e must be chosen.

Below, we rigorously demonstrate the correctness of the RSA cryptosystem by proving that the decryption transformation successfully recovers the exact original plaintext.

Proof

$$m \equiv c^d \pmod{N} \quad \textit{(by congruence 7-8)} \tag{7-9}$$

$$\equiv (m^e \pmod{N})^d \pmod{N} \quad \textit{(by congruence 7-7)} \tag{7-10}$$

$$\equiv m^{ed} \pmod{N} \equiv m^{1 \pmod{\varphi(N)}} \pmod{N} \quad \textit{(by congruence 7-6)} \tag{7-11}$$

$$\equiv m^{k\varphi(N)+1} \pmod{N} \equiv m^{k\varphi(N)} m \pmod{N} \quad \textit{(by Euler's Theorem)} \tag{7-12}$$

$$\equiv m \pmod{N} \tag{7-13}$$

In summary, the public parameters are N, e, and the ciphertext c; the secret parameters are p, q, and d. The encryption process is illustrated in Figure 7-2.

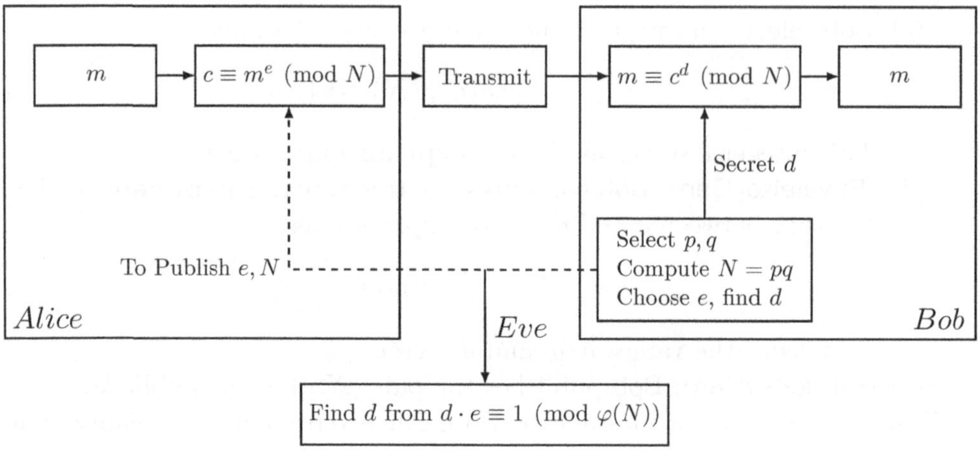

Figure 7-2: RSA Encryption

7.3.2 Examples

Example 7.3.1 Bob chooses two prime numbers $p = 149$ and $q = 311$. He also chooses the encryption exponent $e = 17$. If Alice wishes to send the plaintext message $m = 2022$ to Bob, determine the corresponding ciphertext and demonstrate Bob's decryption process.

Solution: Bob first calculates $N = p \cdot q = 46339$, and the value of $\varphi(N) = (p-1)(q-1) = 45880$.

Since $\gcd(45880, 17) = 1$, the value of e is correct choice. Then he publishes the pair (N, e).

Alice wants to send the plaintext $m = 2022$. Using Bob's public key, she computes the ciphertext c

$$c \equiv m^e \pmod{N} \equiv 2022^{17} \pmod{46339} \equiv 45481 \tag{7-14}$$

Alice transmits c to Bob.

Bob receives the ciphertext c. To decrypt, Bob must first compute the private key exponent d. He solves for d such that

$$d \equiv e^{-1} \pmod{\varphi(N)} \equiv 17^{-1} \pmod{45880} \equiv 16193 \tag{7-15}$$

Using d, Bob decrypts the ciphertext to recover the original message

$$m \equiv c^d \pmod{N} \equiv 45481^{16193} \equiv 2022 \pmod{46339} \tag{7-16}$$

The value that he computes is original message. ■

Example 7.3.2 Bob chooses two prime numbers $p = 53$ and $q = 89$. He also chooses the encryption exponent $e = 119$, then d is 423. If Alice wishes to send the plaintext message $m = 75$ to Bob, determine the corresponding ciphertext and demonstrate Bob's decryption process.

Solution: Alice and Bob Perform all calculations manually without the use of a calculator.

1) Bob first computes the modulus and Euler's totient function

$$N = p \times q = 53 \cdot 89 = 4717 \tag{7-17}$$

$$\varphi(N) = (p-1)(q-1) = 4576 \tag{7-18}$$

Since $\gcd(4576, 119) = 1$, the value of e is correct choice. Then he publishes the pair (N, e).

2) Alice computes the ciphertext $c \equiv m^e \pmod{N}$. To do this efficiently, she employs the *Method of Repeated Squaring*

$$119 = 2^0 + 2^1 + 2^2 + 2^4 + 2^5 + 2^6 = 1 + 2 + 4 + 16 + 32 + 64 \tag{7-19}$$

3) Alice computes the powers of the base $m = 75$ by repeated squaring, as shown in Table 7-1 Therefore,

Table 7-1: RSA Repeated Squaring

k	1	2	4	8	16	32	64
$75^k \pmod{N}$	75	908	3706	3249	4072	929	4547

$$75^{119} \equiv 75 \cdot 908 \cdot 3706 \cdot 4072 \cdot 929 \cdot 4547 \equiv 3500 \pmod{4717} \tag{7-20}$$

4) Using Bob's public key, she computes the ciphertext c

$$c \equiv m^e \pmod{N} \equiv 75^{119} \equiv 3500 \pmod{4717} \tag{7-21}$$

Alice transmits c to Bob.

5) Bob receives $c = 3500$. He then recovers the plaintext

$$m \equiv c^d \pmod{N} \equiv 3500^{423} \equiv 75 \pmod{4717} \tag{7-22}$$

■

To transmit a message, namely a string of characters, we must first map the textual information into a numerical format. Conversely, the decryption process must allow for the rigorous recovery of the original string from the decrypted number.

A standard approach is to treat the letters of the message as digits in a base-26 number system. This method typically employs a standard conversion mapping.

Since any resulting k digit number (base 26) must be less than N, we must have

$$N \geqslant 26^k - 1 \Rightarrow k = \log_{26}(N) \tag{7-23}$$

where k denotes the integer floor value. Here, k represents the maximum number of characters that can be encrypted in a single block. For example, with $N = 131 \cdot 1873 = 245363$, we compute $k = \lfloor \log_{26}(245363) \rfloor = 3$. This means that when using the primes $p = 131$ and $q = 1873$, the system can securely encrypt and transmit messages in blocks of 3 characters at a time.

Example 7.3.3 In RSA, encrypt the plaintext **THE** using the encoding scheme above. Assume $e = 323$, $N = 245363$.

Solution: The encryption proceeds in two stages: message encoding and modular exponentiation.

Map the string **THE** to a numerical integer m

$$m = \mathbf{T} \cdot 26^0 + \mathbf{H} \cdot 26^1 + \mathbf{E} \cdot 26^2 = 19 + 7 \cdot 26 + 4 \cdot 26^2 = 2905 \tag{7-24}$$

We encrypt using $e = 323$ and get the ciphertext $c \equiv 2905^{323} \equiv 13388 \pmod{245363}$. Then we convert the new number into text.

$$\begin{aligned} 13388 &= 24 + 514 \cdot 26 && (7\text{-}25) \\ &= 24 + (20 + 19 \cdot 26) \cdot 26 && (7\text{-}26) \\ &= 24 \cdot 1 + 20 \cdot 26 + 19 \cdot 26^2 && (7\text{-}27) \\ &= \mathbf{Y} \cdot 26^0 + \mathbf{U} \cdot 26^1 + \mathbf{T} \cdot 26^2 && (7\text{-}28) \end{aligned}$$

The plaintext **THE** is encrypted into the ciphertext **YUT**. ■

Example 7.3.4 Let the two primes $p = 127$ and $q = 149$, and known $e = 1261$. Determine the corresponding private decryption exponent d and recover the plaintext underlying the following ciphertext sequence

18110	11222	7659	11236	15240	8290	10958	7661	17370	72
4408	10793	4598	11681	16747	8244	2001	1440	1880	12557
15240	8290	11375	8493	14249	18110	1181	9250	14301	16762
11037	8305	18175	6205	14007	15294	4782	13846	12356	5237
1440	12542	6752	18175	15170	10818	7246	2976	13853	10911
16979	1440	12542	14234	8261	10548	796	4180	5741	16208
12298	11593	2901	4940	10257	2923	11467	13270	5891	18175
6205	14007	12557	11375	1477	16077	9559	16241	12261	12946
18508	13242	18913	11236	13481	3880	15201	6633	1957	2603
10708	13828	12088	14249	18110	11222	7659	11236	15240	8290
17126	9961	5908	302	8794	2001	15107	15610	10793	7217
16172	7074	8549	9628						

The encoding scheme for each block of plaintext is identical to that described in Example 7.3.3. The plaintext is restricted to alphabetic characters only, without spaces, punctuation, or any other symbols.

Solution: Calculate $N = pq = 18923$, then the decryption exponent $d \equiv e^{-1} \equiv 1261^{-1} \equiv 5797 \pmod{18648}$.

We can utilize the following complete Python implementation to execute the block decryption and string reconstruction automatically

```
e = 1261
d = pow(e,-1,126*148)
c = [18110, 11222, 7659, ... ]

for i in c:
    m = pow(i,d,18923)
```

```
    m1 = m%26
    m = (m - m1)/26
    m2 = m%26
    m = (m - m2)/26
    m3 = m%26
    print(chr(int(m3+65)).lower(), '', chr(int(m2+65)).lower(), '',
   chr(int(m1+65)).lower())
```

The original plaintext is: *The turbojet is much simpler than the "piston" engines that it has almost entirely displaced, and it has no reciprocating parts to wear and cause vibrations. Most importantly, it produces very much more thrust for a given weight at high speed. An added advantage is that it will work efficiently close to and beyond the speed of sound, where propellers cannot be used, as described later.* ■

7.4 CRYPTANALYSIS

7.4.1 RSA Security

The security of RSA rests on the fact that, given the encryption function $c \equiv m^e \pmod{N}$, it is computationally infeasible to recover the plaintext m from the ciphertext c when only the public parameters (N, e) are known, unless one can factorize $N = pq$. For sufficiently large values of N, such factorization lies beyond the reach of current algorithms and computational resources.

Suppose an adversary Eve knows the public key (N, e) and a ciphertext c. To break the system completely, Eve may attempt to recover the private decryption exponent d. She must solve the modular congruence

$$d \cdot e \equiv 1 \pmod{\varphi(N)} \tag{7-29}$$

However, computing d requires prior knowledge of $\varphi(N)$. By definition, for $N = pq$, we have

$$\varphi(N) = (p-1)(q-1) = pq - p - q + 1 = N - (p+q) + 1 \tag{7-30}$$

This equation reveals that determining $\varphi(N)$ is computationally equivalent to determining the sum $p + q$. Since $N = pq$ is known, finding $p + q$ allows one to trivially recover p and q. Consequently, computing $\varphi(N)$ without the private factors is as difficult as the **integer factorization problem**. Extracting $\phi(N)$ directly from public channels is therefore classified as computationally unfeasible. Obtaining $\varphi(N)$ therefore requires solving two hard problems

1) The primes p and q are never published and can only be found by factorizing N;
2) Factoring N into two large primes is computationally prohibitive with current technology.

Although RSA is theoretically vulnerable to brute-force factorization, the computational cost depends critically on the size of the modulus N. If N is sufficiently small (e.g., less than 256 bits), it can be factored by a standard personal computer in a relatively short time. However, as the bit-length increases, the difficulty of such attacks grows exponentially. In practice, modern cryptographic systems typically employ a 2048-bit modulus, ensuring that RSA remains secure against current computational capabilities.

Recall the Example 7.3.2, let us examine how the system can be broken using the method of **Quadratic Factoring**. This attack exploits quadratic residues modulo N. The adversary, Eve, attempts to find two distinct integers x and y with $(N-1)/2 \geqslant x > y$, such that

$$x^2 \equiv y^2 \pmod{N}, \quad \text{with } x \not\equiv \pm y \pmod{N} \tag{7-31}$$

If such a pair (x, y) is found, the congruence implies that N divides the difference of squares: $x^2 - y^2 = (x-y)(x+y)$. Since $x \not\equiv \pm y \pmod{N}$, neither $(x-y)$ nor $(x+y)$ is a multiple of N. Consequently, computing the greatest common divisor yields the prime factors

$$p = \gcd(x-y, N) \quad \text{and} \quad q = \gcd(x+y, N) \tag{7-32}$$

The attack proceeds as follows:

1) Randomly select a set of k integers $x_1, x_2, \ldots, x_k$ from the interval $[0, N-1]$.
2) For each integer x_i, compute its square modulo N

$$z_i \equiv x_i^2 \pmod{N} \tag{7-33}$$

3) Check if there exist two distinct indices $i \neq j$ such that $z_i = z_j$. This implies $x_i^2 \equiv x_j^2 \pmod{N}$.
4) If such a collision is found and $x_i \not\equiv \pm x_j \pmod{N}$, compute $\gcd(x_i - x_j, N)$. This operation will reveal a non-trivial factor p or q, thereby breaking the RSA system.

7.4.2 Wiener's Attack

Wiener's attack was introduced by *Michael J. Wiener* in his 1990 IEEE paper [78].

In practical deployments of RSA, the modulus $N = pq$ must be formed from two large primes p and q, and their sizes should not be too close. A common rule of thumb is to choose primes satisfying $p > 2q$, meaning the larger prime is at least twice the smaller. If p and q are close in magnitude and the public exponent e is chosen inappropriately, the system may become susceptible to Wiener's attack, enabling an adversary to infer a short private exponent d.

Wiener proved that if the parameters satisfy

$$3d < N^{1/4} \text{ and } q < p < 2q \tag{7-34}$$

a special type of attack based on continuous fraction expansion of e/N and examining its convergents, Eve can recover the private exponent d in polynomial time $\mathcal{O}(\log(N))$.

First, recall that **continued fractions**. For any real number x, it can be expressed in continued-fraction form

$$x = a_0 + \cfrac{1}{a_1 + \cfrac{1}{a_2 + \cfrac{1}{a_3 + \cfrac{1}{\ddots}}}} \tag{7-35}$$

$$= [a_0, a_1, \ldots, a_n] \tag{7-36}$$

where $a_0 \in \mathbb{R}$ and $a_1, \ldots, a_n \in \mathbb{R}^+$, called **quotients**. If a_i are non-negative integers for $i > 0$ and a_0 be any integer, then we say the continued fraction is **simple**.

Example 7.4.1 Let $x = \frac{111}{26}$, expressed in the form of continued fraction.
Solution:

$$\frac{111}{26} = 4 + \frac{7}{26} = 4 + \cfrac{1}{\frac{26}{7}} \qquad \frac{26}{7} = 3 + \frac{5}{7} = 3 + \cfrac{1}{\frac{7}{5}}$$

$$\frac{7}{5} = 1 + \frac{2}{5} = 1 + \cfrac{1}{\frac{5}{2}} \qquad \frac{5}{2} = 2 + \frac{1}{2}$$

Thus,

$$\frac{111}{26} = 4 + \cfrac{1}{3 + \cfrac{1}{1 + \cfrac{1}{2 + \cfrac{1}{2}}}} \tag{7-37}$$

$$= [4, 3, 1, 2, 2] \tag{7-38}$$

■

Example 7.4.2 To represent the $\sqrt{2}$ as a continued fraction

$$\sqrt{2} = 1 + \cfrac{1}{2 + \cfrac{1}{2 + \cfrac{1}{2 + \cfrac{1}{2 + \ddots}}}}$$

Both rational and irrational numbers can be expressed in the form of continued fractions. For any rational number, its continued fraction terminates after a finite number of steps. In contrast, the continued fractions of irrational numbers are infinite.

If p and q are large, then $N = pq$, $\varphi(N) = (p-1)(q-1)$, then $N \approx \varphi(N)$. The decryption exponent $d \equiv e^{-1} \pmod{\varphi(N)}$, then $ed \equiv 1 \pmod{\varphi(N)} \Rightarrow ed \equiv 1 + k \cdot \varphi(N)$, where $k \in \mathbb{Z}$. Dividing both sides of this linear relation by the scalar product $d \cdot \phi(N)$ yields the absolute underlying fractional error convergence

$$\left|\frac{e}{\varphi(N)} - \frac{k}{d}\right| = \frac{1}{d \cdot \varphi(N)} \tag{7-39}$$

From the theory of continued fractions, assume that $\gcd(e, \varphi(N)) = \gcd(k, d) = 1$. Also $q < p < 2q$, we have $q^2 < pq$, then $q < \sqrt{pq} = \sqrt{N}$. Since $\sqrt{N}/2 < q < p < 2\sqrt{N}$, we have

$$\begin{aligned} N - \varphi(N) &= pq - (p-1)(q-1) && \text{(7-40)}\\ &= p + q - 1 && \text{(7-41)}\\ &< 2q + q && \text{(7-42)}\\ &< 3\sqrt{N} && \text{(7-43)} \end{aligned}$$

Although the attacker does not know $\varphi(N)$, she knows N. Suppose she uses e/N as an approximation to k/d, the following condition hold:

$$\begin{aligned} \left|\frac{e}{N} - \frac{k}{d}\right| &= \left|\frac{ed - kN}{dN}\right| && \text{(7-44)}\\ &= \left|\frac{ed - k\varphi(N) - kN + k\varphi(N)}{dN}\right| && \text{(7-45)}\\ &= \left|\frac{1 - k(N - \varphi(N))}{dN}\right| && \text{(7-46)}\\ &= \left|\frac{1 - k(3\sqrt{N})}{dN}\right| < \frac{3k\sqrt{N}}{dN} = \frac{3k}{d\sqrt{N}} && \text{(7-47)} \end{aligned}$$

Since $e < \varphi(N)$, we have that $k < d \Rightarrow 3k < 3d < N^{1/4}$, hence

$$\left|\frac{e}{N} - \frac{k}{d}\right| < \frac{3k}{d\sqrt{N}} < \frac{N^{1/4}}{d\sqrt{N}} = \frac{1}{dN^{1/4}} < \frac{1}{3d^2} < \frac{1}{2d^2} \tag{7-48}$$

Therefore, by Legendre's continued fraction theorem, the fraction k/d necessarily appears strictly as one of the convergents within the continued fraction expansion of e/N.

In general, the attacker is unknown $\varphi(N)$. Since $N \approx \varphi(N)$, we can rewrite the equation 7-39

$$\begin{aligned} \frac{e}{N} - \frac{k}{d} &= \frac{1}{d \cdot \varphi(N)} && \text{(7-49)}\\ \Rightarrow \frac{e}{N} &\approx \frac{k}{d} && \text{(7-50)} \end{aligned}$$

In other words, if the private exponent d is sufficiently small, k/d is a continued fraction convergent of e/N. Since the public parameters e and N knows, the attack computes the continued fraction expansion of e/N and enumerates its convergents. One of these convergents equals k/d in the Wiener regime. From $ed = 1 + k \cdot \varphi(N)$, once e, d, k are identified, one immediately obtains $\varphi(N) = (ed - 1)/k$.

Finally, using $\varphi(N) = (p-1)(q-1)$ and $N = pq$, Eve has $p+q = N+1-\varphi(N)$. To recover p and q, solve the system below

$$(x-p)(x-q) = x^2 - (p+q)x + pq \tag{7-51}$$

$$= x^2 - (N - \varphi(N) + 1)x + N = 0 \tag{7-52}$$

To verify the correctness of the guessed convergent, the adversary solves Equation (7-52). If the equation yields positive integer solutions, these solutions correspond to the prime factors p and q. The successful extraction of p and q implies that the modulus N has been factored and the RSA system is broken.

We can iterate through the convergents of e/N to determine the decryption exponent d. The procedure is as follows:

1) Given the public key (N, e), compute the continued fraction expansion of the ratio e/N, denoted as $[a_0, a_1, \ldots, a_n]$;
2) Iterate over each convergent in the continued fraction.
3) Check if the convergent is k/d meets the following requirements:
   (a) If d is odd, continue. Otherwise, move on to the next convergent.
   (b) If $3d < N^{1/4}$, continue. Otherwise, move on to the next convergent.
   (c) If $ed \equiv 1 \pmod{k}$, continue. Otherwise, move on to the next convergent.
   (d) Let $\varphi(N) = (ed-1)/k$, find the solutions of $x^2-(N-\varphi(N)+1)x+N = 0$. If the solutions are integers, then the d has been determined. Otherwise, move on to the next convergent.
4) Check all convergents, if we don't find the integers solution, that means the Wiener's attack doesn't work for this RSA cryptosystem.

Example 7.4.3 Suppose Eve intercepted the RSA public key $N = 20532004352107$ 5746592613, $e = 707601359956202812410 19$. Try to break the RSA cryptosystem.
Solution: Compute the continued fraction expansion of e/N, that is

$$\frac{e}{N} = 0 + \cfrac{1}{2 + \cfrac{1}{1 + \cfrac{1}{9 + \ddots}}}$$

There are 40 quotients, the continued fraction expansion of e/N is

$$[0, 2, 1, 9, 6, 54, 5911, 1, \ldots, 4] \approx \frac{k}{d}$$

The first convergent is 0, it does not produce a factorization of N. The second convergent is $0 + 1/2 = \frac{1}{2}$; the third convergent is $1/(2 + 1/1) = \frac{1}{3}$; the fourth convergent is $1/(2 + 1/(1 + (1/9))) = \frac{10}{29}$, and so on. The sixth convergent is $\frac{3304}{9587}$ that produces a factorization of N.

By successively substituting each convergent into the equation $\varphi(N) = (ed-1)/k$, we can test which candidate yields a valid value of $\varphi(N)$. For example, the second convergent $k/d = 1/2$ is invalid since $d = 2$ does not satisfy the required condition, so we move on. The next convergent $k/d = 1/3$ also fails, because $ed \not\equiv 1 \pmod{k}$.

Until the sixth convergent yields $\varphi(N) = (ed-1)/k = 205320043519979308794688$. Solving the Equation 7-52, we can determine the prime factors $p = 239635170197$ and $q = 856802627729$, also we can find the d. This demonstrates that the RSA cryptosystem has been successfully broken. ■

7.4.3 Low Public Exponent Attack

Low Public Exponent Attack is a general term for a class of attacks against RSA systems. Its core idea is to exploit the vulnerabilities caused by using too small an encryption exponent e. Among them, one of the more famous methods is the Coppersmith attack. The American mathematician *Don Coppersmith* first systematically proposed this attack idea in 1997 in the paper [79]. Coppersmith's method relies on the LLL algorithm (see Section 10.3.3); in this section, we introduce a fundamental simplified case to illustrate the underlying vulnerability.

Similar to Wiener's Attack, when RSA parameters are chosen improperly, the system will significantly reduce its security. Suppose the encryption exponent e is too small (for example $e = 3$), and the plaintext m is also small. Once the condition $m^e < N$ is satisfied, the attacker can easily recover the plaintext. According to the encryption formula

$$c \equiv m^e \pmod{N} \tag{7-53}$$

This congruence can be rewritten as an equality over the integers

$$m^e = c + kN \text{ , where } k \in \mathbb{N} \tag{7-54}$$

$$\Rightarrow m = \sqrt[e]{c + kN} \tag{7-55}$$

If $m^e < N$, then necessarily $k = 0$, and the plaintext can be recovered simply as $m = \sqrt[e]{c}$. Consider the case where m^e slightly exceeds N, an attacker can attempt small values of k. For each k, the attacker computes $\sqrt[e]{c + kN}$ and checks if the result is an integer. The first integer solution found reveals the plaintext m, thereby breaking the encryption.

Example 7.4.4 Suppose Eve intercepted the RSA public key $N = 7288176414498$ 01465725885852789917, $e = 3$ and the ciphertext $c = 3719640897611219952668531635$ 5771. Try to break the RSA cryptosystem.

Solution: Try to calculate $m = \sqrt[e]{c + kN}$.

The search for k begins at 0 and increases sequentially. The process until once an integer value of m is obtained. In this case, when $k = 47241$, the plaintext $m = 3253215323532$. The RSA cryptosystem has been successfully broken. ■

Notes, in practical computations, one must account for issues of numerical precision. In certain cases, it may be necessary to apply the `round()` function to ensure correct rounding.

How large should the exponent e be? In general, if $e \geqslant 2^{16} + 1 = 65537$, then RSA is no longer easily vulnerable to small public exponent attacks.

One well-known example of such attacks is the **Broadcast Attack**, which leverages the Chinese Remainder Theorem; readers interested in the details may consult Section 8.5.3. Other variants, including the **Related Message Attack** and the **Short Pad Attack**, also fall under the category of small public exponent attacks [80].

7.5 PRIMALITY TESTS

In the previous section, we analyzed the encryption and decryption protocols of RSA and discussed its attack method. A fundamental prerequisite for implementing RSA is the generation of large prime numbers. While factoring a large composite integer is computationally infeasible, determining whether a given number is prime is a significantly more tractable problem.

This section introduces several widely used primality testing methods. These algorithms generally fall into two broad categories: deterministic and randomized. Deterministic algorithms do not rely on randomness and yield results with absolute certainty, though they are typically slower. In contrast, randomized algorithms employ probabilistic choices to achieve higher efficiency, albeit with a negligible probability of incorrectly classifying a composite number as prime.

7.5.1 Trial Division

Trial division represents the most intuitive deterministic approach. Given an integer n, the method tests for divisibility by all prime numbers less than or equal to $\sqrt{n}$. If a divisor is found, n is identified as composite; otherwise, n is declared prime. The time complexity of this algorithm is approximately $\mathcal{O}(\sqrt{n})$. As n increases, the number of required division operations grows exponentially relative to the number of digits, rendering this approach impractical for the large integers used in modern cryptography.

7.5.2 AKS Primality Test

The AKS primality test (Agrawal–Kayal–Saxena test), introduced in 2002 by Indian mathematicians *Agrawal*, *Kayal*, and *Saxena* [81], was the first algorithm to determine primality in deterministic polynomial time without relying on any unproven assumptions. In other words, it is mathematically rigorous and always correct. Nevertheless, due to its limited efficiency, AKS is seldom used in practice.

The key ideas of AKS are the Freshman's Dream Theorem, also known as the Child's Binomial Theorem.

Theorem 7.5.1 Freshman's Dream Theorem

In any commutative ring of prime characteristic $p > 0$, then for all x, y in a field, that is

$$(x + y)^p = x^p + y^p \tag{7-56}$$

In particular, for all $a, b \in \mathbb{Z}$, that is

$$(a + b)^p \equiv a^p + b^p \pmod{p} \tag{7-57}$$

This result is whimsically called the "Freshman's Dream" because beginners often mistakenly believe that $(x + y)^n = x^n + y^n$. For instance, when $n = 2 : (x + y)^2 = x^2 + 2xy + y^2 \neq x^2 + y^2$.

However, in rings of prime characteristic, all binomial coefficients in the middle terms are divisible by p, so the equality indeed holds.

Proof

The field $\mathbb{F}$ with characteristic prime p, $x, y \in \mathbb{F}$. By the Binomial Theorem, then

$$(x + y)^p = \sum_{k=0}^{p} \binom{p}{k} x^{p-k} y^k \tag{7-58}$$

Observe that, except for the cases $k = 0$ and $k = p$, in the binomial coefficient $\binom{p}{k} = \frac{p!}{k!(p-k)!}$, the numerator $p!$ is always divisible by p. Since neither $k!$ nor $(p - k)!$ contains a factor of p, the denominator cannot cancel out this factor. Hence, each such binomial coefficient necessarily contains p as a factor.

Because binomial coefficients are integers, it follows that in a field $\mathbb{F}$ of characteristic p, all these coefficients vanish modulo p. Therefore, only the two boundary terms remain

$$(x + y)^p = x^p + y^p \tag{7-59}$$

Consequently, for any $a, b \in \mathbb{Z}$ that for prime p, we have

$$(a + b)^p \equiv a^p + b^p \pmod{p} \tag{7-60}$$

Theorem 7.5.2 Child's Binomial Theorem

An integer $n \geqslant 2$ is prime if and only if

$$(x + a)^n \equiv x^n + a \pmod{n} \tag{7-61}$$

in $\mathbb{Z}[x]$, where $\gcd(a, n) = 1$ for some $a \in \mathbb{Z}$.

Example 7.5.1 Test whether the integers $n_1 = 3$ and $n_2 = 4$ are prime numbers using the polynomial congruence identity from Theorem 7.5.2.
Solution: We select an arbitrary integer $a = 2$. We expand the binomial $(x+a)^{n_1}$ and reduce the coefficients modulo n_1

$$(x+a)^{n_1} \pmod{n_1} \equiv (x+2)^3 \pmod 3 \tag{7-62}$$

$$\equiv \left(x^3 + \underbrace{6x^2}_{6 \bmod 3 \equiv 0} + \underbrace{12x}_{12 \bmod 3 \equiv 0} + \underbrace{8}_{8 \bmod 3 \equiv 2} \right) \pmod 3 \tag{7-63}$$

$$\equiv \left(x^3 + 2\right) \pmod 3 \tag{7-64}$$

$$\equiv (x^{n_1} + a) \pmod{n_1} \tag{7-65}$$

Since all intermediate coefficients are divisible by n_1, the identity holds. Thus, $n_1 = 3$ is a prime number.

We select an arbitrary integer $a = 3$. We expand the binomial $(x+a)^{n_2}$ and reduce the coefficients modulo n_2

$$(x+a)^{n_2} \pmod{n_2} \equiv (x+3)^4 \pmod 4 \tag{7-66}$$

$$\equiv \left(x^4 + 12x^3 + 54x^2 + 108x + 81\right) \pmod 4 \tag{7-67}$$

$$\equiv \left(x^4 + 2x^2 + 1\right) \pmod 4 \tag{7-68}$$

Comparing this result to the expected form $x^4 + 3 \pmod 4$, we observe two discrepancies: the constant term is 1 instead of 3, and there is a non-zero intermediate term $2x^2$. Since the congruence does not hold, Theorem 7.5.2 is not satisfied. Therefore, $n_2 = 4$ is composite. ■

The AKS primality test is a deterministic algorithm for determining whether a given integer is prime. The fundamental concept relies on the following polynomial congruence:

$$(x+a)^n - (x^n + a) \pmod n \tag{7-69}$$

The test verifies whether all coefficients of the expanded polynomial vanish modulo n. To gain intuition, one may visualize the binomial coefficients using **Pascal's Triangle**. If n is prime, all intermediate binomial coefficients $\binom{n}{k}$ for $0 < k < n$ are divisible by n. However, when n is large, storing and manipulating a polynomial with up to n terms becomes computationally prohibitive.

To address, the AKS algorithm performs reductions not only modulo n but also modulo a polynomial $x^r - 1$, where r is a small positive integer. Specifically, the test verifies the congruence

$$(x+a)^n \equiv x^n + a \pmod{(n, x^r - 1)} \tag{7-70}$$

Here, the notation $\pmod{(n, x^r - 1)}$ indicates that arithmetic operations are performed within the polynomial ring quotiented by both the integer n and the polynomial $x^r - 1$. Operationally, this involves expanding the polynomial $(x+a)^n$, reducing the resulting coefficients modulo n, and reducing the powers of x modulo $x^r - 1$. This strategy effectively bounds the degree of the polynomials, thereby eliminating the need to store high-degree terms and significantly enhancing computational efficiency.

The AKS primality test can be summarized in the following algorithmic steps:

1) Input an integer $n > 1$.
2) If n is a perfect power, that is the integer n of the form a^k, where $a, k \in \mathbb{Z}$ with $k \geqslant 2$, then n is composite.
3) Determine the smallest integer r such that $ord_r(n) > \log_2^2(n)$.
4) If $2 \leqslant \gcd(a, n) < n$ for some integer $a \leqslant r$, then n is composite.
5) If $n \leqslant r$, then n is prime.
6) For every integer $a \in [1, \lfloor\sqrt{\varphi(r)}\log_2(n)\rfloor]$, check if $(x+a)^n \not\equiv x^n + a \pmod{x^r - 1, n}$ over the ring $\mathbb{Z}_n[x]$, then n is composite. It is also the most time consuming step.
7) If all conditions are satisfied, declare that n is prime.

where $\varphi(r)$ is Euler's totient function, $ord_r(n)$ is the order of $n \pmod r$, defined as the smallest positive integer k such that $n^k \equiv 1 \pmod r$. The time complexity is $\mathcal{O}\left(\log_2^6(n)\right)$.

Example 7.5.2 Examples of the order of $n \pmod r$.
Solution:

- $13^1 \equiv 1 \pmod 4 \Rightarrow ord_4(13) = 1$
- $13^4 \equiv 1 \pmod 5 \Rightarrow ord_5(13) = 4$
- $19^6 \equiv 1 \pmod 7 \Rightarrow ord_7(19) = 6$

■

As the computational steps of the AKS algorithm become unwieldy for even moderately large primes, a detailed example is omitted here. For a relevant code implementation, the reader is referred to [82]. Despite its high computational cost, the AKS algorithm holds significant academic value due to its simplicity and its resolution of the primality testing problem in polynomial time using elementary algebraic methods.

7.5.3 Fermat Primality Test

The Fermat Primality Test [83] is a probabilistic algorithm for primality testing. It is based on randomization and is used to determine whether a given number is likely to be prime or composite [84].

Theorem 7.5.3 Fermat's Little Theorem

If p is prime and $a \in \mathbb{Z}$ with $a^p - a$ is divisible by p, that is

$$a^p \equiv a \pmod p \tag{7-71}$$

For a not divisible by p with $\gcd(a, p) = 1$*, this is clearly*

$$a^{p-1} \equiv 1 \pmod{p} \tag{7-72}$$

The two congruences are equivalent.

Proof

Proof by induction.

The base step, when $a = 1$*, we have* $a^p \equiv 1^p \equiv 1 \pmod{p}$*, is obviously true.*

The induction step, suppose the theorem holds for some positive a*,* $a^p \equiv a \pmod{p}$ *is true.*

We want to prove the statement for $a + 1$*. By the theorem 7.5.1, we have*

$$(a+1)^p \equiv a^p + 1^p \pmod{p} \tag{7-73}$$
$$\equiv a^p + 1 \pmod{p} \tag{7-74}$$
$$\equiv a + 1 \pmod{p} \tag{7-75}$$

Therefore by induction it follows that $a^p \equiv a \pmod{p}$ *for all positive integers* a*.*

Euler's theorem generalizes Fermat's Little Theorem. When n is prime, we have $\varphi(n) = n - 1$. Consequently, Euler's theorem $a^{\varphi(n)} \equiv 1 \pmod{n}$ reduces directly to the formulation of Fermat's Little Theorem

$$a^{\varphi(n)} \equiv a^{n-1} \equiv 1 \pmod{n} \tag{7-76}$$

Although Fermat's Little Theorem can be used for primality testing, it provides only a necessary condition and not a sufficient one. If the theorem fails, then n is certainly composite. In other words, if every $a \in [1, n-1]$ with $a^{n-1} \equiv 1 \pmod{n}$, n is prime. However, verifying this for all a is computationally impractical.

The Fermat primality test is a probabilistic algorithm designed to exploit this property efficiently. The procedure involves selecting several integers a uniformly at random and checking whether the congruence holds. If the condition is satisfied for all chosen bases, n is declared to be a **probable prime**.

If there exists an $a \in [1, n-1]$ with $a^{n-1} \not\equiv 1 \pmod{n}$, then n is certainly composite. The a is called **Fermat witnesses** for the compositeness of n. If n is composite, but the congruence $a^{n-1} \equiv 1 \pmod{n}$ still holds, the base a is called a **Fermat Liar** with respect to n, and n is a Fermat pseudoprime to base a.

A **pseudoprime** is a composite integer that satisfies the congruence property of Fermat's Little Theorem for a specific base, despite not being prime. For example, consider $n = 341$. Although $341 = 11 \times 31$ is composite, it satisfies the congruence $2^{340} \equiv 1 \pmod{341}$. Thus, 341 is termed a pseudoprime to the base 2, and the base 2 is a Fermat liar for 341. This specific pseudoprime was discovered by *Sarrus* in

1819. Later, in 1903, *Malo* proved that if n is a pseudoprime, then $2^n - 1$ is also a pseudoprime, demonstrating the existence of infinitely many such numbers.

Since Fermat witnesses are abundant, we can apply the Fermat Primality Test. Given an odd integer n, the test considers a random number $2 \leqslant a \leqslant n-2$ and $\gcd(a, n) = 1$, if $a^{n-1} \equiv 1 \pmod{n}$, then n is probably prime.

Given an integer n which test to classify as prime or composite, the Fermat Primality Test is the following, repeat k times:

1) Select an integer a uniformly at random from the interval $[2, n-2]$.
2) If $a^{n-1} \not\equiv 1 \pmod{n}$, then n is composite and stop.
3) If there haven't stopped after k times, then n is probably prime.

The Fermat primality test on input n and repeat k times that gives the correct answer "n is composite" with probability at least $1 - 2^{-k}$. If $k = 7$, the probability that it is prime is 99.21875%. Note that there's never any error in the case where n is prime.

The Python code for Fermat primality test is as follows:

```
def gcd(a,b):
    if b==0: return a
    else: return gcd(b, a%b)

def is_prime(num, k=7):
    for _ in range(k):
        a=random.randrange(2,num-2)
        if gcd(a, num)!=1:
            return False
        if pow(a,num-1,num)!=1:
            return False
    return True
```

Example 7.5.3 Determine whether 9949, 48703, 80581 are prime.

1) The Fermat primality test for the choices $a = 2, 3, 4, 5$ and $n = 9949$.
Solution:

$$2^{n-1} \equiv 2^{9948} \equiv 1 \pmod{9949} \tag{7-77}$$
$$3^{n-1} \equiv 3^{9948} \equiv 1 \pmod{9949} \tag{7-78}$$
$$4^{n-1} \equiv 4^{9948} \equiv 1 \pmod{9949} \tag{7-79}$$
$$5^{n-1} \equiv 5^{9948} \equiv 1 \pmod{9949} \tag{7-80}$$

The test provides no evidence that 9949 is composite. Using other deterministic algorithms, we determine 9949 is prime. ■

2) The Fermat primality test for the choices $a = 2$ and $n = 48703$.
Solution:

$$a^{n-1} = 2^{48702} \equiv 11646 \not\equiv 1 \pmod{48703} \tag{7-81}$$

We conclude 48703 is not a prime. 2 is a Fermat witness for 48703. ■

3) The Fermat primality test for the choices $a = 2, 3$ and $n = 80581$.
Solution:

$$2^{80580} \equiv 1 \pmod{80581} \tag{7-82}$$
$$3^{80580} \equiv 76861 \not\equiv 1 \pmod{80581} \tag{7-83}$$

We conclude 80581 is not a prime. The integer 2 is a Fermat liar for 80581. The integer 3 is a Fermat witness for 80581. ■

Example 7.5.4 Determine whether 41041 is prime.
Solution: The Fermat primality test for the choices $a = 3$.

$$3^{41040} \equiv 1 \pmod{41041} \tag{7-84}$$
$$5^{41040} \equiv 1 \pmod{41041} \tag{7-85}$$
$$7^{41040} \equiv 29316 \not\equiv 1 \pmod{41041} \tag{7-86}$$

Because the base 7 fails the congruence, 41041 is strictly composite (factoring explicitly as $41041 = 7 \times 11 \times 13 \times 41$). ■

Determining whether a number is prime or composite is a different task from factoring it. In general, primality testing is much easier than integer factorization.

The Fermat primality test runs in time approximately $\mathcal{O}(k \cdot (\log_2(n))^3)$ where k is the number of tests. This is far more efficient than trial division. However, the algorithm cannot provide an absolute guarantee that n is prime.

Given a composite positive integer n for which $a^{n-1} \equiv 1 \pmod{n}$ for any positive integer a with $\gcd(a, n) = 1$, n is called a **Carmichael number**. The Carmichael numbers are always odd, composed of at least three distinct prime factors, they are square free. The Carmichael numbers are named after *Robert Daniel Carmichael* [85], and there are infinitely many Carmichael numbers that proved by *William Alford* [86]. For this reason, the Fermat primality test is not completely reliable for determining prime numbers.

The first and smallest Carmichael number is $561 = 3 \times 11 \times 17$.

7.5.4 Miller–Rabin Primality Test

Due to the existence of composite numbers with many Fermat liars, we need a new primality test. Unlike the Fermat Primality Test, the **Miller–Rabin Primality Test** [87] [88] works on every number n. The test is a probabilistic primality test. It is derived from a refinement of the converse of Fermat's Little Theorem.

Definition 7.5.1 Modular Square Root

If $a^2 \equiv 1 \pmod{n}$, then a is a square root of 1 mod n.

Thus, if p is prime, then all integer roots of $x^2 \equiv 1 \pmod{p}$ satisfy $x \equiv \pm 1 \pmod{p}$. In other words, given an integer n such that $x^2 \equiv 1 \pmod{n}$. If $x \not\equiv \pm 1 \pmod{n}$, then n is composite.

Let $n \geqslant 3$ be an odd integer, then $n-1$ is an even integer, that can factor the largest power of 2 in $n-1$, that is $2^s \cdot d$, where s is a positive integer and d is a positive odd integer.

Let an integer $a \in [2, n-1]$, for all $0 \leqslant r \leqslant s-1$, if the following conditions hold:

- $a^d \not\equiv 1 \pmod{n}$
- $a^{2^r d} \not\equiv -1 \pmod{n}$

Then n is not a prime, a is called **Miller–Rabin witness** for n. Conversely, if any one of the following congruences hold:

- $a^d \equiv 1 \pmod{n}$, or
- $a^{2^r d} \equiv -1 \pmod{n}$ for some $0 \leqslant r \leqslant s-1$

Then n is probably prime. Thus, suppose n is odd and we wish to know if it is prime. Any positive odd integer n can be expressed as $n-1 = 2^s d$ with $s > 0$, d odd. We choose some $1 < a < n-1$ uniformly at random, and compute $a^d \pmod{n}$, The procedure of the Miller–Rabin primality test is as follows:

1) If $a^d \equiv \pm 1 \pmod{n}$, then n is probably prime, and stop.
2) Otherwise, let $r = [1, 2, \ldots, s-1]$, compute $a^{2^r d} \pmod{n}$, do following steps.
3) Set $r = 1$. Compute $a^{2d} \pmod{n}$.
    - If $a^{2d} \equiv 1 \pmod{n}$, then n is NOT prime, and stop.
    - If $a^{2d} \equiv -1 \pmod{n}$, then n is probably prime, and stop.
4) Otherwise, set $r = 2$. Compute $a^{4d} \pmod{n}$.
    - If $a^{4d} \equiv 1 \pmod{n}$, then n is NOT prime, and stop.
    - If $a^{4d} \equiv -1 \pmod{n}$, then n is probably prime, and stop.
5) Otherwise, set $r = 3$. Compute $a^{8d} \pmod{n}$.
    - If $a^{8d} \equiv 1 \pmod{n}$, then n is NOT prime, and stop.
    - If $a^{8d} \equiv -1 \pmod{n}$, then n is probably prime, and stop.
6) Otherwise, continue in this manner until $r = s-1$ that is $a^{2^{s-1}d} \equiv a^{(n-1)/2} \equiv \pm 1 \pmod{n}$.
    - If $a^{2^{s-1}d} \equiv 1 \pmod{n}$, then n is NOT prime, and stop.
    - If $a^{2^{s-1}d} \equiv -1 \pmod{n}$, then n is probably prime, and stop.
7) Otherwise if neither of these is true then stop, n is NOT prime.

Example 7.5.5 Determine whether $n = 221$ is prime.
Solution: Write $n-1 = 2^s \cdot d = 220 = 2^2 \cdot 55$, yielding $s = 2$, $d = 55$. Let $r \in \{0, 1\}$ and consider the base $a = 125$, we have

$$a^{2^0 d} \pmod{n} \equiv 125^{55} \equiv 31 \not\equiv \pm 1 \pmod{221} \tag{7-87}$$

$$a^{2^1 d} \pmod{n} \equiv 125^{2 \cdot 55} \equiv 77 \not\equiv \pm 1 \pmod{221} \tag{7-88}$$

The test declares $n = 221$ composite. ■

Example 7.5.6 Determine whether $n = 131071$ is prime.
Solution: Write $n - 1 = 2^s \cdot d = 131070 = 2^1 \cdot 65535$, yielding $s = 1$, $d = 65535$. Let $r \in \{0\}$ and consider the base $a = 98$, we have

$$a^{2^0 d} \pmod n \equiv 98^{65535} \equiv 1 \pmod{131071} \tag{7-89}$$

The test concludes that $n = 131071$ is probable prime.
Choose another base a, let $a = 10003$, then

$$a^{2^0 d} \pmod n \equiv 10003^{65535} = 131070 \equiv -1 \pmod{131071} \tag{7-90}$$

The test concludes that $n = 131071$ is probable prime. We might perform more tests before we are convinced that n is in fact prime. Actually, $n = 131071$ is prime. ■

Example 7.5.7 Determine whether $n = 104513$ is prime.
Solution: Write $n - 1 = 2^s \cdot d = 2^6 \cdot 1633$, yielding $s = 6$, $d = 1633$. Let $r \in \{0, 1, 2, 3, 4, 5\}$ and consider the base $a = 3$, we have

$$3^{2^0 \cdot 1633} \equiv 88958 \pmod n \tag{7-91}$$
$$3^{2^1 \cdot 1633} \equiv 88958^2 \equiv 10430 \pmod n \tag{7-92}$$
$$3^{2^2 \cdot 1633} \equiv 10430^2 \equiv 91380 \pmod n \tag{7-93}$$
$$3^{2^3 \cdot 1633} \equiv 91380^2 \equiv 29239 \pmod n \tag{7-94}$$
$$3^{2^4 \cdot 1633} \equiv 29239^2 \equiv 2781 \pmod n \tag{7-95}$$
$$3^{2^5 \cdot 1633} \equiv 2781^2 \equiv -1 \pmod n \tag{7-96}$$

The test concludes that $n = 104513$ is probable prime. ■

In general, the Miller-Rabin Test has an error probability of at most $1/4$. This efficiency makes it the standard algorithm for practical use. By repeating the test with k independently chosen bases, the probability of incorrectly identifying a composite number as prime decreases to 4^{-k}. For instance, repeating the test for 13 rounds reduces the error probability to approximately 1.5×10^{-8}. For industrial-grade applications requiring extremely high confidence, it is common to perform up to 64 rounds, which drives the error probability down to the order of 10^{-39}.

For integers $n < 2^{64}$, testing the fixed bases $a \in \{2,\ 325,\ 9375,\ 28178,\ 450775,\ 9780504,\ 1795265022\}$ with Miller–Rabin is sufficient to deterministically decide primality.

The running time of the Miller–Rabin test is about $\mathcal{O}(k \log_2^3 n)$, where k is the number of rounds and n is the integer being tested. Using fast multiplication techniques (e.g. FFT-based methods) can reduce this to $\mathcal{O}(k \log_2^2 n)$. At present, these implementations are among the primality tests that come closest to linear-time behavior in practice. A sample implementation in Python is provided below.

```
def miller_rabin(n):
    """Return True if n is prime; otherwise return False."""
    if n < 2:
        return False

    small_primes = (2, 3, 5, 7, 11, 13, 17)
    if n in small_primes:
        return True
    if any(n % p == 0 for p in small_primes):
        return False

    d, s = n - 1, 0
    while d % 2 == 0:
        d //= 2
        s += 1

    for a in (2, 325, 9375, 28178, 450775, 9780504, 1795265022):
        if a % n == 0:
            continue

        x = pow(a, d, n)
        if x in (1, n - 1):
            continue

        for _ in range(s - 1):
            x = pow(x, 2, n)
            if x == n - 1:
                break
        else:
            return False

    return True
print(miller_rabin(1000000000061))
```

7.5.5 Solovay–Strassen Primality Test

The Solovay–Strassen primality test was published by *Robert M. Solovay* and *Volker Strassen* in 1977 [89], it is also a randomized algorithm.

The Jacobi symbol is used to test for primality of a given integer n by testing for agreement between two calculations, the Jacobi symbol is a generalization of the Legendre symbol. If n is prime, the Jacobi symbol is equal to the Legendre symbol.

Let n be an odd prime and a be an integer. The Legendre Symbol is defined by

$$\left(\frac{a}{n}\right) = \begin{cases} 0 & \text{if } a \equiv 0 \pmod{n} \\ +1 & \text{if } a \text{ is a quadratic residue mod } n \\ -1 & \text{if } a \text{ is a quadratic non-residue mod } n \end{cases} \tag{7-97}$$

Determine whether $n > 2$ is prime, and if there are some integer $a \in \{1, 2, 3, \ldots, n-1\}$ such that

$$\left(\frac{a}{n}\right) \equiv a^{(n-1)/2} \pmod{n} \tag{7-98}$$

then n is probably prime. The steps of the Solovay–Strassen primality test are the following:

1) Pick k distinct integers a from $[1, 2, \ldots, n-1]$ uniformly at random, that is $a_1, a_2, \ldots, a_k \in \{1, 2, \ldots, n-1\}$.
2) For each a_i, check
   - $(\frac{a}{n}) \equiv a^{(n-1)/2} \pmod{n}$
   - $\gcd(a, n) = 1$
3) If either of the above conditions fails, then n is composite, a is called an **Euler witness**;
4) If both conditions are satisfied for all a_i, then n is probable prime.

The test is a randomized algorithm based on the Jacobi symbol, with a time complexity of $\mathcal{O}(k \cdot log^3(n))$, where k denotes the number of rounds. If the input n is composite, the test gives the output "composite" with probability greater than 1/2. It is less efficient and of lower practical value, and thus is less used in modern cryptographic systems.

Example 7.5.8 Determine whether $n = 109$ is prime.
Solution: Let $a = 50$, then the Legendre symbol is

$$\left(\frac{a}{n}\right) = \left(\frac{50}{109}\right) = -1 \tag{7-99}$$

$$a^{(n-1)/2} \pmod{n} \equiv 50^{54} \equiv 108 \equiv -1 \pmod{109} \tag{7-100}$$

The test concludes that $n = 109$ is probable prime. Actually, $n = 109$ is prime. ■

Example 7.5.9 Determine whether $n = 31659$ is prime.
Solution: Let $a = 101$, then the Legendre symbol is

$$\left(\frac{a}{n}\right) = \left(\frac{101}{31659}\right) = -1 \tag{7-101}$$

$$a^{(n-1)/2} \pmod{n} \equiv 101^{15829} \pmod{31659} \equiv 17303 \pmod{31659} \tag{7-102}$$

The test concludes that $n = 31659$ is composite. ■

Example 7.5.10 Determine whether $n = 7427466391$ is prime.
Solution: Let $a = \{10, 20, 30, 40, 50\}$, then the Legendre symbol is shown in Table 7-2.

Since $(\frac{a_i}{n}) \equiv a_i^{(n-1)/2} \pmod{n}$ holds, $n = 7427466391$ is a prime number with high probability. ■

Table 7-2: Solovay-Strassen Test Process

i	a_i	$\gcd(a_i, n)$	$\left(\frac{a}{n}\right)$	$a^{(n-1)/2} \pmod{n}$
1	10	1	1	1
2	20	1	1	1
3	30	1	-1	-1
4	40	1	1	1
5	50	1	1	1

7.5.6 APRCL Primality Test

The APRCL primality test (Adleman–Pomerance–Rumely–Cohen–Lenstra primality test) [90] is a deterministic primality testing algorithm rooted in algebraic number theory. Originally proposed by *Adleman*, *Pomerance*, and *Rumely* in 1983, it was later simplified and improved by *Cohen* and *Lenstra* in 1986, yielding the more efficient APRCL algorithm [91].

Its theoretical foundation lies in the local–global principle of number theory. By examining certain congruence relations and algebraic structures associated with the candidate number, the algorithm determines whether it is prime. Like the AKS algorithm, APRCL is a deterministic nearly polynomial time algorithm($\mathcal{O}\left(\log(n)^{cloglog\log(n)}\right)$), but in practice its efficiency is much closer to that of the randomized Miller–Rabin test. For this reason, during the 1980s and 1990s it was considered among the most practical deterministic primality tests.

Nevertheless, due to its substantial implementation complexity, and with the emergence of both the Miller–Rabin test and the Elliptic Curve Primality Proving (ECPP) algorithm, APRCL is relatively rarely used in modern cryptography.

7.5.7 Industrial-Grade Primes

The security of RSA rests on the computational hardness of factoring large integers. An RSA modulus is formed as the product of two primes p and q. To generate a 2048-bit modulus, one typically selects two primes of roughly 1024 bits each. But how can we ensure that the generated numbers are indeed prime, particularly large primes? A standard approach is to randomly generate a 1024-bit number, then apply a primality testing algorithm. If the candidate is composite, it is discarded and the process repeats until a prime is found. This procedure is illustrated in Figure 7-3.

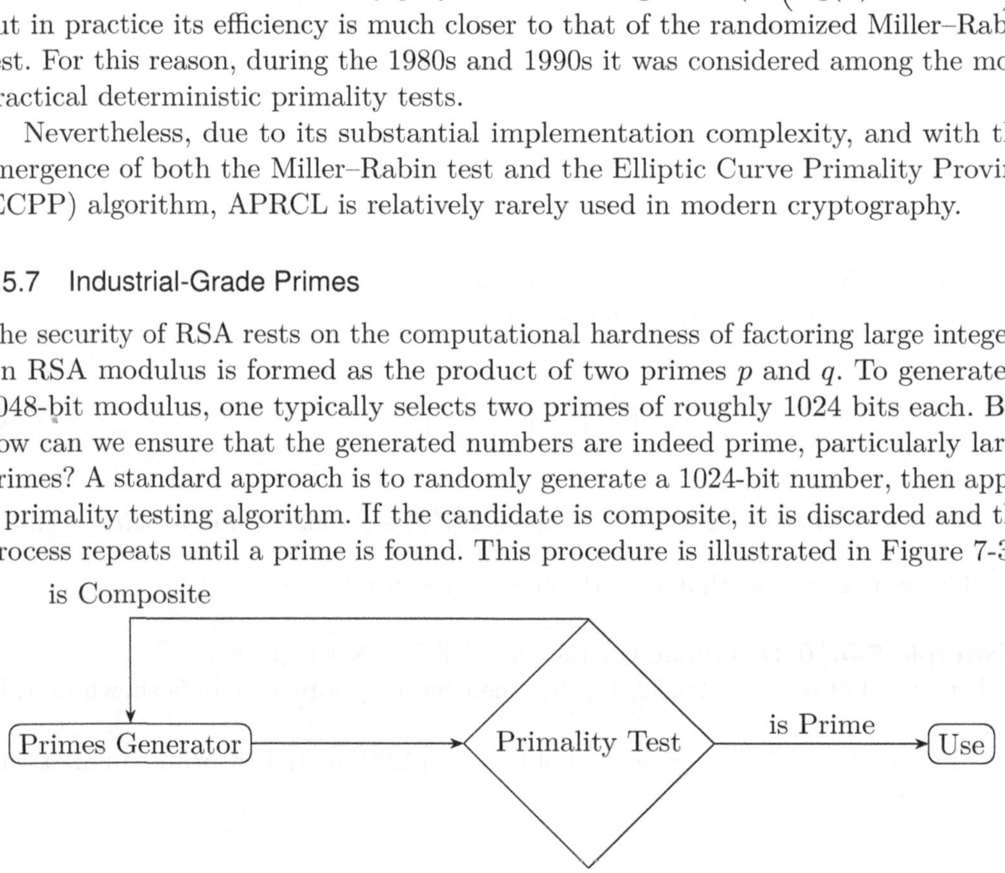

Figure 7-3: Prime Number Generator

Generating large primes requires high entropy random numbers. Since most computers rely on pseudo-random number generators (PRNGs), which are inherently predictable, an adversary who can deduce their generation pattern could compromise the security of RSA. For this reason, one must employ true random number generators (TRNGs) or cryptographically secure pseudo-random number generators (CSPRNGs). Further discussion can be found in Section 13.5.4.

Assuming a CSPRNG is available, how many random numbers must be generated before a prime is found? Is this process efficient? According to the prime number theorem (Theorem 7.2.2), the probability of generating a 1024-bit prime near n is

$$\frac{1}{\ln(n)} = \frac{1}{\ln(2^{1024})} \approx 0.14\% \tag{7-103}$$

This implies that, on average, about $\frac{1}{0.0014} \approx 710$ random trials are needed to obtain a prime. For modern computers, this cost is entirely acceptable and amounts to polynomial-time computation. Moreover, if only odd candidates are generated, the probability of success is roughly doubled.

Primality testing methods can be broadly divided into two categories: Deterministic algorithms and Probabilistic algorithms. In practice, probabilistic methods are favored, by running multiple rounds of testing, the error probability can be driven down to a negligible level.

In computer science, one may think of large prime generation algorithms as factories that manufacture primes, and the resulting products are known as industrial-grade primes. By definition, these integers lack formal deterministic proofs of primality but have successfully passed rigorous probabilistic evaluations, such as the Miller-Rabin test. Consequently, they carry a microscopic, theoretically non-zero probability of being composite. In practical cryptographic applications, however, no such defective composite has ever been encountered.

This approach is not mathematically exact, yet it is extremely fast and, crucially, it never rejects a true prime.

For generating cryptographically secure primes in practical systems, established libraries such as OpenSSL are widely employed. OpenSSL provides certificate and key management, as well as symmetric and asymmetric encryption. As an open-source software library, it is widely deployed in web servers across the Internet.

After 64 rounds of the Miller-Rabin test, the probability that the tested number is composite drops to 2^{-128}. This level of assurance is more than sufficient for cryptographic applications, and there is no practical need to resort to the deterministic but considerably slower primality test.

7.5.8 Large Prime is Not Always Safe

As n increases, the prime number theorem tells us that $\lim_{x\to\infty} \dfrac{1}{\log(x)} = 0$, which means that primes become sparser along the number line as numbers grow larger. In probabilistic terms, one might expect the gaps between consecutive primes to increase without bound. However, observation reveals otherwise. Even among very large numbers, primes can still be found relatively close to each other. This leads to the celebrated **Twin Prime Conjecture**.

The conjecture is simply that there exist infinitely many primes p such that $p+2$ is also prime. Such pairs $(p, p+2)$ are called twin primes, since a gap of 2 is the closest possible between two odd primes. For example, below 100 the twin primes are (3,5), (5,7), (11,13), (17,19), (29,31), (41,43), (59,61), and (71,73), there are exactly eight such pairs less than 100.

In 1849, the French mathematician *Alphonse de Polignac* proposed a generalized conjecture asserting that for every even integer $2k, k \in \mathbb{N}$, there are infinitely many pairs of primes separated by $2k$, i.e., $(p, p+2k)$. This statement is known as **Polignac's Conjecture**. The special case $k = 1$ is precisely the Twin Prime Conjecture. While some credit Polignac as the first to articulate the idea of twin primes, others disagree, and the precise origin of the conjecture remains uncertain.

Although easy to state, the Twin Prime Conjecture is extraordinarily difficult to prove. Countless mathematicians have struggled without resolving it. A landmark breakthrough came in 1966, when the Chinese mathematician *Chen Jingrun* proved what is now called *Chen's Theorem* [92]: There exist infinitely many primes p such that $p+2$ is either a prime or the product of two primes. This result (often referred to as "1+2") represents the most significant theoretical advance toward the Twin Prime Conjecture to date.

In 2013, the Chinese-American mathematician *Yitang Zhang* published his groundbreaking paper [93], establishing that there are infinitely many pairs of primes whose difference is less than 70 million. This was the first unconditional result showing the existence of infinitely many bounded prime gaps

$$\liminf_{n\to\infty} (p_{n+1} - p_n) < 7 \times 10^7 \tag{7-104}$$

where p_n denotes the n-th prime and $p_{n+1} - p_n$ the prime gap. This paper established a weak form of the Twin Prime Conjecture, marking a major advance. It gave mathematicians new optimism: if the bound of 70 million could eventually be reduced to 2, the full conjecture would follow. Building on Zhang's breakthrough, further work by *Terence Tao*, *James Maynard*, and others succeeded in lowering the gap to 246 [94].

The discussion of twin primes in the previous section is not merely theoretical; it has profound implications for the security of RSA. The examples provided earlier represent what is known as "Textbook RSA". If used in real-world Internet applications, such an implementation would be insecure and easily broken.

Selecting primes for RSA requires great care. Even if cryptographically secure primes are used, selecting a twin prime pair as p and q makes the modulus N especially vulnerable. Poor prime selection can render N easy to factor [95] [96]. In particular, analogous to Wiener's attack, if N is formed from two very close primes and the condition

$$|p - q| < 2N^{1/4} \tag{7-105}$$

holds, then N can be factored efficiently [80].

Let p and q be the prime factors of N, with $p < q$. We define $A = (p+q)/2$. If $|p-q| < 2N^{1/4}$, then $\sqrt{N}$ is close to A, with $A - \sqrt{N} < 1$. Since A is an integer, $\sqrt{N}$ needs to round up to approximate A. Consequently, one obtains

$$p < \sqrt{N} < A < q \tag{7-106}$$

which reveals enough information to factor N with ease.

Geometrically, A represents the midpoint between p and q on the number line, so there exists some x with $p = A - x$ and $q = A + x$. Once x is determined, the primes p and q are immediately recovered, giving a factorization of N.

Since $N = pq = (A-x)(A+x) = A^2 - x^2$, it follows directly that $x = \sqrt{A^2 - N}$. The method is called **Fermat's Difference of Squares Method**.

Example 7.5.11 Factorize the following integer N:

$$\begin{aligned} N = \ & 24090918518573421339224533330881775012042001351897292613353317 \\ & 85033733094848800542171145287998065265039099248792513471409 \end{aligned}$$

Solution: Let $A = \lceil \sqrt{N} \rceil$, where "$\lceil \cdot \rceil$" denotes the ceiling function. Since N is large, the **gmpy2** library is required for calculations in Python, for example, `gmpy2.iroot(N,2)`.

$$\begin{aligned} A &= 155212494724440490781129405365328495520831642398052967165271 75 \\ x &= \lceil \sqrt{A^2 - N} \rceil = 96 \\ p &= A - x \\ &= 155212494724440490781129405365328495520831642398052967165270 79 \\ q &= A + x \\ &= 155212494724440490781129405365328495520831642398052967165272 71 \end{aligned}$$

p and q are prime factors of N. ■

To design a secure RSA encryption system, the following guidelines should be observed (among others):

1) The prime numbers p and q must be sufficiently large, they should have a length of at least 512 bits, though 1024-bit primes are recommended for modern applications.
2) The primes should not be too close. In particular, they should satisfy $|p-q| > 2^{11}N^{1/4}$ and $|3p - 2q| > N^{1/4}$.
3) At least one of $p-1$ or $q-1$ must contain a large prime factor.
4) The public exponent should be chosen as $e \geqslant 65537$, which is a commonly adopted secure value.
5) The private exponent must satisfy $d > \frac{1}{3}N^{1/4}$.
6) If the private key d is ever compromised, the entire set of parameters (N, e, d) must all be regenerated immediately.

7) If the bit length of N does not match the prescribed RSA modulus size, the primes p and q must be reselected.
8) The modulus N must never be reused for different key pairs.
9) The plaintexts must adhere to a specified minimum length. If they are too short, proper padding must be applied.
10) The generation of primes requires high-quality entropy. A TRNG or a CSPRNG seeded by a TRNG must be used.
11) The underlying hardware must be reliable.

7.6 EXERCISES

1) Use primality testing methods to determine which of the following numbers are primes:
   (a) 99721
   (b) 99731
   (c) 5006069
   (d) 5017811
   (e) 5017813
2) If n is composite, explain why n must have a prime factor $p \leqslant \sqrt{n}$.
3) If x and y are odd, show that $x^2 + y^2$ cannot be a perfect square.
4) Suppose the sequence n, $n+2$, and $n+4$ consists entirely of prime numbers. Determine the exact value of the integer n.
5) Use the Solovay-Strassen Test to check whether $n = 8911$ is a prime number. Compute the required identities in the algorithm. Summarize the result in the following table:

i	a_i	$\gcd(a_i, n)$	$\left(\frac{a}{n}\right)$	$a^{(n-1)/2} \bmod n$
1				
2				
$\vdots$				

6) Consider the RSA cipher. Let two primes be $p = 113$, $q = 157$, the encryption exponent is $e = 143$, answer the following questions:
   (a) Compute the value of the public modulus N.
   (b) Explain why $d = 14225$ is the decryption exponent?
   (c) Suppose that in addition to knowing the published modulus N and encryption exponent e, Eve also knows the sum $p + q$. Can Eve discover the decrypting factor?
7) Consider the RSA cipher. Let $N = 5183 = 71 \cdot 73$, the encryption exponent is $e = 143$, the decryption exponent is $d = 1727$, answer the following questions:
   (a) Encrypt the plaintext $m = 23423$.
   (b) Decrypt the ciphertext $c = 2$.
8) Consider the RSA cipher. Let $N = 3599$ and the encryption exponent $e = 31$, answer the following questions:
   (a) Find the private key.
   (b) Encrypt the plaintext $m = 100$.

9) Consider the RSA cipher. Let $p = 101, q = 113$, $N = pq$, answer the following questions:
   (a) Let $e_1 = 8765$, $e_2 = 7653$, determine which one is a valid RSA encryption exponent?
   (b) For the valid encryption exponent, compute the decryption exponent.
   (c) Decrypt the ciphertext $c = 3233$.
10) Consider the RSA cipher. Let $N = 12191$, $e = 37$ and $c = 587$. We know that the modulus N is very small, factoring N and decrypting the ciphertext.
11) Consider the RSA cipher. Suppose Eve has obtained $N = 38749709$ through a certain channel, along with two sets of encryption and decryption exponents, which are

$$e_1 = 10988423, d_1 = 16784693$$
$$e_2 = 25910155, d_2 = 11514115$$

    Factor N.
12) Prove that the RSA Cryptosystem is insecure against a chosen ciphertext attack. In other words, given a ciphertext c, describe how to choose a ciphertext $c' \neq c$, such that knowledge of the plaintext $m' = \mathrm{D}_k(c')$ allows $m = \mathrm{D}_k(c)$ to be computed.
13) Consider the RSA cipher, since $c = m^e \pmod{N}$, show that for all $m_1, m_2 \in \mathbb{Z}_n$, we have

$$(c_1 \cdot c_2) \pmod{N} \equiv (m_1 \cdot m_2)^e \pmod{N} \tag{7-107}$$

14) Suppose Bob is communicating using the RSA cipher. His modulus N is sufficiently large that it cannot be factored in polynomial time. Suppose Alice represents each letter as an integer between 0 and 25 (as shown in Table 4-5) and subsequently encrypts the plaintext using the following formula:

$$c \equiv (m_i \pmod{26})^e \pmod{N} \tag{7-108}$$

    Answer the following questions:
   (a) Is this RSA algorithm secure? Please explain the reason.
   (b) Suppose $N = 18721$ and $e = 25$. Attempt to decrypt the following ciphertext:

$$365, 0, 4845, 14930, 2608, 2608, 0$$

15) Prove the following proposition:
   (a) Prove that any natural number n such that $n \equiv 3 \pmod{4}, n \in \mathbb{N}$, has a prime divisor p such that $p \equiv 3 \pmod{4}$.
   (b) Prove that $n! - 1 \equiv 3 \pmod{4}, n > 3$.
   (c) Prove that every prime divisor of $n! - 1$ is bigger than n.
16) Prove that every composite number n has a prime divisor less than or equal to $\sqrt{n}$.
17) Show that 172947529 is a Carmichael number.

18) Show that if $m = \prod p_i^{r_i}$ is composite, then m is a Carmichael number if and only if $r_i = 1$ and $(p_i - 1)|(m - 1)$, where p_i are distinct primes.
19) How many primes would we expect to find between 800000 and 1000000?
20) Consider the RSA cryptosystem with modulus $N = 7978886869909$ and public exponent $e = 3594320245477$. It is known that the private exponent d satisfies $d < 561$. Using Wiener's attack, determine the private exponent d and factor N.
21) Consider the properties of continued fractions and answer the following questions:
    (a) Find a simple continued fraction expansion of $\sqrt{5}$ and $\frac{121}{5}$.
    (b) Suppose $p - q = 2d > 0$ and $N = pq$. Prove that $N + d^2$ is a perfect square.
    (c) Let $N = p \cdot q = 2189284635403183$, where p, q are distinct primes. Given a small positive integer r such that $N + r^2$ is a perfect square, factor N.

CHAPTER 8

ElGamal Cryptosystem

In this chapter, we introduce the ElGamal cryptosystem. This asymmetric encryption scheme is based on the Diffie–Hellman key exchange and serves as a fundamental public-key primitive. The ElGamal cryptosystem offers a significant alternative to RSA for public-key encryption.

The scheme was originally proposed in 1985 by the Egyptian mathematician *Taher ElGamal* in his seminal paper [97]. ElGamal not only provided a concrete realization of public-key encryption but also inspired subsequent digital signature mechanisms, most notably the Digital Signature Algorithm (DSA). In practice, ElGamal is widely used in digital signature protocols and secure email systems.

Recall from the previous chapter that the security of RSA relies on the difficulty of the integer factorization problem. In contrast, ElGamal encryption depends on the difficulty of the discrete logarithm problem over finite groups. More precisely, its semantic security is closely tied to the intractability of the Decisional Diffie–Hellman problem. This distinction provides a security foundation that is structurally different from that of RSA.

A notable advantage of ElGamal encryption is its probabilistic nature, meaning that encrypting the same plaintext multiple times yields different ciphertexts. However, a primary disadvantage is message expansion. Since the ciphertext comprises two group elements, its length is approximately double that of the plaintext. To fully understand the encryption process, we must first review the Diffie–Hellman key exchange and the discrete logarithm problem.

Topics covered in this chapter:

- Diffie-Hellman Key Exchange
- Man-in-the-Middle Attack
- Discrete Logarithm Problem
- ElGamal Encryption and Decryption Process
- Cryptanalysis of the ElGamal Cryptosystem

DOI: 10.1201/9781042011087-8

8.1 DIFFIE-HELLMAN KEY EXCHANGE

The Diffie–Hellman key exchange [7] enables two parties to establish a shared secret over an insecure channel without requiring any prior shared information. It is widely regarded as one of the most significant breakthroughs in public-key cryptography and remains extensively deployed in modern security protocols. Typically, the established shared secret is subsequently used as a symmetric key to encrypt and protect further communications.

While the concept of public-key distribution was first introduced by *Ralph C. Merkle* [98], the concrete method of key exchange was published in 1976 by *Whitfield Diffie* and *Martin Hellman*. This work laid the foundation for modern public-key cryptography.

The Diffie–Hellman scheme represents the first practical method for secure key establishment over an insecure channel. Prior to its invention, key distribution presented a fundamental problem: transmitting keys in plain text risked compromise, while encrypting them required the receiver to already possess a decryption key. The Diffie–Hellman protocol effectively resolved this long-standing circular dependency.

Using this protocol, two parties, denoted as Alice and Bob, can establish a shared secret key over a channel subject to eavesdropping. Crucially, the actual key itself is never transmitted. Modern secure communication protocols, including SSH, TLS, and IPsec, rely heavily on this mechanism or its variants, such as Elliptic-Curve Diffie–Hellman (ECDH).

8.1.1 Key Exchange Steps

1) Alice and Bob agree on a prime number p and a base r that is a primitive root modulo p. Publish r and p.
2) Alice chooses a secret number x such that $1 \leqslant x \leqslant p-2$, computes $A \equiv r^x \pmod{p}$ and sends A to Bob.
3) Bob chooses a secret number y such that $1 \leqslant y \leqslant p-2$, computes $B \equiv r^y \pmod{p}$, and sends B to Alice.
4) Alice computes the key as $K = B^x \pmod{p}$.
5) Bob computes the key as $K = A^y \pmod{p}$.

Alice and Bob can use K as their **private key**, because the two calculations produce the same results

$$\underbrace{B^x \equiv (r^y)^x \equiv r^{xy} \equiv (r^x)^y \equiv A^y}_{\pmod{p}} \tag{8-1}$$

The values of p, r, A, B are public, the values of x, y, K are private. The procedure is illustrated in Figure 8-1.

If Eve were able to solve the discrete logarithm problem, she could readily compute the shared secret K. However, given sufficiently large parameters, recovering the shared secret from r, p, A, and B is computationally infeasible. Using the best known algorithms, such a task would require a time exceeding the lifetime of the universe.

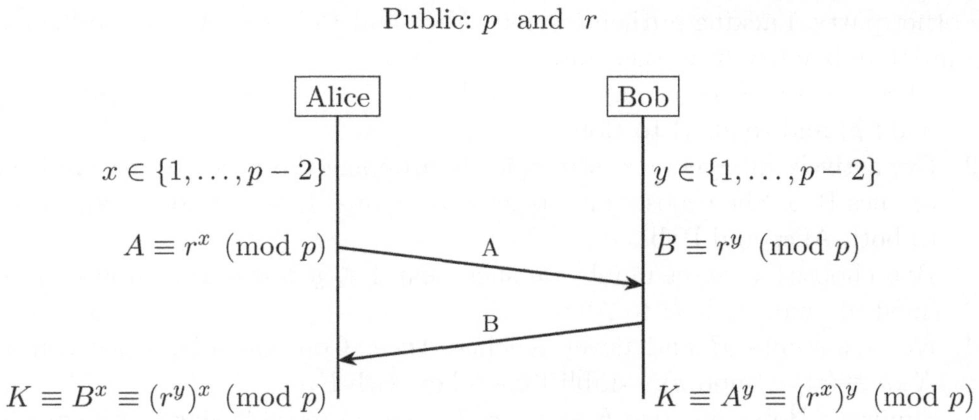

Figure 8-1: The Diffie-Hellman Key Exchange

Example 8.1.1 Suppose Alice and Bob agree on $p = 37$ and $r = 17$. Determine the resulting shared symmetric key.

Solution: Assume Alice and Bob choose secret integers $x = 9$ and $y = 10$. Each party evaluates their respective public component

$$A \equiv r^x \pmod{p} \equiv 17^9 \equiv 6 \pmod{37} \tag{8-2}$$
$$B \equiv r^y \pmod{p} \equiv 17^{10} \equiv 28 \pmod{37} \tag{8-3}$$

Exchange the A, B. Alice computes $K \equiv B^x \equiv 28^9 \equiv 36 \pmod{37}$; Bob computes $K \equiv A^y \equiv 6^{10} \equiv 36 \pmod{37}$.

Then $K = 36$ is the shared key that both Alice and Bob will use to encrypt their messages to each other. ■

As with RSA, prime generation must rely on either a true random number generator (TRNG) or a cryptographically secure pseudorandom number generator (CSPRNG). Moreover, certain system parameters must be chosen with sufficiently large sizes(e.g. 1024 bits) and with appropriate separation. Otherwise, the system may become vulnerable to attacks, compromising the security of the key exchange process.

8.1.2 Man-in-the-Middle Attack

Although the Diffie–Hellman key exchange is secure against passive eavesdropping, it remains vulnerable to a Man-in-the-Middle (MITM) attack [99] if the communicating parties do not authenticate each other's identities. In this scenario, Eve cannot directly compute the shared secret from the public values. However, by intercepting messages and impersonating each party, she can compromise the exchange, preventing Alice and Bob from establishing a genuine shared secret.

The attack proceeds as follows. Eve selects a private exponent t and intercepts the public values: $A \equiv r^x \pmod{p}$ from Alice and $B \equiv r^y \pmod{p}$ from Bob. Since the parameters p, r, A, and B are public, Eve computes her own public value $E \equiv r^t \pmod{p}$. She then sends this value E to both Alice and Bob, masquerading as the other party. Lacking authentication, Alice and Bob accept Eve's value as the legitimate public key from their intended partner.

1) Alice chooses a secret number x such that $1 \leqslant x \leqslant p-2$, computes $A \equiv r^x \pmod{p}$ and sends A to Bob.
2) Eve actively intercepts A, strategically dropping the packet to ensure it never reaches Bob. She chooses an integer t, computes $E \equiv r^t \pmod{p}$ and sends E to both Alice and Bob.
3) Bob chooses a secret number y such that $1 \leqslant y \leqslant p-2$, computes $B \equiv r^y \pmod{p}$, and sends B to Alice.
4) Eve intercepts B and never reaches Alice. Consequently, Alice computes $K_{AE} \equiv (r^t)^x \pmod{p}$, establishing a key with Eve.
5) Similarly, Bob computes $K_{BE} \equiv (r^t)^y \pmod{p}$, establishing a key with Eve.

As a result, Alice and Bob do not share a common secret. Instead, each shares a distinct secret key with Eve. During subsequent communication, Alice and Bob encrypt messages using these respective keys. Eve can intercept these ciphertexts, decrypt them using K_{AE} or K_{BE}, read or modify the content, and then re-encrypt and forward the messages to the intended recipient. This allows Eve to transparently monitor and alter the entire traffic stream without detection, as illustrated in Figure 8-2.

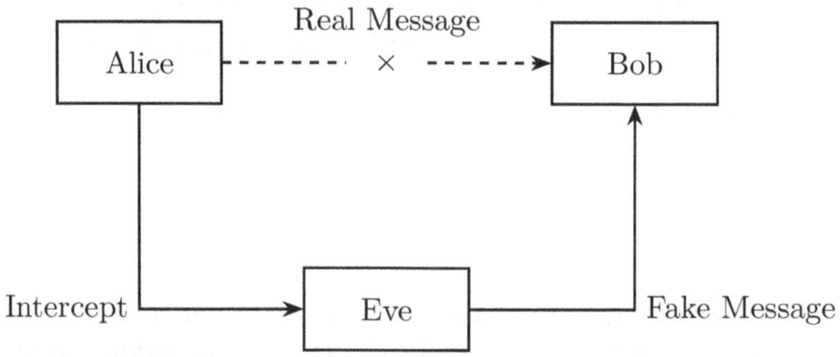

Figure 8-2: Man-in-the-Middle Attack

This vulnerability highlights the necessity of authentication. If Alice and Bob utilize digital signatures or certificates to verify each other's public keys, the Man-in-the-Middle attack can be effectively prevented, as Eve cannot feasibly forge a valid digital signature.

8.1.3 Zero-Knowledge Proof

A classical concept closely tied to signature verification and authentication is the zero-knowledge proof (ZKP). This concept was introduced by *Shafi Goldwasser*, *Silvio Micali*, and *Charles Rackoff* in 1985 [100]. In a zero-knowledge proof, a prover (Alice) demonstrates to a verifier (Bob) that a specific statement is true. The process is designed such that Bob becomes completely convinced of the statement's validity, yet learns nothing else from the interaction. In other words, Bob gains zero knowledge beyond the fact that the statement is true.

At first glance, this seems almost paradoxical. A well-known anecdote from the history of mathematics provides a vivid analogy. In the 16th century, the Italian mathematicians *Fiore* and *Tartaglia* both claimed to possess a method for solving cubic equations, though neither disclosed it publicly. They arranged a mathematical duel in Venice, each giving the other 30 problems. *Tartaglia* effortlessly solved all of *Fiore*'s challenges within an exceptionally short timeframe, whereas *Fiore* completely failed to resolve any of *Tartaglia*'s. Although *Tartaglia* never published his method, the outcome convinced observers that he indeed had a valid solution. While not a formal zero-knowledge proof in the modern sense, this story neatly captures the essence of the idea: proving knowledge of a secret without revealing the secret itself.

Zero-Knowledge proofs have found numerous applications, primarily falling into two categories: identification schemes and the design of cryptographic protocols. These range from classical settings, such as digital signatures and authentication, to more practical modern applications like electronic voting systems and online age verification.

For a proof system to be useful, it must satisfy the following three properties:

1) **Completeness**: an honest prover will be able to convince an honest verifier of the veracity of the claim, if the claim is indeed true.
2) **Soundness**: an honest verifier cannot be tricked into accepting a false statement by a possibly cheating prover.
3) **Zero-Knowledge**: in any interaction with the prover the verifier does not gain any knowledge that it did not possess already.

A classic example is the *Feige-Fiat-Shamir* Authentication Protocol. A single round of this protocol provides a basic proof with a soundness error of 1/2, meaning a cheater has a 50% chance of success. However, this reliability can be amplified to a soundness error of 2^{-n} by repeating the protocol n times. Typically, the number of repetitions is chosen such that $20 \leqslant n \leqslant 40$ [101].

8.2 DISCRETE LOGARITHM PROBLEM

The discrete logarithm is defined in the multiplicative group $(\mathbb{Z}/p\mathbb{Z})^*$ of a prime modulus p, with respect to a chosen base element (often a primitive root). In the Diffie–Hellman key exchange and the ElGamal cryptosystem, the underlying one-way function is modular exponentiation, and the inversion of this function is the Discrete Logarithm Problem (DLP).

Consider a prime p, finite cyclic group G, a primitive element α, and another element β. Solving the following equation:

$$\alpha^x \equiv \beta \pmod{p} \tag{8-4}$$

where $0 \leqslant x \leqslant p-2$. The problem of finding this x is known as the Discrete Logarithm Problem, and the exponent x is said to be the discrete logarithm of β to the base α, modulo p. The uniqueness of x depends on the order of α. If α is a primitive root, the solution is unique modulo $p-1$ (hence unique within $0 \leqslant x \leqslant p-2$). If α is not a primitive root, a solution exists only if β lies in the subgroup generated by α, and the solutions repeat with period $ord(\alpha)$.

For example, $3^x = 11$ has a unique solution $x = \log_3(11)$. However, the congruence $3^x \equiv 11 \pmod{167}$ has more than one solutions $x \equiv 78 \pmod{83}$, which yield $x = 78$ and $x = 161$ within the interval $1 \leqslant x \leqslant 166$.

8.2.1 Order of an Integer Modulo n

Definition 8.2.1 Order of an Integer Modulo n

Let n be a positive integer and let a be an integer satisfying $\gcd(a, n) = 1$. The order of a modulo n is the smallest positive integer k such that

$$a^k \equiv 1 \pmod{n} \tag{8-5}$$

It is denoted by

$$ord_n(a) \tag{8-6}$$

When $n = p$ is prime, write $ord_p(a)$. If $\gcd(a, p) > 1$, then the order is undefined.

Example 8.2.1 Let $p = 7$, $a_1 = 5$, $a_2 = 6$, find $ord_p(a_1)$ and $ord_p(a_2)$.
Solution: Since $a_1 = 5$, and we know that $\varphi(7) = 6$, we have

$$\begin{aligned} 5^1 &\equiv 5 \pmod{7} & 5^4 &\equiv 2 \pmod{7} \\ 5^2 &\equiv 4 \pmod{7} & 5^5 &\equiv 3 \pmod{7} \\ 5^3 &\equiv 6 \pmod{7} & 5^6 &\equiv \mathbf{1} \pmod{7} \end{aligned}$$

Thus, $ord_p(a_1) = 6$.
Since $a_2 = 6$, we have

$$6^1 \equiv 6 \pmod{7} \qquad 6^2 \equiv \mathbf{1} \pmod{7}$$

Thus, $ord_p(a_2) = 2$. ■

If $\gcd(a, p) = 1$ and $p > 0$, then a positive integer k is a solution to the congruence $a^k \equiv 1 \pmod{p}$ if and only if $ord_p a \mid k$.

The equivalent SageMath implementation to compute the multiplicative order of an element over a finite field is elegantly structured as follows:

```
p = 541 #Prime
alpha_val = 5
F = GF(p)
alpha = F(alpha_val)
order = alpha.multiplicative_order()
```

8.2.2 Primitive Root

Definition 8.2.2 Primitive Root

Let a be a positive integer and p be prime, if $\gcd(a, p) = 1$, and $ord_p(a) = \varphi(p)$, we say that a is a primitive root modulo p.

In other words, if $ord_p(a) = p - 1$, we say a is a primitive root modulo p.

Example 8.2.2 Consider $p = 11$ and $p = 13$, find the primitive roots of them.
Solution: To determine the primitive roots of a prime p, we examine the powers of elements in the group. Specifically, we compute $a^b \pmod p$ for $a, b \in \{1, 2, \ldots, p-1\}$, is shown in Table 8-1.

Table 8-1: Table of Powers Modulo 11

a \ b	1	2	3	4	5	6	7	8	9	10
1	**1**	1	1	1	1	1	1	1	1	1
2	2	4	8	5	10	9	7	3	6	**1**
3	3	9	5	4	**1**	3	9	5	4	1
4	4	5	9	3	**1**	4	5	9	3	1
5	5	3	4	9	**1**	5	3	4	9	1
6	6	3	7	9	10	5	8	4	2	**1**
7	7	5	2	3	10	4	6	9	8	**1**
8	8	9	6	4	10	3	2	5	7	**1**
9	9	4	3	5	**1**	9	4	3	5	1
10	10	**1**	10	1	10	1	10	1	10	1

To identify the primitive roots using Table 8-1, we observe the rows corresponding to each base a. Since the group is cyclic, the sequence of powers begins to repeat once the value 1 appears.

In the first row, the value 1 appears immediately, so the sequence is trivial and repeats instantly; in the second row, the value 1 does not appear until the final column, Since $p - 1 = 10$, this indicates that the element 2 generates the entire group without repetition before the end of the period; in the third row, the value 1 occurs already in the fifth column, after which the sequence repeats earlier values, so it does not generate all elements.

The bases a for which the first occurrence of 1 is in the last column are exactly the primitive roots modulo p.

Thus, modulo 11 the primitive roots are $2, 6, 7$, and 8; the remaining elements are not primitive roots.

Similarly, for the prime number 13, its primitive roots are $2, 6, 7$, and 11. ■

Example 8.2.3 Let $p = 7$, are 2 and 3 a primitive root mod p?
Solution: If $a = 2$, since a and p are relatively prime integers, $\varphi(p) = 6$, easy to compute $a^{p-1} \equiv 2^6 \equiv 1 \pmod 7$, however, $2^3 \equiv 1 \pmod 7$, so 2 is not a primitive root modulo 7.

If $a = 3$, since $a^{p-1} \equiv 3^6 \equiv 1 \pmod 7$ and $3^1, 3^2, \cdots, 3^5 \pmod 7 \not\equiv 1$. Therefore, 3 has order 6 = 7-1, so 3 is a primitive root modulo 7. ■

While every prime number possesses a primitive root, this property does not hold for all composite numbers. For example, The set of integers less than 8 and relatively prime to 8 is $\{1, 3, 5, 7\}$. Since $\text{ord}_8(1) = 1$, $\text{ord}_8(3) = 2$, $\text{ord}_8(5) = 2$, $\text{ord}_8(7) = 2$, the maximum order is 2, the number 8 does not possess a primitive root.

The Python implementation to deterministically evaluate the primitive roots modulo p is presented below:

```python
from math import gcd

def countPrimitiveRoots(p):
    p = p -1
    result = 1
    for i in range(2, p, 1):
        if (gcd(i, p) == 1):
            result += 1

    return result
```

The Python code for find the primitive roots modulo p is as follows:

```python
def primRoots(p):
    roots = []
    required_set = set(num for num in range (1, p) if gcd(num, p) ==
    1)

    for g in range(1, p):
        actual_set = set(pow(g, powers) % p for powers in range (1, p
    ))
        if required_set == actual_set:
            roots.append(g)
    return roots
```

Theorem 8.2.1 Primitive Root Test

Let $p > 3$ be a prime, and let $a \geqslant 2$ be an integer such that $\gcd(a, p) = 1$. Then, the integer a is a primitive root if and only if $a^{\varphi(p)/p_i} \not\equiv 1 \pmod{p}$ where p_i are prime divisors $p_i \mid \varphi(p)$.

Proof

(Forward Implication): If a is definitively a primitive root modulo p, then by definition its absolute multiplicative order is exactly $\mathrm{ord}_p(a) = \phi(p) = p-1$. For any distinct prime factor p_i dividing $\phi(p)$, the exponent quotient strictly satisfies $0 < \frac{\phi(p)}{p_i} < \phi(p)$. Because the order is the smallest positive integer k yielding $a^k \equiv 1 \pmod{p}$, it inherently follows that $a^{\phi(p)/p_i} \not\equiv 1 \pmod{p}$.

(Reverse Implication): Suppose for the sake of contradiction that $a^{\phi(p)/p_i} \not\equiv 1 \pmod{p}$ holds for all prime factors p_i, yet a is not a primitive root. Let its actual order be denoted as $\mathrm{ord}_p(a) = l$. Because l must divide the group order $\phi(p)$ by Lagrange's theorem, we have $l \mid \phi(p)$ where $l < \phi(p)$.Consequently, the integer ratio $\frac{\phi(p)}{l} > 1$ must possess at least one prime factor, which we denote as p_i. Thus, $p_i \mid \frac{\phi(p)}{l}$, meaning we can express $\frac{\phi(p)}{p_i} = l \cdot q$ for some positive integer q.Evaluating the modular exponentiation yields

$$a^{\phi(p)/p_i} \equiv a^{l \cdot q} \equiv (a^l)^q \equiv 1^q \equiv 1 \pmod{p} \tag{8-7}$$

This establishes a direct mathematical contradiction against our initial premise that $a^{\phi(p)/p_i} \not\equiv 1 \pmod p$. Hence, our assumption that $l < \phi(p)$ must be false. Therefore, $l = \phi(p)$, explicitly confirming that a is a primitive root modulo p.

This theorem is useful, as it provides an efficient criterion for determining whether a given number is a primitive root modulo a prime.

Example 8.2.4 Find the values of $ord_{17}(5)$, $ord_{17}(39)$ and $ord_{17}(7)$.
Solution: Since $\varphi(p) = p - 1 = 16 = 2^4$, only one prime factor.

1) For $ord_{17}(5)$, since $5^{\varphi(p)/2} \equiv 5^8 \equiv 16 \not\equiv 1 \pmod{17}$, by Theorem 8.2.1, 5 is a primitive root modulo 17, so $ord_{17}(5) = 16$.
2) For $ord_{17}(39)$, since $39 \equiv 5 \pmod{17}$, then $ord_{17}(39) = ord_{17}(5) = 16$.
3) For $ord_{17}(7)$, since $7 \times 5 \equiv 1 \pmod{17}$, $7 \equiv 5^{-1} \pmod{17}$, so the inverse of 7 is 5, thus $ord_{17}(7) = ord_{17}(5) = 16$.

■

8.2.3 Cyclotomic Polynomial

Definition 8.2.3 Cyclotomic Polynomial

The n-th cyclotomic polynomial is defined by

$$\Phi_n(x) = \prod_{d|n}(x^d - 1)^{\mu(n/d)} \tag{8-8}$$

where $\mu(k)$ denotes the classic Möbius function, as rigorously defined in the previous section.

The degree of $\Phi_n(x)$ less than n and relatively prime to n. In other words, the degree of $\Phi_n(x)$ is $\varphi(n)$. $\Phi_n(x)$ is an irreducible polynomial with integer coefficients, the roots of $\Phi_n(x)$ on the unit circle of the complex plane, as shown in Figure 8-3.

For any positive integer n, $x^n - 1 = \prod_{m|n} \Phi_m(x)$. The roots of $x^n - 1$ are precisely the n-th roots of unity. Every n-th root of unity is a primitive m-th root of unity for some divisor m of n, and these are precisely the roots of the product on the right.

$$x - 1 = x - 1 \tag{8-9}$$

$$x^2 - 1 = (x+1)(x-1) \tag{8-10}$$

$$x^3 - 1 = \left(x^2 + x + 1\right)(x-1) \tag{8-11}$$

$$x^4 - 1 = \left(x^2 + 1\right)(x+1)(x-1) \tag{8-12}$$

$$x^5 - 1 = \left(x^4 + x^3 + x^2 + x + 1\right)(x-1) \tag{8-13}$$

$$x^6 - 1 = \left(x^2 - x + 1\right)\left(x^2 + x + 1\right)(x+1)(x-1) \tag{8-14}$$

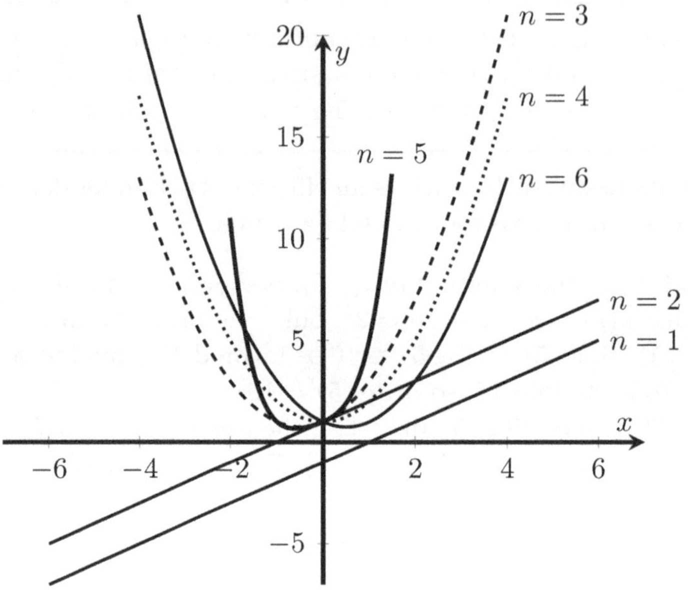

Figure 8-3: Cyclotomic Polynomial

In the factorization of $x^n - 1$, the irreducible factors that arise are known as cyclotomic polynomials. The first few notable cyclotomic polynomials are:

$$\begin{array}{ll}
\Phi_1(x) = x - 1 & \Phi_2(x) = x + 1 \\
\Phi_3(x) = x^2 + x + 1 & \Phi_4(x) = x^2 + 1 \\
\Phi_5(x) = x^4 + x^3 + x^2 + x + 1 & \Phi_6(x) = x^2 - x + 1 \\
\Phi_{10}(x) = x^4 - x^3 + x^2 - x + 1 & \Phi_{12}(x) = x^4 - x^2 + 1 \\
\Phi_{16}(x) = x^8 + 1 & \Phi_{18}(x) = x^6 - x^3 + 1
\end{array}$$

To explicitly construct $\Phi_n(x)$ analytically, we apply the Möbius inversion formula (Equation 8-8). This efficiently synthesizes the target polynomial by aggregating the algebraic fractions strictly across the exact divisors of n, gracefully applying the Möbius weights $\mu(d)$ to isolate the precise minimal polynomial of the primitive n-th roots of unity.

Example 8.2.5 Let $n = 6, 10, 18$, compute the cyclotomic polynomial $\Phi_n(x)$.
Solution:

- Compute $\Phi_6(x)$, since $n = 1 \times 2 \times 3$, so $m \in \{1, 2, 3, 6\}$, then

m	1	2	3	6
$6/m$	6	3	2	1
$\mu(6/m)$	1	−1	−1	1
$1 - x^m$	$1 - x$	$1 - x^2$	$1 - x^3$	$1 - x^6$

Using polynomial long division, we have

$$\Phi_6(x) = \frac{(1-x)(1-x^6)}{(1-x^2)(1-x^3)} = \frac{1+x^3}{1+x} = x^2 - x + 1$$

- Compute $\Phi_{10}(x)$, then

m	1	2	5	10
$10/m$	10	5	2	1
$\mu(10/m)$	1	-1	-1	1
$1-x^m$	$1-x$	$1-x^2$	$1-x^5$	$1-x^{10}$

Using polynomial long division, we have

$$\Phi_{10}(x) = \frac{(1-x^{10})(1-x^1)}{(1-x^5)(1-x^2)} = \frac{1+x^5}{1+x} = x^4 - x^3 + x^2 - x + 1$$

- Compute $\Phi_{18}(x)$, then

m	1	2	3	6	9	18
$18/m$	18	9	6	3	2	1
$\mu(18/m)$	0	0	1	-1	-1	1
$1-x^m$	$1-x$	$1-x^2$	$1-x^3$	$1-x^6$	$1-x^9$	$1-x^{18}$

Using polynomial long division, we have

$$\Phi_{18}(x) = \frac{(1-x^{18})(1-x^3)}{(1-x^9)(1-x^6)} = \frac{1+x^9}{1+x^3} = \frac{(1+x^3)(1-x^3+x^6)}{(1+x^3)} = 1 - x^3 + x^6$$

■

Theorem 8.2.2 Count Primitive Roots

Let p be a prime number. For any prime p, there exist exactly $\varphi(p-1)$ distinct primitive roots modulo p. In fact, a is a primitive root modulo p if and only if

$$\Phi_{p-1}(a) \equiv 0 \pmod{p} \tag{8-15}$$

The proof is shown in [102].

Example 8.2.6 Let $p = 11$, determine whether 2 and 3 are primitive roots modulo p.

Solution: By the Theorem 8.2.2, we have

$$\Phi_{p-1}(2) \equiv \Phi_{10}(2) \equiv 2^4 - 2^3 + 2^2 - 2^1 + 2^0 \equiv 11 \equiv 0 \pmod{11}$$
$$\Phi_{p-1}(3) \equiv \Phi_{10}(3) \equiv 3^4 - 3^3 + 3^2 - 3^1 + 3^0 \equiv 61 \equiv 6 \not\equiv 0 \pmod{11}$$

So 2 is a primitive root modulo p; 3 is not a primitive root modulo p. ■

Theorem 8.2.3 The Set of Primitive Roots

If a is a primitive root modulo p then the set of primitive roots modulo p may be constructed as the set of powers

$$\{a^r \pmod p \mid 1 \leqslant r \leqslant p-1 \text{ and } \gcd(r, p-1) = 1\} \tag{8-16}$$

In other words, if we know one primitive root modulo p, we can derive all primitive roots modulo p.

Example 8.2.7 Find the all primitive roots modulo 11, and known one of primitive root is 2.
Solution: The process is shown in Table 8-2.

Table 8-2: Primitive Root Modulo 11

k	1	2	3	4	5	6	7	8	9	10
$2^k \pmod{11}$	2	4	8	5	10	9	7	3	6	1

Since $k = 1, 3, 7, 9$ and $p - 1 = 10$ are relatively prime integers, so the primitive roots are $2, 6, 7, 8$. ■

Example 8.2.8 If we know the all primitive roots modulo 11, how to solve the congruence $9x \equiv 5 \pmod{11}$?
Solution: The process is shown in Table 8-3.

Table 8-3: Solve $9x \equiv 5 \pmod{11}$

k	1	2	3	**4**	5	**6**	7	8	9	10
$2^k \pmod{11}$	2	4	8	**5**	10	**9**	7	3	6	1

Since 2 is one of primitive roots modulo 11, so $x = 2^y$, then

$$9x \equiv 5 \pmod{11} \tag{8-17}$$
$$2^6 \cdot 2^y \equiv 2^4 \pmod{11} \tag{8-18}$$
$$2^{6+y} \equiv 2^4 \pmod{11} \tag{8-19}$$
$$2^{6+y-4} \equiv 1 \pmod{11} \tag{8-20}$$
$$2^{2+y} \equiv 1 \pmod{11} \tag{8-21}$$

Compute $2 + y \equiv 0 \pmod{\varphi(11)} \equiv 0 \pmod{10} \Rightarrow y = 8$

$$x \equiv 2^8 \pmod{11} \equiv 3 \tag{8-22}$$

■

Example 8.2.9 If we know the all primitive roots modulo 11, how to solve the congruence $7^x \equiv 5 \pmod{11}$?
Solution: We again exploit the primitive root 2 as our foundational algebraic base. From the mapping established in Table 8-2, we substitute the base $7 \equiv 2^7 \pmod{11}$

and the target $5 \equiv 2^4 \pmod{11}$ directly into the congruence

$$7^x \equiv 5 \pmod{11} \tag{8-23}$$
$$2^{7^x} \equiv 5 + 11 \equiv 2^4 \pmod{11} \tag{8-24}$$
$$2^{7x-4} \equiv 1 \pmod{11} \tag{8-25}$$

By the properties of cyclic groups generated by a primitive root, the exponents must strictly satisfy linear congruence modulo the group order $\varphi(11) = 10$

$$7x \equiv 4 \pmod{10} \tag{8-26}$$
$$\Rightarrow x \equiv 7^{-1} \cdot 4 \equiv 3 \cdot 4 \equiv 12 \pmod{10} \tag{8-27}$$
$$\Rightarrow x \equiv 2 \pmod{10} \tag{8-28}$$

■

Definition 8.2.4 Discrete Logarithm Problem(DLP)

Let p be prime and α be a primitive root modulo p, given an integer β, the Discrete Logarithm Problem is the problem of finding x such that

$$\alpha^x \equiv \beta \pmod{p} \tag{8-29}$$

The integer x, where $0 \leqslant x \leqslant p-2$, is called the discrete logarithm of β to the base α, and is denoted by

$$x = \log_\alpha \beta \tag{8-30}$$

Since α is a primitive root modulo p, such an integer x exists and is unique modulo $p-1$.

Given a prime p, finding a primitive root modulo p is significantly easier than solving the Discrete Logarithm Problem, provided the factorization of $p-1$ is known. While generating parameters is feasible, solving the DLP is generally assumed to be hard; there is no known polynomial-time algorithm for solving the DLP in general finite fields on classical computers.

Suppose $p = 941, \alpha = 627, x = 347, y = 781$, then

$$A \equiv \alpha^x \equiv 627^{347} \equiv 390 \pmod{941} \tag{8-31}$$
$$B \equiv \alpha^y \equiv 627^{781} \equiv 691 \pmod{941} \tag{8-32}$$
$$K \equiv \alpha^{xy} \equiv 627^{347 \cdot 781} \equiv 470 \pmod{941} \tag{8-33}$$

Although Eve may intercept A and B, recovering the private exponents x, y and the shared secret key K is computationally infeasible for sufficiently large parameters. Security depends on the computational intractability of reversing the exponentiation within the underlying group. Specifically, unless Eve possesses the computational power to perform operations on the order of $\mathcal{O}(\sqrt{p})$, she cannot break ciphertexts whose security rests on the DLP.

8.3 ELGAMAL

8.3.1 Encryption/Decryption

The security of the ElGamal cryptosystem relies on the asymmetry between the efficiency of modular exponentiation and the computational intractability of the Discrete Logarithm Problem [77].

1) (KeyGen): Alice and Bob agree upon a large prime p and a primitive root r modulo p.
   (a) (PrivateKeyGen): Bob selects a random integer a such that $1 \leqslant a \leqslant p-1$. Bob keeps a secret as his private key.
   (b) (PublicKeyGen): Bob computes

$$\alpha \equiv r^a \pmod p \tag{8-34}$$

   Bob publishes the triple (p, r, α) as his public key.
2) (Encrypt): Suppose Alice wants to send a plaintext as an integer $m \in \{1, 2, 3, \ldots, p-1\}$, and she selects a random integer k such that $1 \leqslant k \leqslant p-1$, then computes the following:

$$U \equiv r^k \pmod p \qquad V \equiv \alpha^k m \pmod p \tag{8-35}$$

   Alice transmits the pair of integers (U, V) to Bob. Typically, a different value of k is used for each plaintext.
3) (Decrypt): Bob decrypts by computing the following:

$$m \equiv U^{-a} V \pmod p \tag{8-36}$$

For correctness, the following proves that the encryption and decryption processes of ElGamal are reversible.

Proof

$$m \equiv U^{-a} V \pmod p \tag{8-37}$$
$$\equiv ((r^k)^{-a} \alpha^k m) \pmod p \tag{8-38}$$
$$\equiv r^{-ak} (r^a)^k m \pmod p \tag{8-39}$$
$$\equiv m \pmod p \tag{8-40}$$

In summary, the public parameters are p, r and α, and the ciphertext (U, V); the secret parameters are a and k. The encryption process is illustrated in Figure 8-4.

Different k is used for each plaintext integer, the reason for this is that then identical plaintext integers will have different corresponding ciphertexts. This property offers several advantages, chief among them being resistance to brute-force attacks and frequency analysis. Even if Eve intercepts the ciphertext (U, V), she cannot perform the calculation above because she doesn't know the key a since $a \equiv log_r(\alpha) \pmod p$.

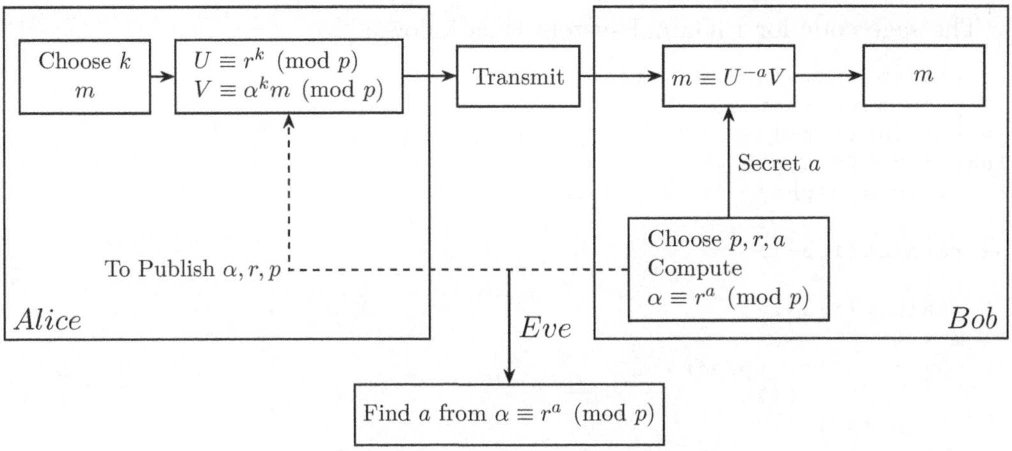

Figure 8-4: ElGamal Encryption

8.4 EXAMPLES

Example 8.4.1 If Alice wants to send a message **LUNCH** to Bob, consider the ElGamal system, how to encrypt the message?

Solution: Do following steps:

1) Suppose Alice and Bob select $p = 11881379$ and $r = 23$;
2) Bob selects $a = 55$ as private key and calculates $\alpha \equiv r^a \equiv 23^{55} \equiv 1308503 \pmod{11881379}$;
3) Bob sends α to Alice;
4) Alice wants to encrypt $m =$ **LUNCH**, encoding the message, starting from 0, in alphabetical order, $L = 11, U = 20, N = 13, C = 2, H = 7$, we have

$$m = 11 \cdot 26^4 + 20 \cdot 26^3 + 13 \cdot 26^2 + 2 \cdot 26^1 + 7 \cdot 26^0 = 5387103 \tag{8-41}$$

then selects $k = 123$.

5) Alice computes the ciphertext

$$U \equiv r^k \pmod p \equiv 23^{123} \equiv 1777907 \pmod{11881379} \tag{8-42}$$

$$V \equiv \alpha^k m \equiv 1308503^{123} \cdot 5387103 \equiv 4944577 \pmod{11881379} \tag{8-43}$$

6) Alice sends $(U, V) = (1777907, 4944577)$ to Bob.
7) Bob decrypts the ciphertext, he computes

$$U^{-a} \equiv U^{-55} \equiv U^{p-1-55} \equiv 1777907^{11881323} \equiv 7112147 \pmod{11881379} \tag{8-44}$$

$$m \equiv U^{-a}V \equiv 7112147 \cdot 4944577 \equiv 5387103 \pmod{11881379} \tag{8-45}$$

Then $m = 5387103 =$ **LUNCH**.

The Python code for modular exponentiation is as follows:

```
pow(1777907, 11881323, 11881379)#a^n%p, pow(a,n,p)
```

■

The sage code for ElGamal system is as follows:

```
p = random_prime(10^20, proof=True)
r = primitive_root(p)
a = randint(1,p-1)
alpha = pow(r,a,p)
print(p,r,a,alpha)

k = randint(1,p-1)

def plain(plain):
    m = 0
    for i in list(plain):
        i = ord(i)
        m += i
    return m

U = pow(r,k,p)
V = pow(alpha,k,p)*m%p

m1 = pow(U,-a,p)*pow(V,1,p)%p
print(m1, m == m1)
```

8.5 CRYPTANALYSIS

Suppose an adversary, Eve, intercepts the ciphertext pair (U, V) transmitted from Alice to Bob. To recover the plaintext m, Eve essentially needs to determine the private exponent. She typically attempts one of the following two strategies:

- Recover Bob's private key a by solving $\alpha \equiv r^a \pmod{p}$
- Recover the ephemeral key k used by Alice from $U \equiv r^k \pmod{p}$

Since the Discrete Logarithm Problem (DLP) is computationally intractable, solving these equations is considered infeasible for sufficiently large primes. Consequently, the confidentiality of the ElGamal cryptosystem relies fundamentally on the hardness of the DLP. The system is based on a one-way trapdoor function. Currently, there is no known algorithm for classical computers that can solve the DLP in polynomial time. However, if p is chosen carelessly, the system may be vulnerable to specific attacks.

A known limitation of the ElGamal cryptosystem is its **malleability**. Even if Eve cannot decrypt the message, she can validly modify the ciphertext. For instance, given a ciphertext (U, V) for a plaintext m, Eve can easily construct a valid ciphertext $(U, 2V)$ that decrypts to $2m$, without ever knowing m. This property implies that ElGamal does not provide integrity or security against chosen-ciphertext attacks.

Example 8.5.1 Recall Example 8.4.1. Suppose Eve wishes to execute an unauthenticated injection attack to deceive Bob. How can she mathematically forge a valid ciphertext without possessing Alice's credentials?

Solution: Assume Eve sends the dummy message $(U', V') = (5387871, 7127763)$ to Bob. Then the dummy message is

$$U'^{-a} \equiv U'^{-55} \equiv U'^{p-1-55} \equiv 5387871^{11881323} \equiv 3552158 \pmod{11881379} \quad (8\text{-}46)$$

$$m' \equiv U'^{-a}V' \equiv 3552158 \cdot 7127763 \equiv 6866650 \pmod{11881379} \quad (8\text{-}47)$$

$$\begin{aligned} 6866650 &= 15 \cdot 26^4 + 12010 && (8\text{-}48)\\ &= 15 \cdot 26^4 + 0 \cdot 26^3 + 17 \cdot 26^2 + 19 \cdot 26^1 + 24 \cdot 26^0 && (8\text{-}49)\\ &= \textbf{PARTY} && (8\text{-}50) \end{aligned}$$

■

In general, one can exhaust all possibilities from $1, 2, \ldots, p$. The time complexity of this approach is $\mathcal{O}(\sqrt{p})$. If p is small, this may be an option. However, Alice will not make such a mistake when sending to Bob, they will both choose a prime of 2048-bit length, which makes the computation time unacceptable.

8.5.1 Baby–Step Giant–Step Method

Eve's objective is to solve the congruence $\alpha \equiv r^a \pmod{p}$ for the private exponent a. Generally, this corresponds to solving the DLP. In 1973, the American mathematician *Daniel Shanks* introduced a method known as the **Baby-Step Giant-Step algorithm**(BSGS) [103]. This is a generic algorithm that applies to any finite cyclic abelian group. It significantly improves upon brute-force search by utilizing a time-memory trade-off, allowing discrete logarithms to be computed in $\mathcal{O}(\sqrt{p})$ time complexity and requires the same space. As the name suggests, the method combines "baby-step" precomputation with "giant-step" searching to gradually approach the target.

Let $m = \lceil \sqrt{p-1} \rceil$, where $\lceil \cdot \rceil$ denotes the ceiling function. By the division theorem, x expressed as $x = im + j$ where $0 \leqslant i, j \leqslant m - 1$, we have

$$\alpha^{im+j} \equiv \beta \pmod{p} \quad (8\text{-}51)$$

$$\alpha^{j} \equiv \beta\alpha^{-im} \pmod{p} \quad (8\text{-}52)$$

If we can identify integers i and j such that a collision occurs, then we have successfully recovered the exponent x. The values $\alpha^j \pmod{p}$ constitute the "baby steps", as they represent the small, incremental powers of α. These pairs (j, α^j) are stored in a lookup table indexed by the value α^j. The values of $\beta(\alpha^{-m})^i \pmod{p}$ constitute the "giant steps", where each subsequent value is obtained by multiplying the previous one by $\alpha^{-m} \pmod{p}$. For each computed giant step $\beta\alpha^{-mi} \pmod{p}$, the algorithm checks for its existence in the precomputed table.

If a match is found between a giant step $\beta\alpha^{-im} \pmod{p}$ and a baby step α^j, then we have $\alpha^j \equiv \beta\alpha^{-mi} \pmod{p}$, which implies $\beta \equiv \alpha^{im+j} \pmod{p}$. The discrete logarithm is then recovered as $x = im + j$.

1) Compute $m = \lceil \sqrt{p-1} \rceil$;
2) Baby steps: compute $\alpha^j \pmod p$ where $j = 0, 1, \ldots, m-1$, store pairs (j, α^j);
3) Giant steps: compute $\beta\alpha^{-im} \pmod p$ where $i = 0, 1, \ldots, m-1$, store the values;
4) Find a match between the two lists, obtain $\alpha^j = \beta\left(\alpha^{-im}\right)$
5) $x = im + j$

Because the algorithm demands substantial memory overhead ($\mathcal{O}(\sqrt{p})$ space) to maintain the baby-steps hash table, it becomes physically prohibitive for modern cryptographic primes. Since the algorithm requires large space, it is less used in practice.

Example 8.5.2 Solve for x in the congruence $89^x \equiv 406 \pmod{787}$.
Solution: $m = \lceil \sqrt{p-1} \rceil = 29$, therefore, the giant-steps and baby-steps tables as shown in Table 8-4.

Table 8-4: Baby-Step Giant-Step Example

index	0	1	2	3	⋯	27	28
$89^j \pmod{787}$	1	89	51	604	⋯	224	261
$406 \cdot 89^{-29 \cdot i} \pmod{787}$	406	1	126	136	⋯	467	604

We need only compute just enough that we find one value in the second row and one value in the third row which are equal. So we obtain a match when $i = 1$ and $j = 0$, we have $89^j \equiv 406 \cdot 89^{-29 \cdot i} \pmod{787}$. Hence, $x = im + j = 29$.

The Python code for BSGS method is as follows:

```
from math import ceil, sqrt
def bsgs(g, h, p):
    '''x = log_g(h) mod p'''
    N = ceil(sqrt(p - 1))

    # L1
    tbl = {pow(g, i, p): i for i in range(N)}

    c = pow(g, N * (p - 2), p)

    # L2
    for j in range(N):
        y = (h * pow(c, j, p)) % p
        if y in tbl:
            return j * N + tbl[y]
    return None
```

■

Example 8.5.3 Solve for x in the congruence $17^x \equiv 438 \pmod{509}$.
Solution: Set $m = \lceil \sqrt{p-1} \rceil = 23$, construct the baby-steps tables is as follow.

Next, compute Giant-Step $\beta\alpha^{-im} \pmod p$.

- $i = 0$, $438 \cdot 17^{-23 \cdot i} \equiv 438 \pmod p$, no value match, continue;
- $i = 1$, $438 \cdot 17^{-23 \cdot i} \equiv 199 \pmod p$, no value match, continue;
- $i = 2$, $438 \cdot 17^{-23 \cdot i} \equiv 238 \pmod p$, match is found.

Table 8-5: Example of the Baby-Step Phase

j	0	1	2	3	4	5	6	7	8	9	10	11
$17^j \pmod p$	1	17	289	332	45	256	280	179	498	322	384	420
j	12	13	14	15	16	17	18	19	20	21	22	
$17^j \pmod p$	14	238	483	67	121	21	357	470	355	436	286	

Hence $i = 2, j = 13$, $x = im + j = 59$. ■

8.5.2 Pollard's Rho Method

Since Baby-Step Giant-Step is that it also requires large storage space. To address this limitation, an improvement known as Pollard's Rho method is often employed [104].

The original version of Pollard's Rho method was introduced by British mathematician *John Pollard* in 1975 for the calculation of discrete logarithms. This method has the same expected run time as the BSGS method, but it only requires a negligible amount of storage, specifically $\mathcal{O}(1)$ space complexity.

A group is a set G with an operation denoted by $\star$. If G has finitely many elements, it is a finite group and the order of G is the number of elements $|G| = n$. A cyclic subgroup of G is all integer powers $\langle\alpha\rangle = \{\alpha^i : 0 \leqslant i \leqslant n-1\}$. If $\langle\alpha\rangle = G$, then α is a primitive root or generator of G, and G is a cyclic group of order n.

Let α be a primitive root of $\mathbb{F}_p$ and let β be a non-zero element of $\mathbb{F}_p$. For solving $\alpha^x \equiv \beta \pmod p$ to find x is the discrete logarithm of β to the base α.

Its idea is to partition G into 3 sets into three subsets S_1, S_2, S_3 of roughly the similar size, and an initial value x_0 is chosen such that $x_0 \equiv 1 \pmod p$ and $x_0 \notin S_2$. The iterating function defined by

$$x_{i+1} = f(x_i) = \begin{cases} \alpha x_i & \text{where } x_i \in S_1 \\ x_i^2 & \text{where } x_i \in S_2 \\ \beta x_i & \text{where } x_i \in S_3 \end{cases} \tag{8-53}$$

where α is a primitive root modulo p and β is an integer.

To generate this sequence $x_i = \alpha^{a_i}\beta^{b_i}$ where $i \in \mathbb{N}$, these sequences are defined using the functions

$$a_{i+1} \equiv \begin{cases} a_i + 1 & \pmod n & \text{where } x_i \in S_1 \\ 2a_i & \pmod n & \text{where } x_i \in S_2 \\ a_i & \pmod n & \text{where } x_i \in S_3 \end{cases} \tag{8-54}$$

$$b_{i+1} \equiv \begin{cases} b_i & \pmod n & \text{where } x_i \in S_1 \\ 2b_i & \pmod n & \text{where } x_i \in S_2 \\ b_i + 1 & \pmod n & \text{where } x_i \in S_3 \end{cases} \tag{8-55}$$

where $n = p - 1$ since $G = \mathbb{F}_p$, and a_0 is randomly selected and $b_0 = 0$. We can select $a_0 = 0$ or $a_0 = 2$, or other small number.

Using **Floyd's cycle-finding algorithm**, we should expect an integer i such that $x_i = x_{2i}$, once we have found a cycle, we have $\alpha^{a_i}\beta^{b_i} \equiv \alpha^{a_{2i}}\beta^{b_{2i}} \pmod p$, and

$$\beta^s \equiv \alpha^t \pmod p \tag{8-56}$$

where $s \equiv b_i - b_{2i} \pmod n$ and $t \equiv a_{2i} - a_i \pmod n$.

Floyd's cycle-finding algorithm was invented by *Robert W. Floyd* in 1969. It is also known as the **Tortoise and Hare algorithm**. Assume there is a path containing a cycle over which a tortoise and a hare are moving, and the hare is twice as fast as the tortoise. If the hare enters a cycle, it will eventually catch up with the tortoise, thus proving that a cycle exists. This method requires only constant space; furthermore, it can determine not only whether a cycle exists but also the starting point and length of the cycle.

Since the group is finite, this sequence must eventually repeat, forming a structure that resembles the Greek letter ρ: a "tail" leading into a cycle. The algorithm maintains two pointers moving through the sequence at different speeds.

- The "Tortoise" moves one step at a time: $x_{i+1} = f(x_i)$.
- The "Hare" moves two steps at a time: $x_{2(i+1)} = f(f(x_{2i}))$.

If a cycle exists, the faster-moving Hare will inevitably catch up to the Tortoise inside the cycle

$$x \cdot s \equiv t \pmod{n} \implies x \equiv t \cdot s^{-1} \pmod{n} \tag{8-57}$$

where $\gcd(s, n) = 1$ and $s \neq 0$.

The Pollard's Rho algorithm is illustrated in Figure 8-5.

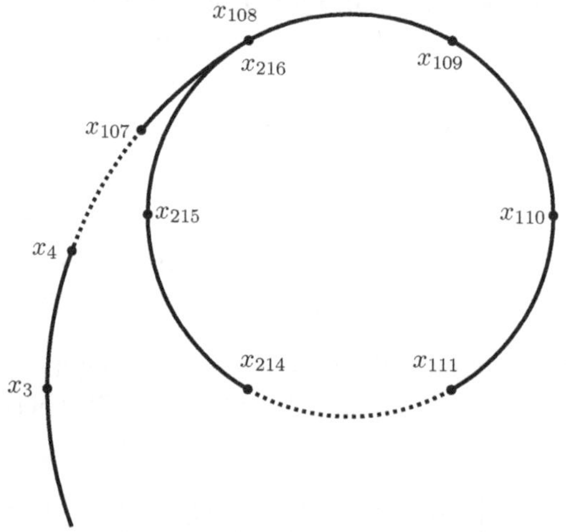

Figure 8-5: Pollard's Rho Algorithm

Example 8.5.4 Let $p = 541$ be a prime, $\alpha = 5$ is a generator of the subgroup G, and $\beta = 449$. Solving $\alpha^x \equiv \beta \pmod{p}$ to find x.
Solution: Partition G into 3 subsets, we set

$$\begin{cases} S_1 = \{x \in G \mid x = 1 \bmod 3\} \\ S_2 = \{x \in G \mid x = 0 \bmod 3\} \\ S_3 = \{x \in G \mid x = 2 \bmod 3\} \end{cases} \tag{8-58}$$

Find the $x_i, a_i, b_i, x_{2i}, b_{2i}, a_{2i}$, as shown in Table 8-6.

Table 8-6: Pollard Rho Algorithm Example

i	x_i	b_i	a_i	$2i$	x_{2i}	b_{2i}	a_{2i}	s	t
1	5	0	1	2	81	1	1	-1	0
2	81	1	1	4	433	4	4	-3	3
3	69	2	2	6	5	4	6	-2	4
4	433	4	4	8	69	10	12	-6	8
5	1	4	5	10	1	20	25	-16	20

Since $x_5 = x_{10} = 1$ as a collision, and α is not a primitive root modulo p, the order n is 135. Since $\gcd(s, n) = \gcd(-16, 135) = 1$, thus $x \equiv \underbrace{ts^{-1} \equiv 20 \cdot (-16)^{-1} \equiv 100.}_{\pmod{135}}$

■

8.5.3 Chinese Remainder Theorem

The Chinese Remainder Theorem (CRT) [105], also known as *Sunzi's theorem*, is a theorem concerning systems of linear congruences in one variable.

The earliest known statement of the problem was introduced by the Chinese mathematician *Sunzi* in the *Sunzi Suanjing* (Master Sun's Mathematical Manual) from the Southern and Northern Dynasties period (420–589). There is the following description: *Now there are an unknown number of things. If we count by threes, there is a remainder 2; if we count by fives, there is a remainder 3; if we count by sevens, there is a remainder 2. Find the number of things* [106].

Sunzi provided the following solution: If we count by threes and there is a remainder 2, put down 140. If we count by fives and there is a remainder 3, put down 63. If we count by sevens and there is a remainder 2, put down 30. Add them to obtain 233 and subtract 210 to get the answer.

Theorem 8.5.1 Chinese Remainder Theorem

Let $m_1, m_2, \ldots, m_n$ be a set of pairwise relatively prime integers, and let $a_1, a_2, \ldots, a_n \in \mathbb{Z}$ be any sequence of target remainders, then set $M = \prod_{i=1}^{n} m_i$.

The system of linear congruences

$$\begin{cases} x \equiv a_1 \pmod{m_1} \\ x \equiv a_2 \pmod{m_2} \\ \quad\vdots \\ x \equiv a_n \pmod{m_n} \end{cases} \tag{8-59}$$

has a unique solution $x \pmod{M}$ for all $1 \leqslant i \leqslant n$.

Proof

Let $M = \prod_{i=1}^{n} m_i$, *for* $1 \leqslant i \leqslant n$, *let* $M_i = M/m_i$. *Since* $m_1, m_2, \ldots, m_n$ *are pairwise relatively prime, we have* $\gcd(M_i, m_i) = 1$. *Suppose*

$$t_i \equiv M_i^{-1} \pmod{m_i} \tag{8-60}$$

Hence, for each i, *there exists an integer* t_i *such that*

$$t_i M_i \equiv 1 \pmod{m_i} \tag{8-61}$$

Define

$$x = \sum_{i=1}^{n} a_i t_i M_i \tag{8-62}$$

For a fixed i, *we reduce* x *modulo* m_i. *Since* M_j *is divisible by* m_i *whenever* $i \neq j$, *we obtain*

$$\begin{aligned} x &\equiv \sum_{j=1}^{n} a_j t_j M_j \pmod{m_i} && (8\text{-}63) \\ &\equiv a_i t_i M_i + \sum_{j \neq i} 0 \pmod{m_i} && (8\text{-}64) \\ &\equiv a_i (t_i M_i) \pmod{m_i} && (8\text{-}65) \\ &\equiv a_i \pmod{m_i} && (8\text{-}66) \end{aligned}$$

Therefore, $x \equiv a_i \pmod{m_i}$ *for* $1 \leqslant i \leqslant n$. *It remains to prove uniqueness modulo M. Suppose that* x *and* y *are two solutions of the system. Then* $x \equiv y \pmod{m_i}$ *for* $1 \leqslant i \leqslant n$.

Hence each m_i *divides* $x - y$. *Since the integers* $m_1, m_2, \ldots, m_n$ *are pairwise relatively prime, their product*

$$M = \prod_{i=1}^{n} m_i \tag{8-67}$$

also divides $x - y$. *Therefore*

$$x \equiv y \pmod{M} \tag{8-68}$$

Thus, the solution is unique modulo M.

Example 8.5.5 Solve the following linear congruence:

$$\begin{cases} x \equiv 6 & \pmod{11} \\ x \equiv 13 & \pmod{16} \\ x \equiv 9 & \pmod{21} \\ x \equiv 19 & \pmod{25} \end{cases} \tag{8-69}$$

Solution: Since $m_1 = 11, m_2 = 16, m_3 = 21, m_4 = 25$ are relatively prime in pairs, thus $M = m_1 \cdot m_2 \cdot m_3 \cdot m_4 = 92400$, and we find the M_1, M_2, M_3, M_4

$$M_1 = M/m_1 = m_2 m_3 m_4 = 8400 \tag{8-70}$$
$$M_2 = M/m_2 = m_1 m_3 m_4 = 5775 \tag{8-71}$$
$$M_3 = M/m_3 = m_1 m_2 m_4 = 4400 \tag{8-72}$$
$$M_4 = M/m_4 = m_1 m_2 m_3 = 3696 \tag{8-73}$$

The inverse of M_1, M_2, M_3, M_4

$$t_1 \equiv M_1^{-1} \equiv 8400^{-1} \equiv 7^{-1} \equiv 8 \pmod{11} \tag{8-74}$$
$$t_2 \equiv M_2^{-1} \equiv 5775^{-1} \equiv 15^{-1} \equiv 15 \pmod{16} \tag{8-75}$$
$$t_3 \equiv M_3^{-1} \equiv 4400^{-1} \equiv 11^{-1} \equiv 2 \pmod{21} \tag{8-76}$$
$$t_4 \equiv M_4^{-1} \equiv 3696^{-1} \equiv 21^{-1} \equiv 6 \pmod{25} \tag{8-77}$$

Thus, a solution of the system is given by

$$x \equiv \sum_{i=1}^{n} a_i t_i M_i \pmod{M} \tag{8-78}$$
$$\equiv a_1 t_1 M_1 + a_2 t_2 M_2 + a_3 t_3 M_3 + a_4 t_4 M_4 \pmod{92400} \tag{8-79}$$
$$\equiv 6 \cdot 8 \cdot 8400 + 13 \cdot 15 \cdot 5775 + 9 \cdot 2 \cdot 4400 + 19 \cdot 6 \cdot 3696 \pmod{92400} \tag{8-80}$$
$$\equiv 89469 \pmod{92400} \tag{8-81}$$

■

8.5.4 Pohlig–Hellman Method

The Pohlig-Hellman method was introduced by the American mathematicians *Stephen Pohlig* and *Martin Hellman* in 1978 [107]. This algorithm applies the Chinese Remainder Theorem to decompose a discrete logarithm problem in a large group into several sub-problems in smaller subgroups, thereby significantly reducing the computational complexity.

Consider the congruence $\alpha^x \equiv \beta \pmod{p}$, where p is a prime and α is a generator of $\mathbb{Z}_p^*$. The goal is to determine the integer x where x is called the discrete logarithm of β to the base α, and is denoted by $x = \log_\alpha \beta$, defined modulo $p-1$ since $|\mathbb{Z}_p^*| = \varphi(p) = p-1$. Let the prime power factorization of the order be $\varphi(p) = p-1 = p_1^{n_1} p_2^{n_2} \cdots p_m^{n_m}$ where the p_i are distinct primes, $n_i \in \mathbb{N}$ and $1 \leqslant i \leqslant m$.

Suppose $q = p_i$ and $n = n_i$ for a fixed index i. If we calculate $y \equiv x \pmod{q^n}$, we can subsequently reconstruct x modulo $p-1$ using the Chinese Remainder Theorem. Let y be expressed in base q representation as

$$y = \sum_{i=0}^{n-1} a_i q^i = a_0 q^0 + a_1 q^1 + \cdots + a_{n-1} q^{n-1} \tag{8-82}$$

where $0 \leqslant a_i \leqslant q-1$. For example, if $q = 2$ and $y = 11$(which is 1011 in base 2), then $y = 11 = 1 \cdot 2^0 + 1 \cdot 2^1 + 0 \cdot 2^2 + 1 \cdot 2^3$.

Since $y \equiv x \pmod{q^n}$, the integer x can be written as

$$x = y + sq^n, \text{where } s \in \mathbb{Z} \tag{8-83}$$

According to the fundamental theorem of cyclic groups, there exists a unique cyclic subgroup of order q^n for each prime power factor. To simplify the problem, we first determine the coefficient a_0. We raise both sides of the congruence $\alpha^x \equiv \beta \pmod{p}$ to the power of $\frac{p-1}{q}$. We have

$$\beta^{\frac{p-1}{q}} \equiv (\alpha^x)^{\frac{(p-1)}{q}} \pmod{p} \tag{8-84}$$

$$\equiv \left(\alpha^{a_0q^0+a_1q^1+\cdots+a_{n-1}q^{n-1}+sq^n}\right)^{\frac{(p-1)}{q}} \pmod{p} \tag{8-85}$$

$$\equiv \left(\alpha^{\frac{a_0(p-1)}{q}}\right) \pmod{p} \tag{8-86}$$

In congruence 8-85, all the remaining terms are of the form $\alpha^{a_jq^j\frac{p-1}{q}}$ $(1 \leqslant j \leqslant n-1)$. By Fermat's Little Theorem, $\alpha^{p-1} \equiv 1 \pmod{p}$, all these terms evaluate to 1 and can be removed from the expression. Then a_0 is determined using the Pollard's Rho method.

Since a_0 known, the next step would be to compute other a_i. These steps can be expressed using a generalized form of congruence 8-86.

To compute a_1,define $\beta_o = \beta$. Let $n = 2$, the congruence $\alpha^x \equiv \beta \pmod{p}$ raise both sides by $\frac{p-1}{q^n}$, we have

$$\beta^{\frac{p-1}{q^2}} \equiv \left(\alpha^{a_0q^0+a_1q^1+\cdots+a_{n-1}q^{n-1}+sq^n}\right)^{\frac{(p-1)}{q^2}} \pmod{p} \tag{8-87}$$

$$\beta^{\frac{p-1}{q^2}} \equiv \left(\alpha^{\frac{a_0(p-1)}{q^2}} \alpha^{\frac{a_1(p-1)}{q}} \alpha^{a_2(p-1)} \cdots \alpha^{sq^{n-2}(p-1)}\right) \pmod{p} \tag{8-88}$$

$$\beta^{\frac{p-1}{q^2}} \equiv \left(\alpha^{\frac{a_0(p-1)}{q^2}} \alpha^{\frac{a_1(p-1)}{q}}\right) \pmod{p} \tag{8-89}$$

$$(\beta\alpha^{-a_0})^{\frac{p-1}{q^2}} \equiv \left(\alpha^{a_1 \cdot \frac{p-1}{q}}\right) \pmod{p} \tag{8-90}$$

$$\beta_1^{\frac{p-1}{q^2}} \equiv \left(\alpha^{a_1 \cdot \frac{p-1}{q}}\right) \pmod{p} \tag{8-91}$$

In the above congruence, $\beta_1 = \beta\alpha^{-a_0}$, we can solve and get a_1. We can keep repeating these steps to get all values from a_2 to a_{n-1}. Let

$$\beta_k = \beta\alpha^{-(a_0q^0+a_1q^1+\cdots+a_{k-1}q^{k-1})} \tag{8-92}$$

where $1 \leqslant k \leqslant n-1$, the recursive formula is

$$\beta_k^{\frac{p-1}{q^{k+1}}} \equiv \alpha^{\frac{a_k(p-1)}{q}} \pmod{p} \tag{8-93}$$

$$\Rightarrow \beta_{k+1} \equiv \beta_k\alpha^{-a_kq^k} \pmod{p} \tag{8-94}$$

We can compute all a_i, then we can get y, by the Chinese Remainder Theorem, we have

$$\begin{cases} x \equiv y_1 \pmod{p_1^{n_1}} \\ x \equiv y_2 \pmod{p_2^{n_2}} \\ \vdots \\ x \equiv y_m \pmod{p_m^{n_m}} \end{cases} \tag{8-95}$$

There is a unique solution. The Pohlig–Hellman algorithm is illustrated in Figure 8-6.

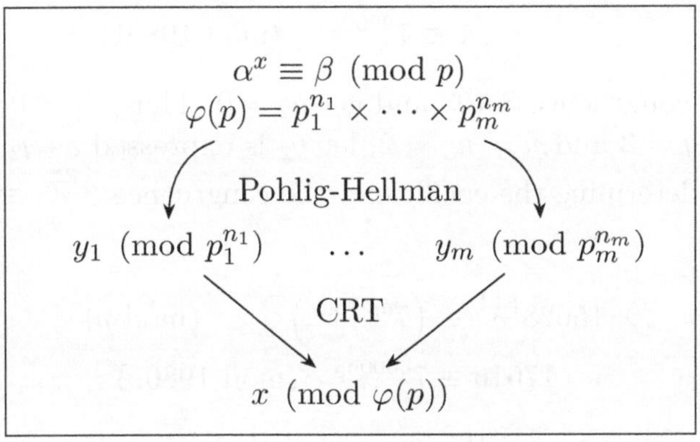

Figure 8-6: Pohlig-Hellman Algorithm

Example 8.5.6 Find the solutions of $7^x \equiv 15628 \pmod{19801}$.
Solution: Since $p - 1 = 19800 = 2^3 \cdot 3^2 \cdot 5^2 \cdot 11$, therefore we need to determine the systems of linear congruences below

$$\begin{cases} x \equiv y_1 \pmod{2^3} \\ x \equiv y_2 \pmod{3^2} \\ x \equiv y_3 \pmod{5^2} \\ x \equiv y_4 \pmod{11} \end{cases} \tag{8-96}$$

We proceed by computing $y_1 \pmod{2^3}$, $y_2 \pmod{3^2}$, $y_3 \pmod{5^2}$, $y_4 \pmod{11}$.

Starting by setting $q = 2$ and $n = n_1 = 3$. First, let y is expressed as $y = a_0 + 2a_1 + 4a_2$ where $a_i \in \{0, 1\}$. To determine the coefficient, the congruence $\beta^{\frac{p-1}{q^n}} \equiv (\alpha^x)^{\frac{p-1}{q^n}} \pmod{p}$ beginning with $n = 1$.

$$15628^{\frac{p-1}{2}} \equiv \left(7^{a_0+2a_1+4a_2}\right)^{\frac{p-1}{2}} \pmod{p} \tag{8-97}$$

$$15628^{9900} \equiv 7^{9900a_0} \pmod{p} \tag{8-98}$$

$$1 \equiv 7^{9900a_0} \pmod{19801} \tag{8-99}$$

We can solve the congruence 8-99 since $a_0 \in \{0, 1\}$ and get $a_0 = 0$, then we can determine a_1, let $n = 2$, we have

$$15628^{\frac{p-1}{2^2}} \equiv \left(7^{2a_1+4a_2}\right)^{\frac{p-1}{2^2}} \pmod p \tag{8-100}$$

$$1 \equiv 7^{9900a_1} \pmod{19801} \tag{8-101}$$

We can solve the congruence 8-101 and get $a_1 = 0$, then we can determine a_2, let $n = 3$, we have

$$15628^{\frac{p-1}{2^3}} \equiv \left(7^{4a_2}\right)^{\frac{p-1}{2^3}} \pmod p \tag{8-102}$$

$$1 \equiv 7^{9900a_2} \pmod{19801} \tag{8-103}$$

We can solve the congruence 8-103 and get $a_2 = 0$. Thus, $y_1 = 0$.

Next, we set $q = 3$ and $n = n_2 = 2$, let y_2 is expressed as $y_2 = a_0 + 3a_1$ where $a_i \in \{0, 1, 2\}$. To determine the coefficient, the congruence $\beta^{\frac{p-1}{q^n}} \equiv (\alpha^x)^{\frac{p-1}{q^n}} \pmod p$ begin with $n = 1$

$$15628^{\frac{p-1}{3}} \equiv \left(7^{a_0+3a_1}\right)^{\frac{p-1}{3}} \pmod p \tag{8-104}$$

$$17616 \equiv 7^{6600a_0} \pmod{19801} \tag{8-105}$$

We can solve the congruence 8-105 since $a_0 \in \{0, 1, 2\}$ and get $a_0 = 1$, then we can determine a_1, let $n = 2$

$$15628^{\frac{p-1}{3^2}} \equiv \left(7^{1+3a_1}\right)^{\frac{p-1}{3^2}} \pmod p \tag{8-106}$$

$$(15628 \cdot 7^{-1}) \equiv 7^{6600a_1} \pmod{19801} \tag{8-107}$$

$$(15628 \cdot 11315) \equiv 7^{6600a_1} \pmod{19801} \tag{8-108}$$

$$7890 \equiv 7^{6600a_1} \pmod{19801} \tag{8-109}$$

We can solve the congruence 8-109 and get $a_1 = 2$. Thus, $y_2 = 1 + 3 \cdot 2 = 7$.

Similarly, we can get $y_3 = 0$ and $y_4 = 0$. Use the Chinese Remainder Theorem to compute the common solution of the congruences

$$\begin{cases} x \equiv 0 \pmod{2^3} \\ x \equiv 7 \pmod{3^2} \\ x \equiv 0 \pmod{5^2} \\ x \equiv 0 \pmod{11} \end{cases} \tag{8-110}$$

Hence, we get $x \equiv 8800 \pmod{19800}$ is the solution. ■

8.5.5 Index–Calculus Method

Let p be a prime. **Index Calculus** is a specialized method for computing discrete logarithms in the multiplicative group $\mathbb{Z}_p^*$ of a finite field. This method is asymptotically faster than generic algorithms such as Baby-Step Giant-Step or Pollard's

Rho. It successfully reduces the computational complexity from exponential time to sub-exponential time. Although it does not achieve the ideal goal of polynomial-time complexity, it is nevertheless highly efficient for specific groups [108].

The process is following:

1) **Factor Base Selection**: Choose a smoothness bound B. Identify the **factor base**, denoted as $S = \{p_1, p_2, \ldots, p_t\}$, which consists of all prime numbers p_i such that $p_i \leqslant B$. Here, t represents the size of the factor base.
2) **Linear Relations Collection**: The goal of this step is to determine the discrete logarithms of the elements in the factor base S. We select random integers k and compute $\alpha^k \pmod{p}$. We then test if the result is B-smooth (i.e., it factors completely over S). If successful, we obtain a relation

$$\alpha^k \equiv \prod_{j=1}^{t} p_j^{c_j} \pmod{p}, \quad \text{where } c_j \geqslant 0. \tag{8-111}$$

Taking the discrete logarithm to the base α on both sides yields a linear congruence

$$k \equiv \sum_{j=1}^{t} c_j \log_\alpha p_j \pmod{p-1}. \tag{8-112}$$

This process is repeated until we collect a sufficient number of linearly independent relations (typically slightly more than t). We then solve the resulting dense system of linear equations to obtain the exact values of $\log_\alpha p_j$ for all $j = 1, \ldots, t$. (Note: Because $p-1$ is even, solving this linear system occurs over a mathematical ring rather than a field. In practice, this requires evaluating the system modulo the prime factors of $p-1$ and synthesizing the results utilizing the Chinese Remainder Theorem).
3) **Individual Logarithm Computation**: To compute the discrete logarithm of a specific target β, we select a random integer $s \in \{1, 2, \ldots, p-1\}$ and compute $\gamma = \beta \cdot \alpha^s \pmod{p}$. We check if γ is B-smooth. If it is, we factor it as

$$\beta \cdot \alpha^s \equiv \prod_{j=1}^{t} p_j^{d_j} \pmod{p}, \quad \text{where } d_j \geqslant 0. \tag{8-113}$$

Taking logarithms yields

$$\log_\alpha \beta + s \equiv \sum_{j=1}^{t} d_j \log_\alpha p_j \pmod{p-1}. \tag{8-114}$$

Since the values of $\log_\alpha p_j$ were computed in Step 2, and s is known, we can easily solve for $\log_\alpha \beta$.

Example 8.5.7 Find the solutions of $79^x \equiv 12604 \pmod{20063}$.
Solution: The element $\alpha = 79$ is the primitive element of $\mathbb{F}_{20063}$, let $S = \{2, 3, 5\}$ as the factor base.

The next step: randomly select k from $[0, 20062]$, and solve at least four such discrete logarithm congruences. The system of congruences

$$\alpha^{3929} \equiv 2^1 \cdot 3^2 \cdot 5^1 \pmod{20063} \quad (8\text{-}115)$$
$$\alpha^{9219} \equiv 2^2 \cdot 3^3 \cdot 5^3 \pmod{20063} \quad (8\text{-}116)$$
$$\alpha^{15687} \equiv 2^1 \cdot 3^1 \cdot 5^1 \pmod{20063} \quad (8\text{-}117)$$

Taking the logarithm to the base α, we have

$$3929 \equiv 1 \cdot \log_\alpha(2) + 2 \cdot \log_\alpha(3) + 1 \cdot \log_\alpha(5) \pmod{20062} \quad (8\text{-}118)$$
$$9219 \equiv 2 \cdot \log_\alpha(2) + 3 \cdot \log_\alpha(3) + 3 \cdot \log_\alpha(5) \pmod{20062} \quad (8\text{-}119)$$
$$15687 \equiv 1 \cdot \log_\alpha(2) + 1 \cdot \log_\alpha(3) + 1 \cdot \log_\alpha(5) \pmod{20062} \quad (8\text{-}120)$$

Solving the system of congruences, we can get

$$\log_\alpha(2) \equiv 17780 \pmod{20062} \quad (8\text{-}121)$$
$$\log_\alpha(3) \equiv 8304 \pmod{20062} \quad (8\text{-}122)$$
$$\log_\alpha(5) \equiv 9665 \pmod{20062} \quad (8\text{-}123)$$

In the final step, we introduce a randomly chosen session scalar s to blind the target ciphertext until the resulting product factors completely over the selected factor base S.

$$\beta \cdot \alpha^s \equiv 2^{d_1} \cdot 3^{d_2} \cdot 5^{d_3} \pmod{20063} \quad (8\text{-}124)$$

Suppose we randomly choose $s = 16673$, we can determine each d_i

$$12604 \cdot 79^{16673} \equiv 9000 \equiv 2^3 \cdot 3^2 \cdot 5^3 \pmod{20063} \quad (8\text{-}125)$$

Taking the logarithm congruence 8-124 to the base α, then we have:

$$x \equiv \log_\alpha \beta \equiv -16673 + 3 \cdot \log_\alpha(2) + 2 \cdot \log_\alpha(3) + 3 \cdot \log_\alpha(5) \pmod{20062} \quad (8\text{-}126)$$
$$\equiv 2022 \pmod{20062} \quad (8\text{-}127)$$

■

The index-calculus method is currently the most effective method for solving the discrete logarithm problem. Its time complexity is sub-exponential, approximately $\mathcal{O}(e^{(\ln p)^{1/2}(\ln \ln p)^{1/2}})$.

8.6 EXERCISES

1) List the orders modulo 13 of the positive integers less than 13.
2) Find the order of the integers 2, 3, and 5:
   (a) modulo 11
   (b) modulo 17
   (c) modulo 23

3) Prove that the following statements below:
   (a) If a has order rk modulo m, then a^r has order k modulo m.
   (b) If a has order $2k$ modulo p where p is an odd prime, then $a^k \equiv -1 \pmod{p}$.
4) Given that 2 is a primitive root modulo 13. List all the primitive roots modulo 13.
5) Show that 3 is a primitive root modulo 17.
6) Let g be a primitive root of p.
   (a) Suppose that $x = a$ and $x = b$ are both integer solutions to the congruence $g^x \equiv h \pmod{p}$. Show that

$$a \equiv b \pmod{p-1}$$

   (b) Show that $\log_g(h_1 h_2) \equiv \log_g(h_1) + \log_g(h_2) \pmod{p-1}$.
   (c) Show that $\log_g(h^n) \equiv n \log_g(h) \pmod{p-1}$.
7) Solve the following congruences:
   (a) $2^x \equiv 13 \pmod{23}$
   (b) $10^x \equiv 22 \pmod{47}$
   (c) $627^x \equiv 608 \pmod{941}$
8) Solve the congruence $8x^5 \equiv 5 \pmod{17}$.
9) Draw the discrete logarithm over $\mathbb{Z}/53\mathbb{Z}$ in Sage.
10) Alice and Bob use the Diffie-Hellman key exchange protocol to communicate in secret. They publicly announce a prime number $p = 29$ and a primitive root $r = 8$ under modulus 29. Alice picks a secret key $A = 13$ and in turn receives the key $B = 27$ from Bob. What is their shared secret?
11) Alice and Bob use the Diffie-Hellman key exchange protocol to communicate in secret. They publicly announce a prime number $p = 23$ and a primitive root $r = 5$ under modulus 23. Alice picks a secret key $A = 6$ and in turn receives the key $B = 19$ from Bob.
   (a) What is the key that Alice sends to Bob?
   (b) What is the shared secret key?
   (c) Can Alice compute Bob's private key using only what she's given?
12) Suppose Alice and Bob want to use Diffie-Hellman method with the published modulus $p = 251$ (which is a prime number) and base $r = 2$. Suppose their private components are $a = 27$ and $b = 28$. Find their shared key.
13) Bob's public ElGamal key is $(p, r, \alpha) = (41, 29, 31)$. Determine Bob's private key.
14) If Bob selects $p = 29$ for ElGamal, how many possible choices does he have for r?
15) Consider the ElGamal cipher. Bob selects the public key $(p, r, \alpha) = (47, 45, 14)$ and transmits to Alice. Encrypt the message $m = 10$, assume Alice selects a random integer $k = 20$.
16) Consider the ElGamal cipher. Bob selects the public key $(p, r, \alpha) = (59, 5, 28)$. Let $a = 13$ be Bob's private key. Answer the following questions:

(a) Suppose Alice wants to send the message $m = 20$. She selects a random integer $k = 6$. Compute the pair (U, V) that she will send to Bob.
(b) Suppose Eve intercepts Alice's message and replaces it with $(U', V') = (46, 34)$. Find the plaintext that Bob would decrypt in this case.

17) Consider the ElGamal cipher. Bob selects the public key $(p, r, \alpha) = (112087, 5, 18074)$. Let $a = 48162$ be Bob's private key. Decrypt the following ciphertext:

(75361, 62572)	(20522, 95281)	(32418, 89253)	(104114, 85855)
(49878, 13114)	(94657, 4967)	(97164, 31973)	(3987, 1579)
(7737, 18493)	(25445, 48799)	(48539, 64181)	(77437, 53546)
(2892, 59591)	(93239, 27521)	(59674, 32712)	(96460, 48275)
(63816, 39829)	(103255, 27773)	(96323, 20644)	(35621, 73493)
(27510, 91731)	(60908, 54057)	(90307, 82549)	(78901, 67192)
(53121, 102954)	(7532, 100687)	(17908, 23068)	(109765, 96997)
(77183, 64881)	(23624, 29173)	(98526, 60655)	

It is known that the encoding method for each plaintext group is as illustrated in Example 7.3.3.

18) Use the Baby-Step Giant-Step method to solve the discrete logarithm problem $3^x \equiv 13 \pmod{29}$.

19) Let $p = 809$. Suppose that the element $\alpha = 89$ has multiplicative order $n = 101$ in the group $\mathbb{Z}_p^*$. Given $\beta = 618$, compute the discrete logarithm $\log_\alpha \beta$ using Pollard's Rho method.

20) Solve the system of linear congruences using Chinese Remainder Theorem.

$$x \equiv 2 \pmod{3} \tag{8-128}$$
$$x \equiv 3 \pmod{7} \tag{8-129}$$
$$x \equiv 4 \pmod{16} \tag{8-130}$$

21) Solve the system of linear congruences using Chinese Remainder Theorem.

$$2x \equiv 6 \pmod{14} \tag{8-131}$$
$$3x \equiv 9 \pmod{15} \tag{8-132}$$
$$5x \equiv 20 \pmod{60} \tag{8-133}$$

22) Let a, b, m, n be integers with $\gcd(m, n) = 1$ and $c \equiv (b - a) \cdot m^{-1} \pmod{n}$. Show that $x = a + cm$ is a solution of $x \equiv a \pmod{m}$ and $x \equiv b \pmod{n}$.

23) Use the Index-Calculus method to solve the discrete logarithm problem $5^x \equiv 1736 \pmod{2017}$. The factorization of $2016 = 2^5 \cdot 3^2 \cdot 7$.

CHAPTER 9

Elliptic Curve Cryptography

This chapter introduces Elliptic Curve Cryptography (ECC). ECC was independently proposed in the mid-1980s by *Miller* [109] and *Koblitz* [110]. Concurrently, *Lenstra* [111] developed an integer factorization algorithm utilizing elliptic curves. Since its inception, the application of elliptic curves in cryptography has expanded rapidly. By exploiting their underlying algebraic structure, elliptic curves allow ECC to provide security levels equivalent to, or even greater than, traditional public-key systems, all while utilizing significantly shorter key lengths.

As a public-key cryptosystem, ECC relies on algebraic operations on points of an elliptic curve to generate key pairs. In contrast to RSA, whose security is founded on the difficulty of integer factorization, the security of ECC rests on the intractability of the Elliptic Curve Discrete Logarithm Problem (ECDLP). Due to its ability to achieve high security levels with reduced key sizes and improved computational efficiency, ECC is widely considered a dominant standard in modern public-key cryptography.

Topics covered in this chapter:

- Elliptic curve arithmetic over the real numbers
- Elliptic curve arithmetic over finite fields
- Elliptic Curve Diffie–Hellman key exchange
- The elliptic-curve variant of the ElGamal encryption and decryption scheme
- The SM2 encryption and decryption scheme
- Cryptanalysis of elliptic curve cryptosystems

9.1 ELLIPTIC CURVES

9.1.1 Elliptic Curves over Real Numbers

Geometrically, an elliptic curve is distinct from an ellipse. The name originates from its historical connection to elliptic integrals, which arise when computing the arc length of an ellipse. In the context of cryptography, an elliptic curve is formally defined as a non-singular curve satisfying the **Weierstrass equation**.

DOI: 10.1201/9781042011087-9

Definition 9.1.1 Weierstrass Equation

An elliptic curve E over a field K is a curve having an equation of the form

$$E : y^2 + a_1xy + a_3y = x^3 + a_2x^2 + a_4x + a_6 \tag{9-1}$$

where the coefficients $a_1, a_2, a_3, a_4, a_6 \in K$ *(no* a_5*), and the discriminant* Δ *of E not equal to zero.*

The discriminant of E is defined by

$$\Delta = -d_2^2d_8 - 8d_4^3 - 27d_6^2 + 9d_2d_4d_6 \tag{9-2}$$

where

$$\begin{cases} d_2 = a_1^2 + 4a_2 \\ d_4 = 2a_4 + a_1a_3 \\ d_6 = a_3^2 + 4a_6 \\ d_8 = a_1^2a_6 + 4a_2a_6 - a_1a_3a_4 + a_2a_3^2 - a_4^2 \end{cases} \tag{9-3}$$

Let K be a field, typically representing $\mathbb{R}$, $\mathbb{C}$, or $\mathbb{F}_p$. The characteristic of the field is denoted by char(K). For $\mathbb{R}$ and $\mathbb{C}$, the characteristic is 0, whereas for a finite field $\mathbb{F}_p$, the characteristic is the prime p.

The general Weierstrass equation is often cumbersome to use in practice. Fortunately, it can be simplified through coordinate transformations. Provided that char$(K) \neq 2$ and char$(K) \neq 3$, we can complete the square and the cube to eliminate the xy, y, and x^2 terms. This process yields the following simplified form:

$$y^2 + \underbrace{\cancel{a_1xy + a_3y}}_{\text{When char}K \neq 2} = x^3 + \underbrace{\cancel{a_2x^2}}_{\text{When char}K \neq 3} + a_4x + a_6 \tag{9-4}$$

$$\Rightarrow y^2 = x^3 + Ax + B \tag{9-5}$$

where $A, B \in K$. The discriminant of this equation is given by $\Delta = -16(4A^3 + 27B^2) \neq 0$. That is one can obtain the commonly seen form of the elliptic curve.

Let L be any extension field of K, denoted $L \supseteq K$, The set of points on the elliptic curve over L, denoted by $E(L)$, is defined as

$$E(L) = \{\mathcal{O}\} \cup \{(x, y) \in L \times L \mid y^2 = x^3 + Ax + B\} \tag{9-6}$$

Here, $\mathcal{O}$ denotes the **point at infinity**. Geometrically, one can visualize $\mathcal{O}$ as being infinitely far up or down the y-axis. It serves as the **identity element** for the group of points on the elliptic curve. Just as parallel train tracks appear to converge at a vanishing point on the horizon, vertical lines on the plane intersect at this point at infinity.

Definition 9.1.2 Elliptic Curve

An elliptic curve over the real numbers is the collection of the points (x, y) *that satisfy the equation*

$$E : y^2 = x^3 + Ax + B, \text{ where } A, B \in \mathbb{R} \tag{9-7}$$

It is required that the curve be non-singular, the condition is equivalent to

$$\Delta = 4A^3 + 27B^2 \neq 0 \tag{9-8}$$

When the discriminant strictly satisfies $\Delta \neq 0$, the elliptic curve is formally designated as **smooth** (or **non-singular**), guaranteeing that all roots of the underlying cubic polynomial are distinct.

Example 9.1.1 There are the graphs of the elliptic curves $y^2 = x^3 - 3x + 3$ and $y^2 = x^3 - 6x + 5$ that is illustrated in Figure 9-1.

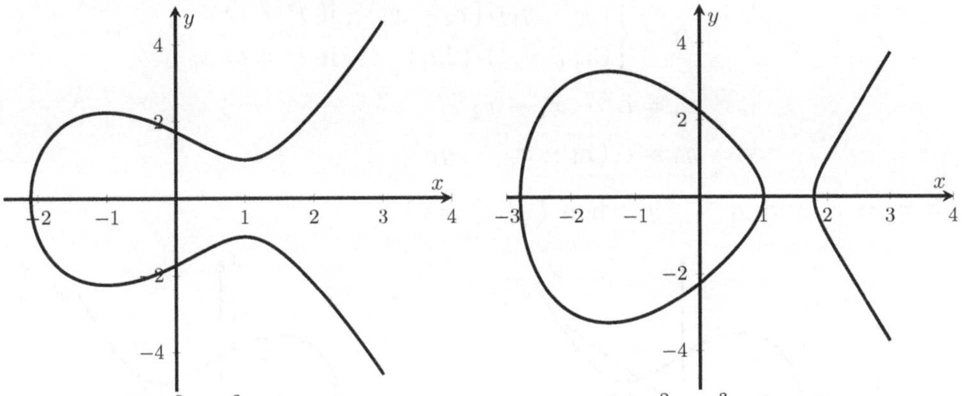

(a) $y^2 = x^3 - 3x + 3$ (b) $y^2 = x^3 - 6x + 5$

Figure 9-1: Graphs of the Elliptic Curves

Obviously, the elliptic curves $y^2 = x^3 - 3x + 3$ has only one real root, however, it has two complex roots. The elliptic curves $y^2 = x^3 - 6x + 5$ has three distinct real roots.

If $\Delta = 4A^3 + 27B^2 = 0$, the elliptic curve has singular point, the point is non-differentiable. Since the elliptic curve has double roots, we discuss the elliptic curve that satisfies $\Delta \neq 0$. Two singular elliptic curve are illustrated in Figure 9-2.

We present the algebraic formulas for computing the sum of two points on an elliptic curve. These operations, **point addition** and **point doubling**, form the building blocks for scalar multiplication.

Let E be an elliptic curve given by the equation $y^2 = x^3 + Ax + B$. The geometric group law can be translated into explicit algebraic formulas. Let $P = (x_1, y_1)$ and $Q = (x_2, y_2)$ be points on $E \setminus \{\mathcal{O}\}$, if $P = -Q$ (meaning $x_1 = x_2$ and $y_1 = -y_2$), the vertical line connecting them intersects the curve strictly at infinity. Thus, $P + Q = \mathcal{O}$.

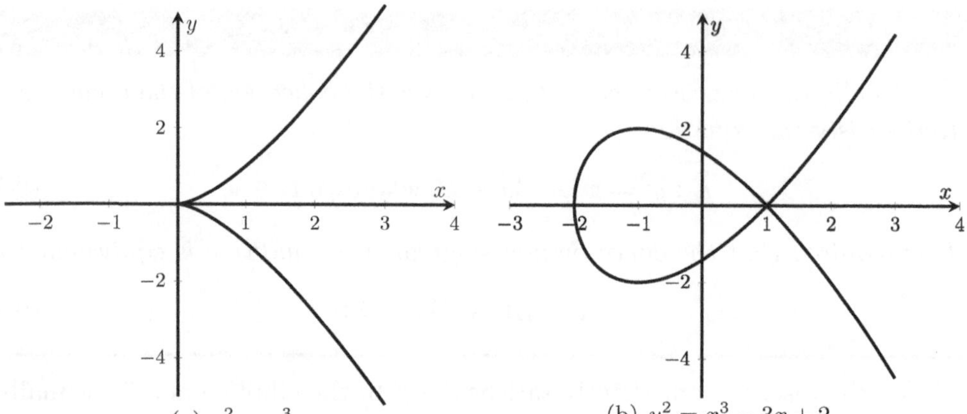

(a) $y^2 = x^3$ (b) $y^2 = x^3 - 3x + 2$

Figure 9-2: Graphs of the Singular Elliptic Curves

The sum $P + Q = (x_3, y_3)$ is calculated as follows:

$$\alpha = \begin{cases} (y_2 - y_1)/(x_2 - x_1) & \text{if } P \neq Q \\ (3x_1^2 + A)/(2y_1) & \text{if } P = Q \end{cases} \tag{9-9}$$

$$x_3 = \alpha^2 - x_1 - x_2 \tag{9-10}$$

$$y_3 = \alpha\,(x_1 - x_3) - y_1 \tag{9-11}$$

If $x_1 = x_2$ and $y_1 = -y_2$, then $P + Q = \mathcal{O}$.

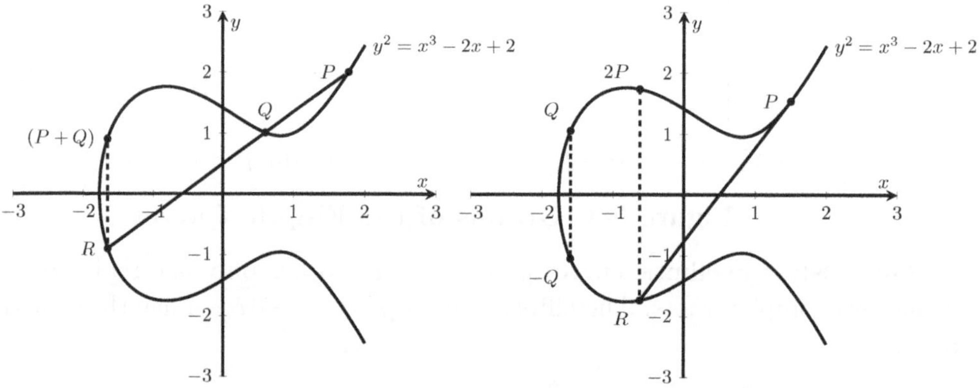

(a) Addition (b) Point Doubling

Figure 9-3: Addition on Elliptic Curve

Example 9.1.2 Given the points $P = (-1, 1)$ and $Q = (4, 9)$ on the elliptic curve $y^2 = x^3 + 3x + 5$, find $P + Q$ and $2P$.
Solution: Find $P + Q$ first.

$$\alpha = \frac{y_2 - y_1}{x_2 - x_1} = 8/5 \tag{9-12}$$

$$x_3 = \alpha^2 - x_1 - x_2 = -11/25 \tag{9-13}$$

$$y_3 = \alpha\,(x_1 - x_3) - y_1 = -237/125 \tag{9-14}$$

$$P + Q = (x_3, -y_3) = (-11/25, -237/125) \tag{9-15}$$

Then we find $2P$.

$$\alpha = \frac{3x_1^2 + A}{2y_1} = \frac{3(-1)^2 + 3}{2(1)} = 3 \tag{9-16}$$

$$x_3 = \alpha^2 - 2x_1 = 3^2 - 2(-1) = 11 \tag{9-17}$$

$$y_3 = \alpha(x_1 - x_3) - y_1 = 3((-1) - 11) - 1 = -37 \tag{9-18}$$

$$2P = (x_3, -y_3) = (11, -37) \tag{9-19}$$

■

9.1.2 Elliptic Curves over GF(p)

The elliptic curves discussed primarily are defined over the field of real numbers $\mathbb{R}$. While geometrically intuitive, curves over $\mathbb{R}$ involve continuous variables and infinitely many points, making them unsuitable for cryptography due to issues with floating-point precision and rounding errors. To ensure reliability and security, ECC operations must be exact. Therefore, curve coefficients and variables are defined over a finite field, commonly denoted as GF(q) or $\mathbb{F}_q$, where $q = p^r$ is a prime power. If $r = 1$, then $\mathbb{F}_q = \mathbb{F}_p$ is called a **prime field**; if $r > 1$, $\mathbb{F}_q$ is called a **extension field**. In this section, we set $r = 1$.

This restriction results in a discrete set of points, as illustrated in Figure 9-4, ensuring that all calculations are exact and computationally feasible.

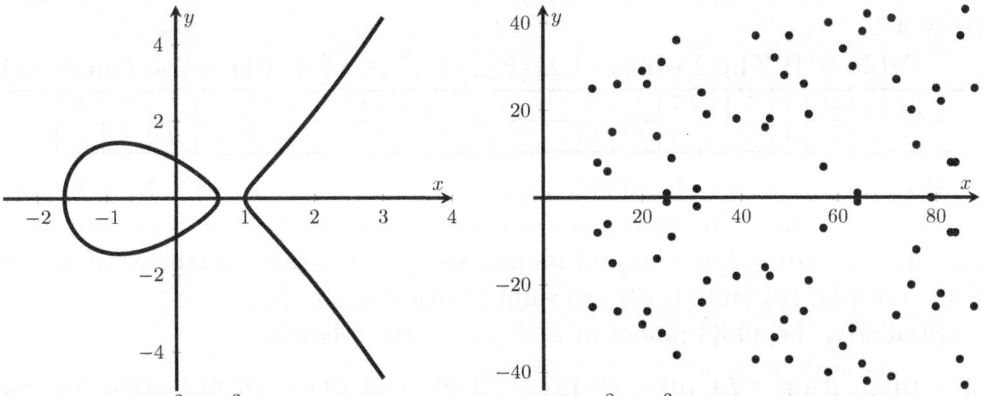

(a) $y^2 = x^3 - 2x + 1$ (b) $y^2 \equiv x^3 - 2x + 1 \pmod{89}$

Figure 9-4: Elliptic Curves over $\mathbb{R}$ and $\mathbb{F}_p$

Over the prime field $\mathbb{F}_p$, the coordinates of the points and the coefficients are integers in the range $[0, p-1]$, and all algebraic operations are performed modulo p.

Definition 9.1.3 Elliptic Curve over $\mathbb{F}_p$

An elliptic curve E over $\mathbb{F}_p$ is defined as the set of solutions (x, y) satisfying the following congruence in affine coordinates:

$$E : y^2 \equiv x^3 + Ax + B \pmod{p} \tag{9-20}$$

where $A, B \in \mathbb{F}_p$, $4A^3 + 27B^2 \not\equiv 0 \pmod{p}$.

$$E(\mathbb{F}_p) = \{(x, y) \in \mathbb{F}_p \times \mathbb{F}_p \mid y^2 \equiv x^3 + Ax + B \pmod{p}\} \cup \{\mathcal{O}\} \quad (9\text{-}21)$$

where $\mathcal{O}$ *is the point at infinity, and* $\mathbb{F}_p$ *is called the* **base field** *or the field of integers modulo p.*

What is the point at infinity over $\mathbb{F}_p$? Let $P_1 = (x_1, y_1)$ and $P_2 = (x_2, y_2)$ be two distinct or identical points residing on $E(\mathbb{F}_p)$, if the line through P_1 and P_2 is vertical, parallel to the y-axis, then their sum to zero that is the point at infinity, $P_1 + P_2 = \mathcal{O}$, since the third intersection with the elliptic curve lies at infinity. Consequently, we formally define $0P = \mathcal{O}$. This transcendent point $\mathcal{O}$ strictly serves as the additive identity element of the discrete elliptic curve group, effectively acting as the zero vector such that $P + \mathcal{O} = P$ for any point on the curve.

The following algebraic properties hold strictly for elliptic curves defined over $\mathbb{F}_p$:

1) $\mathcal{O}$ is the point at infinity, then $\mathcal{O} + \mathcal{O} = \mathcal{O}$;
2) For all $P \in E(\mathbb{F}_p)$, $P + \mathcal{O} = \mathcal{O} + P = P$;
3) For all $P \in E(\mathbb{F}_p)$, there exist $-P = (x, -y) \in E(\mathbb{F}_p)$ such that $P + (-P) = \mathcal{O}$;

Example 9.1.3 Let E is an elliptic curve over $\mathbb{F}_{23}$, consider the elliptic curve $E(\mathbb{F}_{23}) : y^2 \equiv x^3 + 16x + 14 \pmod{23}$, find all points on E.

Solution: The all points on $E(\mathbb{F}_{23}) : y^2 \equiv x^3 + 16x + 14 \pmod{23}$ are shown in Table 9-1.

Table 9-1: The Points of $E(\mathbb{F}_{23}) : y^2 \equiv x^3 + 16x + 14 \pmod{23}$

x	1	2	3	4	5	6	7	8	9	10	11	12	13	14	15	16	17	18	19	20	21	22
y^2	8	8	20	4	12	4	9	10	13	1	3	2	4	15	18	19	1	16	1	8	20	20

For $x = 1$, the right-hand side evaluates to $1^3 + 16 \cdot 1 + 14 = 31 \equiv \mathbf{8} \pmod{23}$. We then solve for y in the congruence $y^2 \equiv 8 \pmod{23}$. The quadratic roots are $y = 10$ (since $10^2 = 100 \equiv 8$) and its inverse $y = 23 - 10 = 13$ (since $13^2 = 169 \equiv 8$). Thus, both $(1, 10)$ and $(1, 13)$ are valid solutions on $E(\mathbb{F}_{23})$.

Similarly, the all 33 points in $E(\mathbb{F}_{23})$ are the following:

$$\begin{array}{ccccccccc} \{(1,10), & (1,13), & (2,10), & (2,13), & (4,2), & (4,21), & (5,9), & (5,14), & (6,2) \\ (6,21), & (7,3), & (7,20), & (9,6), & (9,17), & (10,1), & (10,22), & (11,7), & (11,16) \\ (12,5), & (12,18), & (13,2), & (13,21), & (15,8), & (15,15), & (17,1), & (17,22), & (18,4) \\ (18,19), & (19,1), & (19,22), & (20,10), & (20,13), & \mathcal{O}\} \end{array}$$

How to find the all points of $E(\mathbb{F}_p)$? If p is small, we can use Python to find them.

```
def Elliptic_Curve_points(A,B,p):
    """
    Find all points of y^2 = x^3 + Ax + B mod p
    """
    return [(x, y) for x in range(p) for y in range(p) if (y*y - (x
    **3 + A*x + B)) % p == 0]
#Example
print(Elliptic_Curve_points( A=16, B=14, p=23))
```

■

The elliptic curve over modulo 11 and 13 are shown in Figure 9-5.

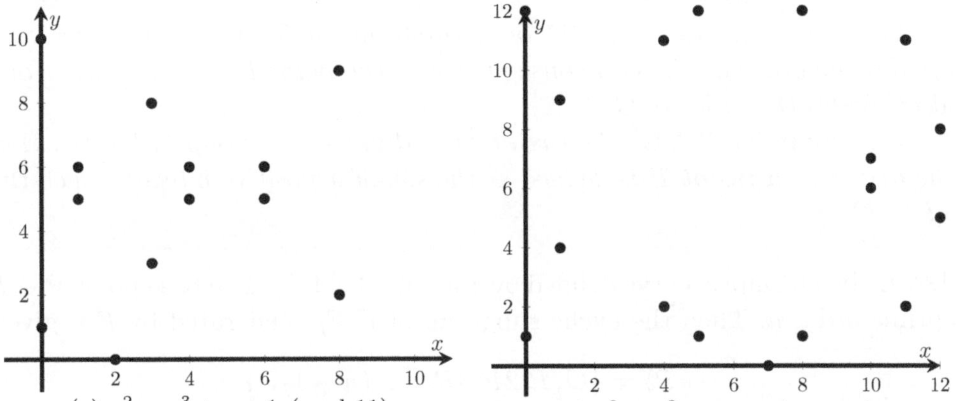

(a) $y^2 \equiv x^3 + x + 1 \pmod{11}$ (b) $y^2 \equiv x^3 + x + 1 \pmod{13}$

Figure 9-5: All Points of $E(\mathbb{F}_{11})$ and $E(\mathbb{F}_{13})$

Theorem 9.1.1 Hasse's Theorem

Let E be an elliptic curve defined over a finite field $\mathbb{F}_p$, given by the equation $y^2 \equiv x^3 + Ax + B \pmod{p}$.

Let N_E denote the number of points on $E(\mathbb{F}_p)$. Then N_E satisfies the inequality

$$|N_E - (p+1)| \leqslant 2\sqrt{p} \tag{9-22}$$

The interval determined by this bound is referred to as the **Hasse interval**. We can write $N_E = p + 1 - t$, where the integer t is called the **trace** of Frobenius of E over $\mathbb{F}_p$. The theorem implies that $|t| \leqslant 2\sqrt{p}$.

The trace t can be expressed in terms of the Legendre symbol

$$t = -\sum_{x \in \mathbb{F}_p} \left(\frac{x^3 + Ax + B}{p} \right) \tag{9-23}$$

where $\left(\frac{x^3 + Ax + B}{p} \right) = \begin{cases} -1 & \text{if } x^3 + Ax + B \text{ is not a square in } \mathbb{F}_p \\ 0 & \text{if } x^3 + Ax + B \equiv 0 \\ 1 & \text{if } x^3 + Ax + B \text{ is a non-zero square in } \mathbb{F}_p \end{cases}$

This result was proved in 1936 by the German mathematician *Helmut Hasse*. Because the proof requires advanced concepts from elliptic curves and algebraic geometry, we will not go into detail here. This means that when p is large, the number of points on the curve is approximately p. The order of the elliptic curve group is close to the size of the prime. In practical applications, to obtain the exact number of points, Schoof's algorithm can be used to compute $|E(\mathbb{F}_p)|$ in polynomial time.

Theorem 9.1.2 Lagrange's Theorem

Let G be a finite group, H be a subgroup of G. Then the order of H divides the order of G. As a consequence, if the point $P \in G$, the order of P also divides the order of G.

For any point $P \in G$, the **order** *of P divides the group order $|G|$. Here, the* **order of a point** *P is defined as the smallest positive integer k such that $kP = \mathcal{O}$.*

Let E_p be an elliptic curve defined over a finite field $\mathbb{F}_p$. The base point $P \in E(\mathbb{F}_p)$ has prime order n. Then the cyclic subgroup of $E(\mathbb{F}_p)$ generated by P is given by

$$\langle P \rangle = \{\mathcal{O}, P, 2P, 3P, \ldots, (n-1)P\} \tag{9-24}$$

The order of P in E_p is defined as the cardinality of $\langle P \rangle$.

Example 9.1.4 Find the order of the point $P = (3, 8)$ on the elliptic curve E_{37} : $y^2 \equiv x^3 - x + 3 \pmod{37}$.

Solution: We compute the multiples of P using the addition law. Since $2P = (3, 29), 3P = \mathcal{O}$, thus $3P$ is the smallest multiple of P. The order of P is 3.

Furthermore, we known the order of elliptic curve Group E_{37} is 42. Since The factor of 42 is $\{1, 2, 3, 6, 7, 14, 21, 42\}$. The computed order of our generator, 3, perfectly divides the group order, confirming the structural integrity of the subgroup. ■

Let N denote the order of the elliptic curve group $E(\mathbb{F}_p)$, representing the total number of points on the curve. In cryptographic applications, we work within a cyclic subgroup of prime order n. Let P be a generator of this subgroup; then n is the smallest positive integer such that $nP = \mathcal{O}$. The integer h defined by $h = \frac{N}{n}$ is called the **cofactor**.

In cryptographic applications, it is highly desirable for the cofactor h to be a very small integer, typically $h \in \{1, 2, 4, 8\}$. We usually set $h = 1$ and the order n is prime. In this case, $N = n$, meaning the group order is prime, and every non-identity point on the curve is a generator.

The following results hold for the elliptic curve over modulo p:

- Curve addition is associative: $(P_1 + P_2) + P_3 = P_1 + (P_2 + P_3)$
- Curve addition is commutative: $P_1 + P_2 = P_2 + P_1$
- For a point $P = (x, y)$ and an integer k, then

$$kP = \underbrace{P + P + \cdots + P}_{\text{k times}} \tag{9-25}$$

- For any two integers k, h, we have

$$h(kP) = (hk)P = k(hP) \tag{9-26}$$

Example 9.1.5 Consider the elliptic curve $E(\mathbb{F}_5) : y^2 \equiv x^3 + 3x \pmod 5$, find the trace of the $E(\mathbb{F}_5)$.
Solution: The points in $E(\mathbb{F}_5)$ are the following, 10 points in total:

$$\{(0,0),(1,2),(1,3),(2,2),(2,3),(3,1),(3,4),(4,1),(4,4),\ \mathcal{O}\} \tag{9-27}$$

Thus, $N_E = 10$. The trace of Frobenius is computed as $t = p+1-N_E = 5+1-10 =$ **-4**. ■

Example 9.1.6 Let $p = 31$, by Hasse's theorem, the Hasse interval is $[31+1-2\sqrt{31}, 31+1+2\sqrt{31}] \approx [21,43]$, if the coefficients (A,B) different, the number of points of E is different that is shown in Table 9-2.

Table 9-2: The Number of Points of $E : y^2 \equiv x^3 + Ax + B \pmod{31}$

n	(A,B)	n	(A,B)	n	(A,B)	n	(A,B)	n	(A,B)
21	(0,7)	26	(1,4)	31	(1,16)	36	(1,7)	41	(1,3)
22	(1,21)	27	(1,12)	32	(1,6)	37	(1,19)	42	(1,10)
23	(1,28)	28	(1,5)	33	(1,15)	38	(2,29)	43	(0,3)
24	(1,2)	29	(1,23)	34	(1,13)	39	(1,14)		
25	(1,17)	30	(1,18)	35	(2,4)	40	(1,29)		

The result of Table 9-2 is not unique.

Definition 9.1.4 Addition on Elliptic Curve over GF(p)

Let $P = (x_1, y_1)$ and $Q = (x_2, y_2)$ be two points on the curve $E_p : y^2 \equiv x^3 + Ax + B \pmod p$. Then $P + Q = (x_3, y_3)$ where

$$\alpha \equiv \begin{cases} (y_2 - y_1)\cdot(x_2 - x_1)^{-1} & \text{if } P \neq Q \\ (3x_1^2 + A)\cdot(2y_1)^{-1} & \text{if } P = Q \end{cases} \tag{9-28}$$

$$x_3 \equiv \alpha^2 - x_1 - x_2 \pmod p \tag{9-29}$$

$$y_3 \equiv \alpha(x_1 - x_3) - y_1 \pmod p \tag{9-30}$$

Here, if $P \neq Q$, then α is the slope of the line through P and Q. If $P = Q$, then α is the slope of the line that is tangent to E at the point P.

Example 9.1.7 Let $p = 23$, given the curve $E : y^2 \equiv x^3 + 13x + 7 \pmod{23}$ and two points $P = (14,9)$ and $Q = (17,14)$, answer the following questions:

1) Check that the curve is valid and that P and Q are two points on the curve?
   Solution: Since $A = 13$, $B = 7$ and $p = 23$, so the discriminant Δ is

$$4A^3 + 27B^2 \equiv 4\cdot(13)^3 + 27\cdot(7)^2 \not\equiv 0 \pmod{23} \tag{9-31}$$

   $P = (14,9)$ and $Q = (17,14)$ satisfy the curve $E : y^2 \equiv x^3 + 13x + 7 \pmod{23}$, thus the points P, Q are on the curve. ■

2) Find $P+Q$.
Solution:

$$\begin{aligned}
\alpha &\equiv (y_2 - y_1)\cdot(x_2 - x_1)^{-1} \equiv (14-9)\cdot(17-14)^{-1} \pmod{23} && \text{(9-32)}\\
&\equiv (5)(3)^{-1} \pmod{23} \equiv 17 \pmod{23} && \text{(9-33)}\\
x_3 &\equiv \alpha^2 - x_1 - x_2 \equiv 5 \pmod{23} && \text{(9-34)}\\
y_3 &\equiv \alpha(x_1 - x_3) - y_1 \equiv 6 \pmod{23} && \text{(9-35)}\\
P+Q &= (x_3, y_3) = (5,6) && \text{(9-36)}
\end{aligned}$$

■

3) Find $2P$.
Solution:

$$\begin{aligned}
\alpha &\equiv (3x_1^2 + A)\cdot(2y_1)^{-1} \equiv (3\cdot 14^2 + 13)\cdot(2\cdot 9)^{-1} \pmod{23} && \text{(9-37)}\\
&\equiv (3)(18)^{-1} \equiv 4 \pmod{23} && \text{(9-38)}\\
x_3 &\equiv \alpha^2 - x_1 - x_1 \equiv 11 \pmod{23} && \text{(9-39)}\\
y_3 &\equiv \alpha(x_1 - x_3) - y_1 \equiv 3 \pmod{23} && \text{(9-40)}\\
2P &= (x_3, y_3) = (11,3) && \text{(9-41)}
\end{aligned}$$

■

4) If $S=(9,5)$, $T=(9,18)$, find $S+T$.
Solution: Because $x_S = x_T$ and $y_S \equiv -y_T \pmod{23}$, the points are additive inverses. Thus, $S+T=\mathcal{O}$. ■

Example 9.1.8 Let $p=29$, given the curve $E: y^2 \equiv x^3+4x+20 \pmod{29}$, answer the following questions:

1) Determine all rational points on the curve $E(\mathbb{F}_{29})$.
Solution: Since $\Delta = -16(4A^3+27B^2) = -176896 \equiv 4 \not\equiv 0 \pmod{29}$, thus the curve is smooth. The complete set of points is as follows below:

$$\begin{array}{llllllll}
\{(0,7), & (0,22), & (1,5), & (1,24), & (2,6), & (2,23), & (3,1), & (3,28)\\
(4,10), & (4,19), & (5,7), & (5,22), & (6,12), & (6,17), & (8,10), & (8,19)\\
(10,4), & (10,25), & (13,6), & (13,23), & (14,6), & (14,23), & (15,2), & (15,27)\\
(16,2), & (16,27), & (17,10), & (17,19), & (19,13), & (19,16), & (20,3), & (20,26)\\
(24,7), & (24,22), & (27,2), & (27,27), & \mathcal{O}\} & & &
\end{array}$$

■

2) Let $P=(5,22)$, $Q=(16,27)$. Find $P+Q$ and $2P$.
Solution:

$$\begin{aligned}
\alpha &\equiv (y_2 - y_1)(x_2 - x_1)^{-1} \equiv (5)(11)^{-1} \equiv 11 \pmod{29}\\
x_3 &\equiv 13 \pmod{29}\\
y_3 &\equiv 6 \pmod{29}\\
P+Q &= (x_3, y_3) = (13,6)
\end{aligned}$$

$$\alpha \equiv \left(3x_1{}^2 + A\right)(2y_1)^{-1} \equiv (3 \times 5^2 + 4) \cdot (2 \times 22)^{-1} \equiv 13 \pmod{29}$$
$$x_3 \equiv 14 \pmod{29}$$
$$y_3 \equiv 6 \pmod{29}$$
$$2P = (x_3, y_3) = (14, 6)$$

■

9.1.3 Elliptic Curves over GF(2^n)

Computes represent data fundamentally as binary strings. While integer arithmetic is standard for prime fields, representing elements as n-bit binary strings is particularly advantageous for hardware implementation. To support cryptographic operations, specifically addition, multiplication, and inversion. We utilize the finite field GF(2^n), also known as a **binary fields.**

In GF(2^n), elements are essentially binary polynomials of degree at most $n - 1$. Arithmetic operations are performed modulo an irreducible polynomial of degree n, rather than modulo an integer 2^n. This distinction is crucial: the field arithmetic is polynomial, not integer. The field contains exactly $q = 2^n$ elements, and the characteristic of the field is 2.

The equation for elliptic curves over GF(p) is not valid for fields of characteristic 2. Instead, for cryptographic applications, we employ **non-supersingular** curves defined by the following generalized Weierstrass equation:

$$E : y^2 + xy = x^3 + Ax^2 + B \tag{9-42}$$

where $A, B \in \text{GF}(2^n)$ and $B \neq 0$. The condition $B \neq 0$ ensures that the curve is non-singular. The set of points on the curve is defined as

$$E(\text{GF}(2^n)) = \{(x, y) \in \text{GF}(2^n) \times \text{GF}(2^n) \mid y^2 + xy = x^3 + Ax^2 + B\} \cup \{\mathcal{O}\} \tag{9-43}$$

For a point $P = (x, y) \in E(\text{GF}(2^n))$, the negative of P, denoted $-P$, is given by

$$-P = (x, x + y) \tag{9-44}$$

Thus, $\mathcal{O} = P + (-P) \Rightarrow P + \mathcal{O} = P$.

Example 9.1.9 Consider the finite field GF(2^3). Let the irreducible polynomial $f(x) = x^3 + x + 1$, and g be a generator of GF(2^3) such that $f(g) = 0$. Since the coefficients of polynomial only 0 and 1, thus $g^3 = g + 1$. There are 8 possibles over GF(2^3) that are shown in Table 9-3.

Since $g^7 = g\,(g^6) = g\,(g^2 + 1) = 1$, thus the powers of g generate all the non-zero polynomials over GF(2^3).

Let $A = g^3$ and $B = g^0$, given the curve $E : y^2 + xy = x^3 + g^3x^2 + 1$, Let us algebraically verify if the specific point $P = (g^3, g^2)$ resides on this curve by

Table 9-3: The Elliptic Curve over GF(2^3)

Generator	Polynomial	Binary	Generator	Polynomial	Binary
0	0	000	g^3	$g+1$	011
g^0	1	001	g^4	$g\,(g^3) = g^2+g$	110
g^1	g	010	g^5	$g\,(g^4) = g^2+g+1$	111
g^2	g^2	100	g^6	$g\,(g^5) = g^2+1$	101

substituting $x = g^3$ and $y = g^2$ into both sides of the equation

$$(g^2)^2 + g^3g^2 = (g^3)^3 + g^3(g^3)^2 + 1$$
$$g^4 + g^5 = g^9 + g^9 + 1$$
$$(g^2+g) + (g^2+g+1) = 1$$
$$1 = 1$$

Given the curve $E : y^2 + xy = x^3 + g^3x^2 + 1$, the all points of E over GF(2^3) are shown in Figure 9-6.

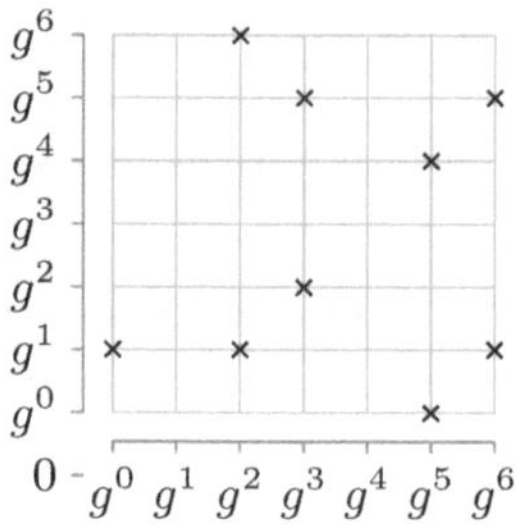

Figure 9-6: All Points of E Over GF(2^3)

Example 9.1.10 Consider the finite field GF(2^4). Let the irreducible polynomial $f(x) = x^4 + x + 1$. Let g be a generator of GF(2^4) such that $f(g) = 0$ also $g^4 = g + 1$. The generator for GF(2^4) is shown in Table 9-4.

Table 9-4: The Elliptic Curve over GF(2^4)

Generator	Polynomial	Binary	Generator	Polynomial	Binary
0	0	0000	g^7	$g(g^6) = g^3+g+1$	1011
g^0	1	0001	g^8	$g(g^7) = g^2+1$	0101
g^1	g	0010	g^9	$g(g^8) = g^3+g$	1010
g^2	g^2	0100	g^{10}	$g(g^9) = g^2+g+1$	0111
g^3	g^3	1000	g^{11}	$g(g^{10}) = g^3+g^2+g$	1110
g^4	$g(g^3) = g+1$	0011	g^{12}	$g(g^{11}) = g^3+g^2+g+1$	1111
g^5	$g(g^4) = g^2+g$	0110	g^{13}	$g(g^{12}) = g^3+g^2+1$	1101
g^6	$g(g^5) = g^3+g^2$	1100	g^{14}	$g(g^{13}) = g^3+1$	1001

Since $g^{15} = g\,(g^{14}) = g\,(g^3+1) = g^4 + g = g + 1 + g = 1$, the powers of g generate all $2^4 - 1 = 15$ non-zero elements of GF(2^4).

The addition rule different because the elliptic curve over different flied.

Definition 9.1.5 The Addition on Elliptic Curve Over GF(2^n)

Let $P = (x_1, y_1)$ and $Q = (x_2, y_2)$ be two points on the curve $E : y^2 + xy = x^3 + Ax + B$ defined over the binary field GF(2^n). Then $P + Q = (x_3, y_3)$ where

$$\alpha = \begin{cases} (y_1 + y_2)\,(x_1 + x_2)^{-1} & \text{if } P \neq \pm Q \\ x_1 + y_1 x_1^{-1} & \text{if } P = Q \end{cases} \tag{9-45}$$

$$x_3 = \begin{cases} \alpha^2 + \alpha + x_1 + x_2 + A & \text{if } P \neq \pm Q \\ \alpha^2 + \alpha + A & \text{if } P = Q \end{cases} \tag{9-46}$$

$$y_3 = \alpha\,(x_1 + x_3) + x_3 + y_1 \tag{9-47}$$

If $P = -Q$ (which algebraically means $x_1 = x_2$ and $y_1 = x_2 + y_2$), then $P + Q = \mathcal{O}$.

We can know that the x-coordinate of $P + Q$ does not involve the y-coordinate of P if $P = Q$.

Example 9.1.11 Let the points $P = (g^2, 1)$ and $Q = (0, 1)$ are on the elliptic curve $E_{23} : y^2 + xy = x^3 + g^3x^2 + 1$, find $P + Q$ and $2P$.
Solution: Because the curve is defined over the binary field GF(2^3), all polynomial coefficients are evaluated modulo 2, with polynomial arithmetic performed modulo the irreducible polynomial

$$\alpha = (y_2 + y_1)\cdot(x_2 + x_1)^{-1} = 2/g^2 = 0/g^2 = 0 \tag{9-48}$$

$$x_3 = g^2 + g^3 = g^2 + (g + 1) = g^5 \tag{9-49}$$

$$y_3 = g^5 + 1 = (g^2 + g + 1) + 1 = g^4 \tag{9-50}$$

Therefore, $P + Q = (g^5, g^4)$.
To find $2P$, since $g^7 = g^2g^5 = 1$, then $g^{-2} = g^5$.

$$\alpha = x_1 + y_1x_1^{-1} = g^2 + g^{-2} = g^2 + g^5 = g^2 + (g^2 + g + 1) = g^3 \tag{9-51}$$

$$x_3 = (g^3)^2 + g^3 + g^3 = g^6 \tag{9-52}$$

$$y_3 = g^3(g^2 + g^6) + g^6 + 1 = g^5 + g^9 + g^6 + 1 = g^5 + g^2 + (g^2 + 1) + 1 = g^5 \tag{9-53}$$

Therefore, $2P = (g^6, g^5)$.
For efficiency in characteristic 2, we utilize the algebraically optimized doubling formula

$$y_3 \equiv x_1^2 + (\alpha + 1)x_3 \tag{9-54}$$

■

9.1.4 Elliptic Curve Discrete Logarithm Problem

The discrete logarithm problem extends naturally to the setting of elliptic curves over finite fields, yielding the **Elliptic Curve Discrete Logarithm Problem** (ECDLP). Analogous to the classical case, the ECDLP is formulated as follows: Given a base point P and a resulting point Q, determine the integer k such that

$$Q = \underbrace{P + P + \cdots + P}_{k \text{ terms}} = kP, \tag{9-55}$$

where the operation is the group law on the elliptic curve. Although denoted by additive notation, the group operation (see Definition 9.1.4) constitutes an algebraic-geometric process that is structurally distinct from standard integer addition.

The security of elliptic curve cryptography relies on the intractability of the ECDLP. Specifically, given points P and Q, it is assumed to be computationally infeasible to recover the scalar k. The most efficient general-purpose algorithms, such as Pollard's ρ method, exhibit a time complexity of approximately $\mathcal{O}(\sqrt{n})$, where n is the order of the subgroup generated by P. For curves defined over large prime fields where $n \approx p$, this exponential complexity renders the problem unsolvable for sufficiently large parameters. Consequently, the ECDLP serves as a robust hardness assumption.

In practice, the scalar multiplication $Q = kP$ is typically computed via the double-and-add algorithm. This method utilizes the binary expansion of k to perform a sequence of point doublings and point additions. In this cryptosystem, the integer k functions as the private key, and the point Q serves as the corresponding public key. Due to the absence of efficient classical algorithms to invert this operation, the ECDLP provides the foundational security guarantee for elliptic curve cryptosystems.

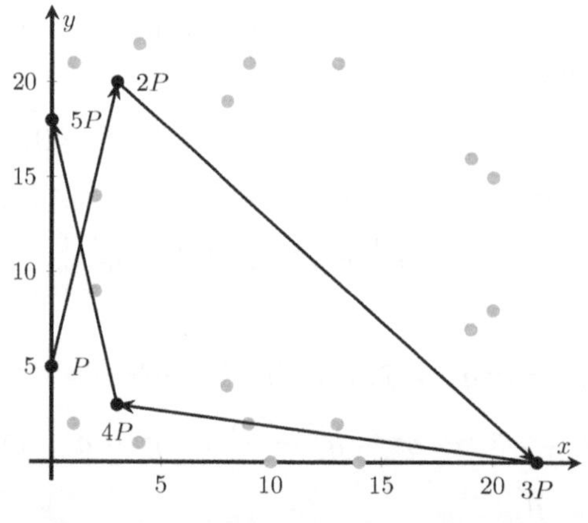

Figure 9-7: Addition on Elliptic Curve Over Finite Fields

Definition 9.1.6 The Elliptic Curve Discrete Logarithm Problem (ECDLP)

Let E be an elliptic curve defined over a finite field $\mathbb{F}_p$, where $p > 3$ is a prime. Let $P, Q \in E(\mathbb{F}_p)$ be points on the curve. The Elliptic Curve Discrete

Logarithm Problem is to determine an integer k satisfying the equation

$$Q = kP. \tag{9-56}$$

If such an integer exists, k is called the discrete logarithm of Q to the base P and is denoted by

$$k = \log_P(Q), \tag{9-57}$$

where $0 \leqslant k < ord(P)$.

Example 9.1.12 Let $E : y^2 \equiv x^3 + 9x + 8 \pmod{113}$, the two points $P = (49, 76), Q = (18, 37)$ and $P, Q \in E(\mathbb{F}_{113})$. Find the integer k such that $Q = kP$.
Solution: We can use brute-force search.

$$\begin{array}{lll} P = (49,76) & 6P = (75,27) & 11P = (11,67) \\ 2P = (14,77) & 7P = (88,54) & 12P = (104,21) \\ 3P = (6,39) & 8P = (107,90) & 13P = (74,62) \\ 4P = (28,105) & 9P = (19,91) & 14P = (46,76) \\ 5P = (52,25) & 10P = (17,21) & 15P = (18,37) \end{array}$$

Thus, $\log_P(Q) = 15$. In practical, k and p both are large numbers.

We can use SageMath to solve some basic ECDLP problems

```
E=EllipticCurve(GF(113),[9,8]) #p A B
P = E(49,76)
Q = E(18, 37)
Q.log(P)
```

■

In general, given k and a base point P, compute $Q = kP$ using scalar multiplication is relatively easy. However, so far there is no definite and efficient algorithm to solve the discrete logarithm problem on elliptic curves. As long as the secret key k is not leaked, the problem remains hard for an attacker.

9.2 ELGAMAL ELLIPTIC CURVE ENCRYPTION

9.2.1 Elliptic Curve Diffie-Hellman Key Exchange

Compared with the basic Diffie–Hellman key exchange [112], the elliptic curve cryptography provides stronger security and better performance.

The procedure is as follows:

1) Let p be prime(or $\text{GF}(2^n)$), Alice and Bob agree on a modulo p and choose a base point P on an elliptic curve $E : y^2 \equiv x^3 + Ax + B \pmod{p}$, where $A, B \in \text{GF}(p)$.
2) Alice chooses a random integer $N_A < n$ and Bob chooses a random integer $N_B < n$. Both keep these choices secret.

3) Alice computes $Q_A = N_A \cdot P$ and transmits it to Bob.
4) Bob computes $Q_B = N_B \cdot P$ and transmits it to Alice.
5) Upon receiving Q_A and Q_B, Alice computes $N_A \cdot Q_B$, Bob computes $N_B \cdot Q_A$.
6) Since

$$N_A \cdot Q_B = N_A(N_B \cdot P) = (N_A \cdot N_B)P = (N_B \cdot N_A)P = N_B(N_A \cdot P) = N_B \cdot Q_A \tag{9-58}$$

they share the secret key $K = N_A \cdot Q_B = N_B \cdot Q_A$.

Notice that N_A and N_B less than n where n is the order of point P on E_p.

The fundamental principle of the Elliptic Curve Diffie–Hellman (ECDH) key exchange is to replace the modular exponentiation used in the classical Diffie–Hellman protocol with scalar multiplication on elliptic curves. Under this group-theoretic analogy, modular multiplication in the multiplicative group corresponds to point addition on the curve, while modular exponentiation corresponds to scalar multiplication.

For an attacker, computing the shared secret K from the public values Q_A, Q_B, and the curve parameters E typically necessitates recovering the private key N_A or N_B. This task is effectively an instance of the Elliptic Curve Discrete Logarithm Problem (ECDLP). The best known generic algorithms for this problem, such as Pollard's ρ method, have a time complexity of approximately $\mathcal{O}(\sqrt{n})$, where n is the order of the subgroup. Consequently, for sufficiently large parameters, the intractability of the ECDLP ensures the computational security of the protocol.

Example 9.2.1 Alice and Bob agree a prime $p = 7211$, the curve $E_{7211} : y^2 \equiv x^3 + x + 7206 \pmod{7211}$ and base point $P = (3, 5)$. How they exchange key using elliptic Diffie–Hellman?

Solution:

1) Alice chooses $N_A = 12$ and computes $Q_A = N_A \cdot P = (1794, 6375)$.
2) Bob chooses $N_B = 23$ and computes $Q_B = N_B \cdot P = (3861, 1242)$.
3) Alice and Bob both keep N_A, N_B secret, publish Q_A, Q_B.
4) Alice receives Q_B and computes $N_A \cdot Q_B = 12 \cdot (3861, 1242) = (1472, 2098)$.
5) Bob receives Q_A and computes $N_B \cdot Q_A = 23 \cdot (1794, 6375) = (1472, 2098)$.

■

However, choosing an appropriate ECC difficulty level is not easy. Since the prime p is typically very large, and the elliptic curve together with the chosen prime must yield a group whose order, these computations are quite involved and therefore challenging in practice. Fortunately, SageMath provides convenient tools for calculating the order.

```
K.<a> = GF(44927)
E = EllipticCurve(K,[0,0,0,7,1])
E.cardinality() # number of points

P = E.lift_x(1) #know x, find y-coordinate of point
P.xy()
```

9.2.2 Encryption/Decryption

We can use the idea of the ElGamal Cryptosystem to construct a new cryptosystem on an elliptic curve [113] [114].

1) (**KeyGen**): Bob chooses a large prime p and an elliptic curve $E_p : y^2 \equiv x^3 + Ax + B \pmod{p}$(or over GF($2^n$)). Bob also chooses a base point P and a positive integer $k < n$.
   (a) (**PublicKey**): Bob computes $Q = k \cdot P$, and publishes the curve E_p, P and Q as his public key.
   (b) (**PrivateKey**): Bob keeps k as his private key.
2) (**Encrypt**): Alice encodes the plaintext as a point $M \in E_p$ and selects a random integer $h < n$. She computes the ciphertext (C_1, C_2)

$$C_1 = h \cdot P, \qquad C_2 = M + h \cdot Q \tag{9-59}$$

   Alice transmits the pair of points (C_1, C_2) to Bob. Typically, a different value of h is used for each plaintext.
3) (**Decrypt**): To decrypt the ciphertext, Bob computes

$$M = C_2 - kC_1 \tag{9-60}$$

For correctness, $C_2 - kC_1 = M + hQ - k(hP) = M + hQ - h(kP) = M + hQ - hQ = M$. The encryption process is illustrated in Figure 9-8.

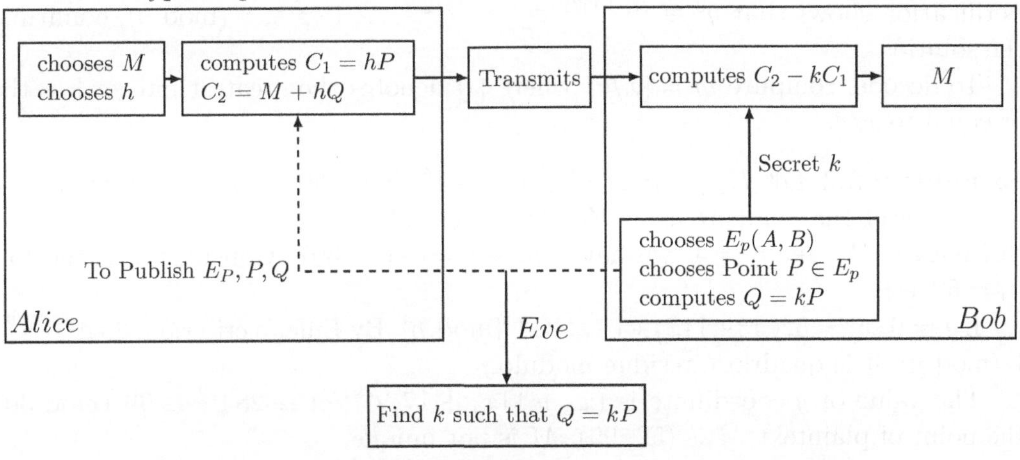

Figure 9-8: ElGamal Elliptic Curve Encryption

Before encryption can proceed, the plaintext m must be encoded as a point M on the elliptic curve E. For a fixed curve defined over $\mathbb{F}_p$, a naive mapping (such as setting the x-coordinate directly to m) is insufficient, as the resulting value may not correspond to a valid point on the curve. Specifically, for a randomly chosen x, the value $z = x^3 + Ax + B$ is a quadratic residue modulo p (see Theorem 2.8.1) with probability approximately $1/2$.

To address this, one may employ a probabilistic encoding scheme known as the **Koblitz method**. The core principle involves introducing a random padding factor to generate multiple candidate x-coordinates for a single message.

Let r be a fixed integer sufficiently large to ensure a high success probability (e.g., $r = 30$). We assume the plaintext is an integer m satisfying the condition $(m + 1)r < p$. The encoding process defines a candidate x-coordinate as

$$x = rm + j, \text{ where } 0 \leqslant j < r \tag{9-61}$$

For $j = 0, 1, \ldots r - 1$, compute $z = x^3 + Ax + B$ and test whether z is a quadratic residue modulo p. If a square root y exists, the process terminates, and the plaintext m is encoded to the point $M = (x, y)$. If z is a non-residue, j is incremented, and the test is repeated.

If no quadratic residue is found for all r, we fail to encode a message to a point, the probability of failure is approximately $(1/2)^r$. For example, when $r = 30$, the probability of total failure is only about 2^{-30}, which is practically negligible. Although the distribution of quadratic residues is not strictly independent, this heuristic provides a sufficient probabilistic assurance for reliable encoding.

Once a valid x is found, we must compute the corresponding y-coordinate. In the specific case where $p \equiv 3 \pmod 4$, this can be done efficiently. Since z is a quadratic residue, Euler's criterion guarantees that $z^{(p-1)/2} \equiv 1 \pmod p$. By Fermat's Little Theorem, the square roots are given explicitly by

$$y \equiv \pm z^{(p+1)/4} \pmod p. \tag{9-62}$$

Verification shows that $y^2 \equiv z^{(p+1)/2} \equiv z^{(p-1)/2} \cdot z \equiv 1 \cdot z \equiv z \pmod p$, confirming the solution.

To decode, compute $m = \lfloor x/r \rfloor$ where $\lfloor \cdot \rfloor$ denotes the greatest integer less than or equal to x/r.

Example 9.2.2 Let $E_{307} : y^2 \equiv x^3 + 11x + 17 \pmod{307}$, the plaintext $m = 13$, how to select the point M using Koblitz's method.
Solution: We set $r = 4$, we have $rm + r = 56 < 307$. Consider x of the form $x_j = 52 + j$.

If $j = 0$, $x_j = 52$, $x_j^3 + 11x_j + 17 \equiv 284 \pmod p$. By Euler's criterion, $284^{(p-1)/2} \equiv 1 \pmod p$, it is quadratic residue modulo p.

The value of y-coordinate is $(x_j^3 + 11x_j + 17)^{(p+1)/4} \equiv 284^{77} \equiv 99 \pmod{307}$, the point of plaintext M is (52, 99). M is not unique. ■

The Python code for Koblitz encode method is as follows:

```
def Encode_ECC(m,p,A,B):
    if m > p/10-1:
        print('Select larger prime')
    else:
        r = len(bin(m)[2:])
        k = len(bin(p)[2:]) - r - 1
        while True:
            b = ''
            for i in range(k):
                b += str(random.randint(0,1))
            binary = '0' + b + bin(m)[2:]
```

```
            integer = int(binary,2)
            x = integer
            residue = (x**3 + A*x+B)%p
            if pow(residue,int((p-1)/2),p) == 1:
                y = pow(residue,int((p+1)/4),p)
                break
        return (x,y)
```

9.2.3 Example

Example 9.2.3 Consider ElGamal Elliptic Curve cryptosystem, Bob selects $p = 100003$ and the curve $E_{100003} : y^2 \equiv x^3 + 3x + 45 \pmod{100003}$, the base point is $P = (4, 11)$. Encrypt the plaintext "**THE**".

Solution: Bob preliminary task requires encoding the plaintext string into a numerical integer. Using a base-26 alphabetical mapping (A=0, ..., Z=25):$m = \mathbf{T} \cdot 26^0 + \mathbf{H} \cdot 26^1 + \mathbf{E} \cdot 26^2 = 19 + 7 \cdot 26 + 4 \cdot 26^2 = \mathbf{2905}$.

1) (Encode:) Encode the plaintext m. Let $r = 10$, we have $rm + r = 29060 < p$. Consider x of the form $x_j = 29050 + j$. For $j = 0, 1, 2, \ldots, 9$, we have
   (a) For $j = 0$, $x_j = 29050$, $x_j^3 + 3x_j + 45 \equiv 73229 \pmod{p}$. By Euler's criterion, $73229^{(p-1)/2} \equiv -1 \pmod{p}$, it is not quadratic residue modulo p.
   (b) For $j = 1$, $x_j = 29051$, $x_j^3 + 3x_j + 45 \equiv 91932 \pmod{p}$. By Euler's criterion, $91932^{(p-1)/2} \equiv -1 \pmod{p}$, it is not quadratic residue modulo p.
   (c) For $j = 2$, $x_j = 29052$, $x_j^3 + 3x_j + 45 \equiv 84935 \pmod{p}$. By Euler's criterion, $84935^{(p-1)/2} \equiv 1 \pmod{p}$, it is quadratic residue modulo p. The value of y-coordinate is $(x_j^3 + 3x_j + 45)^{(p+1)/4} \equiv 84935^{25001} \equiv 91384 \pmod{100003}$, the point of plaintext M is $(29052, 91384)$.
2) (KeyGen:) Suppose Bob chooses an integer $k = 3$, computes $Q = kP = 3(4, 11) = (43378, 26704)$ and sent to Alice. The points P, Q and E_p are his public key. The integer k is his private key.
3) (Encrypt:) Alice receives the point Q, chooses an integer $h = 8$, computes

$$C_1 = h \cdot P = 8(4, 11) = (45696, 30310) \quad (9\text{-}63)$$

$$C_2 = M + h \cdot Q = (29052, 91384) + 8(43378, 26704) = (67479, 24561) \quad (9\text{-}64)$$

   Alice transmits (C_1, C_2) to Bob.
4) (Decrypt:) Bob receives the ciphertext, he computes

$$M = C_2 - kC_1 = (67479, 24561) - 3(45696, 30310) = (29052, 91384) \quad (9\text{-}65)$$

   The plaintext m can be decoded by $m = \lfloor x/r \rfloor = 2905$.

■

9.3 SM2

9.3.1 Introduction

The SM2(ShangMi2) algorithm is a public-key cryptosystem based on ECC. Specifically, the algorithm employs elliptic curves defined over the GF(p).

The SM2 standard was originally published in 2010 by the *Office of State Commercial Cryptography Administration* (OSCCA) managed by the *China's State Cryptography Administration* of China. This cryptosystem is mandated specifically for commercial cryptographic applications within China, as distinct from algorithms reserved for classified or state-secret communications. Following its initial public release in 2010, SM2 was formally standardized in March 2012 as the industry specification GM/T 0003-2012. It was subsequently adopted as the Chinese national standard GB/T 32918-2016 in August 2016 [115].

9.3.2 Encryption/Decryption

SM2 has five different parts: general, digital signature algorithm, key exchange protocol, public key encryption algorithm and parameter definition. In this section, we will introduce public key encryption algorithm.

Let $E(\mathbb{F}_q)$ be the set of rational points on elliptic curves E over $\mathbb{F}_q$ where $\mathbb{F}_q$ be the finite field with q elements, q can be prime fields GF(p) or binary extension fields GF(2^n).

To encrypt the plaintext M, Alice should perform the following procedures:

1) (KeyGen): Generate a random number $d \in [1, n-1]$ with the random number generator where n is the order of the base point G on $E(\mathbb{F}_q)$. Compute $P = dG$.
   (a) (PrivateKey): Bob keeps d as his private key.
   (b) (PublicKey): Bob computes $P = d \cdot G$, and publishes the curve E_p, P and G as his public key.
2) (Encrypt):
   (a) Alice selects a random integer $l \in [1, q-1]$. Compute $C_1 = lG = (x_4, y_4)$ and $lP = (x_s, y_s)$.
   (b) Alice computes $e = \text{KDF}(x_s \| y_s, \text{mlen})$.
   (c) Alice computes $C_2 = M \oplus e$ and $C_3 = \text{H}(x_s \| M \| y_s)$.
   (d) Alice computes the ciphertext $C = C_1 \| C_3 \| C_2$ and transmits to Bob .
3) (Decrypt):
   (a) Bob verifies whether the received C_1 lies on the elliptic curve. If valid, Bob computes $d_B C_1 = (x_5, y_5)$.
   (b) Bob computes $t = \text{KDF}(x_5 \| y_5, \text{mlen})$.
   (c) Bob retrieves the plaintext by computing $M = C_2 \oplus t$.
   (d) Bob computes $u = \text{H}(x_5 \| M \| y_5)$ and verifies whether $u = C_3$. If the equality does not hold, Bob must terminate the process and report an error.
   (e) Bob outputs the plaintext M.

Here, "**H**" is a cryptographic hash function, we introduce it later.

The KDF is to derive key data from a shared secret bit string which outputs a required session key or a key data required by further encryption.

Let $H_v()$ be a cryptographic hash function which outputs a hash value of length v bits. Let Z be bit string input and l be the bit-length of M. The KDF is defined as follows:

1) Initialize a 32-bit counter $ct = \texttt{0x00000001}$;
2) For i from 1 to $\lceil l/v \rceil$ do:
   (a) compute $Ha_i = H_v(Z \| ct)$:
   (b) $ct = ct + 1$
3) If (l/v) is an integer, let $Ha!_{\lceil l/v \rceil} = Ha_{\lceil l/v \rceil}$; otherwise, let $Ha!_{\lceil l/v \rceil}$ be the leftmost $(l - (v \times \lfloor l/v \rfloor))$ bits of $Ha_{\lceil l/v \rceil}$.
4) Let $K = Ha_1 \| Ha_2 \| \cdots \| Ha_{\lceil l/v \rceil - 1} \| Ha_{\lceil l/v \rceil}$.

9.4 FAST SCALAR MULTIPLICATION FOR ELLIPTIC CURVES

9.4.1 Double-and-Add Method

The scalar multiplication of ECC is the most dominant computation part of ECC. In the previous section, we discussed how to compute $2P$. To compute kP for cryptographically massive scalars, naive repeated addition is entirely infeasible. In this case we use **elliptic curve scalar multiplication**. There are many methods. One common method is the **Double-and-Add method**. We write k in binary and then compute. Let k be a positive integer with the binary expansion

$$k = k_0 + 2 \cdot k_1 + 4 \cdot k_2 + 8 \cdot k_3 + \cdots + 2^{n-1} \cdot k_{n-1} \tag{9-66}$$

with $k_0, k_1, \ldots, k_{n-2} \in \{0, 1\}$ and $k_{n-1} = 1$. The Right-to-Left (RTL) Double-and-Add algorithm evaluates kP by systematically scanning the bits from the least significant (k_0) to the most significant (k_{n-1}). We initialize an accumulator $Q = \mathcal{O}$ and a running point $R = P$. For each bit k_i, if $k_i = 1$, we update the accumulator via point addition ($Q \leftarrow Q + R$). Regardless of the bit's value, we continuously double the running point ($R \leftarrow 2R$) for the next iteration. This ensures that each binary power is processed exactly once.

This algorithm ensures that each bit of the scalar k is processed exactly once. Consequently, the computational cost involves exactly n point doublings and at most n point additions.

Example 9.4.1 Consider an elliptic curve $E_{487} : y^2 \equiv x^3 + 4x + 9 \pmod{487}$, let $P = (2, 5)$. Compute $523P$.
Solution: The binary representation of $k = 523$ is

$$523 = 2^0 + 2^1 + 2^3 + 2^9 \tag{9-67}$$

Thus, $523P = Q_0 + Q_1 + Q_3 + Q_9$

$$Q_0 = 2^0 P = 1P = (2, 5) \tag{9-68}$$

$$Q_1 = 2^1 P = 2P = (57, 394) \tag{9-69}$$

$$Q_3 = 2^3 P = 8P = (423, 104) \tag{9-70}$$

$$Q_9 = 2^9 P = 512P = (477, 291) \tag{9-71}$$

Finally, $523P = P + 2P + 8P + 512P = (341, 378)$

To reach $512P$, the algorithm strictly executes 9 point doublings. To aggregate the 4 active terms, it executes 3 point additions. This yields a total of 12 elliptic curve operations. Compared with the plain repeated addition method that needs 522 steps, this saves a lot of time, and the time complexity is about $\mathcal{O}(\log_2 k)$. ■

The SageMath code for scalar multiplication is as follows:

```
E=EllipticCurve(GF(487),[4,9]) #p A B
E.point( [2,5] )*523
```

In addition to the double-and-add method, the **Montgomery ladder** method [116] is another standard algorithm. Unlike the former, it follows a constant execution time strategy. In the double-and-add method, timing variations serve as a side channel because point addition and point doubling require different amounts of time. Consequently, by measuring the time required to compute kP, an attacker can deduce the binary pattern of k. The Montgomery ladder avoids this vulnerability by employing the same operation sequence for each bit of k. For scalars of the same bit length, the computational process is indistinguishable to an observer, thereby improving cryptographic security.

9.4.2 Non-Adjacent Form

In 1997, *Solinas* built on the binary method and formalized the Non-Adjacent form (NAF) [117] for elliptic curve scalar multiplication to improve efficiency. Compared with the usual binary form, the NAF reduces the number of non-zero digits. In this form, the neighbors of every non-zero digit on the left and on the right are 0, so non-zero digits are not next to each other.

Definition 9.4.1 Non-Adjacent Form (NAF)

A non-adjacent form of a positive integer k is an expression

$$k = \sum_{i=0}^{L-1} k_i 2^i, \text{ where } k_i \in \{-1, 0, 1\} \tag{9-72}$$

No two consecutive digits k_i are non-zero such that $k_i \cdot k_{i+1} = 0$. The length of the NAF is L, $k_{L-1} \neq 0$. Each integer k has a unique NAF denoted by NAF(k).

Compute the NAF of a positive integer as follows:

1) Check the parity of integer k
   - If k is odd and $k \equiv 1 \pmod 4$, then write 1, then update $k \leftarrow (k-1)/2$.
   - If k is odd and $k \equiv 3 \pmod 4$, then write $\bar{1}$ (note that $\bar{1}$ denotes -1), then update $k \leftarrow (k+1)/2$.
   - If k is even, then write 0, then update $k \leftarrow k/2$.
2) Prepend the recorded digit $\{\bar{1}, 0, 1\}$ to the NAF sequence.
3) Prepend the extracted digit $k_i \in \{\bar{1}, 0, 1\}$ to the NAF sequence. Repeat step 2 until $k = 0$.

Such a NAF has the fewest non-zero digits.

Example 9.4.2 Let $k = 27$, compute NAF(k).
Solution: Since

$$k \equiv 27 \equiv 3 \pmod 4 \quad \langle \bar{1} \rangle \quad (27+1)/2 = 14 \tag{9-73}$$
$$k \equiv 14 \equiv 2 \pmod 4 \quad \langle 0, \bar{1} \rangle \quad 14/2 = 7 \tag{9-74}$$
$$k \equiv 7 \equiv 3 \pmod 4 \quad \langle \bar{1}, 0, \bar{1} \rangle \quad (7+1)/2 = 4 \tag{9-75}$$
$$k \equiv 4 \equiv 0 \pmod 4 \quad \langle 0, \bar{1}, 0, \bar{1} \rangle \quad 4/2 = 2 \tag{9-76}$$
$$k \equiv 2 \equiv 2 \pmod 4 \quad \langle 0, 0, \bar{1}, 0, \bar{1} \rangle \quad 2/2 = 1 \tag{9-77}$$
$$k \equiv 1 \equiv 1 \pmod 4 \quad \langle 1, 0, 0, \bar{1}, 0, \bar{1} \rangle \quad 1 \tag{9-78}$$

The python code for NAF is as follows:

```
def NAF(k):
    if k == 0:
        return []
    z = 0 if k % 2 == 0 else 2 - (k % 4)
    return NAF( (k-z) // 2 ) + [z]
```

■

NAF method for scale multiplication are following:

1) Set $Q = \mathcal{O}$, let ℓ denote the length of the NAF representation.
2) Process the digits from most significant to least significant, for $i = \ell - 1, \ell - 2, \ldots, 0$, doing:
   (a) Double the accumulator, $Q \leftarrow 2Q$.
   (b) If $k_i = 1$, then $Q \leftarrow Q + P$.
   (c) If $k_i = \bar{1}(-1)$, then $Q \leftarrow Q - P$.
   (d) If $k_i = 0$, no addition or subtraction is performed after the doubling.
3) After all digits have been processed, return the final accumulator Q.

The **Hamming weight** of a representation refers to the number of non-zero digits in its sequence. For the standard binary representation, the average density of non-zero digits is 1/2. In contrast, the Non-Adjacent Form (NAF) reduces this density to approximately 1/3, with a maximum possible density of 1/2. Consequently, the expected Hamming weight for an integer k in NAF is approximately $\frac{1}{3}\log_2 k$.

This reduction has significant implications for scalar multiplication. Since runs of zeros in the scalar expansion require only point doublings and no point additions, a lower Hamming weight directly translates to fewer addition operations. For large scalars, this results in a substantial reduction in computational effort. Although the NAF representation of an ℓ-bit number is at most $\ell + 1$ digits long, the reduction in additions outweighs this minimal overhead for large k. In practice, compared to the standard double-and-add method, the NAF approach yields a performance improvement of approximately 12%.

To further optimize performance, *Solinas* introduced the **Window NAF method** (w-NAF). This generalization employs a window of width w, where typically $w > 2$ (Note that setting $w = 2$ recovers the standard NAF). The w-NAF representation of an integer k is given by the expansion

$$k = \sum_{i=0}^{\ell-1} k_i 2^i \tag{9-79}$$

where each non-zero coefficient k_i is an odd integer, and $|k_i| < 2^{w-1}, k_{\ell-1} \neq 0$. Here, ℓ denotes the length of the expansion. Among any w consecutive digits, at most one is non-zero. For example, if $w = 3$, the set of 3-NAF digits are $\{0, \pm 1, \pm 3\}$, then $NAF_3(27) = \langle 3, 0, 0, 3 \rangle$; if $w = 4$, the set of 4-NAF digits are $\{0, \pm 1, \pm 3, \pm 5, \pm 7\}$, $NAF_4(27) = \langle 1, 0, 0, 0, 0, \bar{5} \rangle$.

The python code for w-NAF is as follows:

```
def mods(k, w):
    windows = pow(2, w)
    M = k % windows
    return M - windows if M >= (windows / 2) else M

def wNAF(k, w):
    i = 0;M = []
    while k > 0:
        if (k % 2) == 1:
            if w == 1:
                M.append(2 - (k % 4))
            else:
                M.append(mods(k, w))
            k -= M[i]
        else:
            M.append(0)
        k //= 2;i += 1
    return M[::-1]
```

Example 9.4.3 Let P be a point on the elliptic curve E_p over the finite field GF(p), set $k = 1013$, and compute kP using the binary method, the NAF, and the 3-NAF, respectively.

Solution: The steps for computing kP are shown in Table 9-5. For $k = 1013$, the binary method needs 16 steps, the NAF needs 13 steps, and the 3-NAF needs 12 steps. As k grows, the saving in steps becomes larger.

Table 9-5: Step-by-Step Comparison of Scalar Multiplication

	$k = 1013$					
Steps	Binary:1111110101		NAF:$10000\bar{1}0101$		3-NAF:$1000000\bar{1}00\bar{3}$	
1	P	1	P	1	P	1
2	$2P$	10	$2P$	10	$2P$	10
3	$3P$	11	$4P$	100	$4P$	100
4	$6P$	110	$8P$	1000	$8P$	1000
5	$7P$	111	$16P$	10000	$16P$	10000
6	$14P$	1110	$32P$	100000	$32P$	100000

Continued on Next Page

Table 9-5: Step-by-Step Comparison of Scalar Multiplication(Continued)

	$k = 1013$					
Steps	Binary:1111110101		NAF:$100000\bar{1}0101$		3-NAF:$1000000\bar{1}00\bar{3}$	
7	$15P$	1111	$64P$	1000000	$64P$	1000000
8	$30P$	11110	$63P$	$100000\bar{1}$	$128P$	10000000
9	$31P$	11111	$126P$	$100000\bar{1}0$	$127P$	$1000000\bar{1}$
10	$62P$	111110	$252P$	$100000\bar{1}00$	$254P$	$1000000\bar{1}0$
11	$63P$	111111	$253P$	$100000\bar{1}01$	$508P$	$1000000\bar{1}00$
12	$126P$	1111110	$506P$	$100000\bar{1}010$	$1016P$	$1000000\bar{1}000$
13	$252P$	11111100	$1012P$	$100000\bar{1}0100$	$1013P$	$1000000\bar{1}00\bar{3}$
14	$253P$	11111101	$1013P$	$100000\bar{1}0101$		
15	$506P$	111111010				
16	$1012P$	1111110100				
17	$1013P$	1111110101				

However, it is structurally imperative to note the engineering trade-off: while the 3-NAF heavily minimizes main-loop operations, it fundamentally necessitates an upfront precomputation overhead to generate and cache the odd multiples of the base point. This demonstrates a classic space-time trade-off in cryptography.

■

9.4.3 Choice of Coordinates

To accelerate the computation of kP, beyond the algorithmic techniques discussed previously, computational efficiency can be significantly enhanced by selecting an appropriate coordinate system. The two most prevalent representations in elliptic curve cryptography are **standard projective coordinates** and **Jacobian projective coordinates**. It is important to note that Jacobian coordinates are not merely a variation of the standard form but constitute a distinct projective scheme that often yields superior performance in practice.

Elliptic curves are typically defined using **affine coordinates**, yet point operation in this form require inverse operation. Inversion is usually done by the extended Euclidean algorithm or other methods, and in large finite fields such as $GF(2^{128})$ it is more costly than a multiplication. To avoid these inverse operations one can use projective coordinates.

The primary strategy is to represent points in a projective space, thereby eliminating the need for inversion during the intermediate steps of scalar multiplication. In these systems, the explicit division operations in the group law formulas are replaced by multiplications. Inversion is required only once at the very end of the computation to convert the final result back to affine coordinates.

An affine point (x, y) can be seamlessly transformed into standard projective coordinates or Jacobian projective coordinates. In the system of standard projective coordinates, a point is represented as the set of triples $(X : Y : Z)$. For $Z \neq 0$, the projective point $(X : Y : Z)$ corresponds to the unique affine point

$$x = X/Z^c, \quad y = Y/Z^d. \tag{9-80}$$

where $c, d \in \mathbb{Z}^+$. The $(X : Y : Z)$ is called a projective point. Let $c = 1$ and $d = 1$, and $\text{char}(K) \neq 2$ and 3, substituting $(X/Z, Y/Z)$ into Equation 9-20 yields the **standard projective equation** of the elliptic curve over GF(p) is

$$E : Y^2Z = X^3 + a_4XZ^2 + a_6Z^3 \tag{9-81}$$

Substituting the point $(X/Z, Y/Z)$ into Equation 9-42, and the standard projective equation of the elliptic curve over GF(2^n) is

$$E : Y^2Z + XYZ = X^3 + a_4X^2Z + a_6Z^3 \tag{9-82}$$

Here, a_4 and a_6 correspond to A and B in Equation 9-20 and Equation 9-42, respectively.

In affine coordinates, the point at infinity $\mathcal{O}$ on an elliptic curve is not well represented and cannot be seen in a plot, as shown in Figure 9-9. In standard projective coordinates, the **point at infinity** corresponds to $(0 : 1 : 0)$, that is the case $Z = 0$, as shown in Figure 9-10. The negative of a point $(X : Y : Z)$ over GF(p) is $(X : -Y : Z)$; over GF(2^n) is $(X : X + Y : Z)$.

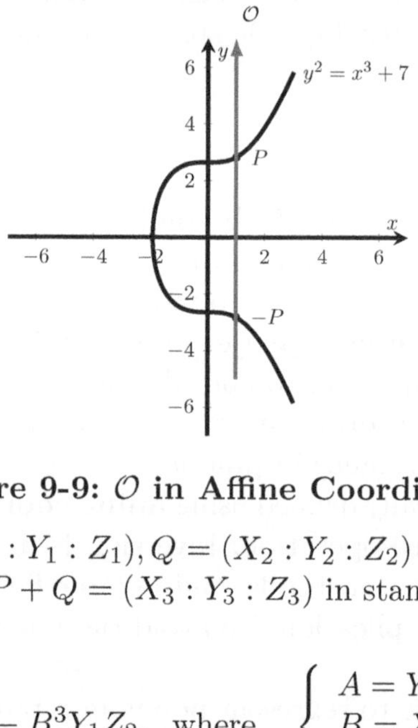

Figure 9-9: $\mathcal{O}$ in Affine Coordinates

Let the points $P = (X_1 : Y_1 : Z_1), Q = (X_2 : Y_2 : Z_2) \in E$ such that $P \neq \pm Q$ and $P, Q \neq \mathcal{O}$. Point addition $P + Q = (X_3 : Y_3 : Z_3)$ in standard projective coordinates over GF(p) is given by

$$\begin{cases} X_3 = BC \\ Y_3 = A(B^2X_1Z_2 - C) - B^3Y_1Z_2, \\ Z_3 = B^3Z_1Z_2 \end{cases} \text{where} \quad \begin{cases} A = Y_2Z_1 - Y_1Z_2 \\ B = X_2Z_1 - X_1Z_2 \\ C = A^2Z_1Z_2 - B^3 - 2B^2X_1Z_2 \end{cases} \tag{9-83}$$

Point doubling $2P = (X_3 : Y_3 : Z_3)$ in standard projective coordinates over GF(p) is given by

$$\begin{cases} X_3 = 2BD \\ Y_3 = A(4C - D) - 8Y_1^2B^2, \\ Z_3 = 8B^3. \end{cases} \text{where} \quad \begin{cases} A = a_4Z_1^2 + 3X_1^2 \\ B = Y_1Z_1 \\ C = X_1Y_1B \\ D = A^2 - 8C \end{cases} \tag{9-84}$$

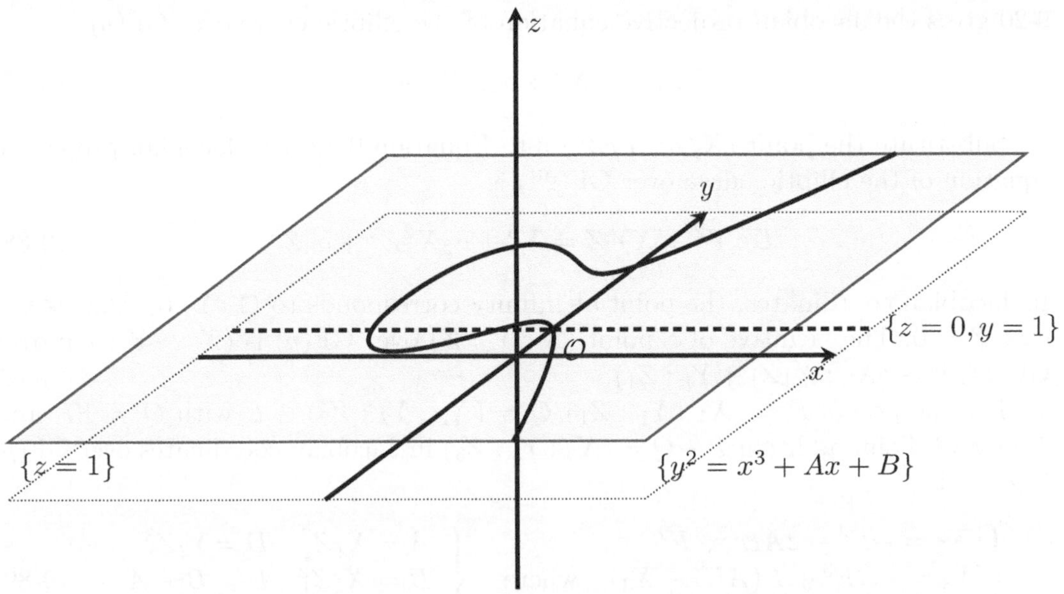

Figure 9-10: $\mathcal{O}$ in Standard Projective Coordinates

Let the points $P = (X_1 : Y_1 : Z_1), Q = (X_2 : Y_2 : Z_2) \in E$ such that $P \neq \pm Q$ and $P, Q \neq \mathcal{O}$. Point addition $P + Q = (X_3 : Y_3 : Z_3)$ in standard projective coordinates over $\mathrm{GF}(2^n)$ is given by

$$\begin{cases} X_3 = BE \\ Y_3 = C(AX_1 + Y_1B)Z_2 + (A+B)E, \\ Z_3 = B^3D. \end{cases} \quad \text{where} \quad \begin{cases} A = Y_1Z_2 + Z_1Y_2 \\ B = X_1Z_2 + Z_1X_2 \\ C = B^2 \\ D = Z_1Z_2 \\ E = (A^2 + AB + a_2C)D + BC \end{cases} \tag{9-85}$$

Point doubling $2P = (X_3 : Y_3 : Z_3)$ in standard projective coordinates over $\mathrm{GF}(2^n)$ is given by

$$\begin{cases} X_3 = CE \\ Y_3 = (B+C)E + A^2C, \\ Z_3 = CD \end{cases} \quad \text{where} \quad \begin{cases} A = X_1^2 \\ B = A + Y_1Z_1 \\ C = X_1Z_1 \\ D = C^2 \\ E = (B^2 + BC + a_2D) \end{cases} \tag{9-86}$$

In projective coordinates, no inversion is needed. The computation times are $12M + 2S$ for an addition and $7M + 5S$ for a doubling over $\mathrm{GF}(p)$. $16M + 2S$ for an addition and $8M + 4S$ for a doubling over $\mathrm{GF}(2^n)$. Here, M and S denote the costs of multiplication and squaring, respectively.

In practice, standard projective coordinates are not always more efficient than affine coordinates, and **Jacobian coordinates** are used more often. In Jacobian coordinates for which $c = 2$ and $d = 3$, the point $(X : Y : Z)$ corresponds to the affine point $(X/Z^2, Y/Z^3)$ with $Z \neq 0$. Substituting $(X/Z^2, Y/Z^3)$ into Equation

9-20 gives the Jacobian projective equation of the elliptic curve over GF(p) is

$$E : Y^2 = X^3 + a_4XZ^4 + a_6Z^6 \tag{9-87}$$

Substitute the point $(X/Z^2, Y/Z^3)$ into Equation 9-42, the Jacobian projective equation of the elliptic curve over GF(2^n) is

$$E : Y^2 + XYZ = X^3 + a_2X^2Z^2 + a_6Z^6 \tag{9-88}$$

In Jacobian coordinates, the point at infinity corresponds to $(1 : 1 : 0)$, that is the case $Z = 0$. The negative of a point $(X : Y : Z)$ over GF(p) is $(X : -Y : Z)$; over GF(2^n) it is $(X_1 : X_1Z_1 + Y_1 : Z_1)$.

Let the points $P = (X_1 : Y_1 : Z_1), Q = (X_2 : Y_2 : Z_2) \in E$ with $Q \neq \pm P$ and $P, Q \neq \mathcal{O}$, Point addition $P+Q = (X_3 : Y_3 : Z_3)$ in Jacobian coordinates over GF(p) is given by

$$\begin{cases} X_3 = -E^3 - 2AE^2 + F^2 \\ Y_3 = -CE^3 + F(AE^2 - X_3), \\ Z_3 = Z_1Z_2E. \end{cases} \text{where} \quad \begin{cases} A = X_1Z_2^2 & D = Y_2Z_1^3 \\ B = X_2Z_1^2 & E = B - A \\ C = Y_1Z_2^3 & F = D - C \end{cases} \tag{9-89}$$

Point doubling $2P = (X_3 : Y_3 : Z_3)$ in Jacobian coordinates over GF(p) is given by

$$\begin{cases} X_3 = -2A + B^2 \\ Y_3 = -8Y_1^4 + B(A - X_3), \\ Z_3 = 2Y_1Z_1. \end{cases} \text{where} \quad \begin{cases} A = 4X_1Y_1^2 \\ B = 3X_1^2 + a_4Z_1^4 \end{cases} \tag{9-90}$$

Let the points $P = (X_1 : Y_1 : Z_1), Q = (X_2 : Y_2 : Z_2) \in E$ with $Q \neq \pm P$ and $P, Q \neq \mathcal{O}$, Point addition $P + Q = (X_3 : Y_3 : Z_3)$ in Jacobian coordinates over GF(2^n) is given by

$$\begin{cases} X_3 = a_2Z_3^2 + FI + E^3 \\ Y_3 = IX_3 + G^2H, \\ Z_3 = GZ_2 \end{cases} \quad \text{where} \quad \begin{cases} A = X_1Z_2^2 & F = C + D \\ B = X_2Z_1^2 & G = EZ_1 \\ C = Y_1Z_2^3 & H = FX_2 + GY_2 \\ D = Y_2Z_1^3 & I = F + Z_3 \\ E = A + B \end{cases} \tag{9-91}$$

Point doubling $2P = (X_3 : Y_3 : Z_3)$ in Jacobian coordinates over GF(2^n) is given by

$$\begin{cases} X_3 = B + a_6C^4 \\ Y_3 = BZ_3 + (A + Y_1Z_1 + Z_3)X_3, \\ Z_3 = X_1C \end{cases} \text{where} \quad \begin{cases} A = X_1^2 \\ B = A^2 \\ C = Z_1^2 \end{cases} \tag{9-92}$$

In the Jacobian coordinate system, point operations are performed without modular inversion. For elliptic curves defined over the prime field $\mathbb{F}_p$, the computational cost is typically $12M + 4S$ for point addition and $4M + 6S$ for point doubling. Over GF(2^n), these costs are approximately $16M + 3S$ for addition and $11M + 3S$ for doubling. Given that the cost of a single inversion (I) can be equivalent to approximately 100 multiplications ($I \approx 100M$) for a 256-bit modulus, avoiding inversion is critical for performance.

Efficiency can be further improved by utilizing **mixed coordinates**. For instance, consider the addition of a point $P = (X : Y : Z)$ in Jacobian coordinates and a point $Q = (X : Y : 1)$ in affine coordinates. In this scenario, the cost of addition reduces significantly to $8M + 3S$ over $\mathbb{F}_p$ and $15M + 3S$ over $\mathbb{F}_{2^n}$.

After the computation, convert back to the affine form if needed. For Jacobian coordinates, the conversion to affine coordinates is $(X : Y : Z) \Rightarrow (X/Z^2, Y/Z^3)$ with $Z \neq 0$.

9.5 CRYPTANALYSIS

Although the elliptic curve discrete logarithm problem (ECDLP) over a finite field is widely seen as hard, its hardness depends on the curve. As shown in Figure 9-1, the parameters A and B shape the curve. On some special curves there are methods that reduce the complexity of solving the ECDLP. General discrete logarithm attacks also apply to elliptic curve groups and lower the time cost, such as the baby step giant step algorithm, Pollard's rho, and the Pohlig–Hellman algorithm described in Section 8.5.

9.5.1 Pohlig-Hellman Method

The Pohlig-Hellman method applied to elliptic curves over finite fields works by factoring the group order. The details of the Pohlig-Hellman method were given in Section 8.5.4, here we will directly describe how to use it on elliptic curves. Let n be the order of the elliptic curve E_p over GF(p), and the two points P and $Q \in E(\text{GF}(p))$ such that $Q = kP$. We want to compute $k = \log_P(Q)$, the Pohlig-Hellman attack proceeds as follows:

1) Check whether the order n of the subgroup generated by P is composite. If it is, take the prime factorization of $n = p_1^{e_1} p_2^{e_2} \cdots p_r^{e_r}$, where the p_i are distinct primes and the e_i ($1 \leqslant i \leqslant r$) are exponents.
2) Compute $k_i \equiv k \pmod{p_i^{e_i}}$ where $1 \leqslant i \leqslant r$. Solve the system of congruences

$$k \equiv k_1 \pmod{p_1^{e_1}} \tag{9-93}$$
$$k \equiv k_2 \pmod{p_2^{e_2}} \tag{9-94}$$
$$\vdots \tag{9-95}$$
$$k \equiv k_r \pmod{p_r^{e_r}} \tag{9-96}$$

where $0 \leqslant k_i < p_i^{e_i}$. Once all k_i are discovered, the master scalar k can be rapidly recovered using the Chinese Remainder Theorem.

3) Representing k_i as a base p_i number such that

$$k_i = a_0 + a_1 p_i + a_2 p_i^2 + \cdots + a_{e_i - 1} p_i^{e_i - 1} \tag{9-97}$$

where each $a_i \in [0, p_i - 1]$, reduce the problem of finding k_i to finding a_i.

4) To compute a_i, let $P_0 = \frac{n}{p_i}P$ and $Q_0 = \frac{n}{p_i}Q$. P_0 has order p_i since $p_i P_0 = nP$, then

$$Q_0 = \frac{n}{p_i}Q = \frac{n}{p_i}kP = k\left(\frac{n}{p_i}P\right) = kP_0 = a_0 P_0 \tag{9-98}$$

since a_0 is the first digit of a base p_i number, $a_0 = \log_{P_0} Q_0$ is found by computing the ECDLP solution in $\langle P_0 \rangle$. Subsequently, to compute a_1, we strip the known a_0 component

$$Q_1 = \frac{n}{p_i^2}(Q - a_0 P) = \frac{n}{p_i^2}(k - a_0)P = \frac{n}{p_i^2}P(a_0 + a_1 p_i - a_0) \tag{9-99}$$

$$= \frac{n}{p_i^2}P(a_1 p_i) = a_1 \frac{n}{p_i}P = a_1 P_0 \tag{9-100}$$

$a_1 = \log_{P_0} Q_1$ is found by computing the ECDLP solution in $\langle P_0 \rangle$.
Similarly, $Q_j = a_j P_0$ where

$$Q_j = \frac{n}{p_i^{j+1}}(Q - a_0 P - a_1 p_i P - a_2 p_i^2 P - \cdots - a_{j-1} p_i^{j-1} P) \tag{9-101}$$

5) After computing each a_i, we determine k_i, and then use the Chinese Remainder Theorem to recover k.

Example 9.5.1 Let E_{8971} be the elliptic curve $y^2 \equiv x^3 + 103x + 25 \pmod{8971}$ defined over GF(8971), suppose the point $P = (6363, 625) \in E$, and $Q = (2533, 1996) \in \langle P \rangle$. Determine the value of $k = \log_P Q$ using the Pohlig-Hellman method.
Solution: First, find the order of P, we can use SageMath, the order $n = 8910 = 2 \times 3^4 \times 5 \times 11$, which factors as $p_i \in \{2, 3, 5, 11\}$.

1) We first determine subgroup of 2. Multiply both sides of $Q = kP$ by $n/2$, and write k as k_1. We obtain $4455Q = 4455k_1P$, where $k_1 \equiv k \pmod 2$. By Lagrange's theorem (Theorem 9.1.2), the order of a subgroup divides the order of the group, hence $4455Q = 4455k_1P = \mathcal{O}$ with $k_1 \in \{0, 1\}$. Since $4455k_1P$ equals the point at infinity, we solve $k_1 = 0$.
2) Determine subgroup of 3^4. $k_2 \equiv k \pmod{3^4}$, representing k_2 as a base-3 expansion $k_2 = a_0 + 3a_1 + 3^2a_2 + 3^3a_3$. Multiply both sides of $Q = kP$ by $n/3$, then

$$\frac{n}{3}Q = \frac{n}{3}a_0 P \Rightarrow 2970Q = 2970a_0P = \mathcal{O} \tag{9-102}$$

where $a_0 \in \{0, 1, 2\}$, hence $a_0 = 0$. Next, multiply both sides of $Q = kP$ by $n/3^2$, then

$$\frac{n}{3^2}Q = \frac{n}{3^2}3a_1P \Rightarrow 990Q = 2970a_1P = (140, 459) \tag{9-103}$$

where $a_1 \in \{0, 1, 2\}$, hence $a_1 = 2$. Next, multiply both sides of $Q = kP$ by $n/3^3$, then

$$\frac{n}{3^3}(Q - 6P) = \frac{n}{3^3}3^2a_2P \Rightarrow 330(Q - 6P) = 2970a_2P = (140, 8512) \tag{9-104}$$

where $a_2 \in \{0, 1, 2\}$, hence $a_2 = 1$. Similarly, $a_3 = 0$. Thus $k_2 = a_0 + 3a_1 + 3^2a_2 + 3^3a_3 = 15$.

3) Determine subgroup of 5. $k_3 \equiv k \pmod 5$, representing $k_3 = a_0$. Multiply both sides of $Q = kP$ by $n/5$, then $1782Q = 1782k_3P = (255, 3783)$, where $a_0 \in \{0, 1, 2, 3, 4\}$, hence $a_0 = 1$. Thus, $k_3 = 1$.
4) Determine subgroup of 11. $k_4 \equiv k \pmod{11}$, representing $k_4 = a_0$. Multiply both sides of $Q = kP$ by $n/11$, then $810Q = 810k_4P = (2166, 1536)$, where $a_0 \in \{0, 1, 2, \ldots, 10\}$, hence $a_0 = 1$. Thus, $k_4 = 1$.
5) Using the Chinese Remainder Theorem on the system of congruences

$$\begin{cases} k \equiv k_1 \pmod 2 \\ k \equiv k_2 \pmod{3^4} \\ k \equiv k_3 \pmod 5 \\ k \equiv k_4 \pmod{11} \end{cases} \Rightarrow \begin{cases} k \equiv 0 \pmod 2 \\ k \equiv 15 \pmod{3^4} \\ k \equiv 1 \pmod 5 \\ k \equiv 1 \pmod{11} \end{cases} \tag{9-105}$$

We find that we obtain the unique solution $k \equiv 8196 \pmod{8910}$ as required, thus $Q = 8196P$. ■

The fundamental reason the ECDLP could be efficiently solved in this example is that all prime factors of the group order are cryptographically small. To guarantee robust security against the Pohlig-Hellman attack, it is absolutely insufficient to merely have a "large order". The chosen elliptic curve must possess an order n that strictly contains a massive prime factor (with length at least 160 bits). The overall time complexity of this attack is mathematically bounded by $\mathcal{O}\left(\sum_{i=1}^{r} e_i \left(\log n + \sqrt{p_i}\right)\right)$.

9.5.2 Pollard's Rho Method

Let n be the order of the elliptic curve E_p over GF(p), and the two points P and $Q \in E(\mathrm{GF}(p))$ such that $Q = kP$. We want to compute $k = \log_P(Q)$, start with a random point $R_0 \in E$ and construct a sequence of points R_i using an iterating function f until a collision occurs. The Pollard's Rho attack proceeds as follows:

1) Splitting E_p into three sets S_1, S_2, S_3 of roughly equal size. In general, the point at infinity $\mathcal{O} \in S_1$, and must $\mathcal{O} \notin S_2$. In Pollard's rho method with three subsets, the partition is commonly determined by the y-coordinate of R_i. Specifically, R_i is placed into one of the three subsets according to whether its y-coordinate belongs to $[0, p/3)$, $[p/3, 2p/3)$, $[2p/3, p)$.
2) Define the original iteration function on a point R_i as follows:

$$R_{i+1} = f(R_i) = \begin{cases} P + R_i & \text{if } R_i \in S_1 \\ 2R_i & \text{if } R_i \in S_2 \\ Q + R_i & \text{if } R_i \in S_3 \end{cases} \tag{9-106}$$

where $R_0 = a_0P + b_0Q$ with a_0 and b_0 independently chosen uniformly at random $\{0, 1, \ldots, n-1\}$.

3) Let $R_i = a_iP + b_iQ$, $i > 1$, update a_i, b_i and make a sequence R_i by using this function until the collision occurs

$$a_{i+1} \equiv \begin{cases} a_i + 1 \pmod{n} & \text{if } R_i \in S_1 \\ 2a_i \pmod{n} & \text{if } R_i \in S_2 \\ a_i \pmod{n} & \text{if } R_i \in S_3 \end{cases} \quad b_{i+1} \equiv \begin{cases} b_i \pmod{n} & \text{if } R_i \in S_1 \\ 2b_i \pmod{n} & \text{if } R_i \in S_2 \\ b_i + 1 \pmod{n} & \text{if } R_i \in S_3 \end{cases} \tag{9-107}$$

where the numbers $0 \leqslant a_i, b_i \leqslant n-1$.

4) To find distinct pairs of integers (a_i, b_i) and (a_{2i}, b_{2i}) modulo n such that $a_iP + b_iQ = a_{2i}P + b_{2i}Q$ using Floyd's cycle-finding algorithm, then compute the value of k as

$$k \equiv \log_P(Q) \equiv (a_{2i} - a_i)(b_i - b_{2i})^{-1} \pmod{n} \tag{9-108}$$

Example 9.5.2 Let E_{659} be the elliptic curve $y^2 \equiv x^3 + 416x + 569 \pmod{659}$ defined over GF(659), suppose the point $P = (23, 213) \in E$, and $Q = (150, 25) \in \langle P \rangle$. Determine the value of $k = \log_P Q$ using the Pollard's Rho method.

Solution: First, find the order of P, we can use SageMath, the point P has prime order $n = 673$.

The partitions of E_{659} as follows:

$$\begin{aligned} S_1 &= \{x \in E_{659} \mid 0 \leqslant x < 219\} \\ S_2 &= \{x \in E_{659} \mid 219 \leqslant x < 439\} \\ S_3 &= \{x \in E_{659} \mid 439 \leqslant x < 659\} \end{aligned}$$

Let $a_0, b_0 \in [1, 672]$ are randomly selected as 104 and 488. Compute $x_i, a_i, b_i, x_{2i}, b_{2i}, a_{2i}$, as shown in Table 9-6. When $i = 14$, $R_{14} = R_{28} = (431, 229)$. Since n is prime and $b_{14} \neq b_{28}$, $b_{14} - b_{28} = 179 - 53 \equiv 126 \pmod{n} \Rightarrow 126^{-1} \equiv 219 \pmod{n}$. Yielding the final discrete logarithm

$$k \equiv (a_{2i} - a_i)(b_i - b_{2i})^{-1} \equiv 587 \times 219 \equiv 10 \pmod{673}$$

Table 9-6: The Steps of Pollard's Rho Method

i	a_i	b_i	R_i	a_{2i}	b_{2i}	R_{2i}
0	104	488	(549,200)	104	488	(549,200)
1	104	489	(104,527)	105	489	(109,495)
2	105	489	(109,495)	107	489	(400,613)
3	106	489	(140,93)	428	610	(637,476)
4	107	489	(400,613)	429	611	(409,158)
5	214	305	(377,539)	186	549	(435,631)
6	428	610	(637,476)	373	425	(598,274)
7	428	611	(98,467)	73	179	(431,229)
8	429	611	(409,158)	146	359	(330,269)

(Continued)

Table 9-6: The Steps of Pollard's Rho Method (Continued)

i	a_i	b_i	R_i	a_{2i}	b_{2i}	R_{2i}
9	185	549	(85,54)	584	90	(68,385)
10	186	549	(435,631)	586	90	(301,380)
11	372	425	(93,509)	500	180	(644,230)
12	373	425	(598,274)	501	181	(435,631)
13	373	426	(289,417)	330	362	(598,274)
14	73	179	(431,229)	660	53	(431,229)

Thus, we conclude $Q = 10P$. ■

When Pollard's rho is used for the ECDLP, the key step after a collision is to solve a congruence modulo n, where n is the order of the subgroup generated by the base point. After a collision one must compute $(b_i - b_{2i})^{-1} \pmod{n}$. This inverse exists if and only if $\gcd(b_i - b_{2i}, n) = 1$.

If n is prime, any non-zero $b_i - b_{2i}$ is coprime to n, so the inverse exists and the method succeeds once a collision is found. If n is composite, the basic behavior of rho does not change, but the system becomes vulnerable to the Pohlig-Hellman attack, which reduces the problem to several subproblems in small prime order subgroups. If all prime factors of n are small, the ECDLP becomes easy.

To resist this, practical systems choose a base point whose subgroup has large prime order. This also makes Pollard's rho infeasible, since its cost is $\mathcal{O}(\sqrt{n})$ group operations, with expected steps $\sqrt{\frac{\pi n}{2}}$. Choosing a prime order subgroup is essential for security and helps defend against both Pohlig-Hellman and Pollard's rho attack.

9.5.3 Key Length

By Theorem 9.1.1, the group order n is approximately equal to the field size p. Since the most efficient generic algorithms for solving the problem have a time complexity of $\mathcal{O}(\sqrt{n})$, which is approximately $\mathcal{O}(\sqrt{p})$, the effective security level is roughly half the bit length of the subgroup order. For example, a curve with an order of $n \approx 2^{512}$, it provides a security level of approximately 2^{256}. This time complexity is the generic cost for the elliptic curve discrete logarithm problem. The computational effort in cryptanalysis can be estimated from the bit length of the key or the subgroup order, as explicitly compared in Table 9-7.

Table 9-7: Comparison of ECC Key Lengths

Symmetric Key	ECC Key	RSA Key	Ratio
56	112	512	1:5
80	160	1024	1:6
112	224	2048	1:9
128	256	3072	1:12
192	384	7680	1:20
256	512	15360	1:30

It can be seen that ECC can use shorter keys while keeping the same security level. Compared with RSA, to reach the same security strength, ECC needs a smaller key length, and in common implementations operations such as key agreement and signature generation are often more efficient. As the target security strength rises, the key length ratio between RSA and ECC widens further. If the RSA key length is 2048 bits, the most efficient method, GNFS, will need 3×10^{20} MIPS-years to factor N. However, if the elliptic curve key length is 234 bits will impose a computational complexity of 1.6×10^{28} MIPS-years. Overall, systems based on the discrete logarithm problem save more resources at equal strength, but they rely on fundamentally distinct mathematical hardness assumptions and do not share a direct evolutionary relationship.

In USA, according to NIST recommendations [118], for security strengths aimed at 2030 and beyond, about 128-bit security usually needs RSA 3072-bit or ECC 256-bit; for about 256-bit security, it needs RSA 15360-bit and ECC about 512 to 521 bits (such as P-521). Therefore, RSA needs larger parameters and consumes more compute. In China, under the guidance of the State Cryptography Administration, elliptic curve algorithms such as SM2 have been widely adopted for commercial applications.

ECC runs over a selected secure elliptic-curve group. In practice we do not choose a curve each time. We set up a library of curves and parameters, define parameter sets for the system, and operate under those sets. The parameters must resist known attacks.

9.6 EXERCISES

1) Prove that the set of points on an elliptic curve forms an abelian group under the operation of point addition.
2) What is the order of the elliptic curve $E(\mathbb{F}_{p^n})$ when the finite field is extended from $\mathbb{F}_p$ to $\mathbb{F}_{p^n}$?
3) Let $E : y^2 \equiv x^3 + Ax + B \pmod{p}$ be an elliptic curve over the finite field $\mathbb{F}_p$. Show that any point on E with y-coordinate equal to zero has order 2.
4) Let $E : y^2 \equiv x^3 + B \pmod{p}$ be an elliptic curve over the finite field $\mathbb{F}_p$. Show that any point on E with x-coordinate equal to zero has order 3.
5) List all points on the following elliptic curves over finite fields:
   (a) $E : y^2 \equiv x^3 + 3x + 2 \pmod{11}$
   (b) $E : y^2 \equiv x^3 + 2x + 7 \pmod{13}$
   (c) $E : y^2 \equiv x^3 + 4x + 5 \pmod{19}$
   (d) $E : y^2 \equiv x^3 + 4x + 20 \pmod{29}$
6) Let $E : y^2 \equiv x^3 + x + 28 \pmod{73}$, answer the following questions:
   (a) Determine the number of points on E.
   (b) Show that E is not a cyclic group.
   (c) What is the maximum order of an element in E?
7) Let $E : y^2 = x^3 + x + 1$, the point $P = (72, 611)$. Compute $2P$.

8) Let $E : y^2 = x^3 - 15x + 18$, answer the following questions:
   (a) Check that it is a valid elliptic curve.
   (b) Check that the point $P = (1, 2)$ is on the curve.
   (c) Let $Q = (1, -2)$, compute $P + Q$.
   (d) Compute $-P$ and $2P$.
   (e) Check that the point $Q = (7, 16)$ is on the curve.
   (f) Compute $-Q$ and $P + Q$.
9) Let $E : y^2 \equiv x^3 + 3x + 5 \pmod{7}$, answer the following questions:
   (a) Find all points of E.
   (b) Compute $2P$ where $P = (1, 3)$.
10) Find all points of the elliptic curve $E : y^2 + xy \equiv x^3 + 1 \pmod{41}$.
11) Use the double-and-add algorithm to compute nP in $E(\mathbb{F}_p)$.
   (a) Let $E : y^2 \equiv x^3 + 23x + 13 \pmod{83}$ and $P = (24, 14)$, compute $19P$.
   (b) Let $E : y^2 \equiv x^3 + 143x + 367 \pmod{613}$ and $P = (195, 9)$, compute $23P$.
   (c) Let $E : y^2 \equiv x^3 + 1828x + 1675 \pmod{1999}$ and $P = (1756, 348)$, compute $11P$.
12) Consider the Elliptic Curve Diffie-Hellman Key Exchange. Let $E_p : y^2 \equiv x^3 + 5x + 8 \pmod{23}$, $N_A = 2$, $Q_B = (3, 2)$. Find the shared key.
13) Let $E_p : y^2 \equiv x^3 + 3x + 17 \pmod{47}$, the point $P = (5, 4)$, $N_A = 3$ and $N_B = 5$, answer the following questions:
   (a) Check that this is a valid curve and the point P is on the curve
   (b) Compute the public key $Q_A = N_A P$.
   (c) Compute the public key $Q_B = N_B P$.
   (d) What is their shared secret key?
   (e) Alice knows the curve E, the prime p, the point P on the curve, her own secret and public keys N_A, Q_A and Bobs public key Q_B. Can she recover Bob's secret exponent N_B?
14) Consider Elliptic Curve Diffie-Hellman Key Exchange. Let $E_p : y^2 \equiv x^3 + 4x + 5 \pmod{2437}$, $P = (28, 111)$, $Q_A = (2192, 975)$ and $N_B = 200$, answer the following questions:
   (a) What point should be sent?
   (b) What is their secret shared key?
   (c) Compute the value of N_A.
15) Suppose Alice and Bob want to communicate using the ElGamal elliptic curve. They agree on the modulus $p = 751$ and the curve $E_p : y^2 \equiv x^3 - x + 188 \pmod{751}$, the base point $P = (0, 376)$. Suppose that Bob's secret key is $k = 85$, answer the following questions:
   (a) What is the public key.
   (b) If Alice wants to send to Bob the message which is encoded as the plaintext point $M = (69, 21)$. Alice selects a random number $k = 113$. Compute the ciphertext pair of points.
   (c) Upon receiving the ciphertext pair of points, Bob uses his private key to compute the plaintext point.

16) Let $k = 12345678$. Provide the binary representation of k and the width-w NAFs of k for $2 \leqslant w \leqslant 6$.
17) Using SageMath code, consider the elliptic curve $E : y^2 = x^3 - 4x$ and answer the following questions:
    (a) Plot the curve over the real numbers $E_{\mathbb{R}}$ and over the finite field E_{11}.
    (b) List all points on E_{31}.
    (c) List the order of each point on E_{31}.
    (d) In the finite field E_{31}, let $P = (1, 11)$ and $Q = (25, 5)$. Given that $Q = nP$, determine the value of n.

CHAPTER 10

Lattice-Based Cryptosystems

Previous chapters explored classical public-key cryptosystems, such as RSA, ElGamal, and ECC. The security of these primitives relies on the intractability of the integer factorization problem or the discrete logarithm problem within classical computing models. However, the advent of quantum computing theory presents a fundamental threat. Shor's algorithm demonstrates that these underlying mathematical problems can be solved efficiently in polynomial time using a quantum computer. Consequently, the realization of large-scale universal quantum computers would render classical public-key cryptosystems insecure. Since merely increasing key parameters is insufficient to withstand quantum attacks, it is imperative to develop new cryptosystems based on alternative mathematical foundations that remain secure in the post-quantum era.

In response to this challenge, research has shifted toward lattice-based cryptography. This chapter focuses on the construction and analysis of such systems. Mathematically, a lattice is defined as a set of discrete points in Euclidean space generated by integer linear combinations of a set of linearly independent vectors. While lattices can be visualized in two dimensions, they are generally defined in an arbitrary n-dimensional space, where n is a positive integer. The mathematical foundation of lattice theory lies at the intersection of linear algebra and high-dimensional geometry.

Topics covered in this chapter:

- Definitions and fundamental properties of lattices
- Computational problems and distance measures in lattices
- Principles of lattice basis reduction algorithms
- GGH public-key cryptosystem: encryption, decryption, and cryptanalysis
- NTRU public-key cryptosystem: encryption, decryption, and cryptanalysis

10.1 LATTICES

Consider the problem of optimally packing identical spheres into a container. In three-dimensional space, the densest arrangement occupies $\pi/\sqrt{18} \approx 74.048\%$ of the volume. This assertion, known as the **Kepler conjecture**, was proposed by

DOI: 10.1201/9781042011087-10

Johannes Kepler in 1611 and marks the origin of lattice theory. While *Gauss* proved in 1831 that this density is maximal for lattice packings, the general proof remained elusive until *Thomas Hales's* computer-aided solution in 1998. Historically, *Gauss* and *Lagrange* applied lattices to problems in number theory, and *Hermann Minkowski* later advanced the field significantly through his work on the geometry of numbers.

Lattice-based cryptography currently stands as one of the most active research areas in modern cryptography. Beyond their cryptographic applications, lattice-based algorithms play a pivotal role in combinatorial optimization and coding theory for wireless communications. The mathematical foundations of this field date back to the 18th century, when Gauss and Lagrange utilized lattice reduction techniques to solve problems in number theory. However, lattice theory did not emerge as a focal point of algorithmic research until the 1980s.

In 1996, Miklós Ajtai published a paper [119] that established a reduction from worst-case lattice problems to average-case lattice problems. This result effectively linked the security of cryptographic schemes to the hardness of solving lattice problems in the worst case, marking the genesis of modern lattice-based cryptography. However, early lattice schemes were often impractical due to large key sizes and low computational efficiency. Furthermore, their complex mathematical structures posed significant challenges for engineering implementation. Consequently, research in this area remained primarily theoretical for an extended period. It was not until the introduction of the NTRU cryptosystem and the formulation of the Learning with Errors (LWE) problem that lattice-based cryptography began to move toward practicality and standardization. In the following section, we provide a detailed mathematical definition of a lattice.

Definition 10.1.1 Lattice

An n-dimensional lattice $\mathcal{L}$ is a **discrete additive** *subgroup of* $\mathbb{R}^n$.

We discuss the properties of being an additive subgroup and being discrete in detail. Recall from Definition 2.9.1 that an additive group is inherently equipped with a vector addition operation. A lattice $\mathcal{L}$ is an **additive** subgroup of $\mathbb{R}^n$ if it contains the identity element $\mathbf{0} \in \mathcal{L}$, and for any $\mathbf{x}, \mathbf{y} \in \mathcal{L}$, we have $\mathbf{x} + \mathbf{y} \in \mathcal{L}$ and $-\mathbf{x} \in \mathcal{L}$.

A lattice is **discrete** if every $\mathbf{x} \in \mathcal{L}$ has a neighborhood in $\mathbb{R}^n$ in which $\mathbf{x}$ is the only lattice point. In other words, for every $\mathbf{x} \in \mathcal{L}$ there exists some $\varepsilon > 0$ such that $(\mathbf{x} + \varepsilon\mathcal{B}) \cap \mathcal{L} = \{\mathbf{x}\}$. Here, $(\mathbf{x} + \varepsilon\mathcal{B})$ denotes a open ball of radius ε centered at $\mathbf{x}$, as shown in the Figure 10-1.

Several examples of lattices and non-lattices.

- The set $\{0\} \subset \mathbb{R}^n$ is a lattice.
- The set $\mathbb{Z}^n \subset \mathbb{R}^n$ is a lattice.
- For any lattice $\mathcal{L}$, if $k \in \mathbb{R}$, then $k\mathcal{L}$ is also a lattice.
- The set $\mathbb{Q}^n \subset \mathbb{R}^n$ is not a lattice since the set of rational numbers is dense and not discrete.

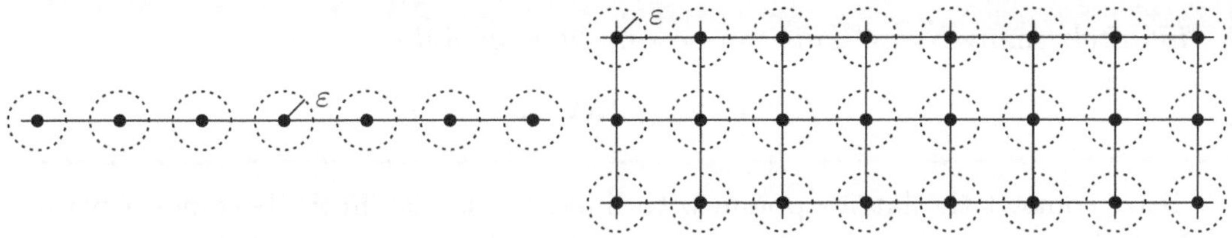

Figure 10-1: Integer Lattices in One Dimension and Two Dimensions

- The set $2\mathbb{Z}+1$ is not a lattice despite being discrete, it does not form an additive subgroup of $\mathbb{R}$.

Except for special cases such as $\{0\} \subset \mathbb{R}^n$, lattices are always infinite sets. To represent them conveniently, we use a finite format called the lattice basis, as shown in Figure 10-2.

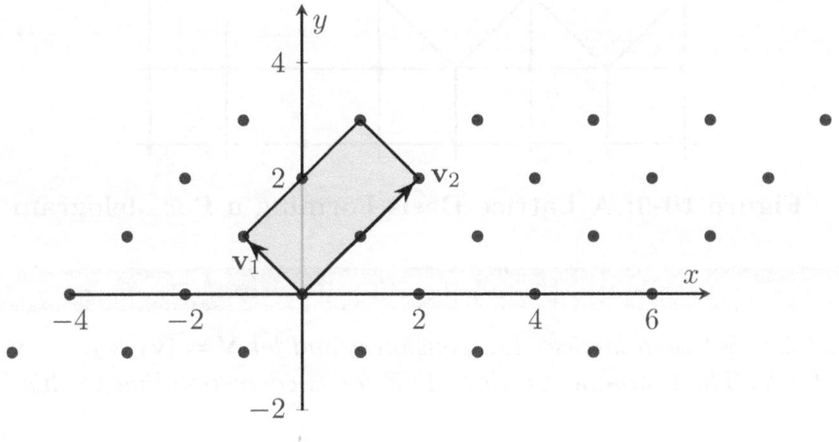

Figure 10-2: Lattice $\mathcal{L}$ in $\mathbb{Z}^2$

Definition 10.1.2 Lattice Bases

In Euclidean space, let $\mathbf{V} = [\mathbf{v_1}, \mathbf{v_2}, \ldots, \mathbf{v_n}]$ *be linearly independent vectors in* $\mathbb{R}^m$ *where* $m \geqslant n$. *The lattice generated by* $\mathbf{V}$ *is the set*

$$\mathcal{L}(\mathbf{V}) = \left\{ \sum_{i=1}^{n} a_i \mathbf{v_i} : a_1, a_2, \ldots, a_n \in \mathbb{Z} \right\} \tag{10-1}$$

of all the integer linear combinations of the vectors in $\mathbf{V}$. *Here, the integer* m *is called the* ***dimension*** *of the lattice, and the integer* n *is called the* ***rank*** *of the lattice,* $n = \dim(\text{span}(\mathcal{L}))$. *If* $m = n$, *the lattice spans the entire ambient space and is called a* ***full-rank*** *lattice. In this book, we discuss full-rank lattices only.*

For convenience, the linear combinations of $[\mathbf{v_1}, \mathbf{v_2}, \ldots, \mathbf{v_n}]$ *are often expressed in matrix form. We write* $\mathcal{L}(\mathbf{V})$ *to denote the lattice generated by the columns of the basis matrix* $\mathbf{V} \in \mathbb{R}^{m \times n}$. *The set of vectors* $\mathbf{v_1}, \mathbf{v_2}, \ldots, \mathbf{v_n}$ *is called a* ***basis*** *for the lattice. The matrix* $\mathbf{V}$ *is non-singular. A lattice has* *infinitely many bases. This can be simplified as follows:*

$$\mathcal{L} = \mathcal{L}(\mathbf{V}) = \{\mathbf{aV} : \mathbf{a} \in \mathbb{Z}^n\} \tag{10-2}$$

If we connect the lattice points with lines, the lattice in $\mathbb{R}^n$ becomes a periodic and infinitely extending grid. In two dimensions, it resembles a tiled wall, as shown in Figure 10-3. How do we describe this grid? We need to use the concept of the fundamental domain:

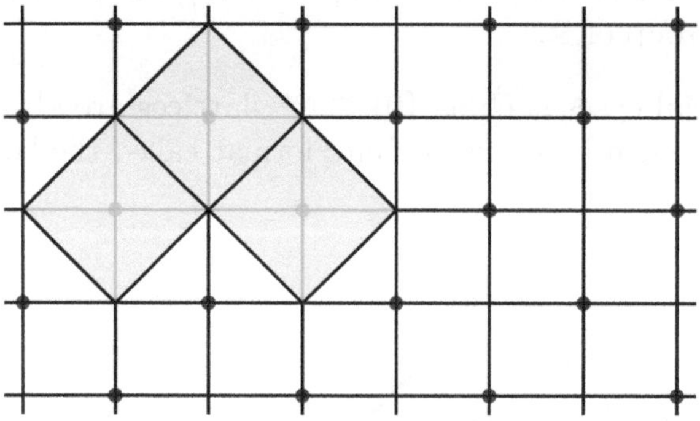

Figure 10-3: A Lattice Basis Forming a Parallelogram

Definition 10.1.3 Fundamental Domain

Let $\mathcal{L} \subset \mathbb{R}^n$ be a lattice of dimension n and let $\mathbf{V} = [\mathbf{v_1}, \mathbf{v_2}, \ldots, \mathbf{v_n}]$ be a basis for $\mathcal{L}$. The fundamental domain $\mathbb{F}$ for $\mathcal{L}$ corresponding to this basis is the set

$$\mathbb{F}(\mathbf{V}) = \left\{ \sum_{i=1}^{n} a_i \mathbf{v_i} | 0 \leqslant a_i < 1 \right\} \tag{10-3}$$

Theorem 10.1.1 Unique Fundamental Domain

Let $\mathcal{L} \subset \mathbb{R}^n$ be a lattice of dimension n and let $\mathbb{F}$ be a fundamental domain for $\mathcal{L}$. Every arbitrary vector $\mathbf{w} \in \mathbb{R}^n$ can be uniquely decomposed and written in the form

$$\mathbf{w} = \mathbf{t} + \mathbf{v} \tag{10-4}$$

For a unique $\mathbf{t} \in \mathbb{F}$ and a unique $\mathbf{v} \in \mathcal{L}$.

Proof

Let $\mathbf{V} = [\mathbf{v}_1, \mathbf{v}_2, \ldots, \mathbf{v}_n]$ be the chosen basis of $\mathcal{L}$ that explicitly defines the fundamental domain $\mathbb{F}$. Because $\mathcal{L}$ is a full-rank lattice, the basis vectors $\mathbf{v}_1, \ldots, \mathbf{v}_n$ are linearly independent in $\mathbb{R}^n$, meaning they also constitute a *basis for the entire continuous space* $\mathbb{R}^n$. *For every* $i \in \{1, \ldots, n\}$, *let* $a_i = \lfloor \alpha_i \rfloor \in \mathbb{Z}$ *and* $t_i = \alpha_i - \lfloor \alpha_i \rfloor \in [0, 1)$.

Consequently, any arbitrary vector $\mathbf{w} \in \mathbb{R}^n$ *can be expressed as a linear combination with real coefficients*

$$\mathbf{w} = \alpha_1 \mathbf{v}_1 + \alpha_2 \mathbf{v}_2 + \cdots + \alpha_n \mathbf{v}_n \quad \text{for } \alpha_1, \ldots, \alpha_n \in \mathbb{R} \tag{10-5}$$

$$= (t_1 + a_1)\mathbf{v}_1 + (t_2 + a_2)\mathbf{v}_2 + \cdots + (t_n + a_n \mathbf{v}_n) \tag{10-6}$$

$$= (t_1 \mathbf{v}_1 + t_2 \mathbf{v}_2 + \cdots + t_n \mathbf{v}_n) + (a_1 \mathbf{v}_1 + a_2 \mathbf{v}_2 + \cdots + a_n \mathbf{v}_n) \tag{10-7}$$

$$= \mathbf{t} + \mathbf{v} \tag{10-8}$$

The coefficients t_i *strictly satisfy* $0 \leqslant t_i < 1$, *which mathematically guarantees that* $\mathbf{t} \in \mathbb{F}$. *Simultaneously, the coefficients* a_i *are strictly integers* ($a_i \in \mathbb{Z}$), *which perfectly defines* $\mathbf{v}$ *as an integer linear combination of the basis, ensuring* $\mathbf{v} \in \mathcal{L}$. *The uniqueness follows naturally from the unique fractional and integer decomposition of real numbers.*

Definition 10.1.4 Integer Lattice

An integer lattice is defined as a lattice in which all vectors have integer coordinates. That is, for $n \geqslant 1$, *an integer lattice is an additive subgroup of* $\mathbb{Z}^n$.

An integer matrix is said to be ***unimodular*** *if its determinant is* ± 1.

Example 10.1.1 Consider the 2-dimensional lattice $\mathcal{L} \subset \mathbb{R}^2$ generated by the two vectors $\mathbf{v}_1 = (3, 5)^T$ and $\mathbf{v}_2 = (8, 9)^T$, then the matrix $\mathbf{V}$ is

$$\mathbf{V} = [\mathbf{v}_1, \mathbf{v}_2] = \begin{bmatrix} 3 & 8 \\ 5 & 9 \end{bmatrix}$$

The matrix $\mathbf{V}$ is also known as a basis matrix or generator matrix of $\mathcal{L}$.

Example 10.1.2 Consider the 3-dimensional lattice $\mathcal{L} \subset \mathbb{R}^3$ generated by the two vectors $\mathbf{v}_1 = (2, 6, 3)^T$, $\mathbf{v}_2 = (1, -2, 5)^T$ and $\mathbf{v}_3 = (3, 4, -5)^T$, then the generator matrix $\mathbf{V}$ is

$$\mathbf{V} = \begin{bmatrix} 2 & 1 & 3 \\ 6 & -2 & 4 \\ 3 & 5 & -5 \end{bmatrix}$$

In the fundamental domains, the **Voronoi Cell** of a lattice is a notable concept. Voronoi Cell is the set of all points in $\mathbb{R}^n$ that are closer to the origin than to any other lattice point

$$\mathcal{V}(\mathcal{L}) = \{\mathbf{x} \in \mathbb{R}^n : \|\mathbf{x}\| < \|\mathbf{x} - \mathbf{v}\|, \forall \mathbf{v} \in \mathcal{L} \backslash \{\mathbf{0}\}\} \tag{10-9}$$

The fundamental domain of a lattice is not unique. However, once a metric is fixed, the Voronoi cell is uniquely determined by the lattice. The Voronoi cell at any lattice point is a translate of the Voronoi cell at the origin.

10.2 COMPUTATIONAL PROBLEMS

10.2.1 Minimum Distance

We begin with a brief review of linear algebra concepts essential to lattice theory. Consider a vector $\mathbf{v}$ in the n-dimensional Euclidean space $\mathbb{R}^n$, represented by its components $(v_1, v_2, \ldots, v_n)$. The Euclidean length, or ℓ_2-norm, of $\mathbf{v}$ is defined as

$$\|\mathbf{v}\| = \sqrt{v_1^2 + v_2^2 + \cdots + v_n^2} \tag{10-10}$$

For a set of basis vectors $\{\mathbf{v}_1, \mathbf{v}_2, \ldots, \mathbf{v}_n\}$ spanning a vector space, the basis is said to be **orthogonal** if the pairwise inner product of distinct basis vectors is zero. That is

$$\mathbf{v}_i \cdot \mathbf{v}_j = 0 \quad \text{if } i \neq j \tag{10-11}$$

Since the lattice $\mathcal{L}$ is discrete, there exists a shortest non-zero vector $\mathbf{v} \in \mathcal{L}$. Its length represents the minimum distance between lattice points. The shortest non-zero vector is not unique, as shown in Figure 10-4.

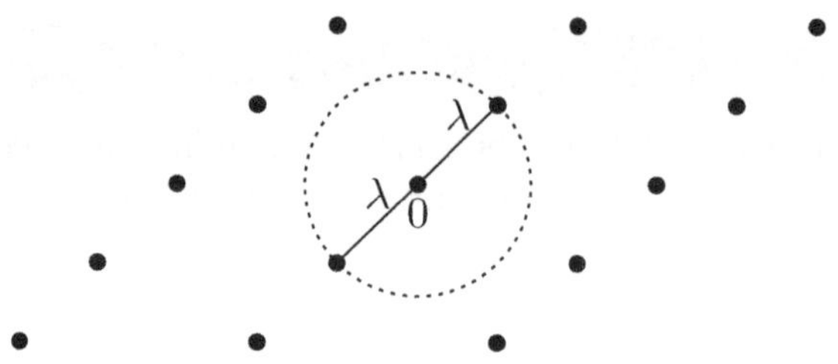

Figure 10-4: Minimum Distance

Definition 10.2.1 Minimum Distance

The minimum distance of a lattice $\mathcal{L}$ is defined as

$$\lambda_1(\mathcal{L}) = \min_{\mathbf{v} \in \mathcal{L}\setminus\{\mathbf{0}\}} \|\mathbf{v}\| = \min_{\text{distinct } \mathbf{x}, \mathbf{y} \in \mathcal{L}} \|\mathbf{x} - \mathbf{y}\| \tag{10-12}$$

where $\|\cdot\|$ denotes the Euclidean norm.

The **determinant** of a lattice $\mathcal{L}(\mathbf{V})$, denoted $det(\mathcal{L}(\mathbf{V})) = \sqrt{det\,(\mathbf{V}^\top\mathbf{V})}$, is defined as $vol(\mathbb{F})$ where $\mathbb{F}$ is any fundamental region of $\mathcal{L}$ and $\mathbf{V}$ is any basis of $\mathcal{L}$. The determinant of $\mathcal{L}$ is also called the **volume** of $\mathcal{L}$.

If the lattice is full-rank, the expression reduces to $det(\mathcal{L}) = |det(\mathbf{V})|$.

Definition 10.2.2 Hadamard Inequality

Let $\mathcal{L} \subset \mathbb{R}^n$ be an n-dimensional lattice, $\mathbf{V} = [\mathbf{v}_1, \mathbf{v}_2, \ldots, \mathbf{v}_n]$ be basis for $\mathcal{L}$, and $\mathbb{F}$ be a fundamental domain for $\mathcal{L}$. Then

$$det(\mathcal{L}) = vol(\mathbb{F}) \leqslant \|\mathbf{v}_1\|\,\|\mathbf{v}_2\|\cdots\|\mathbf{v}_n\| \tag{10-13}$$

Equality is achieved only when the given basis is orthogonal.

Theorem 10.2.1 Minkowski's Convex Body Theorem

Let $\mathcal{L} \subset \mathbb{R}^n$ be an n-dimensional lattice. If $S \subset \mathbb{R}^n$ is a convex, centrally symmetric set, and its volume satisfies

$$\mathrm{vol}(S) > 2^n \cdot \det(\mathcal{L}) \tag{10-14}$$

then S contains a non-zero lattice point. If S is also closed, then it suffices to take

$$\mathrm{vol}(S) \geqslant 2^n \cdot \det(\mathcal{L}) \tag{10-15}$$

Here, we say that a set of numbers is **bounded** if there is a number M so that the size of every element in the set is no more than M. In other words, for any element $s \in S$, there exist $\|s\| \leqslant M$, called an upper bound of S.

Proof

Let $S/2 = \{\mathbf{x} : 2\mathbf{x} \in S\}$ be the set obtained by scaling S by a factor of $1/2$. In n-dimensional space, the volume of $S/2$ mathematically satisfies

$$\mathrm{vol}(S/2) = 2^{-n}\,\mathrm{vol}(S) > \det(\mathcal{L}) \tag{10-16}$$

There exists $\mathbf{z}_1, \mathbf{z}_2 \in S/2$ such that $\mathbf{z}_1 - \mathbf{z}_2 \in \mathcal{L}\backslash\{\mathbf{0}\}$.

By definition, of $S/2 = \{\mathbf{x} : 2\mathbf{x} \in S\}$, so $2\mathbf{z}_1, 2\mathbf{z}_2 \in S$. Since S is symmetric, we have $-2\mathbf{z}_2 \in S$, and S is convexity, we have

$$\mathbf{z}_1 - \mathbf{z}_2 = \frac{2\mathbf{z}_1 - 2\mathbf{z}_2}{2} \in S \tag{10-17}$$

Therefore, there is a non-zero lattice vector contained in the set S.

Based on Minkowski's Convex Body Theorem [120], it is easy to derive Minkowski's First Theorem.

Theorem 10.2.2 Minkowski's First Theorem

Let $\mathcal{L} \subset \mathbb{R}^n$ be an n-dimensional lattice, the length of its shortest non-zero vector strictly satisfies:

$$\lambda_1(\mathcal{L}) \leqslant \sqrt{n} \cdot \det(\mathcal{L})^{1/n} \tag{10-18}$$

Proof

Without loss of generality, assume that $\det(\mathcal{L}) = 1$. This can be achieved by scaling the lattice by a factor of $\det(\mathcal{L})^{-1/n}$, which scales the first successive minimum λ_1 by the same factor. Consider the set $S = \mathcal{B}(\mathbf{0}, \sqrt{n})$, which explicitly represents the closed n-dimensional Euclidean ball of radius $\sqrt{n}$

centered at the origin. Note that the hypercube $[-1,1]^n$*, which has a side length of 2 and volume* 2^n*, is contained within S. Consequently, we have* $\mathrm{vol}(S) \geqslant 2^n$ *(with strict inequality for* $n > 1$*).*

Since S is a convex, symmetric set, by Theorem 10.2.1 that S contains a non-zero lattice point. The derived bound on λ_1 *follows immediately.*

Definition 10.2.3 Gaussian Heuristic

Let $\mathcal{L} \subset \mathbb{R}^n$ *be an n-dimensional lattice, when n is large, the Gaussian expected shortest length is*

$$\|\mathbf{v}_{shortest}\| \approx \sqrt{\frac{n}{2\pi e}}(det(\mathcal{L}))^{1/n} \tag{10-19}$$

Proof

Let the volume of a ball of radius r in $\mathbb{R}^n$ *be* $V_n(r) = \frac{\pi^{n/2} r^n}{\Gamma(n/2+1)}$*. By taking the n-th root of both sides, we obtain:*

$$V_n^{1/n} = \frac{\pi^{\frac{1}{2}} r}{\Gamma\left(\frac{n}{2}+1\right)^{1/n}} \tag{10-20}$$

When the dimension n is sufficiently large, we can mathematically evaluate the asymptotic behavior of the Gamma function using Stirling's approximation (i.e., $\Gamma(x+1) \approx \sqrt{2\pi x}(x/e)^x$*). Ignoring the sub-exponential polynomial terms, the denominator approximates to* $\left((\frac{n}{2e})^{n/2}\right)^{1/n} = (\frac{n}{2e})^{1/2}$*. Substituting this back into the expression yields:*

$$V_n \approx \frac{\pi^{\frac{1}{2}} r}{(n/2e)^{1/2}} = \sqrt{\frac{2\pi e}{n}} r \tag{10-21}$$

$$\Rightarrow r \approx \sqrt{\frac{n}{2\pi e}} V_n^{1/n} \tag{10-22}$$

by setting the expected value to 1, we equate the volume of the Euclidean ball to the volume of the fundamental domain. Consequently, the radius r of this specific ball conceptually approximates the expected length of the shortest vector. Substituting V_n *with* $\det(\mathcal{L})$ *and r with* $\|\mathbf{v}_{\text{shortest}}\|$*, the Gaussian expected shortest length is:*

$$\|\mathbf{v}_{shortest}\| \approx \sqrt{\frac{n}{2\pi e}} det(\mathcal{L})^{1/n} \tag{10-23}$$

10.2.2 Shortest Vector Problem

In this section, we formally define several fundamental computational problems on lattices. Among these, the Shortest Vector Problem (SVP) is of central importance, serving as the foundation for the security of lattice-based cryptosystems.

Definition 10.2.4 Shortest Vector Problem

Given a basis $\mathbf{V}$ *for a lattice* $\mathcal{L}$, *we define the following three variants of the Shortest Vector Problem:*

1) ***Search SVP****: Find a non-zero lattice vector* $\mathbf{v} \in \mathcal{L}$ *such that*

$$\|\mathbf{v}\| = \lambda_1(\mathcal{L}(\mathbf{V})) \tag{10-24}$$

2) ***Decision SVP****: Given a basis* $\mathbf{V}$ *of* $\mathcal{L}$ *and a real number* $d > 0$, *distinguish between the cases* $\lambda_1(\mathcal{L}(\mathbf{V})) \leqslant d$ *and* $\lambda_1(\mathcal{L}(\mathbf{V})) > d$.
3) ***Calculation SVP****: Compute the exact value of* $\lambda_1(\mathcal{L}(\mathbf{V}))$.

Example 10.2.1 In $\mathbb{Z}^2$, the original point to $(0, 1), (0, -1), (1, 0), (-1, 0)$ are all the shortest vectors. As shown in Figure 10-5.

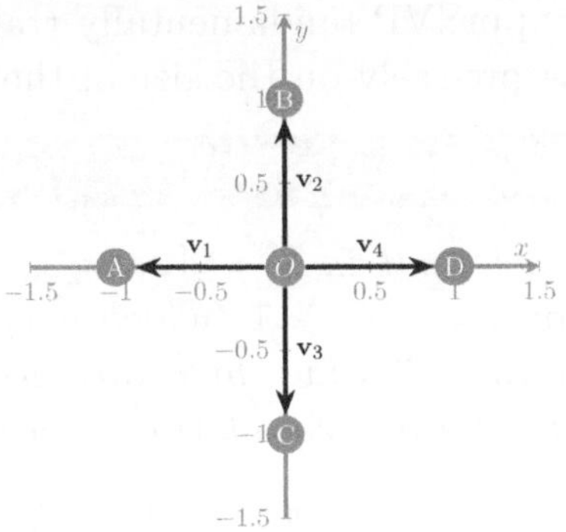

Figure 10-5: Four Shortest Vectors

Example 10.2.2 Figure 10-6 presents another classic example. Given a lattice basis $[\mathbf{v}_1, \mathbf{v}_2]$, we can determine a point closest to the origin, which is represented by $\mathbf{v}_2 - \mathbf{v}_1$.

If the lattice basis is poorly chosen and the dimension of lattice is large, computing λ_1 is not a trivial task. The SVP gets harder as the lattice dimension increases. Although Theorem 10.2.1 states that the shortest distance is upper-bounded by $\lambda_1 \leqslant \sqrt{n}\det(\mathcal{L})^{1/n}$, allowing us to determine its upper and lower bounds, finding the exact value remains difficult. However, cryptosystems based on NP-hard problems often rely on a trapdoor for this problem to facilitate communication between parties. Exact SVP is demonstrably NP-hard under randomized reductions. Consequently, as the lattice dimension n scales to cryptographic sizes (e.g., $n \geqslant 512$), finding the absolute shortest vector requires exponential time, making it computationally intractable. Therefore, the foundational hardness assumption for modern lattice-based cryptography (including NIST Post-Quantum standards) does not rely on exact

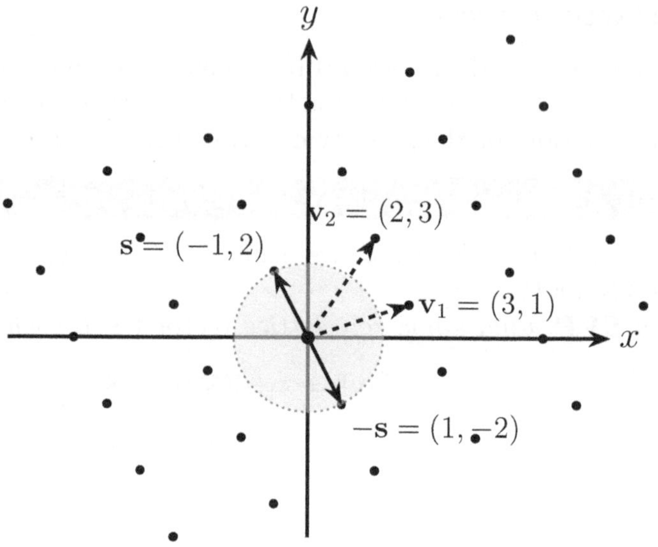

Figure 10-6: Shortest Vector Problem

SVP, but rather on the Approximate Shortest Vector Problem (apprSVP or SVP_γ). The complexity of solving apprSVP fundamentally transitions from exponential to polynomial time depending precisely on the size of the approximation factor γ.

Definition 10.2.5 Approximate Shortest Vector Problem

Given a full-rank basis matrix $\mathbf{V} = [\mathbf{v}_1, \mathbf{v}_2, \ldots, \mathbf{v}_n]$ of a lattice $\mathcal{L}$ and an approximation factor $\gamma = \gamma(n) \geqslant 1$ (which is typically a function of the dimension n), we define the following three variants:

1) ***Search $\mathbf{SVP}_\gamma$*** *: Find a non-zero lattice vector $\mathbf{v} \in \mathcal{L} \setminus \{\mathbf{0}\}$ such that*

$$0 < \|\mathbf{v}\| \leqslant \gamma \cdot \lambda_1(\mathcal{L}(\mathbf{V})) \tag{10-25}$$

2) ***Decision $\mathbf{SVP}_\gamma$****: Given a real number $d > 0$, distinguish between the cases $\lambda_1(\mathcal{L}(\mathbf{V})) \leqslant d$ and $\lambda_1(\mathcal{L}(\mathbf{V})) > \gamma \cdot d$.*
3) ***Estimation $\mathbf{SVP}_\gamma$****: Compute a real number d such that*

$$\lambda_1(\mathcal{L}(\mathbf{V})) \leqslant d \leqslant \gamma \cdot \lambda_1(\mathcal{L}(\mathbf{V})) \tag{10-26}$$

The exact SVP is equivalent to γ-approximate SVP for $\gamma = 1$. Typically, references to SVP or appSVP imply the search version. However, since the search version is often computationally intractable, Decision and Estimation versions were introduced to simplify the problem. The Decision version is also called $\mathbf{GapSVP}_\gamma$ and Estimation version is also called $\mathbf{EstSVP}_\gamma$.

In other words, given the shortest non-zero vector $\mathbf{v}_{\text{shortest}}$ of a lattice $\mathcal{L}$, it suffices to find a non-zero vector $\mathbf{v} \in \mathcal{L}$ that satisfies $\|\mathbf{v}\| \leqslant \gamma \cdot \lambda_1$. As shown in Figure 10-7, when the search range is doubled (i.e., $\gamma = 2$), the number of valid "shortest" vectors increases from 2 to 10. This significantly increases the likelihood of finding a solution.

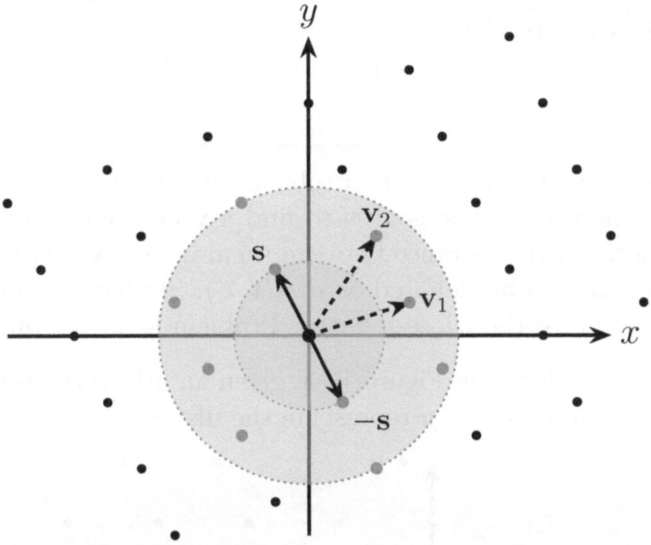

Figure 10-7: Approximate Shortest Vector Problem

Definition 10.2.6 Shortest Independent Vectors Problem(SIVP)

Given a full-rank basis matrix $\mathbf{V} = [\mathbf{v}_1, \mathbf{v}_2, \ldots, \mathbf{v}_n]$ *of a lattice* $\mathcal{L}$*, find a linearly independent set* $\{\mathbf{x}_1, \mathbf{x}_2, \ldots, \mathbf{x}_n\} \subset \mathcal{L}$ *such that*

$$\max_i \|\mathbf{x_i}\| \leqslant \lambda_n(\mathcal{L}(\mathbf{V})) \tag{10-27}$$

Definition 10.2.7 Approximate Shortest Independent Vectors Problem

Given a full-rank basis matrix $\mathbf{V} = [\mathbf{v}_1, \mathbf{v}_2, \ldots, \mathbf{v}_n]$ *of a lattice* $\mathcal{L}$*, and an approximation factor* $\gamma = \gamma(n) \geqslant 1$*, find a linearly independent set* $\{\mathbf{x}_1, \mathbf{x}_2, \ldots, \mathbf{x}_n\} \subset \mathcal{L}$ *such that*

$$\max_i \|\mathbf{x_i}\| \leqslant \gamma \cdot \lambda_n(\mathcal{L}(\mathbf{V})) \tag{10-28}$$

10.2.3 Closest Vector Problem

Another computational problem is the Closest Vector Problem(CVP).

Definition 10.2.8 Closest Vector Problem

Given a full-rank basis matrix $\mathbf{V} = [\mathbf{v}_1, \mathbf{v}_2, \ldots, \mathbf{v}_n]$ *of a lattice* $\mathcal{L}$*, we define the following two variants of the Closest Vector Problem:*

1) ***Search CVP****: Given a target vector* $\mathbf{t} \in \mathbb{R}^n$ *where* $\mathbf{t} \notin \mathcal{L}$*, find a vector* $\mathbf{v} \in \mathcal{L}$ *that is closest to* $\mathbf{t}$ *such that*

$$\min_{\mathbf{v} \in \mathcal{L}} \|\mathbf{t} - \mathbf{v}\| \tag{10-29}$$

> 2) ***Decision CVP**: Given a target vector $\mathbf{t} \in \mathbb{R}^n$ where $\mathbf{t} \notin \mathcal{L}$ and a real number $d > 0$, decide whether or not there is a vector $\mathbf{v} \in \mathcal{L}$ such that $||\mathbf{t} - \mathbf{v}|| \leqslant d$.*

In other words, the Closest Vector Problem involves an arbitrary vector $\mathbf{t} \in \mathbb{R}^n$ that is not contained in $\mathcal{L}$. The goal is to find a vector $\mathbf{v} \in \mathcal{L}$ that is closest to $\mathbf{t}$. The Euclidean norm of the distance between them is $||\mathbf{t} - \mathbf{v}||$. We need to minimize this value. This can also be denoted as $dist(\mathbf{t}, \mathcal{L})$. Similar to the Shortest Vector Problem, the solution to the Closest Vector Problem is not unique.

Example 10.2.3 As shown in Figure 10-8, given an arbitrary vector $\mathbf{t}$ in the space $\mathbb{Z}^2$, we find the vector $\mathbf{v}$, where μ represents the distance.

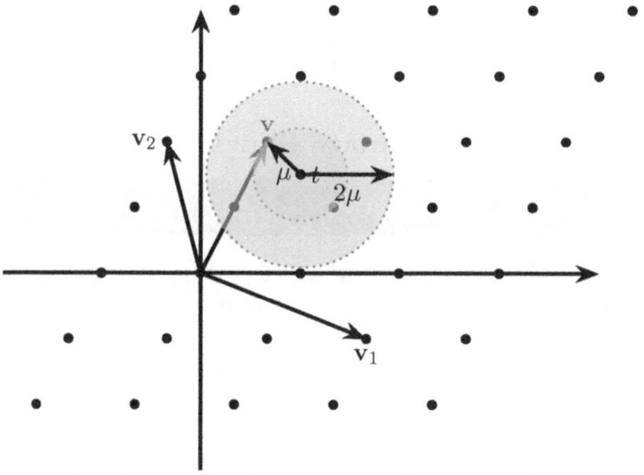

Figure 10-8: CVP and appCVP

Theoretical studies indicate that the exact versions of SVP and CVP are both NP-hard problems. It is worth noting that the SVP can be regarded as a special case of the CVP. In this instance, the target vector is the origin, and the solution requires a non-zero vector. Consequently, there exists a polynomial time reduction from SVP to CVP, denoted as SVP $\leqslant_p$ CVP. This implies that if we can solve the CVP, we can also solve the SVP. Therefore, from the perspective of computational complexity, the CVP is at least as hard as the SVP. In certain algorithmic scenarios, it is considered even more difficult to handle.

Given that solving the exact CVP is computationally infeasible in high-dimensional spaces, modern cryptography typically focuses on the approximate versions of these problems. These are known as the Approximate Closest Vector Problem (CVP$_\gamma$).

Definition 10.2.9 Approximate Closest Vector Problem

Given a full-rank basis matrix $\mathbf{V} = [\mathbf{v}_1, \mathbf{v}_2, \ldots, \mathbf{v}_n]$ of a lattice $\mathcal{L}$ and an approximation factor $\gamma = \gamma(n) \geqslant 1$ (which is typically a function of the dimension n), we define the following two variants

1) ***Search*** $\textbf{CVP}_\gamma$: *Given a target vector* $\mathbf{t} \in \mathbb{R}^n$ *where* $\mathbf{t} \notin \mathcal{L}$*. Find a vector* $\mathbf{v} \in \mathcal{L}$ *such that*

$$\|\mathbf{t} - \mathbf{v}\| \leqslant \gamma \cdot dist(\mathbf{t}, \mathcal{L}) \tag{10-30}$$

where $dist(\mathbf{t}, \mathcal{L}) = \min_{\mathbf{v} \in \mathcal{L}} \|\mathbf{t} - \mathbf{v}\|$ *denotes the distance of* $\mathbf{t} \in \mathbb{R}^n$ *to the closest lattice vector.*

2) ***Decision*** $\textbf{CVP}_\gamma$: *Given a target vector* $\mathbf{t} \in \mathbb{R}^n$ *where* $\mathbf{t} \notin \mathcal{L}$*, and a real number* $d > 0$*, distinguish between the cases* $dist(\mathbf{t}, \mathcal{L}) \leqslant d$ *and* $dist(\mathbf{t}, \mathcal{L}) > \gamma \cdot d$*.*

By introducing an approximation factor γ, the CVP transforms into the Approximate CVP, as illustrated in Figure 10-8, when $\gamma = 2$, the number of feasible solutions increases from 1 to 4. However, the apprCVP remains an NP-hard problem for small approximation factors γ.

Another restricted version of CVP is called the Bounded Distance Decoding (BDD) problem.

Definition 10.2.10 Bounded Distance Decoding

Given a full-rank basis matrix $\mathbf{V} = [\mathbf{v}_1, \mathbf{v}_2, \ldots, \mathbf{v}_n]$ *of a lattice* $\mathcal{L}$*, a distance parameter* $\alpha < 1/2$ *and a target vector* $\mathbf{t} \in \mathbb{R}^n$ *such that* $dist(\mathbf{t}, \mathcal{L}) < \alpha\lambda_1(\mathcal{L})$*. Find a vector* $\mathbf{v} \in \mathcal{L}$ *such that*

$$dist(\mathbf{t}, \mathbf{v}) = dist(\mathbf{t}, \mathcal{L}) < \alpha\lambda_1(\mathcal{L}) \tag{10-31}$$

when the distance between a point and the target vector is less than $\lambda_1(\mathcal{L})/2$, the closest lattice point is unique. Generally, BDD is a difficult problem. However, if the lattice basis is sufficiently good, the BDD problem becomes easy to solve.

In lattice-based cryptosystems, the plaintext is encoded as a lattice point. Small noise is then added to this point. This constitutes a fundamental BDD problem. To decode, only a receiver possessing the correct lattice basis, which serves as the key, can perform the decryption. An attacker without the correct basis will find it difficult to decrypt.

As shown in Figure 10-9, to find the lattice point closest to x, the vectors $\mathbf{v}_1$ and $\mathbf{v}_2$ serve as an excellent basis. We only need to solve a simple system of equations. Conversely, if a poor basis is chosen, such as $\mathbf{b}_1$ and $\mathbf{b}_2$, the task is difficult. These vectors have poor orthogonality and large norms. Using $\mathbf{b}_1$ and $\mathbf{b}_2$ to find the nearest lattice point to x is challenging, although a solution still exists.

Since the exact versions of the SVP and CVP are NP-hard, their computational complexity increases significantly with the dimension of the lattice. Obtaining exact results in polynomial time becomes intractable. When the dimension n is large, for example $n > 100$, known algorithms for solving the exact SVP become computationally prohibitive given current resources. On the other hand, approximate

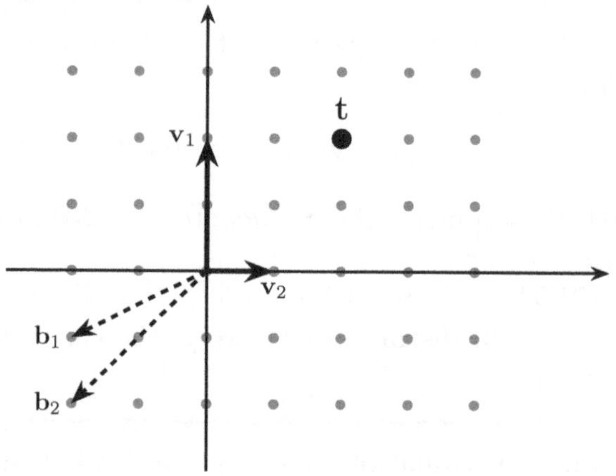

Figure 10-9: The BDD Problem

solutions to the SVP and CVP have significant applications in various fields of pure and applied mathematics.

10.3 LATTICE REDUCTION ALGORITHMS

To date, no polynomial-time algorithm is known that can exactly solve the SVP in arbitrary dimensions. Consequently, when the dimension n is high, computing the exact shortest vector length $\lambda_1(\mathcal{L})$ is computationally infeasible. However, in scenarios where the dimension is small or strict optimality is not required, lattice reduction serves as a powerful practical tool. Unlike exact solvers, lattice reduction does not guarantee finding the shortest non-zero vector. Instead, its objective is to transform a given "bad" basis into a "good" basis. This good basis typically consists of vectors that are relatively short and nearly orthogonal. Through polynomial-time lattice reduction algorithms, we can efficiently find an approximate solution within a factor that is exponential in the dimension n.

10.3.1 Gram-Schmidt Orthogonalization

Let $\mathbf{V}$ be a vector space with an inner product. The Gram-Schmidt Orthogonalization process is an algorithm that transforms a set of linearly independent basis vectors $\mathbf{v}_1, \mathbf{v}_2, \ldots, \mathbf{v}_n$ of an n-dimensional space into a corresponding set of orthogonal basis vectors $\mathbf{v}_1^*, \mathbf{v}_2^*, \ldots, \mathbf{v}_n^*$.

Definition 10.3.1 Orthogonal

A basis $\mathbf{v}_1, \mathbf{v}_2, \ldots, \mathbf{v}_n$ for an inner product space is called an orthogonal basis if

$$\langle \mathbf{v}_i, \mathbf{v}_j \rangle = 0, \text{ where } i \neq j \tag{10-32}$$

After applying the Gram Schmidt process, we obtain an orthogonal basis for the vector space spanned by $\mathcal{L}$, as shown in Figure 10-10. The process is described as follows:

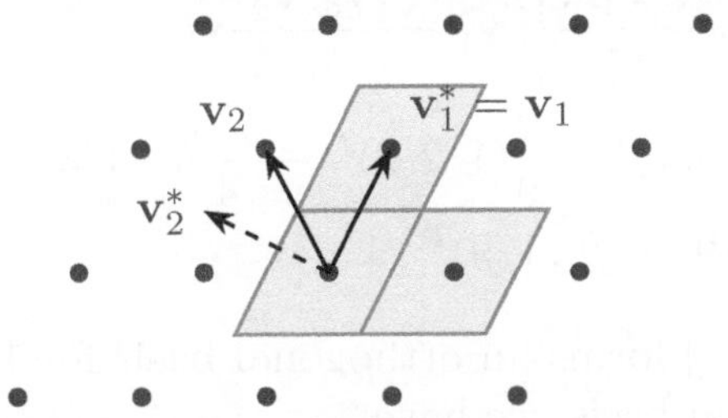

Figure 10-10: Gram-Schmidt Orthogonalization

1) Let $[\mathbf{v}_1, \mathbf{v}_2, \ldots, \mathbf{v}_n]$ of $\mathbb{R}^n$ be a linearly independent list of vectors in $\mathbf{V}$, then set

$$\mathbf{v}_1^* = \mathbf{v}_1 \tag{10-33}$$

2) For $\mathbf{v}_2^*$, we have

$$\mathbf{v}_2^* = \mathbf{v}_2 - \mu_{2,1} \cdot \mathbf{v}_1^* \quad \text{where } \mu_{2,1} = \langle \mathbf{v}_2, \mathbf{v}_1^* \rangle / \langle \mathbf{v}_1^*, \mathbf{v}_1^* \rangle \tag{10-34}$$

3) For $\mathbf{v}_3^*$, we have

$$\mathbf{v}_3^* = \mathbf{v}_3 - \mu_{3,1} \cdot \mathbf{v}_1^* - \mu_{3,2} \cdot \mathbf{v}_2^* \quad \text{where } \mu_{3,1} = \langle \mathbf{v}_3, \mathbf{v}_1^* \rangle / \langle \mathbf{v}_1^*, \mathbf{v}_1^* \rangle \text{ and} \tag{10-35}$$

$$\mu_{3,2} = \langle \mathbf{v}_3, \mathbf{v}_2^* \rangle / \langle \mathbf{v}_2^*, \mathbf{v}_2^* \rangle \tag{10-36}$$

4) For $i = 4, 5, \ldots, n$, to compute $\mathbf{v}_i^*$, we have

$$\mathbf{v}_i^* = \mathbf{v}_i - \sum_{j=1}^{i-1} \mu_{i,j} \cdot \mathbf{v}_j^* \tag{10-37}$$

where $\mu_{i,j} = \left\langle \mathbf{v}_i, \mathbf{v}_j^* \right\rangle / \left\langle \mathbf{v}_j^*, \mathbf{v}_j^* \right\rangle$ for $1 \leqslant j < i$. The number $\mu_{i,j}$ is called the **orthogonal projection coefficient**. $\left\langle \mathbf{v}_i, \mathbf{v}_j^* \right\rangle$ denotes the dot product of the vectors $\mathbf{v}_i$ and $\mathbf{v}_j^*$.

Then $[\mathbf{v}_1, \mathbf{v}_2, \ldots, \mathbf{v}_n]$ is an orthogonal basis for $\mathbf{V}$. Throughout the process, the span of the vectors remains unchanged, that is $\text{Span}(\mathbf{v}_1, \mathbf{v}_2, \ldots, \mathbf{v}_n) = \text{Span}(\mathbf{v}_1^*, \mathbf{v}_2^*, \ldots, \mathbf{v}_n^*)$.

Example 10.3.1 Let $\mathbf{V}$ be the plane in $\mathbb{R}^3$ spanned by vectors $\mathbf{v}_1 = (1, 2, 2)^T$, $\mathbf{v}_2 = (-1, 0, 2)^T$, $\mathbf{v}_3 = (0, 0, 1)^T$, use the Gram–Schmidt process to obtain an orthogonal set of vectors.

Solution: Apply the Gram–Schmidt process, we have

$$\mathbf{v}_1^* = \mathbf{v}_1 = (1, 2, 2)^T \tag{10-38}$$

$$\mathbf{v}_2^* = \mathbf{v}_2 - \frac{\langle \mathbf{v}_2, \mathbf{v}_1^* \rangle}{\langle \mathbf{v}_1^*, \mathbf{v}_1^* \rangle} \mathbf{v}_1^* \tag{10-39}$$

$$= (-1, 0, 2)^T - \frac{3}{9}(1, 2, 2)^T \tag{10-40}$$

$$= (-4/3, -2/3, 4/3)^T \tag{10-41}$$

$$\mathbf{v}_3^* = \mathbf{v}_3 - \frac{\langle \mathbf{v}_3, \mathbf{v}_1^* \rangle}{\langle \mathbf{v}_1^*, \mathbf{v}_1^* \rangle}\mathbf{v}_1^* - \frac{\langle \mathbf{v}_3, \mathbf{v}_2^* \rangle}{\langle \mathbf{v}_2^*, \mathbf{v}_2^* \rangle}\mathbf{v}_2^* \tag{10-42}$$

$$= (0,0,1)^T - \frac{2}{9}(1,2,2)^T - \frac{4/3}{4}(-4/3,-2/3,4/3)^T \tag{10-43}$$

$$= (2/9,-2/9,1/9)^T \tag{10-44}$$

Therefore, $[\mathbf{v}_1^*, \mathbf{v}_2^*, \mathbf{v}_3^*]$ forms an orthogonal basis for $\mathbb{R}^3$. We can normalize the vectors in the orthogonal basis, we have

$$\langle \mathbf{v}_1^*, \mathbf{v}_1^* \rangle = 9 \rightarrow \|\mathbf{v}_1^*\| = 3 \tag{10-45}$$

$$\langle \mathbf{v}_2^*, \mathbf{v}_2^* \rangle = 4 \rightarrow \|\mathbf{v}_2^*\| = 2 \tag{10-46}$$

$$\langle \mathbf{v}_3^*, \mathbf{v}_3^* \rangle = \frac{1}{9} \rightarrow \|\mathbf{v}_3^*\| = \frac{1}{3} \tag{10-47}$$

$$\mathbf{w}_1 = \mathbf{v}_1^* / \|\mathbf{v}_1^*\| = \left(\frac{1}{3}, \frac{2}{3}, \frac{2}{3}\right)^T = \frac{1}{3}(1,2,2)^T, \tag{10-48}$$

$$\mathbf{w}_2 = \mathbf{v}_2^* / \|\mathbf{v}_2^*\| = \left(-\frac{2}{3}, -\frac{1}{3}, \frac{2}{3}\right)^T = \frac{1}{3}(-2,-1,2)^T, \tag{10-49}$$

$$\mathbf{w}_3 = \mathbf{v}_3^* / \|\mathbf{v}_3^*\| = \left(\frac{2}{3}, -\frac{2}{3}, \frac{1}{3}\right)^T = \frac{1}{3}(2,-2,1)^T. \tag{10-50}$$

■

10.3.2 Gaussian Lattice Reduction Algorithm

Similar to how the Euclidean Algorithm computes the greatest common divisor of two integers by iteratively reducing the larger number by the smaller one, the Gaussian Lattice Reduction Algorithm (often called the 2D Lagrange-Gauss Algorithm) finds the shortest basis vectors for a 2-dimensional lattice.

The goal of Gaussian algorithm is to transform an arbitrary basis $[\mathbf{v}_1, \mathbf{v}_2]$ into a basis where the vectors that are not perfectly orthogonal, but is as orthogonal as possible while remaining a valid lattice point.

Given a lattice basis $[\mathbf{v}_1, \mathbf{v}_2] \subset \mathbb{Z}^2$. The algorithm proceeds as follows:

Do While Loop:

1) If $\|\mathbf{v}_1\| > \|\mathbf{v}_2\|$, swap $\mathbf{v}_1$ and $\mathbf{v}_2$ and continue.
2) Compute the nearest integer coefficient μ

$$\mu = \left\lfloor \frac{\mathbf{v}_1 \cdot \mathbf{v}_2}{\|\mathbf{v}_1\|^2} \right\rceil \tag{10-51}$$

where $\lfloor \cdot \rceil$ denotes rounding to the nearest integer.

3) If $\mu \neq 0$, update $\mathbf{v}_2$ by subtracting the projection of $\mathbf{v}_2$ onto $\mathbf{v}_1$

$$\mathbf{v}_2 \leftarrow \mathbf{v}_2 - \mu \mathbf{v}_1 \tag{10-52}$$

and repeat step 2. Otherwise, output $[\mathbf{v}_1, \mathbf{v}_2]$.

Explain why $\mathbf{v}_1$ represents the shortest non-zero vector in the lattice under these conditions. Suppose $||\mathbf{v}_2|| \geqslant ||\mathbf{v}_1|| > 0$ and $\frac{|\mathbf{v}_1 \cdot \mathbf{v}_2|}{||\mathbf{v}_1||^2} \leqslant 0.5$. Let $\mathbf{v} \in \mathcal{L}$ be an arbitrary non-zero lattice vector. We can express $\mathbf{v}$ as an integer linear combination

$$\mathbf{v} = a\mathbf{v}_1 + b\mathbf{v}_2 \tag{10-53}$$

where $a, b \in \mathbb{Z}$, compute $||\mathbf{v}||^2$, we obtain

$$\begin{aligned}
||\mathbf{v}||^2 &= ||a\mathbf{v}_1 + b\mathbf{v}_2||^2 && (10\text{-}54)\\
&= a^2 ||\mathbf{v}_1||^2 + 2ab\,(\mathbf{v}_1 \cdot \mathbf{v}_2) + b^2 ||\mathbf{v}_2||^2 && (10\text{-}55)\\
&\geqslant a^2 ||\mathbf{v}_1||^2 - 2\,|ab| \cdot |\mathbf{v}_1 \cdot \mathbf{v}_2| + b^2 ||\mathbf{v}_2||^2 && (10\text{-}56)\\
&\geqslant a^2 ||\mathbf{v}_1||^2 - |ab| \cdot ||\mathbf{v}_1||^2 + b^2 ||\mathbf{v}_2||^2 \quad \text{since } \frac{|\mathbf{v}_1 \cdot \mathbf{v}_2|}{||\mathbf{v}_1||^2} \leqslant 0.5 && (10\text{-}57)\\
&\geqslant a^2 ||\mathbf{v}_1||^2 - |ab| \cdot ||\mathbf{v}_1||^2 + b^2 ||\mathbf{v}_1||^2 \quad \text{since } ||\mathbf{v}_2|| \geqslant ||\mathbf{v}_1|| && (10\text{-}58)\\
&= \left(a^2 - |a|\,|b| + b^2\right) ||\mathbf{v}_1||^2 && (10\text{-}59)\\
&= \left(\frac{3}{4}a^2 + \left(\frac{1}{2}a - b\right)^2\right) ||\mathbf{v}_1||^2 && (10\text{-}60)
\end{aligned}$$

$\left(\frac{3}{4}a^2 + \left(\frac{1}{2}a - b\right)^2\right) ||\mathbf{v}_1||^2 = 0$ if and only if $a = b = 0$. Therefore, $||\mathbf{v}||^2 \geqslant ||\mathbf{v}_1||^2$ that $\mathbf{v}_1$ is the shortest non-zero vector in $\mathcal{L}$. Figure 10-11 shows a reduced basis in two dimensional space.

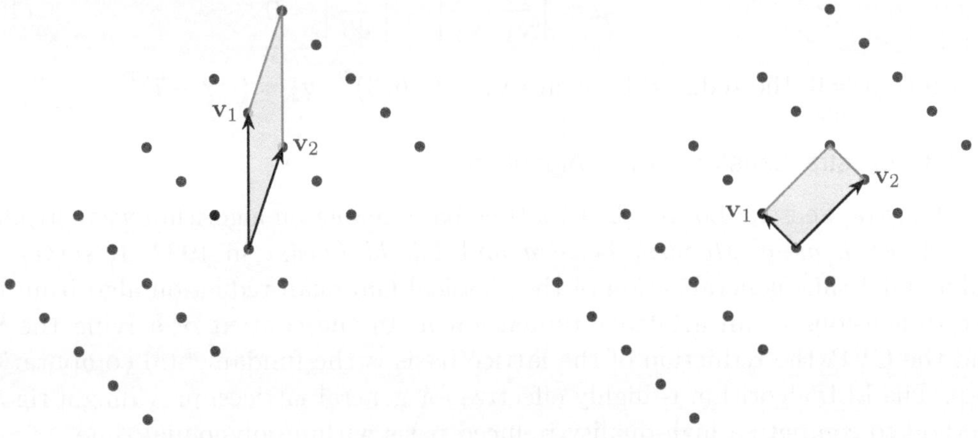

Figure 10-11: Basis Reduction

Example 10.3.2 Let $\mathbf{v}_1 = (90, 123)^T$, $\mathbf{v}_2 = (56, 76)^T$, reduced the basis using Gaussian Lattice Reduction Algorithm.

Solution:

1) Since $||\mathbf{v}_1|| = 3\sqrt{2581}$, $||\mathbf{v}_2|| = 4\sqrt{557}$, therefore, $||\mathbf{v}_1|| > ||\mathbf{v}_2||$. Swap $\mathbf{v}_1$ and $\mathbf{v}_2$, $\mathbf{v}_1 = (56, 76)^T$, $\mathbf{v}_2 = (90, 123)^T$. Then

$$\mu = \left\lfloor \frac{\mathbf{v}_1 \cdot \mathbf{v}_2}{\mathbf{v}_1 \cdot \mathbf{v}_1} \right\rceil = \left\lfloor \frac{56 \cdot 90 + 76 \cdot 123}{56^2 + 76^2} \right\rceil = \left\lfloor \frac{3597}{2228} \right\rceil = 2 \neq 0 \tag{10-61}$$

$$\mathbf{v}_2 = \mathbf{v}_2 - 2\mathbf{v}_1 = (90, 123)^T - 2(56, 76)^T = (-22, -29)^T \tag{10-62}$$

$\|\mathbf{v}_1\| = 4\sqrt{557}$, $\|\mathbf{v}_2\| = 5\sqrt{53}$, therefore $\|\mathbf{v}_1\| > \|\mathbf{v}_2\|$.
Swap $\mathbf{v}_1$ and $\mathbf{v}_2$, $\mathbf{v}_1 = (-22, -29)^T$, $\mathbf{v}_2 = (56, 76)^T$. Then

$$\mu = \left\lfloor \frac{\mathbf{v}_1 \cdot \mathbf{v}_2}{\mathbf{v}_1 \cdot \mathbf{v}_1} \right\rceil = \left\lfloor \frac{(-22) \cdot 56 + (-29) \cdot 76}{(-22)^2 + (-29)^2} \right\rceil = \left\lfloor -\frac{3436}{1325} \right\rceil = -3 \neq 0 \quad (10\text{-}63)$$

$$\mathbf{v}_2 = \mathbf{v}_2 + 3\mathbf{v}_1 = (-10, -11)^T \quad (10\text{-}64)$$

2) Since $\|\mathbf{v}_1\| = 5\sqrt{53}$, $\|\mathbf{v}_2\| = \sqrt{221}$, therefore, $\|\mathbf{v}_1\| > \|\mathbf{v}_2\|$.
Swap $\mathbf{v}_1$ and $\mathbf{v}_2$, $\mathbf{v}_1 = (-10, -11)^T$, $\mathbf{v}_2 = (-22, -29)^T$. Then

$$\mu = \left\lfloor \frac{\mathbf{v}_1 \cdot \mathbf{v}_2}{\mathbf{v}_1 \cdot \mathbf{v}_1} \right\rceil = \left\lfloor \frac{539}{221} \right\rceil = 2 \neq 0 \quad (10\text{-}65)$$

$$\mathbf{v}_2 = \mathbf{v}_2 - 2\mathbf{v}_1 = (-2, -7)^T \quad (10\text{-}66)$$

3) Since $\|\mathbf{v}_1\| = \sqrt{221}$ and $\|\mathbf{v}_2\| = \sqrt{53}$, therefore, $\|\mathbf{v}_1\| > \|\mathbf{v}_2\|$.
Swap $\mathbf{v}_1$ and $\mathbf{v}_2$, $\mathbf{v}_1 = (-2, -7)^T$, $\mathbf{v}_2 = (-10, -11)^T$. Then

$$\mu = \left\lfloor \frac{\mathbf{v}_1 \cdot \mathbf{v}_2}{\mathbf{v}_1 \cdot \mathbf{v}_1} \right\rceil = \left\lfloor \frac{97}{53} \right\rceil = 2 \neq 0 \quad (10\text{-}67)$$

$$\mathbf{v}_2 = \mathbf{v}_2 - 2\mathbf{v}_1 = (-6, 3)^T \quad (10\text{-}68)$$

4) Since $\|\mathbf{v}_1\| = \sqrt{53}$ and $\|\mathbf{v}_2\| = \sqrt{45}$, therefore, $\|\mathbf{v}_1\| > \|\mathbf{v}_2\|$.
Swap $\mathbf{v}_1$ and $\mathbf{v}_2$, $\mathbf{v}_1 = (-6, 3)^T$, $\mathbf{v}_2 = (-2, -7)^T$. Then

$$\mu = \left\lfloor \frac{\mathbf{v}_1 \cdot \mathbf{v}_2}{\mathbf{v}_1 \cdot \mathbf{v}_1} \right\rceil = \left\lfloor \frac{-9}{45} \right\rceil = 0 \quad (10\text{-}69)$$

Since $\mu = 0$, the reduced basis are $\mathbf{v}_1 = (-6, 3)^T$, $\mathbf{v}_2 = (-2, -7)^T$. ■

10.3.3 Lenstra–Lenstra–Lovász Algorithm

The Lenstra–Lenstra–Lovász (LLL) lattice basis reduction algorithm was introduced by *Arjen Lenstra*, *Hendrik Lenstra* and *László Lovász* in 1982. It serves as a polynomial-time generalization of the classical Gaussian reduction algorithm from two dimensions to an arbitrary dimension n. In the context of solving the SVP and the CVP, the reduction of the lattice basis is the fundamental computational step. The LLL algorithm is highly effective for general lattices, providing a rigorous method to compute a high-quality reduced basis within polynomial time.

The LLL algorithm starts with an arbitrary lattice basis and outputs a new basis called the **LLL reduced basis**. Although the vectors in this basis are not necessarily the shortest or closest, they approximate the shortest vector. Therefore, in lattices with low dimensions, it successfully solves the apprSVP. For the standard parameter $\delta = 3/4$, the approximation factor is approximately $2^{(n-1)/2}$ or $(2/\sqrt{3})^n$ with $\delta = 1$. As the dimension n increases, the approximation error also increases. Consequently, the security of lattice-based cryptosystems relies on the inability of the LLL algorithm and other basis reduction algorithms to efficiently solve the apprSVP in high dimensional spaces. In other words, lattice-based cryptosystems must be able to withstand LLL attacks.

Its applications are not limited to solving the apprSVP. It can also be used to attack knapsack cryptosystems (such as the Merkle-Hellman knapsack cryptosystem) and applied in computer science fields like integer programming and polynomial factorization. It is a very powerful algorithm.

Before introducing the LLL algorithm, recall Gram-Schmidt orthogonalization (Section 10.3.1). The Gram-Schmidt process transforms a set of linearly independent vectors into a set of orthogonal vectors. In this context, the subspace is an inner product space described by many linearly independent vectors. The Gram-Schmidt process generates an orthogonal system by calculating the projection of one vector onto another and subtracting it. This process is repeated until all vectors are orthogonal. Note that in the LLL algorithm, we strictly use the Gram-Schmidt process to calculate the orthogonalized vectors $\mathbf{v}_i^*$ to assist in computing projection coefficients. We do not normalize the vectors, that is, we do not force the length to be 1, in order to preserve the original length information.

In the Size Reduction step of the LLL algorithm, we use the projection coefficients $\mu_{i,j} = \frac{\langle \mathbf{v}_i, \mathbf{v}_j^* \rangle}{\|\mathbf{v}_j^*\|^2}$ obtained from Gram-Schmidt orthogonalization to update the lattice basis. If a projection coefficient is found to be too large, specifically satisfying $|\mu_{i,j}| > 0.5$, it indicates that the angle between the two vectors is too small. In this case, we select the integer $k = \lfloor \mu_{i,j} \rceil$ closest to $\mu_{i,j}$ and execute the update

$$\mathbf{v}_i = \mathbf{v}_i - k\mathbf{v}_j \tag{10-70}$$

By subtracting an integer multiple of another lattice basis vector $\mathbf{v}_j$, we ensure that the updated vector $\mathbf{v}_i$ remains within the lattice $\mathcal{L}$ while becoming shorter and more nearly orthogonal.

A lattice basis $\mathbf{V}$ is LLL-reduced if and only if the following two conditions are satisfied:

1) For every $i < j$, we have $|\mu_{i,j}| \leqslant \frac{1}{2}$ where $\mu_{i,j} = \left\langle \mathbf{v}_i, \mathbf{v}_j^* \right\rangle / \left\langle \mathbf{v}_j^*, \mathbf{v}_j^* \right\rangle$.
2) For every $1 \leqslant i < n$, we have $\frac{3}{4} \|\mathbf{v}_i^*\|^2 \leqslant \|\mu_{i+1,i}\mathbf{v}_i^* + \mathbf{v}_{i+1}^*\|^2$.

The first condition is called **Size Condition**, and the second condition is called **Lovász condition** that ensures that the lengths of the Gram-Schmidt vectors do not decrease too quickly. Significantly, the constant $\frac{3}{4}$ is chosen for the simplicity of the paper. This constant is denoted by as δ, the value of δ between 1/4 and 1 can guarantee that the algorithm terminates in polynomial time.

Given a lattice basis $[\mathbf{v}_1, \mathbf{v}_2, \ldots, \mathbf{v}_n]$ of $\mathbb{R}^n$, to get a LLL reduced basis, the LLL algorithm works as below:

1) Reduction Step:
   Set $\mathbf{v}_1^* = \mathbf{v}_1$
   for $i = 2$ to n do
       for $j = i - 1$ downto 1 do
           $\mu_{i,j} = \left\langle \mathbf{v}_i, \mathbf{v}_j^* \right\rangle / \left\langle \mathbf{v}_j^*, \mathbf{v}_j^* \right\rangle$
           $\mathbf{v}_i^* = \mathbf{v}_i^* - \lfloor \mu_{i,j} \rceil \mathbf{v}_j$
2) Swap Step:
   for $i = 1$ to $n - 1$ do
       if $\|\mu_{i+1,i}\mathbf{v}_i^* + \mathbf{v}_{i+1}^*\|^2 < \frac{3}{4} \|\mathbf{v}_i^*\|^2$, then
           swap $\mathbf{v}_{i+1}$ and $\mathbf{v}_i$
           go back to reduction step

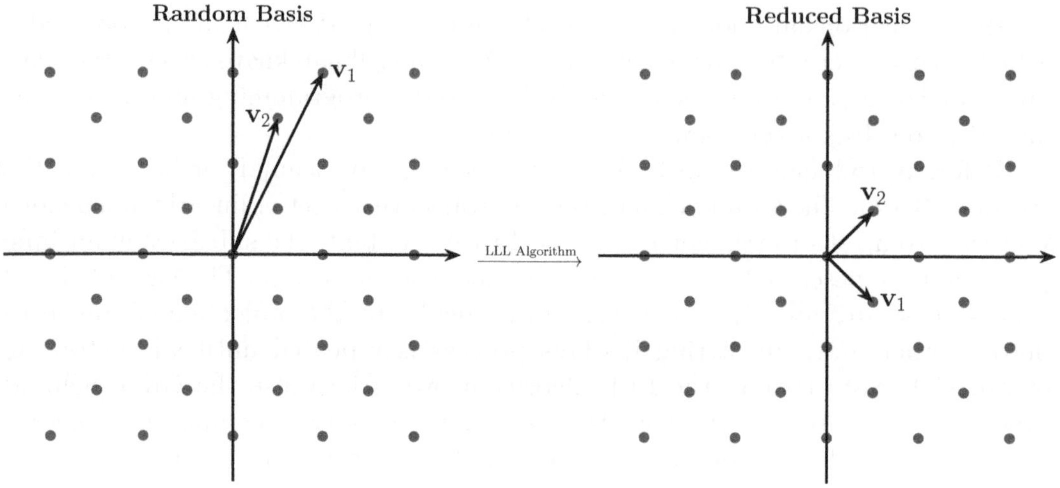

Figure 10-12: LLL Algorithm

The schematic diagram of the LLL algorithm effect is shown in Figure 10-12. For $1/4 < \delta < 1$, the complexity of LLL is $\mathcal{O}\left(n^2 \log n + n^2 \log(max||\mathbf{v}_i||)\right)$.

To evaluate the quality of a reduced basis obtained via the LLL algorithm, we employ a metric known as the **Hadamard ratio.** Recall Definition 10.2.2. Since the volume of the fundamental domain is an invariant property of the lattice, this inequality establishes a fundamental relationship between the lattice determinant and the orthogonality of its basis vectors.

The Hadamard ratio $\mathcal{H}(\mathbf{V})$ of the basis $\mathbf{V}$ is defined by

$$\mathcal{H}(\mathbf{V}) = \left(\frac{det(\mathcal{L})}{\prod_{i=1}^{n} ||\mathbf{v}_i||}\right)^{1/n} \tag{10-71}$$

Obviously, $0 < \mathcal{H}(\mathbf{V}) \leqslant 1$. The more orthogonal are the vectors in the basis, the closer that the value is to 1 because the basis vectors form the sides of the fundamental domain, the volume of the fundamental domain is maximized precisely when the basis vectors are orthogonal to one another.

The following Python code computes the Hadamard ratio:

```
import numpy as np
def hadamard_ratio(V):
    """Return the Hadamard ratio of a lattice basis."""
    V = np.asarray(V, dtype=float)
    n = V.shape[1]

    lattice_det = np.sqrt(np.linalg.det(V.T @ V))
    norm_product = np.prod(np.linalg.norm(V, axis=0))

    return (lattice_det / norm_product) ** (1 / n)

V = np.array([[5, -9, 14],[-4, -19, 15],[2, 3, 9]])
print("Hadamard ratio:", hadamard_ratio(V))
```

Example 10.3.3 Suppose a lattice basis is $\mathbf{V} = \begin{bmatrix} 5 & -9 & 14 \\ -4 & -19 & 15 \\ 2 & 3 & 9 \end{bmatrix}$, apply LLL algorithm to find the reduced basis.

Solution: Do reduction step, we apply the Gram-Schmidt algorithm to find the Gram-Schmidt vectors.

$$\mathbf{v}_1^* = \mathbf{v}_1 = (5, -4, 2)^T \tag{10-72}$$

$$\mathbf{v}_2^* = \mathbf{v}_2 - \frac{\langle \mathbf{v}_2, \mathbf{v}_1^* \rangle}{\langle \mathbf{v}_1^*, \mathbf{v}_1^* \rangle}\mathbf{v}_1^* = (-9, -19, 3)^T - \frac{37}{45}(5, -4, 2)^T \tag{10-73}$$

$$= (-118/9, -707/45, 61/45)^T \tag{10-74}$$

Similarly,

$$\mathbf{v}_3^* = (-17030/9463, 21615/9463, 85805/9463)^T \tag{10-75}$$

The orthonormal basis is $\mathbf{V}^* = \left[\mathbf{v}_1^*, \mathbf{v}_2^*, \mathbf{v}_3^*\right] = \begin{bmatrix} 5 & -118/9 & -17030/9463 \\ -4 & -707/45 & 21615/9463 \\ 2 & 61/45 & 85805/9463 \end{bmatrix}$.

Size Reduction for $\mathbf{v}_2$, since $\mathbf{v}_1^* = \mathbf{v}_1$, we have

$$\mathbf{v}_2 = \mathbf{v}_2 - \lfloor \mu_{2,1} \rceil \mathbf{v}_1 \tag{10-76}$$

$$= (-9, -19, 3)^T - \left\lfloor \frac{\langle \mathbf{v}_2, \mathbf{v}_1^* \rangle}{||\mathbf{v}_1^*||^2} \right\rceil (5, -4, 2)^T \tag{10-77}$$

$$= (-9, -19, 3)^T - \lfloor 0.82 \rceil (5, -4, 2)^T \tag{10-78}$$

$$= (-14, -15, 1)^T \tag{10-79}$$

Update $\mathbf{v}_2$ values. Since $||\mathbf{v}_1^*||^2 = 45$ and $||\mathbf{v}_2^*||^2 \approx 420.58$, $\frac{3}{4} - \mu_{2,1}^2 \approx 0.718$, so $||\mathbf{v}_2^*||^2 \geqslant \left(\frac{3}{4} - \mu_{2,1}^2\right) ||\mathbf{v}_1^*||^2$, Lovász Condition hold. We can compute $\mathbf{v}_3$.

Size Reduction for $\mathbf{v}_3$, we have

$$\mathbf{v}_3 = \mathbf{v}_3 - \lfloor \mu_{3,2} \rceil \mathbf{v}_2 \tag{10-80}$$

$$= (14, 15, 9)^T - \lfloor -0.97 \rceil (-14, -15, 1)^T \tag{10-81}$$

$$= (0, 0, 10)^T \tag{10-82}$$

$$\mathbf{v}_3 = \mathbf{v}_3 - \lfloor \mu_{3,1} \rceil \mathbf{v}_1 \tag{10-83}$$

$$= (0, 0, 10)^T - \lfloor 0.44 \rceil (5, -4, 2)^T \tag{10-84}$$

$$= (0, 0, 10)^T \tag{10-85}$$

Update $\mathbf{v}_3$ values. Since $||\mathbf{v}_2^*||^2 \approx 420.58$, $||\mathbf{v}_3^*||^2 \approx 90.67$, $\frac{3}{4} - \mu_{3,2}^2 \approx 0.75$. Since $||\mathbf{v}_3^*||^2 \ngeqslant \left(\frac{3}{4} - \mu_{3,2}^2\right) ||\mathbf{v}_2^*||^2$, the Lovász Condition fails. Swap $\mathbf{v}_3$ and $\mathbf{v}_2$, we have $\mathbf{V} = \begin{bmatrix} 5 & 0 & -14 \\ -4 & 0 & -15 \\ 2 & 10 & 1 \end{bmatrix}$.

Apply Gram-Schmidt algorithm, update Gram-Schmidt for new $\mathbf{v}_2^*, \mathbf{v}_3^*$ until $||\mathbf{v}_i^*||^2 \geqslant \left(\frac{3}{4} - \mu_{i,i-1}^2\right) ||\mathbf{v}_{i-1}^*||^2$ for all i.

The LLL-reduced basis is $\mathbf{V} = \begin{bmatrix} 5 & 0 & -14 \\ -4 & 0 & -15 \\ 2 & 10 & 1 \end{bmatrix}$.

We can use Hadamard ratio to evaluate the reduced basis. We have

$$\mathcal{H}(\mathbf{V}) = 0.7431 \tag{10-86}$$

$$\mathcal{H}(\mathbf{V}^{LLL}) = 0.9832 \tag{10-87}$$

The reduced basis is more orthogonal. ■

Example 10.3.4 Suppose a lattice basis is $\mathbf{V} = \begin{bmatrix} 12 & 3 & 31 & 45 & 2 & 31 \\ 12 & 41 & 15 & 0 & 4 & 23 \\ 45 & 14 & 0 & 23 & 4 & 15 \\ 21 & 45 & 43 & 0 & 17 & 14 \\ 1 & 41 & 36 & 13 & 49 & 51 \\ 49 & 43 & 22 & 29 & 4 & 25 \end{bmatrix}$, apply LLL algorithm to find the reduced basis.

Solution: The Hadamard ratio of $\mathbf{V}$ is 0.4523, it is a bad basis.

SageMath includes a built in implementation of the LLL algorithm. This allows us to conveniently and quickly obtain the LLL matrix.

```
#LLL Algorithm
A = Matrix(ZZ,6,6,[12,3, 31, 45, 2 ,31,
            12, 41, 15, 0 ,4, 23,
            45, 14 ,0, 23 ,4 ,15,
            21 ,45, 43, 0, 17, 14,
            1 ,41, 36, 13, 49, 51,
            49, 43, 22 ,29, 4 ,25,])
print(A.LLL())# It can also be written as A.BKZ(). The two are
    equivalent.
```

The LLL-reduced basis is $\begin{bmatrix} -8 & -12 & 7 & 6 & -4 & -13 \\ -7 & 0 & 5 & 15 & 22 & -8 \\ -13 & 13 & 1 & 12 & -17 & 6 \\ 9 & 4 & 28 & 0 & 13 & -9 \\ -5 & -12 & 18 & -11 & -3 & 31 \\ 20 & -14 & -14 & 35 & -17 & -2 \end{bmatrix}$. The Hadamard ratio of $\mathbf{V}^{LLL}$ is 0.9301. The effectiveness of the LLL algorithm is remarkable! ■

10.4 GGH PUBLIC-KEY CRYPTOSYSTEM

10.4.1 Encryption/Decryption

The Goldreich-Goldwasser-Halevi(GGH) cryptosystem is a lattice based asymmetric encryption system. Inspired by Ajtai's work along with McEliece's work, three Israeli cryptographers, *Oded Goldreich*, *Shafi Goldwasser*, and *Shai Halevi* proposed this public-key cryptosystem and digital signature scheme in their paper in 1997 [121]. The security of the GGH cryptosystem is based on the intractability of the CVP. Essentially, if the initially chosen basis is poor, calculating the shortest vector becomes difficult. This is especially true as the dimension of the lattice $\mathcal{L}$ increases, making the SVP increasingly difficult to solve.

The GGH cryptosystem is a probabilistic public-key cryptosystem based on lattice theory. Its core is built upon a one way trapdoor function. This function relies on the computational asymmetry of lattice problem. Specifically, the main idea behind GGH encryption is that a public key is a "bad" basis of some lattice, while the corresponding secret key is a "good" basis of the same lattice.

The GGH cryptosystem operates within an n dimensional lattice space. Using a lattice basis composed of n linearly independent vectors, the system can encode a message vector of length n into a ciphertext. However, its public key is an $n \times n$ integer matrix, resulting in a key size as large as $\mathcal{O}(n^2)$. Due to the massive key size and the high computational overhead caused by matrix operations, combined with the fact that its original version has been proven insecure under certain parameters, the GGH system is not practical for real world applications. But it provides an important theoretical foundation for subsequent lattice based cryptographic schemes. The encryption steps of the GGH cryptosystem are introduced below [122]:

1) (KeyGen): Select a security parameter $n \in \mathbb{N}$.
   (a) (PrivateKeyGen): Bob chooses a "good" basis $\mathbf{V} = [\mathbf{v_1}, \mathbf{v_2}, \ldots, \mathbf{v_n}]$ where n is dimension, $\mathbf{V}$ is a full-rank integer matrix. Bob chooses $\mathbf{V}$ as his private key.
   (b) (PublicKeyGen): Bob randomly generates an integer $n \times n$ unimodular matrix $\mathbf{U}$ satisfies $\det(\mathbf{U}) = \pm 1$. Computes $\mathbf{W} = \mathbf{VU}$ where $\mathbf{W} = [\mathbf{w_1}, \mathbf{w_2}, \ldots, \mathbf{w_n}]$ is a "bad" basis, the Hadamard Ratio no larger than 10^{-4}. $\mathbf{W}^{-1}$ is easily to be computed. Bob published $\mathbf{W}$ as his public key.
2) (Encrypt) : Alice wants to send a plaintext, she encodes the plaintext $\mathbf{m} = (m_1, m_2, \ldots, m_n)$ for GGH is an integer vector of the same dimension, and chooses a random small vector uniformly chosen from $\mathbf{r} \xleftarrow{\$} [-\sigma, \sigma]^n$ where $\sigma \in \mathbb{N}$. A typical value is $\sigma = 3$. Then Alice computes

$$\mathbf{c} = \mathbf{Wm} + \mathbf{r} \tag{10-88}$$

   Alice transmits the ciphtertext $\mathbf{c}$ to Bob.
3) (Decrypt): Bob receives the ciphtertext $\mathbf{c}$, and he uses the his private key $\mathbf{V}$ to compute the vector $\mathbf{v} \in \mathcal{L}$ closest to $\mathbf{c}$ by the Babai's algorithm

$$\mathbf{W}^{-1} \cdot \mathbf{v} \approx \mathbf{W}^{-1}(\mathbf{m} \cdot \mathbf{W} + \mathbf{r}) = \mathbf{m} + \mathbf{W}^{-1} \cdot \mathbf{r} \tag{10-89}$$

   If $\mathbf{W}^{-1} \cdot \mathbf{r} \approx 0$, then $\mathbf{m} = \mathbf{W}^{-1} \cdot \mathbf{v}$.

In summary, the good basis $\mathbf{V}$ is the private key, the bad basis $\mathbf{W}$ is the public key, the plaintext is $\mathbf{m}$ and the ciphertext is $\mathbf{c}$. In the last step, we need to compute a vector $\mathbf{v} \in \mathcal{L}$ closest to $\mathbf{c}$ by the Babai's algorithm.

10.4.2 Babai's Algorithm

Babai's algorithm refers to a class of algorithms proposed by the Hungarian mathematician *László Babai* for solving the Approximate CVP [123]. Given a lattice basis

$\mathbf{V}$ and an arbitrary target vector $\mathbf{t} \in \mathbb{R}^n$, the goal of the algorithm is to find a lattice vector $\mathbf{v} \in \mathcal{L}$ such that the distance $||\mathbf{v} - \mathbf{t}||$ is minimized. Note that this does not guarantee finding the global minimum.

Babai's algorithms are primarily categorized into two types: Babai's Nearest Plane Algorithm and Babai's Rounding Algorithm. This book primarily introduces the Rounding Algorithm. Compared to the Nearest Plane Algorithm, the Rounding Algorithm is more intuitive and simpler to implement. It does not require the Gram-Schmidt process recursive iterations associated with the Nearest Plane Algorithm. Instead, it can be executed by calculating the inverse of the matrix and performing simple rounding operations. Its primary drawback is that the error in the output results can be significant.

Let $\mathbf{V} = [\mathbf{v}_1, \ldots, \mathbf{v}_n]$ be the basis for $\mathcal{L} \subset \mathbb{R}^n$, and let $\mathbf{t} \in \mathbb{R}^n$ be an arbitrary vector. If the vectors in the basis $\mathbf{V}$ are sufficiently orthogonal to each other, then the following algorithm solves approximate CVP:

Solve the following equation the real-valued coefficient vector $\boldsymbol{\alpha} = (\alpha_1, \alpha_2, \ldots, \alpha_n)^T \in \mathbb{R}^n$ such that:

$$\mathbf{t} = \mathbf{V}\boldsymbol{\alpha} \implies \boldsymbol{\alpha} = \mathbf{V}^{-1}\mathbf{t} \tag{10-90}$$

The resultant closest lattice vector $\mathbf{u}$ is given by multiplying the basis matrix by the rounded coefficient vector

$$\mathbf{u} = \mathbf{V}\lfloor\boldsymbol{\alpha}\rceil = \mathbf{V}\lfloor\mathbf{V}^{-1}\mathbf{t}\rceil \tag{10-91}$$

where $\lfloor\cdot\rceil$ denotes the rounding to the nearest integer function. However, the quality of the result vector $\mathbf{u}$ from Babai's algorithm depends on how orthogonal the vectors of the basis $\mathbf{V}$ are. If the vectors in the basis are not sufficiently orthogonal to each other, the algorithm might fail to output the correct answer. The Babai's algorithm is illustrated in Figure 10-13.

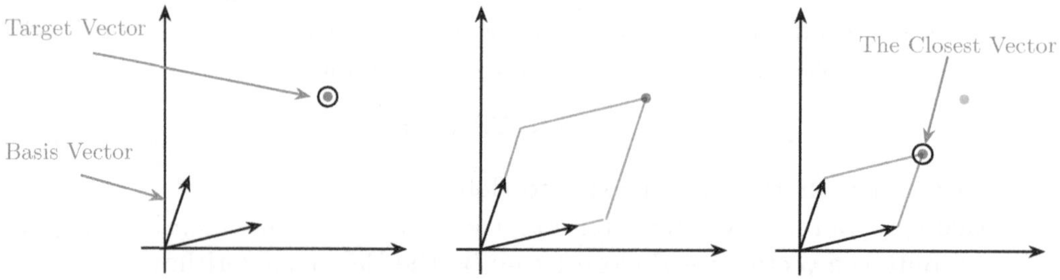

Figure 10-13: Babai's Algorithm for CVP

Example 10.4.1 Let $\mathcal{L} \subset \mathbb{R}^2$ be the lattice given by the basis $\mathbf{v}_1 = (4, 1)^T$ and $\mathbf{v}_2 = (1, 3)^T$, given a target vector $\mathbf{t} = (5, 5)^T$ which does not strictly lie on the lattice. Use Babai's Rounding Algorithm to find a lattice point $\mathbf{v} \in \mathcal{L}$ that is close to $\mathbf{t}$.

Solution: We have $\mathbf{V} = \begin{bmatrix} 4 & 1 \\ 1 & 3 \end{bmatrix}$, $\mathbf{t} = \begin{bmatrix} 5 & 5 \end{bmatrix}^T$. The inverse of $\mathbf{V}$ is $\mathbf{V}^{-1} = \frac{1}{11}\begin{bmatrix} 3 & -1 \\ -1 & 4 \end{bmatrix}$.

Compute $\boldsymbol{\alpha} = \mathbf{V}^{-1}\mathbf{t}$, we have

$$\boldsymbol{\alpha} = \mathbf{V}^{-1}\mathbf{t} = \frac{1}{11}\begin{bmatrix} 3 & -1 \\ -1 & 4 \end{bmatrix}\begin{bmatrix} 5 \\ 5 \end{bmatrix} = \frac{1}{11}\begin{bmatrix} 10 \\ 15 \end{bmatrix} \approx \begin{bmatrix} 0.9091 \\ 1.3636 \end{bmatrix} \tag{10-92}$$

We round each real coefficient α_i to the nearest integer, then $\lfloor \boldsymbol{\alpha} \rceil = \begin{bmatrix} 1 & 1 \end{bmatrix}^T$.

$\mathbf{u} = \mathbf{V}\lfloor \boldsymbol{\alpha} \rceil = \begin{bmatrix} 4 & 1 \\ 1 & 3 \end{bmatrix}\begin{bmatrix} 1 \\ 1 \end{bmatrix} = \begin{bmatrix} 5 \\ 4 \end{bmatrix} \in \mathcal{L}$. The closest vector is $\begin{bmatrix} 5 \\ 4 \end{bmatrix}$. ■

10.4.3 Example

Example 10.4.2 Bob chooses a good basis $\mathbf{V} = \begin{bmatrix} 11 & 0 \\ 0 & 7 \end{bmatrix}$, $\mathbf{U} = \begin{bmatrix} 7 & 5 \\ 4 & 3 \end{bmatrix}$ as his private key and public key.

If Alice want to send Bob a message $\mathbf{m} = (12, 13)^T$, she randomly generates a perturbation vector $\mathbf{r} = (1, 1)^T$, what is the ciphertext?

Solution: Since $\det(\mathbf{U}) = 7 \cdot 3 - 4 \cdot 5 = 1$, the matrix $\mathbf{U}$ is unimodular. Then, Bob computes his public key

$$\mathbf{W} = \mathbf{VU} = \begin{bmatrix} 11 & 0 \\ 0 & 7 \end{bmatrix}\begin{bmatrix} 7 & 5 \\ 4 & 3 \end{bmatrix} = \begin{bmatrix} 77 & 55 \\ 28 & 21 \end{bmatrix} \tag{10-93}$$

The Hadamard Ratios of $\mathbf{V}$ and $\mathbf{W}$ are

$$\mathcal{H}(\mathbf{V}) = 1.0 \tag{10-94}$$

$$\mathcal{H}(\mathbf{W}) = 0.0212 \tag{10-95}$$

Then Bob computes

$$\mathbf{V}^{-1} = \begin{bmatrix} \frac{1}{11} & 0 \\ 0 & \frac{1}{7} \end{bmatrix} \qquad \mathbf{W}^{-1} = \begin{bmatrix} 3/11 & -5/11 \\ -4/11 & 1 \end{bmatrix} \tag{10-96}$$

Alice computes the ciphertext

$$\mathbf{c} = \mathbf{Wm} + \mathbf{r} = (1640, 610)^T \tag{10-97}$$

Alice transmits the ciphertext to Bob. To decrypt the ciphertext, Bob uses Babai's algorithm to compute

$$\boldsymbol{\alpha} = \mathbf{V}^{-1}\mathbf{c} = \begin{bmatrix} 1/11 & 0 \\ 0 & 1/7 \end{bmatrix}\begin{bmatrix} 1640 \\ 610 \end{bmatrix} = \begin{bmatrix} 1640/11 \\ 610/7 \end{bmatrix} \approx \begin{bmatrix} 149.091 \\ 87.143 \end{bmatrix} \tag{10-98}$$

Bob rounds each coefficients to the nearest integer, then $\lfloor \boldsymbol{\alpha} \rceil = (149, 87)^T$, then computes the closest vector $\mathbf{u} = \mathbf{V}\lfloor \boldsymbol{\alpha} \rceil = (1639, 609)^T$.

$$\mathbf{m}' = \mathbf{W}^{-1} \cdot \mathbf{u} = (12, 13)^T = \mathbf{m} \tag{10-99}$$

Bob successfully recovers the plaintext. ■

Example 10.4.3 Bob chooses a good basis $\mathbf{V} = \begin{bmatrix} 58 & 41 & 95 \\ -58 & 82 & 0 \\ 58 & 41 & -32 \end{bmatrix}$ and a matrix $\mathbf{U} = \begin{bmatrix} 98 & 99 & 97 \\ 99 & 100 & 98 \\ 97 & 98 & 97 \end{bmatrix}$. If Alice want to send Bob a message $\mathbf{m} = (52, 25, 99)^T$, she randomly generates a perturbation vector $\mathbf{r} = (13, 39, 19)^T$, what is the ciphertext?

The Hadamard Ratios of $\mathbf{V}$ and $\mathbf{W}$ are

$$\mathcal{H}(\mathbf{V}) = 0.964 \tag{10-100}$$

$$\mathcal{H}(\mathbf{W}) = 0.0047 \tag{10-101}$$

Then Bob computes

$$\mathbf{V}^{-1} = \begin{bmatrix} 32/11049 & -1/174 & 95/11049 \\ 32/15621 & 1/123 & 95/15621 \\ 1/127 & 0 & -1/127 \end{bmatrix} \tag{10-102}$$

$$\mathbf{W}^{-1} = \begin{bmatrix} -0.0951 & 1.3403 & -0.2198 \\ 0.0901 & -1.3461 & 0.2362 \\ 0.0041 & 0.0196 & -0.0190 \end{bmatrix} \tag{10-103}$$

Alice computes the ciphertext

$$\mathbf{c} = \mathbf{Wm} + \mathbf{r} = (3331670, 426647, 1160357)^T \tag{10-104}$$

Alice transmits the ciphertext to Bob. To decrypt the ciphertext, Bob uses Babai's algorithm to compute

$$\lfloor \alpha \rceil = \lfloor \mathbf{V}^{-1}\mathbf{c} \rceil = (17174, 17350, 17097)^T \tag{10-105}$$

$$\mathbf{u} = \mathbf{V} \lfloor \alpha \rceil = (3331657, 426608, 1160338)^T \tag{10-106}$$

$$\mathbf{m}' = \mathbf{W}^{-1} \cdot \mathbf{u} = (52, 25, 99)^T = \mathbf{m} \tag{10-107}$$

Bob successfully recovers the plaintext.

10.4.4 Cryptanalysis

The security of the GGH cryptosystem is established on the difference in lattice basis quality and the computational asymmetry of the CVP. For Alice, she has a good basis characterized by good orthogonality and short vector length. Using this good basis, Babai's algorithm can effectively eliminate noise, thereby recovering the nearest lattice point from the ciphertext $\mathbf{c}$. However, for Eve, she only has a bad basis. It has extremely poor orthogonality and long vector lengths, so she solves the CVP is computationally difficult.

Eve intercepts the ciphertext $\mathbf{c}$. She attempts to recover the plaintext directly using the public key $\mathbf{W}$ and Babai's rounding algorithm without knowledge of the private key $\mathbf{V}$. In Example 10.4.3, Eve calculates $\mathbf{W}^{-1}\mathbf{c}$ and attempts to round it.

Because the public key **W** is extraordinarily skewed, the magnitude of the error term $\mathbf{W}^{-1}\mathbf{r}$ becomes very large. When Eve executes the deterministic rounding operation

$$\mathbf{m}_{\text{Eve}} = \lfloor \mathbf{W}^{-1}\mathbf{c} \rceil \approx \lfloor (98.86, -21.84, 99.46)^T \rceil = (99, -22, 99)^T \qquad (10\text{-}108)$$

Eve finds an incorrect plaintext. We can see that the results are vastly different. Although the third element of $\mathbf{m}_{Eve}$ is coincidentally the same, this does not change the fact that decryption failed. This intuitively demonstrates that using a bad basis fails to correctly eliminate noise and thus fails to restore the plaintext.

The GGH cryptosystem was once considered to possess high security. However, with advancements in lattice theory, the GGH cryptosystem is not secure in all dimensions. Attacks against GGH are primarily divided into two categories: recover the private key **V** and directly recover the plaintext **m**.

Suppose Eve has the public key **W**, which is a bad basis. Although she does not have the private key **V**, she can use a lattice basis reduction algorithm (such as the LLL algorithm) to reduce **W**. If the dimension n of the GGH system is not sufficiently large (for example, $n < 200$), or if the structure of the private key **V** is too simple (for example, composed of very short vectors or diagonal matrices), the LLL algorithm can transform **W** into a set of nearly orthogonal short basis vectors $\mathbf{W}^{LLL}$. This set of basis vectors is often very similar to the private key **V**, differing only by signs or permutations. Consequently, this enables the attacker to completely recover an equivalent private key using only the public key.

Example 10.4.4 Suppose the private key lattice basis is $\mathbf{V} = \begin{bmatrix} -30 & 0 & -83 \\ 60 & 45 & 0 \\ 75 & -89 & -55 \end{bmatrix}$ and the unimodular matrix is $\mathbf{U} = \begin{bmatrix} 1 & 3 & -10 \\ 8 & 25 & -86 \\ -11 & -28 & 81 \end{bmatrix}$. Eve intercepts the public key $\mathbf{W} = \mathbf{VU}$. Attempt to recover **V**.

Solution: Compute the public key **W**

$$\mathbf{W} = \mathbf{VU} = \begin{bmatrix} 883 & 2234 & -6423 \\ 420 & 1305 & -4470 \\ -32 & -460 & 2449 \end{bmatrix} \qquad (10\text{-}109)$$

The Hadamard Ratios of $\mathcal{H}(\mathbf{W}) \approx 0.033$. The vectors in this basis are very long and not orthogonal. Eve uses the LLL lattice basis reduction algorithm on **W** and obtains the reduced basis

$$\mathbf{W}_{LLL} = \begin{bmatrix} -83 & 0 & -30 \\ 0 & 45 & 60 \\ -55 & -89 & 75 \end{bmatrix} \qquad (10\text{-}110)$$

By observing $\mathbf{W}_{LLL}$, we see that the elements of $\mathbf{W}_{LLL}$ and the elements of **V** differ only in the arrangement of row positions and signs. Since the sign of a basis vector does not alter the properties of the lattice, the attacker has successfully found a sufficiently good basis (and even recovered the structure of the private key) in polynomial time using the LLL algorithm. Consequently, the GGH system is broken. ■

In 1999, the French mathematician *Phong Q. Nguyen* presented an in-depth analysis of the flaws in the GGH cryptosystem [124], specifically highlighting the information leakage associated with the error vector $\mathbf{r}$, which is called **Nguyen's attack**. In the encryption process, the ciphertext is given by $\mathbf{c} = \mathbf{Wm} + \mathbf{r}$, where $\mathbf{r}$ is a perturbation vector uniformly chosen from the set $\{-\sigma, \sigma\}^n$, with $n, \sigma \in \mathbb{N}$.

Let a vector $\mathbf{s} = (\sigma, \sigma, \ldots, \sigma) \in \mathbb{Z}^n$, then Eve inserts into the GGH encryption equation, that is

$$\mathbf{c} + \mathbf{s} = \mathbf{Wm} + \mathbf{r} + \mathbf{s} \tag{10-111}$$

$$\Rightarrow \frac{\mathbf{c} + \mathbf{s}}{2\sigma} = \frac{\mathbf{Wm} + \mathbf{r} + \mathbf{s}}{2\sigma} \tag{10-112}$$

$$\Rightarrow \frac{\mathbf{c} + \mathbf{s} - \mathbf{Wm}}{2\sigma} = \frac{\mathbf{r} + \mathbf{s}}{2\sigma} \tag{10-113}$$

Since $\mathbf{r} \in \{-\sigma, \sigma\}^n$ and $\mathbf{s} = \{\sigma\}^n$, then $\mathbf{r} + \mathbf{s} \in \{0, 2\sigma\}^n$. Thus, $\mathbf{r} + \mathbf{s} \equiv \{0\}^n \pmod{2\sigma}$. That is

$$\mathbf{c} + \mathbf{s} - \mathbf{Wm} \equiv 0 \pmod{2\sigma} \tag{10-114}$$

$$\Rightarrow \mathbf{c} + \mathbf{s} \equiv \mathbf{Wm} \pmod{2\sigma} \tag{10-115}$$

If Eve can solve this system then she obtains $\mathbf{m} \bmod 2\sigma$ which Eve denotes by $\mathbf{m}_{2\sigma}$ that is $\mathbf{m} = \mathbf{m}_{2\sigma} + 2\sigma\mathbf{m}'$ where $\mathbf{m}' \in \mathbb{Z}^n$. The congruence is solvable with a few solutions. If certain conditions are satisfied, then a unique solution exists. The solution of the congruences respectively is obtained as the following:

$$\mathbf{m} \equiv \mathbf{m}_{2\sigma} \equiv \mathbf{W}^{-1}(\mathbf{c} + \mathbf{s}) \pmod{2\sigma} \tag{10-116}$$

Let $\mathbf{m}_{2\sigma}$ is multiplied with the public basis $\mathbf{W}$, the vectors $\mathbf{m}_{2\sigma} \cdot \mathbf{W}$ is inserted into the encryption equation

$$\mathbf{c} - \mathbf{W} \cdot \mathbf{m}_{2\sigma} = \mathbf{W}(\mathbf{m} - \mathbf{m}_{2\sigma}) + \mathbf{r} \tag{10-117}$$

$$\mathbf{c} - \mathbf{W} \cdot \mathbf{m}_{2\sigma} = \mathbf{W}(2\sigma\mathbf{m}') + \mathbf{r} \tag{10-118}$$

$$\Rightarrow \frac{\mathbf{c} - \mathbf{W} \cdot \mathbf{m}_{2\sigma}}{2\sigma} = \mathbf{Wm}' + \frac{\mathbf{r}}{2\sigma} \tag{10-119}$$

Since $\mathbf{c}, \mathbf{m}_{2\sigma}, \mathbf{W}$ and 2σ are known $\dfrac{\mathbf{c} - \mathbf{W} \cdot \mathbf{m}_{2\sigma}}{2\sigma}$ is known. The error vector $\dfrac{\mathbf{r}}{2\sigma} \in \left\{\pm\dfrac{1}{2}\right\}^n$ is very small, thus giving the simplified CVP instance with a much smaller error vector, it is possible that algorithms for the CVP that were not successful on the original can succeed on the new CVP. The breaking plaintext is $\mathbf{m} = \mathbf{m}_{2\sigma} + 2\sigma\mathbf{m}'$.

Example 10.4.5 Recall the Example 10.4.2. Suppose Eve knowns the public key $\mathbf{W} = \begin{bmatrix} 77 & 55 \\ 28 & 21 \end{bmatrix}$ and the ciphertext $\mathbf{c} = (1640, 610)^T$. Try to recover the plaintext using Nguyen Attack.

Solution: Let $\sigma = 1$, which implies $\mathbf{s} = (1, 1)$. Add $\mathbf{s}$ to the ciphertext

$$\mathbf{c} + \mathbf{s} = (1641, 611)^T \equiv \mathbf{W} \cdot \mathbf{m}_{2\sigma} \equiv (0, 1)^T \pmod 2 \tag{10-120}$$

$$\Rightarrow \mathbf{m}_{2\sigma} \equiv \mathbf{W}^{-1}(\mathbf{c} + \mathbf{s}) \pmod{2\sigma} \tag{10-121}$$

$$\equiv (\mathbf{W} \pmod 2)^{-1}(0, 1)^T \pmod 2 \tag{10-122}$$

$$\equiv \begin{bmatrix} 1 & 1 \\ 0 & 1 \end{bmatrix} \begin{bmatrix} 0 \\ 1 \end{bmatrix} \equiv (0, 1)^T \pmod 2 \tag{10-123}$$

Checking the actual plaintext $\mathbf{m} = (12, 13)^T$, we observe that $\mathbf{m} \equiv (0, 1)^T \pmod 2$. Thus, Eve has successfully recovered the plaintext modulo 2σ, denoted as $\mathbf{m}_{2\sigma}$. ■

In 2016, the Chinese cryptographer *Yupu Hu* further analyzed multilinear maps constructed upon the GGH framework in his prominent paper [125]. He proposed effective attack methods, which have had a profound impact on various cryptographic applications based on the GGH structure.

10.5 NTRU PUBLIC-KEY CRYPTOSYSTEM

The NTRU public-key cryptosystem was introduced by *Jeffrey Hoffstein*, *Jill Pipher*, and *Joseph H. Silverman* in 1996 [126]. It is one of the most efficient lattice-based public-key cryptosystems currently known, providing both an encryption scheme (NTRUEncrypt) and a digital signature scheme (NTRUSign).

The core operations of NTRU are based on polynomial algebra. Specifically, it is built upon the polynomial quotient ring $R = \mathbb{Z}[x]/(x^N - 1)$, and its operations primarily involve the truncated convolution of polynomials. Its security of NTRU relies on the presumed intractability of the Shortest Vector Problem (SVP) specifically within high-dimensional structured lattices. Because it is distinct from traditional number theory problems, NTRU is recognized as an important representative algorithm in post-quantum cryptography.

The security of traditional public-key cryptosystems such as RSA, ECC, and ElGamal relies on the Integer Factorization Problem or the Discrete Logarithm Problem. Using Shor's Algorithm, these mathematical problems can be solved in polynomial time by a sufficiently powerful quantum computer. In contrast, the security of NTRU is based on the SVP in lattice theory. Currently, no quantum algorithm has been found that can effectively solve this problem in polynomial time.

In 2009, the NTRU cryptosystem was formally standardized by IEEE 1363.1 [127]. As a pioneer of lattice cryptography, NTRU remains an important benchmark for research into lattice-based cryptosystems in both academia and industry.

10.5.1 Convolution Polynomial Rings

Definition 10.5.1 Polynomial Ring

Let $\mathcal{R}$ be a ring. A ***polynomial*** *in the* ***variable*** *x with coefficients in $\mathcal{R}$ is a formal sum of the form*

$$f(x) = \sum_{i=0}^{n} a_i x^i = a_0 + a_1 x + a_2 x^2 + \cdots + a_n x^n \tag{10-124}$$

where $n \geqslant 0$ and $a_0, a_1, \ldots, a_n \in \mathcal{R}$. The set of all such polynomials is called the ***polynomial ring*** *over $\mathcal{R}$ and is denoted by $\mathcal{R}[x]$.*

If n is the largest integer such that $a_n \neq 0$, then n is called the ***degree*** *of $f(x)$, denoted by $\deg(f)$. In this case, the term $a_n x^n$ is called the* ***leading term****, a_n is the* ***leading coefficient****, and a_0 is the* ***constant term****. The generic elements a_i are called a* ***coefficient****.*

The ***zero polynomial*** *is the polynomial with all coefficients equal to zero. Its degree is defined to be $-\infty$.*

Definition 10.5.2 Convolution Polynomial Ring

Let n be a positive integer. The ***convolution polynomial ring****, denoted by R, is defined as the quotient ring*

$$R = \mathbb{Z}[x]/(x^n - 1). \tag{10-125}$$

Each element of R can be represented as

$$f(x) = \sum_{i=0}^{n-1} a_i x^i = a_0 + a_1 x + a_2 x^2 + \cdots + a_{n-1} x^{n-1} \in R \tag{10-126}$$

where $a_i \in \mathbb{Z}$. It is often convenient to identify the polynomial $f(x)$ with its coefficient vector $\mathbf{f} = (a_0, a_1, \ldots, a_{n-1}) \in \mathbb{Z}^n$.

In NTRU, messages are represented as polynomials, the **coefficients are integers modulo** q. Consequently, we use polynomial convolution for representation. Polynomial convolution is also known as polynomial multiplication.

Let $\mathbf{f} = (f_0, f_1, \ldots, f_{n-1})$ and $\mathbf{g} = (g_0, g_1, \ldots, g_{n-1})$. The polynomial multiplication using the convolution formula

$$\mathbf{f} * \mathbf{g} = \sum_{k=0}^{n-1} c_k x^k \tag{10-127}$$

where each coefficient c_k is given by

$$c_k = \sum_{i+j \equiv k \pmod{n}} f_i g_j \tag{10-128}$$

The norm of a polynomial is defined by

$$\|\mathbf{f}\| = \sqrt{\sum_{i=0}^{n-1} f_i^2} \tag{10-129}$$

Example 10.5.1 Let $n = 3$, compute $\mathbf{f} * \mathbf{g}$, where $\mathbf{f}, \mathbf{g} \in R$ be the polynomials are given by

$$f(x) = \sum_{i=0}^{n-1} f_i x^i = -1 + 4x + x^2 \tag{10-130}$$

$$g(x) = \sum_{i=0}^{n-1} g_i x^i = 3 - x + 5x^2 \tag{10-131}$$

Solution: Arrange the coefficients of the terms in ascending order of powers

$$\mathbf{f} = [f_0, f_1, f_2] = [-1, 4, 1] \tag{10-132}$$

$$\mathbf{g} = [g_0, g_1, g_2] = [3, -1, 5] \tag{10-133}$$

Therefore, the convolution product is therefore computed as

$$\begin{bmatrix} c_0 \\ c_1 \\ c_2 \end{bmatrix} = \begin{bmatrix} f_0 & f_2 & f_1 \\ f_1 & f_0 & f_2 \\ f_2 & f_1 & f_0 \end{bmatrix} \begin{bmatrix} g_0 \\ g_1 \\ g_2 \end{bmatrix} = \begin{bmatrix} -1 & 1 & 4 \\ 4 & -1 & 1 \\ 1 & 4 & -1 \end{bmatrix} \begin{bmatrix} 3 \\ -1 \\ 5 \end{bmatrix} = \begin{bmatrix} 16 \\ 18 \\ -6 \end{bmatrix} \tag{10-134}$$

$$\mathbf{f} * \mathbf{g} = 16 + 18x - 6x^2 \tag{10-135}$$

■

The product $f(x) \cdot g(x)$ in R can be expressed in the matrix form

$$\begin{bmatrix} c_0 \\ c_1 \\ \vdots \\ c_{n-1} \end{bmatrix} = \begin{bmatrix} f_0 & f_{n-1} & f_{n-2} & \cdots & f_1 \\ f_1 & f_0 & f_{n-1} & \cdots & f_2 \\ \vdots & \vdots & \vdots & \ddots & \vdots \\ f_{n-1} & f_{n-2} & f_{n-3} & \cdots & f_0 \end{bmatrix} \begin{bmatrix} g_0 \\ g_1 \\ \vdots \\ g_{n-1} \end{bmatrix} \tag{10-136}$$

In the NTRU cryptosystem, operations are performed within convolution polynomial rings modulo p and q. These rings are defined as quotients of polynomial rings over finite fields, given by

$$R_p = \frac{(\mathbb{Z}/p\mathbb{Z})[x]}{(x^n - 1)} \quad \text{and} \quad R_q = \frac{(\mathbb{Z}/q\mathbb{Z})[x]}{(x^n - 1)}. \tag{10-137}$$

The coefficients of polynomials in R_p and R_q lie in $\mathbb{Z}_p$ and $\mathbb{Z}_q$, respectively.

Example 10.5.2 Let $n = 3$, $q = 2$, $f(x) = x + x^2$, $g(x) = 2 + x$. Compute $\mathbf{f} * \mathbf{g}$ (mod q).

Solution: Similar to polynomial multiplication, coefficient arithmetic is performed modulo 2

$$\mathbf{f} * \mathbf{g} \pmod{q} \equiv \underbrace{(x + x^2) * (2 + x)}_{\text{coefficient mod 2}} \tag{10-138}$$

$$\equiv \underbrace{1 + 2x + 3x^2}_{\text{coefficient mod 2}} \tag{10-139}$$

$$\equiv 1 + x^2 \tag{10-140}$$

■

If q is large, we sometimes restrict the coefficients to ensure clarity. Generally, if $\mathbf{f}(x) \in R_q$, the coefficients f_i lie within the interval $(-q/2, q/2]$. This specific and unique integer representation in the base ring R is explicitly called the **centered lift** of $f \pmod{q}$.

Example 10.5.3 Let $n = 3$, $q = 5$, $f(x) = 2 + 4x + 3x^2$, $g(x) = 1 + 2x + x^2$. Compute $\mathbf{f} * \mathbf{g} \pmod{q}$.
Solution:

$$\mathbf{f} * \mathbf{g} \pmod{q} \equiv \underbrace{(2 + 4x + 3x^2) * (1 + 2x + x^2)}_{\text{coefficient mod 5}} \tag{10-141}$$

$$\equiv \underbrace{12 + 11x + 13x^2}_{\text{coefficient mod 5}} \tag{10-142}$$

$$\equiv 2 + x - 2x^2 \tag{10-143}$$

■

Assume that q is a prime number. Then $f(x) \in R_q$ has a multiplicative inverse if and only if

$$\gcd(f(x), x^n - 1) = 1 \in (\mathbb{Z}/q\mathbb{Z})[x] \tag{10-144}$$

If this condition is met, then the inverse $f(x)^{-1} \in R_q$ can be computed by the **Extended Euclidean Algorithm**. To facilitate calculation, we express this as $f(x)u(x) + (x^n - 1)\,v(x) = 1$, where $u(x)$ and $v(x) \in (\mathbb{Z}/q\mathbb{Z})[x]$. Then $u(x) = f(x)^{-1} \in R_q$.

Example 10.5.4 Let $n = 5$, $q = 2$, find the multiplicative inverse of $x^4 + x^2 + 1$ in R_2.
Solution: We employ the Extended Euclidean algorithm to find the gcd of x^4+x^2+1 and the modulus $x^5 - 1$ in R_2. Since we are working in $\mathbb{Z}_2$, subtraction is equivalent to addition (i.e., $-1 \equiv 1 \pmod{2}$). Thus, the modulus becomes $x^5 + 1$. The first step is to divide $x^5 + 1$ by $x^4 + x^2 + 1$

$$\begin{array}{r|l} & \quad\quad\quad\quad\quad x \\ \hline x^4 + x^2 + 1) & x^5 \quad\quad\quad\quad + 1 \\ & - x^5 - x^3 - x \\ \hline & \quad - x^3 - x + 1 \end{array}$$

Using arithmetic modulo 2, the division equation is

$$\begin{aligned} x^5+1 &= (x^4+x^2+1)x + (-x^3-x+1) && (10\text{-}145)\\ &= (x^4+x^2+1)x + (x^3+x+1) && (10\text{-}146)\\ \Rightarrow x^3+x+1 &= (x^5+1) - (x^4+x^2+1)x && (10\text{-}147) \end{aligned}$$

Divide the previous divisor x^4+x^2+1 by the remainder x^3+x+1

$$\begin{array}{r|l} & \quad x \\ \hline x^3+x+1) & x^4+x^2 \qquad +1 \\ & -x^4-x^2-x \\ \cline{2-2} & \qquad\quad -x+1 \end{array}$$

$$\begin{aligned} x^4+x^2+1 &= (x^3+x+1)x + (-x+1) && (10\text{-}148)\\ &= (x^3+x+1)x + (x+1) && (10\text{-}149)\\ \Rightarrow x+1 &= (x^4+x^2+1) - (x^3+x+1)x && (10\text{-}150) \end{aligned}$$

Compute the gcd of x^4+x^2+1 and $x+1$ in R_2

$$\begin{array}{r|l} & x^2 \quad -x+2 \\ \hline x+1) & x^3 \qquad +x+1 \\ & -x^3-x^2 \\ \cline{2-2} & \quad -x^2+x \\ & \quad\ \ x^2+x \\ \cline{2-2} & \qquad\quad 2x+1 \\ & \qquad -2x-2 \\ \cline{2-2} & \qquad\qquad -1 \end{array}$$

The remainder is $-1 \equiv 1 \pmod 2$. Thus, the gcd of polynomial is 1. x^3+x+1 can be wrriten

$$\begin{aligned} x^3+x+1 &= (x+1)(x^2-x+2)+1 && (10\text{-}151)\\ &= (x+1)(x^2+x)+1 && (10\text{-}152)\\ \Rightarrow 1 &= (x^3+x+1) + (x+1)(x^2+x) && (10\text{-}153) \end{aligned}$$

Since their greatest common divisor is 1, the polynomial x^4+x^2+1 has a multiplicative inverse. Let us rewrite the three equations mentioned above using arithmetic modulo 2

$$\begin{aligned}
1 &\equiv (x^3+x+1)+(x+1)(x^2+x)\\
&\equiv (x^3+x+1)+\left[(x^4+x^2+1)+(x^3+x+1)x\right](x^2+x)\\
&\equiv (x^3+x+1)\left[1+x(x^2+x)\right]+(x^4+x^2+1)(x^2+x)\\
&\equiv \left[(x^5+1)+(x^4+x^2+1)x\right](x^3+x^2+1)+(x^4+x^2+1)(x^2+x)\\
&\equiv (x^5+1)(x^3+x^2+1)+(x^4+x^2+1)(x^4+x^3+x+x^2+x)\\
&\equiv (x^5+1)(x^3+x^2+1)+(x^4+x^2+1)(\mathbf{x^4}+\mathbf{x^3}+\mathbf{x^2}) \pmod 2 \quad (\text{Since } 2x\equiv 0)
\end{aligned}$$

Therefore, $f(x)^{-1} = x^4 + x^3 + x^2 \in R_2$.

■

Calculating the multiplicative inverse of a polynomial is not straightforward. Below, we provide code for the fast calculation of the multiplicative inverse of a polynomial. In SageMath, the following code can be used to perform this calculation:

```
q = 2 #prime
N = 5 #dimension
R.<x> = PolynomialRing(Zmod(q))
Mod = x^N-1
f = x^4+x^2+1
inverse_mod(f,Mod)
```

10.5.2 Encryption/Decryption

Before introducing the NTRU encryption, we define a function $\mathcal{T}(d_1, d_2)$. Let $\mathcal{T}(d_1, d_2)$ denote a subset of $\mathcal{T}$ consisting of polynomials that have exactly d_1 coefficients equal to 1, d_2 coefficients equal to -1, and the remaining coefficients equal to 0. In other words, $\mathcal{T}(d_1, d_2)$ is the set of ternary polynomials.

Example 10.5.5 A polynomial of $\mathcal{T}(4, 2)$

$$f(x) = x^7 - x^6 + x^4 + x^3 - x + 1 \in \mathcal{T}(4, 2) \tag{10-154}$$

1) (Setup): Alice and Bob agree the four public parameters N, p, q, d.
   (a) N: Dimension, determines the polynomial ring $R_q = \frac{\mathbb{Z}/q\mathbb{Z}[x]}{(x^n-1)}$, $250 < N < 2500$.
   (b) p, q: Two moduli, they satisfy $\gcd(p, q) = \gcd(N, q) = 1$. Typically, p is fixed to 3 and q will be a power of 2.
   (c) d: A positive integer parameter such that $q > (6d + 1)p$.
2) (KeyGen):
   (a) (PrivateKeyGen): Bob randomly chooses two polynomials

$$\mathbf{f} \in \mathcal{T}(d+1, d), \quad \mathbf{g} \in \mathcal{T}(d, d) \tag{10-155}$$

where $\mathbf{f}$ will need to be invertible in $\frac{\mathbb{Z}[x]}{(x^N-1)}$ modulo p and q respectively. Bob computes $\mathbf{f_p} \equiv \mathbf{f}^{-1} \pmod p$ and $\mathbf{f_q} \equiv \mathbf{f}^{-1} \pmod q$. The polynomial $\mathbf{f}$ and $\mathbf{g}$ are the private key.

(b) (PublicKeyGen): Bob computes

$$\mathbf{h} \equiv \mathbf{f_q} * \mathbf{g} \pmod{q} \tag{10-156}$$

The polynomial $\mathbf{h} \in R_q$ is the public key.

3) (Encrypt): Alice wishes to send a message $\mathbf{m} \in R_p$ to Bob. Alice randomly chooses a small polynomial $\mathbf{r} \in \mathcal{T}(d, d)$, then Alice uses the public key $\mathbf{h}$ to compute

$$\mathbf{c} \equiv p\mathbf{h} * \mathbf{r} + \mathbf{m} \pmod{q} \tag{10-157}$$

Alice transmits the ciphertext $\mathbf{c}$ to Bob.

4) (Decrypt): Bob receives the ciphtertext $\mathbf{c}$, and he uses his private key pair $(\mathbf{f}, \mathbf{g})$ to compute

$$\mathbf{a} \equiv \mathbf{f} * \mathbf{c} \pmod{q} \tag{10-158}$$

Bob performs a **centered lift** of $\mathbf{a}$ to the ring R. This means he identifies the coefficients of $\mathbf{a}$ in the interval from $(-\frac{q}{2}, \frac{q}{2}]$, denotes this lifted polynomial as $\mathbf{b} \in R$. Then, Bob computes the plaintext

$$\mathbf{m} \equiv \mathbf{f_p} * \mathbf{b} \pmod{p} \tag{10-159}$$

For correctness, we have

Proof

$$\begin{aligned} \mathbf{a} &\equiv \mathbf{f} * \mathbf{c} \pmod{q} && (10\text{-}160)\\ &\equiv \mathbf{f} * (p\mathbf{h} * \mathbf{r} + \mathbf{m}) \pmod{q} && (10\text{-}161)\\ &\equiv p\mathbf{f} * (\mathbf{f_q} * \mathbf{g} * \mathbf{r}) + \mathbf{f} * \mathbf{m} \pmod{q} && (10\text{-}162)\\ &\equiv p\mathbf{f} * \mathbf{f}^{-1} * \mathbf{g} * \mathbf{r} + \mathbf{f} * \mathbf{m} \pmod{q} && (10\text{-}163)\\ &\equiv p\mathbf{g} * \mathbf{r} + \mathbf{f} * \mathbf{m} \pmod{q} && (10\text{-}164) \end{aligned}$$

Center lift $\mathbf{a}$ *to* R*, denotes as* $\mathbf{b}$*. Since the congruence contains a small coefficient* p*, by reducing modulo* p*, we obtain:*

$$\begin{aligned} \mathbf{b} &\equiv \mathbf{a} \pmod{p} && (10\text{-}165)\\ &\equiv p\mathbf{g} * \mathbf{r} + \mathbf{f} * \mathbf{m} \pmod{p} && (10\text{-}166)\\ &\equiv \mathbf{f} * \mathbf{m} \pmod{p} && (10\text{-}167) \end{aligned}$$

Thus,

$$\mathbf{f_p} * \mathbf{b} \equiv \mathbf{f}^{-1} * \mathbf{f} * \mathbf{m} \equiv \mathbf{m} \pmod{p} \tag{10-168}$$

We successfully recover the plaintext.

10.5.3 Example

Example 10.5.6 Let $N = 11$, $p = 3$, $q = 79$, $d = 3$. Suppose the plaintext $m(x) = 1 - x + x^2 + x^7 - x^{10}$, what is the ciphertext?

Solution: Alice and Bob use the NTRU cryptosystem with their process below

1) Bob randomly chooses two polynomials:

$$f(x) = -x - x^2 + x^3 + x^4 - x^5 + x^8 + x^{10} \in \mathcal{T}(4,3) \tag{10-169}$$
$$g(x) = x - x + x^2 - x^4 + x^6 - x^8 +^{10} \in \mathcal{T}(3,3) \tag{10-170}$$

Bob computes the multiplicative inverse of f(x):

$$f_q(x) \equiv f(x)^{-1} \pmod q \tag{10-171}$$
$$\equiv 68 + 55x + 76x^2 + 49x^3 + 78x^4 + 24x^5$$
$$+ 60x^6 + 7x^7 + 4x^8 + 25x^9 + 29x^{10} \pmod{79} \tag{10-172}$$
$$f_p(x) \equiv f(x)^{-1} \pmod p \tag{10-173}$$
$$\equiv 2 + x + x^2 + 2x^3 + 2x^6 + x^7 + x^{10} \pmod 3 \tag{10-174}$$

The private key pair is $(\mathbf{f}, \mathbf{g})$.

2) Compute the public key $h(x)$

$$h(x) \equiv \mathbf{f_q} * \mathbf{g} \pmod q \tag{10-175}$$
$$\equiv 19 + 15x + 20x^2 + 51x^3 + x^4 + x^5 + 28x^6$$
$$+ 24x^7 + 8x^8 + 2x^9 + 68x^{10} \pmod{79} \tag{10-176}$$

3) Alice randomly chooses a small polynomial $r(x) = -1 + x - x^5 + x^{10}$ to encrypt the plaintext $m(x)$, then computes the ciphertext

$$c(x) \equiv 30 + 78x + 36x^2 + 62x^3 + 28x^4 + 27x^5 + 25x^6 + 56x^7$$
$$+ 59x^8 + 61x^9 + 13x^{10} \pmod{79} \tag{10-177}$$

Alice then transmits the ciphertext $\mathbf{c}$ to Bob.

4) Bob receices the ciphertext, then he computes

$$\mathbf{a} \equiv \mathbf{f} * \mathbf{c} \pmod q \equiv 77 + 6x + 75x^2 + x^4 + 78x^5$$
$$+ 3x^6 + 74x^7 + 3x^8 \pmod{79} \tag{10-178}$$

Bob performs a centered lift on a to the integer ring R by mapping its coefficients to the interval $(-q/2, q/2]$. He obtains the lifted polynomial $\mathbf{b} = -2 + 6x - 4x^2 + x^4 - x^5 + 3x^6 - 5x^7 + 3x^8$. Then, Bob strictly reduces b modulo p:

$$\mathbf{b} \equiv \mathbf{a} \pmod p \equiv 1 - x^2 + x^4 - x^5 + x^7 \pmod 3 \tag{10-179}$$

Then

$$\mathbf{f_p} * \mathbf{b} \pmod p \equiv 1 + 2x + x^2 + x^7 + 2x^{10} \pmod 3 \tag{10-180}$$
$$\equiv 1 - x + x^2 + x^7 - x^{10} \pmod 3 \tag{10-181}$$
$$\equiv m(x) \tag{10-182}$$

The SageMath code for NTRU is as follows:

```
#Input Parameters
N = 11
p = 3
q = 79
d = 3

R.<x> = PolynomialRing(Zmod(q)) #Set Polynomial ring
Mod = x^N-1

f = x^10+x^8-x^5+x^4+x^3-x^2-x #Polynomial
g = x^10-x^8+x^6-x^4+x^2-x #Polynomial

Fq = (inverse_mod(f,Mod)) #Compute f_q

h = Fq*g%Mod # Compute h
print(h)

h = 68*x^10 + 2*x^9 + 8*x^8 + 24*x^7 + 28*x^6 + x^5 + x^4 + 51*x^3 +
    20*x^2 + 15*x + 19
m = -x^10 +x^7 +x^2 - x + 1 # Plaintext
r = x^10 - x^5 + x -1 # Small Polynomial
e = (ph*r)%Mod + m
print(e)
a = (e*f)%Mod # Compute a
print(a)

R.<x> = PolynomialRing(Zmod(p))
Mod = x^11-1
f = x^10+x^8-x^5+x^4+x^3-x^2-x
g = x^10-x^8+x^6-x^4+x^2-x
Fp = (inverse_mod(f,Mod)) #Compute f_p

b = 3*x^8 -5*x^7 + 3*x^6 -1*x^5 + x^4 -4*x^2 + 6*x -2
print(b)

m =(Fpb)%Mod #
print(m) #Outout
```

■

10.5.4 Cryptanalysis

The security of NTRU is based on the SVP on lattices. The computational hardness of this problem is determined by the parameters N, p, q, d. By imposing certain conditions on these parameters, we can determine the security level of the NTRU cryptosystem.

To cryptanalyze the NTRU cryptosystem, a standard lattice attack attempts to recover a short vector in the NTRU lattice. This attack constructs a $2N$-dimensional lattice from the public key. With currently known attack algorithms against lattice based cryptosystems, if $N < 100$, NTRU can be broken in several minutes on a standard workstation. However, for properly chosen large parameters(e.g., $N > 500$), traditional lattice reduction algorithms do not pose a practical threat. Similar to RSA, if there are undisclosed algorithms that can solve this, then NTRU would become insecure. Below, we discuss the analysis when N is not very large and only the public key is known.

NTRU is a type of lattice-based cryptosystem. Recall the definition of a lattice: $\mathcal{L}(\mathbf{V}) = \left\{\sum_{i=1}^{N} a_i \mathbf{v_i} : a_1, \ldots, a_N \in \mathbb{Z}\right\}$. This is identical to the form of the public key $\mathbf{h} = \mathbf{f_q} * \mathbf{g} \pmod{q} = h_0 + h_1 x + \cdots + h_{N-1}x^{N-1}$. To represent this linear transformation, we transform the public key polynomial $\mathbf{h}$ into a $2N \times 2N$ block matrix $\mathbf{M_h}$. Adhering to the column-vector convention, the basis vectors form the columns of the matrix:

$$\mathbf{M_h} = \begin{bmatrix} \mathbf{I}_{N\times N} & \mathbf{0}_{N\times N} \\ \mathbf{H}_{N\times N} & q\mathbf{I}_{N\times N} \end{bmatrix}$$

where $\mathbf{I}$ is the identity matrix, $\mathbf{0}$ is the zero matrix, and $\mathbf{H}$ is the circulant matrix formed by the cyclic permutations of the coefficients of $\mathbf{h}$. That is

$$\left[\begin{array}{cccc|cccc} 1 & 0 & \cdots & 0 & 0 & 0 & \cdots & 0 \\ 0 & 1 & \cdots & 0 & 0 & 0 & \cdots & 0 \\ \vdots & \vdots & \ddots & \vdots & \vdots & \vdots & \ddots & \vdots \\ 0 & 0 & \cdots & 1 & 0 & 0 & \cdots & 0 \\ \hline h_0 & h_{N-1} & \cdots & h_1 & q & 0 & \cdots & 0 \\ h_1 & h_0 & \cdots & h_2 & 0 & q & \cdots & 0 \\ \vdots & \vdots & \ddots & \vdots & \vdots & \vdots & \ddots & \vdots \\ h_{N-1} & h_{N-2} & \cdots & h_0 & 0 & 0 & \cdots & q \end{array}\right]$$

Applying LLL to this lattice may find a short vector corresponding to the private key.

Example 10.5.7 Suppose Alice and Bob use the NTRU cryptosystem with parameters $N = 7$, $p = 3$, $q = 79$, and $d = 2$.

Bob chooses the private key polynomials

$$f(x) = -x - x^2 + x^3 + x^4 + x^6, \quad g(x) = -x + x^2 - x^4 + x^6 \tag{10-183}$$

Bob calculates and publishes his public key

$$h(x) = 41 + 50x + x^2 + 34x^3 + 53x^4 + 22x^5 + 36x^6 \tag{10-184}$$

Given only the public key $h(x)$ and the system parameters, demonstrate how Eve can recover the private key.

Solution: Eve constructs the NTRU lattice basis matrix $\mathcal{L}_{NTRU}$. This is a $2N \times 2N$ matrix is given by

$$\left[\begin{array}{ccccccc|ccccccc}
1 & 0 & 0 & 0 & 0 & 0 & 0 & 0 & 0 & 0 & 0 & 0 & 0 & 0 \\
0 & 1 & 0 & 0 & 0 & 0 & 0 & 0 & 0 & 0 & 0 & 0 & 0 & 0 \\
0 & 0 & 1 & 0 & 0 & 0 & 0 & 0 & 0 & 0 & 0 & 0 & 0 & 0 \\
0 & 0 & 0 & 1 & 0 & 0 & 0 & 0 & 0 & 0 & 0 & 0 & 0 & 0 \\
0 & 0 & 0 & 0 & 1 & 0 & 0 & 0 & 0 & 0 & 0 & 0 & 0 & 0 \\
0 & 0 & 0 & 0 & 0 & 1 & 0 & 0 & 0 & 0 & 0 & 0 & 0 & 0 \\
0 & 0 & 0 & 0 & 0 & 0 & 1 & 0 & 0 & 0 & 0 & 0 & 0 & 0 \\
\hline
41 & 36 & 22 & 53 & 34 & 1 & 50 & 79 & 0 & 0 & 0 & 0 & 0 & 0 \\
50 & 41 & 36 & 22 & 53 & 34 & 1 & 0 & 79 & 0 & 0 & 0 & 0 & 0 \\
1 & 50 & 41 & 36 & 22 & 53 & 34 & 0 & 0 & 79 & 0 & 0 & 0 & 0 \\
34 & 1 & 50 & 41 & 36 & 22 & 53 & 0 & 0 & 0 & 79 & 0 & 0 & 0 \\
53 & 34 & 1 & 50 & 41 & 36 & 22 & 0 & 0 & 0 & 0 & 79 & 0 & 0 \\
22 & 53 & 34 & 1 & 50 & 41 & 36 & 0 & 0 & 0 & 0 & 0 & 79 & 0 \\
36 & 22 & 53 & 34 & 1 & 50 & 41 & 0 & 0 & 0 & 0 & 0 & 0 & 79
\end{array}\right]$$

Computations can be performed using computational tools such as the Python package `olll` or the `Matrix.LLL`() method in SageMath. Applying the LLL algorithm to the basis $\mathcal{B}$ yields the following reduced basis

$$\begin{bmatrix}
1 & 0 & 0 & -2 & -1 & 1 & 1 & -5 & 5 & -1 & -8 & -8 & -13 & -13 \\
0 & 1 & 0 & 0 & -1 & -1 & -1 & 13 & 5 & -8 & -1 & 13 & 5 & 12 \\
0 & 1 & -1 & 0 & -1 & 0 & 1 & -8 & -13 & 13 & -8 & -5 & 5 & -8 \\
-1 & -1 & -1 & 1 & -1 & 0 & 0 & -1 & 8 & -5 & 13 & -5 & -13 & 0 \\
-2 & -1 & -1 & 0 & -1 & -1 & 0 & -8 & 1 & -5 & -5 & 13 & 8 & 1 \\
0 & 0 & 1 & 0 & -1 & -1 & 1 & 13 & 8 & 13 & -5 & -8 & 1 & 0 \\
0 & -1 & -1 & -1 & -1 & -1 & 1 & -5 & -13 & -8 & 13 & -1 & 8 & 8 \\
-1 & 0 & 0 & 0 & 0 & -1 & -1 & -1 & -6 & 4 & -8 & -9 & -22 & -1 \\
1 & 1 & 1 & 0 & 0 & 0 & 1 & -14 & 1 & -9 & 4 & 22 & -6 & 10 \\
0 & -1 & -1 & 0 & 0 & 0 & 0 & -8 & 14 & 22 & -9 & 6 & 1 & 0 \\
0 & 0 & 0 & -1 & 0 & 1 & 0 & 4 & 8 & 6 & 22 & -1 & 14 & 25 \\
0 & 1 & 1 & 1 & 0 & -1 & -1 & -9 & -4 & -1 & 6 & -14 & 8 & 7 \\
0 & 0 & -1 & 0 & 0 & 0 & 1 & 22 & 9 & -14 & -1 & -8 & -4 & 21 \\
0 & -1 & 0 & 0 & 0 & 1 & 0 & 6 & -22 & -8 & -14 & 4 & 9 & 17
\end{bmatrix}$$

Eve locates the smallest vector in the LLL reduced basis. This column contains only the coefficients 0, −1, and 1. Upon identifying this vector, the first N components represent the coefficients of $\mathbf{f}$, which we called as $\mathbf{f}'$. The subsequent N components represent the coefficients of $\mathbf{g}'$. In this example, $\mathbf{f}'$ and $\mathbf{g}'$ are

$$\mathbf{f}' = x + x^2 - x^3 - x^4 - x^6 \tag{10-185}$$

$$\mathbf{g}' = x - x^2 + x^4 - x^6 \tag{10-186}$$

Observing $\mathbf{f}'$, we notice it differs from Bob's original $\mathbf{f}$. However, due to the cyclic structure of the NTRU lattice, the shortest vector found by LLL is often a **cyclic rotation** (Convolution operation) of the private key. Specifically, $\mathbf{f}'$ is related to $\mathbf{f}$ by the transformation $\mathbf{f}(x) = \pm x^k * \mathbf{f}'(x)$ for some shift k where $1 \leqslant k \leqslant N$.

In this case, multiplying $\mathbf{f}'$ by $-x^7$ recovers the original key

$$\mathbf{f} = -x^7 * \mathbf{f}' = \begin{bmatrix} -1 & 0 & 0 & 0 & 0 & 0 & 0 \\ 0 & -1 & 0 & 0 & 0 & 0 & 0 \\ & & & \vdots & & & \\ 0 & 0 & 0 & 0 & 0 & 0 & -1 \end{bmatrix} \begin{bmatrix} 0 \\ 1 \\ \vdots \\ -1 \end{bmatrix} \tag{10-187}$$

The exact same cyclic rotation automatically applies to g. Once the correct $\mathbf{f}$ is identified which can be verified by checking if it successfully decrypts a test message, the plaintext can be fully recovered. ■

When N is large, if a brute force attack is employed, how many combinations must be attempted? The answer is $\dfrac{N!}{d_1!d_2!\,(N-d_1-d_2)!}$ for $\mathcal{T}(d_1, d_2)$. This involves finding the private key by solving the equation $\mathbf{f} * \mathbf{h} \equiv \mathbf{g} \pmod{q}$. To maximize this search space, one generally selects $d_1 \approx d_2 \approx N/3$, forcing the attacker to spend the maximum amount of time attempting to break the system.

If N is extremely large, the security is significantly enhanced. This is because processing very large matrices is computationally difficult. Most of the computation time is consumed by convolution operations, with a time complexity of $\mathcal{O}(N^2)$.

The selection of the value q also requires careful consideration. If q is too large, the computational complexity increases, which reduces efficiency and is detrimental to real time communication. If q is too small, the security is compromised, leaving a possibility for the plaintext to be recovered via cryptanalysis. The selection of p is much simpler, it is an odd number, generally set to 3. Thus, NTRU achieves a favorable balance between high-security and high-performance.

It is worth noting that *Jaulmes*'paper [128] showed that if NTRU is used without padding, it is vulnerable to chosen ciphertext attacks. What type of padding scheme is suitable? *Howgrave-Graham* et al. introduced a padding scheme in the paper [129]. Interested readers are encouraged to consult the relevant literature [130] [131].

The NTRU cryptosystem has defined different sets of parameters for NTRU providing various security levels. These parameters are shown in Table 10-1.

Table 10-1: NTRU Parameters

Parameters	N	p	q
Standard	251	3	128
High	347	3	128
Very High	503	3	256

These parameters are much smaller than the integer moduli used in RSA, although the resulting key sizes are not directly comparable.

10.6 EXERCISES

1) Let $\mathbf{v}_1 = \begin{bmatrix} 5 \\ 2 \end{bmatrix}, \mathbf{v}_2 = \begin{bmatrix} 7 \\ 3 \end{bmatrix}$ and $\mathbf{u}_1 = \begin{bmatrix} 3 \\ 2 \end{bmatrix}, \mathbf{u}_2 = \begin{bmatrix} 1 \\ 1 \end{bmatrix}$. Find the transformation matrix that converts the basis $[\mathbf{v}_1, \mathbf{v}_2]$ to $[\mathbf{u}_1, \mathbf{u}_2]$.

2) Obtain an orthogonal basis for the subspace of $\mathbb{R}^n$ spanned by
   (a) $\mathbf{v}_1 = (1, 3, 2)^T$, $\mathbf{v}_2 = (4, 1, -2)^T$, $\mathbf{v}_3 = (-2, 1, 3)^T$
   (b) $\mathbf{v}_1 = (4, 1, 3, -1)^T$, $\mathbf{v}_2 = (2, 1, -3, 4)^T$, $\mathbf{v}_3 = (1, 0, -2, 7)^T$
3) Let $\mathcal{L}$ be the lattice generated by

$$\mathbf{v}_1 = (1, 3, -2)^T, \quad \mathbf{v}_2 = (2, 1, 0)^T, \quad \mathbf{v}_3 = (-1, 2, 5)^T$$

   Draw a picture of a fundamental domain for $\mathcal{L}$ and find its volume.
4) Given a lattice basis $[\mathbf{v}_1, \mathbf{v}_2, \ldots, \mathbf{v}_n]$ of $\mathbb{R}^n$ and let $[\mathbf{v}_1^*, \mathbf{v}_2^*, \ldots, \mathbf{v}_n^*]$ be the Gram-Schmidt orthogonalization of $[\mathbf{v}_1, \mathbf{v}_2, \ldots, \mathbf{v}_n]$. Show that it is not true in general that $\lambda_n \mathcal{L} \geqslant max_i \|\mathbf{v}_i^*\|$.
5) Show that a subset of $\mathbb{R}^m$ is a lattice if and only if it is a discrete additive subgroup.
6) Show that for any n, there is an n-dimensional lattice $\mathcal{L}$ such that any point $\mathbf{x} \in \mathbb{R}^n$ is within distance $1.5\lambda_1(\mathcal{L})$ from $\mathcal{L}$, the covering radius of $\mathcal{L}$ is at most $\mu(\mathcal{L}) \leqslant 1.5\lambda_1(\mathcal{L})$.
7) Let $\mathcal{L}_1$ be a full rand sub-lattice of $\mathcal{L}_2$. Show that $\det(\mathcal{L}_2)$ divides $\det(\mathcal{L}_1)$.
8) Let $\mathcal{L}_1$ be a full rand sub-lattice of $\mathcal{L}_2$. Show that $\mathcal{L}_1 = \mathcal{L}_2$ if and only if $\det(\mathcal{L}_1) = \det(\mathcal{L}_2)$.
9) Let $A = \begin{bmatrix} 1 & -1 & 8 \\ 1 & 8 & -4 \\ 1 & 8 & 4 \\ 1 & -1 & 0 \end{bmatrix}$. Find an orthonormal basis for the column space of A.
10) Let $\mathcal{L}$ be a lattice in $\mathbb{R}^m$ of rank n with basis matrix M. Show that $\det(\mathcal{L}) = \sqrt{\det(MM^T)}$.
11) Let $\mathcal{L}^*$ be an LLL-reduced basis. Show that $\|\mathbf{v}_j\|^2 \leqslant 2^i \|\mathbf{v}_i^*\|^2$ for all $0 \leqslant j \leqslant i \leqslant n-1$.
12) Applying LLL algorithm to reduce the following matrix:

$$\text{(a)} \begin{bmatrix} 3 & 9 \\ 12 & 4 \end{bmatrix} \qquad \text{(b)} \begin{bmatrix} 1 & 2 & 14 \\ 3 & 9 & 12 \\ 5 & 7 & 4 \end{bmatrix} \qquad \text{(c)} \begin{bmatrix} 9 & 2 & 3 & 8 \\ 1 & 7 & 4 & 6 \\ 2 & 9 & 4 & 7 \\ 2 & 8 & 4 & 0 \end{bmatrix}$$

13) Consider GGH cryptosystem. Bob selects the private basis

$$\mathbf{v}_1 = (5, 13)^T, \quad \mathbf{v}_2 = (-52, -42)^T$$

   and public basis

$$\mathbf{w}_1 = (-46995, -28987)^T, \quad \mathbf{w}_2 = (-46948, -28958)^T$$

   (a) Compute the determinant of Bob's lattice and the Hadamard ratio of $\mathbf{V}$ and $\mathbf{W}$.
   (b) Alice send the plaintext is $\mathbf{m} = \{1, 2\}$. Computer the ciphertext.
   (c) Try to decrypt Alice's plaintext using Babai's algorithm with the public basis. Is the output equal to the plaintext?

14) Consider GGH cryptosystem. Bob selects the private basis

$$\mathbf{v}_1 = (58, 53, -68)^T, \quad \mathbf{v}_2 = (-110, -112, 35)^T, \quad \mathbf{v}_3 = (-10, -119, 123)^T$$

and public basis

$$\mathbf{w}_1 = (324850, -1625176, 2734951)^T$$
$$\mathbf{w}_2 = (165782, -829409, 1395775)^T$$
$$\mathbf{w}_3 = (485054, -2426708, 4083804)^T$$

(a) Compute the determinant of Bob's lattice and the Hadamard ratio of $\mathbf{V}$ and $\mathbf{W}$.
(b) Alice the encrypted message $\mathbf{c} = \mathbf{Wm} + \mathbf{r} = (8930810, -44681748, 75192665)^T$ to Bob. Use the private basis to decrypt the message and recover the plaintext.
(c) Determine the random vector $\mathbf{r}$.
(d) Try to decrypt Alice's message using Babai's algorithm with the public basis. Is the output equal to the plaintext?

15) Consider the GGH cryptosystem. Suppose Bob uses this scheme to encrypt messages for Alice.
(a) Assume Bob erroneously uses two distinct random error vectors, $\mathbf{r}_1$ and $\mathbf{r}_2$, to encrypt the same plaintext message $\mathbf{m}$. If the adversary Eve intercepts the ciphertexts $\mathbf{e}_1 = \mathbf{Wm} + \mathbf{r}_1$ and $\mathbf{e}_2 = \mathbf{Wm} + \mathbf{r}_2$, is it possible for Eve to recover the plaintext?
(b) Suppose Eve intercepts the ciphertexts $\mathbf{e} = (-9, -29, -48, 18, 48)^T$ and $\mathbf{e}' = (-6, -26, -51, 20, 47)^T$. Determine the number of possible candidates for the random vector $\mathbf{r}$.
(c) Assume Bob erroneously reuses the same random error vector $\mathbf{r}$ to encrypt two distinct plaintext messages, $\mathbf{m}_1$ and $\mathbf{m}_2$. If the adversary Eve intercepts the ciphertexts $\mathbf{e}_1 = \mathbf{Wm}_1 + \mathbf{r}$ and $\mathbf{e}_2 = \mathbf{Wm}_2 + \mathbf{r}$, is it possible for Eve to recover the plaintexts?

16) Compute the polynomial convolution product $\mathbf{f} * \mathbf{g} \pmod{q}$
(a) $N = 3$, $q = 5$, $f(x) = 1 + x + x^2$, $g(x) = -3 + 3x + 2x^2$
(b) $N = 5$, $q = 7$, $f(x) = 1 + x + 2x^2 + x^3 - x^4$, $g(x) = 2x + 2x^2 - 5x^3 + 2x^4$
(c) $N = 6$, $q = 3$, $f(x) = 3x+5x^3-3x^4+2x^5$, $g(x) = -3x+4x^2+3x^3-x^4+3x^5$
(d) $N = 7$, $q = 11$, $f(x) = 3x^2 - 9x^4 + 3x^6$, $g(x) = 2 + x^3 + 2x^5$

17) Find the inverse of $\mathbf{f}(x) \in R_q$ or show that the inverse does not exist
(a) $N = 5$, $q = 13$, $f(x) = 3 + 3x + x^4$
(b) $N = 5$, $q = 13$, $f(x) = -3 + 2x + x^3$
(c) $N = 5$, $q = 19$, $f(x) = -3 + 3x^2 + 2x^4$

18) Consider the NTRU crpytosystem. Alice and Bob select $N = 7, p = 2, q = 29$. The public key is

$$\mathrm{h}(x) = 23x^6 + 24x^5 + 23x^4 + 24x^3 + 23x^2 + 23x + 23$$

The plaintext $\mathrm{m}(x) = 1 + x^5$ and the small vector $\mathrm{r}(x) = x^6 + x^3 + x + 1$.

(a) Compute the ciphertext.
(b) Suppose the secret key is $f(x) = x^5 + x^4 + x^2 + x + 1$, $g(x) = x^5 + x^3 + 1$. Decrypt the message.

19) Consider the NTRU crpytosystem. Alice and Bob select $N = 11, p = 3, q = 32$. Let

$$f(x) = -x^{10} + x^9 + x^6 - x^4 + x^2 + x - 1$$
$$g(x) = -x^{10} - x^8 + x^3 + x^2 + x - 1$$

Answer the following questions:
(a) Compute $\mathbf{f}_p$ and $\mathbf{f}_q$.
(b) Compute the public key $\mathbf{h}$.
(c) Take the plaintext **OK**. To convert this into a polynomial, Alice selects a random polynomial $r(x) = x^7 + x^2 + x + 1$, compute the ciphertext.
(d) Decrypt the ciphertext.

CHAPTER 11

Fully Homomorphic Encryption

This chapter introduces the concept of Fully Homomorphic Encryption (FHE) and explores its practical applications. Fundamentally, fully homomorphic encryption permits computation to be performed directly on ciphertexts. In the contemporary era of big data, privacy and security have garnered significant attention. To comply with stringent laws and regulations, data holders are compelled to encrypt their data. However, the primary utility of data derives from its analysis. While traditional encryption safeguards data in transit and at rest, analytical processes typically necessitate decryption, which introduces a risk of information leakage. Consequently, there is a critical need for a technique that enables arbitrary computation on encrypted data and yields correct results without decryption, effectively distinguishing the utility of data from its visibility. This technique is known as Fully Homomorphic Encryption (FHE).

Topics covered in this chapter:

- Learning with Errors (LWE) Problem
- Definition of Homomorphic Encryption
- Definition of Somewhat Homomorphic Encryption (SHE)
- Definition of Fully Homomorphic Encryption (FHE)
- The Second Generation FHE: The BGV Scheme
- The Second Generation FHE: The DGHV Scheme

11.1 LEARNING WITH ERRORS PROBLEM

11.1.1 Introduction

The Learning with Errors (LWE) problem is a computational problem introduced by the American computer scientist *Oded Regev* in 2005, and it is among his most notable contributions. For his paper [132], he received the Gödel Prize, one of the highest honors in theoretical computer science. Cryptographic schemes based on the

DOI: 10.1201/9781042011087-11

LWE assumption are considered secure against quantum attacks, as there are no known efficient quantum algorithms capable of solving them.

The security of LWE relies on reductions from worst-case lattice problems, which are conjectured to be hard even for quantum computers. Consequently, LWE serves as a versatile foundation for constructing FHE cryptosystems.

To understand LWE, consider the problem of solving a system of linear equations

$$x + 4y = 9 \tag{11-1}$$

$$2x + 6y = 8 \tag{11-2}$$

The system can be solved in polynomial time with **Gaussian Elimination**. Or the system can be solved with linear algebra: $\begin{bmatrix} 1 & 4 \\ 2 & 6 \end{bmatrix}^{-1} \begin{bmatrix} 9 \\ 8 \end{bmatrix} = \begin{bmatrix} -11 \\ 5 \end{bmatrix}$, the solution is found by computing $\mathbf{x} = \mathbf{A}^{-1}\mathbf{b}$.

Furthermore, let q be a prime, $\mathbb{Z}_q$ be integers modulo q in interval $(-q/2, q/2]$. Let $n \in \mathbb{N}$ be number of dimensions, $m \in \mathbb{N}$ be number of samples, $\mathbb{Z}_q^n$ be the vector space of dimension n over $\mathbb{Z}_q$, the ordinary system of equations modulo

$$\mathbf{Ax} \equiv \mathbf{b} \pmod{q} \tag{11-3}$$

where $\mathbf{A} \in \mathbb{Z}_q^{m \times n}$ and $\mathbf{b} \in \mathbb{Z}_q^m$. When $m \geqslant n$ and $\mathbf{A}$ has full rank, the system can be solved in polynomial time using linear algebra over the finite field $\mathbb{Z}_q$.

However, linear equations have a little bit of noise, typically some discrete Gaussian noise, is it still computationally feasible to efficiently recover the unknown vector $\mathbf{x} \in \mathbb{Z}_q^n$?

11.1.2 LWE Problem

The search LWE problem is defined as follows:

Definition 11.1.1 Search $LWE_{n,m,q,\chi}$ Problem, SLWE

Given $(\mathbf{A}, \mathbf{b}^T = \mathbf{s}^T\mathbf{A} + \mathbf{e}^T)$, *the goal is to find the vector* $\mathbf{s}$ *such that*

$$||\mathbf{b}^T - \mathbf{s}^T\mathbf{A}|| \leqslant B \tag{11-4}$$

where $n, m, q, B \in \mathbb{N}$, $\mathbf{A} \in \mathbb{Z}_q^{n \times m}$, $\mathbf{s} \in \mathbb{Z}_q^n$ *is secret,* $\mathbf{e} \in \chi^m$ *is the error that follows a discretized Gaussian distribution. The error distribution is strictly* **B-Bounded**, *that is* $||\mathbf{e}|| \leqslant B$ *where the bound* $B \ll q/2$.

Let $\lambda \in \mathbb{N}$ be the primary security parameter, and $n, m, q, B = poly(\lambda)$ be lattice parameters. The more unknown variables exist in the system, the harder the LWE problem becomes.

In other words, the LWE assumption states that a noisy random linear combinations of n vectors in $\mathbb{Z}^m$ are indistinguishable from random given a matrix $\mathbf{A}$ and a vector $\mathbf{b}^T \equiv \mathbf{s}^T\mathbf{A} + \mathbf{e}^T \pmod{q}$, with an unknown secret vector $\mathbf{s}$ and a noise $\mathbf{e}$ satisfying $||e|| \leqslant B$, recover $\mathbf{s}$. Typically, we take $m \gg n$ to be sufficently large so that the secret vector is uniquely determined.

The selection of LWE parameters is critical for security. Lindner and Peikert [133] suggest the set $(n, m, q, \chi) = (233, 4536, 32749, 2.8)$, whereas Micciancio and Regev [134] propose $(n, m, q, \chi) = (256, 640, 4093, 3.3)$.

The latter set is more representative and widely adopted. The most efficient algorithm for the Search-LWE problem has a time complexity of $2^{\mathcal{O}(n)}$. This complexity renders the problem computationally infeasible for both classical and quantum computers. Despite extensive research, no published algorithm has successfully reduced this exponential complexity.

Definition 11.1.2 Decisional $LWE_{n,m,q,\chi}$ Problem, DLWE

Given m independent samples where every sample is distributed according to either, the LWE distribution or a completely uniform distribution, the goal is to successfully distinguish whether the samples are drawn from

1) $(\mathbf{A}, \mathbf{b}^T = \mathbf{s}^T\mathbf{A} + \mathbf{e}^T)$

2) $(\mathbf{A}, \mathbf{u}^T)$

where $n, m, q, B \in \mathbb{N}$, $\mathbf{A} \in \mathbb{Z}_q^{n\times m}$, $\mathbf{s} \in \mathbb{Z}_q^n$ is secret, $\mathbf{e} \in \chi^m$ is the error that follows a discretized Gaussian distribution. The vector $\mathbf{u} \leftarrow \mathbb{Z}_q^m$ is chosen uniformly at random.

The Decisional LWE problem is structurally similar to the Search version but conceptually simpler. However, decision version becomes much simpler, only to distinguish between a valid LWE problem instance versus some randomly sampled values. Decide if a pair $(\mathbf{A}, \mathbf{b}^T)$ is from the LWE distribution $\mathbf{A}_{\mathbf{s},\chi}$, or uniformly random distribution.

If there is a polynomial time algorithm that solves the decision-LWE problem, then there is a polynomial time algorithm that solves the search LWE problem. Search-LWE is at least as hard as decision-LWE.

Is there a relation between the search LWE problem and the decision LWE problem? If the lattice dimension is n, we write a polynomial in n as $poly(n)$, and the prime q is required to satisfy $q \leqslant 2^{poly(n)}$. When q is polynomial in n, the DLWE problem is equally hard as the SLWE problem, as illustrated in Figure 11-1. Solving it on the average is at least as hard as approximating several lattice problems on n-dimensional lattices in the worst case.

Figure 11-2 illustrates the hierarchy and reduction relationships among computationally hard lattice problems.

The definitions of the specific problems referenced in the figure are as follows:

- $\text{LWE}_{n,m,q,\chi}$ denotes **Learning with Errors Problem** (Definition 11.1.1).
- SVP_γ denotes **Approximate Shortest Vector Problem** (Definition 10.2.5).
- CVP_γ denotes **Approximate Closest Vector** Problem (Definition 10.2.9).
- $\text{BDD}_{1/\gamma}$ denotes **Approximate Bounded-distance Decoding** (Definition 10.2.10).
- SIVP_γ denotes **Approximate Shortest Independent Vectors Problem** (Definition 10.2.6).

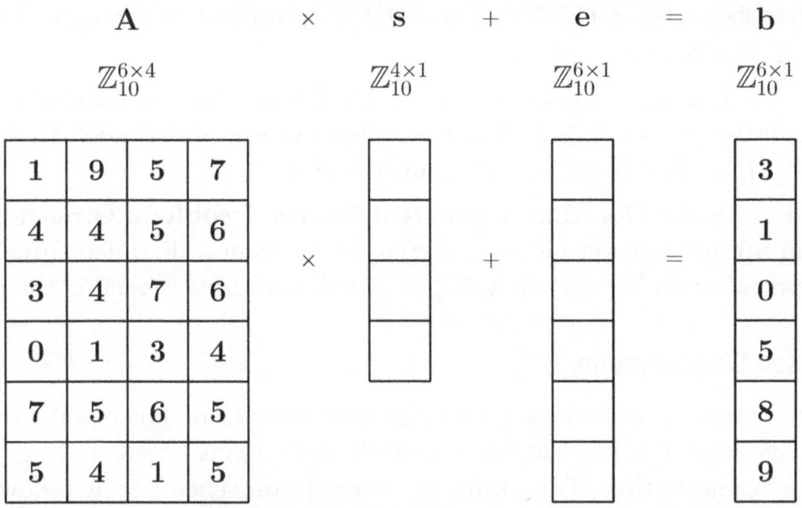

SLWE: Given $\mathbf{A}$, find $\mathbf{s}$

DLWE: Given $\mathbf{A}$, distinguish $\mathbf{b}$ from the $\mathbf{A}_{\mathbf{s},\chi}$ or Uniformly Random Distribution

Figure 11-1: LWE Problem

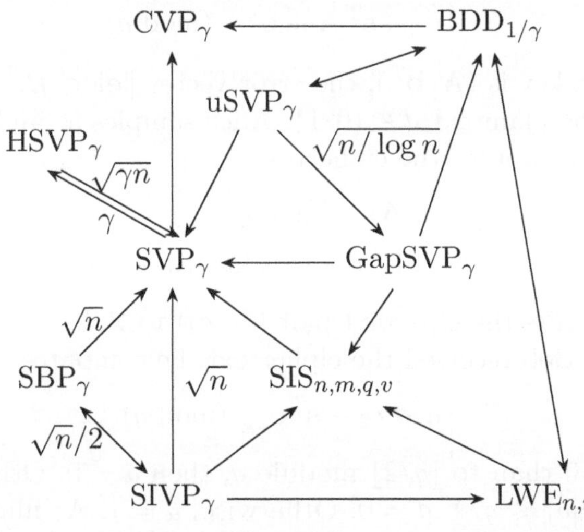

Figure 11-2: The Relationships Between Lattice Problems

- SBP_γ denotes **Shortest Basis Problem**. The goal is to find a basis $\mathbf{V} = [\mathbf{v}_1, \ldots, \mathbf{v}_n]$ for a lattice $\mathcal{L}$ that minimizes the length of the basis vectors according to a specified norm.
- $\text{SIS}_{n,m,q,v}$ denotes **Short Integer Solution Problem**. Given a randomly sampled matrix $\mathbf{A} \in \mathbb{Z}_q^{n\times m}$ such that $m > nlog(q)$, the goal is to find a short non-zero vector $\mathbf{x} \in \mathbb{Z}^m$ such that $\mathbf{Ax} \equiv \mathbf{0} \pmod{q}$ and $\|\mathbf{x}\|_2 \leqslant v$ where $v \in \mathbb{R}$ is the noise bound and $v < q$.
- HSVP_γ denotes **Hermite Shortest Vector Problem**. Given a basis of $\mathcal{L}$ and an approximation factor $\gamma \geqslant 1$, the goal is to find a non-zero vector $\mathbf{x} \in \mathcal{L}$

such that $0 < \|\mathbf{x}\| \leqslant \gamma \cdot \det(\mathcal{L})^{1/n}$, where $\det(\mathcal{L})$ represents the volume of the fundamental parallelepiped of the lattice.

- uSVP_γ denotes **Unique Shortest Vector Problem**. Given a basis of $\mathcal{L}$ and an approximation factor $\gamma \geqslant 1$, find the unique vector $\mathbf{x} \in \mathcal{L}$ such that any $\mathbf{v} \in \mathcal{L}$ with $\|v\| \leqslant \gamma\|x\|$ is an integral multiple of $\mathbf{x}$.
- GapSVP_γ denotes the **Decisional Shortest Vector Problem**. Given a basis of $\mathcal{L}$ and an approximation factor $\gamma = \gamma(n) \geqslant 1$, given a distance threshold $d > 0$, where either $\lambda_1(\mathcal{L}) \leqslant d$ or $\lambda_1(\mathcal{L}) > \gamma(n)d$, determine which is the case.

11.1.3 LWE-Based Cryptosystem

For LWE, we can perform a worst-case to average case reduction. That is, if LWE is hard for the average case it is hard in every case. Regev's LWE based scheme [135] encrypts one bit per encryption. The public key encryption scheme is as follow.

Let $n \in \mathbb{N}$ be a security parameter, $m \in \mathbb{N}$ be number of equations that is public, q be a prime in interval $[n^2, 2n^2]$. The parameters n, m, q such that $m = (1+\epsilon)(n+1)\log(q)$ where $\epsilon \in \mathbb{R}^+$. Let the error distribution χ is a discrete Gaussian over $\mathbb{Z}_q$.

1) (KeyGen): Bob use the key generation algorithm samples $\mathbf{A} \in \mathbb{Z}_q^{n\times m}$, the secret key $\mathbf{s} \in \mathbb{Z}_q^n$ and $\mathbf{e} \in \chi_B^m$. Computes

$$\mathbf{b}^T \equiv \mathbf{s^T A} + \mathbf{e}^T \pmod q \tag{11-5}$$

where the public key is $(\mathbf{A}, \mathbf{b}^T)$, the error vector $\|\mathbf{e}\| \leqslant B$.

2) (Encrypt): Let the plaintext $d \in \{0,1\}$, Alice samples a random binary vector $\mathbf{r} \in \{0,1\}^m$ and computes the ciphertext

$$\mathbf{c}_1 \equiv \mathbf{Ar} \pmod q \tag{11-6}$$

$$c_2 \equiv \mathbf{b}^T\mathbf{r} + \lfloor q/2 \rfloor d \pmod q \tag{11-7}$$

Alice then transmits the cipertext pair $(\mathbf{c}_1, c_2)$ to Bob.

3) (Decrypt): After Bob received the ciphertext, he computes

$$a \equiv c_2 - \mathbf{s}^T\mathbf{c}_1 \pmod q \tag{11-8}$$

If a is closer to 0 than to $\lfloor q/2 \rfloor$ modulo q, then $d = 0$. Otherwise, $d = 1$. In other words, if $\|a\| \leqslant q/4$, $d = 0$. Otherwise, $d = 1$. As illustrated in Figure 11-3.

For correctness, we have

$$\begin{aligned} a \equiv c_2 - \mathbf{s}^T\mathbf{c}_1 &\equiv (\mathbf{s^T A} + \mathbf{e}^T)\mathbf{r} + \lfloor q/2 \rfloor d - \mathbf{s}^T\mathbf{c}_1 \pmod q && (11\text{-}9)\\ &\equiv (\mathbf{s^T A} + \mathbf{e}^T)\mathbf{r} + \lfloor q/2 \rfloor d - \mathbf{s}^T\mathbf{Ar} \pmod q && (11\text{-}10)\\ &\equiv \mathbf{e}^T\mathbf{r} + \lfloor q/2 \rfloor d \pmod q && (11\text{-}11)\end{aligned}$$

Since the error vector $\mathbf{e}$ is neither public key nor secret key, if we have a bound B such that $\|\mathbf{e}\| \leqslant B$, then we have that $\|\mathbf{e}^T\mathbf{r}\| \leqslant mB$ since $\mathbf{r} \in \{0,1\}^m$, the correctness holds if $\|\mathbf{e}^T\mathbf{r}\| < q/4$. The plaintext is recovered by determining whether the result of congruence 11-8 is closer to 0 or $\lfloor q/2 \rfloor$.

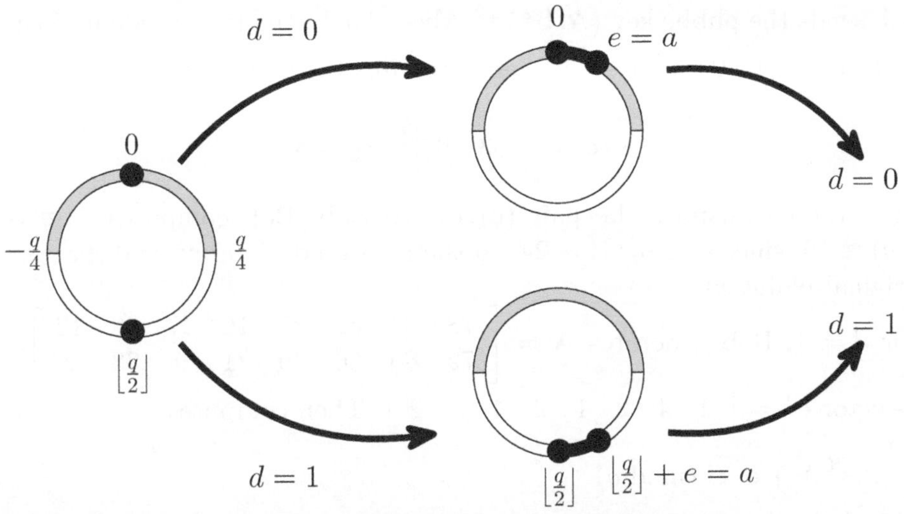

Figure 11-3: LWE Encryption

Example 11.1.1 Alice uses $\mathbf{A} = [75, 70, 71, 74, 28, 76, 82, 4]^T$, $\mathbf{s}^T = [20], \mathbf{e}^T = [2, 4, 2, 3, 4, 1, 3, 3]$, $q = 97$. If Alice wants to send the plaintext $d = 1$ to Bob. Compute the ciphertext.

Solution: The first step, Bob generates the public key $\mathbf{b}^T \equiv \mathbf{s^T A} + \mathbf{e}^T = [47, 46, 64, 28, 79, 66, 91, 83]$, then sends to Alice.

Alice samples a random binary vector $\mathbf{r} = [0, 0, 0, 0, 1, 0, 1, 0]^T$, then computes the ciphertext

$$\mathbf{c}_1 \equiv \mathbf{Ar} \pmod{q} \equiv 28 + 82 \equiv 13 \pmod{97} \tag{11-12}$$

$$c_2 \equiv \mathbf{b}^T\mathbf{r} + \lfloor q/2 \rfloor d \pmod{q} \equiv 79 + 91 + 48 \equiv 24 \pmod{97} \tag{11-13}$$

Alice then transmits the ciphertext pair $(\mathbf{c}_1, c_2)$ to Bob. Bob computes $a \equiv c_2 - \mathbf{c}_1^T\mathbf{s} \pmod{q} \equiv 55$. The distance to $\lfloor q/2 \rfloor = 48$ is $|55 - 48| = 7$, whereas the distance to 0 is 42. Since a is strictly closer to $\lfloor q/2 \rfloor$, the recovered plaintext is deterministically evaluated as 1, which flawlessly matches the original plaintext. ■

Example 11.1.2 Consider Public-Key Encryption from LWE, if Alice wants to send the plaintext **OK** to Bob. Compute the ciphertext.

Solution: Assume we use ASCII for the binary conversion, the binary representation of **OK** is 01001111 01001011.

Bob uses a 2 × 8 matrix, the secret key $\mathbf{s}^T = \begin{bmatrix} 20 & 8 \end{bmatrix}$ and $q = 97$.

For $d = 0$, Alice generates $\mathbf{A} = \begin{bmatrix} 45 & 0 & 34 & 1 & 82 & 42 & 65 & 8 \\ 80 & 69 & 93 & 0 & 33 & 56 & 65 & 17 \end{bmatrix}$ and the error vector $\mathbf{e}^T = \begin{bmatrix} 4 & 4 & 2 & 3 & 2 & 2 & 3 & 2 \end{bmatrix}$. Then computes

$$\mathbf{b}^T \equiv \mathbf{s^T A} + \mathbf{e}^T \pmod{q} \tag{11-14}$$

$$\equiv \begin{bmatrix} 1544 & 556 & 1426 & 23 & 1906 & 1290 & 1823 & 298 \end{bmatrix} \pmod{97} \tag{11-15}$$

$$\equiv \begin{bmatrix} 89 & 71 & 68 & 23 & 63 & 29 & 77 & 7 \end{bmatrix} \pmod{97} \tag{11-16}$$

Bob sends the public key $(\mathbf{A}, \mathbf{b}^T)$ to Alice. Alice samples a random binary vector $\mathbf{r} = \begin{bmatrix} 0 & 1 & 1 & 1 & 0 & 1 & 1 & 1 \end{bmatrix}^T$ and computes the ciphertext

$$\mathbf{c}_1 = \begin{bmatrix} 53 & 9 \end{bmatrix}^T, c_2 = 81 \tag{11-17}$$

Alice then transmits the pair $(\mathbf{c}_1, c_2)$ to Bob. Bob computes $a \equiv c_2 - \mathbf{c}_1^T\mathbf{s} \pmod q \equiv 16$, since $a < \lfloor q/4 \rfloor = 24$, so the recovered plaintext is 0 that is same as the original plaintext.

For $d = 1$, Bob generates $\mathbf{A} = \begin{bmatrix} 78 & 83 & 62 & 37 & 16 & 47 & 28 & 12 \\ 79 & 80 & 56 & 49 & 81 & 9 & 38 & 2 \end{bmatrix}$ and the error vector $\mathbf{e}^T = \begin{bmatrix} 4 & 4 & 2 & 1 & 2 & 4 & 3 & 2 \end{bmatrix}$. Then computes

$$\mathbf{b}^T \equiv \mathbf{s}^\mathbf{T}\mathbf{A} + \mathbf{e}^T \pmod q \tag{11-18}$$

$$\equiv \begin{bmatrix} 2196 & 2304 & 1690 & 1133 & 970 & 1016 & 867 & 258 \end{bmatrix} \pmod{97} \tag{11-19}$$

$$\equiv \begin{bmatrix} 62 & 73 & 41 & 66 & 0 & 46 & 91 & 64 \end{bmatrix} \pmod{97} \tag{11-20}$$

Bob sends the public key $(\mathbf{A}, \mathbf{b}^T)$ to Alice. Alice samples a random binary vector $\mathbf{r} = \begin{bmatrix} 0 & 1 & 1 & 1 & 1 & 1 & 1 & 0 \end{bmatrix}^T$ and computes the ciphertext

$$\mathbf{c}_1 = \begin{bmatrix} 79 & 22 \end{bmatrix}^T, c_2 = 74 \tag{11-21}$$

Alice then transmits the pair $(\mathbf{c}_1, c_2)$ to Bob. Bob computes $a \equiv c_2 - \mathbf{c}_1^T\mathbf{s} \pmod q \equiv 64$, since $a > \lfloor q/4 \rfloor = 24$, so the recovered plaintext is 1 that is same as the original plaintext.

Repeat the calculation in order. The Python code is as follows:

```
import numpy as np
import random
import math

size=8  #Length

s = np.array([[20,8]]) #secret key
q=97 #prime
m = [0,1,0,0,1,1,1,1,0,1,0,0,1,0,1,1] #plaintext

for message in m:
A =  np.array([ random.sample(range(q), size), random.sample(range(q)
    , size)]) matrix A
e=np.array([[random.randint(1,4) for i in range(size)]])  #Error
     vector e
B = np.dot(A.T,s.T)+e.T #compute B = As+e

sample= np.array([[random.randint(0,1) for i in range(size)]])

c1 =  np.dot(A,sample.T)%q #ciphertext 1
c2 = (np.dot(B.T,sample.T) + math.floor(q//2)*message)%q  #ciphertext
    2
```

```
a=(c2-np.dot(s,c1)) % q

if (a>math.floor(q/4)):
  print("Plaintext is: 1")
else:
  print("Plaintext is: 0")
```

■

This scheme is called the **Regev Scheme**. In addition, there are dual Regev Scheme and Multi-bit Scheme [136].

11.1.4 Ring Learning with Errors Problem

To improve the computational efficiency of LWE, a standard approach is to introduce a ring structure, effectively transitioning from general lattices to ideal lattices. Inspired by the NTRU cryptosystem, this method utilizes polynomial rings. In this setting, arithmetic is performed modulo a prime q and modulo a fixed polynomial $f(x)$. Consequently, both the degree and the coefficient size of the polynomials remain bounded, which significantly enhances efficiency. In 2010, *Lyubashevsky*, *Peikert*, and *Regev* systematically proposed and analyzed the Ring Learning with Errors (Ring-LWE) problem in their seminal work [137]. Today, Ring-LWE and its variants serve as the foundation for numerous post-quantum secure cryptosystems.

We proceed with the formal definition. Let n be a security parameter, which is a power of two. Define the polynomial $f(x) = x^n + 1$ of degree n. Let $q \geqslant 2$ be a prime modulus bounded by a polynomial in n denoted as $q \leqslant \text{poly}(n)$ such that $q \equiv 1 \pmod{2n}$. We define the ring R and the quotient ring R_q as follows:

$$R = \mathbb{Z}[x]/(x^n + 1), \quad R_q = \mathbb{Z}_q[x]/(x^n + 1) \tag{11-22}$$

Elements of R_q are typically represented as polynomials with integer coefficients in the range $[0, q-1]$ and degree less than n.

The Ring-LWE distribution, denoted as $\mathcal{A}_{s,\chi}$, is defined over $R_q \times R_q$. Let $s = s(x) \in R_q$ be a secret key sampled uniformly at random. Let χ be an error distribution(a discrete Gaussian distribution) over R from which the error $e \in \chi$ is sampled. The distribution generates samples of the form (a, b), where $a = a(x)$ is chosen uniformly from R_q, and b is computed as

$$b = a \cdot s + e \in R_q \tag{11-23}$$

Here, the multiplication $a \cdot s$ is performed within the ring R_q.

$$\underbrace{\left(a_0 + \cdots + a_{n-1}x^{n-1}\right)}_{a(x)} \underbrace{\left(s_0 + \cdots + s_{n-1}x^{n-1}\right)}_{s(x)} + \underbrace{\left(e_0 + \cdots + e_{n-1}x^{n-1}\right)}_{e(x)} = \underbrace{b_0 + \cdots + b_{n-1}x^{n-1}}_{b(x) = as(x) + e(x)}$$

Example 11.1.3 Let $q = 13$, $n = 4$, then $R_q = \mathbb{Z}_{13}[x]/\left(x^4 + 1\right)$. Assume $a = 5 + 2x + 9x^2 + 11x^3$, $s = 7 + 8x + 11x^2 + 10x^3$, $e = 1 + 2x^2 + x^3$. Compute $b = as + e$

Solution:

$$
\begin{aligned}
b &\equiv as + e \pmod{x^4+1} && \text{(11-24)}\\
&\equiv (5+2x+9x^2+11x^3)(7+8x+11x^2+10x^3)+e \pmod{x^4+1} && \text{(11-25)}\\
&\equiv (-3-x-2x^2)+(1+2x^2+x^3) \pmod{x^4+1} && \text{(11-26)}\\
&\equiv -2-x+x^3 \pmod{x^4+1} && \text{(11-27)}
\end{aligned}
$$

■

Computing $as + e$ is straightforward. However, given only a and b, it is hard to recover s. The Ring LWE problem is defined as follows:

Definition 11.1.3 Ring-LWE Problem

Let $R_q = \mathbb{Z}_q[x]/(x^n+1)$. Let χ be an error distribution over R_q (typically a discrete Gaussian concentrated around zero). For a secret $s \in R_q$ chosen uniformly at random, we define the **RLWE distribution** *$\mathcal{A}_{s,\chi}$ over $R_q \times R_q$ as the distribution of samples (a, b), obtained by sampling a uniformly at random from R_q, sampling e from χ, and computing $b = a \cdot s + e$.*

The Ring-LWE problem comes in two versions:

1) *The* ***Search Version****: Given arbitrarily many pairs (a, b) from the RLWE distribution $\mathcal{A}_{s,\chi}$, the goal is to recover the secret s.*
2) *The* ***Decisional Version****: Given arbitrarily many pairs (a, b) from the RLWE distribution $\mathcal{A}_{s,\chi}$, the goal is to distinguish which is the case:*
   (a) *Samples (a, b) drawn from $\mathcal{A}_{s,\chi}$ where $b = a \cdot s + e$ for a "small" error e.*
   (b) *Samples (a, u) are drawn completely uniformly at random from $R_q \times R_q$.*

11.1.5 Ring LWE-Based Cryptosystem

The encryption scheme based on Ring LWE is a generalization of Regev's LWE scheme. It remains a binary encryption scheme. Its encryption procedure is as follows:

1) (KeyGen): Let n be an integer and a power of 2, the prime $q \geqslant 2$, and set $f(x) = x^n + 1$, $R = \frac{\mathbb{Z}[x]}{(x^n+1)}$, $R_q = \frac{\mathbb{Z}_q[x]}{(x^n+1)}$, χ be an error distribution (such as a discrete Gaussian) over R_q. Bob samples $a = a(x) \in R_q$, $s = s(x) \in R_q$ uniformly at random, $r \in \chi$ according to the error distribution. Computes

$$(a, b = as + r) \in R_q \times R_q \tag{11-28}$$

where s is secret key, the pair (a, b) is public key. The element r can be thrown away.

2) (Encrypt): Let the plaintext $m \in R_{\{0,1\}}$ that is encoded to 0 or 1 coefficients of a polynomial. Alice chooses three random "small" elements $e_1, e_2, e_3 \in \chi$.

Then computes

$$c_1 = ae_1 + e_2 \in R_q \tag{11-29}$$

$$c_2 = \lfloor q/2 \rceil m + be_1 + e_3 \in R_q \tag{11-30}$$

The elements e_1, e_2, e_3 are called temporary elements and can be thrown away. Alice securely transmits (c_1, c_2) sends to Bob.

3) (**Decrypt**): After Bob received the ciphertexts, he computes

$$\begin{aligned} m' = c_2 - c_1 s &= \lfloor q/2 \rceil m + be_1 + e_3 - (ae_1 + e_2)s & (11\text{-}31) \\ &= \lfloor q/2 \rceil m + (as + r)e_1 + e_3 - (ae_1 + e_2)s & (11\text{-}32) \\ &= \lfloor q/2 \rceil m + re_1 - e_2 s + e_3 & (11\text{-}33) \\ &= \lfloor q/2 \rceil m + e' & (11\text{-}34) \end{aligned}$$

Here, $e' = re_1 - e_2 s + e_3$ is is called **noise**, which geometrically remains a very small element within R_q. Rounding each coefficient of m' to 0 or $\lfloor q/2 \rceil$. The plaintext can be recovered successfully if and only if e' less than $q/4$. The plaintext can be recovered by computing the coefficient of m'

$$m' \equiv \lfloor (2/q) \cdot (c_2 - c_1 s) \rceil \pmod 2 \tag{11-35}$$

There are multiple encodings for the plaintext m. As long as e' stays within the **error threshold**, the ciphertext will decrypt correctly.

Example 11.1.4 Consider Public-Key Encryption from Ring LWE, if Alice wants to send the plaintext m to Bob. Compute the ciphertext.

Assume $n = 4$, $q = 17$. $f(x) = x^4 + 1$, then $R_q = \frac{\mathbb{Z}_{17}[x]}{x^4+1}$. The small coefficients, secrets and errors are drawn from $\{-1, 0, 1\}$ since working modulo 17, -1 is represented as 16.

The plaintext bits coefficient wise using $\{0, \lfloor q/2 \rceil\} = \{0, 8\} \longmapsto \{0, 1\}$.

Solution: Bob randomly selects $a = x^2 + 2x + 3 \in R_q$, $s = -x^2 + x + 1 \in R_q$ from R_q uniformly, and the error $r = x^3 - x + 1 \in \chi$. He computes

$$\begin{aligned} b \equiv as + r &\equiv -x^4 + 4x + 4 \pmod{x^4 + 1} & (11\text{-}36) \\ &\equiv 4x + 5 \pmod{x^4 + 1} & (11\text{-}37) \end{aligned}$$

Here, since $f(x) = x^4 + 1$, we have $x^4 \equiv -1 \pmod{x^4 + 1}$.

Then, Bob sends the public key (a, b) to Alice and keeps the secret key s. Alice wants to send the plaintext $m = x^2 + 1$. She samples three random "small" elements $e_1 = x^2 + 1$, $e_2 = x^2 + x$, $e_3 = x^3 + 1$, then computes the ciphertext

$$\begin{aligned} c_1 &\equiv ae_1 + e_2 \equiv 2x^3 + 5x^2 + 3x + 2 \pmod{x^4 + 1} & (11\text{-}38) \\ c_2 &\equiv \lfloor q/2 \rceil m + be_1 + e_3 & (11\text{-}39) \\ &\equiv 8(x^2 + 1) + (5x^5 + 3x^2 + 4x + 6) & (11\text{-}40) \\ &\equiv 5x^3 + 13x^2 + 4x + 14 \pmod{x^4 + 1} & (11\text{-}41) \end{aligned}$$

Alice then transmits (c_1, c_2) sends to Bob. To decrypt, Bob computes

$$m' \equiv c_2 - c_1 s \equiv (5x^3 + 13x^2 + 4x + 14) - (2x^3 + 5x^2 + 3x + 2)(-x^2 + x + 1) \quad (11\text{-}42)$$

$$\equiv (5x^3 + 13x^2 + 4x + 14) - (4x^3 + 6x^2 + 7x + 5) \quad (11\text{-}43)$$

$$\equiv x^3 + 7x^2 - 3x + 9 \pmod{x^4 + 1} \quad (11\text{-}44)$$

Rounding each coefficient of m' back to either 0 or 8. For each $m'_i \in \mathbb{Z}_{17}$, we have

$$m_0 = min(m'_i, 17 - m'_i) \text{ , } m_8 = min(\|m'_i - 8\|, 17 - \|m'_i - 8\|) \quad (11\text{-}45)$$

Declare the plaintext is 1 if $m_8 < m_0$, otherwise declare 0. Applying this to $m' = x^3 + 7x^2 - 3x + 9$ given $x^2 + 1$, which matches the original message.

One more method, computing $m' \equiv \lfloor (2/q) \cdot (c_2 - c_1 s) \rceil \pmod 2$. Since $m' = x^3 + 7x^2 - 3x + 9 = [1, 7, -3, 9]$, then $\lfloor (2/q) \cdot [1, 7, -3, 9] \rceil \equiv \lfloor [0.1176, 0.8235, -0.3529, 1.0588] \rceil \equiv [0, 1, 0, 1] \pmod 2$. Thus, the recovered plaintext is $m = x^2 + 1$. ■

The parameters exploited for implementation are given in follow: n requires at least 512 bits, q requires at least 12289 bits and the standard deviation of the error distribution χ is approximately 4.86 that have high security respectively.

11.2 HOMOMORPHIC ENCRYPTION

Following the publication of the RSA encryption scheme, cryptographers raised a fundamental question: Is it feasible to perform arbitrary arithmetic operations on encrypted data without access to the secret key? Specifically, the goal was to ensure that decrypting the result of operations performed on the ciphertext would yield the same result as if those operations had been performed directly on the underlying plaintext.

To illustrate the utility of such a scheme, consider a scenario involving Alice. She needs to build an AI model from medical data, and her advisor requires running hundreds of cross validation jobs this week. Her laptop is not powerful, so she must send the data to a cloud GPU platform. The data contains patient information, and school policy forbids uploading plaintext.

A viable solution is to encrypt the data locally before transmission. The cloud provider then performs computations on the ciphertext without ever accessing the raw data and returns the encrypted result to Alice. Finally, Alice decrypts this output to obtain the desired result. This paradigm allows for the utilization of cloud computing resources while preserving data privacy. The cryptographic tool possessing such a property is called **Homomorphic Encryption**.

Why is homomorphic encryption essential? In sectors such as healthcare, finance, public services, and the Industrial Internet of Things (IIoT), data processed on external platforms must comply with rigorous privacy laws and industry standards. Homomorphic encryption ensures that data remains computable yet confidential. Furthermore, it allows mutually untrusting parties to encrypt their private data and submit it to a third party to compute shared metrics. This approach eliminates the need to rely on the integrity of the platform or trusted hardware environments and mitigates risks associated with insider threats or cloud security breaches.

However, Homomorphic ciphertexts include noise added for security. Each homomorphic addition or multiplication increases the noise. If the noise grows too large, decryption fails even with the secret key. The key idea in FHE is bootstrapping. It performs a decryption step homomorphically to reduce the noise, so one can keep evaluating deeper circuits. Bootstrapping needs careful parameters and strong engineering, and it is both the main difficulty and the main breakthrough of FHE.

In 1978, *Rivest*, *Adleman*, and *Dertouzos* published a paper [138], introducing the concept of privacy homomorphisms. *Craig Gentry* defined homomorphic encryption as follows: "*A way to delegate processing of your data, without giving away access to it*".

Before delving into the cryptographic details, we must define the underlying mathematical structure. In abstract algebra, a homomorphism is a structure-preserving map between two algebraic structures of the same type. It establishes a connection between two objects of the same type that may have different properties. The previous chapters introduced the basic definitions and properties of groups; this chapter will focus on mappings among group elements, since many algebraic properties are expressed through mappings. A group homomorphism arises from the basic properties of groups. It can be viewed as preserving the underlying binary operation under the mapping. The definition of a group homomorphism is as follows:

Definition 11.2.1 Group Homomorphism

Let G, H be two groups, a homomorphism ϕ from G to H is a mapping $\phi : G \to H$ if the following structural property is strictly satisfied for all $a, b \in G$:

$$\phi(a * b) = \phi(a) * \phi(b) \tag{11-46}$$

The product $a * b$ on the left-hand side takes place in G, while the product $\phi(a) * \phi(b)$ on the right-hand side takes place in H. The two group structures give a relation between these binary operations.

The kernel of a homomorphism $\phi : G \to H$, typically denoted by $\ker \phi$, is defined as the set of elements in G that map exactly to the identity element e_H of H. Formally, $\ker \phi = \{x \in G \mid \phi(x) = e_H\}$.

1) The map $\phi : \mathbb{Z} \to \mathbb{Z}_n$ under addition defined by $\phi(x) = x \pmod n$ is a homomorphism.
2) The map $\phi : \mathbb{Z} \to \mathbb{R}$ under addition defined by $\phi(x) = x$ is a homomorphism.
3) The map $\phi : \mathbb{R}^* \to \mathbb{R}^*$ under multiplication defined by $\phi(x) = x$ is a homomorphism.
4) The map $\phi : \mathbb{R}^* \to \mathbb{R}^*$ under multiplication defined by $\phi(x) = x^2$ is a homomorphism.

5) The map $\phi : \mathbb{Z} \to \mathbb{Z}$ under addition defined by $\phi(x) = 3$ is not a homomorphism since $\phi(1+1) = \phi(2) = 3$, whereas $\phi(1) + \phi(1) = 3 + 3 = 6 \neq 3$.
6) The map $\phi : \mathbb{Z} \to \mathbb{Z}$ under addition defined by $\phi(x) = x + 1$ is not a homomorphism since $\phi(1+2) = \phi(3) = 4$, whereas $\phi(1) + \phi(2) = 2 + 3 = 5 \neq 4$.

Definition 11.2.2 Homomorphic Encryption

An encryption scheme is called ***homomorphic*** *over a plaintext operation "$*$" if there exists a corresponding ciphertext operation "$\star$" such that the following algebraic equation strictly holds:*

$$E(m_1) \star E(m_2) = E(m_1 * m_2), \quad \forall m_1, m_2 \in M \tag{11-47}$$

where E is the encryption algorithm, M is the set of all possible messages, and the decryption algorithm D naturally satisfies $D(E(m_1) \star E(m_2)) = m_1 * m_2$.

An additively homomorphic encryption scheme is homomorphic over addition if there exists a ciphertext operation $\star$ such that:

$$E(m_1) \star E(m_2) = E(m_1 + m_2) \tag{11-48}$$

A multiplicatively homomorphic encryption scheme is homomorphic over multiplication if there exists a ciphertext operation $\star$ such that:

$$E(m_1) \star E(m_2) = E(m_1 \cdot m_2) \tag{11-49}$$

The **RSA cryptosystem** is an early example of Homomorphic Encryption Scheme. Given two ciphertexts $c_1 \equiv m_1^e \pmod N$, $c_2 \equiv m_2^e \pmod N$, we have

$$E(m_1) \cdot E(m_2) = c_1 \cdot c_2 \equiv m_1^e \cdot m_2^e \equiv (m_1 \cdot m_2)^e \pmod N = E(m_1 \cdot m_2) \tag{11-50}$$

Hence, $D(E(m_1) \cdot E(m_2)) = D(E(m_1 \cdot m_2))$. Multiplicatively homomorphic property is present in RSA cryptosystem.

However, since $m_1^e m_2^e \not\equiv (m_1 + m_2)^e \pmod N$, there is no additively homomorphic operation, RSA is only multiplicatively homomorphic.

The **Paillier cryptosystem** is an example of additively Homomorphic Encryption Scheme [139]. The Paillier cryptosystem was developed by *Pascal Paillier* in 1999. Given two ciphertexts $c_1 \equiv g^{m_1} r_1^N \pmod{N^2}$, $c_2 \equiv g^{m_2} r_2^N \pmod{N^2}$ where N is the modulus, g is the base and $r_i \in \mathbb{Z}_N^*$ such that $\gcd(r_i, N) = 1$, we have

$$E(m_1)E(m_2) \equiv c_1 \cdot c_2 \equiv g^{m_1+m_2}(r_1 r_2)^N \pmod{N^2} \equiv E(m_1 + m_2) \tag{11-51}$$

Hence, $D(E(m_1) \cdot E(m_2)) = D(E(m_1 + m_2))$. Additive homomorphic property is present in Paillier cryptosystem.

However, since $g^{m_1+m_2}(r_1 r_2)^N \not\equiv g^{m_1 m_2}(r_1 r_2)^N \pmod{N^2}$, there is no multiplicatively homomorphic operation, Paillier is only additively homomorphic.

RSA and Paillier cryptosystems are called **Partially Homomorphic Encryption (PHE)** that allows only one type of operation with an unlimited number of times, either addition or multiplication. PHE supports operation on ciphertexts, but does not support arbitrary computation on ciphertexts. Apart from the RSA encryption algorithm and the Paillier encryption algorithm, the ElGamal encryption algorithm are both partially homomorphic encryption algorithms.

11.3 FULLY HOMOMORPHIC ENCRYPTION

11.3.1 Definition

Fully Homomorphic Encryption (FHE) allows an unlimited number of operations with unlimited number of times, including additively and multiplicatively. If a homomorphic encryption allows some types of operations with a limited number of times, then it is called **Somewhat Homomorphic Encryption** (SWHE) scheme.

In the 30 years after [138], many cryptographers attempted to design fully homomorphic encryption, yet overall progress was limited. Several proposals achieved partial homomorphism, but their security fell short of full homomorphism or flaws were later found. In 2005, *Dan Boneh, Eu-Jin Goh*, and *Kobbi Nissim* introduced the BGN cryptosystem, which permitted arbitrary number of additions and one multiplication. This was viewed as a key milestone toward fully homomorphic encryption.

In 2009, *Craig Gentry* achieved a historic breakthrough by developing the first Fully Homomorphic Encryption cryptosystem in his paper [140]. It marked a historic breakthrough and resolved a problem that had challenged cryptography for decades.

Gentry's first FHE scheme has major theoretical significance and is often called the first-generation of fully homomorphic encryption. The scheme uses ideal lattices that has low practical efficiency and relies on mathematical tools that are hard to understand, which limits its use. Later work built on it and developed second and third generation FHE schemes.

FHE is an active area in cryptography with applications to outsourced computation, privacy preserving machine learning, secure multi party computation, federated learning, and data exchange and sharing. Its homomorphic property allows one to run arbitrarily complex operations such as search and comparison on encrypted data without decryption and obtain correct results, achieving "usable but not visible" when data and computation are given to a third party. For sensitive data like health care information, FHE enables predictive analysis in a third party environment and lowers privacy risk. If keys are not leaked and the implementation is correct, the data remain confidential even if the service provider is compromised.

Definition 11.3.1 Fully Homomorphic Encryption [141]

A fully homomorphic encryption scheme is an encryption scheme that allows ***evaluation*** *of arbitrarily complex programs on encrypted data. The scheme has four algorithms:* KeyGen, Encrypt, Decrypt, Evaluate, *denoted as* HE = (KeyGen, Enc, Eval, Dec).

1) $\mathsf{KeyGen}(1^\lambda)$: *Let* λ *be a security parameter (represented in unary as* 1^λ*), outputs a key-pair* (pk, sk, evk). *The public key* pk *is used for encryption, the secret key* sk *for decryption, and the evaluation key* evk *for performing homomorphic operations.*
2) $\mathsf{Enc}(pk, m)$: *Given a public key* pk *and a plaintext* $m \in \{0, 1\}$, *outputs a ciphertext* c.
3) $\mathsf{Dec}(sk, c)$: *Given a secret key* sk *and a ciphertext* c, *outputs a plaintext* $m \in \{0, 1\}$.
4) $\mathsf{Eval}(evk, f, [c_1, \ldots, c_n])$: *Given an evaluation key* evk, *a vector of ciphertexts* $[c_1, \ldots, c_n]$ *and a homomorphic function* f *such that* $\{0, 1\}^n \rightarrow \{0, 1\}$, *outputs an evaluated ciphertexts that encrypts the result of applying the function* f *to the original ciphertext vector.*

Compared with traditional encryption schemes, a fully homomorphic encryption scheme includes an additional **evaluation algorithm** (Eval). The homomorphic function f is what Eval executes, and it may be any function, because FHE is designed to enable arbitrary computation on ciphertexts. This algorithm is the core of homomorphic encryption. Computation on ciphertexts is modeled by a layered circuit with the ciphertext as input. A deeper circuit, with more layers, allows more successive computations on the ciphertext.

11.3.2 Circuit

The evaluation algorithm (Eval) systematically executes the homomorphic function f on the input ciphertexts. In fully homomorphic encryption, ciphertexts contain noise and evaluation increases that noise. If we represent f as a circuit, then Eval can correctly handle only circuits up to a finite depth L; circuits deeper than L cannot be evaluated correctly.

Here a circuit means a digital circuit, which is a switching circuit whose inputs and outputs are high or low levels represented by the binary values 0 and 1. The relation between inputs and outputs is a logical causal relation. A circuit has no programmatic control-flow structures such as selection, loops, or tests, so following the design rules keeps ciphertext evaluation simple and convenient. In general, circuits are usually divided into Boolean circuits and arithmetic circuits.

A Boolean circuit is a profound mathematical model for digital logic computation based on two-valued Boolean algebra. Boolean algebra was introduced by the English mathematician *George Boole* for logic operations. When applied to digital circuits it is called switching algebra, and the circuits are called Boolean circuits. The inputs of a Boolean circuit are bits, and the basic logic operations implemented by gates are **AND**, **OR**, and **NOT**, as shown in Figure 11-4.

Arithmetic circuits can represent inputs modulo a larger integer and are built from a sequence of additions and multiplications. If homomorphic encryption is both compact and homomorphic for the class of all arithmetic circuits over $\mathbb{Z}_2$, then the homomorphic encryption is fully homomorphic encryption.

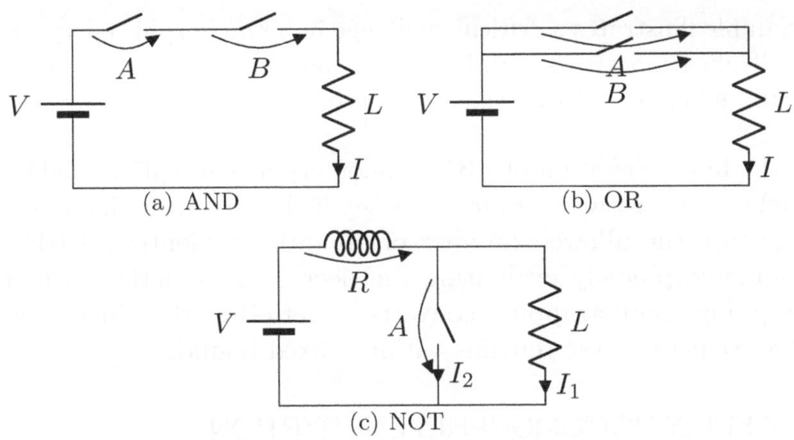

Figure 11-4: Boolean Circuit

Traditional secure computation adopts the circuit model, which processes all inputs in a fixed combinational form and does not reveal extra information. Gentry's fully homomorphic encryption scheme also follows this circuit model. Over $\mathbb{Z}_2$, addition and multiplication form a complete set of operations in practice, with addition corresponding to XOR and multiplication corresponding to AND. Crucially, in theoretical computer science, these gates form a functionally complete set of operations. Hence a fully homomorphic encryption scheme can evaluate any polynomial on ciphertexts [142].

The first generation of fully homomorphic encryption was built on ideal lattices. After encryption, the ciphertext contains noise that masks the plaintext, as in Example 11.3.1. During homomorphic evaluation, each operation increases the noise. When the noise grows beyond a certain level, it covers the plaintext so that even the key holder cannot recover it, as shown in Figure 11-5.

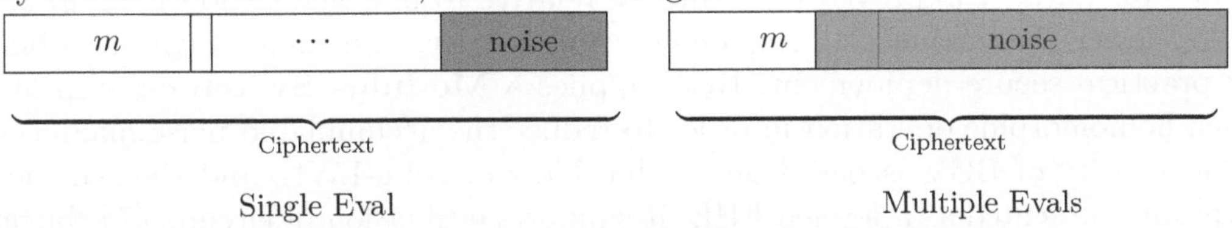

Figure 11-5: Homomorphic Encryption Noise

Example 11.3.1 Let $m_1 = 100$ and $m_2 = 200$ denote the plaintexts, and let the corresponding ciphertexts be $c_1 = 110$ and $c_2 = 220$. The noise terms associated with these ciphertexts are $e_1 = c_1 - m_1 = 10$ and $e_2 = c_2 - m_2 = 20$.

For the additive operation, the sum of the ciphertexts is $c_1 + c_2 = (m_1 + m_2) + (e_1 + e_2)$. In this case, the resulting noise is simply the sum of the individual errors $e_{add} = e_1 + e_2 = 30$.

For the multiplicative operation, expanding the product of the ciphertexts $c_1 \cdot c_2 = (m_1 + e_1)(m_2 + e_2) = m_1m_2 + (m_1e_2 + m_2e_1 + e_1e_2) = 24200$. Thus, $e_{mult} = m_1e_2 + m_2e_1 + e_1e_2 = 4200$.

This example illustrates a critical challenge in homomorphic encryption: the noise term in multiplication grows significantly faster than in addition. If not managed, this accumulated error can eventually cause decryption failures.

Before the first generation of FHE, homomorphic encryption could only support a finite number of operations because of noise. If the growth of the noise is controlled, one can increase the allowed number of operations. Gentry's FHE controls the noise by homomorphically evaluating the decryption function, a method known as bootstrapping. Bootstrapping converts or refreshes the ciphertext into a new ciphertext so that the noise remains within a fixed bound.

11.4 BGV FULLY HOMOMORPHIC ENCRYPTION

Following the first generation of FHE, researchers began to build FHE schemes from Ring-LWE and to exploit the algebraic structure of ideals and fast polynomial algorithms to optimize and implement those schemes. An ideal is a subset of the ring $R = \mathbb{Z}[x]/(f(x))$ that is closed under addition and closed under multiplication by elements of R. Viewing such an ideal as a $\mathbb{Z}$-modulo yields the so called ideal lattice.

First generation FHE can in principle support arbitrary-depth homomorphic evaluation, but only by using bootstrapping to refresh ciphertexts. Bootstrapping is very costly and became the main bottleneck for practical efficiency. In early implementations, homomorphic multiplication was extremely slow, typically ranging from minutes to hours depending on the implementation and parameters. So the first-generation construction was mainly of theoretical interest and was later improved and replaced by a sequence of more efficient FHE schemes.

BGV Fully Homomorphic Encryption, named after *Zvika Brakerski*, *Craig Gentry*, and *Vinod Vaikuntanathan*, introduced a set of effective noise management techniques that substantially improved performance relative to first generation FHE in 2011 [143], lower the engineering implementation barrier, and increase the feasibility of practical secure deployment. BGV applies a **Modulus Switching** step after each homomorphic operation in order to reduce the accumulated noise magnitude. The security of BGV is based on the hardness of Ring-LWE, and the scheme is typically presented as a leveled FHE: it supports evaluation of circuits of arbitrary size provided the circuit depth does not exceed a predetermined bound. This chapter will formalize why the term "leveled" is utilized.

The main contribution of BGV is a method to evaluate circuits of arbitrary polynomial size at a fixed circuit depth. BGV can perform homomorphic evaluation without bootstrapping. Teams at IBM, led by *Halevi* and *Shoup*, subsequently released and maintain the high-performance open-source library HElib, which helped drive the engineering and adoption of FHE. After further optimizations [144], BGV based implementations became prominent among efficient FHE systems. Because homomorphic evaluation in BGV still depends on auxiliary key material, BGV is usually classified as a second-generation FHE scheme.

11.4.1 Homomorphic Encryption

Before studying the BGV algorithm in detail, it is helpful to first understand the process of a basic homomorphic encryption scheme.

1) E.Setup($1^\lambda, 1^\mu, b$): Given the security parameter λ, a functional parameter μ, typically corresponding to the polynomial degree or arithmetic circuit's multiplicative depth L. Let the bit with $b \in \{0,1\}$, with a binary indicator ($b = 0, d = 1$) indicates LWE or ($b = 1, n = 1$) indicates RLWE. Let $R = \mathbb{Z}[x]/(x^d + 1)$, outputs (q, d, n, N, χ), where:
   (a) q denotes prime modulus of length μ bits.
   (b) d denotes degree of $f(x)$, where $d = d(\lambda, \mu, b)$ is power of 2.
   (c) n denotes dimension, where $n = n(\lambda, \mu, b)$.
   (d) N denotes an additional parameter, where $N = \lceil (2n+1)\log q \rceil$.
   (e) χ is a Gaussian error distribution, over R, denoted $\chi(\lambda, \mu, b)$.
2) E.SecretKeyGen($params$): Draw $\mathbf{t} \leftarrow \chi^n$, outputs the secret key $sk = \mathbf{s} \leftarrow (1, \mathbf{t}[1], \ldots, \mathbf{t}[n]) \in R_q^{n+1}$.
3) E.PublicKeyGen($params, sk$): Given the secret key $sk = \mathbf{s}$ and the parameters $params$. Generate a matrix $\mathbf{B} \leftarrow R_q^{N\times n}$ uniformly and a vector $\mathbf{e} \leftarrow \chi^N$ and a set $\mathbf{b} \leftarrow \mathbf{Bt} + 2\mathbf{e}$. Set $\mathbf{A}$ to be the $(n+1)$ column matrix consisting of b followed by the n columns of $-\mathbf{B}$. Outputs the public key $pk = \mathbf{A}$.

$$\mathbf{B} = \begin{bmatrix} B_{11} & B_{12} & \cdots & B_{1n} \\ B_{21} & B_{22} & \cdots & B_{2n} \\ \vdots & \vdots & \ddots & \vdots \\ B_{N1} & B_{N2} & \cdots & B_{Nn} \end{bmatrix}, \quad \mathbf{e} = \begin{bmatrix} e_1 \\ e_2 \\ \vdots \\ e_N \end{bmatrix}, \quad \mathbf{b} = \begin{bmatrix} b_1 \\ b_2 \\ \vdots \\ b_N \end{bmatrix}, \quad \mathbf{A} = [\mathbf{b} \quad -\mathbf{B}]$$

4) E.Enc($params, pk, m$): Given the public key, a plaintext $m \in \{0,1\}$ and the parameters $params$. Let $\mathbf{m} \leftarrow (m, 0, \ldots, 0) \in R_q^{n+1}$, $\mathbf{r} \leftarrow R_2^N$, outputs the ciphertext vector $\mathbf{c} \leftarrow \mathbf{m} + \mathbf{A}^\top \mathbf{r} \in R_q^{n+1}$.
5) E.Dec($params, sk, \mathbf{c}$): Given the secret key, the ciphertext vector $\mathbf{c}$ and the parameters $params$, outputs

$$m \leftarrow \left[[\langle \mathbf{c}, \mathbf{s} \rangle]_q \right]_2 \tag{11-52}$$

Proof

Since $\mathbf{r}$ *and* $\mathbf{e}$ *are very small, therefore* $|m + 2\mathbf{r}^T\mathbf{e}| < q/2$, *we have*

$$\left[[\langle \mathbf{c}, \mathbf{s} \rangle]_q \right]_2 = \left[\left[(\mathbf{m}^T + \mathbf{r}^T\mathbf{A}) \cdot \mathbf{s} \right]_q \right]_2 = \left[\left[m + 2\mathbf{r}^T\mathbf{e} \right]_q \right]_2 = \left[m + 2\mathbf{r}^T\mathbf{e} \right]_2 = m$$

11.4.2 Key Switching

In the BGV scheme, a procedure known as BGV!FHE.SwitchKey plays a pivotal role. Its primary purpose is to perform dimension reduction on the ciphertext, and it serves as a core technique for constructing fully homomorphic encryption from LWE. The FHE.SwitchKey process transforms a ciphertext encrypted under a secret key

$\mathbf{s}_1$ into a new ciphertext encrypted under a different secret key $\mathbf{s}_2$, while strictly preserving the underlying plaintext message. It is important to note that $\mathbf{s}_1$ and $\mathbf{s}_2$ do not necessarily share the same dimension.

To understand why this is necessary, we must examine the algebraic structure of homomorphic operations. Fundamentally, decryption can be viewed as evaluating a linear function. During decryption, one computes the inner product $\langle \mathbf{c}, \mathbf{s} \rangle$. We can express the decryption of a message m as

$$m = \left[[L_{\mathbf{c}}(\mathbf{s})]_q \right]_2 \tag{11-53}$$

where $L_{\mathbf{c}}(\mathbf{s})$ is a ciphertext dependent linear equation over the coefficients of $\mathbf{s}$ given by $\langle \mathbf{c}, \mathbf{s} \rangle$.

Consider two plaintexts m_1 and m_2 encrypted under the same secret key $\mathbf{s}$, yielding ciphertexts $\mathbf{c}_1$ and $\mathbf{c}_2$. Homomorphic addition satisfies the property of linearity

$$L_{\mathbf{c}_1}(\mathbf{s}) + L_{\mathbf{c}_2}(\mathbf{s}) = L_{\mathbf{c}_1+\mathbf{c}_2}(\mathbf{s}) \tag{11-54}$$

However, homomorphic multiplication introduces complexity. The product of two linear functions results in a **quadratic** function

$$Q_{\mathbf{c}_1,\mathbf{c}_2}(\mathbf{s}) = L_{\mathbf{c}_1}(\mathbf{s}) \cdot L_{\mathbf{c}_2}(\mathbf{s}) \tag{11-55}$$

Assuming the noises of $\mathbf{c}_1$ and $\mathbf{c}_2$ are sufficiently small, then the homomorphic multiplication property implies

$$m_1 \cdot m_2 = [[Q_{\mathbf{c}_1,\mathbf{c}_2}(\mathbf{s})]_q]_2 \tag{11-56}$$

Here, $Q_{\mathbf{c}_1,\mathbf{c}_2}(\mathbf{s})$ can be algebraically re-expressed as a linear equation $L^{\text{long}}_{\mathbf{c}_1,\mathbf{c}_2}(\mathbf{s} \otimes \mathbf{s})$ where $\otimes$ is the **tensor product**. For a vector $\mathbf{s}$ of dimension n, the tensor product $\mathbf{s} \otimes \mathbf{s}$ results in a new vector of dimension n^2, containing all possible cross-products of the elements of $\mathbf{s}$.

Let $\mathbf{s} = [2, 4, -3]^T$, then

$$\mathbf{s} \otimes \mathbf{s} = \begin{bmatrix} 4 & 8 & -6 & 8 & 16 & -12 & -6 & -12 & 9 \end{bmatrix}^T \tag{11-57}$$

Each multiplication squares the dimension of the ciphertext and the required secret key. To prevent the parameters from growing unmanageably, the FHE.SwitchKey procedure is employed to switch the key from the expanded form $\mathbf{s} \otimes \mathbf{s}$ back to the original key $\mathbf{s}$, thereby restoring the ciphertext to its original dimension.

There are two functions in FHE.SwitchKey:

1) BitDecomp$(\mathbf{x}, q)$. Given $\mathbf{x} \in R_q^n$ and an odd prime modulus q, decomposes $\mathbf{x}$ into its bit representation

$$\mathbf{x} \equiv \sum_{i=0}^{\lfloor \log q \rfloor} 2^i \cdot \mathbf{u}_i \equiv \mathbf{u}_0 + 2\mathbf{u}_1 + 2^2\mathbf{u}_2 + \cdots + 2^{\lfloor \log q \rfloor}\mathbf{u}_{\lfloor \log q \rfloor} \pmod{q} \tag{11-58}$$

Outputs

$$\left(\mathbf{u}_0, \mathbf{u}_1, \ldots, \mathbf{u}_{\lfloor \log q \rfloor} \right) \in R_2^{n \cdot \lceil \log q \rceil} \tag{11-59}$$

The inverse of BitDecomp is $\sum_{i=0}^{\lfloor \log q \rfloor - 1} 2^i \cdot \mathbf{u}_i \pmod{q}$.

2) Powersof2$(\mathbf{x}, q)$. Given $\mathbf{x} \in R_q^n$ and prime modulus q, outputs

$$\left(\mathbf{x}, 2\mathbf{x}, \ldots, 2^{\lfloor \log q \rfloor}\mathbf{x}\right) \in R_q^{n \cdot \lceil \log q \rceil} \tag{11-60}$$

Powersof2 produces a vector by multiplying $\mathbf{x}$ with 2^i in modulo q, where $i \in [0, \lfloor \log q \rfloor]$.

Example 11.4.1 Consider $q = 16$, $n = 3$ and $\mathbf{x} = (2, 1, 13)^T \in \mathbb{Z}^3$. Find the output of BitDecomp and Powersof2.

Solution: Since $\lfloor \log_2 q \rfloor = \lfloor 4 \rfloor = 4$, we have

$$2 = \mathbf{0} \cdot 2^0 + \mathbf{1} \cdot 2^1 + \mathbf{0} \cdot 2^2 + \mathbf{0} \cdot 2^3 \tag{11-61}$$

$$1 = \mathbf{1} \cdot 2^0 + \mathbf{0} \cdot 2^1 + \mathbf{0} \cdot 2^2 + \mathbf{0} \cdot 2^3 \tag{11-62}$$

$$13 = \mathbf{1} \cdot 2^0 + \mathbf{0} \cdot 2^1 + \mathbf{1} \cdot 2^2 + \mathbf{1} \cdot 2^3 \tag{11-63}$$

Thus

$$\mathbf{u}_0 = (0, 1, 1)^T, \quad \mathbf{u}_1 = (1, 0, 0)^T, \quad \mathbf{u}_2 = (0, 0, 1)^T, \quad \mathbf{u}_3 = (0, 0, 1)^T \tag{11-64}$$

The output of BitDecomp is $\mathbf{u} = (\mathbf{u}_0, \mathbf{u}_1, \mathbf{u}_2, \mathbf{u}_3)^T = (0, 1, 1, 1, 0, 0, 0, 0, 1, 0, 0, 1)^T$. The output of Powersof2 is $(2, 1, 13, 4, 2, 10, 8, 4, 4, 0, 8, 8)^T$. ■

Since the ciphertext vector $\mathbf{c}$ and the secret key vector $\mathbf{s}$ have the same dimension, the following equality holds:

$$\langle \text{BitDecomp}(\mathbf{c}, q),\ \text{Powersof2}\ (\mathbf{s}, q) \rangle = \langle \mathbf{c}, \mathbf{s} \rangle \pmod{q} \tag{11-65}$$

Proof

$$\langle \textit{BitDecomp}(\mathbf{c}, q),\ \textit{Powersof2}\ (\mathbf{s}, q) \rangle \equiv \sum_{i=0}^{\lfloor \log q \rfloor} \left\langle \mathbf{u}_i, 2^i \cdot \mathbf{s} \right\rangle \equiv \sum_{i=0}^{\lfloor \log q \rfloor} \left\langle 2^i \cdot \mathbf{u}_i, \mathbf{s} \right\rangle \tag{11-66}$$

$$\equiv \left\langle \sum_{i=0}^{\lfloor \log q \rfloor} 2^i \cdot \mathbf{u}_i, \mathbf{s} \right\rangle \equiv \langle \mathbf{c}, \mathbf{s} \rangle \pmod{q} \tag{11-67}$$

The key switching procedure in the BGV scheme consists of two distinct algorithms: SwitchKeyGen and SwitchKey.

The first function is SwitchKeyGen$(\mathbf{s}_1, \mathbf{s}_2, n_1, n_2, q)$. Given two vectors $\mathbf{s}_1 \in R_q^{n_1}$ and $\mathbf{s}_2 \in R_q^{n_2}$. Let n_1 and n_2 denote the dimensions of $\mathbf{s}_1$ and $\mathbf{s}_2$ respectively, and let q be the prime modulus. The procedure executes as follows:

1) $\mathbf{A} \leftarrow$ E.PublicKeyGen$(\mathbf{s}_2, N)$, where $N = n_1 \cdot \lceil \log q \rceil$. Generating a public key matrix $\mathbf{A} = \left[\mathbf{b} \quad -\mathbf{A}'\right]$ where $\mathbf{b}$ is the first column vector of $\mathbf{A} \in R_q^{N \times n_2}$.
2) $\mathbf{B} \leftarrow \left[\mathbf{b} + \text{Powersof2}(\mathbf{s}_1) \quad -\mathbf{A}'\right]$. In other words, add Powersof2$(\mathbf{s}_1)$ to $\mathbf{A}$'s first column, outputs the matrix $\mathbf{B} \in R_q^{N \times n_2}$.

The second function is $\mathsf{SwitchKey}(\mathbf{B}, \mathbf{c}_1)$. Given a ciphertext $\mathbf{c}_1 \in \mathbb{Z}_q^{n_1}$ and the matrix $\mathbf{B}$ from SwitchKeyGen, the algorithm outputs

$$\mathbf{c}_2 = \mathbf{B}^T \cdot \mathrm{BitDecomp}(\mathbf{c}_1) \in R_q^{n_2} \tag{11-68}$$

Key switching is essentially the multiplication of a high-dimensional vector by a high-dimensional matrix. The resulting ciphertext $\mathbf{c}_2$ from this operation carries somewhat larger noise than the original ciphertext $\mathbf{c}_1$. By applying key switching, one can reduce the ciphertext dimension, so that a ciphertext whose dimension has expanded after multiplication can be restored to the intended dimension.

For correctness, we have

$$\langle \mathbf{c}_2, \mathbf{s}_2 \rangle \equiv 2 \langle \mathsf{BitDecomp}(\mathbf{c}_1), \mathbf{e}_2 \rangle + \langle \mathbf{c}_1, \mathbf{s}_1 \rangle \pmod q \tag{11-69}$$

11.4.3 Modulus Switching

Modulus Switching is a technique based on modular arithmetic that lets one convert approximate linear relations modulo q into another modulo p. Modulus Switching can achieve leveled FHE without bootstrapping, that is a noise reduction technique.

Consider a ciphertext vector $\mathbf{c}$ is a valid encryption of m under the secret key $\mathbf{s}$ modulo q, that is $m \equiv [\langle \mathbf{c}, \mathbf{s} \rangle]_q \pmod 2$. Let a vector $\mathbf{c}'$ be the closest to $(p/q) \cdot \mathbf{c}$ such that $\mathbf{c}' \equiv \mathbf{c} \pmod 2$, where p, q are integers and $q > p > m$. We have $m \equiv [\langle \mathbf{c}', \mathbf{s} \rangle]_p \equiv [\langle \mathbf{c}, \mathbf{s} \rangle]_q \pmod 2$, this transformation changes the modulus q to p while keeping the plaintext m and the secret key $\mathbf{s}$ unchanged.

Let $\mathbf{c}$ be an integer vector, and let p, q, r be integers. The function $\mathsf{Scale}(\mathbf{c}, q, p, r)$ outputs a vector closest to $(p/q) \cdot \mathbf{c}$ that satisfies $\mathbf{c}' \equiv \mathbf{c} \pmod r$. We usually set $r = 2$ since BGV is a binary encryption scheme.

Example 11.4.2 Consider $p = 13$, $q = 17$, and $r = 2$, then the scale of the vector $\mathbf{c} = (8, 10)^T$ is $\mathbf{c}' = (13/17) \cdot (8, 10)^T \equiv (6, 8)^T \pmod 2$. ■

Let d be the degree of the polynomial ring $R = \mathbb{Z}[x]/(x^d + 1)$. Let p, q, r be positive integers satisfying $q > p > r$ and $q \equiv p \equiv 1 \pmod r$. Let $\mathbf{c} \in R^n$ and $\mathbf{c}' = \mathsf{Scale}(\mathbf{c}, q, p, r)$. Then, for any secret key $\mathbf{s} \in R^n$ with $\left|[\langle \mathbf{c}, \mathbf{s} \rangle]_q\right| < q/2 - (q/p) \cdot (r/2) \cdot \sqrt{d} \cdot \gamma_R \cdot \ell_1^{(R)}(\mathbf{s})$, we have

$$[\langle \mathbf{c}', \mathbf{s} \rangle]_p \equiv [\langle \mathbf{c}, \mathbf{s} \rangle]_q \pmod r \tag{11-70}$$

$$\left\| [\langle \mathbf{c}', \mathbf{s} \rangle]_p \right\| < (p/q) \cdot \left\| [\langle \mathbf{c}, \mathbf{s} \rangle]_q \right\| + \gamma_R \cdot (r/2) \cdot \sqrt{d} \cdot \ell_1^{(R)}(\mathbf{s}) \tag{11-71}$$

where γ_R is the expansion factor of R, $\ell_1^{(R)}(\mathbf{s})$ denotes the ℓ_1-norm of $\mathbf{s}$.

Proof

Let $e_q = [\langle \mathbf{c}, \mathbf{s} \rangle]_q$. By definition, there exists an integer $k \in \mathbb{Z}$ such that $[\langle \mathbf{c}, \mathbf{s} \rangle]_q = \langle \mathbf{c}, \mathbf{s} \rangle - kq \in [-q/2, q/2)$. Let noise be $e_p = \langle \mathbf{c}', \mathbf{s} \rangle - kp \in \mathbb{Z}$, that is

$e_p \equiv [\langle \mathbf{c}', \mathbf{s} \rangle]_p \pmod{p}$. *Assuming* $\|e_p\|$ *very small that can withdraw modulus* p, *we have*

$$\|e_p\| = \| -kp + \langle (p/q) \cdot \mathbf{c}, \mathbf{s} \rangle + \langle \mathbf{c}' - (p/q) \cdot \mathbf{c}, \mathbf{s} \rangle \| \tag{11-72}$$

$$\leqslant \| -kp + \langle (p/q) \cdot \mathbf{c}, \mathbf{s} \rangle \| + \| \langle \mathbf{c}' - (p/q) \cdot \mathbf{c}, \mathbf{s} \rangle \| \tag{11-73}$$

$$\leqslant (p/q) \cdot \| [\langle \mathbf{c}, \mathbf{s} \rangle]_q \| + \gamma_R \cdot \sum_{j=1}^{n} \|\mathbf{c}'[j] - (p/q) \cdot \mathbf{c}[j]\| \cdot \|\mathbf{s}[j]\| \tag{11-74}$$

$$\leqslant (p/q) \cdot \| [\langle \mathbf{c}, \mathbf{s} \rangle]_q \| + \gamma_R \cdot (r/2) \cdot \sqrt{d} \cdot \ell_1^{(R)}(\mathbf{s}) \tag{11-75}$$

$$< p/2 \tag{11-76}$$

It remains to show that $e_p \equiv e_q \pmod{r}$. *Recall that* ***Scale*** *ensures* $\mathbf{c}' \equiv \mathbf{c} \pmod{r}$. *Since* $\mathbf{s}$ *is an integer vector, this implies* $\langle \mathbf{c}', \mathbf{s} \rangle \equiv \langle \mathbf{c}, \mathbf{s} \rangle \pmod{r}$. *Furthermore, the condition* $p \equiv q \equiv 1 \pmod{r}$ *implies that* $kp \equiv k \cdot 1 \equiv kq \pmod{r}$. *We obtain:*

$$e_p = \langle \mathbf{c}', \mathbf{s} \rangle - kp \equiv \langle \mathbf{c}, \mathbf{s} \rangle - kq \pmod{r} \equiv e_q \pmod{r} \tag{11-77}$$

Example 11.4.3 Let $\mathbf{s} = (3, 5)^T$, $\mathbf{c} = (45, 22)^T$ and $r = 2$, then $\langle \mathbf{c}, \mathbf{s} \rangle = 45 \times 3 + 22 \times 5 = 135 + 110 = 245$. Suppose $q = 97$ and $p = 19$, we have $[\langle \mathbf{c}, \mathbf{s} \rangle]_q \equiv 51 \pmod{97}$, the vector closest to $(p/q) \cdot \mathbf{c} = (19/97) \cdot \mathbf{c} \approx (8.81, 4.31)^T$.

Round the $p/q \cdot \mathbf{c}$, yields the new ciphertext is $\mathbf{c}' = (9, 4)^T$. Compute $\langle \mathbf{c}', \mathbf{s} \rangle = 47$, we have $[\langle \mathbf{c}', \mathbf{s} \rangle]_p \equiv 9 \pmod{p}$. The magnitude of the noise has been reduced from 51 to 9. Crucially, the underlying plaintext message is perfectly preserved, as the new parity remains mathematically unchanged: $9 \equiv 1 \pmod{2}$. ■

The example above illustrates a fundamental property of the BGV scheme: the ability to reduce the magnitude of the noise term by switching to a smaller modulus. While the relative noise ratio remains approximately constant ($51/97 \approx 9/19$), the absolute value of the noise decreases significantly. This reduction is vital because the accumulation of noise in homomorphic multiplication depends on the absolute magnitude of the input noise.

Through modulus switching, the BGV scheme effectively manages noise growth. Instead of allowing noise to grow indefinitely until decryption fails, BGV suppresses the noise after each operation by consuming a portion of the modulus budget. This structure allows BGV to perform a sequence of homomorphic operations up to a predetermined circuit depth without relying on the computationally expensive bootstrapping procedure. This paradigm, known as **Leveled FHE**, represents a significant advancement over first-generation schemes, offering a practical pathway for secure computation in real-world applications.

11.4.4 BGV Algorithm

The BGV scheme proceeds as follows. Let $R = \mathbb{Z}[x]/(x^d + 1)$ and $params = (q, d, n, N, \chi)$:

1) FHE.Setup$(1^\lambda, 1^L, b)$: Given a security parameter λ (typically $\lambda > 100$ and have 2^λ secure), a circuit multiplicative depth L and $b \in \{0,1\}$(selecting between LWE and RLWE). Furthermore, define a bit-length parameter $\mu = \mu(\lambda, L, b) = \Theta(\log\lambda + \log L)$ that decides the size of the modulus q. Let $i = L, L-1, \ldots, 0$, generates a sequence of parameter sets

$$params_i \leftarrow \mathsf{E.Setup}(1^\lambda, 1^{(i+1)\mu}, b) \tag{11-78}$$

This process produces a chain of moduli $\{q_L, \ldots, q_0\}$ whose bit-lengths decrease from $(L+1)\cdot\mu$ bits to μ bits. These moduli are utilized in the modulus switching procedure to effectively manage ciphertext noise growth. Outputs (q, d, n, N, χ).

2) FHE.KeyGen$(params_i)$: Given the parameters of FHE.Setup. For $i = L$ to 0, each parameter group generates a sequence of secret key sk:
   (a) Set $\mathbf{s}_i \leftarrow \mathsf{E.SecretKeyGen}(params_i)$ where $\mathbf{s}_i = (1, \mathbf{t}) \in R_{q_i}^{n_i+1}$.
   (b) Set $\mathbf{A}_i \leftarrow \mathsf{E.PublicKeyGen}(params_i, \mathbf{s}_i)$ where $\mathbf{A}_i \in R_{q_i}^{N\times n_i}$ is a matrix.
   (c) Set $\mathbf{s}'_i \leftarrow \mathbf{s}_i \otimes \mathbf{s}_i \in \mathbb{Z}_{q_i}^{(n_i+1)^2}$. Here, $\mathbf{s}'_i$ is the result of tensor product $\mathbf{s}_i \otimes \mathbf{s}_i$.
   (d) Set $\tau_{\mathbf{s}'_{i+1}\to\mathbf{s}_i} \leftarrow \mathsf{SwitchKeyGen}(\mathbf{s}'_{i+1}, \mathbf{s}_i)$. Skip this step when $i = L$. Here, $\tau_{\mathbf{s}'_{i+1}\to\mathbf{s}_i}$ is called the auxiliary information.

   Output the secret key $sk = \{\mathbf{s}_i\}$ and the public key $pk = \{\mathbf{A}_L, \ldots, \mathbf{A}_0, \tau_{\mathbf{s}'_L\to\mathbf{s}_{L-1}}, \ldots, \tau_{\mathbf{s}'_1\to\mathbf{s}_0}\}$.

3) FHE.Enc$(params, pk, m)$: Given the parameters, the public key and the plaintext $m \in \{0,1\}$. Set $\mathbf{c} \leftarrow \mathsf{E.Enc}(params_L, \mathbf{A}_L, m)$, outputs the ciphertext $\mathbf{c}$.

4) FHE.Dec$(params, sk, \mathbf{c})$: Given the parameters, the ciphertext vector $\mathbf{c}$ under the secret key $\mathbf{s}_i$. Set $m \leftarrow \mathsf{E.Dec}(params_i, \mathbf{s}_i, \mathbf{c}) \equiv [\langle \mathbf{c}, \mathbf{s}_i\rangle]_{q_i} \pmod 2$, outputs the plaintext m.

5) FHE.Add$(sk, \mathbf{c}_1, \mathbf{c}_2)$: Given two ciphertext vectors $\mathbf{c}_1, \mathbf{c}_2$ that are encrypted under the same $\mathbf{s}_i$. Homomorphic addition

$$\mathbf{c}_3 \leftarrow \mathbf{c}_1 + \mathbf{c}_2 \pmod{q_i} \tag{11-79}$$

$$\mathbf{c}_4 \leftarrow \mathsf{FHE.Refresh}(\mathbf{c}_3, \tau_{\mathbf{s}'_i\to\mathbf{s}_{i-1}}, q_i, q_{i-1}) \tag{11-80}$$

where $\mathbf{c}_3$ is a ciphertext vector. Because addition is strictly linear, the intermediate ciphertext $\mathbf{c}_3$ is decryptable directly under the original secret key $\mathbf{s}_i$. Interpret $\mathbf{c}_3$ as a ciphertext under $\mathbf{s}'_i = \mathbf{s}_i \otimes \mathbf{s}_i$ and $\mathbf{s}'_i$ first coefficient is 1.

6) FHE.Mult$(sk, \mathbf{c}_1, \mathbf{c}_2)$: Given two ciphertext vectors $\mathbf{c}_1, \mathbf{c}_2$ that are encrypted under the same $\mathbf{s}_i$. Homomorphic multiplication

$$\mathbf{c}_3 \leftarrow \mathbf{c}_1 \otimes \mathbf{c}_2 \pmod{q_i} \tag{11-81}$$

$$\mathbf{c}_4 \leftarrow \mathsf{FHE.Refresh}(\mathbf{c}_3, \tau_{\mathbf{s}'_i\to\mathbf{s}_{i-1}}, q_i, q_{i-1}) \tag{11-82}$$

where $\mathbf{c}_3$ is a ciphertext vector, it can be decrypted by the secret key $\mathbf{s}'_i = \mathbf{s}_i \otimes \mathbf{s}_i$.

7) FHE.Refresh$(\mathbf{c}, \tau_{\mathbf{s}'_i\to\mathbf{s}_{i-1}}, q_i, q_{i-1})$: Given a ciphertext encrypted under $\mathbf{s}'_i$, the auxiliary information $\tau_{\mathbf{s}'_i\to\mathbf{s}_{i-1}}$ and two moduli q_i, q_{i-1}. Do the following:

$$\mathbf{c}_{temp} \leftarrow \mathsf{SwitchKey}(\tau_{\mathbf{s}'_i\to\mathbf{s}_{i-1}}, \mathbf{c}, q_i) \tag{11-83}$$

$$\mathbf{c}_{out} \leftarrow \mathsf{Scale}(\mathbf{c}_{temp}, q_i, q_{i-1}, 2) \tag{11-84}$$

To demonstrate the correctness of homomorphic addition and multiplication, suppose Alice encrypts two plaintexts, m_1 and m_2, under the same secret key $\mathbf{s}$ to obtain the corresponding ciphertexts $\mathbf{c}_1$ and $\mathbf{c}_2$.

For **homomorphic addition**, we verify the decryption of the sum of the ciphertexts as follows:

$$\begin{aligned}\langle \mathbf{c}_1 + \mathbf{c}_2, \mathbf{s}\rangle &= \langle \mathbf{c}_1, \mathbf{s}\rangle + \langle \mathbf{c}_2, \mathbf{s}\rangle && \text{(11-85)}\\ &\equiv \left[\mathbf{b}^T\mathbf{r}_1 + m_1 - (\mathbf{Bt})^T\mathbf{r}_1\right] + \left[\mathbf{b}^T\mathbf{r}_2 + m_2 - (\mathbf{Bt})^T\mathbf{r}_2\right] \pmod q && \text{(11-86)}\\ &\equiv (2\mathbf{e}^T\mathbf{r}_1 + m_1) + (2\mathbf{e}^T\mathbf{r}_2 + m_2) \pmod q && \text{(11-87)}\\ &\equiv m_1 + m_2 + \mathcal{O}(E) \pmod q. && \text{(11-88)}\end{aligned}$$

Applying the modulo 2 operation recovers the sum of the messages

$$m_1 + m_2 + \mathcal{O}(E) \equiv m_1 + m_2 \pmod 2 \qquad \text{(11-89)}$$

As long as the noise is well controlled and does not wrap around the modulus q_i, decryption produces the correct plaintext.

Similarly, for **homomorphic multiplication**, we have

$$\begin{aligned}\langle \mathbf{c}_1 \otimes \mathbf{c}_2, \mathbf{s} \otimes \mathbf{s}\rangle &= \langle \mathbf{c}_1, \mathbf{s}\rangle \cdot \langle \mathbf{c}_2, \mathbf{s}\rangle && \text{(11-90)}\\ &= (m_1 + E) \cdot (m_2 + E) && \text{(11-91)}\\ &= m_1 m_2 + \mathcal{O}(E^2) && \text{(11-92)}\end{aligned}$$

After analyzing the noise growth for homomorphic addition and multiplication, a homomorphic addition increases the noise to roughly $\mathcal{O}(E)$, while a single homomorphic multiplication increases it to roughly $\mathcal{O}(E^2)$. Therefore, after L successive multiplications the noise grows to about E^{2^L}. Without noise reduction, at most about $L \approx \log_2(\log_E(q))$ multiplication layers can be evaluated, otherwise the noise would exceed $q/2$ and decryption would fail.

Because multiplication causes far greater noise growth than addition, the core of BGV is to control multiplication-induced noise. The scheme does this by shrinking both ciphertexts and moduli, using two key operations: Key Switching and Modulus Switching. Key switching primarily preserves the key structure but introduces a small additional noise term; modulus switching is the operation that actually reduces the noise.

Concretely, multiplying two ciphertexts modulo q generates an expanded noise term approximating E^2. Switching the underlying modulus from q down to a smaller modulus p scales this absolute noise by the factor p/q, resulting in a scaled noise term of $(p/q)E^2$. By explicitly selecting $p \approx q/E$, the scaled noise drops back to roughly E modulo p. This transformation maintains the noise to modulus ratio while critically preventing the absolute magnitude from compounding.

Hence, choosing a large initial modulus $q_0 \gg E$ supports multiple modulus switches. By performing a modulus switch after each multiplication and choosing $q_i \approx \frac{q_{i-1}}{E}$, one can prevent excessive noise growth, continuing this process until

$q_L/2 < E$. Using this mechanism, BGV reduces exponential noise growth to a polynomial regime, roughly $E \cdot \text{poly}(n)$, and thereby substantially increases the feasible circuit depth and overall efficiency.

Example 11.4.4 Consider the BGV encryption scheme where the base noise bound of an encrypted ciphertext is denoted by E. A leveled homomorphic scheme is constructed using a chain of moduli defined by the parameter E. Let the initial (largest) modulus be $q_0 = E^{10}$, and let the subsequent moduli for $i > 0$ be $q_i = E^{10-i}$. Using the BGV noise-control technique, what is the maximum multiplicative depth the scheme can support? If no noise control is used, what is the maximum multiplicative depth?

The noise growth throughout the levels. We start with initial ciphertexts at Level 0, which have noise $B_0 \approx E$. Consider two ciphertexts $\mathbf{c}_1$ and $\mathbf{c}_2$, each having been "refreshed" by the modulus switch, so their noise is $B_i \approx \mathcal{O}(E)$. For Homomorphic Multiplication, we perform $\mathbf{c}_1 \times \mathbf{c}_2$. $B_{\text{mult}} \approx B_i \times B_i \approx E^2$. For this operation to be valid, the resulting noise must be less than the current modulus

$$B_{\text{mult}} < q_i/2, \quad \text{or} \quad E^2 < E^{10-i}/2 \tag{11-93}$$

After multiplication, the scheme scales the ciphertext $\mathbf{c}_{\text{mult}}$ which has noise $B_{\text{mult}} \approx E^2$, from modulus q_i to q_{i+1}. The new noise B_{new} is approximately

$$B_{\text{new}} \approx \frac{q_{i+1}}{q_i} \cdot B_{\text{mult}} + B_{\text{switch}} \tag{11-94}$$

$$= \left(\frac{E^{9-i}}{E^{10-i}}\right) \cdot E^2 + E \tag{11-95}$$

$$= \left(\frac{1}{E}\right) \cdot E^2 + E \tag{11-96}$$

$$= 2E \tag{11-97}$$

where B_{switch} represents the small additive noise introduced by the switching procedure itself, typically on the order of E. Thus, with BGV's modulus switching, the noise is "reset" from a quadratic growth of $\mathcal{O}(E^2)$ back to a linear $\mathcal{O}(E)$ level after each multiplication. The cost of this reduction is the consumption of one level in the modulus chain.

If no noise control is used, all operations are performed under the initial modulus $q_0 = E^{10}$. The noise grows exponentially with the multiplicative depth L. After L levels of multiplication, the noise B_L is

$$B_L \approx E^{2^L} \tag{11-98}$$

To find the maximum depth L, we must satisfy the decryption condition

$$B_L < q_0/2 \quad \text{and} \quad E^{2^L} < \frac{E^{10}}{2} \tag{11-99}$$

Testing integer values for L, we find that the maximum integer satisfying the condition is $L = 3$. The result as shown in Table 11-1.

Table 11-1: Comparison of Noise Growth (Noise vs. Modulus)

Level (i)	Controlled Noise (B_{mult} vs. q_i)	Uncontrolled Noise (B_L vs. q_0)
0	$E^2 < E^{10}$	$E < E^{10}$
1	$E^2 < E^9$	$E^2 < E^{10}$
2	$E^2 < E^8$	$E^4 < E^{10}$
3	$E^2 < E^7$	$E^8 < E^{10}$
4	$E^2 < E^6$	$E^{16} \not< E^{10}$ (Fail)
...	...	...
7	$E^2 < E^3$	-
8	$E^2 \not< E^2$ (Fail)	-

Thus, if we control the noise, the last valid multiplication occurs at Level 7. Since we started at Level 0, the total depth is $L = 0$ to $L = 7$, the scheme can support a maximum multiplicative depth of 8. Without noise control, the scheme can support a maximum multiplicative depth of 3.

However, as the circuit depth L increases, the modulus gradually decreases, since reducing noise also reduces the modulus. When L becomes sufficiently large, the modulus can no longer be made smaller, and the plaintext will eventually be drowned by the accumulated noise. This limitation explains why BGV is considered a leveled FHE scheme.

To use BGV correctly, the modulus must be chosen according to the expected circuit depth L so that the noise remains below the threshold throughout computation. When the circuit depth cannot be determined in advance, this becomes problematic. In such cases, BGV is not suitable, and one should choose another scheme.

11.5 DGHV FULLY HOMOMORPHIC ENCRYPTION

In addition to the BGV scheme, the DGHV scheme is another prominent second-generation fully homomorphic encryption framework. It was proposed in 2010 by *Marten van Dijk*, *Craig Gentry*, *Shai Halevi* and *Vinod Vaikuntanathan*, with the acronym DGHV derived from the authors' surnames [145]. The security of the DGHV scheme relies on the hardness assumption of the **Approximate Greatest Common Divisor** (AGCD) problem. Notably, it was the first construction to achieve fully homomorphic encryption using basic arithmetic operations over integers.

11.5.1 Approximate Greatest Common Divisor Problem

Recall the standard Greatest Common Divisor (GCD) problem: given two or more integers $a_1, a_2, \ldots, a_n$, not all zero, find their GCD, which is the largest positive integer d that divides all a_i. This problem is computationally tractable. The **Euclidean Algorithm**, known for millennia, computes the GCD of two integers a and b in time polynomial in the number of bits required to represent them.

Consider introducing a perturbation component to this formulation. The Approximate GCD (AGCD) problem is a computational challenge that asks for the recovery of a hidden common divisor from a set of numbers that are near-multiples of it [146].

Definition 11.5.1 Approximate Greatest Common Divisor (AGCD) Problem

Let p be a secret odd integer. Given a set of integers $x_0, x_1, \ldots, x_n \in \mathbb{Z}$ sampled from a specific distribution, where each x_i is of the form: $x_i = p \cdot q_i + r_i$ with q_i being a large random integer and r_i a small noise integer, the goal is to find p.

The problem is believed to be computationally hard, provided that the noise bound is large enough to hide divisibility, but small enough to allow decryption correctness. For the problem to be hard, let $\rho, \eta, \gamma \in \mathbb{N}$ denote the bit-lengths of the parameters. Let $\rho \ll \eta \ll \gamma$, the target p be an η-bit odd integer, the integer q_i uniformly at random from $[0, 2^\gamma/p]$, the small noise r_i uniformly at random from $(-2^\rho, 2^\rho)$ and $r_i \neq 0$. Therefore, the size of $|r_i| < p < q_i$.

For example, let $p = 13$, $x_1 = 13 \times 17 + 3 = 224$ and $x_2 = 13 \times 22 + 2 = 288$. The GCD of $(224, 288) = 32$, Since 32 is not a multiple of 13, it is evident that the small noise hides p.

Let $x_0 = q_0 \cdot p + r_0$ and $x_1 = q_1 \cdot p + r_1$, compute

$$p \mid \gcd((x_0 - r_0), (x_1 - r_1)) \tag{11-100}$$

We need to guess their associated noise values. This method has a running time of $\mathcal{O}(2^\rho)$. If the noise parameter ρ is large, the brute-force attack becomes computationally inefficient.

The Approximate GCD Problem is of great interest because it is conjectured to be computationally hard. That is, no efficient algorithm is known to solve it for suitably large parameters in polynomial time. Since the DGHV scheme is built on the hardness of the AGCD problem. In other words, if the AGCD problem were to be solved efficiently, the DGHV scheme would be broken.

11.5.2 Homomorphic Encryption

The construction below has many parameters, controlling the number of integers in the public key and the bit-length of the various integers. The security parameter λ refers to the number of bits of security of the scheme.

- γ is the bit-length of the integers in the public key.
- η is the bit-length of the secret key.
- ρ is the bit-length of the noise.
- ρ' is the bit-length of the secondary noise.
- τ is the number of integers in the public key.

These parameters must be set under the following constraints:

- $\rho = \omega(\log_2 \lambda)$, to protect against brute force attacks on the noise. In general, set $\rho = \lambda$.
- $\rho' = \rho + \omega(\log_2 \lambda)$. In general, set $\rho' = 2\lambda$.
- $\eta \geqslant \rho \cdot \Theta(\lambda \log_2^2 \lambda)$, in order to support homomorphism for deep enough circuits to evaluate. In general, set $\eta = \mathcal{O}(\lambda^2)$.
- $\gamma = \omega(\eta^2 \log_2 \lambda)$ to thwart various lattice-based attacks on the underlying AGCD problem. In general, set $\gamma = \mathcal{O}(\lambda^5)$.
- $\tau \geqslant \gamma + \omega(\log_2 \lambda)$, in order to use the leftover hash lemma in the reduction to AGCD. In general, set $\tau = \gamma + \lambda$.

Here Θ denotes a quantity that grows on the order of $\lambda \log_2^2 \lambda$. Thus, the condition means that η must be at least on the order of $\rho\lambda \log_2^2 \lambda$. There exists $\rho \approx \rho' < \eta < \gamma$. The four different levels of security parameters are shown in Table 11-2:

Table 11-2: DGHV Parameters

Parameters	λ	ρ	η	γ	τ	l_{pk}
Toy	42	16	1088	1.6×10^5	158	5.75MB
Small	52	24	1632	8.6×10^5	527	100.91MB
Medium	62	32	2176	42×10^5	2110	2.04 GB
Large	72	39	2652	190×10^5	7659	33.70 GB

The DGHV fully homomorphic encryption scheme consists of the following steps:

1) KeyGen(λ): Given a security parameter λ. Let the secret key p be an odd integer and generated by $[2^{\eta-1}, 2^{\eta})$. Sample independent quotients q_i uniformly from $\mathbb{Z} \cap [0, 2^{\gamma}/p)$ and noise integers r_i from $\mathbb{Z} \cap (-2^{\rho}, 2^{\rho})$, compute

$$x_i = pq_i + r_i, \text{where } 0 \leqslant i \leqslant \tau \tag{11-101}$$

Relabel so that x_0 is the largest. If $x_0 \equiv 1 \pmod 2$ and $r_0 \equiv 0 \pmod 2$, output the secret key $sk = p$ and the public key $pk = \mathbf{x} = \langle x_0, x_1, \ldots, x_\tau \rangle$. Otherwise, resample.

2) Encrypt(pk, m): Given the public key pk and the plaintext $m \in \{0, 1\}$. Let a random subset $S \subseteq \{1, 2, \ldots, \tau\}$ and a random integer $r' \in (-2^{\rho'}, 2^{\rho'})$. Output the ciphertext c

$$c \equiv (m + 2r') + 2\sum_{i \in S} x_i \pmod{x_0} \tag{11-102}$$

3) Decrypt(sk, c): Given the secret key sk and the ciphertext c, output

$$m' \equiv (c \bmod p) \pmod 2 \tag{11-103}$$

where $c \bmod p$ is required to lie within the interval $[-p/2, p/2]$.

4) Evaluate($pk, C, c_1, \ldots, c_t$): Given the public key pk, a circuit C with t inputs and a tuple of ciphertexts $\mathbf{c} = \{c_1, c_2, \ldots, c_t\}$. Apply the integer addition and multiplication gates of C to the ciphertexts, performing all the operations over the integers, and output the resulting integer.

For correctness, we have

Proof

The decryption procedure is defined by $m \equiv (c \bmod p) \pmod 2$. *Since* $c \equiv (m + 2r' + 2\sum_{i\in S} x_i) \pmod{x_0}$, *the ciphertext implies the existence of an integer* $k \in \mathbb{Z}$ *such that*

$$c = m + 2r' + 2\sum_{i\in S}(pq_i + r_i) + kx_0 \tag{11-104}$$

$$= m + 2r' + 2\sum_{i\in S}(pq_i + r_i) + k(pq_0 + r_0) \tag{11-105}$$

$$= 2p\sum_{i\in S} q_i + m + 2r' + 2\sum_{i\in S} r_i + kpq_0 + kr_0. \tag{11-106}$$

By regrouping the terms that are multiples of the secret key p, *we obtain*

$$c = p\underbrace{\left(2\sum_{i\in S} q_i + kq_0\right)}_{Q} + \underbrace{\left(m + 2r' + 2\sum_{i\in S} r_i + kr_0\right)}_{B}. \tag{11-107}$$

The term Q *is strictly divisible by* p, *which implies* $Q \equiv 0 \pmod p$. *Also* r_0 *is even, if the noise term* $B \in (-p/2, p/2 - 1)$, *then*

$$(c \bmod p) \pmod 2 = (Q + B \bmod p) \pmod 2 \tag{11-108}$$

$$= (0 + B) \pmod 2 \tag{11-109}$$

$$= m \pmod 2 \tag{11-110}$$

Thus, the reduction modulo p *hides* Q, *leaving the noise* B. *The modulo 2 operation hides the noise* B, *revealing the message* m.

For **homomorphic addition**, given two plaintexts $m_1, m_2 \in \{0, 1\}$ and $r'_1, r'_2 \in \left(-2^{\rho'}, 2^{\rho'}\right)$, then the ciphertexts are

$$c_1 \equiv \left(m_1 + 2r'_1 + 2\sum_{i\in S} x_i\right) \pmod{x_0} \tag{11-111}$$

$$c_2 \equiv \left(m_2 + 2r'_2 + 2\sum_{i\in S'} x_i\right) \pmod{x_0} \tag{11-112}$$

To verify the additively homomorphic property, summing the ciphertexts yields, we have

$$c_{\text{add}} \equiv (m_1 + 2r_1' + 2\sum_{i\in S} x_i) + (m_2 + 2r_2' + 2\sum_{i\in S'} x_i) \pmod{x_0} \tag{11-113}$$

$$= (m_1 + m_2) + 2(r_1' + r_2') + 2\sum_{i\in S\cup S'} x_i + 2\sum_{i\in S\cap S'} x_i \tag{11-114}$$

$$= (m_1 + m_2) + 2r_{\text{add}}' + 2\sum_{i\in T} x_i \pmod{x_0}, \tag{11-115}$$

for some combined index set T.

We use the decryption function on the sum of the two ciphertexts to obtain

$$\text{Dec}(c_1 + c_2) \equiv \left[\left[\left(m_1 + m_2 + 2r_{\text{add}}' + 2\sum_{i\in T} x_i\right) \bmod x_0\right] \bmod p \bmod 2\right. \tag{11-116}$$

$$\equiv \left[\left(m_1 + m_2 + 2r_{\text{add}}' + 2\sum_{i\in T}(pq_i + r_i) + kx_0\right) \bmod p\right] \bmod 2 \tag{11-117}$$

$$\equiv \left[\left(m_1 + m_2 + 2r_{\text{add}}' + 2\sum_{i\in T}(pq_i + r_i) + k(pq_0 + r_0)\right) \bmod p\right] \bmod 2 \tag{11-118}$$

where $k \in \mathbb{Z}$. Assuming the parameters are set such that the accumulated noise term $(m_1 + m_2 + 2r_{\text{add}}' + 2\sum_{i\in T}(pq_i + r_i) + k(pq_0 + r_0))$ strictly resides within the interval $(-p/2, p/2]$, the modulo p reduction acts identically, entirely eliminating all multiples of p:

$$\text{Dec}(c_1 + c_2) \equiv \left(m_1 + m_2 + 2r_{\text{add}}' + 2\sum_{i\in T} r_i + kr_0\right) \pmod 2 \tag{11-119}$$

Since the fundamental parameter r_0 is defined as even, the term kr_0 is also even. All remaining noise terms prominently feature a factor of 2. Applying the modulo 2 reduction perfectly strips away these even integers:

$$\text{Dec}(c_1 + c_2) = m_1 + m_2 \tag{11-120}$$

For **homomorphic multiplication**, we consider the product of two ciphertexts $c_{\text{mult}} = c_1 \cdot c_2$. We express a ciphertext as

$$c = m + p\underbrace{\left(2\sum_{i\in S} q_i + kq_0\right)}_{Q} + \underbrace{\left(2r' + 2\sum_{i\in S} r_i + kr_0\right)}_{B}. \tag{11-121}$$

where Q is a multiple of p, and B represents the even noise term. Consequently, the product is given by

$$\begin{aligned} c_{\text{mult}} &= c_1 \cdot c_2 & \text{(11-122)} \\ &= (m_1 + Q_1 + B_1)(m_2 + Q_2 + B_2) & \text{(11-123)} \\ &= m_1 m_2 + (m_1 Q_2 + m_2 Q_1 + Q_1 Q_2 + Q_1 B_2 + B_1 Q_2) \\ &\quad + (m_1 B_2 + m_2 B_1 + B_1 B_2). & \text{(11-124)} \end{aligned}$$

Applying the decryption function to the product of the two ciphertexts, and strictly assuming the magnitude of the resulting cross-multiplied noise term still lies within $(-p/2, p/2]$, we evaluate:

$$\begin{aligned} \text{Dec}(c_1 \cdot c_2) &\equiv m_1 m_2 + m_1 Q_2 + m_1 B_2 + m_2 Q_1 + Q_1 Q_2 \\ &\quad + Q_1 B_2 + m_2 B_1 + B_1 Q_2 + B_1 B_2 \pmod p \pmod 2 & \text{(11-125)} \\ &\equiv m_1 m_2 + m_1 B_2 + m_2 B_1 + B_1 B_2 \pmod 2 & \text{(11-126)} \\ &\equiv m_1 m_2 \pmod 2 & \text{(11-127)} \end{aligned}$$

Hence, the scheme satisfies the multiplicative homomorphism property $\text{Dec}(c_1 \cdot c_2) = m_1 \cdot m_2$.

11.5.3 Examples

Example 11.5.1 Consider DGHV scheme, suppose Bob chooses a security parameter $\lambda = 30$, $\eta = 10$, $\tau = 30$, and a private key $p = 1009$. Then, he generates uniformly random public key $\mathbf{x} = (x_0, \ldots, x_\tau)$ where $x_i = pq_i + r_i$ and $q_i \in [0, 2^{30}/1009) = [0, 1064164)$, $r_i \in [-5, 5]$. The plaintext is 10 in decimal, computer the ciphertext [147].

Solution: Bob computes the public key $x_i = pq_i + r_i$, that is

$$\begin{aligned} x_0 &= 73057656 = 1009 \cdot 72406 + 2 & \text{(11-128)} \\ x_1 &= 513644568 = 1009 \cdot 509063 + 1 & \text{(11-129)} \\ x_2 &= 876699925 = 1009 \cdot 8688805 & \text{(11-130)} \\ &\vdots \\ x_{29} &= 59196010 = 1009 \cdot 58668 - 2 & \text{(11-131)} \\ x_{30} &= 374983754 = 1009 \cdot 3716393 & \text{(11-132)} \end{aligned}$$

Bob then relabels the elements so that x_0 is the largest. The public key is listed below:

1062750437	1036204653	993094119	928855135	876699925	874765669
832867956	832138444	792882286	771791167	754977188	747537832
727545508	700696016	732311006	652857310	569802485	513644568
491291182	434812407	422865849	374983754	366088407	360464238
273495507	228386138	118759302	73057656	59196010	26031189
12080758					

Alice converts $m = 10$ to binary $m =$ 00001010. She generates a secondary noise term $r'_i \in [-7, 7]$ and computes the ciphertext. She also generates a random bit string of length τ in order to create a random subset of the public key. Let the first bit string be a 30-bit vector $\mathbf{z} = [x_1, x_2, \ldots, x_{30}]$ =[11 1011 0111 0010 1001 0101 1111 0110]. Thus, the first ciphertext is:

$$c_0 \equiv (m + 2r' + 2\sum_{i \in S} x_i) \pmod{x_0} \tag{11-133}$$

$$\equiv \left(0 + 2(-5) + 2\sum_{i=1}^{\tau} z_i x_i\right) \equiv 21424837616 \pmod{x_0} \tag{11-134}$$

$$\equiv 169828876 \pmod{1062750437} \tag{11-135}$$

Table 11-3: DGHV Process

Index	Plaintext	$m + 2r' + 2\sum_{i \in S} x_i$	c mod x_0	Ciphertext
0	0	21424837616	169828876	0
1	0	10918318430	290814060	0
2	0	14177339966	361584285	1
3	0	31650412938	830650265	1
4	1	26981114085	412353160	0
5	0	31802590340	982827667	1
6	1	25586250283	80239795	1
7	0	6166451046	852698861	1

It can be observed that the parity of the ciphertext does not consistently correspond to that of the plaintext, thereby preventing Eve from eavesdropping on the information. Alice transmits the ciphertext to Bob.

To decrypt, Bob first computes

$$m_0 \equiv (c_0 \bmod p) \pmod{2} \tag{11-136}$$

$$\equiv 50 \pmod{2} \tag{11-137}$$

$$\equiv 0 \pmod{2} \tag{11-138}$$

Here, $c \bmod p$ is called **centered modular reduction** and centered value between $(-p/2, p/2]$. Bob decrypts the other bits in the same way. ■

11.6 OTHER FHE ALGORITHMS

In 2013, *Gentry*, *Sahai*, and *Waters* published the paper [148]. They proposed a fully homomorphic encryption algorithm based on matrix approximate eigenvectors, which belongs to the third generation of fully homomorphic encryption schemes. Since the ciphertexts are matrices, the product of ciphertexts does not suffer from the expansion of the ciphertext vector. Consequently, leveled fully homomorphic encryption can be achieved without key switching or modulus switching techniques. The security of this scheme is based on the LWE problem.

The fourth generation of FHE is the CKKS algorithm [149]. Four Korean scholars proposed this approximate arithmetic homomorphic encryption algorithm in their 2017 paper "*Homomorphic Encryption for Arithmetic of Approximate Numbers*". Its specific construction is based on the BGV algorithm. It also supports homomorphic operations on floating-point numbers.

Table 11-4 presents a comparison of classic fully homomorphic encryption schemes.

Table 11-4: Comparison of Classic Fully Homomorphic Encryption Schemes

FHE Scheme	Mathematical Basis	Security Assumption	Key Technique
Gentry Scheme	Ideal Lattices	Sparse Subset Sum Problem	Bootstrapping
BGV Scheme	Polynomial Rings	RLWE Assumption	Modulus & Key Switching
DGHV Scheme	Integers	ApprGCD Problem	Bootstrapping
GSW Scheme	Matrices over $\mathbb{Z}_q$	LWE Assumption	Flattening
CKKS Scheme	Polynomial Rings	RLWE Assumption	Rescaling & Canonical Encoding

11.7 EXERCISES

1) Let p and q be two odd moduli, and let $\mathbf{c}$ be an integer vector. Define $\mathbf{c}'$ to be the integer vector closest to $(p/q) \cdot \mathbf{c}$ such that $\mathbf{c}' = \mathbf{c} \bmod 2$.
Show that for any $\mathbf{s}$ with $|[\langle \mathbf{c}, \mathbf{s} \rangle]_q| < q/2 - (q/p) \cdot \ell_1(\mathbf{s})$, we have

$$\langle \mathbf{c}', \mathbf{s} \rangle]_p = [\langle \mathbf{c}, \mathbf{s} \rangle]_q \bmod 2 \quad \text{and} \quad |[\langle \mathbf{c}', \mathbf{s} \rangle]_p| < (p/q) \cdot |[\langle \mathbf{c}, \mathbf{s} \rangle]_q| + \ell_1(\mathbf{s})$$

where $\ell_1(\mathbf{s})$ is the ℓ_1-norm of $\mathbf{s}$.

2) Let $\mathbf{s}_1, \mathbf{s}_2, q, n_1, n_2, \mathbf{A}, \mathbf{B} = \tau_{\mathbf{s}_1 \to \mathbf{s}_2}$ be as in $\mathsf{SwitchKeyGen}(\mathbf{s}_1, \mathbf{s}_2)$, and let $\mathbf{A} \cdot \mathbf{s}_2 = 2\mathbf{e}_2 \in R_q^N$. Let $\mathbf{c}_1 \in R_q^{n_1}$ and $\mathbf{c}_2 \leftarrow \mathsf{SwitchKey}(\tau_{\mathbf{s}_1 \to \mathbf{s}_2}, \mathbf{c}_1)$. Show that the following equation holds:

$$\langle \mathbf{c}_2, \mathbf{s}_2 \rangle = 2 \langle \text{BitDecomp}(\mathbf{c}_1), \mathbf{e}_2 \rangle + \langle \mathbf{c}_1, \mathbf{s}_1 \rangle \pmod q$$

3) Let d be the degree of the ring (e.g., $d = 1$ when $R = \mathbb{Z}$). Let $q > p > r$ be positive integers satisfying $q = p = 1 \bmod r$. Let $\mathbf{c} \in R^n$ and $\mathbf{c}' \leftarrow \mathsf{Scale}(\mathbf{c}, q, p, r)$. Then, for any $\mathbf{s} \in R^n$ with

$$\|[\langle \mathbf{c}, \mathbf{s} \rangle]_q\| < q/2 - (q/p) \cdot (r/2) \cdot \sqrt{d} \cdot \gamma(R) \cdot \ell_1^{(R)}(\mathbf{s})$$

Show that the following equations hold:

$$[\langle \mathbf{c}', \mathbf{s} \rangle]_p = [\langle \mathbf{c}, \mathbf{s} \rangle]_q \pmod r$$
$$\|[\langle \mathbf{c}', \mathbf{s} \rangle]_p\| < (p/q) \cdot \|[\langle \mathbf{c}, \mathbf{s} \rangle]_q\| + (r/2) \cdot \sqrt{d} \cdot \gamma(R) \cdot \ell_1^{(R)}(\mathbf{s})$$

4) Write SageMath code for the **BitDecomp** and **Powersof2** functions.

5) Let q be a prime, n be a positive integer, and χ be an error distribution over $\mathbb{Z}_q$. Assume there exists a PPT algorithm $\mathcal{A}$ that solves the Decision-LWE problem with non-negligible advantage. Construct a PPT algorithm $\mathcal{B}$ that uses $\mathcal{A}$ as a subroutine to solve the Search-LWE problem. Show how to recover $\mathbf{s}$ coordinate-wise using the decision oracle.
6) Consider the cyclotomic ring $R_q = \mathbb{Z}_q[x]/\langle x^n + 1\rangle$ where n is a power of 2. For an RLWE sample $(a, b = a \cdot s + e) \in R_q \times R_q$, let $\mathbf{a}, \mathbf{s} \in \mathbb{Z}_q^n$ be the coefficient vectors of a and s respectively.
   (a) Define the matrix $\mathbf{M}_a \in \mathbb{Z}_q^{n\times n}$ such that the coefficient vector of the product $a \cdot s$ satisfies $\text{coeff}(a \cdot s) = \mathbf{M}_a \cdot \mathbf{s}$.
   (b) Write down the explicit form of $\mathbf{M}_a$. Explain how this circulant-like structure reduces the computational complexity of the sample generation compared to standard LWE, and discuss its potential impact on the security reduction from the Shortest Independent Vectors Problem (SIVP).
7) Consider LWE public-key cryptosystem, prove that for any $k = poly(n)$, the following computational indistinguishability holds:

$$(pk, \text{PKE.Enc}(pk, \mu_1), \ldots, \text{PKE.Enc}(pk, \mu_k)) \overset{c}{\approx} (pk, \text{PKE}\cdot\text{Enc}(pk, 0), \ldots, \text{PKE}\cdot\text{Enc}(pk, 0))$$

   where "$\overset{c}{\approx}$" denotes computational indistinguishability.
8) Consider Regev's LWE-based scheme with parameters $n = 2$, $q = 17$, and a secret key $\mathbf{s} = (3, 5)^T \in \mathbb{Z}_{17}^2$. Given the following public key matrix $\mathbf{A}$ and error vector $\mathbf{e}$:

$$\mathbf{A} = \begin{bmatrix} 2 & 10 & 4 \\ 7 & 1 & 13 \end{bmatrix}, \quad \mathbf{e} = [1, -1, 0]^T.$$

   (a) Compute the public key vector $\mathbf{b}^T \equiv \mathbf{s^T A} + \mathbf{e}^T \pmod{17}$.
   (b) Encrypt the bit $m = 1$ using the randomness vector $\mathbf{r} = [1, 0, 1]^T$. Compute the ciphertext $(\mathbf{c}_1, c_2) \in \mathbb{Z}_{17}^2 \times \mathbb{Z}_{17}$.
   (c) Show the decryption process by computing $a \equiv c_2 - \mathbf{s}^T\mathbf{c}_1$ and determine if the result correctly maps to $m = 1$.
9) Consider the Regev's LWE-based scheme with parameters $q = 101$, a ciphertext $(\mathbf{c}_1, c_2)$ is received. The decryption formula yields $a \equiv c_2 - \mathbf{s}^T\mathbf{c}_1 \equiv 56 \pmod{101}$. If the decoding rule is $m = 0$ if $a \in [-\lfloor q/4\rfloor, \lfloor q/4\rfloor]$ and $m = 1$ otherwise, determine the decrypted bit.
10) Let $n = 4$ and the ring be $R_{13} = \mathbb{Z}_{13}[x]/\langle x^4 + 1\rangle$. Given a secret polynomial $s(x) = x^2 + 1$ and a public polynomial $a(x) = 2x^3 + 5x$. Compute the noise-free product $t(x) = a(x) \cdot s(x)$ in R_{13}. If the error polynomial is $e(x) = x - 1$, provide the RLWE sample $(a(x), b(x))$ where $b(x) = a(x)s(x) + e(x)$.
11) Let the ring be $R_{17} = \mathbb{Z}_{17}[x]/\langle x^4 + 1\rangle$. Given the secret polynomial $s(x) = x^3 + 2x$ and the public polynomial $a(x) = 3x^2 + 1$.
   (a) Compute the polynomial product $p(x) = a(x) \cdot s(x) \in R_{17}$.
   (b) Given the error polynomial $e(x) = x^2 - 1$, compute the RLWE public key component $b(x) = a(x)s(x) + e(x) \pmod{17}$.

12) Consider the Regev's RLWE-based scheme with $n = 4, q = 17$ and $R_{17} = \mathbb{Z}_{17}[x]/\langle x^4+1\rangle$. The public key is (a, b) and the secret key is s. Let $s(x) = x^2+1$, $a(x) = 2x$, and $e(x) = 1$. Encryption: To encrypt a single bit $m = 1$, we choose a small random polynomial $e_1(x) = x$ and small error polynomials $e_2(x) = 1, e_3(x) = 0$. Compute the ciphertext (c_1, c_2).
13) Consider a BGV ciphertext $(\mathbf{c}_0, \mathbf{c}_1) = (15, 15)$ at level L with modulus $Q = 1021$. The plaintext is $m \in \{0, 1\}$ and the secret key is s. The decryption relation is $[\langle \mathbf{c}, \mathbf{s}\rangle]_Q = m+2e$, where the current noise is $e = 15$. To reduce noise for further operations, we perform a modulus switching to $q = 101$. Answer the following questions:
    (a) Compute the scaled ciphertext $\mathbf{c}' = \text{Round}(\frac{q}{Q} \cdot \mathbf{c})$.
    (b) Calculate the new noise e' such that $[\langle \mathbf{c}', \mathbf{s}\rangle]_q = m + 2e'$, and verify that the plaintext is preserved by showing that $[\langle \mathbf{c}', \mathbf{s}\rangle]_q \bmod 2 = m$.
    (c) Verify that $|e'| < \frac{q}{Q}|e| + \frac{1}{2}(1 + |s|)$ given $s = 1$. Show that the decryption remains correct.
14) Let the plaintext space be $\mathbb{Z}_2$. After a homomorphic multiplication of two ciphertexts $(\mathbf{c}_0, \mathbf{c}_1)$ and $(\mathbf{d}_0, \mathbf{d}_1)$, we obtain a linearized 3-element ciphertext (C_0, C_1, C_2) such that $m_1 m_2 \equiv C_0 + C_1 s + C_2 s^2 \pmod{Q}$. We use a switching key $swk = (A, B) = (A, -As+2e+s^2) \in \mathbb{Z}_Q^2$ to transform it back to a standard 2-element ciphertext (c_0', c_1'). Answer the following questions:
    (a) Given the modulus $Q = 1021$, a 3-element ciphertext $(C_0, C_1, C_2) = (350, 800, 400)$, and the switching key components $(A, B) = (100, 550)$, compute the new reduced components:

$$c_0' \equiv C_0 + B \cdot C_2 \pmod{Q}$$
$$c_1' \equiv C_1 + A \cdot C_2 \pmod{Q}$$

    (b) Prove that the standard decryption of (c_0', c_1'), defined as $[c_0' + c_1' s]_Q \pmod{2}$, correctly yields the product $m_1 m_2$, and mathematically calculate the exact additional noise term introduced by this key switching process.
15) Consider the DGHV fully homomorphic encryption. Show that for any $C \in Enc(m)$ is valid if and only if the image of the noise map is contained in $2\mathbb{Z} \cap (-p/2, p/2 - 1)$.
16) Consider the DGHV fully homomorphic encryption. Let $x_0 = pq_0 + r_0$ be the largest element of the public key. Show that the encryption function produces valid ciphertexts only if r_0 is even.
17) Consider GSW encryption scheme.
    (a) **(KeyGen)**: Set pk $= A \in \mathbb{Z}_q^{n \times m}$ and sk $= s \in \mathbb{Z}_q^n$ where $s^\top A = e^\top$ such that $e \leftarrow \chi^m$.
    (b) **(Encrypt)**: Compute $C \leftarrow AR + \mu \cdot G$.
    (c) **(Decrypt)**: Compute $s^\top C$ and round.

Prove the correctness of the above GSW encryption scheme.

IV

Data Integrity

In the digital era, data integrity is a paramount concept for maintaining information security. As the transmission, storage, and processing of large-scale data become ubiquitous, ensuring integrity is critical. Data integrity guarantees that information remains unaltered by accidental errors or malicious tampering, thereby preserving its accuracy and reliability. To address these requirements, cryptographers employ specific primitives: hash functions, Message Authentication Codes (MACs), and digital signatures.

A hash function is an algorithm that maps an input of arbitrary length to a fixed-length output, commonly referred to as a hash value or message digest. Acting as a digital fingerprint, a secure hash function exhibits properties of pre-image resistance and collision resistance. Consequently, integrity is verified by comparing these hash digests, allowing for the detection of any data corruption or manipulation.

Building upon basic integrity, a Message Authentication Code (MAC) utilizes a secret key to generate a cryptographic checksum, known as an authentication tag. The MAC algorithm takes both the message and the shared secret key as inputs to produce this fixed-length tag. The sender transmits the message alongside the tag to the receiver. Upon receipt, the receiver recomputes the tag using the same key and the received message, then compares it with the transmitted tag. A match confirms two critical properties: the data has not been modified (integrity) and the sender possesses the valid secret key (data origin authentication). Consequently, MACs are widely deployed in network protocols to detect unauthorized tampering and verify authenticity.

Furthermore, digital signatures represent a sophisticated method for ensuring integrity and legal validity. By integrating hash functions with asymmetric cryptography, this technology offers a unique security property: non-repudiation. In practice, the sender computes a hash of the data and encrypts this digest using their private key to generate the digital signature. The receiver subsequently verifies the signature using the sender's public key. This validation process not only guarantees data integrity and authenticity but also strictly prevents the sender from denying their authorship (non-repudiation). Consequently, digital signatures are foundational to e-commerce, electronic contracts, and Public Key Infrastructure (PKI), enabling trusted data exchange.

Data integrity is the cornerstone of information security, and it safeguards user data. Hash functions, Message Authentication Codes, and digital signatures provide reliable protection for achieving data integrity. However, as technology continues to develop, attackers constantly upgrade their methods. Consequently, systems must continuously strengthen and improve data integrity measures to cope with increasingly complex security challenges. This ensures that data remains secure at all times.

CHAPTER 12

Hash Functions

This chapter introduces hash functions. Biological fingerprints are renowned for their stability and distinctiveness. Exhibiting unique ridge patterns across individuals, they serve as reliable identifiers in identity verification and criminal investigations. Consequently, these biological markers significantly enhance the efficiency of forensic analysis and the accuracy of suspect identification.

Hash functions act as digital "fingerprints" that compress messages of arbitrary length to fixed-length hash values. The most common cryptographic applications of hash functions are in digital signatures and in ensuring data integrity without requiring byte-by-byte comparison. While collisions theoretically exist, cryptographic hash functions are designed to make finding them computationally infeasible. This chapter introduces their definitions, properties, and security implications.

Topics covered in this chapter:

- Definition of hash functions
- MD4 hash function
- SHA family of hash function
- SM3 hash function
- Attacks against hash functions
- Applications of hash functions

12.1 INTRODUCTION TO HASH FUNCTION

Hash functions, variously referred to as **message digest function**, **hash algorithm**, or digital fingerprint function, denoted by $H(m)$ or $\text{hash}(m)$. These functions generate a fixed-length "fingerprint" for a given data. Consequently, verifying the identity of two messages does not necessitate a byte-by-byte comparison of the original data; comparing their respective fingerprints is sufficient. Formally, a hash function maps an input of arbitrary length to a fixed-length output digest. In an ideal model, these outputs appear uniformly distributed and unpredictable. The term "hash function" describes a broad class of algorithms; those specifically designed for security and integrity purposes are known as **cryptographic hash**

DOI: 10.1201/9781042011087-12

functions. A defining characteristic of these functions is that the resulting hash value is significantly shorter than the input data.

To illustrate the efficiency of this mapping, consider the analogy of locating a book in a library. Scanning books one by one requires roughly $\mathcal{O}(m)$ work, where m is the number of titles, and is inefficient. In practice a fixed-length call number organized by category and number is used to locate a book quickly, giving an average lookup close to $\mathcal{O}(1)$. No matter how thick a book is, it maps to a fixed-length code. This "code then locate" idea resembles hash lookup, although the two are not identical. The cryptographic hash functions discussed here do not use a secret key. Examples of a hash function are shown in Figure 12-1.

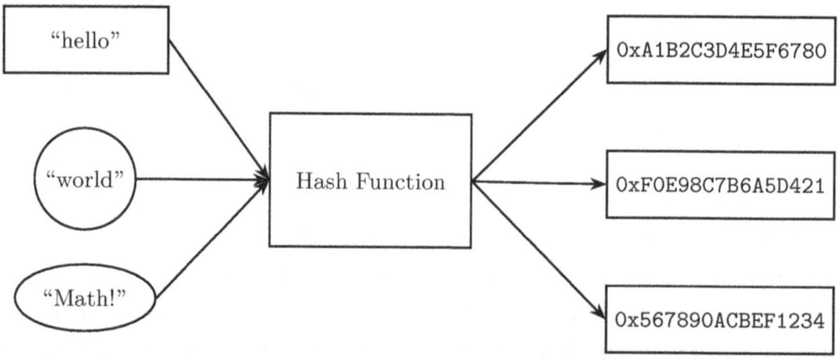

Figure 12-1: Simplified Examples of a Hash Function

A common practical example is cloud storage. To speed up uploads, some services perform an instant upload check: the server computes a quick fingerprint of the file (for example the file digest or a fixed chunk) and, if a file with the same fingerprint already exists in the backend, the service links to the existing copy instead of requiring a full upload. This improves large-file user experience, reduces storage by deduplication, and helps identify known malicious samples.

From a mathematical perspective, a simplistic hash function can be constructed using modular arithmetic. Consider the reduction modulo q: for any integer input m, we define the function as $H(m) = m \pmod q$. A slight variant might be defined as $H(m) = m(m+3) \pmod q$. However, such constructions are cryptographically insecure due to their lack of **collision resistance**. For instance, with $q = 10$, it is trivial to observe that $H(31) = 1 \pmod{10}$ and $H(41) = 1 \pmod{10}$.

An unkeyed hash function is defined as $H : \mathcal{M} \rightarrow \mathcal{Y}$ where $\mathcal{M}$ represents the set of inputs and $\mathcal{Y}$ represents a finite set of outputs that are called digests. A well-designed hash function should satisfy the following properties:

1) **Efficient**: A hash function should be computationally efficient.
2) **One-way**: It should be computationally infeasible to reconstruct the original message from its hash value. This does not mean absolute impossibility, but that the time required to reverse it would be impractically long.
3) **Fixed Output Length**: The output of a hash function has a constant length regardless of the input size.
4) **Avalanche Effect**: Even a minor change in the input, such as flipping one bit, should produce a completely different and unpredictable output.

5) **Collision Resistance**: It should be computationally infeasible to find two distinct inputs m_1 and m_2 that yield the same hash value.
6) **Uniform Distribution**: Hash outputs should be approximately uniformly distributed over the entire output space to avoid statistical bias that could otherwise enable prediction or analysis.

These robust properties are fundamental to the operation of secure communications and modern blockchain systems. High computational efficiency in evaluating the hash is essential for network nodes; without it, processing delays in verifying time-sensitive blockchain transactions could result in financial losses due to price volatility. Furthermore, blockchain employs a pseudonymous addressing mechanism where each user's address is deterministically derived from the hash of their public key. The strict one-wayness of the hash function renders it computationally infeasible to reverse-engineer the public key from the visible address, thereby preserving user privacy on the public ledger until a transaction is initiated.

Collision resistance is equally critical. Suppose Alice transfers one bitcoin to Bob, and the system computes the hash value H_1 for the instruction. If the hash function lacks collision resistance, a malicious party could generate a fraudulent instruction "transfer ten bitcoins to Alice" with an identical hash value H_2, such that $H_1 = H_2$. Consequently, the valid signature on H_1 would also validate H_2. This scenario demonstrates how hash collisions can directly compromise the integrity of digital signatures.

For this reason, hash functions are indispensable in digital signature systems. Public-key signature algorithms such as RSA and ECDSA are sensitive to input length, so signing a long message directly would be computationally expensive. A hash function compresses messages of arbitrary length into fixed-length digests, enabling efficient and secure signing. Moreover, due to the avalanche effect, even a single-bit change in the input produces a completely different output, allowing hash functions to detect data tampering effectively.

Suppose a sender, Alice, computes a plain message hash and transmits it alongside the data to verify integrity as illustrated in Figure 12-2. If the transmission occurs over a noisy but benign channel, Bob can recompute the hash upon receipt; if the hashes match, the message is deemed unaltered. However, this provides zero security against an active attacker. If an attacker, Eve, intercepts the transmission, she can trivially modify the message, compute a new valid hash for the forged message, and forward

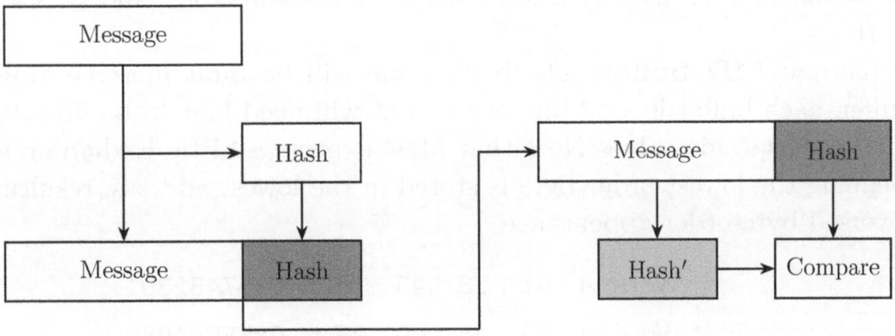

Figure 12-2: Message Integrity Using a Hash Function

the new pair to Bob. Bob's verification would succeed, and he would accept the forged data. To achieve true integrity and authentication against malicious actors, a plain unkeyed hash function is insufficient to provide authentication against active attackers. Authentication requires a keyed construction, such as a digital signature scheme.

12.2 EXAMPLES OF HASH FUNCTIONS

12.2.1 MD4

The Message-Digest 4 (MD4) algorithm [150] is a cryptographic hash function developed by Professor *Ron Rivest* at MIT in 1990. Designed to offer enhanced efficiency and security compared to its predecessor, MD2, MD4 represented a significant evolution in hash function architecture suitable for 32-bit processors. Although MD4 retains the 128-bit output size of MD2, its internal structure differs substantially. Notably, there is no "MD3" algorithm; it is widely understood that MD3 was an experimental precursor abandoned prior to publication due to early identified vulnerabilities.

The MD4 algorithm accepts a message of arbitrary length as input and produces a fixed 128-bit message digest. The computation proceeds through the following steps:

1) **Append padding bits**: Let M be the input message. The message M is padded so that its length is congruent to 448 modulo 512 in bits, that is, a single "1" bit is appended to the message, and then enough zero bits are appended so that the length in bits of the padded message becomes congruent to 448, modulo 512. Suppose the message M with a length of n bits, the number of k is the smallest, non-negative solution satisfying the congruence

$$n + 1 + k \equiv 448 \pmod{512}. \tag{12-1}$$

2) **Append Length**: Since the previous step has 448 bits, this step will fill the remaining 64 bits of the last block that reach a perfect size of 512 bits by blocks. The length of the message before padding (64 bits) is appended.
If $n > 2^{64}$, then only the low-order 64 bits of n are used.
After padding message is a multiple of the 512-bit block size, or a multiple of 32 bit word size. Let N be number of 32-bit words, the padded message $M = (m_0, m_1, \ldots, m_{N-1})$ where each m_i is a 32-bit word, and N is a multiple of 16.
3) **Initialize MD buffer**: The hash value will be built incrementing 4-word buffer, each buffer is a 32 bits word, that will need first to be initialized with the below specific values Note that MD4 expects a Little-Endian architecture, meaning the lowest-order byte is stored in the lowest address, resulting in the reversed byte-order appearance

$$\text{Word } A : \texttt{01} \quad \texttt{23} \quad \texttt{45} \quad \texttt{67} \Rightarrow \texttt{0x67452301} \tag{12-2}$$

$$\text{Word } B : \texttt{89} \quad \texttt{AB} \quad \texttt{CD} \quad \texttt{EF} \Rightarrow \texttt{0xEFCDAB89} \tag{12-3}$$

$$\text{Word } C : \texttt{FE} \quad \texttt{DC} \quad \texttt{BA} \quad \texttt{98} \Rightarrow \texttt{0x98BADCFE} \tag{12-4}$$

$$\text{Word } D : \texttt{76} \quad \texttt{54} \quad \texttt{32} \quad \texttt{10} \Rightarrow \texttt{0x10325476} \tag{12-5}$$

4) **Process Message Blocks**: Define three auxiliary functions that each take as input three 32-bit words and produce as output one 32-bit word

$$F(x, y, z) = (x \wedge y) \vee (\neg x \wedge z) \tag{12-6}$$

$$G(x, y, z) = (x \wedge y) \vee (x \wedge z) \vee (y \wedge z) \tag{12-7}$$

$$H(x, y, z) = x \oplus y \oplus z \tag{12-8}$$

where "$\wedge$" denotes the bitwise AND operation, "$\vee$" denotes the bitwise OR operation, and "$\neg X$" denotes the bitwise complement of X.
The function F takes three binary inputs x, y and z, each of which is either 0 or 1. It outputs y when $x = 1$, and outputs z when $x = 0$.

```
    return ((x & y) | ((~x) & z))
```

The function G takes three binary inputs x, y and z, each being 0 or 1. It outputs 1 if at least two of the input bits are 1, otherwise it outputs 0.

```
    return ((x & y) | (x & z) | (y & z))
```

The function H takes three binary inputs x, y and z, each being 0 or 1. It performs a bitwise parity check, returning the XOR sum of the three inputs.

```
    return x ^y ^ z
```

Selected computation results are shown in Table 12-1.

Table 12-1: The Result of Selected Auxiliary Functions

x	y	z	Function F Value	Function G Value	Function H Value
0	0	0	0	0	0
0	0	1	1	0	1
0	1	1	1	1	0
1	1	0	1	1	0
1	1	1	1	1	1

Then, split each 512 bits into a 16 words and update A, B, C, D, as shown in Figure 12-3. The Python of MD4 Algorithm as follow

```
h = [0x67452301, 0xEFCDAB89, 0x98BADCFE, 0x10325476]

def MD4_Process(blocks):
    for block in blocks:
        X, h = list(struct.unpack("<16I", block)), h.copy()

        # Round 1.
        Xi = [3, 7, 11, 19]
        for n in range(16):
            i, j, k, l = map(lambda x: x % 4, range(-n, -n + 4))
            K, S = n, Xi[n % 4]
            hn = h[i] + F(h[j], h[k], h[l]) + X[K]
            h[i] = lrot(hn & mask, S)

        # Round 2.
        Xi = [3, 5, 9, 13]
```

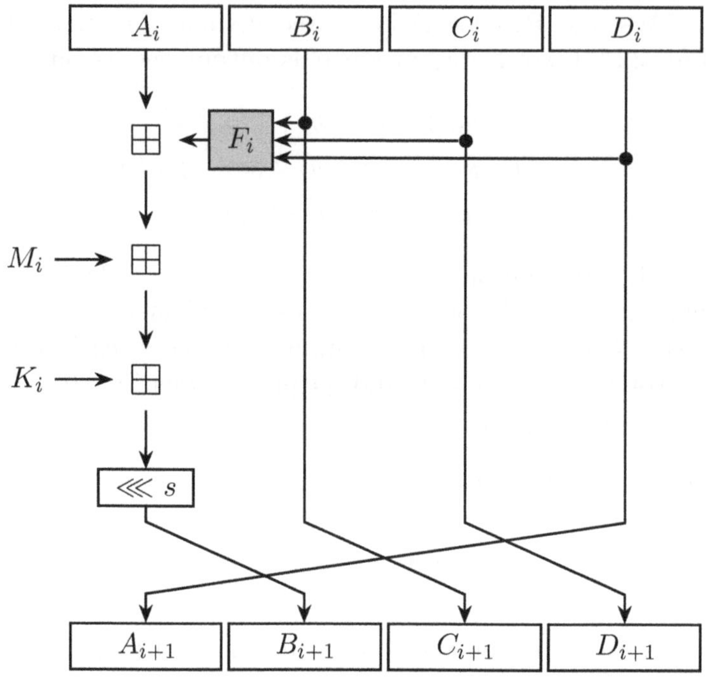

Figure 12-3: MD4 Step Function

```
        for n in range(16):
            i, j, k, l = map(lambda x: x % 4, range(-n, -n + 4))
            K, S = n % 4 * 4 + n // 4, Xi[n % 4]
            hn = h[i] + G(h[j], h[k], h[l]) + X[K] + 0x5A827999
            h[i] = lrot(hn & mask, S)

        # Round 3.
        Xi = [3, 9, 11, 15]
        Ki = [0, 8, 4, 12, 2, 10, 6, 14, 1, 9, 5, 13, 3, 11, 7,
    15]
        for n in range(16):
            i, j, k, l = map(lambda x: x % 4, range(-n, -n + 4))
            K, S = Ki[n], Xi[n % 4]
            hn = h[i] + H(h[j], h[k], h[l]) + X[K] + 0x6ED9EBA1
            h[i] = lrot(hn & mask, S)

        h = [((v + n) & mask) for v, n in zip(h, h)]

def F(x, y, z):
    return (x & y) | (~x & z)

def G(x, y, z):
    return (x & y) | (x & z) | (y & z)

def H(x, y, z):
    return x ^ y ^ z

def lrot(value, n):
    lbits, rbits = (value << n) & mask, value >> (width - n)
    return lbits | rbits
```

5) **Output**: The output is A, B, C, D. Begin with the low-order byte of A, and end with the high-order byte of D, then convert it into the hexadecimal.

Example 12.2.1 Compute the MD4 hash of the following poem. The lines of the poem: "**Since ancient times can run from death no men, I will leave in history a staunch fame then.**"

Solution: The example of the MD4 process is given as follows:

1) **Append padding bits**. The length of message is 91 bytes, 728 bits, so $n = 728$. The total length after padding $(n+1+k)$ satisfies $(n+1+k) \bmod 512 \equiv 448$, therefore, $k \equiv (448 - n - 1) \equiv 231 \pmod{512}$. The padded message as shown in Table 12-2.

Table 12-2: MD4 Append Padding

	0	1	2	3	4	5	6	7	8	9	10	11	12	13	14	15
k_0	83	105	110	99	101	32	97	110	99	105	101	110	116	32	116	105
k_1	109	101	115	32	99	97	110	32	114	117	110	32	102	114	111	109
k_2	32	100	101	97	116	104	32	110	111	32	109	101	110	44	32	73
k_3	32	119	105	108	108	32	108	101	97	118	101	32	105	110	32	104
k_4	105	115	116	111	114	121	32	97	32	115	116	97	117	110	99	104
k_5	32	102	97	109	101	32	116	104	101	110	46	**128**	0	0	0	0
k_6	0	0	0	0	0	0	0	0	0	0	0	0	0	0	0	0
k_7	0	0	0	0	0	0	0	0								

2) **Append Length**. Since the length of message is 728 bits, so 728 will be the value and append at the end of the message within a 64 bits representation. 728 translated into its binary form is 00000010 11011000. According to the endianness convention, the conversion begins with the low-order byte (least significant byte first), as illustrated in Figure 12-4.

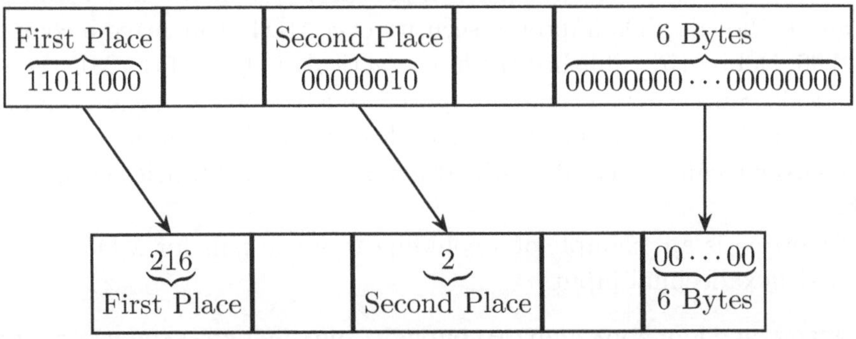

Figure 12-4: MD4 Append Length

Then, append the message length to the table, as shown in Table 12-3.

Table 12-3: MD4 Append Length

k_7	0	0	0	0	0	0	0	0	216	2	0	0	0	0	0	0

3) **Initialize MD Buffers**. Built incrementing 4-word buffer A, B, C, D, as shown in the Equation 12-2 to 12-5. Then update A, B, C, D. The first four characters of the poem, "**Sinc**", are converted into their ASCII codes, corresponding to columns 1 through 4 of row k_1 in Table 12-2. These values are then listed, expressed in binary, reordered in little-endian format, and finally converted back to a decimal number, as illustrated in Figure 12-5.

Character	S	i	n	c
Decimal	83	105	110	99
Binary	01010011	01101001	01101110	01100011

01100011	01101110	01101001	01010011	$\Rightarrow$	1668180307

Figure 12-5: MD4 Convert to Decimal

4) **Output**. The hash value is `0x9784B1BBA4D5A45FCD96778C7F6E7DB9`.

■

Following the development of MD2 and MD4, *Rivest* introduced MD5 [151] and subsequently MD6 [152] to address security vulnerabilities. MD5 retains the architectural foundation of MD4. The initial operations, including padding, length appending, and buffer initialization, remain identical. However, MD5 introduces critical security enhancements over MD4. First, the main compression loop is expanded from three rounds to four rounds. The newly added fourth round employs a distinct auxiliary boolean function $I(x, y, z) = y \oplus (x \vee \neg z)$. Most significantly, MD5 systematically injects a unique additive constant $T[i]$ into every single one of its 64 steps across all four rounds (where $T[i] = \lfloor 2^{32} \times |\sin(i)| \rfloor$). This continuous injection of non-linear constants fundamentally disrupts symmetrical patterns and mathematically strengthens the avalanche effect, distinguishing MD5 from its vulnerable predecessor.

Initially, MD5 was widely adopted in protocols for file integrity and password verification. Although MD5 improved security over MD4, it incurred a computational cost. In 1996, Dobbertin published the first practical analysis of the MD5 compression function [153]. Subsequent research exposed severe vulnerabilities, leading to the deprecation of MD5. Its 128-bit digest length is insufficient against collision attacks. Indeed, collisions can be readily verified using standard libraries such as Python's `hashlib`.

The following is an example of a colliding message pair for MD5:

The first hexadecimal input

4DC968FF0EE35C209572D4777B721587D36FA7B21BDC56B74A3DC0783E7B9518A

FBFA2**02**A8284BF36E8E4B55B35F427593D849676DA0D1**D5**5D8360FB5F07FEA2

The second hexadecimal input

4DC968FF0EE35C209572D4777B721587D36FA7B21BDC56B74A3DC0783E7B9518A

FBFA2**00**A8284BF36E8E4B55B35F427593D849676DA0D1**55**5D8360FB5F07FEA2

They have the same MD5 hash value: `0x008EE33A9D58B51CFEB425B0959121C9`.

MD5 is no longer considered collision-resistant and has gradually been replaced by the SHA family of hash functions.

12.2.2 SHA-1

Beyond the MD family, the Secure Hash Algorithm (SHA) family plays a pivotal role in modern cryptography. Developed by the U.S. National Security Agency (NSA), this family includes SHA-0 [154], SHA-1 [155], SHA-2 [156]. The initial version, SHA-0, contained critical flaws and was rapidly superseded by SHA-1 [157]. Subsequent research by *Xiaoyun Wang* on SHA-0 collisions vindicated this replacement [158]. SHA-1 generates a 160-bit digest and became ubiquitous in digital signature schemes.

However, SHA-1 eventually proved vulnerable [159] [160]. Given its architectural similarities to the compromised MD5, researchers correctly anticipated its insecurity. Consequently, NIST deprecated SHA-1 after 2010, transitioning to the SHA-2 family. SHA-2 offers variants such as SHA-256 and SHA-512, with output lengths ranging from 224 to 512 bits. These longer digests substantially improve resistance against collision attacks. In 2015, responding to advances in cryptanalysis, NIST standardized SHA-3 [156] as the next-generation algorithm. A comparison of these iterations appears in Table 12-4.

Table 12-4: Comparison of SHA Functions

Algorithm	Input Size	Output Size	Block Size
SHA-0	$2^{64}-1$	160	512
SHA-1	$2^{64}-1$	160	512
SHA-2-224	$2^{64}-1$	224	512
SHA-2-256	$2^{64}-1$	256	512
SHA-2-512	$2^{128}-1$	512	1024
SHA-3-512	Unbounded	512	576

This subsection details the operational principles of SHA-1. Unlike SHA-3, the members of the SHA-2 family retain the architectural framework of SHA-1. This group, which includes SHA-224, SHA-256, SHA-384, and SHA-512, differs from SHA-1 primarily in internal parameters and security enhancements designed to resist cryptanalysis. The digest computation process for SHA-1 is outlined below:

1) **Padding the Message**: Let M be a message with a length of l bits, append a single bit "1" followed by k zero bits, and finally, a 64-bit block representing the integer l in binary. The number k is the smallest, non-negative solution such that $l+1+k \equiv 448 \pmod{512}$.
2) **Dividing the Padded Message**: The padded message is divided into N 512-bit blocks $M^{(1)}, M^{(2)}, \ldots, M^{(N)}$. Each 512-bit input block can be subdivided into sixteen 32-bit words and can be represented as $M_0^{(i)}, M_1^{(i)}, \ldots, M_{15}^{(i)}$ for $1 \leqslant i \leqslant N$.

3) **Initialize Hash Buffer**: Initialize five 32-bit hexadecimal hash values, known as buffers. These values are set to the following initial constants:

$$H_0^{(0)} = \texttt{0x67452301}$$
$$H_1^{(0)} = \texttt{0xEFCDAB89}$$
$$H_2^{(0)} = \texttt{0x98BADCFE}$$
$$H_3^{(0)} = \texttt{0x10325476}$$
$$H_4^{(0)} = \texttt{0xC3D2E1F0}$$

4) **Message Schedule Expansion**: For each message block $M^{(i)}(1 \leqslant i \leqslant N)$, the sixteen 32-bit words are expanded into 80 words, denoted by $W_0, W_1, \ldots, W_{79}$. The expansion is performed as follows:

$$W_t = M_t^{(i)}, \qquad 0 \leqslant t \leqslant 15 \tag{12-9}$$
$$W_t = (W_{t-3} \oplus W_{t-8} \oplus W_{t-14} \oplus W_{t-16})_{\lll 1}, \qquad 16 \leqslant t \leqslant 79 \tag{12-10}$$

where $_{\lll s}$ indicates a circular left shift of the word by s bit positions.

5) **Variable Initialization**:

$$A = H_0^{(i-1)}, \quad B = H_1^{(i-1)}, \quad C = H_2^{(i-1)}, \quad D = H_3^{(i-1)}, \quad E = H_4^{(i-1)}$$

A hash value H_i consists of five 32-bit words: $H_0^{(i)}, H_1^{(i)}, H_2^{(i)}, H_3^{(i)}, H_4^{(i)}$. Initially, the hash value is set to the predefined initial vector H_0. After processing each message block, this value is updated to produce a new hash value. Once all message blocks have been processed, the final hash value $H^{(N)}$ represents the output $H(M)$ of the SHA-1 algorithm.

6) **Step Functions and Constants**: The 80 rounds of SHA-1 are not uniform in structure. The entire process is divided into four stages of 20 rounds each, and every stage uses a distinct logical function f_t together with some constant k_t. Let t denote the round index, where $0 \leqslant t \leqslant 79$. In each round, f_t takes three 32-bit words B, C, and D as input and produces a 32-bit output. The specific logical functions f_t and constants differ across the four stages and are defined as follows:

$$f_t(B,C,D) = \begin{cases} (B \wedge C) \vee (\neg B \wedge D) & , 0 \leqslant t \leqslant 19 \\ B \oplus C \oplus D & , 20 \leqslant t \leqslant 39 \\ (B \wedge C) \vee (B \wedge D) \vee (C \wedge D) & , 40 \leqslant t \leqslant 59 \\ B \oplus C \oplus D & , 60 \leqslant t \leqslant 79 \end{cases} \tag{12-11}$$

Here, $\wedge, \vee, \neg$, and $\oplus$ denote bitwise AND, OR, NOT, and XOR operations, respectively. The constant k_t is defined as follows:

$$k_t = \begin{cases} \texttt{0x5A827999}, & 0 \leqslant t \leqslant 19 \\ \texttt{0x6ED9EBA1}, & 20 \leqslant t \leqslant 39 \\ \texttt{0x8F1BBCDC}, & 40 \leqslant t \leqslant 59 \\ \texttt{0xCA62C1D6}, & 60 \leqslant t \leqslant 79 \end{cases} \tag{12-12}$$

7) **Round Function**: The operation of a single round is illustrated in Figure 12-6. In each round t, the working variables are updated. Let T be a temporary variable defined as

$$T = (A \lll 5) + f_t(B, C, D) + E + W_t + k_t \tag{12-13}$$

The variables are then updated for the next round as follows:

$$E \leftarrow D, \quad D \leftarrow C, \quad C \leftarrow (B \lll 30), \quad B \leftarrow A, \quad A \leftarrow T \tag{12-14}$$

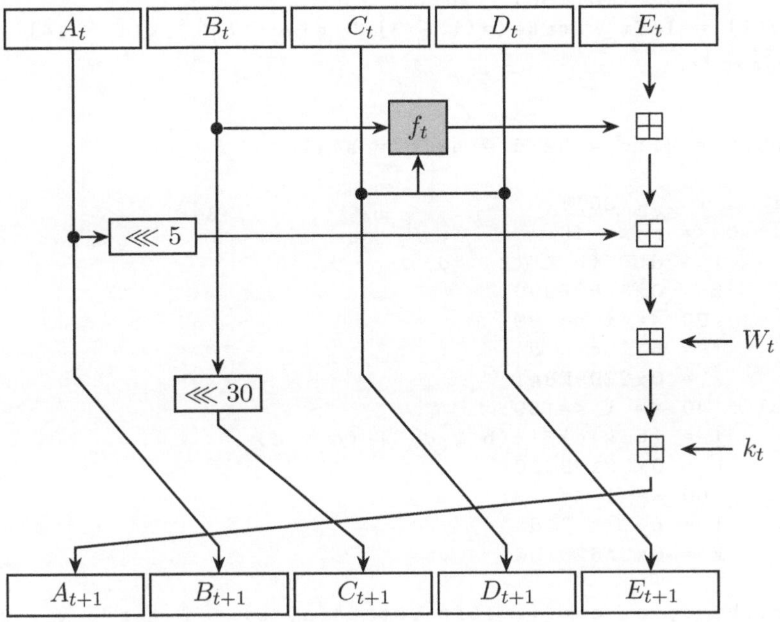

Figure 12-6: Structure of a Single Step in SHA-1

In other words, in each round the five 32-bit registers A, B, C, D, and E are updated in sequence according to the following rules:

(a) Calculate T: Add the value of A rotated left by 5 bits, the output of $f_t(B, C, D)$, variable E, the message word W_t, and the constant k_t.
(b) Update E: Set E to the current value of D.
(c) Update D: Set D to the current value of C.
(d) Update C: Set C to the current value of B rotated left by 30 bits.
(e) Update B: Set B to the current value of A.
(f) Update A: Set A to the value of T.

After processing all 80 rounds for block $M^{(i)}$, $1 \leqslant i \leqslant N$, the hash values are updated as follows:

$$H_0^{(i)} = A + H_0^{(i-1)} \tag{12-15}$$
$$H_1^{(i)} = B + H_1^{(i-1)} \tag{12-16}$$
$$H_2^{(i)} = C + H_2^{(i-1)} \tag{12-17}$$
$$H_3^{(i)} = D + H_3^{(i-1)} \tag{12-18}$$
$$H_4^{(i)} = E + H_4^{(i-1)} \tag{12-19}$$

The Round function of the SHA-1 algorithm is implemented in Python as follows:

```
w = [0] * 80
#W_t = M_t
for i in range(16):
    w[i] = struct.unpack(b'>I', chunk[i * 4:i * 4 + 4])[0]

  #W_t =(W_{t-3}  XOR W_{t-8} XOR  W_{t- 14}  XOR W_{t-16}) \111
    1
for i in range(16, 80):
    w[i] = left_rotate(w[i - 3] ^ w[i - 8] ^ w[i - 14] ^ w[i -
    16], 1)

  # Initialize hash value
a = h0;b = h1;c = h2;d = h3;e = h4;

for i in range(80):
    if 0 <= i <= 19:
        f = d ^ (b & (c ^ d))
        k = 0x5A827999
    elif 20 <= i <= 39:
        f = b ^ c ^ d
        k = 0x6ED9EBA1
    elif 40 <= i <= 59:
        f = (b & c) | (b & d) | (c & d)
        k = 0x8F1BBCDC
    elif 60 <= i <= 79:
        f = b ^ c ^ d
        k = 0xCA62C1D6

    a, b, c, d, e = ((_left_rotate(a, 5) + f + e + k + w[i]) & 0
    xffffffff,
                        a, _left_rotate(b, 30), c, d)
h0 = h0 + a
h1 = h1 + b
h2 = h2 + c
h3 = h3 + d
h4 = h4 + e
```

8) **Output**. After repeating steps one through four a total of N times, the resulting 160-bit hash value of the M is

$$H_0^{(N)} \| H_1^{(N)} \| H_2^{(N)} \| H_3^{(N)} \| H_4^{(N)} \tag{12-20}$$

Example 12.2.2 Compute the SHA-1 hash of the message: "**missile**".
Solution: First, convert the word into its binary form using ASCII encoding

01101101 01101001 01110011 01110011 01101001 01101100 01100101

Then padding the message, "missile" consisting of seven 8-bit ASCII characters with a total length of $l = 56$ bits, so the message is padded $448 - 56 = 392$ bits in total, a one bit followed by 391 zero bits. After that, append the 64-bit value which contains the length of message. The padded message is then given by

$$\underbrace{\underbrace{01101101}_{\text{m}}\quad\underbrace{01101001}_{\text{i}}\quad\cdots\quad\underbrace{01100101}_{\text{e}}\quad 1\quad\overbrace{00\cdots00}^{391\text{ bits}}\quad\overbrace{00\cdots0\underbrace{111000}_{56}}^{64\text{ bits}}}_{512\text{ bits}}$$

Convert the padded message in hexadecimal

```
6D697373 696C6580 00000000 00000000
00000000 00000000 00000000 00000000
00000000 00000000 00000000 00000000
00000000 00000000 00000000 00000038
```

The message block in hexadecimal form consists of 128 hexadecimal characters, which corresponds to 512 bits in binary. Since there is only one block, $N = 1$. This block is divided into sixteen 32-bit words, denoted $M_0^{(1)}, M_1^{(1)}, \ldots, M_{15}^{(1)}$, as shown below:

$$\begin{array}{llll}
M_0^{(1)} = \texttt{6D697373} & M_4^{(1)} = \texttt{00000000} & M_8^{(1)} = \texttt{00000000} & M_{12}^{(1)} = \texttt{00000000} \\
M_1^{(1)} = \texttt{696C6580} & M_5^{(1)} = \texttt{00000000} & M_9^{(1)} = \texttt{00000000} & M_{13}^{(1)} = \texttt{00000000} \\
M_2^{(1)} = \texttt{00000000} & M_6^{(1)} = \texttt{00000000} & M_{10}^{(1)} = \texttt{00000000} & M_{14}^{(1)} = \texttt{00000000} \\
M_3^{(1)} = \texttt{00000000} & M_7^{(1)} = \texttt{00000000} & M_{11}^{(1)} = \texttt{00000000} & M_{15}^{(1)} = \texttt{00000038}
\end{array}$$

For $0 \leqslant t \leqslant 15$, $W_t = M_t$. For $16 \leqslant t \leqslant 79$, $W_t = (W_{t-3} \oplus W_{t-8} \oplus W_{t-14} \oplus W_{t-16})_{\lll 1}$. The Table 12-5 presents several sample values of W_t.

Table 12-5: SHA-1 Sample Values of W_t

W_0 = 6D697373	W_{16} = DAD2E6E6	···	W_{76} = D3C2409D
W_1 = 696C6580	W_{17} = D2D8CB00	···	W_{77} = C83C102B
W_2 = 00000000	W_{18} = 00000070	···	W_{78} = 9988035D
···	···	···	W_{79} = 93A0802D

Initial value H_0. Let $A = H_0^{(0)}, B = H_1^{(0)}, C = H_2^{(0)}, D = H_3^{(0)}, E = H_4^{(0)}$ and update A, B, C, D, E. Table 12-6 presents the values of A, B, C, D, E for selected rounds.

Table 12-6: SHA-1 Sample Values of A, B, C, D, E

Round	A	B	C	D	E
0	67452301	EFCDAB89	98BADCFE	10325476	C3D2E1F0
1	0D1E0C26	67452301	7BF36AE2	98BADCFE	10325476
19	AC1A3627	263A2F49	62A48F28	5E4B17CC	771AA4ED
20	84EAD0D4	AC1A3627	498E8BD2	62A48F28	5E4B17CC
39	CA7D219D	7DF7811A	35EB9E19	8C46EAE5	B05D93F9
40	C9FD0AFF	CA7D219D	9F7DE046	35EB9E19	8C46EAE5

Continued on Next Page

Table 12-6: SHA-1 Sample Values of A, B, C, D, E (Continued)

Round	A	B	C	D	E
59	C0D48C83	7986E0CE	6E270F78	DB273C51	6B62B8CD
60	C658AD1B	C0D48C83	9E61B833	6E270F78	DB273C51
79	9AEB82ED	F48B797C	AA977770	E78E0B69	75C0BD51
80	EAC6626C	9AEB82ED	3D22DE5F	AA977770	E78E0B69

In the final round, the updated registers are $A =$ `0xEAC6626C`, $B =$ `0x9AEB82ED`, $C =$ `0x3D22DE5F`, $D =$ `0xAA977770`, $E =$ `0xE78E0B69`.

Block 1 has been processed. These values are added to their corresponding initial hash values $H_0^{(0)}$, $H_1^{(0)}$, $H_2^{(0)}$, $H_3^{(0)}$, $H_4^{(0)}$. We have

$$H_0 = H_0^{(0)} + A = \texttt{0x520B856D} \tag{12-21}$$

$$H_1 = H_1^{(0)} + B = \texttt{0x8AB92E76} \tag{12-22}$$

$$H_2 = H_2^{(0)} + C = \texttt{0xD5DDBB5D} \tag{12-23}$$

$$H_3 = H_3^{(0)} + D = \texttt{0xBAC9CBE6} \tag{12-24}$$

$$H_4 = H_4^{(0)} + E = \texttt{0xAB60ED59} \tag{12-25}$$

Finally, by concatenating H_0, H_1, H_2, H_3, and H_4 as $H_0 \| H_1 \| H_2 \| H_3 \| H_4$, the final hash value is

`0x520B856D8AB92E76D5DDBB5DBAC9CBE6AB60ED59`

■

Example 12.2.3 Let the message be "I am a rocket engineer", the hash value of SHA-1 is

`0xD8D25328850C60365334350E24B99D0734C694B8` ■

It is important to note that the design and standardization of the SHA-1 and SHA-2 families involved significant participation by the NSA. These algorithms were subsequently released as public standards under the FIPS 180 series. Although the specifications were made public, the internal design criteria were not fully disclosed. To date, no reliable evidence indicates that the NSA intentionally inserted hidden backdoors to compromise the algorithms' security. Nevertheless, both the public and segments of the developer community remain wary of intelligence agency involvement. This skepticism, fueled by subsequent controversies in the broader cryptographic landscape, has prompted many non-governmental organizations and open-source projects to adopt a cautious stance, often favoring alternative algorithms or advocating for the transition to SHA-3.

In information security, the term *backdoor* refers to a concealed mechanism or logic covertly integrated into hardware or software. A backdoor may exist as a standalone program, an inserted code fragment, or a system-level feature. When exploited by a malicious actor or an authorized insider, it can circumvent security controls to allow unauthorized access, data tampering, or the subversion of cryptographic protections. Such mechanisms are designed to be extremely difficult to detect or trace.

12.2.3 SM3

Given that widely used international hash function algorithms (such as MD5 and SHA-1) successively exposed security vulnerabilities, NIST initiated a public competition for the new generation hash function standard, SHA-3, between 2007 and 2012. After five years of rigorous selection, the KECCAK algorithm distinguished itself due to its elegant structure, sufficient security margin, excellent overall performance, and high efficiency in software and hardware implementation, and it was finally established as the SHA-3 standard. Concurrently with the international SHA-3 competition, China publicly solicited standards for hash functions. The SM3 cryptographic hash algorithm was adopted as the Chinese cryptographic industry standard in 2012 and as the national standard in 2016. Furthermore, achieving a monumental milestone in international recognition, SM3 was formally published as an international standard by the International Organization for Standardization (ISO/IEC 10118-3) in 2018. This chapter describes the design principles and technical features of the SM3 algorithm.

SM3 is a cryptographic hash function, it takes a message of arbitrary length as input, processes the data in fixed 512-bit blocks, and outputs a 256-bit hash value. The following steps are performed to compute the hash value of the input [161].

We begin by defining the constants and boolean functions utilized in the SM3 algorithm. The Initial Value (**IV**) of SM3 is defined as the following 256-bit string, represented as eight 32-bit big-endian integers:

$$\begin{aligned}\mathbf{IV} = {} & \texttt{0x7380166F 0x4914B2B9 0x172442D7 0xDA8A0600} \\ & \texttt{0xA96F30BC 0x163138AA 0xE38DEE4D 0xB0FB0E4E}\end{aligned}$$

The constants of SM3 are

$$T_j = \begin{cases} \texttt{0x79CC4519}, & \text{for } 0 \leqslant j \leqslant 15 \\ \texttt{0x7A879D8A}, & \text{for } 16 \leqslant j \leqslant 63 \end{cases} \tag{12-26}$$

The boolean functions of SM3 are

$$FF_j(X,Y,Z) = \begin{cases} X \oplus Y \oplus Z, & \text{for } 0 \leqslant j \leqslant 15 \\ (X \wedge Y) \vee (X \wedge Z) \vee (Y \wedge Z), & \text{for } 16 \leqslant j \leqslant 63 \end{cases} \tag{12-27}$$

$$GG_j(X,Y,Z) = \begin{cases} X \oplus Y \oplus Z, & \text{for } 0 \leqslant j \leqslant 15 \\ (X \wedge Y) \vee (\neg X \wedge Z), & \text{for } 16 \leqslant j \leqslant 63 \end{cases} \tag{12-28}$$

where X, Y, Z are 32-bit words, "$\wedge$" denotes the bitwise AND operation, "$\vee$" denotes the bitwise OR operation, and "$\neg X$" denotes the bitwise complement of X.

The permutations of SM3 are

$$P_0(X) = X \oplus (X \lll 9) \oplus (X \lll 17) \tag{12-29}$$

$$P_1(X) = X \oplus (X \lll 15) \oplus (X \lll 23) \tag{12-30}$$

1) **Padding**: Let M be the input has l bits. Append a single bit "1" followed by k zero bits and finally the 64-bit Big-Endian binary representation of the length l. The number of k is the smallest, non-negative solution such that $l + 1 + k \equiv 448 \pmod{512}$. After padding, the length of the padded message is a multiple of 512.
2) **Iterative Compression**: The padded message m' is split into 512-bit blocks, and denoted as $m' = B^{(0)}B^{(1)}\ldots B^{(n-1)}$, where $n = (l + k + 65)/512$. The iteration procedure for m' is as follows:

$$V^{(i+1)} = CF\left(V^{(i)}, B^{(i)}\right), \text{ for } 0 \leqslant i \leqslant n-1 \tag{12-31}$$

where CF is the compression function, $V^{(0)}$ is the 256-bit **IV**, and $B^{(i)}$ is the i-th message block after padding. The result after iterative procedure is $V^{(n)}$.
3) **Message Expansion**: The message block $B^{(i)}$ is expanded to 132 words $W_0, W_1, \ldots, W_{67}, W'_1, \ldots, W'_{63}$, which are applied to compression function CF. The message expansion structure as shown in Figure 12-7.

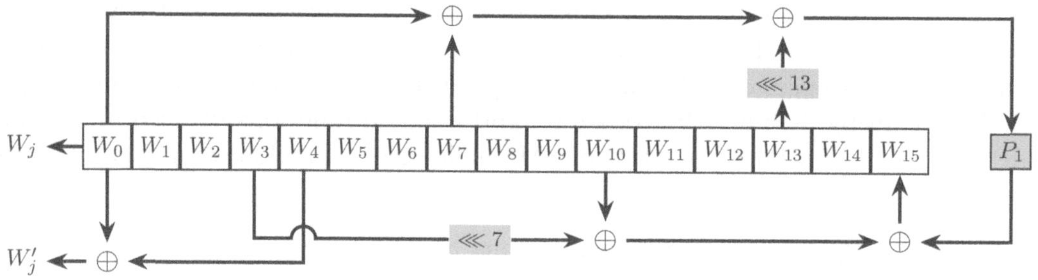

Figure 12-7: SM3 Message Expansion Structure

(a) Split message block $B^{(i)}$ into 16 words $W_0, W_1, \ldots, W_{15}$.
(b) For $16 \leqslant j \leqslant 67$, compute

$$W_j \leftarrow P_1\left(W_{j-16} \oplus W_{j-9} \oplus (W_{j-3} \lll 15)\right) \oplus (W_{j-13} \lll 7) \oplus W_{j-6} \tag{12-32}$$

(c) For $0 \leqslant j \leqslant 63$, compute

$$W'_j = W_j \oplus W_{j+4} \tag{12-33}$$

4) **Compression Function**: Let A, B, C, D, E, F, G, H be eight word registers, $SS1, SS2, TT1, TT2$ be four intermediate variables, and the compression function $V^{(i+1)} = CF\left(V^{(i)}, B^{(i)}\right)$ where $0 \leqslant i \leqslant n-1$, as shown in Figure 12-8. The computation procedure is described as following:
   (a) $ABCDEFGH \leftarrow V^{(i)}$
   (b) For $j = 0$ to 63, do following step:

$$SS1 \leftarrow ((A \lll 12) + E + (T_j \lll (j \bmod 32))) \lll 7 \tag{12-34}$$

$$SS2 \leftarrow SS1 \oplus (A \lll 12) \tag{12-35}$$

$$TT1 \leftarrow FF_j(A, B, C) + D + SS2 + W'_j \tag{12-36}$$

$$TT2 \leftarrow GG_j(E, F, G) + H + SS1 + W_j \tag{12-37}$$

$$D \leftarrow C \tag{12-38}$$

$$C \leftarrow B \lll 9 \tag{12-39}$$

$$B \leftarrow A \tag{12-40}$$

$$A \leftarrow TT1 \tag{12-41}$$

$$H \leftarrow G \tag{12-42}$$

$$G \leftarrow F \lll 19 \tag{12-43}$$

$$F \leftarrow E \tag{12-44}$$

$$E \leftarrow P_0(TT2) \tag{12-45}$$

(c) $V^{(i+1)} \leftarrow ABCDEFGH \oplus V^{(i)}$

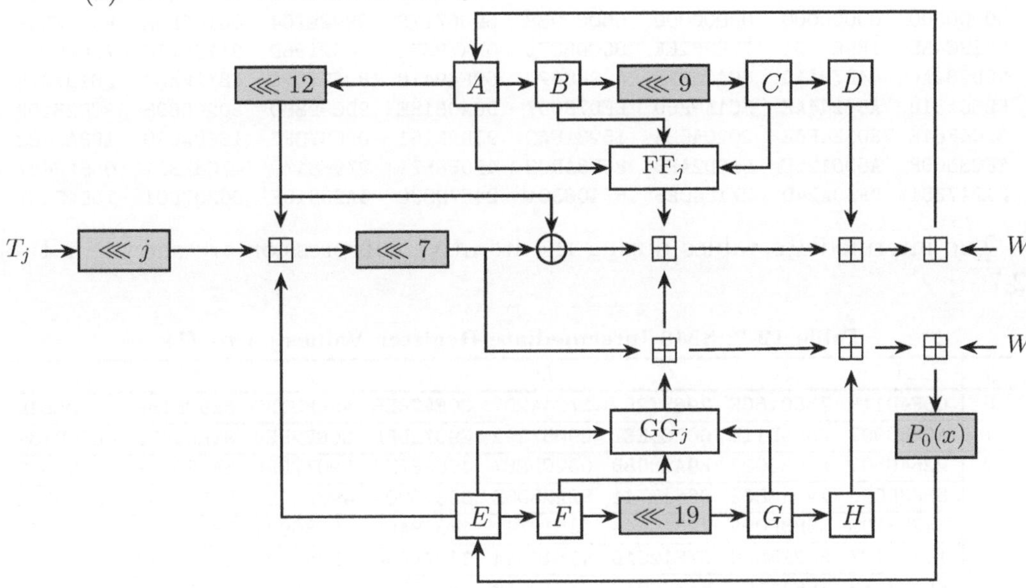

Figure 12-8: SM3 Message Compression Structure

5) **Output**: After the n rounds iteration completion, we let $A, B, C, D, E, F, G, H \leftarrow V^n$. Output a 256-bit hash value

$$y = A\|B\|C\|D\|E\|F\|G\|H \tag{12-46}$$

Example 12.2.4 Compute the SM3 hash of the message: "**missile**".
Solution: Since the message padding process is identical to that of SHA-1, the padded message in hexadecimal notation corresponds exactly to the result in Example 12.2.2.

```
6D697373 696C6580 00000000 00000000
00000000 00000000 00000000 00000000
00000000 00000000 00000000 00000000
00000000 00000000 00000000 00000038
```

The expanded message words $W_0, W_1, \ldots, W_{67}$ are listed below:

6D697373	696C6580	00000000	00000000	00000000	00000000	00000000	00000000
00000000	00000000	00000000	00000000	00000000	00000000	00000000	00000038
6D66717E	9B98E704	001C0E0E	FA7AF577	B35DB52B	80038035	77FE6CE0	7AB7190C
BCFA235A	C4819958	E6E76B96	00038036	912817F7	8036284A	6AAB0D6F	429B06C4
F8DC83EC	32595EB6	01B9E708	9482A1BA	A3B42BF7	99DB1A18	EDA37868	7A55216D
7E149A79	0412C295	BD8FA0FD	F6E710B6	FCD06C67	342C8DFB	9DAF0547	E3C40F14
6F029D06	EB77F10D	86C2A5EE	FA4E7B97	80C1C10D	4BE1E351	DC0F8F16	7CFDD655
CFCA442C	6C7F6228	9BCC6487	79A722D2	7EBE3A7D	B3D6C065	BCD42862	1EE741D3
5A59E2ED	F9F6916A	BAE45563	63B3CB14				

Similarly, the expanded words $W'_0, W'_1, \ldots, W'_{63}$ are derived as follows:

6D697373	696C6580	00000000	00000000	00000000	00000000	00000000	00000000
00000000	00000000	00000000	00000038	6D66717E	9B98E704	001C0E0E	FA7AF54F
DE3BC455	1B9B6731	77E262EE	80CDEC7B	0FA79671	4482196D	91190776	7AB4993A
2DD234AD	44B7B112	8C4C66F9	429886F2	69F4941B	B26F76FC	6B12EA67	D619A77E
5B68A81B	AB8244AE	EC1A9F60	EED780D7	DDA0B18E	9DC9D88D	502CD895	8CB231DB
82C4F61E	303E4F6E	2020A5BA	15231FA2	93D2F161	DF5B7CF6	1B6DA0A9	198A7483
EFC35C0B	A096125C	5ACD2AF8	86B3ADC2	4F0B8521	279E8179	47C3EB91	055AF487
B1747E51	DFA9A24D	27184CE5	67406301	24E7D890	4A20510F	06307D01	7D548AC7

The intermediate values during the iterative compression are shown in Table 12-7.

Table 12-7: SM3 Intermediate Register Values (A to H)

j	A	B	C	D	E	F	G	H
0	C5F4D11E	7380166F	29657292	172442D7	CCEE2BEB	A96F30BC	C550B189	E38DEE4D
1	A0E33093	C5F4D11E	002CDEE7	29657292	F9072BFF	CCEE2BEB	85E54B79	C550B189
2	2254B503	A0E33093	E9A23D8B	002CDEE7	498FE7E7	F9072BFF	5F5E6771	85E54B79
3	55B3F096	2254B503	C6612741	E9A23D8B	693E6904	498FE7E7	5FFFC839	5F5E6771
4	542F3ED8	55B3F096	A96A0644	C6612741	4F34BADD	693E6904	3F3A4C7F	5FFFC839
5	15F411C7	542F3ED8	67E12CAB	A96A0644	9487A9C4	4F34BADD	482349F3	3F3A4C7F
6	EB50BBF3	15F411C7	5E7DB0A8	67E12CAB	0BB128A1	9487A9C4	D6EA79A5	482349F3
7	CB7F7F12	EB50BBF3	E8238E2B	5E7DB0A8	37809873	0BB128A1	4E24A43D	D6EA79A5
8	532878BC	CB7F7F12	A177E7D6	E8238E2B	388D8A04	37809873	45085D89	4E24A43D
9	F78F4041	532878BC	FEFE2596	A177E7D6	2E3514E2	388D8A04	C399BC04	45085D89
10	4E9A4512	F78F4041	50F178A6	FEFE2596	6F9D0978	2E3514E2	5021C46C	C399BC04
⋮	⋮	⋮	⋮	⋮	⋮	⋮	⋮	⋮
60	F1ED90EA	34EA8530	B0E7F34A	3F5D52A2	32233974	DE658F0A	2585C6AB	F2E2849A
61	D2CDC3CE	F1ED90EA	D50A6069	B0E7F34A	09CEA652	32233974	7856F32C	2585C6AB
62	1367CEA3	D2CDC3CE	DB21D5E3	D50A6069	5B1F15CA	09CEA652	CBA19119	7856F32C
63	002586CF	1367CEA3	9B879DA5	DB21D5E3	1FF9ACBD	5B1F15CA	32904E75	CBA19119

Since the initial value $V^{(0)} = \mathbf{IV}$, we compute the final output $V^{(1)}$ by XORing the output of round 63 with $V^{(0)}$

$$A_{63} \oplus V_0^{(0)} = \texttt{0x73A590A0} \quad B_{63} \oplus V_1^{(0)} = \texttt{0x5A737C1A} \tag{12-47}$$

$$C_{63} \oplus V_2^{(0)} = \texttt{0x8CA3DF72} \quad D_{63} \oplus V_3^{(0)} = \texttt{0x01ABD3E3} \tag{12-48}$$

$$E_{63} \oplus V_4^{(0)} = \texttt{0xB6969C01} \quad F_{63} \oplus V_5^{(0)} = \texttt{0x4D2E2D60} \tag{12-49}$$

$$G_{63} \oplus V_6^{(0)} = \texttt{0xD11DA038} \quad H_{63} \oplus V_7^{(0)} = \texttt{0x7B5A9F57} \tag{12-50}$$

Finally, let $A, B, C, D, E, F, G, H \leftarrow V^{(1)}$. By concatenating the components $A\|B\|C\|D\|E\|F\|G\|H$, the resulting hash value is

0x73A590A05A737C1A8CA3DF7201ABD3E3B6969C014D2E2D60D11DA0387B5A9F57

■

The Python implementation of the SM3 algorithm is presented below.

```
IV = "7380166f 4914b2b9 172442d7 da8a0600 a96f30bc 163138aa e38dee4d
    b0fb0e4e"
IV = [int(x, 16) for x in IV.split()]
T_j = [0x79cc4519] * 16 + [0x7a879d8a] * 48

def rotate_left(a, k):
    k = k % 32
    a = a & 0xFFFFFFFF
    left_part = (a << k) & 0xFFFFFFFF
    right_part = (a >> (32 - k)) & 0xFFFFFFFF
    return (left_part | right_part) & 0xFFFFFFFF

def bytes_to_list(data):
    return [int.from_bytes(data[i:i+4], 'big') for i in range(0, len(
    data), 4)]

def list_to_bytes(lst):
    return b''.join(x.to_bytes(4, 'big') for x in lst)

def FF_j(X, Y, Z, j):
    if 0 <= j < 16:
        return X ^ Y ^ Z
    else:
        return (X & Y) | (X & Z) | (Y & Z)

def GG_j(X, Y, Z, j):
    if 0 <= j < 16:
        return X ^ Y ^ Z
    else:
        return (X & Y) | ((~X) & Z)

def P_0(X):
    return X ^ rotate_left(X, 9) ^ rotate_left(X, 17)

def P_1(X):
    return X ^ rotate_left(X, 15) ^ rotate_left(X, 23)

def CF(V_i, B_i):
    W = []
    for j in range(16):
        W.append(int.from_bytes(B_i[j*4:(j+1)*4], 'big'))
    for j in range(16, 68):
        W_j = P_1(W[j-16] ^ W[j-9] ^ rotate_left(W[j-3], 15)) ^
    rotate_left(W[j-13], 7) ^ W[j-6]
        W.append(W_j)
    W_1 = [W[j] ^ W[j+4] for j in range(64)]
```

```
    A, B, C, D, E, F, G, H = V_i
    for j in range(64):
        SS1 = rotate_left((rotate_left(A, 12) + E + rotate_left(T_j[j], j)) & 0xFFFFFFFF, 7)
        SS2 = SS1 ^ rotate_left(A, 12)
        TT1 = (FF_j(A, B, C, j) + D + SS2 + W_1[j]) & 0xFFFFFFFF
        TT2 = (GG_j(E, F, G, j) + H + SS1 + W[j]) & 0xFFFFFFFF
        D = C
        C = rotate_left(B, 9)
        B = A
        A = TT1
        H = G
        G = rotate_left(F, 19)
        F = E
        E = P_0(TT2)
    return [x ^ y for x, y in zip([A, B, C, D, E, F, G, H], V_i)]


def sm3(msg_bytes):
    msg_len = len(msg_bytes)
    msg_list = []
    for i in range(msg_len // 64):
        msg_list.append(msg_bytes[i*64:(i+1)*64])
    rest_len = msg_len % 64
    if rest_len < 56:
        padding = b'\x80' + b'\x00' * (55 - rest_len) + (msg_len * 8).to_bytes(8, 'big')
        msg_list.append(msg_bytes[-(rest_len):] + padding)
    else:
        padding1 = b'\x80' + b'\x00' * (63 - rest_len)
        padding2 = b'\x00' * 56 + (msg_len * 8).to_bytes(8, 'big')
        msg_list.append(msg_bytes[-(rest_len):] + padding1)
        msg_list.append(padding2)
    V = IV.copy()
    for msg in msg_list:
        V = CF(V, msg)

    return list_to_bytes(V)
```

12.3 SECURITY OF HASH FUNCTIONS

12.3.1 Three Central Properties

Both the MD family and the SHA family of hash functions (excluding SHA-3) are built upon the Merkle–Damgård construction [162], as shown in Figure 12-9. The fundamental concept of this structure is to iteratively apply a compression function to messages of arbitrary length, producing a fixed-size digest while extending the collision resistance of the compression function to the entire hash function. The following attack methods are applicable to all hash functions that employ the **Merkle–Damgård construction**.

To formally analyze these functions, we define the standard terminology. For a hash value $y = \mathrm{H}(m)$, the input message m is referred to as the **preimage** of y. The

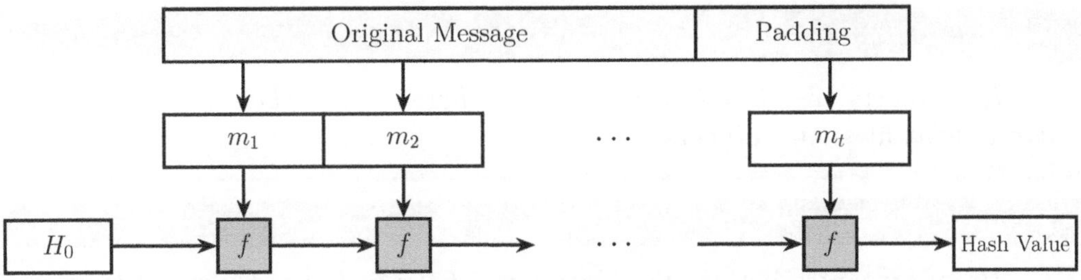

Figure 12-9: The Merkle–Damgård Construction

output generated by the function is known as the **message digest**, **fingerprint**, or simply the **image**. The architecture of a typical hash function is depicted in Figure 12-10. To ensure security and prevent the fabrication of valid messages by adversaries, a cryptographic hash function must satisfy three essential properties.

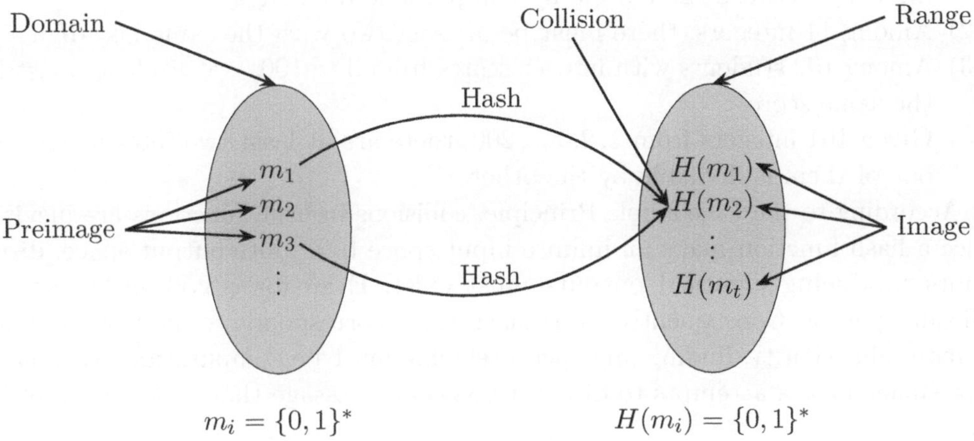

Figure 12-10: Mapping of a Hash Function

1) **Preimage Resistance**. Given a hash output $y = H(m)$, it is computationally infeasible to find any input message m such that $H(m) = y$. This property implies that the hash function is a one-way function.
2) **Second Preimage Resistance**. Given a message m_1, it is computationally infeasible to determine a second input message m_2 such that $H(m_1) = H(m_2)$, where $m_1 \neq m_2$.
3) **Collision Resistance**. It is computationally infeasible to determine a pair of distinct messages (m_1, m_2) such that $H(m_1) = H(m_2)$.

Attacker Eve will attempt the three challenge types in turn.

For the preimage and second preimage problems, the relevant threats are the preimage attack and the second preimage attack, respectively. As with other cryptosystems, attacks on hash functions fall into two broad classes: brute-force attacks and cryptanalysis. The feasibility of a brute-force attack against a hash function is determined primarily by the hash value. By definition, a hash function maps inputs of arbitrary length to a fixed-size digest. For example, SHA-256 maps arbitrary length messages to 256-bit digests. When the set of possible inputs is effectively unbounded but the output space contains only 2^{256} possible values, the pigeonhole principle guarantees that distinct inputs must collide under the hash.

Theorem 12.3.1 The Pigeonhole Principle

If n objects are placed into m boxes, where $m < n$, then at least one box contains at least two objects.

Proof

Proof by contradiction. *Suppose none of the m boxes has more than one object. Then the total number of objects would be at most m. This contradicts the statement that we have n objects.*

Examples of the pigeonhole principle

1) Among any company of 367 people, there must be at least two with the same birthday because there are only 366 possible birthdays.
2) Among 11 integers, there must be at least two with the same last digit.
3) Among 102 students with integer scores from 0 to 100, two students must have the same score.
4) Given 101 integers from $1, 2, \ldots, 200$, there are at least two integers such that one of them is divisible by the other.

According to the Pigeonhole Principle, collisions in hash functions are inevitable. Since a hash function maps an infinite input space to a finite output space, distinct inputs producing identical outputs must exist. Even for a 256-bit digest, such collisions persist. Consequently, every hash value corresponds to multiple preimages. To maintain security, finding any such preimage must be computationally infeasible. A preimage attack attempts to discover a specific message that yields a target hash value.

In theory, for a 256-bit output, an exhaustive search requires a time complexity of $\mathcal{O}(2^{256})$. However, if an attacker possesses immense computational power and exploits structural features, such as using a **meet-in-the-middle attack** (MITM) [163], this complexity may be reduced. In 2008, Thomsen proposed an improved preimage attack on MD2 that reduced the complexity to $\mathcal{O}(2^{73})$ [164]. Similarly, in 2009, researchers presented a theoretical preimage attack on SHA-256 with a complexity of $\mathcal{O}(2^{251.7})$ [165]. Although these results remain purely theoretical, they highlight the necessity of accounting for potential preimage attacks in hash function design. Continuous analysis ensures that no exploitable weaknesses exist in current algorithms.

A second major threat is the **Collision Attack** [166]. Since collisions are unavoidable, finding two distinct messages m_1 and m_2 such that $H(m_1) = H(m_2)$ within feasible time compromises the integrity of the function. Unlike preimage search, collision search does not target a specific output. Therefore, its computational cost is typically lower than that of preimage search.

To illustrate the severe conceptual risk of collision attacks, suppose Alice, the victim, needs to digitally sign a contract. An attacker, Eve, generates two distinct contracts with the exact same hash value: a benign contract m_1 ("Alice agrees to pay Eve 100 dollars") and a malicious contract m_2 ("Alice agrees to transfer her entire estate to Eve"). Eve presents the benign m_1 to Alice. Alice reviews it, computes the hash, and securely signs the digest. Later, Eve takes Alice's valid mathematical signature and maliciously attaches it to m_2. Because $H(m_1) = H(m_2)$, the signature verification algorithm will accept m_2 as fully legitimate and authorized by Alice.

This example is illustrative, yet collisions occur more frequently than intuition suggests. The *Birthday Paradox* demonstrates that in a group of thirty people, the probability that two share a birthday exceeds 70%. Analogously, for an n-bit hash function, approximately $2^{n/2}$ trials suffice to find a collision with high probability. Consequently, the cost of collision attacks grows as the square root of the preimage search space, rendering them far more efficient than exhaustive preimage attacks.

12.3.2 Birthday Attack

In a collision attack, the question can be reformulated as follows: how many randomly generated messages are required before the probability that at least two of them produce the same hash value exceeds 50%? This approach is known as the **Birthday Attack** [167]. In other words, finding a collision for a hash function is fundamentally equivalent to finding shared birthdays among a group.

In the birthday attack, the probability space extends from 365 possible birthdays to 2^n possible hash values, where n represents the bit length of the hash output. How many messages must be generated before a collision is likely to occur? The answer is approximately $\sqrt{2^n} = 2^{n/2}$. We now examine why this result holds.

According to the birthday paradox, let λ be the probability of at least one collision, if l distinct messages are hashed, we have

$$\lambda = 1 - P(\text{no collision}) = 1 - \frac{P(2^n, l)}{(2^n)^l} \tag{12-51}$$

$$= 1 - \frac{2^n \cdot (2^n - 1) \cdots (2^n - l + 1)}{(2^n)^l} \tag{12-52}$$

$$= 1 - 1 \cdot \left(1 - \frac{1}{2^n}\right) \cdot \left(1 - \frac{2}{2^n}\right) \cdots \left(1 - \frac{l-1}{2^n}\right) \tag{12-53}$$

$$= 1 - \prod_{i=1}^{l-1} \left(1 - \frac{i}{2^n}\right) \tag{12-54}$$

According to the Taylor series expansion, e^x can be expressed as

$$e^x = \sum_{k=0}^{\infty} \frac{x^k}{k!} = 1 + x + \frac{x^2}{2!} + \frac{x^3}{3!} + \cdots + \frac{x^k}{k!} + \cdots \quad \forall x \tag{12-55}$$

Then

$$e^{-x} = \sum_{k=0}^{\infty} \frac{(-x)^k}{k!} = 1 - x + \frac{x^2}{2!} - \frac{x^3}{3!} + \cdots + \frac{x^k}{k!} - \cdots \quad \forall x \tag{12-56}$$

Thus, $1 - x$ can be approximated by e^{-x}, that is, $e^{-x} \approx 1 - x$. Substituting this approximation into Equation 12-54

$$\lambda = 1 - \prod_{i=1}^{l-1}\left(1 - \frac{i}{2^n}\right) \approx 1 - \prod_{i=1}^{l-1}\left(e^{-\frac{i}{2^n}}\right) \tag{12-57}$$

$$= 1 - \left(e^{-\frac{1+2+\cdots+l-1}{2^n}}\right) \tag{12-58}$$

$$= 1 - \left(e^{-\frac{l(l-1)}{2^{n+1}}}\right) \quad \text{(Arithmetic series)} \tag{12-59}$$

$$\Rightarrow ln(1-\lambda) \approx -\frac{l(l-1)}{2^{n+1}} \tag{12-60}$$

$$ln\left(\frac{1}{1-\lambda}\right) \approx \frac{l(l-1)}{2^{n+1}} \tag{12-61}$$

$$2^{n+1} ln\left(\frac{1}{1-\lambda}\right) \approx l(l-1) = l^2 - l \tag{12-62}$$

If l is very large, $l^2 - l \approx l^2$, and thus

$$l \approx 2^{(n+1)/2}\sqrt{ln\left(\frac{1}{1-\lambda}\right)} \tag{12-63}$$

Assuming a collision probability of 50%, that is, $\lambda = 0.5$, substitution into Equation 12-63 yields $l \approx 2^{(n+1)/2} \times 0.83 \approx 2^{n/2}$. Therefore, for a hash function with an n-bit output, approximately $2^{n/2}$ messages are needed to obtain a collision with constant probability.

The steps of a birthday attack are as follows:

1) An attacker Eve first prepares a malicious message E, for example "Please Alice transfer 1 bitcoin to Eve". Eve wants Alice to sign this malicious instruction, but a prudent Alice will not sign it directly.
2) Eve then prepares a harmless message M that Alice is likely to sign, for example, "please answer 'Are you currently in China?"'. Because the message is trivial, Alice is more likely to sign or approve it, and Eve can thus obtain a legitimate signature.
3) Eve then generates large sets of semantically equivalent variants of each message type that differ in form but not in meaning, producing two candidate lists:

$$M_1, M_2, \ldots, M_L \text{ and } E_1, E_2, \ldots, E_L \tag{12-64}$$

with L on the order of $2^{n/2}$, where n is the hash output length. Variants can be created by adding meaningless whitespace, small comments, or different metadata formats. The goal is to expand the set of inputs so that the birthday paradox can be exploited to find a hash collision.
4) Eve computes the hashes of all variants in both lists and compares them, using the birthday paradox to seek a pair with $\mathrm{H}(M_i) = \mathrm{H}(E_j)$. When a colliding pair is found, Eve submits the harmless variant M_i to Alice for signing. Perceiving

M_i as harmless, Alice signs the message. Because the signature is tied to the hash value, the same signature is valid for the colliding malicious variant E_j. Eve attaches the signature to E_j and presents it to the verifier, who may then accept the forged authorization, for example by executing a transfer.

Consequently, if Eve identifies a distinct pair of messages M_1 and M_2 such that $\mathrm{H}(M_1) = \mathrm{H}(M_2)$, she has effectively compromised the collision resistance property of the hash function. To achieve this, Eve conducts a probabilistic search by randomly generating candidate inputs and comparing their hash values against previously computed entries to locate a match.

For the SHA-256 hash function, a birthday attack reduces the attacker's time complexity to $\mathcal{O}(2^{256/2}) = \mathcal{O}(2^{128})$. From Eve's point of view, compared with a preimage attack, this is a huge improvement. This is not merely halving the work, but an exponential decrease. To achieve 256-bit collision security, a hash output length of 512 bits is required.

12.4 EXERCISES

1) For the F function in MD4, determine whether the following statements are true:
   (a) $F(x, y, z) = F(\neg x, y, z)$ if and only if $x = z$.
   (b) $F(x, y, z) = F(x, \neg y, z)$ if and only if $x = y$.
   (c) $F(x, y, z) = F(x, y, \neg z)$ if and only if $x = z$.
2) Convert the pseudocode for updating A, B, C, and D in MD4 into Python code.
3) Using MD4, hash the message "I am a rocket engineer" and calculate the output of the first round.
4) In MD5, the auxiliary function I is defined as

$$I(x, y, z) = y \oplus (x \vee \neg z)$$

   Determine the value of I for all combinations of $x, y,$ and z equal to 0 or 1.
5) Consider the message **abc**, answer the following questions:
   (a) Perform the MD4 padding procedure and write down the resulting 512-bit message block.
   (b) Parse the padded message into sixteen 32-bit words, denoted as $X_0, X_1, \ldots, X_{15}$.
   (c) Compute the hexadecimal values of X_0 and X_1.
6) A single step in Round 1 of MD4 is defined as:

$$A = (A + F(B, C, D) + X[i] + K)_{\lll s}$$

   Assume the following initial state $A = \texttt{0x67452301}, B = \texttt{0xEFCDAB89}, C = \texttt{0x98BADCFE}, D = \texttt{0x10325476}$, message word $X[0] = \texttt{0x00000000}$, constant $K = 0$ and circular shift $s = 3$. Compute the updated value of register A after this single step.

7) The MD4 auxiliary function employs three different logic functions (F, G, and H) for each of the three rounds. Answer the following questions:
   (a) Let X, Y, and Z be 32-bit words. Prove that the function $F(X, Y, Z) = (X \wedge Y) \vee (\neg X \wedge Z)$ acts as a conditional multiplexer. Specifically, show that for each bit position, the output bit is equal to the corresponding bit of Y if the bit of X is 1, and equal to the bit of Z if the bit of X is 0.
   (b) Compute the output of $G(X, Y, Z) = (X \wedge Y) \vee (X \wedge Z) \vee (Y \wedge Z)$ where $X =$ 0x0F0F0F0F, $Y =$ 0x33333333, $Z =$ 0x55555555.
   (c) Compute the output of $H(X, Y, Z) = X \oplus Y \oplus Z$ where $X =$ 0x0F0F0F0F, $Y =$ 0x33333333, $Z =$ 0x55555555.
8) What is the process for solving the preimage problem?
9) What is the process for solving the second preimage problem, and what is the success rate?
10) The SHAppening and SHAttered attacks proved that SHA-1's practical security is lower than its theoretical bound.
   (a) Based on the Birthday Paradox, what is the theoretical number of hash operations required to find a collision in SHA-1?
   (b) The SHAttered attack (2017) found a collision in approximately 2^{63} operations. Express the ratio of the theoretical complexity to the actual attack complexity as a power of 2. What does this ratio imply about the mathematical "shortcuts" found in the SHA-1 compression function?
11) Determine the relationship between the bit-length of a hash value and the computational workload required for a birthday attack.
12) Consider a simplified hash function H that produces an n-bit output. The probability $P(n, k)$ that at least one collision occurs after hashing k distinct messages is approximated by

$$P(n, k) \approx 1 - e^{-\frac{k(k-1)}{2^{n+1}}}$$

   For a "toy" hash function with an 8-bit output, calculate the probability of a collision occurring if an attacker hashes $k = 20$ random messages. How many messages k must be hashed to ensure the probability of finding a collision is at least 0.5?
13) Consider the SHA-1 function, let the initial vectors be defined as $A = H_0^{(0)}, B = H_1^{(0)}, C = H_2^{(0)}, D = H_3^{(0)}, E = H_4^{(0)}$. Calculate the output of the logical function f_i for the first round.
14) Consider the SHA-1 function, the expansion is performed as follows:

$$W_t = M_t, \qquad 0 \leqslant t \leqslant 15$$
$$W_t = (W_{t-3} \oplus W_{t-8} \oplus W_{t-14} \oplus W_{t-16}) \lll 1, \qquad 16 \leqslant t \leqslant 79$$

   Assume $W_0 =$ 0x00000080, and $W_1 = \cdots = W_{15} =$ 0x00000000.
   (a) Compute W_{16}.
   (b) Explain why a single nonzero bit in W_0 influences multiple later words.
   (c) Let T be a temporary variable defined as

$$T = (A \lll 5) + f_t(B, C, D) + E + W_t + k_t$$

where A, B, C, D, E are initial constants. Set $t = 0$, compute the value of A for the next step $t + 1$. Use the standard SHA-1 initial hash values. Show all intermediate values.

15) Consider the SHA-1 function, if W_t were defined without the 1-bit left rotation ($\lll 1$), show that each bit of W_t would be a simple XOR sum of bits from the original 512-bit message block. Explain the mathematical purpose of the 1-bit rotation in terms of coupling different bit positions (columns) and improving diffusion during the expansion process.
16) Assume a hash function generates a hash value of length l bits. Describe the implementation of a brute-force attack for finding a preimage and determine the expected work factor.
17) MD2, MD4, and SHA-1 are all based on the Merkle-Damgård construction. Describe the properties of the Merkle-Damgård construction.
18) The permutation functions of SM3 are defined as follows:

$$P_0(X) = X \oplus (X \lll 9) \oplus (X \lll 17)$$
$$P_1(X) = X \oplus (X \lll 15) \oplus (X \lll 23)$$

  (a) Given an input word $X =$ `0x00000100`, compute the hexadecimal output of $P_1(X)$.
  (b) In the compression function, P_1 is applied to a temporary variable derived from the message expansion. Explain why a mathematician would consider P_0 and P_1 to be linear transformations over the vector space $\mathrm{GF}(2)^{32}$.

19) A single step of the SM3 compression function updates eight 32-bit registers A, B, C, D, E, F, G, H. One of the most critical updates is for register E

$$TT2 \leftarrow GG_j(E, F, G) + H + SS1 + W_j$$

where GG_j is the boolean function for rounds $16 \leqslant j \leqslant 63$. Given the following intermediate values at a specific step j: $E =$ `0xFFFFFFFF`, $F =$ `0x00000000`, $G =$ `0xAAAAAAAA`, $H =$ `0x00000000`, $SS_1 =$ `0x00000001`, $W_j =$ `0x00000001`. Compute the value of register E for step $j + 1$.

20) Describe the procedure an attacker would employ to execute a collision attack against HMAC.
21) What measures can be taken to prevent exhaustive search attacks against hash functions?
22) How many attempts, on average, are needed to find a person the same age as you, given a group of people born after 1970?

CHAPTER 13

Message Authentication Codes

In the previous chapter, we observed that hash functions allow users to verify message integrity but do not facilitate message authentication. In other words, while a hash value can reveal whether a message was altered during transmission, it cannot confirm the identity of the sender. To enable verification of both integrity and message origin, a new cryptographic primitive is introduced: the **Message Authentication Code** (MAC).

Historically, many developers fell into the dangerous cryptographic trap of assuming that standard symmetric encryption implicitly guaranteed authenticity. They believe that if a ciphertext successfully decrypted, it must have come from the legitimate sender. This is a profound fallacy. Due to ciphertext malleability, an adversary can easily alter intercepted ciphertexts to produce forged, yet technically decryptable, plaintexts.

True message authentication is fundamentally achieved through mechanisms that mandate the possession of a shared secret key. Formally, a MAC function takes both a target message and a secret key as input to produce a strictly compressed verification code. This mathematically binds the message to the specific parties possessing the key. Modern MACs are practically constructed using two primary approaches: hash-based constructions and cipher-based constructions.

Topics covered in this chapter:

- Definition of MACs
- MACs Based on Hash Functions
- MACs Based on Block Ciphers
- Pseudorandom Number Generation

13.1 MAC

Two fundamental objectives of modern cryptography are ensuring the **integrity** and **authenticity** of messages. To simultaneously guarantee both properties and prevent an adversary from tampering with, deleting, forging, or impersonating the source of a

DOI: 10.1201/9781042011087-13

message, the sender and the receiver typically employ a **Message Authentication Code** (MAC). A MAC, often referred to as an authentication tag, is a concise bit string derived from a symmetric cryptographic algorithm and a shared secret key. Its primary function is to verify that a message has not been altered and was genuinely issued by an authorized party.

Message integrity ensures that the information remains unmodified during transmission. For example, when Alice instructs Bob to transfer funds, integrity is preserved if Bob can confirm that the received instruction is identical to what Alice originally sent. Message authenticity, by contrast, allows the receiver to verify the identity of the originator. In this scenario, authenticity ensures that Bob can be confident the transfer request indeed originated from Alice, rather than an imposter.

To counter this threat, the use of a secret key is essential. A MAC algorithm takes both a secret key K and a message M as input, producing an authentication tag denoted as $\text{MAC}_K(M)$ (or simply the tag). This tag is intrinsically bound to the message, allowing the receiver to verify both its integrity and origin. Without knowledge of K, an adversary cannot compute a valid tag for a forged or modified message. Consequently, successful verification assures the receiver that the message was generated by a legitimate party possessing the shared key.

In practice, message authentication is primarily realized through two categories of constructions: MACs based on hash functions (e.g., HMAC) and MACs based on block ciphers (e.g., CBC-MAC or CMAC). In both scenarios, the symmetric secret key shared between Alice and Bob underpins the security of the exchange, ensuring that no unauthorized third party can forge a valid tag.

There are various methodologies for generating a MAC. A MAC constructed from a cryptographic hash function is known as an **HMAC** (Hash-based Message Authentication Code). This algorithm was first defined in RFC 2104 in 1997, later standardized by NIST in 2002 as FIPS PUB 198, and subsequently updated to FIPS 198-1 in 2008 [168].

Alternatively, MACs can be derived from block ciphers, with common examples including CBC-MAC and CMAC. Regardless of the underlying construction, a MAC outputs a fixed-length string independent of the message size, analogous to a hash function. The critical distinction remains that while a standard hash function provides only integrity verification, a MAC guarantees both integrity and authenticity by validating the message's origin.

A MAC has the following properties:

1) It accepts messages of arbitrary length as input.
2) It can be computed efficiently.
3) It generates fixed-size output value.
4) It provides message integrity; any unauthorized modification can be detected.
5) It provides message authentication, the receiver can verify the message source.
6) It is based on secret symmetric keys.
7) It is computationally infeasible to recover the message or key from the MAC value.
8) It is computationally infeasible to find two different messages $M_1 \neq M_2$ such that their MAC values are equal.

A MAC is a cryptographic checksum based on a security function of the message M and the symmetric key K. The authentication code is computed as

$$\text{MAC} = C(M, K) \tag{13-1}$$

where "C" denotes the MAC algorithm, "M" represents a message of arbitrary length, and "K" is the shared secret key.

During communication, Alice computes the MAC for her message M and transmits both M and the resulting MAC value to Bob. Upon receiving the transmission, Bob recomputes the MAC using the same secret key K and compares it with the received value. If the two values match, Bob can be confident that the message has not been altered and genuinely originates from Alice. Otherwise, the message is rejected as having been tampered with or forged. Even if an attacker, Eve, intercepts and modifies the transmission, she cannot generate a valid MAC for the modified message without knowledge of the secret key K. This ensures that the verification process fails. The message authentication process is illustrated in Figure 13-1.

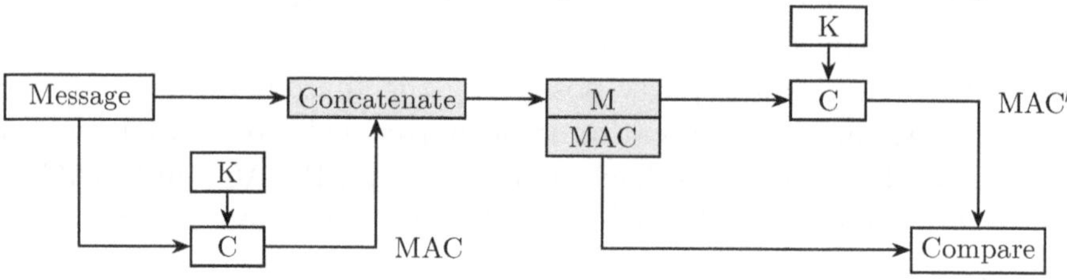

Figure 13-1: Principle of MACs

It is important to distinguish MACs from conventional encryption algorithms. Encryption is fundamentally a reversible transformation: plaintext is converted into ciphertext and can be fully recovered using the corresponding decryption key. In contrast, a MAC function is designed to be irreversible. Its primary purpose is not to obscure the message for confidentiality or to allow for reconstruction, but rather to verify its integrity and authenticity. This distinction constitutes the essential difference between encryption and message authentication.

A MAC function is a many-to-one mapping, meaning that distinct messages under the same key may yield identical MAC, and collisions are therefore theoretically possible. For two different messages M_1 and M_2, where $M_1 \neq M_2$, the probability that they produce the same MAC value is approximately 2^{-L}, where L represents the bit length of the MAC.

The domain of a MAC function comprises all possible messages of arbitrary length, whereas its range is restricted to fixed-length MAC outputs. Consider a scenario where the message length is fixed at n bits and the MAC output length is L bits. The input space contains 2^n possible messages, while the output space contains only 2^L possible values. Typically, $n \gg L$. According to the pigeonhole principle, each MAC value corresponds, on average, to approximately 2^{n-L} different messages. While this many-to-one mapping makes collisions theoretically unavoidable, locating such collisions remains computationally infeasible provided that L is sufficiently large.

MACs are widely employed across diverse application domains. In broadcast communications, where messages are often transmitted in plaintext, a MAC ensures authenticity and prevents tampering without the overhead of encryption. In large-scale information systems, receivers utilize MACs for selective verification to rapidly detect unauthorized modifications. Furthermore, numerous critical security protocols rely on MACs for message authentication and integrity protection, including the SWIFT interbank transaction system, SSL/TLS, and IPsec [169].

13.2 SECURITY ANALYSIS OF MACS

The security of a MAC primarily depends on its resistance to forgery and cryptanalytic attacks. A secure MAC function should satisfy the following requirements:

1) Given one or more valid message-tag pairs (M, MAC) observed over the network, it must be computationally infeasible for an adversary to construct a valid tag MAC' for any new, unqueried message M' such that $C(M', K) = \text{MAC}'$. This rigors standard universally prevents the forgery of authentication codes under any circumstance.
2) The MAC outputs should be statistically close to a uniform distribution. That is, if an n-bit MAC is used, for any two randomly chosen messages M and M', the probability that $C(M, K) = C(M', K)$ is approximately 2^{-n}.
3) A secure MAC must also be a pseudorandom function. For an n-bit MAC, given any two distinct messages M and M', even if their relationship is known, the outputs $C(M, K)$ and $C(M', K)$ will appear to be two independently and uniformly chosen n-bit strings, the probability of an accidental collision, $P(C(M, K) = C(M', K))$ is 2^{-n}. The primary security goal for a MAC is **existential unforgeability**.

In practical network communication, potential threats such as system faults, masquerading, active attacks, and human errors can compromise message delivery, leading to loss, alteration, or unauthorized disclosure. To ensure robust security, secure communication protocols must satisfy the following requirements:

1) **Confidentiality**: During transmission, neither the plaintext message nor the cryptographic key should be exposed to unauthorized entities. While message authentication ensures integrity, confidentiality is typically achieved through symmetric or asymmetric encryption to prevent information leakage.
2) **Source Authentication**: Adversaries may attempt to masquerade as legitimate participants. Message Authentication Codes (MACs) effectively mitigate this threat by verifying the origin of the message, ensuring it was generated by a holder of the shared key.
3) **Data Integrity**: Any unauthorized modification, insertion, or deletion of the message content must be detectable. Such alterations will cause the MAC verification algorithm to fail, thereby revealing that the message integrity has been compromised.

4) **Sequence Integrity**: An adversary may attempt to capture and reorder or replay transmitted messages. By incorporating sequence numbers or monotonic counters into the MAC computation, the system can detect and reject out-of-order or replayed messages.
5) **Timestamp Protection**: Adversaries may replay old messages to falsify transaction timing. Synchronization mechanisms or the inclusion of timestamps ensure message freshness, preventing the acceptance of expired or delayed data.
6) **Defense against Denial-of-Service**: Flooding or blocking attacks aim to disrupt communication. While cryptographic primitives alone cannot prevent DoS, they are often deployed alongside firewalls, intrusion detection systems, and traffic analysis tools to mitigate such threats.

Brute-force attacks against MACs are generally more computationally demanding than collision attacks against hash functions. In the context of a hash function, an attacker aims to find a collision, which is susceptible to the birthday attack with a complexity of approximately $\mathcal{O}(2^{n/2})$.

The brute-force resistance of a MAC depends on its key length, output length, and the attacker's computational power. For an n-bit MAC with a k-bit key, the brute-force attack on this MAC has cost related to $\mathcal{O}(\min(2^k, 2^n))$. Hence, both the key and the MAC should be sufficiently long, and secure key management practices must be implemented to prevent compromise.

To ensure robustness, only well-analyzed and standardized algorithms such as HMAC (Hash-based MAC) and CMAC (Cipher-based MAC) should be employed, supported by secure key management and proper implementation practices.

In summary, the security of a MAC relies on a combination of algorithmic soundness, adequate parameter sizes, and disciplined operational protocols. When correctly implemented, MACs provide a foundational layer for authentication and integrity in modern cryptographic systems.

13.3 HMAC

A widely adopted construction for MACs based on cryptographic hash functions is the **Keyed-Hash Message Authentication Code** (HMAC). HMAC provides greater computational efficiency, simpler implementation, and broader compatibility with existing systems. Hash functions are easy to implement, fast to compute, and generally public, which greatly reduces the cost of deployment and maintenance. More importantly, HMAC features a modular structure, allowing easy replacement of the underlying hash function in the event that faster or more secure hash functions are later available. For example, migrating from SHA-1 to SHA-3 once the former becomes insecure. This flexibility has made HMAC one of the most widely used authentication mechanisms in modern cryptographic protocols.

HMAC was first introduced in 1996 by *Bellare*, *Canetti*, and *Krawczyk* who provided a rigorous proof of security for the construction [170]. It was subsequently standardized and integrated into major Internet protocols, serving as a cornerstone for network security systems such as SSL/TLS and IPsec.

Implementations of HMAC are denoted by the underlying hash function employed. For example, constructions based on MD5, SHA-1, SHA-256, and SHA-3-512 are referred to as HMAC-MD5, HMAC-SHA-1, HMAC-SHA-256, and HMAC-SHA3-512, respectively. These constructions preserve the performance characteristics of the underlying hash functions while enhancing cryptographic robustness through the incorporation of a secret key. Specifically, the nested design of HMAC effectively immunizes the system against Length Extension Attacks that is a catastrophic vulnerability that compromises naive implementations attempting to simply concatenate a key and a message.

In March 2002, the NIST officially standardized HMAC in FIPS PUB 198, which was later revised in 2008 as FIPS PUB 198-1. Other national standards, such as China's GB/T 15852.2-2024 [171], have also formalized this mechanism. These standards define a nested construction that combines an inner hash and an outer hash to secure the message.

The fundamental concept of HMAC [172] [173] is straightforward. Suppose Alice and Bob share a secret key K and wish to authenticate a message M. Rather than encrypting the hash output, the key is integrated directly into the hash input specifically to produce a secure authentication tag. The workflow of HMAC is illustrated in Figure 13-2.

The HMAC can be expressed as

$$\mathbf{HMAC}(K, M) = H\left((K' \oplus opad) \| H\left((K' \oplus ipad) \| M\right)\right) \tag{13-2}$$

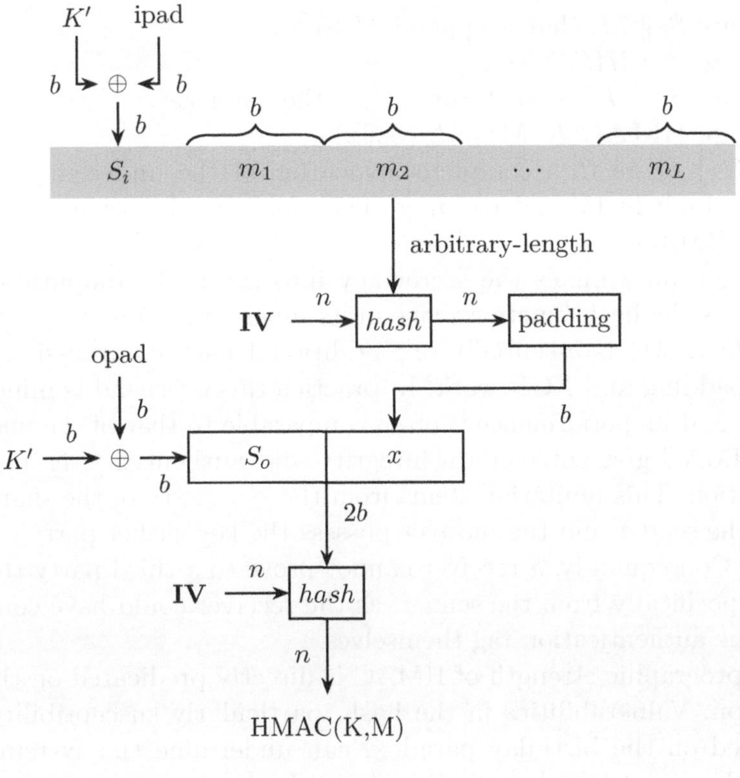

Figure 13-2: The Process of HMAC

where H is the embedded hash function; M is the message input; K is the secret key shared between Alice and Bob; and $||$ denotes concatenation. b is the number of bits in a block length, for HMAC-SHA-256, $b = 512$ and $n = 256$ bits.The key K' is derived from K by padding it with zeros to match the block size b of the hash function if needed.

ipad and *opad* are two fixed b-bits constants. *ipad* is Inner Padding. *opad* is Outer Padding. They are

$$ipad = \underbrace{00110110 \quad 00110110 \quad \cdots \quad 00110110}_{b\text{-bit}} = \underbrace{\texttt{0x36}}_{\text{repeated } b/8 \text{ times}}$$

$$opad = \underbrace{01011100 \quad 01011100 \quad \cdots \quad 01011100}_{b\text{-bit}} = \underbrace{\texttt{0x5c}}_{\text{repeated } b/8 \text{ times}}$$

The HMAC process is as follows:

1) Let K be the shared secret key. We first derive a block-sized key K' of length b bits:
   (a) If the length of $K = b$, set $K' = K$.
   (b) If the length of $K < b$, padding K with zeros on the right so that the result is b bits in length.
   (c) If the length of $K > b$, apply $H(K)$ down to less than or equal to b bits first, then padding with zeros on the right so that the result is b bits in length such that $K' = H(K)||000...000$.
2) Compute $S_i = K' \oplus ipad$. Here, S_i is the inner key.
3) Compute $S_i \parallel M$, that is append M to S_i.
4) Compute $x = H(S_i \parallel M)$.
5) Compute $S_o = K' \oplus opad$. Here, S_o is the outer key.
6) Compute $\mathbf{HMAC}(K, M) = H\left(S_o \| x\right)$.

Note that $H()$ refers to a complete invocation of the underlying hash function, including its built-in IV and padding. Therefore, we do not need to mention IV explicitly in HMAC.

This design fully mixes the secret key into the hash computation. Although HMAC applies the hash function twice in its inner and outer stages, the extra cost over a single $H(M)$ is essentially one additional hash compression plus a small amount of padding and XOR work. In practice this overhead is minor, so HMAC remains fast and its performance is often comparable to that of the underlying hash.

While HMAC guarantees data integrity and authenticity, it inherently lacks non-repudiation. This limitation stems from the symmetry of the shared secret key: since both the sender and the receiver possess the key, either party can generate a valid MAC. Consequently, a receiver cannot prove to a third party that a message originated specifically from the sender, as the receiver could have computationally generated the authentication tag themselves.

The cryptographic strength of HMAC is directly predicated on the underlying hash function. Vulnerabilities in the hash, particularly susceptibility to collision attacks based on the birthday paradox, can undermine the system. For a hash function with output length n, finding a collision typically requires approximately $2^{n/2}$ operations; thus, selecting a hash with a sufficiently large n is critical for practical security. Despite this dependency, HMAC is generally more robust than the underlying unkeyed hash function alone. Because the secret key is intimately mixed into the computation, attackers cannot easily exploit hash collisions to forge valid tags without knowledge of the key.

Example 13.3.1 Consider HMAC-SHA1 algorithm with block size 512 bits(64 bytes) and output szie 160 bits(20 bytes). Let the secret key be the ASCII string K ="key" and the message be the ASCII string M = "missile". Compute the HMAC.
Solution: We show every value in hexadecimal. The message is 0x6D697373696C65, the key is 0x6B6579.

1) Since the length of key is 3 bytes, less than block size 64 bytes. We need to pad zeros on the right until the length of key equals the block size. So new key is $K' = K \| \texttt{0x00} \| \ldots \| \texttt{0x00} = \texttt{0x6B6579} \| \texttt{0x00} \| \ldots \| \texttt{0x00}$ (61 zeros).
2) Create inner pad. The ipad = 0x36 repeated 64 times, $S_i = \texttt{ipad} \oplus K' =$ 0x5D534F3636...36 (the last 61 bytes are 0x36).
3) Create Outer pad. The opad = 0x5C repeated 64 times, $S_o = \texttt{opad} \oplus K' =$ 0x3739255C5C...5C (the last 61 bytes are 0x5C).
4) Append the message to S_i that is $S_i \| M =$ 0x5D534F36...366D697373696C65.
5) Compute $x = H(S_i \| M) =$ 0x5E3F7A14DECDF36744250839EC07CD71633F4F27.
6) Compute $\mathbf{HMAC}(K, M) = H(S_o \| x) =$ 0xB79EC4E2031ABC5B9EDA5A30517B67A84525B760.

If the secret key be the ASCII string K = "keykeykeykey...key" ("key" repeated 25 times), the length of key greater than block size. Hash the key, and then pad zeros on the right until its length becomes 64 bytes.

Compute $H(K)$ = 0x765317EA24585A513D828CF172FCA34F495E73B0. The length of $H(K)$ is 20 bytes, so we need to pad zeros on the right until the length becomes 64 bytes. Therefore, K' = 0x765317EA24585A513D828CF172FCA34F495E73B0 $\|$0x00 (repeated 44 times).

The rest of the steps are similar and will not be repeated. ■

Example 13.3.2 Consider HMAC-SHA256 algorithm with block size 512 bits (64 bytes) and output size 256 bits (32 bytes). Let the secret key be provided as the hexadecimal string K = 00112233445566778899AABBCCDDEEFF and the message be the ASCII string M = "A very good reference for people interested in applied cryptography". Compute the HMAC.
Solution: HMAC can be easily computed using Python.

```
import hashlib

BLOCK_SIZE = 64
def hmac_sha256_manual(key, message):
    # Convert key to bytes
    if isinstance(key, str):
        key = key.encode()

    if isinstance(message, str):
        message = message.encode()
```

```
    # Step 1: Normalize key
    if len(key) > BLOCK_SIZE:
        key = hashlib.sha256(key).digest()

    if len(key) < BLOCK_SIZE:
        key = key + b'\x00' * (BLOCK_SIZE - len(key))

    # Step 2: Define ipad and opad
    ipad = bytes([0x36] * BLOCK_SIZE)
    opad = bytes([0x5c] * BLOCK_SIZE)

    # Step 3: Inner hash
    inner_key = bytes([k ^ i for k, i in zip(key, ipad)])
    inner_hash = hashlib.sha256(inner_key + message).digest()

    # Step 4: Outer hash
    outer_key = bytes([k ^ o for k, o in zip(key, opad)])

    hmac_value = hashlib.sha256(outer_key + inner_hash).hexdigest()
    return hmac_value

key = "00112233445566778899AABBCCDDEEFF"
message = 'A very good reference for people interested in applied cryptography'

result = hmac_sha256_manual(key,message)
print(result)
```

The results is

0x54088711FB86701273F322B9A8944AE49E2BCBE04917F3AF1A584BEFB097B5EC

If the output is considered too long, it can be truncated as needed. Truncation is performed from left to right, keeping only the desired number of bits. For example, HMAC-SHA256-80 means that the output of HMAC-SHA256 is truncated to the first 80 bits from the left. This operation is called the **Most Significant Bit** (MSB) operation, so $\text{MSB}_s(M)$ is the s leftmost bits of the bit string M. ■

13.4 CBC-MAC

Beyond hash based constructions, MACs can also be built from block ciphers. There are several standard block cipher based MAC constructions. According to the Chinese national standard GB/T 15852.1-2020 [174], which corresponds to the international standard ISO/IEC 9797-1, eight block cipher based MAC algorithms are defined: CBC-MAC, EMAC, ANSI Retail MAC, MacDES, CMAC, LMAC, TrCBC, and CBCR.

Among these, CBC-MAC (Cipher Block Chaining Message Authentication Code) is one of the most widely used designs. Historically, it appears in FIPS PUB 113 (1985) and in the financial security standards ANSI X9.9/X9.19. CBC-MAC also served as the basis for later schemes such as CMAC, EMAC, and XCBC, which refine its ideas to improve security and performance.

In this subsection, we detail the operation of CBC-MAC. Let the underlying block cipher size be exactly b bits, the input message be M, and the ultimate output be an n-bit MAC. In general cryptographic practice, $n \leqslant b$. The basic computation of CBC-MAC can be summarized in the following seven steps:

1) **Padding**: As CBC-MAC operates on fixed-size blocks, the input message M must be padded so that its length is an exact multiple of the block size b. If the length of M is already a multiple of b, a full b-bit block (typically consisting of all zeros or a specific padding value) is appended. This ensures that the length of the padded message M' is a multiple of b.
2) **Message Splitting**: The padded message M' is divided into q blocks $M' = m_1 \| m_2 \| \ldots \| m_q$, each m_i is b bits long.
3) **Initialization**: Set the Initialization Vector (**IV**) to the b-bit zero string.
4) **Iterative Chaining**: The algorithm processes the blocks using the block cipher E_K. The chaining variables H_i are computed as follows:

$$H_1 = E_K(m_1 \oplus \mathbf{IV}) \tag{13-3}$$

$$H_i = E_K(m_i \oplus H_{i-1}) \quad \text{for } i = 2, \ldots, q \tag{13-4}$$

5) **Transform**: Set $G := H_q$.
6) **Truncation**: To produce the final n-bit MAC, the block G is truncated to its n most significant bits

$$\text{MAC} = \text{MSB}_n(G) \tag{13-5}$$

7) **Verification**: Upon receiving the message M and MAC, the receiver validates the message using the same shared key K. Recompute a new MAC. The receiver compares the received tag MAC with his locally computed MAC. If the values are identical, the message is verified as authentic; otherwise, it is rejected.

In general, the block size depends on the block cipher selected. If DES is used as the block cipher, it has a 64-bit block size and a 56-bit key size. The resulting MAC output should not exceed 64 bits, yet for collision resistance, it should generally be no less than 16 bits. If AES-128 is used, the cipher operates with a 128-bit block size and a 128-bit key size, and the maximum MAC output length is 128 bits.

Example 13.4.1 Consider CBC-MAC algorithm using a simplified "toy" block cipher. The block size $b = 16$ bits, the secret key $K =$ `0xA1B2`. For simplicity, we define the encryption as a key-XOR followed by a 3-bit left rotation:

$$E_K(M) = \text{rol}(M \oplus K, 3) \tag{13-6}$$

The message $M =$ `0xABCDEF`. Compute the final 8-bit MAC ($n = 8$).

Solution:

1) Padding. Append a single "1" bit, then append "0" bits as needed to reach the b-bit block boundary. Ensure that the padded message M' has length that is a multiple of b.

   The message M in binary is 1010 1011 1100 1101 1110 1111, the padded message M' is 1010 1011 1100 1101 1110 1111 1000 0000.

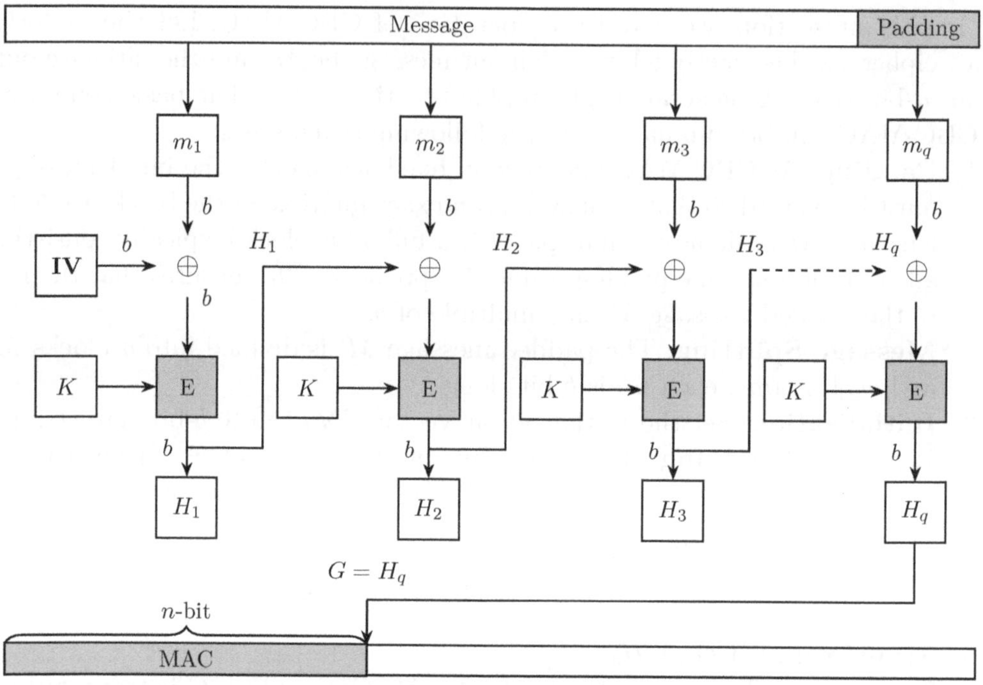

Figure 13-3: CBC-MAC Algorithm

2) Message splitting. Divide the message into $q = 2$ blocks: $m_1 = \texttt{0xABCD}$ and $m_2 = \texttt{0xEF80}$.
3) Set the initialization vector to IV = 0x0000.
4) Iterative chaining. We have

$$H_1 = E_K(m_1 \oplus \mathbf{IV}) = E_K(\texttt{0xABCD} \oplus \texttt{0x0000}) \quad (13\text{-}7)$$
$$= rol(\texttt{0x0A7F}, 3) = \texttt{0x53F8} \quad (13\text{-}8)$$
$$H_2 = E_K(m_2 \oplus H_1) = E_K(\texttt{0xEF80} \oplus \texttt{0x53F8}) \quad (13\text{-}9)$$
$$= rol(\texttt{0x1DCA}, 3) = \texttt{0xEE50} \quad (13\text{-}10)$$

5) Let $G = H_2 = \texttt{0xEE50}$.
6) The MAC is $\text{MSB}_n(G) = \text{MSB}_8(\texttt{0xEE50}) = \texttt{0xEE}$.

■

The procedure above describes the most basic form of CBC-MAC, but it is insecure in that raw form. If the padding rule simply appends zeros until the message length reaches a multiple of the block size b, an attacker can mount a simple forgery. In that case an attacker Eve may add or remove trailing zeros without changing the CBC-MAC value. Consequently, zero padding is safe only when the message length L is known in advance by the MAC user, or when different numbers of trailing zeros are semantically equivalent for the application.

To counter this weakness, a common remedy is to use bit padding of the form "one followed by zeros". Append a single bit with value one to the right end of the message and then append zeros so that the total length is a multiple of b.

Even with that padding, CBC-MAC can still be vulnerable to an exclusive or forgery attack. When the MAC output length equals the block cipher block size, the linear properties of the chaining may be exploited to forge tags, and using the key only once does not prevent this. To protect against exclusive or forgery, use the following scheme. First pad the message on the right with zeros so that the padded message length is a multiple of b. Next, strictly prepend a dedicated length block B_L directly to the beginning of the padded message. Construct this length block B_L from the binary representation of the true original message length L, systematically left-padding it with zeros until B_L is exactly b bits long.

Prepending this length block prevents messages that differ only by trailing zeros or by simple concatenation from producing the same CBC-MAC, and thus strengthens the scheme against both simple forgery and exclusive or forgery.

Example 13.4.2 Assume the block size is $b = 128$ bits. Consider the message "**This is the test message for mac**" for the MAC computation. First, represent the message in hexadecimal. Then, perform padding using the three different padding methods described previously.

Solution: Method 1: Zero Padding: Append zero bits such that after padding the length of message is equal to a multiple of 128 bits. The result is shown in Table 13-1.

Table 13-1: CBC-MAC Padding Method 1

m_1	54	68	69	73	20	69	73	20	74	68	65	20	74	65	73	74
m_2	20	6D	65	73	73	61	67	65	20	66	6F	72	20	6D	61	63
m_3	00	00	00	00	00	00	00	00	00	00	00	00	00	00	00	00

Method 2: Bit Padding: Append a single "1" followed by k zero bits such that after padding the length of message is equal to a multiple of 128 bits. The result is shown in Table 13-2.

Table 13-2: CBC-MAC Padding Method 2

m_1	54	68	69	73	20	69	73	20	74	68	65	20	74	65	73	74
m_2	20	6D	65	73	73	61	67	65	20	66	6F	72	20	6D	61	63
m_3	80	00	00	00	00	00	00	00	00	00	00	00	00	00	00	00

Method 3: Length Prepending: Append zero bits on the right such that after padding the length of message is equal to a multiple of 128 bits. Then prepend one b-bit block L, where L is the binary encoding of the original length, left-padded with "0" as needed, the right-most bit of L is the least significant bit of M. The result is shown in Table 13-3.

Table 13-3: CBC-MAC Padding Method 3

m_1	00	00	00	00	00	00	00	00	00	00	00	00	00	00	01	00
m_2	54	68	69	73	20	69	73	20	74	68	65	20	74	65	73	74
m_3	20	6D	65	73	73	61	67	65	20	66	6F	72	20	6D	61	63

■

13.5 RANDOM NUMBER GENERATORS

13.5.1 True Random and Pseudorandom Numbers

While deterministic algorithms ensure the precise verification of structures like MACs, the overarching security of all such cryptosystems is intrinsically dependent on the unpredictability of their cryptographic parameters. From the generation of shared secret keys to initialization vector (IV), securing these components heavily relies on high-quality random numbers.

Commonly, "random" is understood as a phenomenon that does not follow any pattern and is completely unpredictable. However, in a mathematical sense, a random process is a collection of random variables driven by uncertain factors and changing over time or other parameters, whose values follow some probability distribution.

Fundamental to this concept is probability. To any possible future event, we assign a real number between 0 and 1, known as the probability, which quantifies the likelihood that the event will occur. A probability of 1 implies certainty that the event will happen, while a probability of 0 implies certainty that it will not. Values strictly between 0 and 1 indicate uncertainty. Formally, probability is a function that maps events to real numbers within the interval $[0, 1]$.

What is a random number? Consider a random variable X that follows a distribution function $F(x)$, if $\{X_1, X_2, \dots\}$ are independently and identically distributed according to $F(x)$, then the numerical values $\{x_1, x_2, \dots\}$ from one observation of $\{X_1, X_2, \dots\}$ are called **Random Number**. Random numbers are an important fundamental computing resource. They are in wide demand not only in cryptography but also in fields like information security and simulation, as well as in daily production and life. Random numbers are divided into two types: **True Random Number** and **Pseudorandom Number**.

True random numbers rely on physical random phenomena, that is, uncertain events in natural or artificial processes, generated by the combined action of multiple uncontrollable factors. Such phenomena can only be analyzed for their statistical properties, and their specific results cannot be accurately predicted. Therefore, the generated numerical sequences are non-repeatable. For example, the result of a coin toss is affected by random factors such as initial velocity, angular velocity, wind speed, projection angle, ground material, and gravity. Other typical random sources include dice rolling, thermal noise, nuclear decay, raindrop distribution, electron thermal motion, and radiation intensity. Numerical sequences generated using these physical processes are called true random numbers.

To generate random numbers, most computers have a built-in function called a **pseudorandom number generator** (PRNGs), whose output is a sequence of **pseudorandom numbers**. These random numbers are generated by deterministic algorithms and are sequences that seem random but are reproducible. Most random number generators depend on an initial value, called the **seed**. Once the algorithm and the seed are determined, the subsequent "random sequence" generated is also determined. The seed is similar to a key in an encryption system and needs to be kept secret to prevent the random sequence from being predicted or reproduced.

Although pseudorandom numbers are not random in the rigorous sense, they can replace true random numbers in the vast majority of applications, provided that their output statistically approximates an independent and identically distributed sequence and that recovering the generation rule is computationally infeasible. Particularly in computing and cryptography, pseudorandom numbers are typically derived using PRNGs or **pseudorandom functions** (PRFs). These are utilized to generate keys, **initialization vectors**, padding data, and other cryptographic parameters.

A good pseudorandom number sequence should possess the following properties:

1) **Uniformity:** The output bitstream must be uniformly distributed over the discrete set $\{0, 1\}$. No single bit value or sequence pattern should occur statistically more frequently than others.
2) **Independence:** The output should behave as if it is independent of all previous outputs, exhibiting no detectable correlation.
3) **Long Period:** The generator should produce an extremely long sequence before repeating, ensuring that cycles are practically unreachable.
4) **Unpredictability:** Given any prefix of the output sequence, it should be computationally infeasible to predict any future numbers.
5) **Efficiency:** The generator should produce outputs rapidly, utilizing minimal computational resources.
6) **Reproducibility:** The same seed should always yield the same output sequence, facilitating debugging and controlled experimentation.
7) **Forward Secrecy:** Observing any continuous segment of the output sequence must never allow an adversary to computationally deduce the internal state of the generator.

To ensure that a generated pseudorandom sequence exhibits the statistical properties of true randomness, it must undergo rigorous randomness testing. Common examples include the frequency test, the runs test, and Maurer's universal statistical test. In particular, the **Chi-squared test** is frequently employed to verify uniformity, while other tests are designed to assess the independence of the sequence.

The property that the next random number cannot be predicted from a certain segment of the sequence also is called **unpredictability**. In simpler terms, when a user uses a pseudorandom number generator to generate random numbers, even if Eve has obtained many pseudorandom sequences, she still cannot predict the next random number. If this condition is met, it can be called a **strong pseudorandom number**. Conversely, it is called a **weak pseudorandom number**.

The applications of pseudorandom numbers are widespread. For example, in public-key encryption algorithms, pseudorandom numbers are needed for the selection of the parameter k in the ElGamal cryptosystem, the selection of the parameter k in the ECC cryptosystem, the selection of the lattice basis in the GGH cryptosystem, and when cryptanalyzing hash functions. In symmetric algorithms, pseudorandom numbers are also used to generate the initialization vector. Some optimization algorithms also require the use of pseudorandom numbers. For example, stochastic gradient descent in artificial neural networks, randomly generating the initial ant colony in ant colony algorithms, and randomly generating the initial population in genetic algorithms, all use pseudorandom numbers. Sometimes when a phone plays songs on shuffle, it might be playing in a pseudorandom form; if you listen long enough, it is very possible to discover a repeating cycle. In programming languages, whether Python, Matlab, R, C++, or Java, they all have built-in random number generators with good performance.

Can a computer generate true random numbers? The answer is yes. Using a **Hardware Random Number Generator** (HRNG), it can generate random numbers through physical processes rather than algorithms, such as through thermal noise, atmospheric noise, or mouse movements. However, for most computer programs, using pseudorandom numbers is sufficient, because their probability distribution is not significantly different from a true random distribution. However, certain special scenarios, such as secure communication, require the use of true random numbers to prevent analysis by attackers.

Consider a very simple method for generating pseudorandom numbers. We generate pseudorandom numbers that follow a uniform distribution on the interval from 0 to 1. Suppose X is a random variable with distribution $X \sim U(0,1)$, and let x be a possible value of X, where U denotes the uniform distribution and $(0,1)$ is the interval of the distribution. Its **probability density function**(PDF) of X is given by

$$f(x) = \begin{cases} 1, & 0 < x < 1 \\ 0, & \text{otherwise} \end{cases} \tag{13-11}$$

The probability density function f is shown in Figure 13-4.

Its **cumulative distribution function**(CDF) of X is given by

$$F(x) = \begin{cases} 0, & x \leqslant 0 \\ x, & 0 < x < 1 \\ 1, & x \geqslant 1 \end{cases} \tag{13-12}$$

The cumulative distribution function F is shown in Figure 13-5.

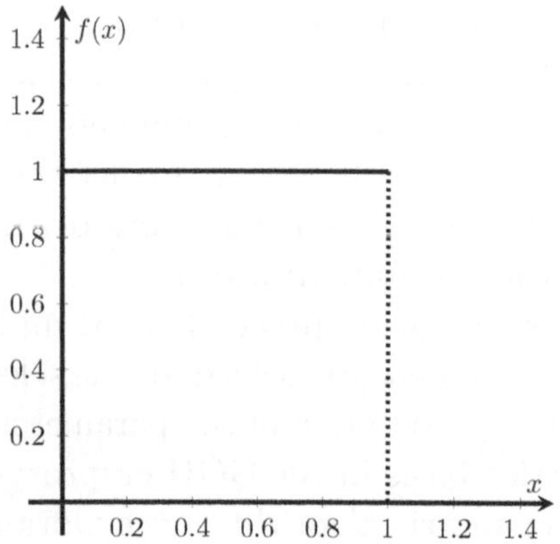

Figure 13-4: Graph of the PDF $f(x)$

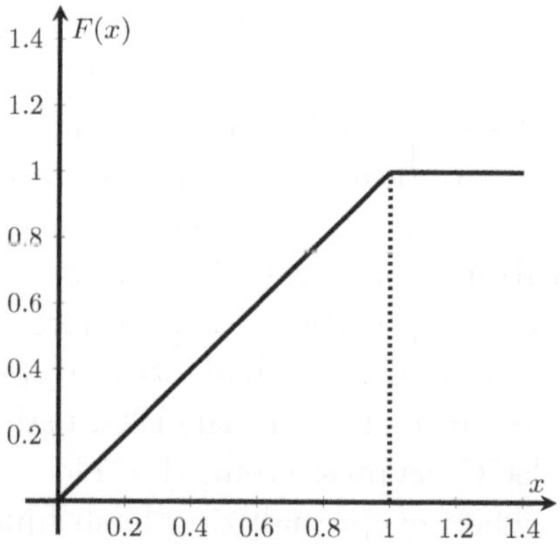

Figure 13-5: Graph of the CDF $F(x)$

In discrete computing environments, a pseudorandom decimal exhibiting a uniform distribution over the interval $[0,1)$ is typically derived by generating a uniformly distributed pseudorandom integer and dividing it by a massive modulus m. The foundational methods for generating such uniformly distributed pseudorandom integers include the following four techniques:

1) Middle-Square method.
2) Middle-Product method.
3) Linear congruential method.
4) Multiplicative congruential method.

13.5.2 Middle-Square and Middle-Product Methods

The **Middle-Square Method** is a foundational algorithm for pseudorandom number generation, proposed by *John von Neumann* in 1946 [175]. Let S_0 be an n-digit integer (typically in base 2 or base 10), referred to as the **seed**. The algorithm generates a sequence of numbers $S_0, S_1, S_2, \ldots$, where the next state S_{k+1} is derived from the current state S_k.

Let $X = S_k^2$. If X has fewer than $2n$ digits, it is padded with leading zeros to achieve a total length of $2n$ digits. The new state S_{k+1} is then defined as the middle n digits extracted from this $2n$-digit representation of X.

Example 13.5.1 Suppose an initial seed is 1234 and generate a sequence.
Solution:

$$\begin{aligned} 1234^2 &= 1522756 \Rightarrow 01\mathbf{5227}56 \\ \Rightarrow 5227^2 &= 27321529 \Rightarrow 27\mathbf{3215}29 \\ \Rightarrow 3215^2 &= 10336225 \Rightarrow 10\mathbf{3362}25 \\ \Rightarrow 3362^2 &= 11303044 \Rightarrow 11\mathbf{3030}44 \\ \Rightarrow 3030^2 &= 9180900 \Rightarrow 09\mathbf{1809}00 \end{aligned} \tag{13-13}$$

■

A primary flaw of the Middle-Square Method is its short **period length**. After a sufficient number of iterations, the sequence will inevitably enter a **cycle**, causing the same series of numbers to be generated repeatedly. For instance, the sequence $2916 \to 5030 \to 3009 \to 0540 \to 2916 \ldots$ forms one such short, inescapable loop.

Due to this tendency to degenerate rapidly into short cycles, the method is considered statistically weak. Consequently, it is no longer in practical use, serving primarily as a historical example.

The **Constant Multiplier method** is similar to the middle-square method. This method generates the next number by multiplying the previous number. Let S_0 be an n-digit seed and A be a fixed n-digit constant multiplier. The iteration formula is

$$S_{k+1} = [A \times S_k]_n \tag{13-14}$$

The product is padded to $2n$ digits, and the middle n digits become S_{k+1}.

The method is statistically weak compared to modern algorithms and is no longer used.

13.5.3 Linear Congruential Method

The foundational concept of congruence-based random number generation was pioneered by *D. H. Lehmer* in 1951, and subsequently generalized into the Linear Congruential Method by *W. E. Thomson* and *A. Rotenberg* in 1958. It is also known as the **Linear Congruential Generator** (LCG) and is a classic algorithm for generating random numbers [176]. The iterative formula for this method is

$$S_{k+1} \equiv (AS_k + C) \pmod{M} \tag{13-15}$$

where the integer $M \in \mathbb{Z}^+$ is called modulus, the integer $A \in (0, M)$ is called multiplier, and the integer $C \in [0, M)$ is called increment. In computer programs, A, C, and M are fixed constants. When $k = 0$, $S_0 \in [0, M)$ is called random seed. The general term for S_k is

$$S_k \equiv \left(A^k S_0 + \frac{A^k - 1}{A - 1} \cdot C\right) \pmod{M} \tag{13-16}$$

where A and M are given positive integers, and strictly $A > 1$.

We now prove that congruence 13-16 is correct.

Proof

Proof by Induction. First, let $k = 1$. Then $S_1 \equiv AS_0 + C \pmod{M}$ is clearly true.

Let $k = n$. Assume that $S_n \equiv \left(A^n S_0 + \frac{A^n - 1}{A - 1} \cdot C\right) \pmod{M}$ holds.

Let $k = n + 1$. Then we have

$$\begin{aligned}
S_{n+1} &\equiv AS_n + C \pmod{M} && \text{(13-17)}\\
&\equiv A\left(A^n S_0 + \frac{A^n - 1}{A - 1} \cdot C\right) + C \pmod{M} && \text{(13-18)}\\
&\equiv \left(A^{n+1} S_0 + \frac{A^{n+1} - A}{A - 1} \cdot C\right) + C \pmod{M} && \text{(13-19)}\\
&\equiv \left(A^{n+1} S_0 + \frac{A^{n+1} - 1 - (A - 1)}{A - 1} \cdot C\right) + C \pmod{M} && \text{(13-20)}\\
&\equiv \left(A^{n+1} S_0 + \left(\frac{A^{n+1} - 1}{A - 1} - 1\right) \cdot C\right) + C \pmod{M} && \text{(13-21)}\\
&\equiv \left(A^{n+1} S_0 + \frac{A^{n+1} - 1}{A - 1} \cdot C\right) \pmod{M} && \text{(13-22)}
\end{aligned}$$

Therefore, by mathematical induction, the general term holds for all $k \geqslant 1$.

Since the result of each iteration in the LCG depends only on the previous term, and there are only M possible values, a repeated value must occur after generating at most M elements. However, the period is usually less than M. Let L be the number of bits in the computer system (typically 64 bits). To absolutely guarantee that the LCG achieves the maximum theoretical period of 2^L, the parameters must rigidly satisfy the conditions derived from the renowned Hull-Dobell Theorem:

- C and M are coprime.
- $A = 4q + 1$, where q is a positive integer.

Example 13.5.2 Consider the sequence defined by the linear congruence relation $S_{k+1} \equiv (7S_k + 7) \pmod{10}$ where $k \geqslant 0$ and the initial seed is $S_0 = 1$. Determine the sequence generated by this relation.
Solution: Computing the first few terms yields the following periodic sequence $(4, 5, 2, 1, 4, 5, 2, 1, \dots)$ which repeats with a period of 4. Note that this does not achieve the maximum possible period of 10. ■

Example 13.5.3 Consider the sequence defined by the linear congruence relation $S_{k+1} \equiv (17S_k + 5) \pmod{64}$ where $k \geqslant 0$ and the initial seed is $S_0 = 1$. Determine the sequence generated by this relation.
Solution: Computing the first few terms yields the following periodic sequence: (**22**, 59, 48, 53, 10, 47, 36, 41, 62, 35, 24, 29, 50, 23, 12, 17, 38, 11, 0, 5, 26, 63, 52, 57, 14, 51, 40, 45, 2, 39, 28, 33, 54, 27, 16, 21, 42, 15, 4, 9 ,30, 3, 56, 61, 18, 55, 44, 49, 6, 43, 32, 37, 58, 31, 20, 25, 46, 19, 8, 13, 34, 7, 60, 1, **22**, 59).

The period is 64. Since $64 = 2^6$, if this were running on a 6-bit architecture, it would have reached the maximum theoretical period.

Note that the sequence visits every integer from 0 to 63 exactly once before repeating. This is a desirable property for a random number generator known as maximal period.

The Python code for the Linear Congruential Method is as follows:

```python
import time

def LCG(m, a, c, seed):
    """Generator for the Linear Congruential Method."""
    x = seed
    while True:
        yield x
        x = (a * x + c) % m

def random_int_samples(n_samples, seed=None, upper=1000, lower=1):
    """Generates a list of scaled pseudorandom integers."""
    # CRITICAL FIX: Never use time() as a default argument in the function signature,
    # as it evaluates only once upon module import, destroying randomness across calls.
    if seed is None:
        seed = int(time.time() * 1000)  # Use millisecond precision for seed

    m = 2**64
    a = 594156893
    c = 0 # Note: Setting c=0 reduces this to a Multiplicative Congruential Generator

```

```
    gen = LCG(m, a, c, seed)
    sequence = []

    for _ in range(n_samples):
        rand_float = next(gen) / m
        rand_int = int((upper - lower) * rand_float) + lower
        sequence.append(rand_int)

    return sequence
```

■

In the Linear Congruential Method, if the increment parameter C is set to zero, the algorithm reduces to the Multiplicative Congruential Method, also known as the **Multiplicative Congruential Generator** (MCG). First proposed by *Lehmer* in 1951 [177], its iterative formula is defined as

$$S_{k+1} \equiv AS_k \pmod{M} \tag{13-23}$$

Although the MCG computationally requires one less addition than the standard LCG, the algebraic properties of the two differ significantly. This distinction is particularly pronounced when the modulus M is set to the computer word size, $M = 2^L$. Under these conditions, the maximum period of the MCG is limited to 2^{L-2}. When working with power-of-two modulo, the LCG offers a period length four times that of the MCG.

From a cryptographic perspective, however, the Linear Congruential Method is fundamentally insecure. Since its generation mechanism relies on a simple linear recurrence relation, the output sequence exhibits a predictable lattice structure in high-dimensional space. An attacker can efficiently deduce the internal state of the generator and predict all future outputs by solving a system of linear equations. Notably, this can often be achieved by observing only a short segment of the output sequence, even without prior knowledge of the parameters A, C, or M. Therefore, despite their potentially long periods, LCGs must not be used to generate keys or nonces in security protocols, as illustrated in Figure 13-6 and Figure 13-7.

Figure 13-6: Short Period

Figure 13-7: Long Period

For non-cryptographic applications, such as Monte Carlo simulations, an LCG implemented on a 64-bit architecture can achieve a period of $2^{64} \approx 1.84 \times 10^{19}$, which is generally sufficient for basic statistical modeling. Nevertheless, practitioners must exercise caution in selecting the seed. If a random seed is not explicitly provided, libraries often default to using the current system timestamp. Since attackers can easily estimate the approximate time of generation, the timestamp represents a low-entropy source susceptible to brute-force attacks. Consequently, in any security-sensitive context, relying solely on system time for seeding is unsafe and exposes the system to predictability attacks.

Due to its inherent linear recurrence structure, the output sequence of the Linear Congruential Method is predictable. Furthermore, its period is relatively short compared to modern computing standards. Consequently, the LCG is unsuitable for key generation and other cryptographically secure applications. To address these limitations regarding period length and statistical properties, modern programming languages such as Python, SageMath, R, and MATLAB have widely adopted the Mersenne Twister(MT) algorithm in their standard libraries.

The **Mersenne Twister** was developed by *Makoto Matsumoto* and *Takuji Nishimura* in 1998 [178]. Based on a matrix linear recurrence over the binary field, this algorithm offers high computational efficiency and generates pseudorandom numbers with excellent statistical properties. Its most common variant, MT19937, derives its name from its vast period length of $2^{19937} - 1$, which is a Mersenne prime.

While MT19937 effortlessly passes stringent statistical randomness tests and possesses an almost inexhaustible period, it is fundamentally NOT a Cryptographically Secure Pseudorandom Number Generator (CSPRNG). Because its state transitions consist entirely of linear operations (bitwise XORs and bit shifts), an adversary only needs to observe 624 consecutive 32-bit outputs to completely reconstruct the generator's internal state array. Once the state is cloned, all past and future outputs are 100% predictable. Therefore, the Mersenne Twister must never be used to generate cryptographic keys.

To generate pseudorandom numbers that follow a standard Uniform Distribution $U(0,1)$ using the LCG method, the integer state S_k must be normalized. By computing $U_k = S_k/M$, we obtain a floating-point number in the interval $[0,1)$. Building on this, a random number X uniformly distributed over an arbitrary interval $[a,b]$ can be generated via the following linear transformation:

$$X = a + (b-a)\frac{S_k}{M} \tag{13-24}$$

If a sequence of uniformly distributed integers within a closed interval $[a,b]$ is required, the floor function is typically applied to the normalized state derived from the generator. The transformation is given by

$$I = a + \left\lfloor (b-a+1)\frac{S_k}{M} \right\rfloor \tag{13-25}$$

Beyond uniform distributions, it is also possible to construct pseudorandom numbers that follow a Normal distribution. According to the **Central Limit Theorem**

(CLT), if $Y_1, Y_2, \ldots, Y_n$ are n independent and identically distributed random variables, the distribution of their sum approaches a Normal distribution as n becomes sufficiently large.

A classic implementation of this principle is to set $n = 12$ for computational simplicity. We generate 12 independent samples y_i from the standard uniform distribution $U(0,1)$. Since the expectation of $U(0,1)$ is $\mu = 1/2$ and the variance is $\sigma^2 = 1/12$, the sum of 12 such variables has a variance of $12 \times (1/12) = 1$. We can standardize the sum as follows to obtain a value $z = \frac{\sum_{i=1}^{n} y_i - n\mu}{\sqrt{n\sigma^2}} = \frac{\sum_{i=1}^{12} y_i - 12(0.5)}{\sqrt{12 \cdot (1/12)}} = \sum_{i=1}^{12} y_i - 6$.

The resulting value z is a pseudorandom number that approximately follows the standard normal distribution $N(0,1)$. While this "Sum of 12" method is highly computationally efficient and intuitively demonstrates the CLT, it possesses a fundamental statistical limitation: because $0 < y_i < 1$, the maximum possible value of z is $12 - 6 = 6$, and the minimum is $0 - 6 = -6$. Consequently, this approximation completely truncates the infinite tails of a true Gaussian curve, strictly bounding all outputs within the interval $(-6, 6)$. When higher mathematical precision and true unbounded distribution tails are required, advanced techniques such as Inverse Transform Sampling or the Box-Muller Transform are mandatorily preferred.

13.5.4 Cryptographically Secure Pseudorandom Number Generators

Although modern software development environments provide convenient methods for generating random numbers, this does not imply that their output satisfies cryptographic security requirements. Standard pseudorandom number generators are fundamentally deterministic algorithms. Their output sequence is mathematically determined entirely by the initial seed. Furthermore, in the absence of external entropy, these generators often default to using the current system timestamp as the seed. In practice, this implementation can be catastrophic.

The security of an encryption scheme is critically dependent on the quality of the random number generators it employs. Fortunately, there exist pseudorandom number generators (PRNGs) that meet rigorous cryptographic security requirements. These algorithms typically rely on computational hardness assumptions from complexity theory. This section introduces two classic Cryptographically Secure Pseudorandom Number Generators (CSPRNGs): the RSA Pseudorandom Generator and the Blum-Blum-Shub (BBS) Generator.

To illustrate this vulnerability, consider an online card game with a flawed shuffling mechanism. If an attacker understands the underlying dealing algorithm and synchronizes their local clock with the server's time, they can compute the seed used for the current session. This allows the attacker to predict the opponent's hand in real-time, thereby compromising the integrity of the game. Consequently, for any application involving security protocols or sensitive data, a **Cryptographically Secure Pseudorandom Number Generator** (CSPRNG) is mandatory.

A CSPRNG must satisfy stricter criteria than merely passing statistical randomness tests. First, it must meet computational security requirements, specifically the **Next-bit Test**. This test dictates that given the first k bits of the generator's output, there exists no polynomial-time algorithm that can predict the $(k+1)$-th bit with a probability greater than 1/2. If an algorithm's predictive advantage over random guessing is rendered negligible, it passes the test. Additionally, a CSPRNG must possess **backtracking resistance**, often referred to as irreversibility. This property ensures that even if an attacker compromises the current internal state of the generator, it remains computationally infeasible to derive the random sequence generated in the past.

The linear congruential method (LCG) fails to meet these security standards. Its security is extremely fragile due to its linearity:

1) **Partial Parameters Are Known**. If the parameters S_0, A, and M are known, the system is trivially broken, as any future state can be calculated via $S_{k+1} \equiv (AS_k + C) \pmod{M}$. Even if the increment C is unknown, an attacker who intercepts two consecutive outputs S_0 and S_1 can uniquely determine C by solving the linear congruence $C \equiv S_1 - S_0 A \pmod{M}$. Similarly, if only the modulus M and three consecutive outputs S_0, S_1, S_2 are known, the parameters A and C can be recovered by solving a system of two linear congruences.
2) **All Parameters Are Unknown**. This is the most challenging case. The attacker can only observe the sequence $S_0, S_1, S_2, \ldots$ but does not know any information about A, C, M. In this context, directly establishing a system of linear congruences for S_i is often hindered by an **underdetermined system**

$$S_1 \equiv AS_0 + C \pmod{M} \tag{13-26}$$
$$S_2 \equiv AS_1 + C \pmod{M} \tag{13-27}$$
$$\vdots$$
$$S_i \equiv AS_{i-1} + C \pmod{M} \tag{13-28}$$

However, by exploiting the algebraic structure of the LCG, we can eliminate some variables. Let us define a difference sequence $R_i = S_{i+1} - S_i$. Utilizing the linear property of the LCG, we derive

$$\begin{aligned} R_i &= S_{i+1} - S_i && (13\text{-}29)\\ &\equiv (AS_i + C) - (AS_{i-1} + C) \pmod{M} && (13\text{-}30)\\ &\equiv A(S_i - S_{i-1}) \pmod{M} && (13\text{-}31)\\ &\equiv AR_{i-1} \pmod{M} && (13\text{-}32) \end{aligned}$$

Observe that the difference sequence R_i forms a geometric progression modulo M. We can use this property to construct an identity that eliminates the unknown multiplier A. Consider three consecutive terms R_i, R_{i+1}, R_{i+2}. By substituting the relation $R_{k+1} \equiv AR_k \pmod{M}$, we have

$$\begin{aligned} R_{i+2}R_i - R_{i+1}^2 &\equiv (AR_{i+1})R_i - R_{i+1}^2 \pmod{M} && (13\text{-}33)\\ &\equiv A(AR_i)R_i - (AR_i)^2 \pmod{M} && (13\text{-}34)\\ &\equiv A^2R_i^2 - A^2R_i^2 \pmod{M} && (13\text{-}35)\\ &\equiv 0 \pmod{M} && (13\text{-}36) \end{aligned}$$

Congruence 13-36 reveals a critical weakness. The computed value $T_i = |R_{i+2}R_i - R_{i+1}^2|$ must be a multiple of the modulus M, here $T_i = kM$ for some integer k. By collecting sufficient samples and calculating multiple T_i values, we can recover the modulus M with high probability using the Euclidean algorithm to find the Greatest Common Divisor $M \approx \gcd(T_0, T_1, T_2, \cdots)$. Once M is determined, the problem reduces to Case 1. The attacker can subsequently solve for A and C, thereby achieving a complete break of the pseudorandom number generator.

Example 13.5.4 Suppose a sequence is known to be generated using the Linear Congruential Generator. The sequence is $[17, 1, 16, 15, 10, 4]$. Determine the completely hidden parameters M, A, and C of this LCG.
Solution: Given the sequence $[17, 1, 16, 15, 10, 4]$, let $S_0 = 17$. First, we calculate the difference sequence $R_i = S_{i+1} - S_i$:

$$R_0 = S_1 - S_0 = -16 \tag{13-37}$$

$$R_1 = S_2 - S_1 = 15 \tag{13-38}$$

$$\vdots$$

$$R_4 = S_5 - S_4 = -6 \tag{13-39}$$

This yields the difference vector $R = [-16, 15, -1, -5, -6]$. Next, we calculate the determinant values $T_i = R_{i+2}R_i - R_{i+1}^2$. Based on Eq. 13-36, these values must be exactly congruent to 0 modulo M. Computing these three determinants yields $[-209, -76, -19]$. The absolute modulus M is fundamentally the greatest common divisor (GCD) of the absolute values of these results: $M = \gcd(209, 76, 19) = 19$.

With $M = 19$ determined, we proceed to find A. With $M = 19$ definitively established, we proceed to analytically recover the multiplier A. Since the difference sequence satisfies $R_1 \equiv A \cdot R_0 \pmod{M}$, we can mathematically isolate A by computing the modular multiplicative inverse of R_0:

$$A \equiv R_1 \cdot R_0^{-1} \pmod{M} \equiv 15 \times (-16)^{-1} \pmod{19} \tag{13-40}$$

Since $-16 \equiv 3 \pmod{19}$, and the modular inverse of 3 modulo 19 is exactly 13, we derive:

$$A \equiv 15 \times 13 \equiv 195 \equiv 5 \pmod{19} \tag{13-41}$$

Having successfully recovered $A = 5$, solving for the final parameter C is trivial. Utilizing the initial state transition equation $C \equiv S_1 - AS_0 \pmod{M}$:

$$C \equiv 1 - 5(17) \equiv -84 \equiv 11 \pmod{19} \tag{13-42}$$

This linear congruential method is $S_k \equiv \left(5^k S_0 + \frac{5^k - 1}{5 - 1} \cdot 11\right) \pmod{19}$.

The Python code for breaking the Linear Congruential Method is as follows:

```
from functools import reduce
import math

def break_LCG(LCG_list):
    """
    Recovers the M, A, and C parameters of an LCG from an observed sequence.
    """
    # Step 1: Compute the difference sequence R_i
    R_i = [s1 - s0 for s0, s1 in zip(LCG_list, LCG_list[1:])]

    # Step 2: Construct the determinant values T_i that are multiples of M
    zeroes = [t2 * t0 - t1 * t1 for t0, t1, t2 in zip(R_i, R_i[1:], R_i[2:])]

    # Step 3: Extract the Modulus M via GCD of absolute values
    M = abs(reduce(math.gcd, zeroes))

    # Step 4: Recover Multiplier A using modular multiplicative inverse
    # WARNING: pow(x, -1, M) requires gcd(x, M) == 1.
    # For prime M this is trivial, but for power-of-two moduli, you must dynamically
    # search the R_i list for an invertible difference.
    R_0_inv = pow(R_i[0] % M, -1, M)
    A = (R_i[1] * R_0_inv) % M

    # Step 5: Recover Increment C
    C = (LCG_list[1] - A * LCG_list[0]) % M

    return M, A, C

recovered_M, recovered_A, recovered_C = break_LCG([17, 1, 16, 15, 10, 4])
print(f"Broken Parameters: M={recovered_M}, A={recovered_A},
C={recovered_C}")
```

■

The security of an encryption scheme is critically dependent on the quality of the random number generators it employs. Fortunately, there exist pseudorandom number generators (PRNGs) that meet rigorous cryptographic security requirements. These algorithms typically rely on computational hardness assumptions from complexity theory. This section introduces two classic Cryptographically Secure Pseudorandom Number Generators (CSPRNGs): the RSA Pseudorandom Generator [179] and the Blum-Blum-Shub (BBS) Generator [180].

The **RSA Pseudorandom Generator** utilizes the one-way property of the RSA function, demonstrating the intrinsic link between public-key cryptography and pseudorandom number generation. The construction of the algorithm proceeds as follows:

1) **(Setup)**: Let L be the bit length of the modulus that is the security parameter of RSA. Select two distinct large primes p and q of length $L/2$, and calculate the modulus $N = pq$. Next, choose an integer e that satisfies $1 < e < \varphi(N)$ and $\gcd(e, \varphi(N)) = 1$, where $\varphi(N) = (p-1)(q-1)$ is the Euler φ function. Finally, publish the parameters (N, e), and keep p and q secret. This process is identical to the key generation of the RSA encryption scheme.
2) **(Initialization)**: Select a random integer S_0 as the seed, such that $1 \leqslant S_0 < N$, and preferably satisfying $\gcd(S_0, N) = 1$.
3) **(Generation)**: Suppose we need to generate a random sequence of m bits. For $k = 0, 1, \ldots, m-1$, do the following steps:
   (a) Update the internal state using the RSA function

$$S_{k+1} \equiv S_k^e \pmod{N} \tag{13-43}$$

   (b) Compute the output bit

$$z_{k+1} = S_{k+1} \pmod{2} \tag{13-44}$$

4) **(Output)**: The resulting pseudorandom binary sequence is $(z_1, z_2, \ldots, z_m)$.

From a security perspective, the robustness of the RSA generator relies on the RSA Assumption. Predicting the next bit z_{k+1} in the sequence is equivalent to inverting the RSA function, which is considered computationally infeasible for sufficiently large values of L.

Example 13.5.5 Assume that $p = 331$ and $q = 997$, generate a 10 bit pseudorandom number using RSA generator.
Solution: First, definitively compute the modulus $N = pq = 330007$ and Euler's totient function $\varphi(N) = (p-1)(q-1) = 330 \times 996 = 328680$. Select the public exponent $e = 23521$ since $\gcd(23521, 328680) = 1$. Next, initialize the system with the secret seed $S_0 = 235252$ which safely satisfies $\gcd(235252, 330007) = 1$.

$$z_1 \equiv S_1 \equiv S_0^e \equiv 161562 \pmod{N} \implies z_1 \equiv \mathbf{0} \pmod{2} \tag{13-45}$$
$$z_2 \equiv S_2 \equiv S_1^e \equiv 120556 \pmod{N} \implies z_2 \equiv \mathbf{0} \pmod{2} \tag{13-46}$$
$$z_3 \equiv S_3 \equiv S_2^e \equiv 6488 \pmod{N} \implies z_3 \equiv \mathbf{0} \pmod{2} \tag{13-47}$$
$$\vdots$$
$$z_{10} \equiv S_{10} \equiv S_{10}^e \equiv 197849 \pmod{N} \implies z_{10} \equiv \mathbf{1} \pmod{2} \tag{13-48}$$

The binary pseudorandom number is 0001101011, 107 in decimal. ■

Then we introduce another CSPRNG that is called Blum-Blum-Shub Generator (BBS) after the names of its three inventors. The unconditional security of the BBS generator is fundamentally based on the computational intractability of the Quadratic Residuosity Problem. The procedure is as follows:

1) (Setup): Let L be the bit length of the modulus that is the security parameter of BBS. Select two distinct large primes p and q of length $L/2$, that both have a remainder of 3 when divided by 4. That is

$$p \equiv q \equiv 3 \pmod 4 \tag{13-49}$$

   Calculate the modulus $N = pq$. A composite number N formed by the product of two such primes is known in number theory as a Blum Integer. Next, choose an integer r which is coprime to N.
2) (Initialization): Compute $S_0 \equiv r^2 \pmod N$.
3) (Generation): Suppose we need to generate a random sequence of m bits. For $k = 0, 1, \ldots, m-1$, do the following steps:
   (a) Update the internal state using the following function:

$$S_{k+1} \equiv S_k^2 \pmod N \tag{13-50}$$

   (b) Compute the output bit

$$z_{k+1} = S_{k+1} \pmod 2 \tag{13-51}$$

4) (Output): The resulting pseudorandom binary sequence is $(z_1, z_2, \ldots, z_m)$.

Example 13.5.6 Assume that $p = 4943$ and $q = 2131$, generate a 10 bit pseudorandom number using BBS generator.
Solution: Since $p \equiv q \equiv 3 \pmod 4$, so $N = pq = 10533533$. Let $r = 125$, then the seed is $S_0 \equiv r^2 \equiv 15625 \pmod N$. We have

$$\begin{aligned}
S_1 \equiv S_0^2 &\equiv 1869366 \pmod N \implies z_1 \equiv 1869366 \equiv \mathbf{0} \pmod 2\\
S_2 \equiv S_1^2 &\equiv 8602140 \pmod N \implies z_2 \equiv 8602140 \equiv \mathbf{0} \pmod 2\\
S_3 \equiv S_2^2 &\equiv 7278560 \pmod N \implies z_3 \equiv 7278560 \equiv \mathbf{0} \pmod 2\\
S_4 \equiv S_3^2 &\equiv 535136 \pmod N \implies z_4 \equiv 535136 \equiv \mathbf{0} \pmod 2\\
S_5 \equiv S_4^2 &\equiv 5910358 \pmod N \implies z_5 \equiv 5910358 \equiv \mathbf{0} \pmod 2\\
S_6 \equiv S_5^2 &\equiv 7800863 \pmod N \implies z_6 \equiv 7800863 \equiv \mathbf{1} \pmod 2\\
S_7 \equiv S_6^2 &\equiv 446875 \pmod N \implies z_7 \equiv 446875 \equiv \mathbf{1} \pmod 2\\
S_8 \equiv S_7^2 &\equiv 2547011 \pmod N \implies z_8 \equiv 2547011 \equiv \mathbf{1} \pmod 2\\
S_9 \equiv S_8^2 &\equiv 9666010 \pmod N \implies z_9 \equiv 9666010 \equiv \mathbf{0} \pmod 2\\
S_{10} \equiv S_9^2 &\equiv 6823278 \pmod N \implies z_{10} \equiv 6823278 \equiv \mathbf{0} \pmod 2
\end{aligned}$$

The binary pseudorandom number is `0000011100`, 28 in decimal. ■

Both the RSA and BBS pseudorandom number generators utilize the modulus $N = pq$. Consequently, the security of these algorithms relies heavily on the difficulty of the **integer factorization problem**. As discussed in the introduction to the RSA cryptosystem, integer factorization is considered computationally intractable. Provided that the modulus N is sufficiently large, the generated sequence is cryptographically unpredictable. Therefore, compared to standard statistical generators, both the RSA and BBS generators offer provable security, thereby meeting the rigorous requirements for cryptographic applications.

13.6 EXERCISES

1) Explain what difference between message integrity and message authentication.
2) Let the message consist of three 32-bit blocks $M = M_1||M_2||M_3$ where

$$M_1 = \texttt{0x12345678}$$
$$M_2 = \texttt{0x9ABCDEF0}$$
$$M_3 = \texttt{0x0F1E2D3C}$$

The block cipher under key (K) is defined as

$$E_K(X) = X \oplus \texttt{0xA5A5A5A5}$$

The initial chaining value is $C_0 = \texttt{0x00...00}$ with 32-bit block size. Answer the following questions:
   (a) Compute the CBC-MAC value of M.
   (b) Show the intermediate chaining values C_1, C_2 and C_3.
3) Consider two messages $M = M_1||M_2$ and $M' = M_1||M_2||M_3$. Answer the following questions:
   (a) Write the CBC-MAC computation equations for both M and M'.
   (b) Compare the final MAC values symbolically.
   (c) Based on your computation, explain why CBC-MAC is secure only for fixed-length messages.
4) CBC-MAC utilizes a block cipher in Cipher Block Chaining mode, where the final ciphertext block serves as the authentication tag. For these problems, assume a 4-bit "Mini-Cipher" $E_K(X)$ where the encryption process is a simple XOR with the key K followed by a left circular shift of 1 bit ($\lll 1$). The formula is shown below:

$$E_K(X) = (X \oplus K) \lll 1$$

Answer the following questions:
   (a) Consider a message M consisting of two 4-bit blocks $M_1 = 1010$ and $M_2 = 1100$. Using the key $K = 0011$ and an initial vector $IV = 0000$. Compute the first intermediate block $C_1 = E_K(M_1 \oplus IV)$.
   (b) Compute the final 4-bit MAC tag $T = E_K(M_2 \oplus C_1)$.
   (c) Let $T = \text{CBC-MAC}(K, M_1)$. Show that the attacker can immediately produce a valid MAC tag for a two-block message $(M_1||M_2)$ without knowing K, provided they can choose M_2 based on T.
   (d) If $M_1 = 0101$ and $T = 1011$, what should the value of M_2 be such that the tag for $(M_1||M_2)$ is also T?
5) $HMAC(K, M) = H((K' \oplus opad)||H((K' \oplus ipad)||M))$. For these problems, assume H is a toy hash function that outputs 4 bits, and the block size b is also 4 bits. Let $ipad = 0110$ and $opad = 1010$. Answer the following questions:
   (a) If the secret key is $K = 11$, and the required block size is $b = 4$, the key is padded with zeros to the right. Determine K'.

(b) Compute the inner key $S_i = K' \oplus ipad$ and the outer key $S_o = K' \oplus opad$.
(c) From a bitwise logic perspective, explain why HMAC uses two distinct constants, *ipad* and *opad*. What security issue would arise if these two constants were identical?

6) Let $H(X)$ be a simple hash that returns the XOR sum of all 4-bit blocks in the input. Given: $M = 1101$, $S_i = 1010$, and $S_o = 0110$. Compute the inner hash value $V = H(S_i||M)$ and the final MAC tag $T = H(S_o||V)$.
7) Let $H(X)$ be a simple hash that is treated as a black-box hash function with 32 bits output length and 64 bits block length. Let a simplified HMAC construction is defined as

$$HMAC_K(M) = H((K \oplus opad)||H((K \oplus \text{ipad})||M))$$

where $ipad = \underbrace{\texttt{0x36}}_{\text{repeated}}$ and $opad = \underbrace{\texttt{0x5c}}_{\text{repeated}}$. Let the secret key be $K = \texttt{0x1A2B3C}$, which is shorter than the hash block size. Answer the following questions:
(a) Pad K to the block length.
(b) Compute $K \oplus ipad$.
(c) Compute $K \oplus opad$.
(d) Let $M = \texttt{0xCAFEBABE}$. Compute the input $(K' \oplus ipad) \parallel M$ to the inner hash.

8) Apart from those mentioned in the text, what other sources of true randomness exist? True Random Number Generators (TRNGs) built into computer CPUs primarily generate random numbers by amplifying thermal noise within circuits. What is the specific working principle behind this mechanism?
9) Consider the Middle-Square method, let $n = 4$, the seed value be $X_0 = 2026$. Compute the next two numbers in the sequence X_1 and X_2.
10) A critical weakness of the Middle-Square Method is its tendency to enter short cycles or degenerate to zero. Consider a 2-digit version of the algorithm. Start with the seed $X_0 = 50$. Answer the following questions:
(a) Perform the iterations. What is the value of X_1? What does this imply about the period of the generator for this specific seed?
(b) Start with the seed $X_0 = 10$. Compute X_1, X_2, and X_3. Identify the behavior of the sequence at X_3.

11) Consider the Linear Congruential Method defined by $S_k \equiv \left(A^k S_0 + \frac{A^k - 1}{A - 1} \cdot C\right)$ (mod M). Let $k = 1$ and $S_0 = -\frac{C}{A-1}$, show that the period of the LCG is 1.
12) Consider the Middle-Square Method, with the iteration formula

$$S_{k+1} = [S_k \times S_k]_n$$

Assuming the seed is 2345, what is the random number generated after 5 iterations?

13) Consider the Linear Congruential Method, given by

$$S_{k+1} \equiv (97S_k + 3) \pmod{101}$$

Let $S_0 = 1$. What is the period of this generator?
14) Consider the Linear Congruential Method. If the computer word size is 5 bits, it follows that the maximum period is $2^5 = 32$. Let $A = 13$, $C = 5$, and $S_0 = 1$. Calculate the generated sequence of random numbers.
15) Consider the Linear Congruential Method. Given a segment of a random sequence $[18, 2, 11, 9, 7, 17, 6]$, is it possible to determine the parameters of this Linear Congruential Generator?
16) What is the method for generating a pseudo-random sequence that follows a negative exponential distribution?
17) Let i, j, k, and M be integers. If $ik \equiv jk \pmod{M}$, prove that

$$i \equiv j \left(\bmod \frac{M}{\gcd(M, k)} \right)$$

18) What are the methods for generating non-uniform random numbers?
19) Assume the existence of a pseudorandom generator with variable output length. Construct a variable-length encryption scheme and prove that this scheme possesses indistinguishable encryptions in the presence of an eavesdropper.

CHAPTER 14

Digital Signatures

In traditional commerce and social interactions, handwritten signatures or seals serve as the primary mechanism for authenticating documents. These physical signatures signify the signer's assent and establish a chronology. Consequently, they provide key evidence in legal disputes involving tampering or denial of action, thereby ensuring authenticity, integrity, and non-repudiation. However, traditional signatures cannot meet the demands of modern digital communication. While Message Authentication Codes (MACs) effectively detect tampering and verify sources, they rely on symmetric cryptography where the receiver also possesses the key to generate valid tags. Thus, MACs fail to provide non-repudiation.

To address this, cryptographers introduced **Digital Signature** technology based on public-key cryptography. This technology employs asymmetric key pairs: a private key for signing and a public key for verification. This mechanism replicates traditional signatures in the digital realm and provides a mathematical proof of the sender's identity.

Topics covered in this chapter:

- Definition of Digital Signature
- RSA Digital Signature Scheme
- ElGamal Digital Signature Scheme
- Elliptic Curve Digital Signature Scheme

14.1 INTRODUCTION

Digital signature technology emerged in the 1970s. As computer networks expanded, issues concerning data security and authentication became increasingly prominent. In 1976, *Whitfield Diffie* and *Martin Hellman* introduced the concept of digital signatures in their seminal paper [7]. However, they did not provide a concrete construction at that time. It was not until 1978 that *Ron Rivest, Adi Shamir*, and *Leonard Adleman* presented the first practical implementation of a digital signature alongside the RSA public-key encryption system.

Early signature schemes contained vulnerabilities that made them susceptible to forgery. In 1988, *Shafi Goldwasser, Silvio Micali*, and *Ron Rivest* published the influential paper [181]. Widely regarded as a watershed miles[]tone in modern

DOI: 10.1201/9781042011087-14

signature theory. This work established the first rigorous security definitions for digital signatures, formally introducing the gold standard of security: Existential Unforgeability under Chosen-message Attacks (EUF-CMA).

Modern digital signature schemes universally adopt the **Hash-then-Sign** strategy. Alice first computes the hash of the message using a secure hash function, such as SHA-3-512. She then generates a digital signature on this hash value using her private key and transmits it to Bob. Upon receipt, Bob uses Alice's public key to verify the signature. He determines the validity of the signature by checking its consistency with the locally computed hash of the received message. This approach has significantly enhanced security and efficiency, serving as the cornerstone of trust for internet security, e-commerce, and financial systems.

14.1.1 Applications

Digital signatures primarily provide the following three types of security services:

1) **Authentication**: Similar to traditional handwritten signatures, digital signatures verify the identity of the message sender. Since the private key is held exclusively by the signer, any signature successfully verified by the corresponding public key provides computational proof that it was generated by the signer. This mechanism relies on the asymmetry of public-key cryptography to ensure reliable identity binding.
2) **Integrity**: Digital signatures ensure that data remains unaltered by unauthorized parties during transmission. This property is primarily guaranteed by the use of cryptographic hash functions. Due to the collision resistance of these functions, any modification to the message content results in a different hash digest, causing the signature verification process to fail.
3) **Non-repudiation**: This feature is the most significant distinction between digital signatures and Message Authentication Codes (MACs). MACs rely on shared keys, allowing both sender and receiver to generate valid authentication tags. Consequently, a receiver cannot prove to a third party that a message originated from the sender. In contrast, digital signatures employ asymmetric key pairs. As only the sender possesses the private key, only she can generate a valid signature. This prevents the sender from denying her actions and irrefutably establishes the identity of the signatory.

14.1.2 Basic Properties of Digital Signatures

Implementing a digital signature mechanism necessitates the establishment of an asymmetric key infrastructure. Let the key pair be denoted as (pk, sk), where pk represents the Public Key and sk represents the Secret Key. The secret key sk must be held strictly confidential by Alice. If sk is compromised, Eve could forge Alice's signature, leading to a collapse of system trust. For instance, in banking scenarios, if Alice's private key is leaked, Eve could forge transfer instructions to illicitly move funds. Since the bank cannot distinguish whether the signature was generated by Alice or by the adversary, it would accept the forged instruction as valid.

A secure and practical Digital Signature Scheme typically consists of three polynomial-time algorithms: Key Generation (**Gen**), Signing (**Sign**), and Verification (**Vrfy**). It must satisfy the following core properties:

1) **Efficiency of Signing**: For any message m and private key sk, the signing algorithm must be executable in polynomial time. This efficiency depends largely on the underlying hash function and asymmetric encryption primitives.
2) **Efficiency of Verification**: For a given message m, signature σ, and public key pk, the verification algorithm must be able to efficiently determine the validity of the signature.
3) **Unforgeability**: Without possession of the private key sk, an attacker even after intercepting an arbitrary number of historical message-signature pairs, he cannot computationally generate a valid new signature σ' for any unqueried message m' with a non-negligible probability in polynomial time. This property, known as Existential Unforgeability under Chosen-message Attacks (EUF-CMA), is the absolute primary security requirement.

We now introduce two methods of digital signatures

1) **Direct Signing on Plaintext**:
   (a) Alice generates a key pair and uses her private key to sign the file.
   (b) Alice transmits the signature, the file, and the public key to Bob.
   (c) Bob inputs Alice's public key, the received file, and the signature into the verification algorithm.
   (d) The verification algorithm performs the corresponding asymmetric mathematical operations. Bob compares the recovered file with the received file. If they are consistent, the verification succeeds; otherwise, it fails.
2) **Hash-then-Sign**:
   (a) Alice uses a cryptographic hash function to perform a hash operation on the file, obtaining a hash value.
   (b) Alice uses her private key to sign this hash digest, generating the signature σ.
   (c) Alice transmits the signature, the file, and the public key to Bob.
   (d) Upon receipt, Bob independently hashes the received file using the exact same hash function to obtain a new hash value.
   (e) Bob compares the recovered hash value with the hash value he calculated. If they are consistent, the verification succeeds; otherwise, it fails. As shown in Figure 14-1.

The integration of hash functions into digital signature schemes is primarily driven by the need for computational efficiency. Since digital signatures rely on asymmetric cryptographic primitives, their operational speed is significantly slower than symmetric counterparts. Without hash functions, a long original file would require conversion into binary sequences and processing via multiple block-wise signing operations. This incurs prohibitive computational costs. By utilizing a cryptographic hash function, an input of arbitrary length is mapped to a fixed-length digest. Signing this short digest instead of the entire file drastically reduces computational overhead, thereby enhancing system performance and broadening the applicability of digital signatures.

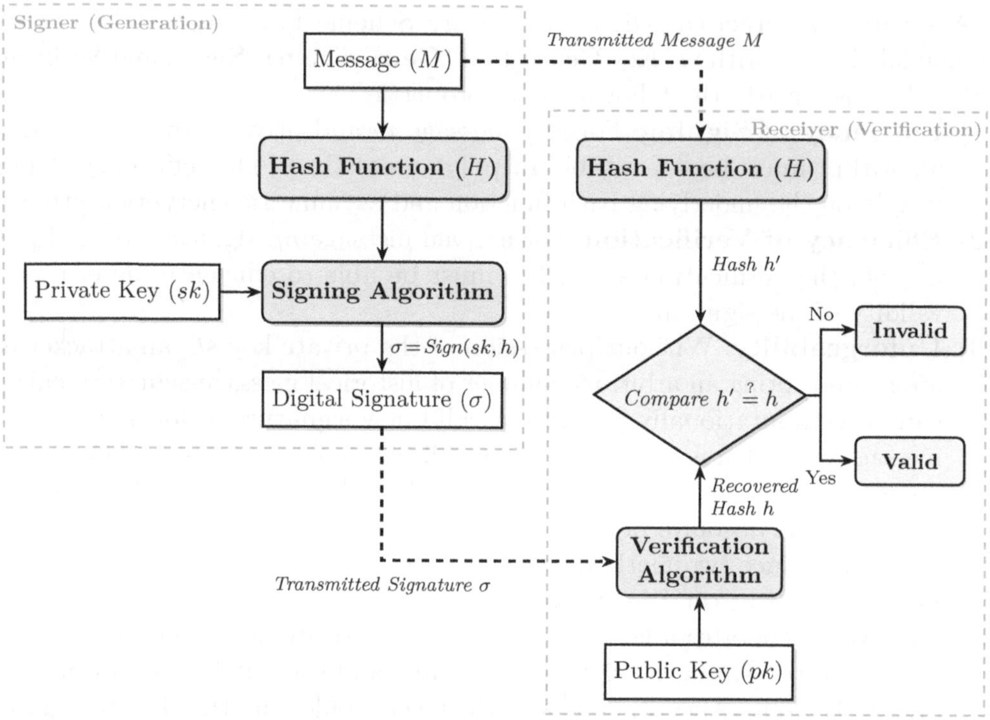

Figure 14-1: Digital Signature Process

Another reason for introducing Hash algorithms is to maintain the structural integrity of the message and defend against tampering attacks. Suppose Hash functions are not used, for a long message M, it must be split into data blocks $m_1, m_2, \ldots, m_k$ and signed individually. The data sequence sent to Bob would appear as follows:

$$m_1 \parallel m_2 \parallel \cdots \parallel m_k \parallel S(m_1) \parallel S(m_2) \parallel \cdots \parallel S(m_k) \tag{14-1}$$

Here, "$\parallel$" denotes the concatenation operator, and $S(m_k)$ represents the signature of data block m_k.

This fragmented structure introduces a catastrophic cryptographic vulnerability known as a Block Reordering Attack. Eve could maliciously intercept the transmission and alter the sequence of both the message blocks and their corresponding signatures simultaneously. For instance, she could swap block 1 and block 6, altering the sequence to the form shown in Equation 14-2:

$$m_6 \parallel m_3 \parallel \cdots \parallel m_{k-3} \parallel S(m_6) \parallel S(m_3) \parallel \cdots \parallel S(m_{k-3}) \tag{14-2}$$

Because each individual signature σ_i remains mathematically valid for its correspondingly isolated block m_i, the signature verification process for every single block will blindly succeed. However, the semantic structure of the reconstructed message M is entirely destroyed, allowing Eve to arbitrarily manipulate the document's meaning without forging any underlying cryptography. By integrating a cryptographic hash function within the Hash-then-Sign paradigm, the signature algorithm targets the globally unique digest of the entire message, drastically simplifying the transmitted data structure to:

$$M \parallel S(H(M)) \tag{14-3}$$

In this case, Eve cannot disrupt the message structure through reordering means. Simultaneously, based on the collision resistance of Hash functions, this mechanism effectively prevents forgery attacks against the file content.

14.2 RSA DIGITAL SIGNATURE SCHEME

The RSA digital signature scheme was the first proposed public-key digital signature system. It builds the signing and verification processes directly upon the RSA public-key cryptographic algorithm. Thanks to its strong security and non-repudiation properties, the RSA digital signature has been widely applied in fields such as e-commerce and e-government. However, its use may be limited in scenarios with constrained computational resources or extremely high real-time requirements.

While the standard RSA encryption algorithm ensures data confidentiality, it does not inherently provide identity authentication. To address this, the creators of RSA cleverly adapted the underlying trapdoor permutation. Rather than utilizing the private key to decrypt a ciphertext, the signer utilizes their private exponent to calculate an inverse mathematical trapdoor over the message, thereby establishing a deterministic mechanism for digital signatures. To understand the evolution of this scheme, we first introduce the Textbook RSA Signature. While conceptually foundational, it is cryptographically insecure for practical use. The specific construction process of this raw form is defined as follows:

1) (**KeyGen**): Alice chooses two large primes p and q such that $2^{L-1} < p, q < 2^L$ where $1024 \leqslant L \leqslant 2048$. Alice computes $N = p \cdot q$ and $\varphi(N) = (p-1)(q-1)$. She then selects a public exponent e such that $\gcd(e, \varphi(N)) = 1$. Finally, she computes a private exponent d such that $ed \equiv 1 \pmod{\varphi(N)}$ and keeps d secret.
2) (**Signing**): To sign a message M, where $M \in \mathbb{Z}_N$, Alice computes
$$S \equiv M^d \pmod{N} \tag{14-4}$$
and publishes the message M and the signature S.
3) (**Verifying**): Bob receives the pair (M, S). Bob uses Alice's public key (N, e) to compute
$$M' \equiv S^e \pmod{N}. \tag{14-5}$$
Bob then compares M' with the received message M. If $M' = M$, the signature is accepted as valid; otherwise, it is rejected.

The RSA digital signature process is shown in Figure 14-2. The proof is identical to that of RSA encryption (Proof 7.3.1) and is not repeated here.

Example 14.2.1 Suppose that Alice chooses $p = 463$ and $q = 997$, then calculates $N = 461611$ and $\varphi(N) = (p-1)(q-1) = 460152$. Assume Alice chooses $e = 571$, the message $M = 10000$. Show the signature and verification process.

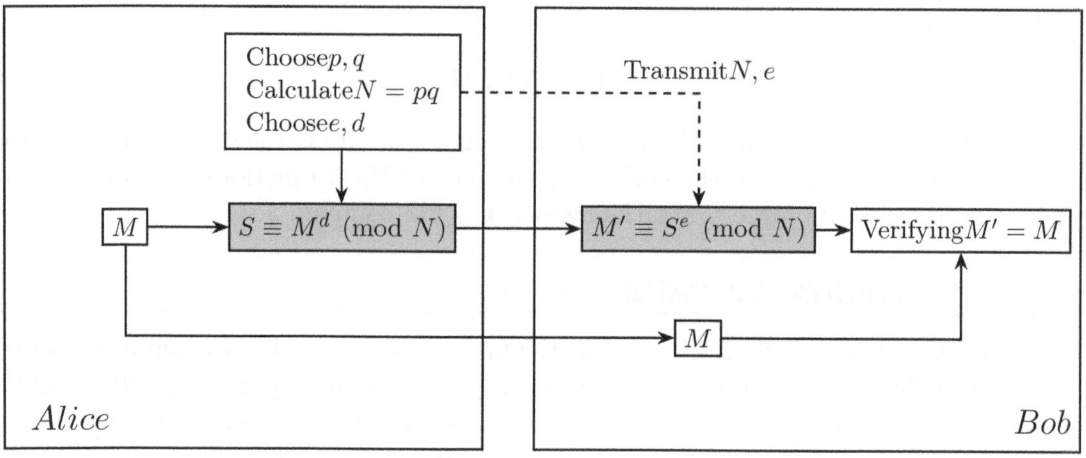

Figure 14-2: RSA Digital Signature Scheme

Solution: First, Alice computes the private exponent d such that $ed \equiv 1 \pmod{\varphi(N)}$

$$d \equiv e^{-1} \pmod{\varphi(N)} \tag{14-6}$$
$$\equiv 416635 \pmod{460152} \tag{14-7}$$

Using this private exponent, Alice generates the signature S

$$S \equiv M^d \pmod{N} \tag{14-8}$$
$$\equiv 10000^{416635} \pmod{461611} \tag{14-9}$$
$$\equiv 234362 \pmod{461611} \tag{14-10}$$

Alice transmits the message M and the signature S to Bob. Upon receipt, Bob verifies the signature by calculating

$$M' \equiv S^e \pmod{N} \tag{14-11}$$
$$\equiv 234362^{571} \pmod{461611} \tag{14-12}$$
$$\equiv 10000 \pmod{461611} \tag{14-13}$$

Since $M' = M$, Bob accepts the signature as valid. ■

It is important to note the distinction between the RSA signature scheme described earlier and the general digital signature process shown in Figure 14-1. This is because the original RSA signature scheme does not use a Hash function. Consequently, it has flaws regarding resistance to forgery and the practicality of processing long messages. To improve computational efficiency and fix security flaws, practical applications usually employ secure Hash functions, such as SHA-512, to compute a digest of the message, and then sign the digest.

The security of the RSA digital signature is identical to that of the RSA encryption system, both are established on the assumption that the integer factorization problem is hard. If an attacker can factor the modulus N into prime factors in polynomial time, they can easily calculate Alice's signature private key d and subsequently forge a valid signature for any message.

14.3 ELGAMAL DIGITAL SIGNATURE SCHEME

The ElGamal public-key cryptosystem encompasses not only an encryption scheme but also a distinct digital signature algorithm. This signature scheme was proposed by *Taher Elgamal* in 1985. Introduced subsequently to RSA, the ElGamal signature scheme initially saw less widespread adoption. It is crucial to note that while the ElGamal digital signature and encryption algorithms share the same authorship and nomenclature, their computational procedures are fundamentally different. The primary connection between the two is that their security is based on the assumption of the difficulty of the Discrete Logarithm Problem over finite fields.

Suppose Alice and Bob intend to utilize the ElGamal digital signature scheme for authentication. The specific construction process is strictly defined as follows:

1) (**KeyGen**): Alice selects a large prime p, and let r be a primitive root of p. Alice selects her private key a such that $a \in [2, p-2]$. She then calculates $v \equiv r^a \pmod{p}$. The public key is (v, r, p).
2) (**Hash**): To sign a message M, Alice applies the hash function to compute the hash value $m = H(M)$ such that $m \in [0, p-1]$.
3) (**Sign**): Alice selects a secret random integer k such that $k \in [1, p-1]$ and $\gcd(k, p-1) = 1$. Then, she calculates the signature

$$S_1 \equiv r^k \pmod{p} \tag{14-14}$$
$$S_2 \equiv (m - aS_1)k^{-1} \pmod{p-1} \tag{14-15}$$

Alice transmits the hash value m and the signature (S_1, S_2).

4) (**Verify**): Bob receives m and (S_1, S_2), then he computes

$$v^{S_1} {S_1}^{S_2} \equiv r^m \pmod{p} \tag{14-16}$$

If the Verification congruence 14-16 is congruent, the signature is valid. Otherwise, Bob rejects the signature.

For correctness, we have

$$v^{S_1} {S_1}^{S_2} \equiv (r^a)^{S_1} (r^k)^{S_2} \pmod{p} \tag{14-17}$$
$$\equiv r^{aS_1} r^{kS_2} \pmod{p} \tag{14-18}$$
$$\equiv r^{aS_1 + kS_2} \pmod{p} \tag{14-19}$$
$$\equiv r^{aS_1 + k(m - aS_1)k^{-1}} \pmod{p} \tag{14-20}$$
$$\equiv r^{aS_1 + m - aS_1} \pmod{p} \tag{14-21}$$
$$\equiv r^m \pmod{p} \tag{14-22}$$

To summarize, the prime p and the primitive root r are public parameters. In contrast, the private key a and the secret integer k are confidential and known only to Alice. The ElGamal signature process is illustrated in Figure 14-3.

Example 14.3.1 Suppose that Alice selects $p = 467, r = 2, a = 127$, the hashed message $m = 100$. Show the signature and verification process.

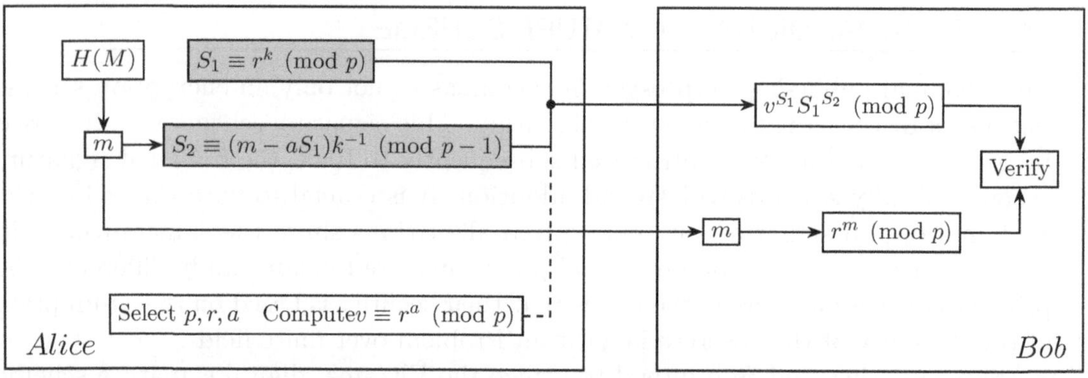

Figure 14-3: ElGamal Digital Signature Scheme

Solution: Alice selects a secret random integer k from $\{1, 2, \ldots, 466\}$, assumes $k = 11$ since $\gcd(11, 466) = 1$. First, she computes the public component v:

$$v \equiv r^a \pmod{p} \equiv 2^{127} \equiv 132 \pmod{467} \tag{14-23}$$

She then calculates the signature

$$S_1 \equiv r^k \pmod{p} \equiv 2^{11} \equiv 180 \pmod{467} \tag{14-24}$$
$$S_2 \equiv (m - aS_1)k^{-1} \pmod{p-1} \tag{14-25}$$
$$\equiv (100 - 127 \times 180)11^{-1} \tag{14-26}$$
$$\equiv -22760 \times 339 \tag{14-27}$$
$$\equiv 388 \pmod{466} \tag{14-28}$$

Alice transmits the hashed message m and the signature (S_1, S_2) to Bob. Bob receives m and (S_1, S_2). He computes

$$v^{S_1} {S_1}^{S_2} \pmod{p} \equiv 132^{180} \times 180^{388} \equiv 189 \pmod{467} \tag{14-29}$$
$$r^m \equiv 2^{100} \equiv 189 \pmod{467} \tag{14-30}$$

Since $v^{S_1} {S_1}^{S_2} \equiv r^m \pmod{p}$, the signature is valid. ■

If Eve can deploy a sufficiently advanced algorithm to solve the Discrete Logarithm Problem (DLP), they can completely break the ElGamal digital signature scheme by extracting the absolute private key a. This would seamlessly allow the adversary to forge mathematically perfect signatures for any arbitrary message, successfully deceiving Bob into accepting them. For more information regarding the security of the ElGamal digital signature scheme, please refer to Section 14.8.5 of this chapter.

14.4 SCHNORR DIGITAL SIGNATURE SCHEME

The Schnorr Digital Signature Scheme was invented by *Claus Schnorr* in 1991 [182]. It is similar to the ElGamal signature scheme, as the security of both is based on the difficulty of the Discrete Logarithm Problem. The Schnorr digital signature scheme is known for its simplicity and efficiency. While providing the same level of security as the ElGamal signature scheme, the length of a Schnorr signature is significantly shorter, which greatly reduces the computational load.

The Schnorr signature scheme proceeds as follows:

1) (KeyGen): Alice selects two large primes p and q such that $p-1 \equiv 0 \pmod{q}$, $q \geqslant 2^{160}$, $p \geqslant 2^{1024}$. Alice then selects an integer a such that $a^q \equiv 1 \pmod{p}$ and $a \neq 1$.
   (a) (PrivateKeyGen): Alice selects a random integer d with $0 < d < q$, the secret key is d.
   (b) (PublicKeyGen): Alice computes $v \equiv a^{-d} \pmod{p}$, the public key is (p, q, v, a).
2) (Sign): To sign a message M, Alice selects a random integer r with $0 < r < q$ and computes $x \equiv a^r \pmod{p}$, concatenates M with x, and hashes the result to obtain S_1

$$S_1 = H(M\|x) \tag{14-31}$$
$$S_2 \equiv r + dS_1 \pmod{q} \tag{14-32}$$

   where H can be any cryptographic hash function, such as SHA-3-512. Alice transmits the message M and the signature (S_1, S_2).
3) (Verify): Bob receives M and (S_1, S_2), he computes

$$x' \equiv a^{S_2} v^{S_1} \pmod{p} \tag{14-33}$$
$$S' = H\left(M\|x'\right) \tag{14-34}$$

   If $S_1 = S'$, the signature is valid. Otherwise, Bob rejects the signature.

For correctness, we have

$$x' \equiv a^{S_2} v^{S_1} \equiv a^{S_2} a^{-dS_1} \equiv a^{S_2 - dS_1} \equiv a^r \equiv x \pmod{p} \tag{14-35}$$
$$\Rightarrow S_1 = H(M\|x) = H(M\|x') = S' \tag{14-36}$$

To forge a Schnorr signature, an adversary must solve the DLP and breach the collision or preimage resistance of the hash function. Consequently, for equivalent key lengths, this scheme is generally considered to offer stronger provable security guarantees than the standard ElGamal signature scheme.

Example 14.4.1 Suppose that Alice selects $p = 2837, q = 709$, and wishes to sign the message $M = 100$. Show the signature and verification process.

Solution: Observe that $p - 1 = 2836 \equiv 0 \pmod{q}$. Since $256^q \equiv 1 \pmod{p}$, Alice selects an integer $a = 256$ and the secret key $d = 500$. She then computes $v \equiv a^{-d} \equiv 2687 \pmod{p}$. The public key is $(p, q, v, a) = (2837, 709, 2687, 256)$.

Alice selects a random integer $r = 88$ and computes $x \equiv a^r \equiv 13 \pmod{p}$. Assuming the hash of the concatenated message and x is $H(M\|x) = 300$, she computes

$$S_1 = H(M\|x) = 300 \tag{14-37}$$
$$S_2 \equiv r + dS_1 \equiv 489 \pmod{q} \tag{14-38}$$

Alice transmits the message M and the signature (S_1, S_2) to Bob. Bob receives M and (S_1, S_2), he computes

$$x' \equiv a^{S_2} v^{S_1} \equiv 13 \pmod{p} \tag{14-39}$$

Bob then calculates $H(M \parallel x')$. Since $H(M \parallel x') = H(100 \parallel 13) = 300$, the signature is valid. ■

14.5 DIGITAL SIGNATURE ALGORITHM

The **Digital Signature Algorithm** (DSA) is a variant of the ElGamal and Schnorr signature schemes. In 1994, the NIST adopted this scheme as the **Digital Signature Standard** (DSS), specified in FIPS-186. The security of DSA relies on the intractability of the Discrete Logarithm Problem. Upon its initial release, the scheme faced significant controversy. NIST has subsequently revised the standard multiple times, culminating in the publication of FIPS 186-5 in February 2023. In this subsection, we focus on the original formulation of DSA.

Its process is as follows:

1) (KeyGen): Alice selects two large primes p and q such that $p - 1 \equiv 0 \pmod{q}$, where $2^{L-1} < p < 2^L$ for $512 \leqslant L \leqslant 1024$ and L a multiple of 64, $2^{159} < q < 2^{160}$. She then computes

$$g \equiv h^{(p-1)/q} \pmod{p} \tag{14-40}$$

where h is any integer with $1 < h < p - 1$ such that $h^{(p-1)/q} \pmod{p} > 1$. Modern implementations under FIPS 186-5 mandate $L \geqslant 2048$ and $q \geqslant 256$ bits to resist advanced cryptanalysis

   (a) (PrivateKeyGen): Alice selects a random integer x with $0 < x < q$, the secret key is x.

   (b) (PublicKeyGen): Alice calculates $y \equiv g^x \pmod{p}$, the public key is (p, q, y, g).

2) (Sign): To sign a message M, Alice selects a random integer k such that $0 < k < q$. She computes the signature pair (S_1, S_2)

$$S_1 \equiv \left(g^k \bmod p\right) \pmod{q} \tag{14-41}$$

$$S_2 \equiv \left[k^{-1}(H(M) + xS_1)\right] \pmod{q} \tag{14-42}$$

where $H(M)$ denotes hash of M using any cryptographic hash function. Alice publishes the message M and the signature (S_1, S_2).

3) (Verify): Bob receives M and (S_1, S_2). Let M', S_1' and S_2' be the received versions of M, S_1 and S_2. Bob first verifies that $0 < S_1', S_2' < q$. If not, he rejects the signature. Otherwise, he computes

$$w \equiv (S_2')^{-1} \pmod{q} \tag{14-43}$$

$$u_1 \equiv [H(M')\, w] \pmod{q} \tag{14-44}$$

$$u_2 \equiv S_1' w \pmod q \tag{14-45}$$
$$v \equiv [(g^{u_1} y^{u_2}) \bmod p] \pmod q \tag{14-46}$$

If $v = S_1'$, the signature is valid. Otherwise, Bob rejects the signature.

Example 14.5.1 Suppose that Alice chooses $p = 9817$, $q = 409$ and $h = 135$. The hashed message $H(M) = 500$. Show the signature and verification process.
Solution: Since $p - 1 \equiv 9816 \equiv 0 \pmod q$, Alice computes $g \equiv h^{24} \equiv 4857 \pmod p$.

Alice selects $x = 279$ as the private key and computes $y \equiv 4857^{279} \equiv 6450 \pmod p$. The public key is $(p, q, y, g) = (9817, 409, 6450, 4857)$.

Alice selects a random integer $k = 188$, the signature is

$$S_1 \equiv \left(g^k \bmod p\right) \equiv 279 \pmod q \tag{14-47}$$
$$S_2 \equiv \left[k^{-1}(H(M) + xS_1)\right] \equiv 284 \pmod q \tag{14-48}$$

Although $H(M) = 500 > q$, the modulo arithmetic seamlessly reduces it within the $\pmod q$ operation. In formal FIPS implementation, the leftmost bits of the hash are algorithmically truncated if its bit-length exceeds that of q. Bob receives M and (S_1, S_2). Let M', S_1' and S_2' be the received versions of M, S_1 and S_2. Since $0 < S_1', S_2' < q$, he then computes

$$w \equiv (S_2')^{-1} \equiv 373 \pmod q \tag{14-49}$$
$$u_1 \equiv [H(M')\, w] \equiv 405 \pmod q \tag{14-50}$$
$$u_2 \equiv S_1' w \equiv 181 \pmod q \tag{14-51}$$
$$v \equiv [(g^{u_1} y^{u_2}) \bmod p] \equiv 279 \pmod q \tag{14-52}$$

Since $v = S_1'$, the signature is valid. ■

To ensure the security of DSA, NIST specified four sets of lengths, as shown in Table 14-1.

Table 14-1: Selection of Parameter Sizes For DSA

L (bit-length of p)	N (bit-length of q)	Hash Function
1024	160	SHA-1
2048	224	SHA-224
2048	256	SHA-256
3072	256	SHA-256

DSA has been removed from the latest standard, FIPS 186-5, and replaced by ECDSA and EdDSA.

14.6 ELLIPTIC CURVE DIGITAL SIGNATURE ALGORITHM

The **Elliptic Curve Digital Signature Algorithm** (ECDSA) is the elliptic curve analogue of the DSA. The concept of Elliptic Curve Cryptography (ECC) was independently proposed by *Neal Koblitz* and *Victor Miller* in 1985, establishing the mathematical groundwork for ECDSA [183].

As one of the most prevalent public-key signature schemes, ECDSA has been incorporated into numerous international standards, including ANSI X9.62, FIPS 186-2, IEEE 1363-2000, and ISO/IEC 15946-2. In the latest Digital Signature Standard, FIPS 186-5, released by NIST in February 2023, ECDSA retains a central role. A primary advantage of ECDSA over traditional algorithms like RSA is its ability to provide equivalent security with substantially shorter key lengths. This characteristic effectively reduces storage requirements and enhances computational efficiency.

ECDSA and deterministic ECDSA are defined for two finite fields: $\mathrm{GF}(2^m)$ and $\mathrm{GF}(p)$ with p is an odd prime. We consider prime curves, the ECDSA procedures are described below:

1) (KeyGen): Alice selects a large prime p and an elliptic curve $E_p : y^2 \equiv x^3 + Ax + B \pmod{p}$, the coefficients $A, B \in \mathbb{Z}_p$. To ensure rigorous cryptographic security, the curve must satisfy the non-singularity condition: $4A^3 + 27B^2 \not\equiv 0 \pmod{p}$. Let G be a base point on the curve with prime **order** n.
   (a) (PrivateKeyGen): Alice selects a random integer d with $0 < d < n$. The secret key is d.
   (b) (PublicKeyGen): Alice computes $Q = dG$. The public key is the point Q.
2) (Sign): To sign a message M, Alice selects another random integer k with $0 < k < n$, then computes $P = kG = (x, y)$ where x is the x-coordinate of the affine representation of the point P. The signature is

$$S_1 \equiv x \pmod{n} \tag{14-53}$$

$$S_2 \equiv k^{-1}(H(M) + dS_1) \pmod{n} \tag{14-54}$$

   If $S_1 = 0$ or $S_2 = 0$, Alice reselects k and recompute. Here, $H(M)$ is hash of M using SHA-3. Alice transmits the message M and the signature (S_1, S_2).
3) (Verify): Bob receives M and (S_1, S_2). Bob first verifies that $0 < S_1, S_2 < n$. If not, he rejects the signature. Otherwise, he computes

$$u_1 \equiv H(M)S_2^{-1} \pmod{n} \tag{14-55}$$

$$u_2 \equiv S_1 S_2^{-1} \pmod{n} \tag{14-56}$$

$$R = u_1 G + u_2 Q = (x_R, y_R) \tag{14-57}$$

   If $R = \mathcal{O}$, Bob rejects the signature else Bob computes $v \equiv x_R \pmod{n}$. If $v = S_1$, the signature is valid. Otherwise, Bob rejects the signature. The ECDSA process is illustrated in Figure 14-4.

For correctness, we have

$$S_2 \equiv k^{-1}(H(M) + dS_1) \pmod{n} \tag{14-58}$$

Then

$$k \equiv S_2^{-1}(H(M) + dS_1) \pmod{n} \tag{14-59}$$

$$\equiv H(M)S_2^{-1} + dS_1 S_2^{-1} \pmod{n} \tag{14-60}$$

$$\equiv u_1 + du_2 \pmod{n} \tag{14-61}$$

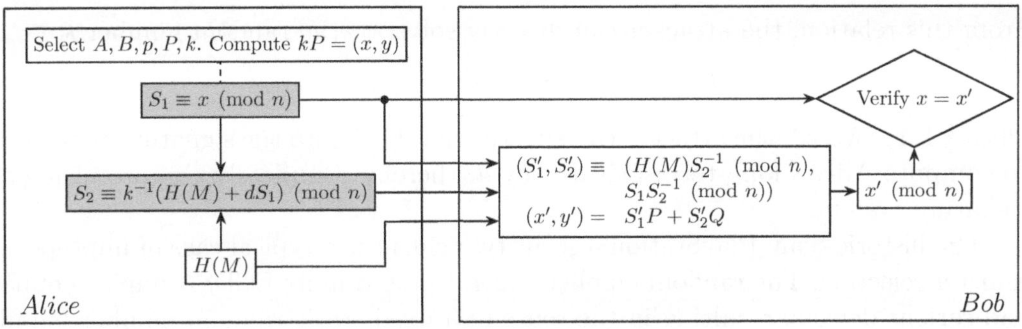

Figure 14-4: ECDSA Process

Thus

$$u_1G + u_2Q = u_1G + u_2(dG) = (u_1 + du_2)G = kG \tag{14-62}$$

Let $R' = kG = (x_1, y_1)$, the x-coordinate of R' is x_1 must exactly equal x. Recall that the verification variable is defined as $v \equiv x_R \pmod{n}$. Therefore, the value v computed by the verifier mathematically perfectly satisfies $v \equiv x \equiv S_1 \pmod{n}$, unequivocally confirming the validity of the signature.

In the ECDSA digital signature verification protocol, the primary step is to verify whether the signature components S_1 and S_2 both fall within the interval $[1, n-1]$. If this step is omitted, the ECDSA scheme is exposed to **trivial forgery attacks**.

Furthermore, the security of ECDSA relies fundamentally on the primality of the group order n. The generation of the signature component s requires the computation of a modular inverse modulo n. If n is composite, the **Pohlig-Hellman attack** can be employed to decompose the Discrete Logarithm Problem into subproblems over subgroups of smaller order. This decomposition significantly reduces the computational complexity required to break the system. Consequently, standard ECDSA implementations must utilize subgroups of prime order.

During the signature generation process, the selection of the random number k is crucial. The number k must be generated using a cryptographically secure method and remain strictly secret. A catastrophic failure occurs if the same k is reused to sign two distinct messages, M and M', with hash values e and e'. Since the value $S_1 = x \bmod n$ depends solely on k, the resulting signatures will take the form (S_1, S_2) and (S_1, S_2'). An attacker observing the identical S_1 component can algebraically recover the private key d.

Given that the ephemeral key k is identical, the linear relationships for the two signatures are

$$S_2 \equiv k^{-1}(e + dS_1) \pmod{n} \tag{14-63}$$
$$S_2' \equiv k^{-1}(e' + dS_1) \pmod{n} \tag{14-64}$$

Subtracting the second congruence from the first eliminates the term involving the private key d

$$S_2 - S_2' \equiv k^{-1}(e + dS_1) - k^{-1}(e' + dS_1) \pmod{n} \tag{14-65}$$
$$\equiv k^{-1}(e - e') \pmod{n} \tag{14-66}$$

From this relation, the attacker can directly solve for the random number k

$$k \equiv (e - e')(S_2 - S_2')^{-1} \pmod{n} \tag{14-67}$$

Once k is recovered, the attacker can substitute it back into the signature congruence to compute Alice's long-term private key d, thereby completely compromising the signature system.

The historic Sony PlayStation 3 security incident is a typical case of improper parameter selection. The random number generator used in its ECDSA implementation had serious defects, resulting in the reuse of a fixed static random number (similar to $k = 4$) across different signing processes. Hackers used the algebraic relationship described above to quickly recover the private key, leading to a complete system compromise and huge economic losses. This vulnerability was not fixed until the PlayStation 4 era.

This demonstrates that improper curve parameters, base point selection, or low-quality random number generators can all lead to the collapse of ECDSA security. Therefore, it is essential to ensure that the random number k is strictly random and used only once per signature. Any form of reuse or leakage will directly lead to the exposure of the private key.

Example 14.6.1 Suppose that Alice chooses an elliptic curve $E_{23} : y^2 \equiv x^3 - 2x + 15 \pmod{23}$ with order $n = 23$. The hashed message $H(M) = 10$. She then selects a base point $G = (4, 5)$. Show the signature and verification process.
Solution: Alice selects $d = 3$ as her secret key and calculates $Q = dG = (13, 22)$.

To sign the hashed message M, Alice selects $k = 19$, then computes $P = kG = (9, 17)$. Therefore

$$S_1 \equiv 9 \pmod{23} \tag{14-68}$$
$$S_2 \equiv k^{-1}(H(M) + dS_1) \equiv 19^{-1}(10 + 3 \cdot 9) \equiv 8 \pmod{23} \tag{14-69}$$

Alice transmits the message M and the signature (S_1, S_2) to Bob.

Bob receives M and (S_1, S_2). Since $0 < S_1, S_2 < n$, he then computes

$$\begin{aligned}(u_1, u_2) &\equiv (H(M)S_2^{-1} \pmod{n}, S_1S_2^{-1} \pmod{n}) && (14\text{-}70)\\ &\equiv (10 \cdot 8^{-1} \pmod{n}, 9 \cdot 8^{-1} \pmod{n}) && (14\text{-}71)\\ &\equiv (10 \cdot 3 \pmod{23}, 4 \pmod{23}) && (14\text{-}72)\\ &\equiv (7, 4) \pmod{23} && (14\text{-}73)\end{aligned}$$

Then

$$R = u_1G + u_2Q = 7(4, 5) + 4(13, 22) = (17, 8) + (10, 12) = (9, 17) \tag{14-74}$$

Since $v \equiv x_R \equiv 9 \equiv S_1 \pmod{n}$, the signature is valid. ■

Due to the slow computational speed of ECDSA and the requirement to store large amounts of signature data, the high costs made service providers reluctant to use it. Consequently, in 2021, ECDSA was upgraded to the elliptic curve version of the Schnorr digital signature scheme, known as EC-Schnorr. This upgrade significantly improved efficiency.

14.7 GGH DIGITAL SIGNATURE SCHEME

In 1997, *Goldreich*, *Goldwasser*, and *Halevi* proposed the first framework for constructing digital signatures based on lattice theory, commonly referred to as the GGH signature scheme. This scheme established the fundamental paradigm of utilizing the geometric properties of lattices to design digital signatures. However, the GGH scheme did not establish a rigorous security proof in theory. Specifically, its unforgeability cannot be mathematically reduced to any specific hard lattice problem. From an algorithmic perspective, the signature generation process of the GGH scheme is equivalent to solving the Approximate Closest Vector Problem on a lattice. The output digital signature corresponds to an approximate solution to this problem.

Its process is as follows:

1) (KeyGen): Let n be the security parameter that is the dimension of the lattice.
   (a) (PrivateKeyGen): Alice selects a set of n linearly independent vectors $\mathbf{v}_1, \mathbf{v}_2, \ldots, \mathbf{v}_n \in \mathbb{Z}^n$ that are short and nearly orthogonal. These vectors form the "good" basis, represented as $\mathbf{V} = [\mathbf{v}_1, \ldots, \mathbf{v}_n]$. The lattice $\mathcal{L}$ is defined as

$$\mathcal{L}(\mathbf{V}) = \{\mathbf{V}\mathbf{x} \mid \mathbf{x} \in \mathbb{Z}^n\} \tag{14-75}$$

   The secret key is the "good" basis $\mathbf{V}$.
   (b) (PublicKeyGen): Alice selects a unimodular matrix $\mathbf{U}$ satisfying $\det(\mathbf{U}) = \pm 1$, and computes $\mathbf{W} = \mathbf{V}\mathbf{U}$ where $\mathbf{W} = [\mathbf{w_1}, \mathbf{w_2}, \ldots, \mathbf{w_n}]$ for $\mathcal{L}$ is a "bad" basis. The "bad" basis is as her public key.
2) (Sign): To securely sign an arbitrary message m, Alice first applies a hash function H that maps the message directly into the n-dimensional Euclidean space, obtaining a target vector $\mathbf{M} = H(m) \in \mathbb{Z}^n$. Alice uses Babai's algorithm with her private basis $\mathbf{V}$ to compute a lattice point $\mathbf{t} \in \mathcal{L}$ that is close to $\mathbf{M}$. Alice expresses this lattice point $\mathbf{t}$ as a linear combination of the public basis $\mathbf{W}$. She solves for integers $s_1, s_2, \ldots, s_n$ such that

$$\mathbf{t} = s_1\mathbf{w}_1 + s_2\mathbf{w}_2 + \cdots + s_n\mathbf{w}_n \tag{14-76}$$

   Alice transmits the message $\mathbf{M}$ and the signature $\mathbf{s} = (s_1, s_2, \ldots, s_n)$.
3) (Verify): Bob receives m and the signature vector $\mathbf{s}$. He first independently recomputes the target vector $\mathbf{M} = H(m)$. He then uses the public basis $\mathbf{W}$ and the received coefficients to reconstruct the lattice point:

$$\mathbf{M}' = s_1\mathbf{w}_1 + s_2\mathbf{w}_2 + \cdots + s_n\mathbf{w}_n \tag{14-77}$$

   If $\mathbf{M}'$ is sufficiently close to $\mathbf{M}$ such that $\|\mathbf{M}' - \mathbf{M}\| < \epsilon$, the signature is valid. Otherwise, Bob rejects the signature.

The choice of threshold ϵ is not a fixed constant. Instead, ϵ is selected accordingly based on the lattice basis and the vectors. If the lattice dimension n is large, the threshold ϵ can be set to

$$\epsilon = \sqrt{n}\sigma(\mathcal{L}) \approx \frac{n(\det \mathcal{L})^{1/n}}{\sqrt{2\pi e}} \tag{14-78}$$

If the lattice dimension n is small, the threshold ϵ is derived from the volume formula of the n-dimensional ball

$$\epsilon = \sqrt{n}\sigma(\mathcal{L}) = \sqrt{n}\left(\frac{det(\mathcal{L})}{C_n}\right)^{1/n} \tag{14-79}$$

where for even numbers $n = 2k$, $C_n = \frac{\pi^k}{k!}$. For odd numbers $n = 2k+1$, $C_n = \frac{2^{2k+1}k!\pi^k}{(2k+1)!}$. The GGH digital signature process is illustrated in Figure 14-5.

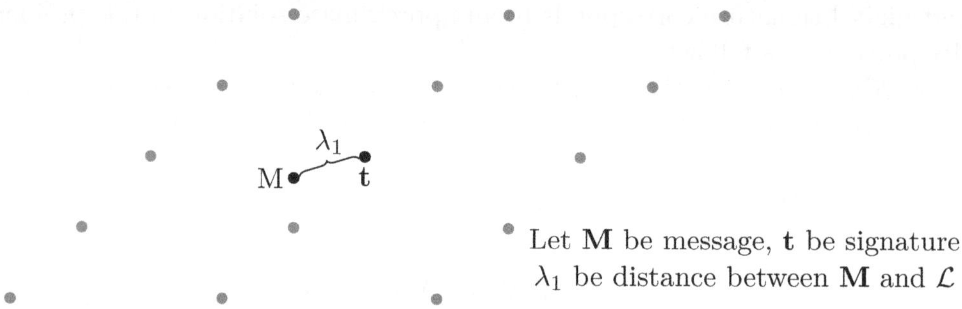

Figure 14-5: GGH Digital Signature Scheme

Example 14.7.1 Suppose that Alice selects a good basis $\mathbf{V} = \begin{bmatrix} 13 & 16 & 93 \\ 92 & 2 & 30 \\ 4 & 78 & 25 \end{bmatrix}$ and a bad basis $\mathbf{W} = \begin{bmatrix} -11 & -47 & 102 \\ 4 & 17 & 37 \\ 3 & 12 & 28 \end{bmatrix}$. The hashed message $\mathbf{h} = (23523, 42125, 11412)$. Show the signature and verification process.

Solution: Alice uses Babai's algorithm to find a vector $\mathbf{t} \in \mathcal{L}$ that is close to $\mathbf{h}$

$$\lfloor \mathbf{hV}^{-1} \rceil \approx \begin{bmatrix} -106 & 247 & 556 \end{bmatrix}$$
$$\mathbf{t} = \lfloor \mathbf{hV}^{-1} \rceil \times \mathbf{V} = \begin{bmatrix} 23570 & 42166 & 11452 \end{bmatrix}$$

She then expresses $\mathbf{t}$ in terms of the bad basis

$$\mathbf{s} = \mathbf{tW}^{-1} = \begin{bmatrix} 677718 & 1981040 & -148564 \end{bmatrix}$$

Since $n = 3$, the threshold $\epsilon = \sqrt{n}\sigma(\mathcal{L}) = \sqrt{3}\left(\frac{3det(\mathcal{L})}{4\pi}\right)^{1/3} \approx 90.72$.

Alice sends the hashed message $\mathbf{h}$ and the signature $\mathbf{s}$ to Bob. Bob receives $\mathbf{h}$ and $\mathbf{s}$ and calculates

$$\mathbf{M}' = \mathbf{sW} = \begin{bmatrix} 23570 & 42166 & 11452 \end{bmatrix}$$
$$||\mathbf{M}' - \mathbf{h}|| \approx 74.09 < \epsilon$$

Since $||\mathbf{M}' - \mathbf{h}|| \approx 74.09 < \epsilon$, the signature is valid. ■

The GGH signature scheme is considered broken and is no longer used due to Nguyen's attack in 1999. It has been superseded by modern, secure lattice-based standards like FALCON or Dilithium, which use techniques like Gaussian sampling to prevent this information leakage.

14.8 SECURITY ANALYSIS OF DIGITAL SIGNATURES

Digital signature mechanisms are ubiquitous in critical domains such as internet security, e-commerce, and financial transactions. Their primary objectives are to ensure **identity authentication**, **data integrity**, and **non-repudiation**. However, like all cryptographic primitives, digital signature schemes are susceptible to various categories of attacks. A successful compromise can undermine the foundation of trust between communicating parties, potentially leading to severe information security breaches and financial losses.

It is crucial to clarify that the design intent of digital signature technology is to *detect* tampering rather than to physically *prevent* it. While Eve may possess the capability to intercept and modify the message or signature during transmission, a robust scheme ensures that such tampering is inevitably detected during the verification phase. If the message or signature has been altered, the verification algorithm outputs a failure result, prompting the receiver to reject the data. Even if the attacker attempts to modify both the message and the signature simultaneously, the strict **avalanche effect** of the cryptographic hash function ensures that even a minute alteration in the input results in a drastically different digest. Without access to the private key, it is computationally infeasible for the attacker to compute a valid signature for this new digest. Consequently, the hash function employed must exhibit strong collision resistance to preclude substitution attacks.

Common attack patterns against digital signature systems are classified as follows:

1) **Brute-force Attack**. The attacker exhaustively traverses the entire key space, attempting to discover the correct private key. Given the key length of modern standards, this is generally computationally infeasible.
2) **Key-only Attack**. The attacker only knows the public key released by Alice. The attacker makes use of this fact and tries to forge the signature of Alice and Alice cannot deny signing it. However, this is the scenario with the highest difficulty for the attacker.
3) **Known-message Attack**. The attacker has access to a set of message-signature pairs. He tries to create a new message and a valid signature for it.
4) **Chosen-message Attack**. The attacker can force the signer to sign specific messages selected by the attacker. He tries to create a new message and a valid signature for it. By analyzing the generated signatures, the adversary attempts to extract the private key or forge a signature for a target message they did not explicitly query. Resisting this attack is the gold standard for modern schemes, known formally as Existential Unforgeability under Chosen-message Attacks (EUF-CMA).

5) **Man-in-the-Middle Attack**. The attacker impersonates a trusted third party in the communication process, then steals, tampers with, or forges communication content without detection by either communicating party.
6) **Key Theft Attack**. Without cryptanalysis, the attacker directly steals the private key file from the user through physical intrusion, Trojan horse implantation, or social engineering.
7) **Replay Attack**. The attacker intercepts a signed message and subsequently sends this signed message repeatedly with malicious or fraudulent intent, causing the receiver to accept the verification, such as duplicate fund transfers.
8) **Fault Attack**. The attacker deliberately introduces faults during the signature generation or verification process, causing the signature to be invalid or leading to the forgery of a new signature.
9) **Dictionary Attack**. The attacker repeatedly tries different words or phrases, attempting to determine the private key since these keys are generated from or protected by a weak password.

Next, we will provide a detailed mathematical analysis of representative key attack methods.

14.8.1 Key-only Attack

In the Key-only Attack, Eve has access only to Alice's public key and cannot obtain any historical signature samples. For the RSA digital signature scheme, if Eve attempts to recover the private key d from the public key (N, e) to achieve a Total Break, she must solve the Integer Factorization Problem. It is known that the generation of the RSA private key relies on Euler's totient function $\varphi(N)$, the formula for which is given by

$$\varphi(N) = (p-1)(q-1) = pq - p - q + 1 = N - (p+q) + 1 \tag{14-80}$$

The above equation tells us that computing $\varphi(N)$ is mathematically identical to factoring N. If Eve somehow obtains $\varphi(N)$, she instantaneously derives the sum of the primes $p + q = N - \varphi(N) + 1$. Since their product $N = pq$ is public knowledge, Eve can trivially recover the absolute prime factors p and q by finding the roots of the simple quadratic equation $x^2 - (p+q)x + pq = 0$.

If Eve can successfully factor the modulus N into two prime factors p and q, she can directly calculate $\varphi(N)$. Subsequently, she can use the Extended Euclidean Algorithm to determine the private key exponent d, thereby gaining the ability to impersonate Alice and sign arbitrary messages. However, as long as the key length selected by Alice complies with security standards, the Integer Factorization Problem is computationally infeasible.

Similarly, for the ElGamal digital signature scheme and the ECDSA, their resistance to Key-only Attacks is based on the intractability of the Finite Field Discrete Logarithm Problem and the Elliptic Curve Discrete Logarithm Problem. As long as users strictly adhere to parameter selection standards and manage keys properly, Key-only Attacks usually do not pose a substantial threat to modern digital signature schemes.

14.8.2 Man-in-the-Middle Attack

Digital signature schemes are vulnerable to Man-in-the-Middle (**MITM**) attacks during the public key distribution phase. In this model, Eve fully controls the communication channel between Alice and Bob. By substituting the public keys exchanged between the parties, Eve can impersonate Alice to Bob and Bob to Alice, thereby manipulating the communication without detection.

A simplified example of a Man-in-the-Middle attack is as follows:

1) Eve intercepts the network channel, cutting off direct communication between Alice (a user) and Bob (a bank). All data packets pass through Eve.
2) Alice attempts to send her public key to Bob. Eve intercepts this key and transmits her own public key to Bob, claiming it belongs to Alice. Consequently, Bob mistakenly binds Eve's public key to Alice's identity.
3) Alice uses her private key to sign a transaction instruction M ("transfer \$100 to Nicole") and sends the signature to Bob.
4) Eve intercepts and discards Alice's message. She then creates a forged instruction M' ("transfer \$10,000 to Eve") and generates a valid signature using her own private key.
5) Eve transmits the forged pair to Bob. Bob verifies the signature using the public key he received (Eve's key). Since the signature corresponds to that key, the verification algorithm succeeds. Relying on the non-repudiation property, Bob executes the fraudulent transfer.

Ultimately, Alice suffers financial loss while Eve gains illicit profit. Note that Eve does not break Alice's private key; rather, she attacks the trust model of public key distribution. Simply attaching a hash of the public key is insufficient, as the adversary can also replace the hash. To prevent MITM attacks, a trusted third party, such as a Certificate Authority (CA), is required to cryptographically bind public keys to user identities via digital certificates.

14.8.3 Known-message Attack

In the Known-message Attack model, the adversary Eve intercepts k valid message-signature pairs (M_i, S_i) signed by Alice, where $1 \leqslant i \leqslant k$. Using this data, Eve attempts to construct a new valid signature without knowledge of the private key.

For the *Textbook* RSA signature scheme, Eve can exploit its multiplicative property. If Eve collects k signatures, she calculates $M \equiv \prod_{i=1}^{k} M_i \pmod N$ and $S \equiv \prod_{i=1}^{k} S_i \pmod N$. The validity of the forged signature is derived as follows:

$$S \equiv S_1 \times S_2 \times \cdots \times S_k \pmod N \tag{14-81}$$

$$\equiv M_1^d \times M_2^d \times \cdots \times M_k^d \pmod N \tag{14-82}$$

$$\equiv (M_1 \times M_2 \times \cdots \times M_k)^d \pmod N \tag{14-83}$$

$$\equiv M^d \pmod N \tag{14-84}$$

This derivation proves that S is a valid digital signature for the message M. Consequently, Eve can transmit the forged pair (M, S) to Bob. The verification algorithm will accept the signature, leading Bob to attribute the message M to Alice. This attack demonstrates that textbook RSA is vulnerable to *existential forgery*. Although the constructed message M may lack semantic meaning, this vulnerability is sufficient to undermine the scheme's security guarantees.

14.8.4 Chosen-message Attack

The Chosen-message Attack represents a more powerful threat model than the Known-message Attack. In this scenario, the adversary, Eve, possesses access to a *signing oracle*. This allows her to obtain valid digital signatures for specific messages of her choice. By analyzing the mathematical correlation between these chosen messages and their signatures, Eve aims to either extract the private key directly or construct a valid signature for a new, unqueried message.

Furthermore, Eve can exploit the homomorphic properties inherent in certain schemes to combine multiple message-signature pairs. Consequently, she can synthesize a valid signature for a new message, deceiving Bob into accepting the verification.

In practical scenarios, Eve often employs deceptive tactics to induce Alice into signing arbitrary, structured data. To mitigate such risks, it is essential to strictly regulate signing operations. Specifically, users should refuse to sign or authenticate raw data of unknown origin, preventing attackers from exploiting the mathematical structure of the signature scheme.

14.8.5 Forgery Attack

The ElGamal digital signature scheme is susceptible to distinct forgery attacks if implemented incorrectly. To break the ElGamal signature, it is typically necessary to find a solution that satisfies the following congruence:

$$v^{S_1} {S_1}^{S_2} \equiv r^M \pmod{p} \tag{14-85}$$

Alternatively, an attacker could attempt to recover the private key by solving the DLP

$$S_2 = \log_{S_1}(r^M v^{-S_1}) \tag{14-86}$$

where p is prime, $v \equiv r^a \pmod{p}$, a is the private key, r is a primitive root modulo p, M is the message, (S_1, S_2) is signature. Given the intractability of the DLP, directly solving for the private key is computationally infeasible. However, if the signature scheme does not implement a hash function, Eve can utilize the algebraic relationships between parameters to construct a forged signature.

Suppose Eve has intercepted a valid signature pair (S_1, S_2) generated by Alice for an unhashed message M. Eve can construct a set of valid signatures for a new message M' without knowledge of the private key [184].

Eve selects three integers $i, j, k \in \mathbb{Z}$ satisfying $0 \leqslant i, j, k \leqslant p-2$ and $\gcd(iS_1 - kS_2, p-1) = 1$, then computes

$$x \equiv S_1^i r^j v^k \pmod{p} \tag{14-87}$$

$$y \equiv S_2 x (iS_1 - kS_2)^{-1} \pmod{p-1} \tag{14-88}$$

$$M' \equiv x(iM + jS_2)(iS_1 - kS_2)^{-1} \pmod{p-1} \tag{14-89}$$

Then the (x, y) are a valid signature pair on message M'. To determine x, y, M', since $x \equiv S_1^i r^j v^k \pmod{p}$, if (x, y) is a valid signature pair on message M', then it should satisfy

$$r^{M'} \equiv v^x x^y \pmod{p} \tag{14-90}$$
$$\equiv v^x (S_1^i r^j v^k)^y \pmod{p} \tag{14-91}$$
$$\equiv v^{x+ky} S_1^{iy} r^{jy} \pmod{p} \tag{14-92}$$

To ensure the verification equation holds, we need to find a parameter t such that $v^{x+ky} S_1^{iy} \equiv (v^{S_1} S_1^{S_2})^t \equiv r^{Mt} \pmod{p}$. By comparing the coefficients in the exponent of the primitive root r, we establish the following system of linear congruence equations:

$$v^{x+ky} S_1^{iy} = r^M = (v^{S_1} S_1{}^{S_2})^t \tag{14-93}$$

To ensure the verification congruence holds, we need to find a parameter t such that:

$$v^{x+ky} S_1^{iy} \equiv (v^{S_1} S_1^{S_2})^t \equiv r^{Mt} \pmod{p} \tag{14-94}$$

By comparing the coefficients in the exponent of the primitive root r modulo $p-1$, we establish the following system of linear congruence:

$$x + ky \equiv S_1 t \pmod{p-1} \tag{14-95}$$
$$iy \equiv S_2 t \pmod{p-1} \tag{14-96}$$

To eliminate the parameter t and solve for y, we multiply congruence 14-96 by S_2 and substitute $S_2 t$ with iy:

$$S_2(x + ky) \equiv S_2(S_1 t) \pmod{p-1} \tag{14-97}$$
$$\equiv S_2 t S_1 \pmod{p-1} \tag{14-98}$$
$$\equiv iy S_1 \pmod{p-1} \tag{14-99}$$
$$\Rightarrow S_2 x \equiv (iS_1 - kS_2)y \pmod{p-1} \tag{14-100}$$
$$\Rightarrow y \equiv (S_2 x)(iS_1 - kS_2)^{-1} \pmod{p-1} \tag{14-101}$$

Eve solves for the coefficient t utilizing congruence 14-96:

$$t \equiv iy S_2^{-1} \equiv ix(iS_1 - kS_2)^{-1} \pmod{p-1} \tag{14-102}$$

Once the parameter t is determined, she then finds the value of M' by congruence 14-92:

$$r^{M'} \equiv v^{x+ky} S_1^{iy} r^{jy} \pmod{p} \tag{14-103}$$
$$\equiv (r^M)^t r^{jy} \pmod{p} \tag{14-104}$$
$$\Rightarrow M' \equiv tM + jy \pmod{p-1} \tag{14-105}$$
$$\equiv M[(ix)(iS_1 - kS_2)^{-1}] + j[(S_2 x)(iS_1 - kS_2)^{-1}] \pmod{p-1} \tag{14-106}$$
$$\equiv (x(iM + jS_2))(iS_1 - kS_2)^{-1} \pmod{p-1} \tag{14-107}$$

Here the (x, y) is a valid signature pair on message M'. In addition to the forgery attack described above, the ElGamal signature scheme imposes extremely high requirements on the uniqueness of the random number k. If Alice reuses the same random number k when signing two different messages M_1, M_2, Eve can directly recover the private key a, even if a hash function is used.

Suppose Alice generates two signature pairs (S_1, S_2) and (S_1, S_2') with the same k. Since the random number k is the same, the first component of the signature $S_1 \equiv r^k \pmod p$ must be identical. The signature congruences are:

$$S_2 \equiv k^{-1}\left(H\left(M_1\right) - aS_1\right) \pmod{p-1} \tag{14-108}$$

$$S_2' \equiv k^{-1}\left(H\left(M_2\right) - aS_1\right) \pmod{p-1} \tag{14-109}$$

where H denotes the hash function. Subtracting the two congruences eliminates the private key a:

$$(S_2 - S_2')k \equiv H(M_1) - H(M_2) \pmod{p-1} \tag{14-110}$$

If $\gcd(S_2 - S_2', p-1) = 1$, the random number k can be directly solved:

$$k \equiv \left(H\left(M_1\right) - H\left(M_2\right)\right)\left(S_2 - S_2'\right)^{-1} \pmod{p-1} \tag{14-111}$$

Once k is obtained, Eve can substitute it into congruence 14-108 or congruence 14-109 to calculate the private key a:

$$a \equiv \left(H\left(M_1\right) - S_2k\right)(S_1)^{-1} \pmod{p-1} \tag{14-112}$$

If $\gcd(S_1, p-1) \neq 1$, the inverse S_1^{-1} does not strictly exist. Instead, the linear congruence yields exactly d mathematically valid candidates for the private key a. Since d is typically a very small integer, Eve can trivially brute-force these candidates to pinpoint the true private key.

At this point, the private key is completely compromised, allowing Eve to impersonate Alice and sign any message. Therefore, in ElGamal, the random number k must possess high entropy and must strictly never be reused. Furthermore, strict checks on boundary conditions, such as $0 < S_1 < p$, are required to prevent other types of forgery threats, such as the Bleichenbacher's attack [185].

14.9 CERTIFICATES

14.9.1 Certificate Usage Process

Digital signature technology effectively provides identity authentication, message integrity verification, and non-repudiation services, encompassing the key elements of an information security assurance system. This significantly reduces trust costs in network communication environments and improves interaction efficiency. However, an absolute prerequisite for the security of a digital signature is that the public key held by Bob must truly belong to the claimed Alice. If the public key distribution channel lacks an authentication mechanism, leading Bob to acquire a forged public key replaced by an attacker, the system is vulnerable to Man-in-the-Middle attacks, causing the digital signature scheme to fail completely.

Therefore, on top of the basic process shown in Figure 14-1, a public key verification phase must be introduced. The core idea to solve this problem is to treat the public key as a data file to be authenticated and submit it to a trusted third-party organization for a digital signature, thereby providing an endorsement of the authenticity of the public key's source. This mechanism is known as **digital certificate** technology. A digital certificate is essentially a digitally signed file containing public key information and the owner's identity information, aimed at providing a mathematical proof of the public key's legitimacy.

Digital certificates are issued by a Certificate Authority (CA). The CA is a third-party authoritative organization mutually trusted by all communicating parties in the network environment. A certificate containing a user's public key issued by a CA is usually referred to as a Public-key Certificate (PKC). When Bob verifies the validity of the certificate, he can be assured that the public key contained therein indeed belongs to Alice.

The application flow for certificate-based digital signatures is as follows:

1) Alice runs the key generation algorithm to obtain a public key and a private key.
2) Alice sends a Certificate Signing Request, containing her public key and identity information, generating a formal Certificate Signing Request (CSR), to the Certificate Authority (CA).
3) The CA authenticates Alice's identity.
4) Upon successful verification, the CA signs Alice's public key and identity using its own private key, issuing a digital certificate.
5) Bob obtains the certificate and verifies its validity using the CA's public key. If the verification passes, Bob accepts Alice's public key as authentic.

14.9.2 Entity Authentication Schemes

During the process of public key registration and certificate application, to prevent Eve from executing Man-in-the-Middle attacks or forging identities, the CA must perform strict entity authentication on the applicant Alice upon receiving the public key, in accordance with the **Certification Practice Statement** (CPS). The strength and method of verification typically depend on the intended application of the certificate and the security level requirements of relevant laws and regulations. The entity authentication mechanism mainly encompasses the following two core dimensions:

1) **Identity Verification**: Ensures the legitimacy of the applicant and strictly binds the identity to the public key holder.
2) **Liveness Detection**: Confirms the entity is active in real-time to effectively prevent replay attacks.

Common authentication schemes are generally categorized into *knowledge-based*, Possession-Based and *biometric-based* verification.

Verification based on Passwords is the most widespread method and can be subdivided into static passwords and one-time passwords. For static passwords such as login passwords, their security depends highly on the entropy of the character combination. To defend against dictionary attacks and social engineering attacks, the system should strictly prohibit the use of pure number sequences such as 1357924680, birth dates such as 950101, simple increasing sequences such as 123456, or the user's name. An ideal static password design should strike a balance between ease of memorization and resistance to guessing, typically the use of pseudo-random sequences with mixed character types.

One-Time Passwords (OTP) enhance security by introducing dynamic change factors. Common implementations include sending SMS verification codes to the user's mobile phone or sending email verification codes to a registered mailbox. This method verifies not only the user's identity but also the user's control over a specific communication terminal.

Furthermore, Biometrics technology utilizes unique physiological characteristics of the user, such as fingerprints, faces, and irises, for identity authentication. These characteristics are intrinsic to the user and cannot be easily forgotten, misplaced, or forged. These technologies can prove the legitimacy of the entity's identity to the verifier without revealing the secret information itself. As shown in Figure 14-6, these schemes collectively constitute a multi-level entity authentication system.

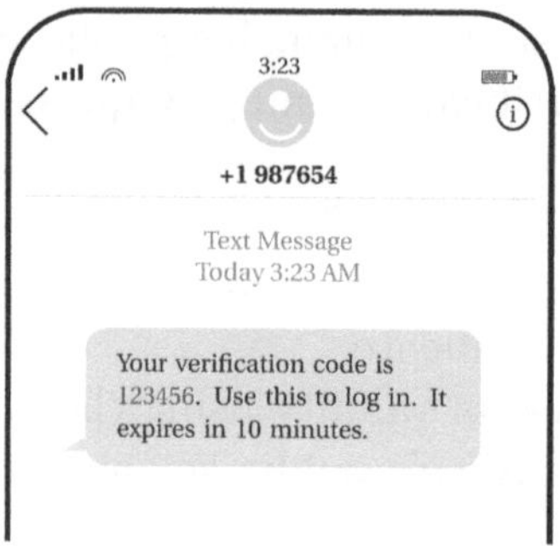

(a) Phone Code

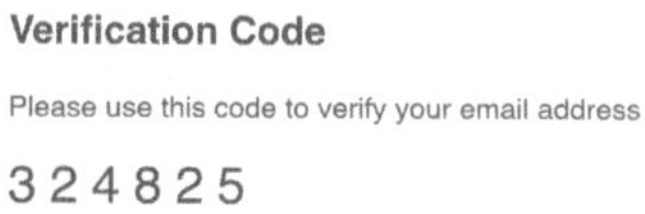

(b) Email Code

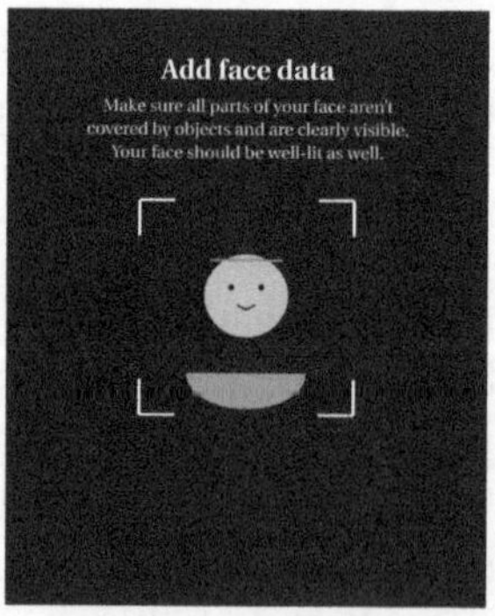

(c) Face Verification

Figure 14-6: Authentication

14.9.3 SSL and TLS

In an open Internet environment, plaintext transmission leaves data highly vulnerable to eavesdropping and tampering. To address this, *Netscape* introduced the **SSL**

(Secure Sockets Layer) protocol in 1994, aiming to establish an encrypted channel between the application layer and the TCP/IP layer. As cryptanalysis advanced, the security defects of the SSL protocol were gradually exposed. The IETF (Internet Engineering Task Force) subsequently took over the standard and published a significantly upgraded successor, namely the **Transport Layer Security** (TLS) protocol. Currently, the mainstream TLS 1.3 standard serves as the absolute core cornerstone for ensuring network communication security globally. Although the term SSL is still colloquially widely used, modern secure networks effectively run exclusively on the TLS protocol.

HTTPS (Hypertext Transfer Protocol Secure) is essentially the implementation of the HTTP protocol built on top of the SSL/TLS protocol, also known as HTTP over SSL/TLS. Its core mechanism involves achieving server identity authentication through digital certificates, utilizing asymmetric encryption to negotiate session keys, and subsequently using symmetric encryption to safeguard the confidentiality and integrity of the data.

The process by which the SSL/TLS protocol establishes a secure connection is called a Handshake. Its simplified flow is as follows:

1) **Negotiation Stage**: The client initiates a connection request to the server, and both parties negotiate the supported TLS versions and cipher suites.
2) **Authentication Stage**: The server sends a digital certificate containing its public key to the client. The client uses a trusted root certificate to verify the validity of the server's certificate, thereby completing identity authentication.
3) **Key Exchange**: Once verification is successful, the client uses the server's public key to encrypt a random number or employs the Diffie-Hellman algorithm to negotiate with the server and generate a temporary session key.
4) **Encrypted Communication**: The handshake concludes, and both parties use the session key to perform encrypted communication for all subsequent application-layer data transmission.

The entire handshake process is completed within milliseconds and is transparent to the user. When a padlock icon appears in the browser's address bar, it indicates that the current HTTP session is being protected by the SSL/TLS protocol.

To view the credential details of the current secure connection, one can access the certificate viewing interface through the security status icon in the browser's address bar. A valid SSL/TLS digital certificate typically contains the following core metadata:

1) **Subject Common Name**: The primary domain name or server identifier bound to the certificate.
2) **Subject Entity Information**: Specific identity information of the certificate holder, including the individual's name, organization, or device name.
3) **Issuer Information**: The name of the CA that issued the certificate.
4) **Digital Signature**: The digital signature value generated by the CA using its private key over the certificate content, used to verify the integrity of the certificate.
5) **Subject Alternative Name**: A list of other domain names or subdomains associated with the certificate.

6) **Validity Period**: The effective date and expiration date of the certificate.
7) **Public Key Information**: The public key data of the certificate holder.
8) **Public Key Algorithm Identifier**: The type of mathematical algorithm used to generate the public key, such as RSA or ECC.
9) **Signature Algorithm Identifier**: The combination of the hash function and signature algorithm used by the CA when signing the certificate, such as SHA256 with RSA.

14.9.4 Necessity of SSL and TLS Deployment

The core purpose of deploying SSL/TLS certificates for network services is to ensure the confidentiality of data transmission, verify the authenticity of the server identity, and maintain the integrity of communication content. When network interactions involve user authentication, financial payments, or the retrieval of personal private data, encrypted channels must be used to ensure that information is not eavesdropped upon. SSL/TLS certificates utilize digital signature technology to provide identity endorsement for websites, establishing a trust anchor between the user and the server.

In modern internet architecture, HTTPS has become the security baseline for network communication. Current mainstream browsers have implemented strict security policies, flagging HTTP sites that have not deployed SSL/TLS certificates as "Not Secure". This mechanism indicates that traffic to the site has not undergone encryption processing and carries an extremely high risk of data leakage, thereby compelling service providers to migrate their operations to the HTTPS protocol.

In practical application scenarios, SSL/TLS protocols are primarily used to protect the following categories of sensitive information:

1) User login credentials and account passwords
2) Credit card transaction data
3) Personal identity information
4) Electronic documents
5) Electronic medical records
6) Intellectual property
7) Physical addresses and contact details

The validity of digital certificates strictly depends on the authority of the issuing CA. Only certificates issued by CAs that are pre-configured as trusted root certificates by mainstream operating systems and browsers possess global recognition.

14.10 EXERCISES

1) Consider the RSA signature scheme, let $p = 809$, $q = 751$ and $d = 23$. Compute the value of the public key e. Find the value of S if $m = 100$.
2) Consider the RSA signature scheme. Let S_1 and S_2 denote the signatures of messages m_1 and m_2, respectively, generated using the same key pair. Let $m = m_1 \cdot m_2$. If S denotes the signature of m, determine whether the relation $S \equiv S_1 \cdot S_2 \pmod{N}$ holds.

3) Consider the RSA signature scheme. The signature is computed by $S \equiv M^d \pmod{N}$. Show that it is possible to forge signatures for some messages in the scheme.
4) Explain the purpose of the collision-resistance requirement for the hash function used in a digital signature scheme.
5) Consider the ElGamal signature scheme, let $p = 3119$, $r = 2$, $a = 127$ and $k = 307$. Find the value of (S_1, S_2) if $H(M) = 320$.
6) Consider the ElGamal signature scheme. Suppose Eve obtains the random integer k used in a signature generation. Determine whether it is possible for Eve to forge a valid signature.
7) Consider the ElGamal signature scheme. Suppose Alice has to sign a contract with Bob, Bob has managed to find 40 distinct places where he can make a slight change in the contract: adding a space at the end of line, adding a comma, replacing with equivalent words (like replacing "agreed to pay" with "is obliged to pay"), etc. If Alice does not object any such minor change in the contract and is willing to sign a contract with any of these minor changes.
   (a) How many possible versions of the contract can Bob generate that Alice would be willing to sign?
   (b) Bob creates a fraudulent contract reflecting a substantial increase in amount that Alice owes to Bob. He computes the hash of the fraudulent contract as $H(f)$ and finds a version of the good contract that hashes to the same value $H(f)$. What is a minimum safe output size for the hash function to make these collisions unlikely?
8) Consider the Schnorr signature scheme, let $p = 997$, $q = 83$, $d = 23$ and $r = 13$. Find the value of a and v. Find the value of (S_1, S_2) if $H(m) = 100$.
9) Consider the Schnorr signature scheme. Suppose Eve obtains the random integer r used in a signature generation. Determine whether it is possible for Eve to forge a valid signature.
10) Consider the Schnorr signature scheme, suppose that under this verification key, (S_1, S_2) is a valid signature on m and (S_1', S_2') is a valid signature on m' where $m \neq m'$. Suppose further that

$$a^{S_2} v^{S_1} \equiv a^{S_2'} v^{S_1'} \pmod{p}$$

Explain why the existence of these two signatures suggests a malfunction in random number generation, and show how to recover the signing key corresponding to v using only a handful of arithmetic operations.
11) Show that the Verifier in an execution of the Schnorr Signatures scheme does accept the proof when the Prover follows the steps correctly.
12) Consider the Digital Signature Algorithm, let $p = 6823, q = 379$ and $h = 140$. Find the value of (S_1, S_2) if $H(m) = 100$.
13) Consider the Digital Signature Algorithm, let $p = 59, q = 29$ and $g = 3$. The private key is $x = 23$. Answer the following questions:
   (a) Compute the public key.
   (b) Generate a signature for a message M with hash value $H(M) = 17$. Use the per-message random secret $k = 10$. Calculate the pair (S_1, S_2).

14) Consider the Digital Signature Algorithm, a verifier receives a message M' with hash $H(M') = 25$ and a signature pair $(S_1, S_2) = (20, 4)$. The signer's public key is $y = 3$. The public parameters are $p = 59, q = 29, g = 3$. Answer the following questions:
    (a) Compute the modular inverse $w \equiv (S_2)^{-1} \pmod{q}$
    (b) Compute $u_1 \equiv [H(M')\, w] \pmod{q}$ and $u_2 \equiv S_1' w \pmod{q}$.
    (c) Compute the verification value $v \equiv [(g^{u_1} y^{u_2}) \bmod p] \pmod{q}$ and determine if the signature is valid.
15) Consider the ECC signature scheme, let $E_p : y^2 = x^3 + 2x + 2$, $p = 17$. The base point $G = (5, 1)$ which has prime order $n = 19$. Let the private key $d = 7$, $H(m) = 10$ and $k = 3$.
    (a) Compute the public key $Q = dG$.
    (b) Compute the elliptic curve point kG.
    (c) Compute (S_1, S_2).
16) Consider the ECC signature scheme, let $E_p : y^2 = x^3 + 231x + 473$, $p = 17389$. The base point $P = (11259, 11278)$ has prime order $n = 1321$. Show that the point is on the E_p. Find the value of (S_1, S_2) if $k = 542$, $H(m) = 644$, $d = 847$.
17) Consider the GGH signature scheme, let the basis $\mathbf{V} = \begin{bmatrix} 3 & 0 \\ 0 & 4 \end{bmatrix}$ and the unimodular matrix $\mathbf{U} = \begin{bmatrix} 2 & 1 \\ 5 & 3 \end{bmatrix}$. Answer the following questions:
    (a) Compute the public basis.
    (b) Prove that $\mathbf{U}$ is indeed unimodular by calculating its determinant.
18) Consider the GGH signature scheme, let the basis $\mathbf{V} = \begin{bmatrix} 4 & -2 \\ 1 & 3 \end{bmatrix}$ and the hashed message $\mathbf{m} = (15, 12)$. Answer the following questions:
    (a) Compute the exact coordinates in the basis $\mathbf{V}$ by calculating $t = m\mathbf{V}^{-1}$.
    (b) Apply Babai's algorithm, round the components of t to the nearest integers to get vector $\mathbf{z}$.
    (c) Compute the signature lattice point $\mathbf{s} = \mathbf{z}\mathbf{V}$. This point s is the approximation of m within the lattice.
19) Consider the GGH signature scheme, let the basis $\mathbf{V} = \begin{bmatrix} 177 & 5 & -7 \\ 8 & 155 & 3 \\ -2 & 0 & 136 \end{bmatrix}$ and the basis $\mathbf{W} = \begin{bmatrix} 2814 & -11782 & 11775 \\ -650 & 2731 & -2728 \\ -168 & 678 & -542 \end{bmatrix}$. Find the value of signature if $\mathbf{M} = [214153, 532556, 372454]$.
20) Consider the GGH signature scheme, let the basis

$$\mathbf{W} = \begin{bmatrix} 3712318934 & -14591032252 & 11433651072 \\ -1586446650 & 6235427140 & -4886131219 \\ 305711854 & -1201580900 & 941568527 \end{bmatrix}$$

The hashed message is $\mathbf{M} = [5269775, 7294466, 1875937]$ and the signature is $S = [6987814629, 14496863295, -9625064603]$. If the maximum allowed distance from the signature to the document is 70, verify that Alice's signature is valid.

Bibliography

[1] Fukang Liu, Willi Meier, Santanu Sarkar, Gaoli Wang, Ryoma Ito, and Takanori Isobe. New cryptanalysis of ZUC-256 initialization using modular differences. Cryptology ePrint Archive, Paper 2021/1104, 2021.

[2] T. Cleary and S. Tzu. *The Art of War*. Shambhala, 2024.

[3] Ralph D Sawyer. *The Seven Military Classics of Ancient China*. Hachette UK, 2020.

[4] E. Marshall and Z Gongling. *Complete Essentials for the Military Classics: Wujing Zongyao, Story Collection, Volume One*. Daybreak Studios, 2024.

[5] Claude Elwood Shannon. A Mathematical Theory of Communication. *The Bell System Technical Journal*, 27(3):379–423, 1948.

[6] Claude E Shannon. Communication theory of secrecy systems. *The Bell System Technical Journal*, 28(4):656–715, 1949.

[7] Whitfield Diffie and Martin E Hellman. New directions in cryptography. In *Democratizing Cryptography: The Work of Whitfield Diffie and Martin Hellman*, pages 365–390. 2022.

[8] Ronald L Rivest, Adi Shamir, and Leonard Adleman. A method for obtaining digital signatures and public-key cryptosystems. *Communications of the ACM*, 21(2):120–126, 1978.

[9] Peter J Eccles. *An Introduction to Mathematical Reasoning: Numbers, Sets and Functions*. Cambridge University Press, 2013.

[10] Kenneth H Rosen. *Elementary Number Theory*. Pearson Education London, 2011.

[11] Joseph A Gallian. *Contemporary Abstract Algebra*. Chapman and Hall/CRC, 2021.

[12] Helmut Hasse. Zur theorie der abstrakten elliptischen funktionenkörper iii. die struktur des meromorphismenrings. die riemannsche vermutung. 1936.

[13] René Schoof. Elliptic curves over finite fields and the computation of square roots mod p. *Mathematics of Computation*, 44(170):483–494, 1985.

[14] Claude E Shannon. Prediction and entropy of printed english. *Bell System Technical Journal*, 30(1):50–64, 1951.

[15] Thomas Cover and Roger King. A convergent gambling estimate of the entropy of english. *IEEE Transactions on Information Theory*, 24(4):413–421, 1978.

[16] William J Teahan and John G Cleary. The entropy of english using ppm-based models. In *Proceedings of Data Compression Conference-DCC'96*, pages 53–62. IEEE, 1996.

[17] Ioannis Kontoyiannis. *The Complexity and Entropy of Literary Styles*. Department of Statistics, Stanford University Stanford, CA, USA, 1997.

[18] Fabio G Guerrero. A new look at the classical entropy of written english. *arXiv preprint arXiv:0911.2284*, 2009.

[19] John D. Cook. Chinese character frequency and entropy.

[20] David A Huffman. A method for the construction of minimum-redundancy codes. *Proceedings of the IRE*, 40(9):1098–1101, 1952.

[21] T.H.G. Megson. *Aircraft Structures for Engineering Students*. Aerospace Engineering. Elsevier Science, 2012.

[22] Lester S Hill. Cryptography in an algebraic alphabet. *The American Mathematical Monthly*, 36(6):306–312, 1929.

[23] Ralph Merkle and Martin Hellman. Hiding information and signatures in trapdoor knapsacks. *IEEE Transactions on Information Theory*, 24(5):525–530, 1978.

[24] Adi Shamir. A polynomial time algorithm for breaking the basic merkle-hellman cryptosystem. In *23rd Annual Symposium on Foundations of Computer Science (sfcs 1982)*, pages 145–152. IEEE, 1982.

[25] Ernest F Brickell. Breaking iterated knapsacks. In *Workshop on the Theory and Application of Cryptographic Techniques*, pages 342–358. Springer, 1984.

[26] Arjen K Lenstra, Hendrik Willem Lenstra, and László Lovász. Factoring polynomials with rational coefficients. *Mathematische annalen*, 261(ARTICLE):515–534, 1982.

[27] Shinya Kiuchi, Yasuyuki Murakami, and Masao Kasahara. New multiplicative knapsack-type public key cryptosystems. *IEICE TRANSACTIONS on Fundamentals of Electronics, Communications and Computer Sciences*, 84(1):188–196, 2001.

[28] Horacio Hideki Yanasse and Nei Yoshihiro Soma. A new enumeration scheme for the knapsack problem. *Discrete Applied Mathematics*, 18(2):235–245, 1987.

[29] Andrew M Odlyzko. The rise and fall of knapsack cryptosystems. *Cryptology and Computational Number Theory*, 42(2), 1990.

[30] David Kahn. *The Codebreakers: The Comprehensive History of Secret Communication from Ancient Times to the Internet.* Simon and Schuster, 1996.

[31] J.O. Mauborgne. *An Advanced Problem in Cryptography and Its Solution.* Press of the Army Services Schools, 1914.

[32] Alan G Konheim. Cryptanalysis of adfgvx encipherment systems. In *Workshop on the Theory and Application of Cryptographic Techniques*, pages 339–341. Springer, 1984.

[33] Ronald L Rivest and Jacob CN Schuldt. Spritz—a spongy rc4-like stream cipher and hash function. *Cryptology ePrint Archive*, 2016.

[34] Eli Biham and Orr Dunkelman. Cryptanalysis of the a5/1 gsm stream cipher. In *International Conference on Cryptology in India*, pages 43–51. Springer, 2000.

[35] Miia Hermelin and Kaisa Nyberg. Correlation properties of the bluetooth combiner. In *International Conference on Information Security and Cryptology*, pages 17–29. Springer, 1999.

[36] Jovan Dj Golic. Linear statistical weakness of alleged rc4 keystream generator. In *Advances in Cryptology—EUROCRYPT'97: International Conference on the Theory and Application of Cryptographic Techniques Konstanz, Germany, May 11–15, 1997 Proceedings 16*, pages 226–238. Springer, 1997.

[37] Hal Finney. An rc4 cycle that can's happen. 1994.

[38] Lars R Knudsen, Willi Meier, Bart Preneel, Vincent Rijmen, and Sven Verdoolaege. Analysis methods for (alleged) rc4. In *Asiacrypt*, volume 1514, pages 327–341. Springer, 1998.

[39] Scott Fluhrer, Itsik Mantin, and Adi Shamir. Weaknesses in the key scheduling algorithm of rc4. In *International Workshop on Selected Areas in Cryptography*, pages 1–24. Springer, 2001.

[40] Andrei Popov. Prohibiting rc4 cipher suites. Technical report, 2015.

[41] State Cryptography Administration of the People's Republic of China. GM/T 0001.1—2012 zuc stream cipher algorithm - part 1: Description of the algorithm. *Beijing: China Standards Press*, 2012.

[42] Standardization Administration of the People's Republic of China. GB/T 33133—2016 zuc stream cipher algorithm - part 1: Description of the algorithm. *Beijing: China Standards Press*, 2016.

[43] Fukang Liu, Willi Meier, Santanu Sarkar, Gaoli Wang, Ryoma Ito, and Takanori Isobe. New cryptanalysis of ZUC-256 initialization using modular differences. Cryptology ePrint Archive, Paper 2021/1104, 2021.

[44] Feng XiuTao. The zuc stream cipher algorithm. *Journal of Information Security Research*, 2(11):1028–1041, 2016.

[45] DU Hong-hong and ZHANG Wen-ying. Security analysis on zuc stream cipher. *Journal of Information Security Research*, 22(6):151–155, 2012.

[46] A Gersho. Unclassified summary: Involvement of nsa in the development of the data encryption standard. *IEEE Communications Society Magazine*, 16(6):53–55, 1978.

[47] Joan Daemen and Vincent Rijmen. *The Design of Rijndael*, volume 2. Springer, 2002.

[48] Victor L Voydock and Stephen T Kent. Security mechanisms in high-level network protocols. *ACM Computing Surveys (CSUR)*, 15(2):135–171, 1983.

[49] Whitfield Diffie and Martin E Hellman. Privacy and authentication: An introduction to cryptography. *Proceedings of the IEEE*, 67(3):397–427, 1979.

[50] Horst Feistel. Cryptography and computer privacy. *Scientific American*, 228(5):15–23, 1973.

[51] Niels Ferguson and Bruce Schneier. *Practical Cryptography*, volume 141. Wiley, New York, 2003.

[52] Don Coppersmith. The data encryption standard (DES) and its strength against attacks. *IBM Journal of Research and Development*, 38(3):243–250, 1994.

[53] Lauren De Meyer, Begül Bilgin, and Bart Preneel. Extended analysis of DES s-boxes. In *Proceedings of the 34rd Symposium on Information Theory in the Benelux*, pages 30–31, 2013.

[54] Dan Boneh Christopher Dunworth and Richard J Lipton. Breaking DES using a molecular computer. *DNA Based Computers*, 27:37, 1996.

[55] David McNett. US government's encryption standard broken in less than a day, 1999.

[56] Paul C Van Oorschot and Michael J Wiener. Parallel collision search with application to hash functions and discrete logarithms. In *Proceedings of the 2nd ACM Conference on Computer and Communications Security*, pages 210–218, 1994.

[57] J. Daemen and Rijmen. Aes proposal: Rijndael, version 2. submission to niste, 1999.

[58] Daniel J Bernstein. Cache-timing attacks on aes. 2005.

[59] David Gullasch, Endre Bangerter, and Stephan Krenn. Cache games–bringing access-based cache attacks on aes to practice. In *2011 IEEE Symposium on Security and Privacy*, pages 490–505. IEEE, 2011.

[60] Standardization Administration of the People's Republic of China. GB/T 33133—2016 information security technology—SM4 block cipher algorthm. *Beijing: China Standards Press*, 2016.

[61] Lv Shuwang, Su Bozhan, Wang Peng, Mao Yingying, and Huo Lili. Overview on SM4 algorithm. *Journal of Information Security Research*, 2(11):995–1007, 2016.

[62] Taehyun Kim, Jongsung Kim, Seokhie Hong, and Jaechul Sung. Linear and differential cryptanalysis of reduced sms4 block cipher. *Cryptology ePrint Archive*, 2008.

[63] Ming-Jie Liu and Jia-Zhe Chen. Improved linear attacks on the chinese block cipher standard. *Journal of Computer Science and Technology*, 29(6):1123–1133, 2014.

[64] Lei Zhang, Wentao Zhang, and Wenling Wu. Cryptanalysis of reduced-round sms4 block cipher. In *Australasian Conference on Information Security and Privacy*, pages 216–229. Springer, 2008.

[65] Dong XiaoLi. *Cryptanalysis of the AES and SMS4 Block Ciphers*. PhD thesis, Xidian University, 2011.

[66] Wentao Zhang, Wenling Wu, Dengguo Feng, and Bozhan Su. Some new observations on the sms4 block cipher in the chinese wapi standard. In *International Conference on Information Security Practice and Experience*, pages 324–335. Springer, 2009.

[67] ZB Du, Z Wu, M Wang, and JT Rao. Improved chosen-plaintext power analysis attack against SM4 at the round-output. *Journal on Communications*, 36(10):85–91, 2015.

[68] Siyang Yu, Kenli Li, Keqin Li, Yunchuan Qin, and Zhao Tong. A vlsi implementation of an SM4 algorithm resistant to power analysis. *Journal of Intelligent & Fuzzy Systems*, 31(2):795–803, 2016.

[69] John M Pollard. Theorems on factorization and primality testing. In *Mathematical Proceedings of the Cambridge Philosophical Society*, volume 76, pages 521-528. Cambridge University Press, 1974.

[70] Peter W Shor. Algorithms for quantum computation: discrete logarithms and factoring. In *Proceedings 35th Annual Symposium on Foundations of Computer Science*, pages 124–134. Ieee, 1994.

[71] Ronald L Rivest, Martin E Hellman, John C Anderson, and John W Lyons. Responses to nist's proposal. *Communications of the ACM*, 35(7):41–54, 1992.

[72] J Barkley Rosser and Lowell Schoenfeld. Approximate formulas for some functions of prime numbers. *Illinois Journal of Mathematics*, 6(1):64–94, 1962.

[73] Jacques Hadamard. Sur la distribution des zeros de la fonction zeta (s) et ses consequences arithmetiques. *Bulletin de la Societe mathematique de France*, 24:199–220, 1896.

[74] Charles-Jean De la Vallee Poussin. *Recherches analytiques sur la theorie des nombres premiers.* Hayez, Imprimeur de l'Academie royale de Belgique, 1897.

[75] Paul Erdös. On a new method in elementary number theory which leads to an elementary proof of the prime number theorem. *Proceedings of the National Academy of Sciences*, 35(7):374–384, 1949.

[76] Atle Selberg. An elementary proof of the prime-number theorem. *Annals of Mathematics*, pages 305–313, 1949.

[77] Jeffrey Hoffstein, Jill Pipher, Joseph H Silverman, and Joseph H Silverman. *An Introduction to Mathematical Cryptography*, volume 1. Springer, 2008.

[78] Michael J Wiener. Cryptanalysis of short rsa secret exponents. *IEEE Transactions on Information theory*, 36(3):553–558, 1990.

[79] Don Coppersmith. Small solutions to polynomial equations, and low exponent rsa vulnerabilities. *Journal of Cryptology*, 10(4):233–260, 1997.

[80] Dan Boneh et al. Twenty years of attacks on the rsa cryptosystem. *Notices of the AMS*, 46(2):203–213, 1999.

[81] Manindra Agrawal, Neeraj Kayal, and Nitin Saxena. Primes is in p. *Annals of Mathematics*, pages 781–793, 2004.

[82] Motaz Muhammad. aks: An implementation of the AKS primality test. `https://github.com/motazmuhammad/aks`, 2019. Accessed: 2026-03-20.

[83] Keith Conrad. The Fermat primality test, 2026.

[84] Albert H Beiler. *Recreations in the Theory of Numbers: The Queen of Mathematics Entertains.* Courier Corporation, 1964.

[85] Robert D Carmichael. Note on a new number theory function. *Bulletin of the American Mathematical Society*, 16(5):232–238, 1910.

[86] William R Alford, Andrew Granville, and Carl Pomerance. There are infinitely many carmichael numbers. *Annals of Mathematics*, pages 703–722, 1994.

[87] Gary L Miller. Riemann's hypothesis and tests for primality. *Journal of Computer and System Sciences*, 13(3):300–317, 1976.

[88] François Arnault. Rabin-miller primality test: composite numbers which pass it. *Mathematics of Computation*, 64(209):355–361, 1995.

[89] Robert Solovay and Volker Strassen. A fast monte-carlo test for primality. *SIAM Journal on Computing*, 6(1):84–85, 1977.

[90] Leonard M Adleman. On distinguishing prime numbers from composite numbers. In *21st Annual Symposium on Foundations of Computer Science (sfcs 1980)*, pages 387–406. IEEE, 1980.

[91] Jean-Jacques Quisquater. *Advances in Cryptology, EUROCRYPT'89: Proceedings*. Springer, 1990.

[92] Chen Jing-Run. On the representation of a larger even integer as the sum of a prime and the product of at most two primes. *Goldbach Conjecture*, 4:253, 1984.

[93] Yitang Zhang. Bounded gaps between primes. *Annals of Mathematics*, pages 1121–1174, 2014.

[94] DHJ Polymath. Variants of the selberg sieve, and bounded intervals containing many primes. *Research in the Mathematical Sciences*, 1(1):12, 2014.

[95] Paul Kocher, Joshua Jaffe, and Benjamin Jun. Differential power analysis. In *Annual International Cryptology Conference*, pages 388–397. Springer, 1999.

[96] Don Coppersmith. Finding a small root of a bivariate integer equation; factoring with high bits known. In *International Conference on the Theory and Applications of Cryptographic Techniques*, pages 178–189. Springer, 1996.

[97] Taher ElGamal. A public key cryptosystem and a signature scheme based on discrete logarithms. *IEEE Transactions on Information Theory*, 31(4):469–472, 1985.

[98] Ralph C Merkle. Secure communications over insecure channels. *Communications of the ACM*, 21(4):294–299, 1978.

[99] Franco Callegati, Walter Cerroni, and Marco Ramilli. Man-in-the-middle attack to the https protocol. *IEEE Security & Privacy*, 7(1):78–81, 2009.

[100] Shafi Goldwasser, Silvio Micali, and Chales Rackoff. The knowledge complexity of interactive proof-systems. In *Providing Sound Foundations for Cryptography: On the Work of Shafi Goldwasser and Silvio Micali*, pages 203–225. 2019.

[101] Yvo Desmedt, Claude Goutier, and Samy Bengio. Special uses and abuses of the fiat-shamir passport protocol. In *Conference on the Theory and Application of Cryptographic Techniques*, pages 21–39. Springer, 1987.

[102] Mike Zabrocki. Cyclotomic polynomials and primitive roots, 2010.

[103] Daniel Shanks. Class number, a theory of factorization, and genera. In *Proc. of Symp. Math. Soc., 1971*, volume 20, pages 41–440, 1971.

[104] J. M. Pollard. A monte carlo method for factorization. *BIT*, 15(3):331–334, September 1975.

[105] Dingyi Pei, Arto Salomaa, and Cunsheng Ding. *Chinese Remainder Theorem: Applications in Computing, Coding, Cryptography.* World Scientific, 1996.

[106] Lay Yong Lam and Tian Se Ang. *Fleeting footsteps: Tracing the conception of arithmetic and algebra in ancient China.* World scientific, 2004.

[107] S Pohtig and M Hellman. An improved algorithm for computing logarithms over gf (p) and its cryptographic siginificance. *IEEE Transactions on Information Theory*, 1978.

[108] Leonard Adleman. A subexponential algorithm for the discrete logarithm problem with applications to cryptography. In *20th Annual Symposium on Foundations of Computer Science (SFCS 1979)*, pages 55–60. IEEE Computer Society, 1979.

[109] Victor S Miller. Advances in cryptology—crypto'85 proceedings. *Use of Elliptic Curves in Cryptography*, pages 417–426, 1986.

[110] Neal Koblitz. Elliptic curve cryptosystems. *Mathematics of Computation*, 48(177):203–209, 1987.

[111] Hendrik W Lenstra Jr. Factoring integers with elliptic curves. *Annals of Mathematics*, pages 649–673, 1987.

[112] Elaine Barker, Lily Chen, Sharon Keller, Allen Roginsky, Apostol Vassilev, and Richard Davis. Recommendation for pair-wise key-establishment schemes using discrete logarithm cryptography. Technical report, National Institute of Standards and Technology, 2017.

[113] Debabrat Boruah and Monjul Saikia. Implementation of elgamal elliptic curve cryptography over prime field using c. In *International Conference on Information Communication and Embedded Systems (ICICES2014)*, pages 1–7, 2014.

[114] Douglas R Stinson. *Cryptography: Theory and Practice.* Chapman and Hall/CRC, 2005.

[115] Standardization Administration of the People's Republic of China. Gb/t 32918-2016 information security technology—public key cryptographic algorithm sm2 based on elliptic curves. *Beijing: China Standards Press*, 2016.

[116] Peter L Montgomery. Speeding the pollard and elliptic curve methods of factorization. *Mathematics of Computation*, 48(177):243–264, 1987.

[117] Jerome A Solinas. An improved algorithm for arithmetic on a family of elliptic curves. In *Advances in Cryptology—CRYPTO'97: 17th Annual International Cryptology Conference Santa Barbara, California, USA August 17–21, 1997 Proceedings 17*, pages 357–371. Springer, 1997.

[118] Elaine Barker and Quynh Dang. Nist special publication 800-57 part 1, revision 4. *NIST, Tech. Rep*, 16, 2016.

[119] Miklós Ajtai. Generating hard instances of lattice problems. In *Proceedings of the Twenty-Eighth Annual ACM Symposium on Theory of Computing*, pages 99–108, 1996.

[120] Jiri Matousek. *Lectures on Discrete Geometry*, volume 212. Springer Science & Business Media, 2013.

[121] Oded Goldreich, Shafi Goldwasser, and Shai Halevi. Public-key cryptosystems from lattice reduction problems. In *Annual International Cryptology Conference*, pages 112–131. Springer, 1997.

[122] Arif Mandangan, Hailiza Kamarulhaili, and Muhammad Asyraf Asbullah. A security upgrade on the ggh lattice-based cryptosystem. *Sains Malaysiana*, 49(6):1471–1478, 2020.

[123] László Babai. On lovász'lattice reduction and the nearest lattice point problem. *Combinatorica*, 6(1):1–13, 1986.

[124] Phong Nguyen. Cryptanalysis of the goldreich-goldwasser-halevi cryptosystem from crypto'97. In *Annual International Cryptology Conference*, pages 288–304. Springer, 1999.

[125] Yupu Hu and Huiwen Jia. Cryptanalysis of ggh map. In *Annual International Conference on the Theory and Applications of Cryptographic Techniques*, pages 537–565. Springer, 2016.

[126] Jeffrey Hoffstein, Jill Pipher, and Joseph H Silverman. Ntru: A ring-based public key cryptosystem. In *International Algorithmic Number Theory Symposium*, pages 267–288. Springer, 1998.

[127] Maureen Robinson. Security innovation acquires ntru cryptosystems, a leading security solutions provider to the embedded security market, 2009.

[128] Éliane Jaulmes and Antoine Joux. A chosen-ciphertext attack against ntru. In *Annual International Cryptology Conference*, pages 20–35. Springer, 2000.

[129] Nick Howgrave-Graham, Joseph H Silverman, Ari Singer, and William Whyte. Naep: Provable security in the presence of decryption failures. *Cryptology ePrint Archive*, 2003.

[130] Nick Howgrave-Graham. A hybrid lattice-reduction and meet-in-the-middle attack against ntru. In *Annual International Cryptology Conference*, pages 150–169. Springer, 2007.

[131] Jeffrey Hoffstein, Nick Howgrave-Graham, Jill Pipher, Joseph H Silverman, and William Whyte. Ntrusign: Digital signatures using the ntru lattice. In *Cryptographers' Track at the RSA Conference*, pages 122–140. Springer, 2003.

[132] Oded Regev. On lattices, learning with errors, random linear codes, and cryptography. *Journal of the ACM (JACM)*, 56(6):1–40, 2009.

[133] Richard Lindner and Chris Peikert. Better key sizes (and attacks) for lwe-based encryption. In *Topics in Cryptology–CT-RSA 2011: The Cryptographers' Track at the RSA Conference 2011, San Francisco, CA, USA, February 14-18, 2011. Proceedings*, pages 319–339. Springer, 2011.

[134] Daniele Micciancio and Oded Regev. Lattice-based cryptography in post quantum cryptography, Bernstein DJ, Buchmann J., Dahmen E, 2009.

[135] Oded Regev. On lattices, leaning with errors, random linear codes, and cryptography. *Proc. STOC 2005*, 2005.

[136] Akinori Kawachi, Keisuke Tanaka, and Keita Xagawa. Multi-bit cryptosystems based on lattice problems. In *International Workshop on Public Key Cryptography*, pages 315–329. Springer, 2007.

[137] Vadim Lyubashevsky, Chris Peikert, and Oded Regev. On ideal lattices and learning with errors over rings. In *Annual International Conference on the Theory and Applications of Cryptographic Techniques*, pages 1–23. Springer, 2010.

[138] Ronald L Rivest, Len Adleman, Michael L Dertouzos, et al. On data banks and privacy homomorphisms. *Foundations of Secure Computation*, 4(11):169–180, 1978.

[139] Pascal Paillier. Public-key cryptosystems based on composite degree residuosity classes. In *International Conference on the Theory and Applications of Cryptographic Techniques*, pages 223–238. Springer, 1999.

[140] Craig Gentry. Fully homomorphic encryption using ideal lattices. In *Proceedings of the Forty-First Annual ACM Symposium on Theory of Computing*, pages 169–178, 2009.

[141] CHEN Zhigang. *Research and Design of Fully Homomorphic Encryption Based on Lattice.* PhD thesis, Ph. D. dissertation], Nanjing University of Aeronautics and Astronautics, 2015.

[142] Vinod Vaikuntanathan. Computing blindfolded: New developments in fully homomorphic encryption. In *2011 IEEE 52nd Annual Symposium on Foundations of Computer Science*, pages 5–16. IEEE, 2011.

[143] Zvika Brakerski, Craig Gentry, and Vinod Vaikuntanathan. (leveled) fully homomorphic encryption without bootstrapping. *ACM Transactions on Computation Theory (TOCT)*, 6(3):1–36, 2014.

[144] Shai Halevi and Victor Shoup. Faster homomorphic linear transformations in helib. In *Annual International Cryptology Conference*, pages 93–120. Springer, 2018.

[145] Marten van Dijk, Craig Gentry, Shai Halevi, and Vinod Vaikuntanathan. Fully homomorphic encryption over the integers. In *Annual International Conference on the Theory and Applications of Cryptographic Techniques*, pages 24–43. Springer, 2010.

[146] Nathanael David Black. *Homomorphic Encryption and the Approximate GCD Problem*. PhD thesis, Clemson University, 2014.

[147] Melanie Pabstel. *Parameter Constraints on Homomorphic Encryption over the Integers*. PhD thesis, 04 2017.

[148] Craig Gentry, Amit Sahai, and Brent Waters. Homomorphic encryption from learning with errors: Conceptually-simpler, asymptotically-faster, attribute-based. In *Annual Cryptology Conference*, pages 75–92. Springer, 2013.

[149] Jung Hee Cheon, Andrey Kim, Miran Kim, and Yongsoo Song. Homomorphic encryption for arithmetic of approximate numbers. In *International Conference on the Theory and Application of Cryptology and Information Security*, pages 409–437. Springer, 2017.

[150] Ronald L Rivest. Md4 message digest algorithm. Technical report, 1990.

[151] Ronald Rivest. Rfc 1321: The md5 message-digest algorithm, april 1992. *Status: Informational*, 2014.

[152] Ronald L Rivest, Benjamin Agre, Daniel V Bailey, Christopher Crutchfield, Yevgeniy Dodis, Kermin Elliott Fleming, Asif Khan, Jayant Krishnamurthy, Yuncheng Lin, Leo Reyzin, et al. The md6 hash function–a proposal to nist for sha-3. *Submission to NIST*, 2(3):1–234, 2008.

[153] Hans Dobbertin. Cryptanalysis of md5 compress. *rump Session of Eurocrypt*, 96:71–82, 1996.

[154] QH Dang. Secure hash standard;(no. federal inf. process. stds.(nist fips)-180-4). *National Institute of Standards and Technology: Gaithersburg, MD, USA*, 2015.

[155] Bruce Schneier. Schneier on security: cryptanalysis of sha-1. *Schneier.com*, 2005.

[156] Wouter Penard and Tim van Werkhoven. On the secure hash algorithm family. *Cryptography in Context*, pages 1–18, 2008.

[157] Florent Chabaud and Antoine Joux. Differential collisions in sha-0. In *Annual International Cryptology Conference*, pages 56–71. Springer, 1998.

[158] Xiaoyun Wang, Hongbo Yu, and Yiqun Lisa Yin. Efficient collision search attacks on sha-0. In *Annual International Cryptology Conference*, pages 1–16. Springer, 2005.

[159] Marc Stevens, Pierre Karpman, and Thomas Peyrin. The shappening: Freestart collisions for sha-1, 2015.

[160] Marc Stevens, Elie Bursztein, Pierre Karpman, Ange Albertini, and Yarik Markov. The first collision for full sha-1. In *Annual International Cryptology Conference*, pages 570–596. Springer, 2017.

[161] Wang Xiaoyun and Yu Hongbo. Sm3 cryptographic hash algorithm. *Journal of Information Security Research*, 2(11):983–994, 2016.

[162] Ivan Bjerre Damgard. A design principle for hash functions. In *Conference on the Theory and Application of Cryptology*, pages 416–427. Springer, 1989.

[163] Stephane Moore. Meet-in-the-middle attacks. *Retrieved from Stephane Moore*, 2010.

[164] Søren S Thomsen. An improved preimage attack on md2. *Cryptology ePrint Archive*, 2008.

[165] Yu Sasaki, Lei Wang, and Kazumaro Aoki. Preimage attacks on 41-step sha-256 and 46-step sha-512. *Cryptology ePrint Archive*, 2009.

[166] Gaëtan Leurent and Thomas Peyrin. From collisions to chosen-prefix collisions application to full sha-1. In *Annual International Conference on the Theory and Applications of Cryptographic Techniques*, pages 527–555. Springer, 2019.

[167] Marc Girault, Robert Cohen, et al. A generalized birthday attack. In *Workshop on the Theory and Application of of Cryptographic Techniques*, pages 129–156. Springer, 1988.

[168] National Institute of Standards and Technology. Fips pub 198-1: The keyed-hash message authentication code (hmac). 2008.

[169] Charles Cresson Wood. Security for computer networks : D.w. davies and w.l. price new york: John wiley and sons, 1984. 386 + xix pages, $19.50. *Comput. Secur.*, 4:248–249, 1985.

[170] Mihir Bellare, Ran Canetti, and Hugo Krawczyk. Keying hash functions for message authentication. In *Annual International Cryptology Conference*, pages 1–15. Springer, 1996.

[171] State Cryptography Administration of the People's Republic of China. GB/T 15852.2-2024 network security technology - message authentication code - part 2: Mechanism using specially designed hash functions. *Beijing: China Standards Press*, 2024.

[172] Hugo Krawczyk, Mihir Bellare, and Ran Canetti. Hmac: Keyed-hashing for message authentication. Technical report, 1997.

[173] Hugo Krawczyk, Mihir Bellare, and Ran Canetti. Rfc2104: Hmac: Keyed-hashing for message authentication, 1997.

[174] State Cryptography Administration of the People's Republic of China. GB/T 15852.1-2020 information technology—security techniques—message authentication codes—part 1: Mechanisms using a block cipher. *Beijing: China Standards Press*, 2020.

[175] John Von Neumann. Various techniques used in connection with random digits. *John von Neumann, Collected Works*, 5:768–770, 1963.

[176] WE Thomson. A modified congruence method of generating pseudo-random numbers. *The Computer Journal*, 1(2):83–83, 1958.

[177] Derrick H Lehmer. Mathematical methods in large-scale computing units. *Annu. Comput. Lab. Harvard Univ.*, 26:141–146, 1951.

[178] Makoto Matsumoto and Takuji Nishimura. Mersenne twister: a 623-dimensionally equidistributed uniform pseudo-random number generator. *ACM Transactions on Modeling and Computer Simulation (TOMACS)*, 8(1):3–30, 1998.

[179] Adi Shamir. On the generation of cryptographically strong pseudorandom sequences. *ACM Transactions on Computer Systems (TOCS)*, 1(1):38–44, 1983.

[180] Lenore Blum, Manuel Blum, and Mike Shub. A simple unpredictable pseudo-random number generator. *SIAM Journal on Computing*, 15(2):364–383, 1986.

[181] Shafi Goldwasser, Silvio Micali, and Ronald L Rivest. A digital signature scheme secure against adaptive chosen-message attacks. *SIAM Journal on Computing*, 17(2):281–308, 1988.

[182] Claus-Peter Schnorr. Efficient signature generation by smart cards. *Journal of Cryptology*, 4:161–174, 1991.

[183] Don Johnson, Alfred Menezes, and Scott Vanstone. The elliptic curve digital signature algorithm (ecdsa). *International Journal of Information Security*, 1(1):36–63, 2001.

[184] Hing Che Chan. *On Forging ElGamal Signature and Other Attacks.* PhD thesis, Chinese University of Hong Kong, 2000.

[185] Daniel Bleichenbacher. Generating eigamal signatures without knowing the secret key. In *Advances in Cryptology—EUROCRYPT'96: International Conference on the Theory and Application of Cryptographic Techniques Saragossa, Spain, May 12–16, 1996 Proceedings 15*, pages 10–18. Springer, 1996.

Index

For Product Safety Concerns and Information please contact our
EU representative GPSR@taylorandfrancis.com Taylor & Francis
Verlag GmbH, Kaufingerstraße 24, 80331 München, Germany